INTERMEDIATE MICROECONOMICS

D0322646

Yuxi Heluo

"Robert Mochrie presents modern microeconomics in its full beauty: insightful, clear, rigorous, and broadened to include all of human behaviour. Both students and scholars will gain from this intuitive and masterly development of economic theory, with its expression of ideas in mathematical form, and real world perspective introduced through illustrative examples. If you want to convince with economic arguments, you must master the foundations. This book, studied with care and time, will help you get there."

Stephanie Rosenkranz, Utrecht University, the Netherlands

"*Intermediate Microeconomics* is a great book, set to become a staple for those of us teaching at this level. We finally have a text that combines both traditional theory with a substantive amount of game theory and also ventures into behavioural economics. It puts the development of the student's understanding and acquisition of analytical skills proactively at its core with an excellent fusion of technical rigor and clear, intuitive exposition."

Anne Gasteen, Glasgow Caledonian University, UK

"This book introduces a wide variety of rich and complex theories of microeconomics, with many useful tools designed to assist student learning. These include help with mathematical notation, clearly articulated explanations of core concepts and numerous problem sets to help build on the material introduced in each section. I recommend this as a valuable resource for all students learning about microeconomics at an intermediate level."

Joe Cox, Portsmouth University, UK

"Robert Mochrie has done a remarkable job at presenting the key theoretical principles in a very accessible and rigorous/accurate way. The book deals brilliantly with both the intuitive as well as the analytical side of microeconomics and aims at students that already have some intuitive understanding of microeconomics. The very elegant and simple presentation as well as the extensive coverage of resource allocation in an intermediate microeconomics textbook is rare and forms an excellent foundation for teaching on an intermediate level."

Anna Göddeke, Reutlingen University, Germany

"The textbook is a very valuable addition to the existing ones. It combines basic concepts, lots of examples, and applications with mathematical rigor and exercises in a very effective way."

Martin Kocher, University of Munich, Germany

ROBERT MOCHRIE

INTERMEDIATE MICROECONOMICS

 palgrave

© 2016

All rights reserved. No reproduction, copy or transmission of this publication may be made without written permission.

No portion of this publication may be reproduced, copied or transmitted save with written permission or in accordance with the provisions of the Copyright, Designs and Patents Act 1988, or under the terms of any licence permitting limited copying issued by the Copyright Licensing Agency, Saffron House, 6–10 Kirby Street, London EC1N 8TS.

Any person who does any unauthorized act in relation to this publication may be liable to criminal prosecution and civil claims for damages.

The author has asserted his right to be identified as the author of this work in accordance with the Copyright, Designs and Patents Act 1988.

First published 2016 by
PALGRAVE

Palgrave in the UK is an imprint of Macmillan Publishers Limited, registered in England, company number 785998, of 4 Crinan Street, London, N1 9XW.

Palgrave Macmillan in the US is a division of St Martin's Press LLC, 175 Fifth Avenue, New York, NY 10010.

Palgrave is the global imprint of the above companies and is represented throughout the world.

Palgrave® and Macmillan® are registered trademarks in the United States, the United Kingdom, Europe and other countries.

ISBN 978–1–137–00844–2

This book is printed on paper suitable for recycling and made from fully managed and sustained forest sources. Logging, pulping and manufacturing processes are expected to conform to the environmental regulations of the country of origin.

A catalogue record for this book is available from the British Library.

A catalog record for this book is available from the Library of Congress.

Printed in China

Dedication

To Milos Bartosek, Katie Trolan, and Tsveti Yordanova:
the students whose engagement with my teaching and whose
thirst for knowledge have been the greatest encouragement to
write this book.

Brief contents

Long contents

List of figures

List of tables

List of essential maths

About the author

Dr Robbie Mochrie is a Senior Lecturer in Economics at Heriot-Watt University, Edinburgh. His main research interests are in the economics of religion and the history of economic thought. He has served as the Executive Director of the Association for the Study of Religion, Economics and Culture. Before entering academia, he worked in the Law Department of Bank of Scotland.

Acknowledgements

The origin of this book was a discussion with Jaime Marshall, now Managing Director of Palgrave Macmillan, back in 1998. After several attempts, Jaime persuaded me to write this book. I would like to thank him for his support and belief in the project throughout this long process. The book has involved many staff at Palgrave: Aleta Bezuidenhout helped to refine the concept while it was in development; Amy Grant provided editing support; Kirsty Reade supervised the editing; and Nikini Jayatunga managed all of the processes required to turn the initial draft into the final product. Working with Palgrave has been a pleasure; everyone who has contributed to the book has been unfailingly optimistic about it, while providing me with very good advice and all the support needed to convert my rather diffuse and woolly ideas into a final text. I am sure that there are many people at Palgrave whose names and contributions to this project I simply do not know, and for all of their efforts also I am extremely grateful.

I have to thank Leo Goretti, the editor of the book, separately and at rather greater length. Leo's unstinting support and care in guiding me through several revisions of the manuscript is largely responsible for the emergence of the text in its final form. He has read every word that I have written, working his way through three drafts. Frequently, he has had to wade through a mass of text, sifting it for useful ideas, yet has nonetheless remained invariably courteous, gentle and persistent in suggesting how I might both simplify and clarify the writing, cut out extraneous material, and develop arguments that are more immediately intelligible. As with the staff of Palgrave, my debt to him is very large and I cannot really thank him adequately here.

The book has also benefited from comments by students at Heriot-Watt University who have been exposed to the development of my ideas. I have dedicated the book to three students whose enthusiastic response to the approach to teaching that I was developing was instrumental in my agreeing to write the book. They are representative of the many students at Heriot-Watt University who have shaped my thoughts through ongoing debate.

I would also like to thank the many colleagues at Heriot-Watt University who have allowed me to rehearse arguments, especially about what the content of a microeconomics textbook might be; and the staff of the Institute for the Study of Religion, Economics and Society, at Chapman University, where I spent a period of study leave in 2012 and where I drafted the first half of the manuscript. In addition, many academics have reviewed the manuscript and have helped to refine arguments in many places.

Lastly, I have to thank my wife, Jane, who has been a constant source of support and encouragement while I have been writing.

Robbie Mochrie

The author and publishers would like to thank the many reviewers for their helpful comments and suggestions throughout the writing process. These include, but are not limited to:

Massimo Antonini, University of Oxford, UK
Frank Bohn, Radboud University, the Netherlands
David Bjerk, Claremont McKenna College, USA
Vivien Burrows, University of Reading, UK
Phoebe Chan, Wheaton College, USA
Rachel Connelly, Bowdoin College, USA
Arnaud Dellis, Laval University, Canada
Spyros Galanis, University of Southampton, UK
José Manuel Giménez-Gómez, Rovira i Virgili University, Spain
Floris Heukelom, Radboud University, the Netherlands
Ali Kabiri, University of Buckingham, UK
Kanika Kapur, University College Dublin, Ireland
Klaus Kultti, University of Helsinki, Finland
Manfredi La Manna, University of St Andrews, UK
Scott Ogawa, Northwestern University, USA
Lucy O'Shea, University of Bath, UK
Indrajit Ray, Cardiff University, UK
Santiago Sanchez-Pages, University of Edinburgh, UK
Emanuela Sciubba, Birkbeck, University of London, UK
Omari Swinton, Howard University, USA

Finally, the author and publishers are grateful for permission to reproduce the following copyright material:

Exercises 27.18–27.21 are adapted from *Cognitive Psychology*, Vol. 5 Issue 2, Amos Tversky and Daniel Kahneman, 'Availability: A heuristic for judging frequency and probability', 207–232, Copyright (1973), with permission from Elsevier.

Message to students

My intention has been to provide a text that will set out the essential principles of micro-economics, and then apply them in a variety of situations. There are only a few principles, but they support a theory that is rich, subtle, and, for those who take the time necessary to master its intricacies, deeply satisfying.

Much of economic theory is best stated in formal language and arguments. These need to be studied carefully, and can be assimilated only slowly. Economics is like a rich stew that cannot be prepared in a hurry. You may find this frustrating, especially when theories are presented in a very abstract form which lends itself naturally to the mathematical expression of ideas. Furthermore, since the financial crisis of 2008–09 there has been substantial concern that economics has become detached from reality. This has long been a problem for economists.

Alfred Marshall, whose *Principles of Economics* was the first book to set out much of what is now the standard theory, constructed his book so that it would be of use to 'men of commerce'. Himself a formidable mathematician, Marshall wrote to his colleague A. L. Bowley in 1906:

> *I had a growing feeling in the later years of my work at the subject that a good math-ematical theorem dealing with economic hypotheses was very unlikely to be good economics: and I went more and more on the rules – (1) Use mathematics as a short-hand language, rather than as an engine of inquiry. (2) Keep to them till you have done. (3) Translate into English. (4) Then illustrate by examples that are important in real life. (5) Burn the mathematics. (6) If you can't succeed in 4, burn 3. This last I did often.*

There will be plenty of mathematics in this book: this is one of the ways in which econom-ics has advanced in the last century, as its arguments have become steadily more complex. But Marshall's rule will be very helpful. We should never reach the end of a mathematical argument, breathe a sigh of relief at reaching that point, and immediately start a new argu-ment. Instead, we must always pause, reflect upon what we have done, and think how we might explain it to people who are not so skilled in using microeconomics. Only then can we claim to understand the subject.

The design of the book

In writing this book, I had several objectives in mind. I wanted to cover much of the tradi-tional material of a microeconomics textbook. I also wanted to add in some more recent developments, specifically in game theory and the widening of the scope of economics to include all of human behaviour. Above all, though, I wanted to integrate the use of math-ematical techniques with the development of microeconomic theory. To do this, I have designed the text quite carefully.

- Each chapter is introduced by a **What we do in this chapter** section and ends with a **Summary** section. These features set out the content discussed in the chapter and highlight how it fits into the larger picture of microeconomic theory.

- There is a substantial **Essential Maths** commentary. This is found in boxes at the bottom of pages, generally with several on successive pages. They are only a brief statement of the mathematics that you will need to assimilate, but each appears where a mathematical technique is used for the first time.
- The exercises in the **By yourself** boxes feature many problems chosen to emphasize the need for student readers to understand formal arguments. The placing of the questions within the text is intended to encourage you to stop and think about the argument. The text surrounding these boxes offers some guidance on how to solve the problems (and answers are available on the companion website), but require you to undertake the working yourself, as a helpful way to see whether you've understood the underlying principles. In terms of Marshall's process, solving these problems will often represent steps 1 and 2; and sometimes, along with discussion in the text, steps 3 and 4 as well. (I leave you to do step 5 for yourself; and like Marshall, I have often had recourse to step 6.)
- The terminology of economic theory is placed in boxes of **Key terms** throughout the text. Like the Essential Maths, these definitions, repeated in the Glossary, appear where you will encounter the terms for the first time.
- Where there are **Propositions** and **Assumptions**, of general applicability, these are highlighted in boxes at relevant points in the text.
- From time to time I direct you to additional **Student essay** material available on the companion website.

How to use this book

You might now see that the book is designed to enable you to develop the skill of *thinking like a microeconomist.* That means understanding how to analyse problems of resource allocation, using and interpreting the outcomes of a range of techniques. It involves assimilating a particular worldview, in effect finding an Archimedean point from which we can not only see the whole world, but also work out how to move it. You will find that it begins with an abstract analysis of resource allocation, but its scope gradually expands so that by the end it covers much of human decision making.

As you develop your understanding of economics, the book and the companion website should be a resource to which you return repeatedly as you become increasingly skilled in constructing economic arguments. Sometimes pressure of time means that even good students decide that, instead of working through an argument from its assumptions to their logical conclusion, they will simply learn the conclusion. With simple arguments, little harm may result from doing this; but as arguments become more complex, the weaknesses of such an approach become steadily more apparent. As many of the arguments in the book have been set out as problems for you to solve, you should find it relatively easy to identify what you do and do not understand in an argument, and so gradually deepen your understanding of the key principles. In many ways, this can be described as a time allocation problem, as it involves deciding how best to use your time in order to achieve the objective of passing an exam – and this is a good example of a resource allocation problem of the sort that we shall analyse in considerable detail in Part II of the book.

Structure of the book

Taking Parts I–III of the book together, we will meet the concept of the perfect market and examine the outcomes of market behaviour, given that no single buyer or seller has the ability to change either the quantity traded or the price at which the good is traded. We show that when such a market is in equilibrium, it is impossible to find a buyer and a seller willing to enter into a transaction at the existing market price. All feasible (welfare-improving) transactions take place, and so there is no final allocation of goods that could improve on the market outcome. Such a market therefore serves as a benchmark: throughout the remainder of the book, as we extend and qualify our market analysis, we will repeatedly compare the outcomes achieved under alternative assumptions about market behaviour with the outcome that would have emerged had the market been perfect. This allows us to estimate the costs, if any, of deviations from the assumptions necessary for perfect markets.

We complete our discussion of perfect markets in Part V, where we consider the economy as a system. We define a general equilibrium – a situation in which there is simultaneously an equilibrium in every product and in every input market – as a set of market-clearing prices, at which, without making someone worse off, it is impossible: (1) to alter the use of factors of production within a firm; or (2) to reallocate resources between firms in an industry; or (3) to reallocate resources between industries so as to change the mix of outputs across firms; or (4) to allow consumers to exchange goods in any sort of private (non-market) exchange. In a system in which all markets are perfect, all inputs are used with maximum efficiency.

In spite of all this effort devoted to the analysis of perfect competition, it describes an idealized market structure, which we never expect to observe. An important assumption, necessary for the derivation of the result that in the long run all supernormal profits will be eliminated, is that there are no impediments to setting up (or closing down) a business. The opposite of perfect competition, at least with respect to the extent of competition among producers, is monopoly, which we discuss at the start of Part IV. In a monopoly, there is only one firm producing the good. We show that a monopolist, seeking to make as much profit as possible, will always produce a less than optimal output, selling it for a higher price than if there were to be perfect competition in the industry. As a result of the monopoly being in place, people who buy, or who wish to buy, the good certainly feel worse off than they would if there were perfect competition.

The second half of Part IV asks what might happen were only a small number of firms able to engage in production. This is oligopoly, an intermediate case between monopoly and perfect competition, and perhaps one that seems immediately relevant to analysis of markets as they exist in practice. After showing how we can adapt our analysis of monopoly markets to conditions of oligopoly, we introduce tools of game theory to explore further how firms respond in situations where they have only a few competitors. Game theory is a branch of mathematics that allows us to examine how a group of decision makers should behave when the decisions that each makes have an impact on the well-being of other members of the group.

The remainder of the book does not set aside the standard model, but should be understood as an exploration of some important extensions. Part VI examines individual behaviour, including an introduction to recent developments in behavioural economics; while Part VII extends our use of game theory. In Part VI, we ask a series of questions, and answer them using the techniques developed in the derivation of the standard model in order to demonstrate the flexibility of the approach. We think about the demand for goods that are staple products, but also the value of goods that might be consumed to demonstrate wealth. We consider whether it might be sensible to replace money as the resource that limits consumption with time, which can be transformed into money through work. In Part VII, we develop game theoretic models that help us understand the nature of the interactions between the members of a group when some of them have information that would benefit others. We show how uninformed participants might use observation of others' behaviour to infer something about the underlying state of the world, thereby demonstrating that someone who has information which has value in the market might be willing to use up resources simply to convey this information credibly.

We conclude with a brief review in which we suggest that economics may gradually become less concerned with analysis of resource allocation than with the methods used in allocating resources. The utilitarian concept of rationality, central to this book, will be modified, as a result of which optimization will no longer be such a clearly defined goal as it might seem to students who read only the first few chapters of this book. Economists may even find that they are able to offer normative advice, telling people about how they should choose in order to live the good life, in which case the gap between economics and moral philosophy would shrink substantially. None of this is new: Adam Smith did exactly that in his two greatest works, *The Theory of Moral Sentiments* and *The Wealth of Nations*, written well over 200 years ago.[1]

Online learning resources

The companion website (www.palgrave.com/mochrie) contains further resources, which you should also find helpful:

- In the **Student essay bank** you will find selected essays written by students on interesting real-world topics. The essays act as examples of good writing to inspire your own academic work, and also help shed light on the relevance and applicability of microeconomics to everyday life.
- Summary answers to the **By yourself** questions in the book are given in a **Solutions manual**.
- As well as the questions in this book, there is a **Multiple choice question bank** on the website to allow you to confirm the extent of your understanding of the chapter content.
- The **Glossary** is a compilation of all of the **Key terms** introduced in the book.

Thanks to this design, you should find the book to be rather like an extended conversation with someone who already understands economics; or at least, to extend the stew metaphor, it should provide you with your own recipe book. Just as you need to do much more than read a few recipe books to be a good cook, so you need to develop problem-solving skills to be a good economist.

---

1   One issue of ethical concern, on which several economists have written, is the emergence of Fairtrade certification. Scott Galbraith's piece in the online student essay bank is quite a sympathetic treatment, and sets out many of the principles while being alert to the limitations of these arrangements. You will find Scott's essay (and those of other students) on the companion website for this book, at: **www.palgrave.com/mochrie.**

Online student essay bank

There are a wide range of student essays both integrated into and offered as an additional resource for this book. These essays, written by undergraduate students, act as examples of good academic writing, relating economic principles to aspects of everyday life, and thereby shedding light on the wider relevance and usefulness of microeconomics.

All the student essays are available to read in full on the companion website for the book (www.palgrave.com/mochrie). They are also tied to the book content, with footnotes explaining their relevance to theories and topics discussed on specific pages (see below).

Essay title	Page reference in book
With the rapid growth of the Fair Trade movement, how do rational consumers allow ethics to influence their decisions when maximising utility, through the consumption of Fair Trade coffee? (*Scott Galbraith*)	p. xxx
Why do consumers spend more on gasoline than they have to? (*Fredrik Hansen*)	p. 10
Time allocation and the importance of volunteering (*Lukas Gotzelmann*)	p. 39
Flat rate taxation in Bulgaria (*Anastasia Stoyanova*)	p. 52
Giving to the homeless (*Conor Morgan-Hughes*)	p. 80
What are the differences in consumer theory between consumers who regularly update their mobile handsets and those consumers who choose to wait and upgrade their handsets every few years? (*Tristan Blümli*)	p. 129
Carrier bags minimum pricing effect on consumers (*Calum MacPherson*)	p. 135
Does National Minimum Wage reduce poverty? (*Anne-Marie Gardner*)	p. 182
Why do restaurants in the United States offer significantly larger serving sizes than those provided by their counterparts in the United Kingdom? (*Andrew Turton*)	p. 235
Why do governments nationalize failing businesses at the tax payer's expense? (*Stephen Ricca*)	p. 246
Why is mobile money (M-PESA) a huge success in Kenya? (*Vivian Wanjiku*)	p. 279
How does the new music economy work? (*James Murray*)	p. 282
Why do budget airlines offer free loyalty cards to regular customers? (*Charlotte Lovell*)	p. 295
Why do rail companies offer such a large range of tickets and prices for the same journey? (*Jeremy Cottingham*)	p. 297
Students in Assessed Workshops: An analysis of their behaviour as economic agents (*Andreea Piriu*)	p. 335
Employees' differing payment choices on bank holidays; an economic analysis (*Connor Godsell*)	p. 463
Rental prices in Norway (*Malin Bjaroy*)	p. 469
Utility maximization over time in regard to durable and consumable goods (*Witu Willmann*)	p. 474
Whatever happened to the students who would quote the great novelists at each other in arguments? (*Diarmuid Cowan*)	p. 493

(Continued)

Message to lecturers

The organization of the material

The book is divided into seven parts, and is intended to provide enough material for a two-semester course. The arguments contained in the book and the accompanying material can only be absorbed through the most careful, active reading. Typically, only the outline of an argument being presented is to be found in the text. Wherever I have deemed it useful and appropriate, important points in arguments are left as exercises so that students must develop their understanding by completing these. While the companion website has guidance to all of these questions, my expectation is that students should be able to follow the arguments in the text up to the point where the exercises are presented; that they should then be able to complete the majority of the exercises (perhaps with some hints); and that they will then be able to reflect fully on what they have done by reading the commentary that follows as the text continues. Very often the exercises will require students to complete numerical examples or to explore the mathematical properties of applied models. These take students to the point at which I felt I could 'burn the mathematics', with the commentary intended to place the mathematical argument within the broader, conceptual modelling of economic theory.

To achieve this more effectively, I have tried to integrate the acquisition of mathematical knowledge with the development of economic theory. I assume familiarity with the basics of algebraic manipulation, but introduce the main concepts – especially the measurement of rates of change and elasticities, and the solution of optimization problems using differential calculus – which everyone studying economics at this level needs to understand. I do not claim that the book can replace textbooks in mathematics, but by placing 'just in time' primers in the text, at the point where students first meet the ideas, I have tried to reduce as far as possible the gap between the development of economic theory and the expression of ideas in mathematical form. While there is some use of constant elasticity of substitution functions rather than the special case of the Cobb–Douglas functions, I have generally sought to find a path that avoids use of mathematical complexity. For example, I make very limited use of exponential and logarithmic functions, even though this restricts the functional forms that I can use in problem sets. In effect, I have consciously decided to restrict the range of mathematical tools that we introduce, in order to use those that do appear in some depth.

In my own teaching, I frequently tell students that I will know that they understand an economic argument well if they are able to draw me a diagrammatic representation. From time to time students admit to me that while they are able to draw the diagram that I wish to see, and that they can pick out two or three points in it, they are then surprised when I talk about the diagram in class and they realize just how much they have missed out. The diagrams in the textbook are very important, but even more important is that students should learn how to construct and interpret them by themselves. It is only then, I find, that it becomes clear that they have truly passed through the stage of developing the mathematical argument and started to think in terms of economic concepts once again.

The structure of the book

The division into seven parts follows a relatively standard pattern.

- Part I (Chapters 1–2) introduces many of the essential concepts of economic theory, develops examples of markets, and demonstrates some characteristics of behaviour in perfect markets.
- Part II (Chapters 3–9) develops a model of economic decision making for people.
- Part III (Chapters 10–14) firstly replicates this for firms, and then concludes by applying our model of individual decision making in understanding behaviour in markets.
- Part IV (Chapters 15–19) introduces principles of game theory in the context of strategic interaction between firms.
- Part V (Chapters 20–23) covers material on general equilibrium and welfare.
- Part VI (Chapters 24–27) looks at developments of the theory of individual behaviour, including the incorporation of risk, and also behavioural economics.
- Part VII (Chapters 28–30) features more advanced game theory, including the analysis of games with imperfect information, spatial differentiation, and auctions.

This sequence follows the way I currently structure my own course over two semesters. I have attempted to ensure that each chapter has enough content for it to be introduced satisfactorily in a two-hour lecture. I cover almost all of Parts I–IV in the first semester (setting a few topics from later Parts as end-of-semester student projects), and leaving the more advanced Parts V–VII for the second semester. (The one part of the argument that I consider to be optional is Chapter 9, which contains a mathematical summary of the core argument, and so is more technically demanding than the rest of the argument.) My experience has been that allowing for some revision of principles covered in the first semester, this material is more than sufficient for a very comprehensive teaching programme. However, there are many other ways to use the book to suit the structure of your course (as illustrated in Figure P.1).

The book is conceived as comprising a very compact core and a range of topics that might be treated in more or less detail. The core of the argument consists of all of Parts I–III, as well as chapters selected from Parts IV and VII (to cover the analysis of partial equilibrium in a single, competitive market, along with techniques of game theory). There is more emphasis on game theory in the core, as defined here, than is perhaps ordinarily the case, but this reflects my conviction that game theoretic concepts are now so central to economic theory that their introduction should be brought forward as far as possible. Material outside the core does not extend the range of techniques, but instead demonstrates the extent to which the key techniques can be applied to more realistic problems.

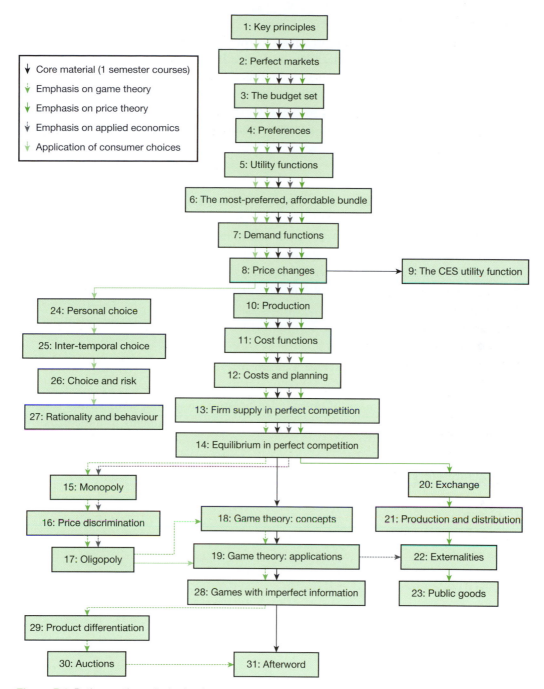

Figure P.1 Pathways through the book

Single-semester courses

A single-semester course could be designed to cover the core material of the book. This pathway (denoted by the solid black line in Figure P.1) would introduce the concept of the mixed strategy, emphasizing that such strategies are probability distributions over actions. It would also touch on the refinement of sub-game perfection within extensive games. I would conclude the course with a discussion of games of imperfect information, illustrating some simple examples of Bayesian equilibria; and this would draw on Chapter 28 from Part VII.

Courses with a specific focus

While I have generally chosen to cover the whole of Parts I–III, as Figure P.1 suggests, I can conceive of many different ways of ordering the remaining material. For example, discussion of all of Part VI (Chapters 24–27) could follow on from lectures on Part II as a series of applications of consumer choice, as shown by the pale green line; while the green dashed line (with all of Part VII following Part IV directly) shows a more suitable route for a course with more emphasis on game theory. Similarly there are possible pathways that highlight price theory and applied economics.

Additional teaching resources

The companion website (www.palgrave.com/mochrie) offers a range of further materials to support your teaching, including:

- **Lecturer testbank** – a set of open-ended questions requiring short answers, which could be assigned for assessments and which encourage students to understand the underlying theory.
- **Lecturer manual** – guideline answers to the testbank questions.
- **Lecture slides** – chapter by chapter.

part

I

Markets in context

We are immersed in economic activity. Every time we make a decision about how to use limited resources – our money, or our time, for example – that choice is potentially a matter for economic analysis. Chapter 1 therefore begins by setting out a simple, but abstract, argument about how we might usefully analyse individual decisions. As well as individual decisions, economic activity also involves interactions involving several decision makers in markets for goods and services. We consider several simple examples of realistic markets, in which we should be able to imagine ourselves participating, which demonstrate the variety of market environments. We develop the simple, but abstract, economic concept of a market, defined as a mechanism for the exchange of resources.

Throughout this book, we will repeatedly switch between thinking about individual decision makers and thinking about their market interactions. Our arguments will often be abstract, but they should always allow us to understand real behaviour rather better. In Part I, we will think more about market interactions than about individual decision making, partly because in Parts II and III we shall analyse the standard model of resource allocation within microeconomics before turning back to market behaviour at the end of Part III. Without this preliminary discussion of markets, in which we introduce the concepts of supply and demand, it would be very easy to overlook the fact that the ultimate purpose of our analysis of individual decision making is to prepare us for a more complete analysis of market outcomes than we are able to present at the moment.

1

Key principles

What we do in this chapter

Throughout this book, we will treat *economics* as the study of how people allocate resources. In this chapter, we start off by thinking what that might mean – how we use our time, and how we might start to develop useful arguments. As soon as possible, we introduce a very important rule to which we shall return repeatedly: the *equi-marginal principle*. This is a condition that must hold when people have solved their resource allocation problem, applying their resources to their most productive uses.

Resource allocation frequently takes place within *markets*, with buyers and sellers exchanging goods and services for money. We outline principles for the economic analysis of a market, defining the concept of *market clearing*, which occurs when the quantity that sellers offer equals the amount that buyers demand. To illustrate how markets might operate, we conclude the chapter with examples of the variety of *market structures* in which goods and services can be traded, using examples that will often be familiar from everyday life.

1.1   The value of microeconomics

Why are you reading this? Only a few people open up a textbook and start reading it from the beginning. Perhaps you are engaged in displacement activity just now, on an evening when you are trying to avoid completing an assignment. Or maybe you are panicking on the night before you sit an exam, having persuaded yourself that you know nothing about economics, and so have at last opened the book that you bought in the first week of the course. Or maybe you are simply curious to read this introductory material as it precedes sections that you have been assigned as reading. Whichever of these it might be, the important point is that *you have made a choice* to read this paragraph. And we shall argue throughout this book that wherever people choose one action from all those which are available to them, then this choice is potentially a subject for microeconomic analysis.

I begin with a bold claim, which I will not justify: that among the social sciences, economics is unique in its conviction that *human behaviour is always purposeful*. In thinking about why you choose to read this paragraph, we may assume that you have chosen freely. Economics claims that your chosen action stems from a belief that there is no better way to spend your time at this precise moment than to read these exact words. Perhaps in five minutes' time, something will have changed – a friend might have phoned and you might have put the book down once again to talk or to go out to meet him or her. But just for now, reading this introduction is what you have decided to do.

We should perhaps add that reading this book is the best thing that you can do in the context of being required to complete a course in microeconomic theory. Your decision to study economics is here a part of the environment that shapes the payoffs to your actions. Given the book's content and format, it is likely to make considerable intellectual demands on you – enough, certainly, to deter all but the most determined amateur. Without the prospect of an examination in the subject, almost everyone would consider the *cost* of reading this book to exceed the *benefits* from doing so. Only economics students, specifically those who have been told that they must read this book, act *rationally* in reading it, in the sense that it is only they who can identify potential benefits that are greater than the costs. We can generalize from this simple observation: *people choose actions that maximize benefits (net of costs)*.

This is not a complete explanation of your choice to read this page. Not every student's interest in economics is purely instrumental, beginning and ending with its value as a source of academic credit. I have had countless discussions with students about how to use economic principles to understand a wide variety of social phenomena. Although it is thirty years since I first picked up an economics textbook, I can still remember the argument in it – about the nature of sunk costs – that first caught my attention. Consider this example.

> *Suppose that a firm bought a machine tool for £750,000 last year, but that a new method of production has now been developed, so that the machine has no resale value and new machines can produce the same output more cheaply. The purchase price is then a sunk cost in the sense that it cannot be recovered. It should play no part in the firm's decisions about how to use the machine. It would be wrong for the firm to argue thus: since the money was spent recently, we should not mothball or scrap the machine, but instead recover the investment costs by using it to make and sell output. Such an argument would fail to take into account that, looking to the future, the firm should write off its investment as soon as the purchase and use of new machinery would increase profits. The concept of sunk costs leads us to the conclusion that in economics, what has been done cannot be undone: bygones are bygones.*

When I first read this argument, it immediately seemed entirely obvious to me, yet before that moment it had never occurred to me – or at the very least, it had never occurred to me in the way that it was then presented. It seemed at once quite mundane and yet entirely novel that when we make a decision we should always look to the future, to what our actions might change, rather than to the past, so that our actions justify past decisions. That was the meaning of the conclusion, 'Let bygones be bygones.' I still remember that moment because it demonstrated exactly what a good economic argument does, transforming the way that we think about particular problems.

Coming back to why you are reading these pages, let me suggest one reason for writing this book. I want to present an introduction to microeconomic theory in such a way that, for at least a few readers, it will be the start of a lifetime of engagement with microeconomics and the economic way of looking at the world; and that somewhere in this textbook there will be arguments memorable enough to capture their attention and imagination. I hope that you might find this happening as you read these pages; and, even if you don't, that you will at least find the material you require to enable you to approach your exams feeling confident that you will pass them.

1.1.1   Microeconomics and resource allocation

Assuming that behaviour is purposeful, we shall explore economics as a way of thinking about the behaviour of people, businesses, and organizations. We do not seek to define what those purposes are, or indeed what they should be: those are more typically concerns of psychology or moral philosophy. Nor are economists, unlike sociologists or political scientists, typically interested in the social factors that might affect choice. Instead, economists tend to assume quite general objectives – perhaps that people wish to be as happy as possible, or that firms wish to maximize profits. They then consider the resources that people or firms might possess and use to enable them to achieve those objectives. Lastly, they investigate how those resources should best be used.

We might say that microeconomics is the study of choice. You have chosen to read this book, which is a choice in the sense that we use the term in microeconomics. But it may be more fruitful to define microeconomics as the study of resource allocation. You have only a finite amount of time available in a day or a week, or even a year. There are many ways in which you can spend, or allocate, that time, of which reading this book is only one. According to the theory of resource allocation that we shall develop, every chosen resource allocation should be economically *efficient*, in the sense that there should be no alternative that might enable people to achieve their objectives more fully.

1.1.2 The equi-marginal principle

We shall assume that there is some measure of both benefits and costs associated with every action or activity that we might choose or engage in. We shall assume that both benefits and costs can be measured on a single scale, such as monetary or time values. We shall also assume that activities are variable in intensity, so that it is possible to alter their level very slightly. For example, suppose that there are only two activities open to you just now: surfing the Web or reading this book. You can choose to vary the amount of time that you spend on each by a few seconds. We refer to these small changes in the level of an activity, increasing or reducing it by a few seconds, as being **changes at the margin**. Generally, in microeconomic analysis, we are interested in changes in both benefits and costs at the margin. For the moment, though, let us say that we are only interested in the marginal benefit of participation in an activity. If we know how the marginal benefits of time spent surfing the Web and reading this book change as we vary the time spent on each, then we can work out how intensely to engage in each of them.

> **Changes at the margin** Very small changes in the level of an activity.

Suppose that starting from your current time allocation, you expect to benefit more from increasing time spent surfing the Web than from increasing time spent reading this introduction. You should then reduce your engagement in reading the book (and/ or increase your time surfing the Web). The gain from increased time surfing the Web outweighs the loss from reading less. Similarly, if the marginal benefit from surfing the Web is less than the marginal benefit from reading this introduction, then you should allocate more time to reading the book (and/or reduce your time on the Web). If the marginal benefit of time spent on both activities is equal, though, you should find that any alteration in your time allocation reduces the total benefits derived from these activities, and so you have no reason to change your participation in either. The **equi-marginal principle** here takes the form that the marginal benefits of alternative uses of a resource should be equal.

> **Equi-marginal principle** A rule that, when the resource is being used as effectively as possible, the ratio of marginal benefits to costs will be the same across all alternative uses of the resource.

We can extend the discussion by allowing for activities having costs as well as benefits. Suppose that reading a page on the Web takes one minute, while reading a page of this textbook takes five minutes. These are the (time) costs of the activities. How should we now apply the equi-marginal principle? If the benefit from reading a Web page and reading a page of the book were equal, then in the time taken to read one page of the book, you might read five Web pages, and browsing would yield more benefits. But if the benefit from reading one more page of the book were to be five times the benefit of accessing a Web page, then the benefit from a minute spent reading the textbook would be equal to the benefit of a minute spent surfing. At the margin, the return to each unit of time is equal, and, intuitively, this seems equivalent to the outcome of the previous argument. This is not the place to set out the detail of the argument, but we can summarize the equi-marginal principle as follows (Principle 1.1):

Principle **1.1**

When the ratio of the marginal benefit to the marginal cost is equal across all uses of a resource, it is impossible to reassign resources and increase the total benefits of activity.

The equi-marginal principle is extremely important. Developing our understanding of how it affects choice will take up most of Parts II, III, and V, where we consider the insights that it provides into the behaviour of consumer, the cost-minimizing behaviour of firms and the organization of the economy. In the other parts of the book, where it is not obviously central, it is still present in the background, understood as being important without attention needing to be drawn to it.

1.1.3   Markets

The application of the equi-marginal principle is central to the explanation of individual decision making in economics. In microeconomics, we are also very interested to understand more about the interactions between decision makers that involve the mutually beneficial exchange of resources. The standard modelling tool for such analysis is the **market**.

> **Market** An abstraction from the physical concept of a place and a time at which buyers and sellers of a good or a service meet to take part in exchanges.

Simply carry out a Websearch for images of markets and you will find many examples of people meeting for one of two purposes: either to buy or to sell a relatively narrow range of goods, typically fruit and vegetables. In economics, we abstract from the concept of a market as a physical location bringing together willing buyers and sellers, and instead treat the market as a way of understanding transactions involving the purchase and sale of a single good. The typical image of a market stall shows it laden with many different types of fruit: apples, bananas, citrus fruits, tomatoes, and so forth. In our economic analysis, though, there will be distinct markets for each of these. In each market, there will be two sides: buyers seeking the goods and sellers bringing those goods to market. Thinking about the market for apples, for example, we might expect it to be very closely related to the market for pears – as apples and pears have very similar uses, someone might choose to buy pears instead of apples. Equally, we might consider it sensible not to talk about a single market for apples, but rather a market for a specific variety of apples, since there are over 8,000 varieties grown around the world. We also have considerable freedom in defining the geographical limits of the market. We may identify the market for apples in a single town, in a region of a country, in the whole country, or even globally. How we define *the market* simply depends upon the nature of the analysis which we wish to carry out.

Just as the equi-marginal principle is an important concept in analysis of individual behaviour, so the concept of **market clearing** is essential to understanding market behaviour. In ideal, or perfect, markets, all transactions will take place at a single price, and the total quantity of the good that sellers bring to the market will match exactly the total quantity that buyers seek to purchase. We will derive

> **Market clearing** A situation in which potential sellers offer the quantity of a good that buyers wish to purchase.

the property of market clearing more formally in Chapter 2. Intuitively, though, it is reasonable to expect that in every market buyers will try to pay the lowest possible price, while sellers will charge the highest possible price. While buyers try to push the price down, sellers try to push the price up. Market clearing occurs where those forces cancel each other out.

Suppose that there is a single price charged for all transactions, but that some sellers cannot find willing buyers at that price. The quantity supplied to the market is greater than the quantity demanded. These sellers who cannot find buyers will reduce the price that they charge, and so will make sales. But this will leave other sellers unable to make sales, and so they too will cut the price that they charge.

In the same way, if there are some buyers who cannot find willing sellers at the single price ruling in the market, then the quantity *supplied* to the market is less than the quantity *demanded*. These buyers who cannot find sellers will increase the price that they offer to pay until they find willing sellers. But this will leave other buyers unable to make their desired purchase, and so they too will increase the price that they offer.

The higher the price of a good, the more costly it is to acquire, and the greater its value when measured in terms of other goods. The logic of the equi-marginal principle is that people will want to use less of an expensive good. As its price rises, demand for it in the market will fall, while the quantity brought to the market will increase. **Excess supply** causes the price of the good to fall, reducing the excess supply. **Excess demand** causes the price to rise, reducing the excess demand. We now have the basis for our definition of market clearing (Principle 1.2).

> **Excess supply** A situation in which potential sellers offer more of a good than buyers wish to purchase.
>
> **Excess demand** A situation in which potential sellers offer less of a good than buyers wish to purchase.

---

*Principle **1.2***

All transactions in a specific market take place at a single **market price***, for which the quantity of the good brought to market will be exactly equal to the quantity that potential buyers wish to purchase, so that there is neither excess supply of the good nor excess demand.*

The market-clearing principle is fundamental to the analysis of Parts III and IV, and also underpins much of the material presented in Part VII. Quite simply, there is almost no argument in the book that does not rely at some point on one or other of the equi-marginal and market-clearing principles, or indeed on both of them.

> **Market price** The price at which all transactions completed in a market take place.

1.2   Market environments

Images of markets make us think of situations in which many buyers and sellers of goods come together, so that many exchanges can take place at the same time. There can be substantial differences, especially in the supply side of market environments, which can affect both buyers' and sellers' behaviour, and hence the nature of the market-clearing outcome. On the basis that everyone participates in markets regularly, at least as a purchaser, we set out the principles of organization of several types of market.

From Chapter 3 onwards we shall develop a very abstract model of decision making. We do this only so that we can better understand the ordinary behaviour in which we all engage.

1.2.1   Example: the fruit market

The central fruit market in a large city has more than fifty stalls. Many of these are almost exactly identical: they sell the same range of fruit and vegetables as each other. Members of the public are able to walk around the stalls, stopping from time to time to think about making purchases. Customers will typically point out what they want to buy, with the stall owner selecting items and putting them into a bag.

Let us consider the behaviour in the fruit market during one specific day. We assume that the stall owners purchased supplies from a wholesale market earlier in the day, and so have fixed quantities that they can sell. We shall also assume that they choose prices to ensure that when they close up their stalls at the end of the day there will be no goods left over that they have not been able to sell. That is, there are no supplies wasted because no willing buyers can be found.

By yourself

X1.1   The fruit market is a location in the city.

(a) When considering pairs of goods from the viewpoint of a consumer, it is often useful to distinguish between those that are *substitutes* because either can be used to meet a particular need, and those that are *complements* because they tend to be used together. Give examples of pairs of goods traded in the fruit market that seem likely to be strongly substitutable and pairs that are strongly complementary.

(b) How might a consumer approach the problem of identifying from which of the 50 sellers she wishes to buy goods? We consider here consumers who are making a single visit to the market. In what ways might people's approach differ if they are: (i) very experienced shoppers, who have used the market for several years; and (ii) newly arrived in the city, and visiting for the first time?

(c) How easy might it be for stallholders to give their stalls unique identities? How might experienced shoppers distinguish between stalls?

(d) Suppose that the market is owned by the city council, which rents space to stallholders. What extent of variation in rents might there be?

(e) How easy would you expect it to be for new stalls to set up in the market?

1.2.2   Example: bakeries on an island

Two bakeries provide all of the bread sold in a small town, located on an island. Each of the bakeries owns a general store, and there is nowhere else that the local inhabitants can buy bread. The bakeries use the same technology, and both make exactly the same range of goods. Every night, the bakers decide how many loaves to bake, with the intention of charging prices the next day to ensure that by late afternoon every loaf has been sold: there will be no waste in production. To emphasize the extent of uniformity in supply, the general stores are next door to each other, with the bakery counters set out in exactly the same way.

By yourself

X1.2   We assume that the bakeries produce a single standard 800 g loaf and that they use the same technology. Presented with a loaf from each bakery, consumers would not be able to distinguish between them.

    (a) How easy would it be for someone recently arrived in the town to confirm whether the experience of buying bread is almost identical at both locations?

    (b) To what extent do you think that each bakery would have loyal customers, who would prefer buying bread from that bakery rather than from its competitor? Would your answer be different if the two shops were at opposite ends of the main shopping street?

    (c) Suppose that one bakery were to increase the price of a loaf by £0.10. Before the price change, both bakeries were selling 1,000 loaves per day. How might sales (at each bakery) change as a result of the price change? What do you conclude about the prices that the two shops will set?

    (d) There are two firms in this market. What characteristics of the market might prevent other bakeries from setting up in business?

1.2.3 Example: cafés in a small town

Suppose two cafés face each other across the main street in the small town where I live. They are the only places there in which I can buy a cup of coffee. Both brew fresh coffee on demand. While the cafés have to maintain a stock of raw materials for making coffee, they do not keep a stock of the finished product, instead producing it to order. There is no limit to the number of cups of coffee that the cafés can sell in any day, so long as they do not run through their stock of supplies. We assume that they set prices at which they can expect to operate close to their physical (seating) capacity, at least during the peak hours for business, between 10.30 a.m. and 3.00 p.m. This town lies about five kilometres from neighbouring villages and their nearest potential competitors.

By yourself

X1.3   We assume that the cafés sell a standard cup of coffee.

    (a) How would someone newly arrived in the town determine the price that they would be willing to pay for a coffee at each café? If there is no difference between the willingness-to-pay measures for the two cafés, what do you conclude about the price that the cafés will set?

    (b) Were one café to reduce its price by £0.10, what would you expect to happen to sales of coffee in the two cafés?

    (c) Suppose that one café decides to differentiate itself from the other one by using certified coffee. (Certification schemes for coffee cover organic production, environmental protection, and fair trade.) Explain how this might affect the cost incurred in making a cup of coffee, but also the price that potential customers might be willing to pay.

    (d) This market is served by two cafés. What characteristics of the market might ensure that no one else decided to set up a third café?

1.2.4   Example: petrol stations in a city

Three petrol stations lie on the route that I usually take while driving to work. Each one is a separate business and each is affiliated to one of the major oil companies, which act as distributors throughout the country. Whichever petrol station I use, I know that the fuel will have been refined at a single plant, owned by a specialist company. While there might be small differences in the range of additives that each of the oil companies insists should go into their fuel, differences in performance are so slight that I have never been able to detect them. Like most drivers, I am free to choose a different petrol station every time I need to buy petrol. All three petrol stations are situated on major roads close to the edge of my town. They therefore all have several competitors within five kilometres. Each petrol station also has large reservoirs of fuel. Given the prices that they charge for petrol, an order to refill these reservoirs can be completed well before they are emptied.[1]

> **By yourself**
>
> **X1.4**   In this case:
> (a) How might we define the market?
> (b) I regularly use all three petrol stations on this route because I find this to be convenient. How might someone who has never driven on this route make decisions about which petrol station to use?
> (c) How might the willingness to pay for fuel at a given petrol station differ between the time when I plan my journey and the time when I turn off the road onto that petrol station's forecourt?
> (d) Suppose that I usually buy about 40 litres of petrol at a time and I notice as I pull onto the forecourt that the petrol station has increased its price by £0.05 per litre. How might that affect my decision about which petrol station I use?
> (e) Suppose that I see no difference in price from the last time I used a particular petrol station. How might this affect my decision making?
> (f) How do you think two petrol stations might sustain a difference in price of £0.05 per litre over a period of a year?

1.2.5   Example: hairdressing in a small town

In the town in which I live there are five hairdressing salons. All offer a similar range of services, but each has a distinctive character. Whether or not there are differences in quality between the services they provide, there are certainly substantial differences in the prices each charges for services that seem to be very similar. Customers tend to make appointments a few days or a few hours in advance. The capacity limit of the businesses will be reached when their diaries for any day are completely filled.

---

1   While it might seem that in this case the law of one price should definitely hold, Fredrik Hansen, a student, demonstrates in his essay that there are in fact persistent differences in prices at different petrol stations, and argues that these are so large that they cannot easily be explained by an argument based on time savings. You can read Fredrik's argument (and other student essays) on the companion website for this book, at **www.palgrave.com/mochrie.**

X1.5   While the range of services provided by the hairdressers is essentially the same, we expect the method of delivery to differ across salons. We say that there is product differentiation across the salons.

(a) To what extent might these salons face competition from businesses in other towns?

(b) Thinking of the measures of willingness to pay and willingness to accept, what might be the effects of allowing product differentiation on choice?

(c) How important do you consider repeat business will be to the success of a salon?

(d) Suppose that the price charged in a salon increases by 10%. What effect might this have on the business of the salon?

(e) Suppose that all five salons cut their prices by 10%. What effect might this have on their business?

(f) Salons might charge different prices for men and women. Why?

1.2.6: Example: rail travel

Once I have made the decision to travel from my house to Edinburgh by train, the only choice that I can make is the time of travel. There is one railway track, and only one company runs trains on it. Of course, on any given train passengers might be paying different prices. Compared with the price that I would pay travelling early in the morning to work when the train is busiest, children, students, older people, more regular travellers, and even I, were I to travel after 9.30 a.m., all pay less. Yet all passengers enjoy the same service. If anything, those travelling during the peak period, who may be obliged to stand in cramped conditions, might experience the lowest quality of service while paying the highest price.

X1.6   Consider the railway service between two cities.

(a) Between most pairs of cities, there is only one train operator. How might the lack of alternative suppliers affect the price that potential buyers will have to pay?

(b) Once a train operator has made a decision to run a service, what is the lowest ticket price that the operator might set for carrying an additional passenger?

(c) Given that there are periods of the day in which there are capacity constraints, how might train operators manage demand at these times? In this case, what might lead to differences in the amounts that passengers would pay to travel on a particular train?

(d) Assume that the operating company sets a standard price for travel on the same day. Give examples of discounts that might be offered to different types of passengers, and discuss the rationale for offering these.

1.2.7 Market structures

The structure of the market is different in each of the examples we have considered here, and in some cases the difference is substantial. For example, with the train company there is very limited direct competition. I do have alternatives when making the journey: I could drive, or take a bus, or cycle, or even run. But there is only one train company. With the petrol stations, there is no uncertainty over the number of suppliers or the quality of the fuel that they sell, but when visiting a given petrol station I cannot know for certain whether the others are selling fuel at the same price, more cheaply, or at a higher price. Once I am on the forecourt of any petrol station, though, it would be unusual were I to change my mind and buy fuel elsewhere. With this example, I have to make a decision without being fully informed about the alternatives.

In comparison, when buying bread or going out for a cup of coffee, the situation is quite different. I can easily become fully informed about prices, and so it might seem reasonable that I should expect to see the same prices. However, there are subtle differences in the production processes. The bakeries cannot change their output during the day, so if one bakery cuts the price without increasing the quantity of bread baked in advance, that bakery will make all of its sales at the start of the day. The other bakery will make its sales at the full price later in the day, when the first bakery has sold all its loaves. Price cutting here has few benefits for the bakeries. For the cafés, the situation is rather different. They wait until an order is placed before producing their output. Neither café wants to set the higher price, so price competition will be very intense.

We therefore see from these examples that we should not expect all markets to be the same. We should also note that the bulk of the differences across the market are likely to be found among the sellers – we would expect individual consumers to have very limited market power. It does not matter much to a local bakery whether I purchase a loaf from that bakery or from its competitor – I have very little effect on the total sales. In the same way, the train operator, the petrol station, the local café, the hairdresser, and the stallholder in the fruit market do not consider it particularly important that they have my custom. However, I would certainly notice the difference if my local train station closed, or if the petrol station that I have used most regularly for the last 18 months closed because of competition from a nearby supermarket that was able to undercut it substantially, or if price competition between the bakeries were eventually to lead to one closing, or even if my preferred hairdresser finally decided that the time had come to shut his shop and spend more time with his grandchildren. When we consider the assumptions required for a perfect market (in Chapter 2), we shall see there are several assumptions about the behaviour of firms, but only one about the people who demand goods and services.

The discussion also suggests that the intensity of competition within a market can differ substantially. It seems reasonable that the train operator, which has a monopoly of supply, should have considerable power in the market and so should be able to make profits. It also seems reasonable that the cafés, even though each has only a single competitor, should face quite intense price competition. The petrol stations, the hairdressers, and the bakery all seem to be in an intermediate stage. The most competitive market, though, is the fruit market. There are many sellers; their prices and goods can be inspected very easily, so buyers should be fully informed; and on any day, suppliers are interested in selling a fixed quantity of output. All of this seems likely to push prices down and to make the market highly competitive. In Chapter 2, such a market will be our starting point.

Summary

In microeconomics, we assume that all behaviour has a purpose, which is to enable the achievement of some objective.

Decision makers choose the actions that maximize benefits (net of costs). We formalize this in the equi-marginal principle, that when the ratio of the marginal benefit to the marginal cost is equal across all uses of a resource, it is impossible to reassign resources and to increase the total benefits of activity.

We analyse the exchange of goods and services in markets. Typically, we wish to identity the market-clearing condition, defined as the price at which goods and services are bought and sold, such that the quantity brought to the market equals the quantity demanded. With market clearing, the good is neither in excess demand nor in excess supply.

We consider markets to be competitive when there are many buyers and sellers, all of whom are perfectly informed.

We consider that sellers have market power if they are able to affect the price charged or the quantity traded. This will often mean that there is limited competition in supply.

Visit the companion website at **www.palgrave.com/mochrie** to access further teaching and learning materials, including lecturer slides and a testbank, as well as guideline answers and student MCQs.

2

Perfect markets

Within microeconomic theory, markets are fundamental structures. We use them to analyse the exchange of goods and services for money between groups of potential sellers, typically businesses, and potential buyers, typically people.

We assume that the buyer and the seller in any transaction act under their own volition. We can therefore rely on the principle of *voluntary exchange*: an exchange will take place only if it makes neither buyer nor seller worse off. The seller's valuation, the *willingness to accept*, can be no greater than the price; while the buyer's valuation, the *willingness to pay*, cannot be less than the price.

We define a *perfect market* in terms of a set of assumptions, which are sufficient to rule out frictions caused by costs of entry into, or exit from, the market, or from the assimilation of information. It follows that in perfect markets the people buying goods and services value them most; and, to that extent, we argue that all markets are *efficient*. We derive four propositions relating to the behaviour of firms supplying a good to a market, the behaviour of the people seeking to buy the good, the price at which all transactions take place, and the quantity of the good which will be traded in the market. These four propositions characterize the *equilibrium* in a perfect market.

2.1 The structure of a market

We have introduced the market as the mechanism by which individual decision makers exchange resources. In this chapter, we define more precisely what we mean by a perfect market, introducing a set of restrictive assumptions, which largely affect the supply of the good and information flows within the market. We consider the interaction between the supply of, and demand for, goods within such a market, confirming that market clearing will occur, given our assumptions.

2.1.1 Consumers and producers

To keep our initial analysis simple, we make many assumptions. This first set of assumptions limits the scope of our analysis:

- We consider markets for final goods and services, which are consumed at the time of purchase. This excludes many markets, including those for:
  - durable goods, such as cars, used over a period of time;
  - inputs used in production, including the labour services provided by workers;
  - intermediate goods and services (produced by one firm, then sold to another firm and used in further production processes); and
  - financial assets, held to generate income or capital gains in future.

- The potential buyers of a particular good or service are individual people.
  - People are purely consumers of goods. They are self-interested, and have a vaguely defined objective of obtaining the greatest possible satisfaction from consumption.
  - We ignore purchases made by groups of people, or by one person on behalf of others. (In particular, there will be no role for families, in which people engage in purchasing and consumption collectively.) People buy goods, and then consume those goods, on their own.
- Goods are brought to the market by firms, or businesses, with each business specializing in the production of a single good.
  - Firms, which produce goods and services, are only interested in making profits.
  - Firms generate income, or *revenue*, from sales (to consumers), but have to pay production costs. Profits are the difference between revenue and costs.
  - We ignore the distribution system for most goods and assume that people buy directly from the producer. (For example, we disregard supermarkets, which sell a wide range of products bought wholesale from manufacturers.)

By yourself

X2.1   Consider the following goods and services. Discuss the extent to which there is likely to be a violation of the assumptions made above when they are traded. (We consider these examples from the perspective of the consumer, or buyer. Remember to include discussion of production by the seller.)

(a) Filling the fuel tank of a car with petrol.

(b) Buying a loaf of bread.

(c) Having a haircut.

(d) Buying a pair of trousers.

(e) Buying a car.

(f) Booking a holiday.

(g) Buying greeting cards, such as for birthdays or Christmas.

(h) Registering for a university degree.

(i) Buying a copy of a creative work, such as a novel, a film, or a music album.

(j) Buying seeds which, when sown, might grow into decorative (rather than edible) plants.

Consideration of the markets for the goods and services in Exercise X2.1 show how much we are abstracting from reality. Our restrictive assumptions are not intended permanently to exclude discussion of such markets. Instead, we start off from the most straightforward examples of markets, obtaining useful predictions about the likely outcome of behaviour in them. Only then will it be possible to extend our analysis.

2.2   The perfect market: assumptions

A perfect market is an environment for the exchange of resources, in which participants, being fully informed about the alternatives open to them, and choosing freely to engage with any one of a large set of potential partners, actively pursue their own interests.

Perfect market A market in which the assumptions of perfect competition all hold.

We understand perfection to be a theoretical formulation, with reality always departing from it in some ways, so that in analysing behaviour in an actual market we do not expect to observe perfection. The two important categories of imperfection, which we explore later in the book, are:

- a small number of participants on one or both sides of the market; and
- barriers to the acquisition of information relevant to market activity.

We shall adopt the set of Assumptions A2, which are sufficient to ensure the elimination of all imperfections in the exchange process.

Assumptions A2

The assumptions of perfect competition:

A2.1 *Product uniformity:* All firms produce a single good or service, and there are no differences in quality between firms' products.

A2.2 *Unrestricted access to technology:* There are many firms that have the ability to enter a market.

A2.3 *Unrestricted scale of activity:* With freedom of entry into, and exit from, the market, new firms can set up operations, and existing firms can change their output or shut down operations without penalty.

A2.4 *(Eventually) diminishing returns to scale:* For every firm, the cost of production increases more quickly than the level of production. (Alternatively, repeatedly increasing output by a set amount, the additional cost of production becomes steadily larger.)

A2.5 *Insignificance of individual demands:* All potential customers have demands that are small relative to the size of the market.

A2.6 *Free access to information:* The cost of acquiring information, both for firms and people, is zero.

Market power A situation in which market participants, by their actions, can affect the quantity traded or the market price.

Taken together, the set of Assumptions A2 seeks to ensure that all sources of market imperfection are eliminated. Note that Assumptions A2.1–A2.4 relate to the nature of the supply of goods rather than to demand for them. This is typical of the market structures, which we analyse. Where participants have **market power**, and so can materially affect the outcome of the exchange process, they will be firms. The demand side will generally be simpler to model because it represents the individual demands of many people.

2.2.1 Product uniformity: implications

Product uniformity The situation in which all units of a good are identical.

We have already discussed in Chapter 1 the assumption of **product uniformity**, arguing that it is necessary to avoid even the perception of difference in quality across suppliers. In the café example, we might think of a standard cup of coffee: there will be no alternatives, and no diversification into the provision of baked goods to go with the coffee. Across all cafés, a customer's experience of ordering a coffee, paying for it while it is made, and then drinking it will be exactly the same.

Uniformity here covers the whole of the experience of consumption. Consider the sales of fuel at a petrol station: because the underlying product is identical, the costs of driving past one petrol station and on to the next alternative may be too high to be worth bearing. Even in the example of the fruit market, there are two obvious ways in which stalls can have some identity: their position and their signage. A stall that is close to the main entrance or perhaps one that is in the centre of the market seems likely to have many more potential customers passing it than one that is close to a wall. In contrast, in the market for hair-dressing, some degree of product differentiation, possibly based on perceived differences in quality of service, seems essential.

By yourself

X2.2   We define fast-moving consumer goods (FMCGs) as items that are purchased repeatedly but in small quantities. There are no long-run contracts, so people are free to switch supplier every time that they make a purchase.
  (a) Discuss the extent to which the market environments discussed in Section 2.2.1 are likely to involve the sale of such goods, and the potential value to the firms in the market of securing regular repeat purchases.
  (b) There are many FMCG industries – such as those for detergents, carbonated water, and toiletries – where firms have established strong brand identities, supported by extensive marketing activity. Why might FMCG markets be particularly susceptible to this form of activity? (Think of the role of repeat purchasing, but also of the impact on consumers of disappointment if they are dissatisfied with their purchase.)
  (c) Tobacco companies have argued against restrictions on marketing activity on the basis that such activity is designed to encourage existing users to switch brands rather than to encourage new users. How reasonable do you consider this claim to be?

2.2.2   Unrestricted access to technology: implications

Even in a simple retail business, such as a market stall, there is a production process – in this case, one involving the purchase of goods in bulk at a wholesale market, their transportation to the retail market, and activities involving the display and sale of goods. In the same way, the owner of a petrol station buys fuel from an oil company and has to be able to store it safely and to deliver it from tanks. Between hair salons, on the other hand, there might easily be substantial differences in the production process, especially in services such as hair colouring.

We shall use the term **technology of production** to denote the exact combination of inputs that are transformed, through the production process, into a quantity of output. As we use the term, 'technology' is rather like the ingredient list for a recipe. Using the example of making a cup of coffee, the inputs will include the building, its fixtures and fittings, the espresso machine for making the coffee, the serving staff, and of course coffee beans, water, and the cup. The **state of technology** describes the firm's capacity to transform such inputs into output: the quantity of inputs required to produce a set level of outputs. As time passes, we expect firms to utilize methods of production that are more efficient. We say that with **advances in technology (technological progress)** firms are able to produce a given level of output with fewer inputs; or that the productivity of the inputs increases.

Technology of production The combination of inputs used in producing a (unit) quantity of output.

State of technology A measure of the inputs required at any time to produce an output unit.

Advances in technology (technological progress) Changes in the state of technology over time.

Profits The difference between revenues and costs.

Costs of production The expenditure that is necessary in order to make sales.

Revenues The income that the seller obtains from sales of goods and services.

We shall argue throughout this book that firms are interested only in maximizing profits. We can think of a firm starting off with a sum of money, using this to purchase inputs, turning those inputs into outputs, and then selling those outputs. At the end of the process, the firm should have recouped its original outlays and be able to start again, preferably with an additional sum of money, its **profits**. The expenditure on inputs constitutes the **costs of production**, while the income received from sales is the firm's **revenues**. Profits are simply the difference: revenues less costs of production. In this approach, the cost of producing a target output depends on the state of technology. Advances in the state of technology reduce the cost of the necessary inputs, so that if the firm can generate the same sales revenue as it did before, its profits will increase.

By yourself

X2.3 Advances in technology rarely occur by accident. Suppose that a firm expects that an advance in technology will not be copied by other firms.
   (a) What effect might we expect more efficient use of resources to have on a firm's production plans?
   (b) How might the advance in technology used by only one firm affect other firms?
   (c) Why might we expect a firm to be willing to pay for the ability to make a technological advance? If we consider technological advances to be a good, how much might firms be willing to pay to achieve them?

X2.4 Suppose that a firm expects that any advance in technology will immediately be disseminated across all other firms in the industry.
   (a) How might we expect firms' production plans to respond?
   (b) Compared with the situation in X2.3, what might happen to the output of the firm that had originated the technological advance?
   (c) How might this affect firms' willingness to pay for the investment need for technological advances?
   (d) What might we conclude about the rate of technological advance in an industry in which all firms obtain unrestricted access to technology, compared with one in which firms are able to use proprietary technology that they can prevent competitors from using?

We might think of firms as facing a choice between: (1) producing a high level of current output and generating immediate profits; and (2) producing a low level of current output in the expectation of higher future profits. The market structure also seems likely to have some effect on each firm's willingness to engage in innovation. From Exercises X2.3 and X2.4, we might conclude that if market imperfections allow firms to restrict access to their own technological advances, they may be able to increase their future profits compared with the situation in which the advances are copied immediately. While perfect markets ensure that all feasible transactions take place, allowing firms to profit from innovations might then increase the number of feasible transactions in future. Recognizing that innovation has benefits beyond the increase in the innovator's profits, society might enable innovators to restrict access to technological advances for a limited period of time. Such arguments are the basis for a variety of intellectual property rights, such as patents and copyright, which in this context constitute market imperfections.

2.2.3 Unrestricted scale of activity: implications

When this assumption holds, firms should be able to adjust both the type and the volume of the inputs that they use without any restrictions. For example, one firm might decide to sell all of its assets, quitting the market entirely. Other firms, believing that the market presents an opportunity to make profits, might choose to start up production and enter the market. It must also be the case that adjusting the scale of activity is costless. In effect, it is not only the market for the products, but also all of the markets for the inputs that firms use, that must be perfect.

To see the difficulties with this, suppose that a petrol station has two storage tanks. The firm can sell both petrol and diesel, but could not simply decide to enter the market for 'advanced' fuel without building a third reservoir. Once built, this reservoir, which is little more than a carefully constructed hole, would sit under the ground. The petrol station could not easily sell it to another firm. The reservoir simply remains in the ground until it is scrapped. The firm would then bear the costs of its removal and destruction. In contrast, the owner of a market stall who believes that there is a sudden increase in consumers' *WTP* for tomatoes can easily increase the proportion of tomatoes in daily purchases and allocate more space on the stall to display this particular product. Even so, we shall assume that the stallholder cannot easily increase the stall's size. The stallholder will have signed a lease and will not immediately be able to change the floor area used for the display of goods.

In a perfect market, we exclude any possibility of fixed costs, which are paid irrespective of the level of input used. The lease of a market stall and the construction (and maintenance) costs of a fuel reservoir are examples of these. Instead, we shall assume that firms will face variable costs for all inputs. We shall also assume that all inputs are perfectly divisible, so that the firm can vary output by very small quantities. This assumption ensures that firms can hire the exact quantity of inputs needed to produce their desired output, given the state of technology.

> **By yourself**
>
> **X2.5**   Suppose that an opportunity arises for a firm to enter a market and start trading, but that the firm is aware that the opportunity is transient. Explain why the existence of entry costs might mean that some opportunities could not be exploited.
>
> **X2.6**   Every summer, soft fruits come into season. Explain how the price that consumers would pay for these goods might change during the summer; how the price that stallholders charge might change; and what happens at the end of the season.

2.2.4 Diminishing returns to scale: implications

We have argued that firms must hire inputs in order to produce outputs. This assumption states that once output reaches a particular level, the addition to inputs necessary for a given increase in output will become larger and larger. For the moment, we shall assume that this assumption holds for all levels of output. If we consider two firms, one of which is already selling more output than the other, the firm that is producing more will use more resources per unit of output, and so will have to charge a higher price per unit to cover its costs. More generally, in these circumstances, we may expect that the price that a firm will charge to cover its costs will increase as it expands its output.

By yourself

X2.7   Assume that Assumptions A2.1–A2.4 hold.
   (a) Explain why smaller firms will always have a lower breakeven price than larger firms, and that larger firms can reduce their breakeven price by reducing their size.
   (b) Assume that firms want to achieve the lowest possible breakeven price. Confirm that with entry being possible, the market will come to be served by a very large number of very small businesses.

The assumption of eventually diminishing returns to scale has an important role to play in our discussion of the standard model of market behaviour. We generally justify it by arguing that there are difficulties in coordinating the use of inputs, which mean that it is possible for a firm to be too large. Where it holds, it ensures that markets cannot easily be dominated by a single firm. In the context of technology of production available to market traders, this assumption seems perfectly reasonable. Retail markets typically are dominated by a few very large firms, rather than very small businesses. The largest of these, such as Walmart and Carrefour, have developed global distribution networks in which there is no obvious problem of diminishing returns to scale.

2.2.5   Insignificance of individual demands: implications

As noted already, the role that people play in a perfect market is much simpler than the role played by firms. We simply assume that there are many people in the market, none of whom has any market power. Where there might be only one train operator serving a pair of cities, the passengers will typically book a few seats on a single train rather than the whole service. In all of the other examples that we have considered so far we expect there to be a constant turnover of customers, with each transaction contributing only a small amount to that firm's total revenues.

2.2.6   Free access to information: implications

Perfect information
A situation in which a person has all the information she or he needs to make a decision.

Frequently, this assumption is stated as **perfect information**. Allowing people to acquire information costlessly, we expect them to find out everything that might guide their behaviour, so that they become perfectly informed. Specifically:

- firms will know how much every potential customer would be willing to pay for a unit of the good;
- people will know how much every firm needs to charge if it is to cover its costs;
- there will be immediate diffusion of every technological advance.

In the set of Assumptions A2, this is probably the assumption that is least credible, at least at the level of descriptive accuracy. The presence of competition in supply ensures that firms have no market power and so cannot try to charge any customer a higher price than that charged by any of its competitors. Were a firm to do this, it would lose sales to other suppliers.

By yourself

X2.8   Consider the two cafés located opposite each other in the main street of a small town. Every day their proprietors, Aimee and Bianca, set boards outside their premises announcing the price at which they intend to sell cups of coffee.

They can set different prices every day.

(a) Given our assumptions, what might we infer about the price that each café would want to charge for a cup of coffee?

(b) How reasonable do you consider it to be that the cost of making each additional cup of coffee will remain constant as output increases?

(c) Suppose that Bianca sees the price that Aimee intends to charge before she sets her own price, and realizes that Aimee's price is higher than the price she herself planned to charge. What might Bianca do? (Bianca wants to make the greatest possible profits.)

(d) Given Bianca decision, what might Aimee notice? How might she respond?

(e) Why might Bianca and Aimee end up competing very intensely with each other? What would you expect to be the outcome of this competition?

The market in Exercise X2.8 is very simple:

- the two cafés have constant and identical costs of making a cup of coffee (at least until they reach some capacity constraint);
- there is uniformity of product (and experience) between the cafés;
- there are many potential customers, all of whom are fully informed and face no costs in switching between cafés;
- both cafés announce the price at which they will make an exchange (avoiding the need for prolonged negotiation over price).

Even with two firms, this structure brings about intense competition in supply. If Aimee announces a price above the minimum that Bianca would charge, then Bianca can undercut it and still make profits. Every potential customer (at least until Bianca's capacity constraint is met) will see that Bianca's coffee is cheaper and will therefore go to Bianca's café. The only way for Aimee to prevent this from happening is to announce that she will charge a price at which Bianca will only just break even, since Bianca will then only match the price (not undercut it). Given that the alternatives are identical, customers will select one randomly. We would then expect the cafés to share the market equally.

In Exercise X1.3, we considered one way in which cafés might be able to differentiate their product: by using certified products. We have also discussed how consumption might be considered to be an experience. Design, for example the use of more informal seating, can add to the experience a little more luxury. Some cafés diversify by using their walls as an art gallery. Others promote live music. Such efforts, intended to allow cafés to differentiate themselves from each other, both reduce the intensity of competition and increase the price that potential customers might pay. Café owners are willing to pay for such activities because they believe that these will lead to an increase not just in revenues but also in profits. As in our discussion of technological advances, it is possible that while outcomes in a perfect market will meet the criteria specified in terms of efficiency, in thinking of the social benefits of exchange it may be desirable to have product differentiation rather than uniformity. Such differentiation makes it more difficult to compare products, however, and also makes the market environment much more complex. Under these circumstances, the presumption that it is possible to assimilate information about the market costlessly becomes still more strained.

2.3   Market clearing: *WTA* = *WTP*

In any transaction, such as the sale of a kilogram of apples or a cup of coffee, a firm provides goods to a person in return for a payment (the price, *p*, defined in terms of money). The higher the price, the more profit made by the firm supplying the good: but the lower the price, the more money the purchaser will still have to buy other goods. All transactions are voluntary, so if the firm insists on receiving a high price, potential buyers might refuse to buy from that firm; while someone who insists on paying only a low price might not be able to find a firm willing to supply goods at that price. We define:

Willingness to accept (*WTA*) The minimum price for which a seller will sell one unit of a good.

- the willingness to accept (*WTA*) as the minimum price at which the firm would bring the good to the market, which cannot be greater than the transaction price, *p*:

$$WTA \leq p \tag{2.1}$$

Willingness to pay (*WTP*) The maximum price that a consumer will pay for one unit of a good.

- the willingness to pay (*WTP*) as the maximum price at which a particular person would buy the good, which cannot be less than the transaction price:

$$WTP \geq p \tag{2.2}$$

Economic surplus The difference between *WTP* and *WTA*; the social benefit from a transaction.

- the economic surplus associated with this transaction as the difference between the buyer's and the seller's value of the good, so that if Conditions 2.1 and 2.2 are satisfied:

$$WTP - WTA \geq 0 \tag{2.3}$$

We expect to find economic surplus every time that a buyer and a seller complete a transaction. Expressions 2.1–2.3 emphasize the requirement in voluntary exchange that both buyer and seller will be better off – or, at the very least, no worse off – on completing it. Otherwise, transactions would happen in which people acted against their own interests.

We have considered a single transaction, perhaps giving the impression that potential buyers and sellers typically negotiate the price. This might be necessary if market participants have to seek out partners or if the good being traded is unique. Consider websites such as Craigslist or Gumtree, which exist to make it easier for potential buyers to find sellers. Some potential sellers use such sites because they are not businesses and do not regularly make sales. Although sellers will often indicate a price that they would definitely accept, a buyer can make a lower offer and probe whether or not the announced price is really the seller's willingness to accept.

2.3.1   The apple market example

Consider a very simple market for apples. It is close to the end of the day, and there are five farmers, each of them with 1 kg of apples left to sell. There are also five potential buyers, each wishing to buy 1 kg of apples.

By yourself

X2.9   Suppose that the *WTA* for each farmer is different: 0.5, 0.75, 1, 1.5, and 2. Similarly, suppose that for the potential buyers the *WTP* values are: 1.75, 2.25, 2.5, 3, and 3.25.

(a) Suppose that potential buyers are matched to potential sellers in the order listed. Explain why all five transactions will take place.

(b) If all sales took place at a single price, $p = 1.8$, what would the outcome be?

(c) Suppose that, after matching, it is possible for any of the buyers to engage in resale. What opportunities, if any, might there be? After resale, what characterizes the valuations of the people who have apples compared with those who do not?

(d) Why is it credible that all transactions might take place at the price $p = 1.8$?

We do not usually expect prices simply to be announced, or that bargains will be matched through a mechanism of the form suggested in Exercise X2.9a. The exercise suggests an important rule: if transactions, including resale, continue until all feasible transactions have taken place, then across the market, after all feasible sales have taken place, the people who end up owning (and consuming) the apples will be those who place the highest (monetary) value on them. Every transaction that would yield an economic surplus occurs, but no other transaction does. This is consistent with market activity leading to a socially optimal distribution of goods. And in this particular exercise, this occurs even when we try to limit opportunities to seek out the best trading partner, making the outcome more difficult to realize.

Building on this example, consider Figure 2.1, which illustrates exchange in a similar situation. Suppose 12 firms each offer to sell exactly 1 kg of apples, and 12 potential buyers each seek to buy that quantity. We order firms by ascending *WTA*, and people by descending *WTP*. The first transaction is feasible, since $WTP(1) > WTA(1)$: the highest *WTP* exceeds

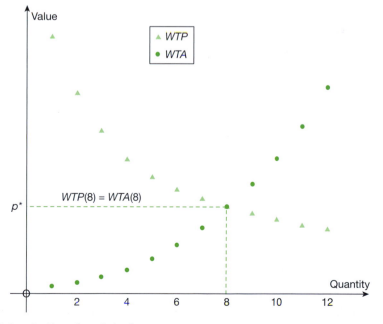

Figure 2.1 Determination of market price

the least *WTA*. We can confirm the following results, assuming that the buyer and seller in each transaction will negotiate the sales price between them:

- Exactly 8 transactions will take place.
- All 8 transactions occur at price $p^* = WTP(8) = WTA(8)$.
- The seller for whom $WTA = p^*$ obtains no surplus.
- The buyer for whom $WTP = p^*$ obtains no surplus.
- If more than 8 transactions take place, then, allowing resale, we could increase the total surplus from trade.

Notation: The '*' symbol will appear throughout the book to indicate that a variable quantity or value is at its equilibrium (or optimal) value.

A note on method. We use the technique of proof by contradiction. This means assuming an outcome that we do not expect, and then showing that it is actually impossible for it to occur.

- *Suppose that all transactions take place at a price $p > p^*$.*
  - There can no more than 7 willing buyers (and so 7 transactions).
  - An 8th transaction cannot take place at a higher price than $p^* = WTP(8)$.
  - There is at least one farmer, for whom $WTA \leq p^*$, who has still to sell her apples.
  - An 8th transaction will definitely take place, at price, $p \leq p^*$.
  - It is therefore not possible that all transactions take place at price $p > p^*$.

By yourself

X2.10 Confirm that the following statements are false. (You may use the technique of proof by contradiction.)
(a) All transactions take place at a price $p < p^*$.
(b) There will be some transactions that take place at price $p > p^*$.
(c) There will be some transactions that take place at price $p < p^*$.

X2.11 Suppose that people and firms agree to exchanges at a range of prices. Some prices are higher than p^* and some are lower. The transactions have still to conclude.
(a) Show that there is at least one buyer who can find a better bargain.
(b) Show that there is at least one seller who can find a better bargain.
(c) Hence confirm that no buyer whose $WTP < p^*$, and no seller whose $WTA > p^*$, will complete the proposed transaction.

In these exercises, we must assume that there are very few frictions in the market: in Exercise X2.11c, for example, it has to be possible to observe the prices being agreed in other transactions, and to respond to these immediately. With perfect information, both buyers and sellers, made any offer, know whether or not they should accept it and whether they will find a better one. Once again, a set of exchanges take place at the market-clearing price, p^*, and these are the only ones that will be completed. In Figure 2.1, we might think of 8 firms and 8 people coming to the market. The total quantity supplied in the market, given the market price, will just equal the total quantity demanded. The market will clear.

By yourself

X2.12 Given the market price, p^*, suppose that one seller, for whom $WTA < p^*$, insists on a price just above the market price. What would you expect to happen? Why do you think that no seller would do this?

X2.13 Repeat X2.12 for a seller considering accepting a price just below p^*.

2.4 Individual demand

We have defined people's willingness to pay for a single unit of a good or service. It is much more realistic to allow people to demand any quantity of a good – not just a whole number of units, but also fractions of a unit. We define the individual demand for a good as the quantity that one person will seek to purchase at a given price.

Think of one person's demands for cups of freshly roasted coffee, which we suppose sell at a price of €2.50 in the café that one particular consumer frequents. In Figure 2.2, we can see both individual demand and *WTP*. The consumer, Zahra, will purchase more and more cups of coffee so long as her *WTP* for another cup is at least the market price. From the diagram, we can see that Zahra would be willing to pay €5.00 for the first cup of coffee, €4.00 for a second one, €3.00 for a third one, and only €2.00 for a fourth one. Given that the café that she frequents has set a price of €2.50, we predict that Zahra will buy 3 cups of coffee every day.

In Figure 2.2, we show Zahra's *WTP* for each cup of coffee by a green circle, emphasizing that in this case she cannot buy a fraction of a cup of coffee. The vertical line starting from the dot shows the range of prices at which Zahra will demand a particular number of cups of coffee. In this case, if the café set any price between €2.01 and €3.00, Zahra would demand exactly 3 cups. Her demand for cups of coffee therefore appears in the diagram as a series of steps, with demand decreasing by 1 cup in each. Note that whereas we calculate *WTP* only for the standard unit, here a cup of coffee, we can calculate the quantity that the consumer will demand for any fixed price. In the diagram, consumer demand takes us from the vertical (price, or value) to the horizontal (quantity) axis, as illustrated by the line showing that Zahra demands 3 cups of coffee when the price is set to €2.50. Note that we can also define the willingness to pay for an additional cup of coffee, so that here the value of the 4th cup of coffee (or 1 more cup after consuming 3) may be written $WTP(4) = 2.00$.

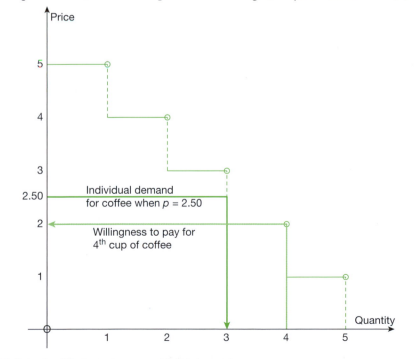

Figure 2.2 Zahra's willingness to pay and total demand

By yourself

X2.14 Consider the situation facing Yvonne, who is considering how many loaves of bread to purchase on a shopping trip. She can purchase any quantity of bread at a price of £1.50 per loaf. Her willingness to pay for each (additional) loaf may be written as $WTP = 2.5 - 0.5b$, where b is the number of loaves that the consumer would then be purchasing.
(a) Explain why Yvonne will choose to purchase 3 loaves.
(b) Suppose that the bakery offers 5 loaves for £7.00. How should Yvonne respond?

X2.15 We define Yvonne's consumer surplus as the amount of money she would be willing to pay in excess of the total cost of purchases.
(a) Showing the number of loaves purchased on the horizontal axis and her *WTP* on the vertical axis, sketch a graph of Yvonne's *WTP* as a function of the number of loaves.
(b) Show her consumer surplus on the diagram as the difference between the total valuation of the loaves purchased and the cost of purchase.
(c) Sketch Yvonne's demand for bread on the diagram.

X2.16 Now consider a small economics class in which there are 5 students, each willing to purchase one and only one copy of a textbook. Students are respectively willing to pay £100, £75, £60, £40, and £30. The campus bookstore has set a price for the text of £40.
(a) Draw a diagram showing the willingness to pay across students. Explain why the bookshop will sell 4 copies of the textbook, and calculate the total consumer surplus across all the students.
(b) Adapt your diagram so that the vertical axis now measures the (variable) price that the campus bookstore charges. Show how the number of books sold varies with the price that the bookstore sets.

X2.17 A new producer of smartphones has to decide the price that it should set for handsets. After conducting some market research, it concludes that the demand for its product can be written as $q = 100 - 0.5p$, where q is the quantity of handsets and p is the price that the firm can charge.
(a) Explain why the firm would be unable to give away more than 100 handsets free of charge.
(b) Explain why there cannot be any consumer with a *WTP* greater than 200.
(c) Sketch the demand curve for the firm.

X2.18 Go back to the discussion of the café, recalling the assumption that any consumer can buy any number of cups of coffee for a fixed price:
(a) Does this maximize the sales revenue that the café might obtain from the consumer?
(b) Describe a mechanism that might increase revenue further. Do you consider that the café could reasonably introduce such a mechanism?

X2.19 We have assumed that consumers will display a diminishing *WTP*. Suppose that assumption were not true. What sort of behaviour might we expect to observe?

2.4.1   Individual demands and WTP

In these examples we have started to introduce algebraic expressions, relating the quantity which consumers demand to the market price. This allows us to treat the quantity demanded as a continuous variable, so that a small change in price will always lead to a small change in demand. This may seem entirely natural for any commodity that is sold by weight or volume, but is different from our treatment of Zahra's demand for coffee, which we have assumed must be expressed as a whole number of cups of coffee.

It is possible, though, to redefine Zahra's demand as the rate at which she consumes cups of coffee over time. In Figure 2.2, we showed her demand on one particular day. On the following day, she might be willing to pay more for each cup of coffee, and so the steps would be higher above the vertical axis. Her demand for coffee would therefore shift from day to day. Over the course of a week, or a month, we could measure her average daily demand for coffee, and we would expect that average to be a continuous, rather than a discrete, variable. A small change in price would lead to a small change in demand.

From here on we shall treat goods as being perfectly divisible, so that **individual demands** can take any value. The *WTP* can then be defined for any level of consumption, q. In the same way, the (individual) demand for the good, q, can be defined for any price, p. With a fixed price for the good, everyone will purchase the quantity of the good for which their *WTP* is equal to the fixed price, so that:

> **Individual demand**
> The quantity of a good purchased at a given price.

$$WTP(q) = p \qquad\qquad [2.4]$$

In Figure 2.3, we measure quantity on the horizontal axis, and price (or value) on the vertical axis. As indicated, there are two ways of interpreting the diagram:

- Given any quantity, q, the height of the curve above the horizontal axis is the willingness to pay, $WTP(q)$.
- Given any price, p, the distance that the curve lies to the right of the vertical axis is the individual demand for the good, $q(p)$.
- Starting from quantity q^* we obtain $WTP(q^*)$. Then if firms set a price $p^* = WTP(q^*)$, this demand $q^* = q(p^*)$. *WTP* and individual demand are inversely related.

We can rewrite Expression 2.4 so that demand, q, is a function of the market price, p:

$$q = q(p) \qquad\qquad [2.5]$$

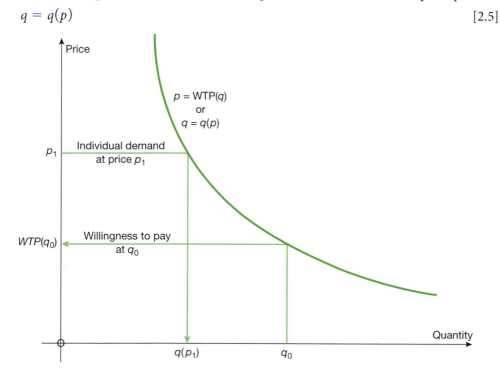

Figure 2.3 Inverse relation between willingness to pay and individual demand

Throughout the book, we will illustrate demand curves with the quantity shown on the horizontal axis and the price shown on the vertical axis, as in Figure 2.3. It would perhaps be more accurate to say that with this arrangement of axes we are drawing *WTP* curves, or inverse demand curves, but the convention of showing demand curves in this way is very well established in economics.

By yourself

X2.20   How might we best interpret *WTP* when the quantity consumed is a continuous variable, and not just a whole number? [*Hint:* It may be useful to start by thinking in terms of the change in consumer surplus associated with a one unit increase in consumption.]

2.4.2   Individual and market demands

Market demand The total quantity of a good purchased in a market at a given price.

Expression 2.5 defines demand for a single consumer. Suppose that in a market there are only two consumers, Yvonne and Zahra, who have individual demands for coffee, $q_Y(p)$ and $q_Z(p)$. We write the **market demand**, $q^D(p)$, at any price, p, as the sum of the individual demands:

$$q_X(p) + q_Y(p) = q^D(p) \qquad [2.6]$$

Generalizing this definition, given that all consumers pay the same price p, we write the total market demand for a market with N consumers as:

$$q^D(p) = \sum_{c=1}^{N} q_c(p) \qquad [2.7]$$

where the operator Σ indicates that we obtain the market demand by adding together the individual demands of all N consumers. We illustrate the market demand for coffee in Figure 2.4, adding a third consumer, Xiu. In Figure 2.4a, the lines show the individual demands, $q_X(p)$, $q_Y(p)$, and $q_Z(p)$. The market demand, $q^D(p)$, adds these demands together at each price, giving us the kinked market demand curve, $q^D(p)$, with the kinks occurring

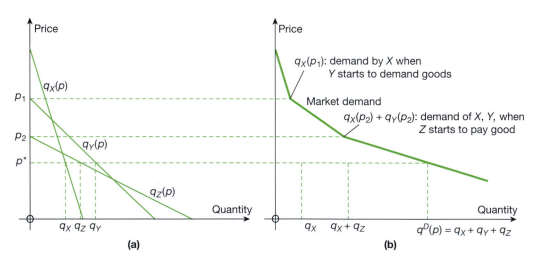

Figure 2.4 Market demand is the sum of individual demands

at each consumer's maximum *WTP*. (Above their maximum *WTP*, individual demands $q(p) = 0$.) The shape of the demand curve results from differences in the position of individual demand curves.

By yourself

X2.21	Draw two individual demand curves that are downward-sloping straight lines that intersect the price axis of your diagram at different prices. Show that the market demand for these two consumers is kinked when the price is equal to the maximum willingness to pay of the second consumer, and that the lower segment of the market demand is flatter than the upper segment.
X2.22	Define the individual linear demand functions $q_A = 60 - 0.25p$ and $q_B = 50 - 0.5p$.

    (a) Calculate the values of q_A and q_B when $p = 0$. How would you interpret a price of zero?

    (b) Calculate the values of p for which (i) $q_A = 0$ and (ii) $q_B = 0$. How would you interpret a demand of zero?

    (c) Sketch the individual demand curves, which are straight lines that intersect the horizontal axis at the values found in (a) and the vertical axis at the values found in (b).

    (d) Calculate: (i) the quantity of the good that will be demanded in the market when $p = 0$; and (ii) the quantity of the good demanded when $p = 100$. Hence or otherwise, sketch the market demand curve.

    (e) If the price is less than 100, by how much will demand increase if the price falls by one (euro)?

We say that the market demand can be obtained from individual demand curves by adding up demand horizontally. If we were to draw individual demand curves on separate diagrams (to the same scale), then we could simply add up the individual demands at any market price to obtain the market demand. The market demand will decrease if the price of the good increases, just as the individual demands do, and the effect on market demand of a given change in price will be the sum of the effects on individual demands.

2.5 Firm and market supply

Turning to market supply, we can largely repeat the argument that we have presented for the derivation of market demand. Given the market price, p, then a firm's *WTA* for any level of output, q_f, will be chosen so that:

$$WTA(q_f) = p \qquad [2.8]$$

From this implicit definition, we can define **individual firm supply** explicitly as a relation between the market price and the output that a firm decides to produce:

$$q_f = q_f(p) \qquad [2.9]$$

Lastly, we can sum up the quantity that each firm would be willing to supply at any given price to obtain the market supply for that price. Note that while we have argued that individual *WTP* must fall as consumption increases, we cannot assert that *WTA* always increases with firm output. However, in the context of Assumption A2.4 of eventually diminishing returns to scale, as a firm increases its output, its costs of producing additional output also

Individual (firm) supply The quantity of output produced by a firm at a given price.

increase. To cover its costs and make profits, the firm will have to obtain a higher price when it has a larger output. Given the set of Assumptions A2, *WTA* will never decrease with output.

By yourself

X2.23   Recall Exercise X2.16, in which we explored the relationship between *WTP* and consumer surplus. Sketch a diagram that shows a firm's *WTA* as increasing with output, which is perfectly divisible. Show how the *WTA* can be related to changes in producer surplus as output increases.

A very simple way of modelling *WTA* is to assume that it will remain constant until the firm reaches a fixed production capacity, at which point it becomes infinitely large. When the firm reaches its production capacity, no matter how much a consumer might offer to pay the firm would be unable to increase output in order to meet that demand.

By yourself

X2.24   Consider the markets for bread on an island where the market is supplied by two bakeries, and the market for freshly brewed coffee in a small town where the market is supplied by two cafés. We argued that coffee shops respond to demand when brewing each cup, but that bakeries fix the number of loaves available for sale the day before they sell them.
(a) What is the cost of making one additional cup of coffee? How reasonable would it be to expect a café's *WTA* to remain constant?
(b) Consider the situations where (i) the baking process has been completed and loaves have to be sold that day; and (ii) the baking process is about to start. How might the bakery's *WTA* differ between these two situations?
(c) Assume that the bakery has a fixed production capacity of 1,000 loaves, and that its willingness to accept an offer for a loaf of bread is £1.50 until that limit is reached. Sketch a diagram showing its *WTA* as a function of quantity.

2.5.1   Market supply

Market supply The total quantity of a good brought to market at a given price.

We return to the cafés operated by Aimee and Bianca. Their firms' supply can be written as $q_A(p)$ and $q_B(p)$. Then, defining firm supply as a function of the market price, **market supply** is the sum of the firms' supply at the market price. With two firms, the market supply, $q^S(p)$, is the sum of the two individual quantities:

$$q_A(p) + q_B(p) = q^s(p) \qquad [2.10]$$

It follows that, given the market price p, the firms will supply quantities q_I and q_{II}. Adding these quantities together, we find the total market supply at price p, which we have denoted as $q^S(p)$. In general, given that all firms receive the same price, p, the total market supply for a market with M firms might be written:

$$q^s(p) = \sum_{f=1}^{M} q_f(p) \qquad [2.11]$$

As with demand, we define the market supply by adding together the quantities that every firm will supply, given that they are all able to sell any quantity at some common price p. From our previous discussion of market demand, it is now possible for us to illustrate the market supply in a situation where there are three firms.

By yourself

X2.25 A third café (Caroline's) opens. Assume that the cafés have maximum outputs (measured by cups of coffee per day): $m_A = 500$, $m_B = 750$ and $m_C = 1,000$. The *WTA* for each firm is constant until it achieves its production limit. $WTA_A = 1.2$, $WTA_B = 1.5$ and $WTA_C = 2.0$.

(a) What happens to a café's *WTA* at its maximum output?

(b) Sketch diagrams showing each café's *WTA* (output on the horizontal axis and *WTA* on the vertical axis). How much output will each café be willing to produce given market price p: (i) $p < WTA$; (ii) $p = WTA$; and (iii) $p > WTA$?

(c) Sketch a diagram showing the market supply of the three cafés, assuming that they are each able to sell as much of the good as they wish at a given price p. Discuss how the market supply increases with the price that firms are able to obtain for their output.

In Exercise X2.25 we derived a market supply curve, which is a series of steps. As the market price, p, rises, the quantity of coffee supplied remains constant, increasing only when it reaches the *WTA* for another, larger café. The market supply never decreases, and the step function captures the inability of firms to increase output once they have reached their production capacity. Of course, the market supply need not necessarily be a series of steps. In general, we will expect it to be increasing in the price that the firms are offered, as illustrated in Figure 2.5.

In Figure 2.5a, firms A and B supply the good to the market for any price above p_A, but firm C requires a market price above p_C. For $p > p_C$, firm C is the most responsive to further price increases, so that for the market price, $p = p^*$, its output, q_C, is higher than the others'. Figure 2.5b shows the market supply. For very low prices, there is no supply to the market. When firms A and B enter the market, the market supply is the total output of firms A and B. As the price passes p_C and firm C enters the market, the market supply curve flattens, reflecting the fact that with further price increases all three firms increase their output.

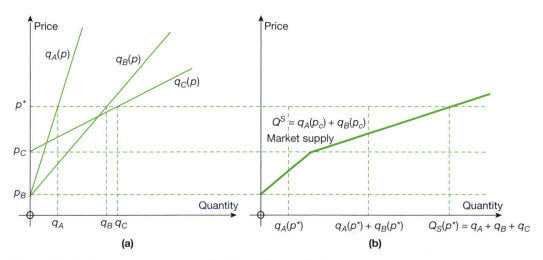

Figure 2.5 Market supply is the sum of individual firms' output

2.6   Market clearing: when supply equals demand

On the basis that *WTP* will decrease with consumption, we have argued that individual and market demands will decrease with price. Similarly, relying on Assumption A2.4 we have argued that individual and market supply are never decreasing in price. In Figure 2.6 we show market supply, $q^S(p)$, increasing, and market demand, $q^D(p)$, decreasing, as the market price, p, increases. The market clears, so that it is in equilibrium at price p^*, where the market supply and demand curves intersect. Supply equals demand: $q^D(p^*) = q^S(p^*) = q^*$. We can summarize the argument of the chapter in four propositions, all of which we have discussed already.

---

*Propositions **P2***

Propositions about market outcomes in perfect competition

P2.1   All transactions in the market take place at a single price, the market price, p^M.

P2.2   The total demand for the good or service (the market demand, Q^D) depends on the market price, p^M. If the market price, p^M, increases, then the market demand, Q^D will not increase.

P2.3   The total supply of the good or service (the market supply, Q^S) depends on the market price, p^M. If the market price, p^M, increases, then the market supply, Q^S will not decrease.

P2.4   For the market price $p^M = p^* : Q^D(p^*) = Q^S(p^*) = Q^*$. The market equilibrium is (p^*, Q^*). At the equilibrium, there is market clearing, and all feasible transactions take place. The sum of producer surplus and consumer surplus is maximized.

So long as all market participants are perfectly informed, we would expect all markets to clear, in the sense that supply will equal demand. In our model of perfect competition, small firms are able to enter and exit the market without facing any costs. This is essential if

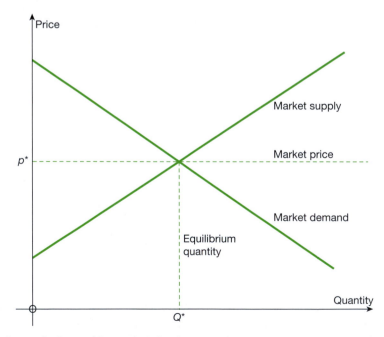

Figure 2.6 Supply equals demand for market clearing

Propositions P2.3 and P2.4 are to hold, for otherwise firms would have market power and could restrict output or manipulate prices to increase their profits.

By yourself

X2.26 Suppose that every firm that might enter the market can produce up to 100 units of a good at a cost of €10.00 each, and that each of 1,000 potential consumers will demand a quantity $q_c = 10 - 0.5p^M$.

(a) For any firm, what is the WTA for the first unit of the good, WTA(1)? And for the hundredth, WTA(100)?

(b) Confirm that if the market price, p^M, is less than 10 ($p^M < 10$), then the market supply, Q^S, equals 0 ($Q^S = 0$).

(c) Explain why all firms will enter the market as soon as $p^M = 10$, and why they will be willing to produce to their production capacity of 100 units at that price.

(d) Sketch a graph showing, for any single firm, the quantity of output that will be brought to market as the market price changes.

(e) On a single diagram, show how the market supply will change if there are: (i) 25 firms; (ii) 50 firms; and (iii) 100 firms in the market.

(f) Calculate the quantities of the good that each consumer will demand if the market price is: (i) 20; (ii) 15; (iii) 10; and (iv) 5. Sketch the relation between market price and individual demand.

(g) To the diagram showing the relationship between market price and supply, add a line illustrating the relationship between market price and demand.

(h) On this diagram, identify the market-clearing price and quantity when there are: (i) 25 firms; (ii) 50 firms; and (iii) 100 firms in the market. Explain why the market price will not fall below €10.00, and outline the circumstances under which it will be higher than €10.00.

In Exercise X2.26, we see the effect of allowing the number of firms in the market to vary. We find that the market supply, Q^S, has three components:

- for market price $p^M < 10$, which is the WTA for all firms, $Q^S = 0$;
- for $p^M > 10$, all firms produce at full capacity, so with F firms in the market, $Q^S = 100F$; and
- for $p^M = 10$, firms obtain an equal share of the market, so $0 < Q^S < 100F$.

In a graph, the market supply curve is firstly vertical, then horizontal, then once again vertical, with the position of the second vertical segment depending on the number of firms in the market. The market equilibrium will occur where market demand equals market supply. As shown in Figure 2.6, with 50 (or more) firms in the market, then the market supply is large enough that the market equilibrium $(p^*, Q^*) = (10, 5,000)$. With fewer than 50 firms in the market (so $F < 50$), the market-clearing price $p^* > 10$ and the market-clearing quantity $Q^* = 100F$.

2.7 Conclusions

Chapters 1 and 2 set out the nature of interactions between potential buyers and potential sellers in a perfect market. The set of Assumptions, A2, are sufficient to ensure that there will be perfect competition. We have identified two properties that underpin these assumptions: free access to information among all market participants, and the smallness of individual participants relative to the size of the market. From these assumptions, in this chapter, we have formulated a set of Propositions, P2, that define the nature of the equilibrium in a perfect market.

Perfect markets have very desirable properties as a mechanism for the exchange of resources. All transactions that are feasible at a single market price are completed, and it is impossible to increase the sum of the consumer and producer surplus from exchange by setting any other price. But we have had to make very restrictive assumptions about the market environment, which do not correspond well to what we observe regularly in market interactions. We shall therefore gradually lay these assumptions aside as we develop our arguments later in the book.

In discussing examples, we have simply made assumptions about individual and market demand, and also about individual and market supply. We have already claimed that a theory of resource allocation is an important component of microeconomic analysis. Our analysis will allow us to obtain measures of how people's individual demands for a good, and also firms' individual supply, change with the price of the good. Aggregating across all firms and all people, as we have done in this chapter, we will obtain measures of market supply and market demand, and so develop a much more complete characterization of the market-clearing equilibrium in a perfect market.

Summary

A market is a mechanism for the exchange of resources. Firms bring a quantity of a good to the market, seeking to sell it to people who will consume it.

In a perfect market, there will be a large number of people seeking to buy the good, but also a large number of firms seeking to supply it. There are no barriers to entry and exit, and all relevant information can be assimilated costlessly.

With these assumptions, it is reasonable to expect that all firms will adopt the same methods of production, so that the quality of the good will be uniform. There will be no incentive for firms to engage in product development or to seek to create brand identity.

People want to acquire goods as cheaply as possible. To make profits, firms want to sell goods for the highest price possible.

Willingness to pay (*WTP*) is the highest price that a person will pay for a particular unit of the good. We do not expect *WTP* to increase as consumption increases. The quantity of the good that any person demands increases as the price of the good falls. Both individual and market demand curves slope downwards.

Willingness to accept (*WTA*) is the lowest price that a firm will accept for a particular unit of the good. We assume that *WTA* will fall as output increases. The quantity of the good that any firm supplies will never fall as the price of the good rises. Neither individual nor market supply curves slope upwards.

In a perfectly competitive market, no firm will wish to be undercut by its competitors since it would lose sales, so all transactions take place at a single price. At this market-clearing price, the quantity of the good that firms supply equals the quantity that people demand. All feasible transactions take place and the sum of producer and consumer surplus is maximized.

Visit the companion website at **www.palgrave.com/mochrie** to access further teaching and learning materials, including lecturer slides and a testbank, as well as guideline answers and student MCQs.

Resource allocation for people

On 4 March 2012, Alex Hope, a 23-year-old self-proclaimed foreign exchange trading expert, spent nearly £204,000 in a Liverpool nightclub. Of this total, £125,000 was spent on a single, very large, bottle of champagne. Mr Hope did not consume all of his purchases by himself, and according to media reports he appeared to remain sober while distributing the alcohol to other customers. Sadly, a month after running up what had been widely reported as the world's largest-ever bill in a nightclub, Mr Hope's name again appeared in news media, in reports that he had been arrested for running an unlicensed foreign exchange trading operation. His operations were immediately closed down, amid allegations that he had been using clients' funds to finance his lavish lifestyle.

Mr Hope seems to have decided that he could ignore the rules of resource allocation that apply to all of us. Generally, we assume that people have only a limited amount of money to spend: Mr Hope's bill was approximately eight times the median earnings of men in full-time employment in the UK; and it may well have been settled with money that was not strictly his. We might note, though, that he chose only to buy one bottle, suggesting that there were some constraints on his expenditure. Giving away so much of what he bought does not fit in well with the framework for resource allocation sketched in Chapter 1, where we assumed that in general people finance purchases that they themselves then consume. Furthermore, if we assume that all purchasing decisions are purposeful, we should ask why someone would choose to make gifts to people who were apparently strangers. In the absence of facts, there was no shortage of speculation online.

We have already introduced the problem of resource allocation as it applies to people, emphasizing the equi-marginal principle. We shall develop a model so that we can derive this principle quite formally, concentrating on examples in which people have a fixed amount of money with which they buy a quantity of two goods; for Mr Hope, visiting a nightclub, these would be vodka and champagne. We will not think about the source of the money, but will simply assume that people set themselves a budget, whether that is £200,000 or £20, and then stick firmly to it. People will also treat the prices of the two goods as fixed. In terms of our discussion of perfect markets in Chapter 2, this is simply a result of every person's demand being a very small part of the market demand.

Calculating someone's expenditure is relatively straightforward, and we do this in Chapter 3. But when people buy goods, it is to obtain benefits from their consumption, and these benefits are not easily observable. We need to develop a theory about how to measure the payoffs from consumption that takes account of its very private nature. Strictly, as in Chapter 4, all we can say is that people are able to compare any pair of combinations of goods which they might buy, and to decide which one of the pair they prefer. Then, in Chapter 5, we develop a rule that assigns numbers to bundles, with the numbers increasing with a person's ranking of the bundles (so that the most-preferred bundle is assigned the highest number). This is enough for us to address, in Chapter 6, the challenge of identifying the most-preferred, affordable consumption bundle, given the money available to finance consumption and the prices of all goods. This most-preferred consumption bundle gives us the demand for each good. In solving this problem, the equi-marginal principle has a crucial role.

In Chapter 2, we defined both individual and market demands, arguing that people demand less of a good when its price increases. In Chapter 7, we show this to be a property of the mathematical functions that needed to represent preferences. Then, in Chapters 8 and 9, we explore some important properties of individual demand. These introduce a more technical analysis of demand, related to the effects of the change in the relative price of a good, and the effect on demand for goods of changes in the amount of money available to finance consumption; and so we present our arguments using a mixture of mathematical formulation, diagrammatic illustration, and verbal explanation. Preparing for the analysis of firms' resource allocation problems in Part III, we also show that it is possible, instead of finding the most-preferred affordable consumption bundle, for someone to choose the least costly, acceptable bundle. Thinking for the last time here of Mr Hope in the nightclub, perhaps his objective was to generate a certain level of publicity for his business, for which he may have reckoned that he had to spend at least £204,000.

Our subject here has often been called price theory, or the theory of choice; or, referring specifically to the material of Part II, the theory of the consumer. The name *price theory* emphasized the importance of prices in the decisions that people make; while *theory of choice* reflected the fact that people are free to change their decisions at any time. The *theory of the consumer* emphasized that here we are only interested in people as consumers. We shall usually refer to the *standard theory of resource allocation*, to emphasize firstly that the decisions people make as consumers typically involve deciding how to allocate limited resources – often, but not necessarily, money – to purchase quantities of all of the goods and services available at that time. We will often simply refer to the *standard theory*, recognizing that economists have developed and relied upon it for more than 100 years.

The budget set

What we do in this chapter

In economic theory, we frequently use everyday words in a very particular way. In this chapter, we begin by talking about the economic meaning of the word *scarcity*, which means that there is less of a commodity available than people would like. We shall explain how scarcity leads to commodities having *prices*, usually expressed in monetary terms. This leads on to a discussion of *opportunity cost* – that is to say, the amount of one good that must be given up in order to purchase a unit of another good.

We then outline briefly our model of *resource allocation*. We assume that anyone purchasing goods and services has a finite amount of money available. Since goods are scarce, they all have prices in monetary terms: there is a limit to the quantity of goods and services that

might be purchased. We consider a special case where only two goods exist, but allow consumers to select any quantity of each. We define a *consumption bundle* as a list of the quantities of each good selected (here the lists are short, since there will be two quantities on them).

We classify the *acquisition cost* for all consumption bundles and distinguish between *affordable* and *unaffordable* bundles. Those bundles that are just affordable – because their acquisition cost is exactly equal to amount of money available to finance consumption – are said to lie on the *affordability constraint* (also known as the *budget constraint*). We show that if the prices of the two goods are fixed, the budget constraint has a constant gradient, which is the opportunity cost of the goods.

3.1   Scarcity

If economic behaviour has an essential underpinning, it is *scarcity*. Rather than try to define scarcity just now, it may be easiest to begin with an example of a resource that is not scarce: air. Wherever we are, we are able to breathe air without paying for it. We therefore say that air is abundant. In contrast, while water may also seem to be abundant, particularly to people who live in countries where there is very high rainfall, it is in fact a scarce resource. In advanced societies, every house will have taps that can be opened to provide a plentiful supply, seemingly without any restrictions. This ignores the process of storage and purification of water, and its distribution through an extensive physical network. We may not be charged every time we open a tap, but there has to be some way of paying for the substantial costs associated with collecting the water, purifying it, and maintaining the distribution network.

Clean water is an essential resource, which people need in order to live. That does not prevent it being scarce; indeed scarcity is the usual state of affairs. It is, in fact, the abundance of air that is unusual. Almost all of the goods and services that we rely upon are scarce. Housing, heat and light, food, clothing, and transport are essentials, but all have to be purchased. This is the usual sign of scarcity.

Scarcity The situation in which the quantity of a good or service that is sought is less than the amount that is available.

It reflects the fact that the quantity of most goods and services that people seek to consume is less than the amount that they would consume were the goods free; but also that goods and services are produced using resources that are themselves scarce.

By way of contrast, if a good is abundant, it is in such plentiful supply that no one has to purchase it. Its price is effectively zero. Whenever a good is scarce, its price will be greater than zero. In terms of understanding resource allocation, the price of a good is a measure of what is given up in order to consume that good and not simply the amount of money paid for the good. For example, suppose that you decide to buy a new laptop that costs £400. You then have that much less money in your bank account. But you could have done many other things with that £400. You might have gone on holiday, or paid your share of that month's rent, or bought new clothes. The fact is that you decided instead to buy a laptop, and so the price reflects the value of what you chose *not* to do – to go on holiday, to pay the rent, or to buy clothes.

Opportunity cost
The quantity of goods forgone in order to increase consumption of some specific good.

The relevant economic concept is opportunity cost: the quantity of one good or service that is given up, or forgone, in order to buy a unit of another good or service. In the examples listed above, different items have the same monetary value, £400. We might note that none of them are examples of the relatively simple goods introduced in Chapter 2 as being likely to be traded in a perfect market, which we argued should be purchased and then consumed instantaneously. One of the pleasures of a week's holiday is the anticipation of going away, so it might be argued that consumption begins from the time of booking, possibly weeks or even months in advance of the event. The laptop is probably not a source of pleasure in itself. Instead, it is in using it that the laptop becomes valuable: you pay for it in order to obtain access to those services. Similarly, paying the monthly rent is probably not a source of pleasure for most people, but a house provides many services – a place to eat and sleep, a place to store possessions, and a place to meet friends.

We can relate opportunity cost to financial cost quite easily because most goods have a price in money. This is one of the important roles of money. Without money to act as a unit of account, it would be necessary to work out opportunity costs between each pair of goods. A loaf of bread might be exchanged for a kilogram of apples. A boxed set of DVDs might be exchanged for a simple dress, or 25 loaves of bread. A small house in the country might be exchanged for a garage in central London or for 4,000 dresses. Money gives us a common reference, making pairwise comparisons unnecessary. (I had in mind £1.40 for a loaf of bread, £35 for a dress, and £140,000 for the small house in the country.) In the analysis that follows, we assign all goods money prices so that we can calculate the opportunity costs, measured in terms of other goods. We shall show that there is nothing special about the price level itself – if all prices increased by the same proportion, the opportunity costs would remain constant.

Money is the most common unit of account used in setting prices. There are some activities, however, where it may be more useful to measure prices in terms of other resources, and probably the next most common method of pricing goods and services is the cost in terms of time. If you have a meal with friends, then you could express its cost in terms of the amount of money that you spend, but you might also express the cost in terms of the time spent, thinking of the activities forgone (because time is a scarce resource). The time that you will spend studying for your end-of-course exam – let's say

40 hours – might instead be devoted to watching your favourite film 20 times, or sleeping normally throughout a week, or working weekend shifts for a month in your part-time job as a waiter. Time, like money, is a scarce resource, and so its allocation can be represented by opportunity costs.[1]

> **By yourself**
>
> **X3.1**   What are the opportunity costs of visiting a free public museum (such as the National Gallery or the British Museum if you are in the UK)?
>
> **X3.2**   What are the opportunity costs of completing a university degree?
>
> **X3.3**   What are the opportunity costs of reading this chapter?
>
> **X3.4**   What is the opportunity cost of money?
>
> **X3.5**   Estimate the opportunity cost of a litre of milk in terms of litres of petrol.

3.2   Outline of the standard theory

We might say that scarcity motivates resource allocation decisions, with opportunity cost allowing us to measure its extent. Opportunity cost underpins economists' understanding both of how prices are set in a market, and of how people respond to changes in the prices that they must pay for goods and services. In Chapters 6 and 7 we will derive the equimarginal principle, introduced in Chapter 1 as the crucial solution concept in theories of individual resource allocation, as an equality between the opportunity cost, as defined here in terms of market prices, and personal opportunity costs, measured in terms of private (and implicitly unobservable) valuations of the good.

As it relates to resource allocation decisions made by people, we here specify a conceptual model embodying the assumptions of the standard theory, which we keep as simple as possible by assuming that the resource allocation involves deciding how to spend a fixed sum of money to buy some quantity of each of two goods. The decision to restrict attention to models with two goods is itself a resource allocation decision. While it is relatively straightforward to analyse more complex problems using mathematical tools, if choice, or resource allocation, involves the acquisition of a consumption bundle containing quantities of only two goods, it is possible to illustrate the analysis graphically, allowing for a relatively intuitive explanation of the principles.

To analyse the model, we make the following assumptions:

- The choice is made by one person.
- This person has a simple objective, which we define for now as 'to do as well as possible'. (We shall examine two closely related specifications of this objective in Chapters 4 and 5.)
- The person 'does well' by purchasing a *consumption bundle*, consisting of quantities of the different goods that are available.
- The purchase is financed from a fixed sum of money, often called *income*.

---

1   We typically assume that goods cost money, but, in an essay in the online student essay bank, Lukas Gotzelmann has written about volunteering as an activity that has time costs, explaining that this activity must have some characteristics that allow participants to treat it as a good. You can read Lukas's argument (and other students' essays) on the companion website for this book, at **www.palgrave.com/mochrie.**

- All money must be spent now. (We do not consider problems where a person might spend money at different times, saving up from time to time or borrowing money for large purchases.)
- There are only two goods available, both of which are traded on perfectly competitive markets, as defined in Chapter 2. The chosen consumption bundle will contain non-negative quantities of the two goods, and its purchase cost will not exceed the available income.

This standard model is simply a useful way of framing discussion of the wider principles that might underlie resource allocation. We have carefully chosen examples designed to elucidate important principles that we can apply to a wide variety of more complex problems, some of which we consider later in this book. Starting from this high degree of abstraction, we can concentrate fully on developing those important principles.

3.2.1 Consumption bundles

For simplicity of notation, the two goods in our examples will be bread and cheese. We might describe combinations of quantities of bread and cheese in two ways. Firstly, we can write a list of the amounts of bread and cheese, (b, c): b is the number of loaves of bread in the bundle, and c the mass of cheese in kilograms. We call such a list a *consumption bundle*. Our objective is to understand why someone acquires one particular consumption bundle out of all the bundles that might possibly exist.

Consumption bundle
A combination of quantities of the goods available to the consumer.

In using the formulation (b, c) we represent the **consumption bundle** by an ordered list, or vector, of quantities. Since we are only considering two goods, we can also depict consumption bundles graphically, as in Figure 3.1. We start from the intersection of

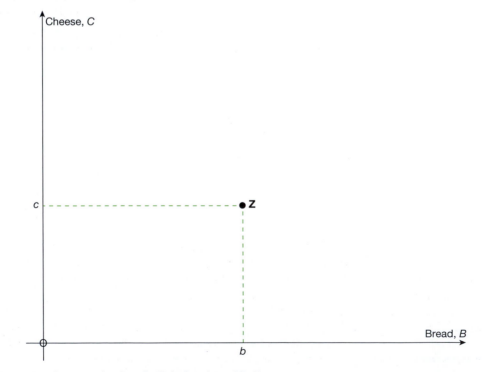

Figure 3.1 Consumption bundle Z depicted graphically

the axes, which represents the zero bundle, which contains no bread and no cheese. The distance we move to right of that point shows us the quantity of bread in the consumption bundle, while the distance we move vertically shows us the quantity of cheese. The point **Z**: (b, c) in Figure 3.1 represents the consumption bundle with b loaves and c kilograms of cheese. The two dimensions of the diagram represents the two quantities in the consumption bundle.

Note that we assume that all loaves are identical and that all cheese is of the same quality. This is consistent with the definitions of a good introduced in Chapters 1 and 2. Introducing quality differences between types of bread or types of cheese is not difficult, but we would then treat each type of bread and each type of cheese as distinct goods in our analysis, violating the two-commodity assumption.

To understand which consumption bundle someone will choose, we are going to ask two questions. Firstly, which consumption bundles can this person afford to buy? Secondly, which one(s) of the affordable consumption bundles does this person like the most? In this chapter, we only answer the first question. To resolve the second issue, we have to explore how people might achieve their assumed objective, of 'doing as well as possible'.

3.2.2   Affordability

Whether or not a particular consumption bundle is affordable depends on the cost of buying it. We have assumed that people face fixed prices so that, irrespective of the quantity of a good in a consumption bundle, the price paid per unit remains the same. (This need not be the case: businesses often offer quantity discounts or special offers.) For consumption bundles containing loaves of bread and a quantity of cheese, we write the price of a loaf of bread as p_b, and the price of a kilogram of cheese as p_c. The total cost of the consumption bundle (b, c) is then $p_b b + p_c c$. In this expression, $p_b b$ is the total cost of buying b loaves, each of which costs p_b; while $p_c c$ is the total cost of buying c loaves, each of which costs p_c. The total cost of the bundle is simply the sum of the expenditures on each good.

Essential Maths 3.1: A Cartesian diagram

Set a sheet of paper on a table. Draw two lines on it, one parallel to the bottom edge of the paper, and one parallel to the left-hand edge of the paper. Mark the point where they cross with the letter 'O'. Mark the right-hand end of the line parallel with the bottom edge with an arrow, and label that line 'x'. Mark the left-hand end of the line parallel with the left edge with an arrow and the letter 'y'.

You have just drawn the axes for a Cartesian diagram. We can identify every point on the diagram by two coordinates: the distance that it lies to the right of the origin and the distance that it lies above the origin. We call these the x and y coordinates, and usually write them as (x, y). We do not restrict our interpretation of these points to the purely physical; if there is any object that can be represented by having two numerically measurable characteristics (such as simple consumption bundles), then we are able to capture those characteristics in terms of these Cartesian coordinates. For example, we might be interested in the volume and mass of objects; or the maximum speed and fuel consumption of cars; or the age and height of trees.

We assume that it is impossible to borrow money to finance consumption. To be able to *afford* a consumption bundle, the amount of money, m, that a person has available to spend cannot be less than the cost of acquiring the bundle. Using our algebraic notation, a consumption bundle is affordable if:

$$m - p_b b - p_c c \geq 0 \qquad [3.1]$$

Expression 3.1 simply says that expenditure cannot exceed income. Placing a maximum value on expenditure limits the actions that a person can choose with the chosen consumption bundle being affordable.

Let us suppose that the constraint is just satisfied – in mathematical terminology, we say that such a constraint is *binding*. Then the cost of the bundle is exactly equal to this person's income. If this happens, then the constraint in Expression 3.1 holds with equality, so that $m = p_b b + p_c c$. In Figure 3.2, this condition is satisfied for all points on the downward-sloping straight line passing through consumption bundle **Z**. We usually call such a line a **budget constraint** (or **affordability constraint**), because it shows all consumption bundles whose purchase cost is equal to this person's income.

> **Budget (affordability) constraint** Those consumption bundles that cost the full amount of money available.

Now, consider the area above and to the right of consumption bundle **Z**, which is not specifically defined in the diagram. Every consumption bundle in this region contains at least as much bread and as much cheese as bundle **Z**. Since the price of every good is fixed, however, these bundles all cost more than bundle **Z**. It is easy to confirm that every consumption bundle represented by a point in the diagram above (or to the right of) the budget constraint *must* cost more than the consumption bundles on the budget constraint. In other words, this region represents the set of unaffordable consumption bundles.

In contrast, the shaded area contained within the budget constraint contains all of the affordable consumption bundles – that is, all consumption bundles that satisfy

Essential Maths 3.2: Convex sets

On the sheet of paper with the Cartesian diagram, draw a loop. We can classify all points in the plane according to whether they lie in the area enclosed by the loop or outside the loop. We can define two *sets* of points: those in the loop and those outside it.

We have to decide whether or not points that lie *on* the loop should be counted as being inside or outside the loop. Unless stated otherwise, we shall typically assume that the boundary of the loop is part of the loop – that is, the set of points *inside* the loop includes the boundary, and is said to be closed.

Now choose two points within the loop. Draw a line between those two points. If the line between those points, and indeed every line between any two points within the loop, lies entirely within the set, then the set is *convex*. Squares, right-angled triangles, circles, and ellipses all form closed, convex sets. Heart shapes, doughnuts, and crescents do not: we can draw a line connecting two points within any of these sets that strays outside it. For this chapter, we note that budget sets with constant prices are triangular, so they are always convex.

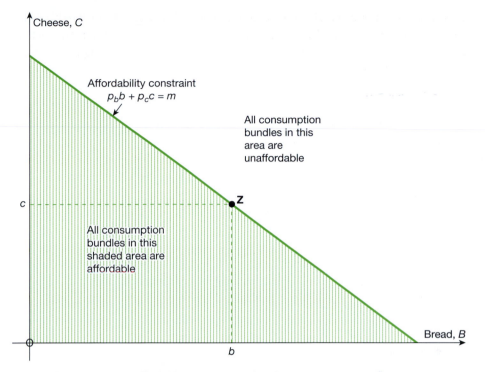

Figure 3.2 Affordable and unaffordable consumption bundles

Expression 3.1. These bundles are the **budget set** (or **affordable set**). The consumption bundle that the person chooses must lie within, or on the edge of, this triangular region. In later chapters we shall explore where in the affordable set the chosen bundle will lie. For now, there are only a few points that we need to make about the budget set. These will be very important in later analysis. They relate the budget set to the acquisition cost of bundles, and use the concept of convexity set out in Essential Maths 3.4.

> **Budget (affordable) set** All the consumption bundles that can be acquired for a cost less than income.

By yourself

X3.6 For each of the following situations, sketch graphs showing the budget constraints and the affordable set.
(a) The price of a loaf of bread is £1.20; the price of cheese is £6.00 per kilogram; income is £30.
(b) Prices are £1.50 and £9.00; income is £27.
(c) Price are £1.40 and £9.80; income is £39.20.

The budget constraint forms the boundary of the affordable set, and allows us to divide the space of all possible consumption bundles in two – in the diagram, the region consisting of affordable bundles, and the region consisting of unaffordable bundles. It is perhaps not too surprising that when we analyse choice, we can restrict attention to bundles that lie in the affordable set. For the moment, we shall not consider choice further, and instead set out some properties of the budget constraint.

The triangular budget set in Figure 3.2 is *closed* and *convex*. It is closed because the boundary of the set, the budget constraint, consists of bundles that are just afford-able, and the boundary of the budget set therefore lies within the set. It is convex because, choosing any two points in the budget set and drawing a line between them, the line lies entirely within the set. In particular, note that the line connecting any pair of points on the boundary of the budget set is the budget constraint, which lies within the budget set.

Essential Maths 3.3: Functions of two variables (1)

For the point P(x, y) in the Cartesian diagram, suppose that we can define a further characteristic, z, whose value depends on the values of x and y. That is, the value z is not independent, but can be calculated if we know the values of x and y. For example, given any point, we can calculate its distance from the origin; or given height and weight, we can calculate someone's body mass index; or given the height and age of a tree, we can work out its average annual growth.

Such rules are known as *functions*. We can identify three elements of every function. Firstly, there is the *domain* set, which forms the inputs to the function. Here the domain consists of all possible pairs (x, y) – in other words, every point in the diagram. Secondly, there is the *range*, or *image*, which forms the outputs of the function. Here this is the number z, whose value depends on the values of x and y. Thirdly, there is the *functional relation*, the mechanism that allows us to work out the value of z from any given pair of inputs (x, y). Here, we can write a function f in the form:

$$z : (x, y) \rightarrow z(x, y) \qquad \text{[M3.1]}$$

Essential Maths 3.4: Functions of two variables (2)

The functions that we consider here use two numbers as inputs, and so we call them *functions of two variables*. The function defines calculations that we complete for any pair of input values to obtain a third number, $z(x, y)$, which is the (unique) image value of the function.

It is relatively easy to sketch graphs illustrating the functional relationship when z depends on only one variable. For example, were we to hold y constant, so that $y = y_0$, but allow the value of x to vary, then we might write:

$$f : (x, y_0) \rightarrow z(x, y_0) \qquad \text{[M3.2]}$$

Since x is the only variable input, we can draw a Cartesian diagram, with the domain value, x, measured on the horizontal axis, and the range value, $z(x)$, measured on the vertical axis, with the graph of the function showing how z changes with the value of x. If we allow the values of both x and y to change, we require two dimensions to show the domain set, say D = $\{(x, y): x, y \geq 0\}$, and a third dimension to show the image, z.

To simplify graphical presentations in such cases, we tend to show a selection of contours, curves for which the value of $z(x, y) = z_0$.

3.3   The acquisition cost of a bundle

We can present much of the standard theory simply by considering properties of closed sets. However, many important results are derived more easily by examining the properties of functions of consumption bundles directly. We therefore define affordability in terms of an acquisition cost function: a rule that takes the quantities of bread and cheese in a consumption bundle (more generally the quantities b and c of two goods) and assigns a value to the bundle. We write:

$$A(b, c) = p_b b + p_c c \tag{3.2}$$

calling this function, $A: (b, c) \rightarrow A(b, c)$, the *acquisition cost*. The function is a rule for working out how much money must be spent to acquire consumption bundle (b, c). From Expression 3.1, for someone with an amount of money, m, available to finance consumption, the bundle is affordable if:

$$A(b, c) \leq m \tag{3.3}$$

We now define the budget set, B:

$$B = \{(b, c) : A(b, c) \leq m\} \tag{3.4}$$

and the budget constraint C as the subset of the affordable set for which the constraint holds with equality:

$$C = \{(b, c) : A(b, c) = m\} \tag{3.5}$$

Essential Maths 3.5: Contour maps

In Figure M3.1, we show such a selection. The domain set is the $x-y$ plane. The contour, $z = z_0$, represents the level set of ordered pairs, $I(z_0) = \{(x, y): z = z_0\}$.

Think of a physical contour map. The domain is all pairs of coordinates, measuring distances East and North from a given origin. The image is height above sea level. Contour lines on the map indicate all points that are the same height above sea level. If we think of a particular hill, then the contour lines will be loops, enclosing the part of the hill that lies above that contour line.

We define the set, $P(z_0) = \{(x, y): z(x, y) \geq z_0\}$, which consists of all pairs for which $z(x, y)$ is no less than z_0. In Figure M3.1, $P(z_0)$ is convex for all z_0. In addition, the level set $I(z_0)$ forms the boundary of $P(z_0)$, so that it is a *closed* set.

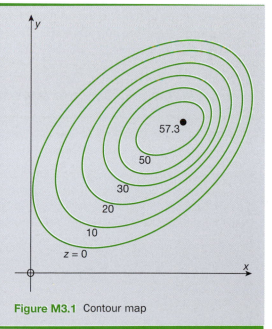

Figure M3.1 Contour map

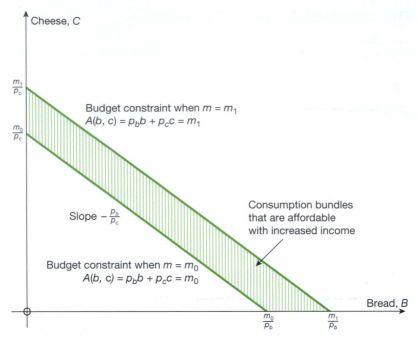

Figure 3.3 Characteristics of the budget line

3.3.1 Convexity

Now suppose that the money available to finance consumption increases from an amount m_0 to m_1. We illustrate this in Figure 3.3. Previously, the most expensive, affordable bundles cost m_0, with associated budget constraint, $A(b, c) = m_0$. In the new budget set, all bundles that cost up to m_1 are affordable, and the budget constraint becomes $A(b, c) \leq m_1$. The new budget set contains all the bundles in the original budget set plus all those bundles that were previously unaffordable but are now affordable: those in the shaded region of Figure 3.3, for which:

$$m_0 < A(b, c) \leq m_1 \qquad [3.6]$$

Essential Maths 3.6: Concave and convex functions

A function, $z: (x, y) \to z(x, y)$, is *concave* if for every possible value of the image, $z = z_0$, the set $P(z_0) = \{(x, y): z(x, y) \geq z_0\}$ is convex and closed. The contours in Figure M3.1 illustrate this property.

On a physical contour map, think of a hill with smooth sides, so that the contours are a similar shape to those in Figure M3.1. The hill is concave. Suppose though that the contours instead measured the depth of a lake, again with smooth sides. A contour showing the depth of the water below the surface at any point would enclose the part of the lake where the water is deeper.

Suppose that we measure depth as a negative number. We define the level set $I(z_0) = \{(x, y): z = z_0\}$, which can be represented by a contour and the set $P(z_0) = \{(x, y): z(x, y) \leq z_0\}$, bounded by the level set, and represented by the area of deeper water in the lake. $P(z_0)$ is convex and closed.

The function, $z: (x, y) \to z(x, y)$, is *convex* if for every possible value of the image, $z = z_0$, the set $P(z_0) = \{(x, y): z(x, y) \leq z_0\}$ is convex and closed. The depth of water in the lake can therefore be represented by a convex function.

By yourself

X3.7   Consider these three cases:
(1) prices $p_b = 1.5$ and $p_c = 7.5$, with money available to finance consumption, $m = 30$;
(2) $p_b = 2$, $p_c = 12$, $m = 24$; and
(3) $p_b = 4$, $p_c = 16$, $m = 40$.
  (a) Write down expressions for the acquisition cost, A, for bundle (b, c) and the budget constraint, C, for which $A(b, c) = m$.
  (b) Sketch separate diagrams showing the budget set, B, and the budget constraint, C.
  (c) Confirm that that the budget sets in cases (2) and (3) are subsets of the budget set in case (1).

X3.8   Show the effect on the budget sets in your diagrams of an increase in the money available to finance consumption, to: (a) $m_1 = 36$; (b) $m_1 = 40$; and (c) $m_1 = 60$.

X3.9   Using the diagrams in X3.8, demonstrate that the acquisition function is convex.

Since the budget set is convex, and the acquisition cost of bundles in the interior of the budget set is less than the acquisition cost on its boundary, the acquisition cost function is convex. This is important. We shall see that the predictions of the standard theory rely on the acquisition cost having this property.

3.3.2 Some properties of the budget constraint

The budget constraint consists of all consumption bundles that are just affordable, given the amount of money available for consumption, so that, as defined in Expression 3.5, it is the boundary of the budget (or the affordable) set, such that $p_b b + p_c c = m$. It is quite straightforward to rewrite this equality in the form:

Subtract $p_b b$ from both sides

$$c = \frac{m - p_b b}{p_c}$$ [3.7]

And divide both sides by p_c

Expression 3.7 is the *explicit form* of the budget constraint. A person with income m, after buying b loaves of bread (and so spending $p_b b$) has $m - p_b b$ to spend on cheese. To spend all the money available for consumption, she buys c kg of cheese.

We can quickly work out properties of the budget constraint, making three simple calculations:

1. Someone who buys only cheese (and no bread), but still spends all her money would buy m/p_c kg of cheese.

2. Someone who buys only bread (and no cheese), but still spends all her money would buy m/p_b loaves.

3. Someone who spends all her money (so that she is *budget-constrained*), but who decides to buy an extra loaf of bread, has to give up p_b/p_c kg of cheese.

The first two statements simply tell us where the budget constraint intersects the bread and cheese axes in Figures 3.3 and 3.4. We obtain the first intersection from Expression 3.7 by setting b to zero; and the second in a similar way by setting c to zero and then solving the equation $m - p_b b = 0$. Statement 3 is more important, because it defines the *opportunity cost* of a loaf of bread. It allows us to calculate the amount of cheese that someone who is already spending all her money would have to give up in order to buy a loaf of bread.

By yourself

X3.10   Suppose that a person with income m_1 only uses m_0 to finance consumption. What difficulties might this pose for calculating the opportunity cost of bread? How would your answer differ if income received today was also used to finance consumption tomorrow? What if goods other than bread and cheese could be chosen?

A person with income m_1 who chooses to spend only m_0 can afford to buy any of the consumption bundles in the shaded region of Figure 3.4 but has chosen not to do so. It must be that such a person can see no advantage in buying a more expensive bundle. But if this is the case, we cannot easily apply the concept of opportunity cost. Say that this person has enough money to buy an extra kilogram of cheese. Since it is possible to buy that cheese without giving up any bread, its opportunity cost can only be expressed in terms of the fact that this money cannot now be used for any other purpose.

We might argue that in deciding to spend the remaining money on cheese, people have to forgo some bread, in which case the comparison should not be with the original

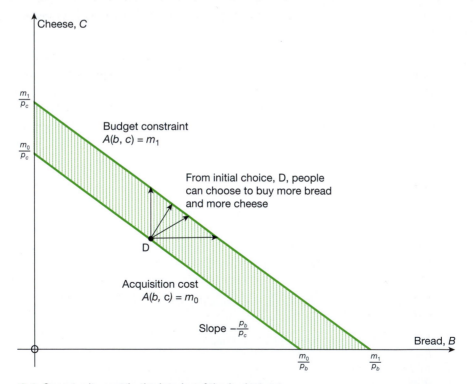

Figure 3.4 Opportunity cost in the interior of the budget set

consumption bundle but with the alternative bundle in which the remaining money was spent on bread rather than cheese. This is not a very strong argument, because deciding to buy more cheese only excludes the possibility of buying more bread if all the remaining income is spent on cheese. From a point in the interior of the budget set, different people might decide to buy different mixtures of bread and cheese. It is only when *all* of someone's money has been spent that a purchase has a clearly defined opportunity cost.

Scarcity drives economic analysis because it implies opportunity costs. We have claimed that opportunity costs exist only when resources are fully allocated – in this case, when an individual has no money to spare. In other words, the budget constraint limits behaviour only for those people who choose a consumption bundle on the constraint, so that they would have to give up some of one good in order to buy more of the other one. Rather than consider all affordable consumption bundles, we only consider the ones on the constraint, whose acquisition cost is equal to the available income.

3.3.3 Changes in prices and income

In the preceding diagrams, we have measured the number of loaves in a consumption bundle on the horizontal axis and the mass of cheese on the vertical axis. The opportunity cost is the slope of the budget constraint, and is defined as the relative price of bread, p_b/p_c. If this number is small, the cost of a loaf of bread is low compared to that of a kilogram of cheese, and only a small amount of cheese need be given up should another loaf be purchased. In this case, the budget constraint has a shallow slope. On the other hand, if the budget constraint has a steep slope, the price of a loaf of bread relative to the price of a kilogram of cheese is large, and the opportunity cost of a loaf of bread is high.

Often, we are interested to find out how behaviour changes when there is a change in the situation in which people have to make choices. The only things that can change in our budget constraint are the price of bread, p_b, the price of cheese, p_c, and the amount of money, m, that someone has to spend. We consider the effects of changing each of these parameters in the following examples, illustrating the outcomes graphically in Figure 3.5.

(1) In Figure 3.5a, the price of a loaf of bread doubles, rising from p_b to $2p_b$.

    (a) A person who only buys cheese can afford m/p_c kilograms. This amount does not depend on the price of bread, so the intercept on the cheese (vertical) axis is unaffected by the price change.

    (b) Similarly, someone who buys only bread can afford m/p_b loaves originally, so after the price increase he can afford $m/2p_b$ loaves, or half the previous amount. Before the price increase, total expenditure was $p_b(m/p_b) = m$. After the price increase, total expenditure is $2p_b(m/2p_b) = m$. Total expenditure is still equal to income. In our diagram, the intercept on the bread (horizontal) axis is closer to the origin.

    (c) Lastly, the opportunity cost of a loaf of bread increases from $-p_b/p_c$ to $-2p_b/p_c$. Since the price of a loaf has doubled, the amount of cheese that someone has to give up in order to buy a loaf of bread has also doubled. As a result, in the diagram the budget constraint is now twice as steep as it was before.

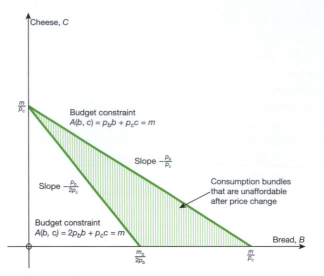

(a) Increase in the price of bread

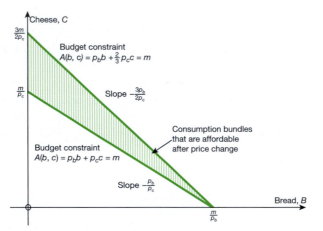

(b) Decrease in the price of cheese

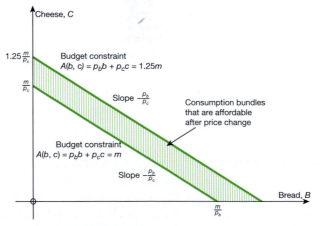

(c) Increase in income

Figure 3.5 Effects of price and income changes

By yourself

X3.11   In Figure 3.5b, we show a situation in which the price of a kilogram of cheese falls from p_c to $\frac{2}{3} p_c$. Calculate the effect:
(a) on someone who only buys bread;
(b) on someone who only buys cheese;
(c) on the opportunity cost of bread.

X3.12   In Figure 3.5c, we show a situation in which the money available to finance consumption, m, increases by 25%. Repeat X3.11.

X3.13   Why might we consider that a price increase makes someone worse off, while a price fall makes someone better off?

It is usual to talk about the budget constraint *shifting* as the result of an income change and *pivoting* as the result of a price change. As shown in Figure 3.5c, the parallel shift resulting from a change in income is quite straightforward. As income falls, the budget constraint moves in towards the origin, while if income rises, the constraint moves away from the origin. Its slope, which is the relative price, or opportunity cost, of the good whose consumption is measured on the horizontal axis, is unchanged.

The pivot as the result of a price change is a little more complex. Firstly, the fixed point of the pivot is the intersection of the budget constraint with the axis measuring consumption of the good whose price does not change. Secondly, where there is an increase in the relative price of the good whose consumption is measured on the horizontal axis, the pivot is clockwise and the budget constraint becomes steeper. This occurs in Figures 3.5a and 3.5b, with both an increase in the price of bread and a fall in the price of cheese. Were the price of cheese to increase, or the price of bread to fall, the relative price of bread would fall and the budget constraint would pivot anti-clockwise.

By yourself

X3.14   Sketch graphs showing the budget constraints and the affordable set before and after prices and income change. State how the relative prices of bread and cheese change.
(a) Initially, $p_b = 1.20$, $p_c = 6.00$, and $m = 30$. After price and income changes, $p_b = 1.50$, $p_c = 6.00$, and $m = 36$.
(b) Initially, $p_b = 1.50$, $p_c = 9.00$, and $m = 27$. After price and income changes, $p_b = 1.80$, $p_c = 12.00$, and $m = 27$.
(c) Initially, $p_b = 1.40$, $p_c = 9.80$, and $m = 39.20$. After price and income changes, $p_b = 1.20$, $p_c = 8.40$, and $m = 37.80$.

X3.15   Suppose that both the price of bread and the price of cheese, p_b and p_c, rise by 10%, and the amount of money available to finance consumption, m, also increases by 10%. Demonstrate that the budget set is the same before and after the price rise.

We interpret Exercise X3.15 as indicating that there is a sense in which people are not concerned about how much money they have, except in so far as that amount affects the affordable set and the possibilities for consumption. We should distinguish between nominal measures of purchasing capacity, such as the amount of money available, m, and real measures, defined by the ability to purchase consumption bundles. Some consumption bundles that lie in the affordable set before a price change will lie outside it afterwards. Before the price change some people could afford those bundles, but after the price change they cannot. We have asserted that with scarcity people will choose consumption bundles that lie on the budget constraint, which means that after a price increase they will not be able to afford their previous choice. A price increase is then a fall in real *income*, defined as the ability to purchase specific consumption bundles. In addition, given the objective of seeking to do as well as possible, anyone who chose a consumption bundle that is now unaffordable will have to purchase a consumption bundle that was previously affordable but not chosen, given the initial budget constraint.[2]

3.4 Endowments

Up to this point, we have considered the situation in which a person has a fixed amount of money to finance the purchase of a consumption bundle. We might talk about everyone having an *endowment* in the form of a sum of money. Suppose instead that the endowment takes the form of an initial allocation of goods, distributed somehow across the population, and which people can trade to 'do better'.

The value of the endowment can be expressed in terms of the prices of the goods that are consumed. Continuing with our two goods example, the endowment of bread and cheese can be represented by the ordered pair (b^E, c^E), or by point E in Figure 3.6, whose market value is equivalent to the money available to finance consumption, $m = p_b b^E + p_c c^E$.

Trade consists of exchanging units of one good for units of another. As before, the opportunity cost of bread is the relative price, $-\frac{p_b}{p_c}$. In Figure 3.6, allowing for exchange, we obtain a budget constraint, which passes through the endowment, E, and whose slope is the opportunity cost of bread. The chosen consumption bundle, shown at point A in the diagram, involves this person giving up bread from the endowment to enable greater consumption of cheese. (Note that this implies the presence of people willing to make the counterpart exchange, giving up cheese to increase their consumption of bread.) Given the prices of bread and cheese, the market value of consumption bundle A is the same as the market value of consumption bundle E. We can write this relation as:

$$p_b b^A + p_c c^A = p_b b^E + p_c c^E \qquad [3.8]$$

where the left-hand side is the market value of the bundle that is consumed, and the right-hand side is the market value of the endowment. The market value of the endowment then takes on the role of money income in the previous analysis.

By yourself

X3.16   Sketch diagrams showing the budget constraint for someone with the given endowments, given the opportunity cost of cheese:

(a) Endowment: 12 loaves of bread plus 3 kg of cheese, where 1 kg of cheese can be traded for 3 loaves.

---

2   Governments are able to affect both prices and incomes by varying tax rates (and the structure of taxation). In an essay in the online student essay bank, Anastasia Stoyanova has demonstrated that major simplifications of the income tax regime in Bulgaria have had substantial distributional effects, increasing the post-tax income of relatively well-off workers. You can read Anastasia's argument (and other students' essays) on the companion website for this book, at **www.palgrave.com/mochrie.**

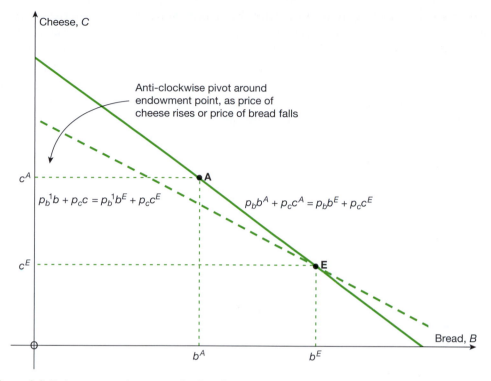

Figure 3.6 Endowment and consumption bundles

(b) Endowment: 20 loaves of bread plus 2 kg of cheese, where 1 kg of cheese can be traded for 8 loaves.

(c) Endowment: 18 loaves of bread plus 4 kg of cheese, where 1 kg of cheese can be traded for 6 loaves.

We can make some additional points about trade, though. Firstly, we can rewrite the relationship between the endowment and the consumption bundle:

| Subtract $p_c c^E$ from both sides | Subtract $p_b b^A$ from both sides |

$$p_c(c^A - c^E) = p_b(b^E - b^A)$$ [3.8a]

Collect terms together

| Divide both sides by p_c and $(b^A - b^E)$ |

$$\frac{c^A - c^E}{b^A - b^E} = -\frac{p_b}{p_c}$$ [3.8b]

or

$$c^A = c^E - \frac{p_b}{p_c}(b^A - b^E)$$ [3.8c]

From Expression 3.8a, we conclude that the market value of the bread that is traded is equal to the market value of the cheese that is traded. In Expression 3.8b, we recognize the right-hand side as the opportunity cost, or the relative price from previous analysis. The left-hand side of the expression is the ratio of the quantities traded: the higher the relative price of a commodity, the less of it that will be traded. Lastly, in Expression 3.8c, we obtain the explicit form of the affordability constraint, showing how much cheese can be consumed, given the amount of bread that is traded, and the endowment of cheese. This is the boundary of the set of affordable consumption bundles.

Starting from an endowment of goods, rather than an endowment of money, the budget constraint is a line with slope equal to the relative price of the two goods, and the budget set is convex. Analysing a change in relative prices, the fixed point of the budget set is no longer one of the intersections with the axis, but the endowment point. When prices change, the physical endowment stays the same, but the terms on which it can be traded do change. Hence in Figure 3.6 we show the effect of a decrease in the relative price p_b/p_c as an anti-clockwise pivot around the endowment point, E.

It may seem that discussion of endowments is just a theoretical curiosity. In fact, there are many places in this book where we think about people having to plan consumption, given endowments. It is particularly important in the general equilibrium models of Part V, as well as in developing the theory of inter-temporal choice, the analysis of risk, and in understanding how families make consumption decisions, all in Part VI.

3.5   Conclusions

When people set out to 'do as well as they can', they do so in the face of resource constraints. The form of constraint used here is very simple: that people have a fixed amount of money to spend. This will be the usual form of endowment throughout Part II, since an endowment of goods can always be sold to turn it into an endowment of money. Money and prices are entirely conventional, though, in the sense that they allow us to do away with the need to exchange pairs of goods. Doubling the amount of money available to finance consumption and all prices, the budget set remains unchanged. In addition, since we think only about the decision to use the money available to finance consumption, the endowment appears without any further explanation of its origin, but we might reasonably expect it to take the form of income from work, or else the returns from savings or investment.

In terms of developing the standard model, it is useful for us to think of the affordable set in terms of its diagrammatic representation, with the boundary line consisting of the set of all consumption bundles whose acquisition cost is equal to the sum of money available to finance consumption. This acquisition cost is an increasing, convex function, ensuring firstly that all budget sets are convex, and secondly that any increase in the amount of money available to finance consumption leads to an expansion of the affordable set.

By yourself

X3.17   Sketch the budget constraint facing someone with an income of £84, who can buy up to 60 litres of petrol or 70 bottles of beer.
   (a) What are the prices of a litre of petrol and a bottle of beer?
   (b) Now suppose that anyone buying more than 40 l of petrol is given a 10% quantity discount. What is the discounted price of a litre of petrol?
       (i) How many bottles of beer can someone buying 40 l of petrol afford?
       (ii) How much petrol can someone who buys no beer afford?
       (iii) How many bottles of beer can someone buying 41 l of petrol afford?

(c) Sketch a diagram showing the original budget constraint, and the new section of the budget constraint that reflects the discount. Why might it be very unusual for someone to buy 40l of petrol?

X3.18 Reading books and going to a concert both require time and money. Suppose that a book costs £10 and takes six hours to read, while going to a concert costs £20 and takes 3 hours. For someone who is willing to spend £80 and 18 hours on these activities:

(a) How many concerts can this person go to, without reading any books?

(b) How many books can this person read, without going to any concerts?

(c) Sketch the money and the time budget constraints for this person.

(d) On your sketch, indicate the budget set.

X3.19 How would you interpret a negative price for a good? Sketch the budget constraint and budget set for consumption bundles with one good with a positive price and one with a negative price.

Summary

We denote a consumption bundle by an ordered list consisting of the quantities of the various goods that an individual might purchase and consume. Each good is sold at a fixed price; the cost of the consumption bundle can be obtained by multiplying the quantity of each good by its price, and summing together these products.

A consumer with a fixed sum of money to finance consumption can afford any consumption bundle that costs no more than that income.

Where there are only two goods, it is possible to depict the set of affordable bundles by a triangular area, bounded by the axes and a downward-sloping budget constraint. The slope of the budget constraint is the opportunity cost of the good whose quantity in the consumption bundle is measured on the horizontal axis. The slope is also the relative price of that good.

An increase in price of the good whose quantity is measured on the horizontal axis leads to the budget constraint pivoting in towards the origin. (The fixed point for the pivot is the intercept on the axis measuring the quantity of the good whose price remains constant.) An increase in income leads to the budget constraint shifting outwards, with the slope of the budget line remaining the same.

A consumer who has an endowment of goods can trade with other consumers, giving away units of one good in exchange for units of the other. The terms of this trade are given by the relative price, which is again the slope of the budget constraint. On the budget constraint, the value of the goods given away equals the value of the goods acquired during trade.

Visit the companion website at **www.palgrave.com/mochrie** to access further teaching and learning materials, including lecturer slides and a testbank, as well as guideline answers and student MCQs.

4

Preferences

We have examined the concept of the consumption bundle and considered its acquisition cost. The cost is the first of two properties of a consumption bundle in which we are interested: the other is how strongly the person whose behaviour we are studying actually *likes* the bundle. We will define this in terms of strength of preference in a comparison of pairs of consumption bundles.

People usually choose from among more than just a pair of consumption bundles, and so we develop rules for pairwise comparisons across bundles. If, in principle, it is possible to make a comparison between every pair of bundles and if these comparisons are consistent, then we can define what is known as a *weak preference relation*. If, in addition, the preference relation is such that having more of any good is always

preferred, and that bundles comprising a mixture of goods are typically preferable to mixtures consisting almost completely of one good, then we can say that preferences are *well behaved*.

We discuss how all bundles about which someone is indifferent can then be depicted by a single *indifference curve*, with the preference relation being illustrated by an indifference curve map. If the preference relation is well behaved, then indifference curves will never touch, but will slope downwards, becoming flatter as we move from left to right. Weakly preferred sets are then *convex*; and so, where preference relations are well behaved, we can identify graphically the *most strongly preferred, affordable consumption bundle*, which is this person's optimal consumption bundle.

4.1   Ordering preferences

In Chapter 3, while we concentrated on the affordability of consumption bundles, we assigned people the objective of seeking to do as well as possible. We now need to understand that statement more fully within the context of our model in which someone uses a sum of money to buy a consumption bundle made up of quantities of two goods. After purchase, the bundle is consumed fully – in the case of our working example of bread and cheese, simply by being eaten – so that none of it is saved. For any consumer, 'doing well' in this context simply means choosing the best of the affordable consumption bundles, and in this chapter we use the standard model to explore how people might identify this bundle.

Preference A ranking of two outcomes based on which one is considered better.

The concept of a **preference** relation is not complex by itself, but we have to define it quite precisely, so that it has the characteristics necessary for us to develop our theory satisfactorily. Preference relations should be defined over all consumption bundles and are binary. We use them to rank pairs of consumption bundles.

Suppose that we specify pairs of consumption bundles, which are identical except that:

- one includes a season ticket for a gym, and the other a season ticket for a spa; *or*

- one includes an iPhone, and the other a Nokia Windows Phone; *or*
- one includes a subscription to *The Economist*, and the other a subscription to the *Financial Times*; *or*
- one includes a family holiday, and the other a holiday with friends.

In these examples, each pair consists of two alternative consumption bundles, between which a person has to choose. We shall call these alternatives A and B, writing:

- A: *a bundle of goods* plus a season ticket for a gym;
- B: *the same bundle of goods* plus a season ticket for a spa.

If someone tells us that they like A more than B, then we say that for that person, 'A is preferred to B', writing this in symbols, A > B. Other people may express different preferences when faced with this comparison. We would say that 'B is preferred to A', writing this either as B > A or A < B, if our informant tells us that they like B more than A. If we ask many people which of the various alternatives listed above they like more, we do not expect to find universal agreement: such rankings are subjective, and there cannot be a unique, objectively correct **ordering of preferences**.

> **Preference ordering** A complete ranking of all consumption bundles.

It may seem that these two statements about rankings exhaust the possibilities. Suppose, though, that someone considers A to be just as good as, but no better than, B. Neither statement is then true, so we have to rely on a statement such as 'A and B are equally preferred'. For what follows, we call this situation **indifference**, writing this in symbols, A ~ B. Indifference is not the result of an inability to evaluate the alternatives, for anyone who is unable to rank the alternatives simply cannot express a preference between A and B; whereas someone who is indifferent between them considers that they are wholly equivalent.

> **Indifference** Equal ranking of outcomes, so that neither is seen as better than the other.

Working with preference and indifference is possible, but in the theoretical model that we shall analyse, it is generally more satisfactory to use the concept of **weak preference**. Instead of simply saying that 'A is preferred to B', as we did initially, we might describe a preference for A in negative terms, saying that 'B is not preferred

> **Weak preference** Ranking two outcomes based on one being considered at least as good as the other.

to A'. The person whose preferences we are analysing might say something like, 'I like A at least as much as B.' In symbols, we can write, A ≥ B. The difference between this statement and a stronger statement such as 'I like A more than B' is that only the 'weak' statement is true for someone who is indifferent between A and B. In other words, a weak preference for A over B means that A is liked as much as, or more than, B.

Using weak preference, we assume that at least one of the statements 'A is (weakly) preferred to B' and 'B is (weakly) preferred to A' must be true. Both are true whenever someone is indifferent between A and B. So long as a person is able to rank bundles A and B, these are the only possible outcomes:

- A ≥ B, or A is weakly preferred to B;
- A ≤ B, or B is weakly preferred to A;
- A ~ B, or A and B are ranked equally (so that this person is indifferent between A and B).

Weak preference is therefore a binary relation that allows us to express a person's ranking of every conceivable pair of consumption bundles. We shall use it to identify the most-preferred, affordable consumption bundle, rather than the alternative (strict) preference relation. For this reason, unless specified otherwise, we should always read the statement 'A is preferred to B' as being broadly equivalent to 'A is at least as good as B' rather than 'A is better than B'.

4.1.1 (Weakly) preferred sets

If choices involved only two consumption bundles, there would be nothing more to say. When there are more than two consumption bundles available, however, developing a preference ordering through successive pairwise comparisons of bundles may still seem to be possible, if rather complex.

We will normally allow consumption bundles to contain any (non-negative) quantity of two goods. There will be no upper limit to the quantity of either good in these consumption bundles, and we will also assume that goods are infinitely divisible.

(Weakly) preferred set All consumption bundles that are ranked at least as highly as the reference bundle.

These assumptions make it impossible simply to write down a preference ordering that ranks all possible consumption bundles. Instead, we define the **(weakly) preferred set** for each consumption bundle, which contains all consumption bundles that the person whom we are studying likes at least as much as the reference bundle.

For example, suppose that once again we make a comparison between two consumption bundles, each containing a quantity b of bread and c of cheese. Then we have bundles, A: (b_A, c_A), and B: (b_B, c_B). Now, if $A \succ B$, the preferred set of B, $P(B) = \{A\}$, while the preferred set of A, $P(A) = \varnothing$. (This is the symbol for the empty set, meaning that there is no consumption bundle preferred to A.) Should a third bundle, C: (b_C, c_C), become available, with $A \sim C$ and $B \prec C$, then we obtain a preferred set for B, $P(B)$, where $P(B) = \{A, C\}$, while the weakly preferred set for A, $P(A)$, is given by $P(A) = \{C\}$ and $P(C) = \{A\}$.

By yourself

X4.1 Write out the weakly and strongly preferred sets for the alternatives A, B, C, D, E, and F, where A is weakly preferred to B, B is strongly preferred to C, which is at least as good as D, but better than E, and F is not (weakly) preferred to any other alternative.

X4.2 Three football fans have different preferences over the outcome of a game in which the team that they support, the Reds, play against their local rivals, the Blues.
   (i) Fan A simply cares about the outcome: a win is better than a draw, which is better than a defeat.
   (ii) Fan B also cares about the goal difference, d, defined as the number of goals the Reds score, r, less the number of goals that the Blues score, b. [That is: $d = r - b$.]
   (iii) Fan C cares about the number of goals that the Reds score, but also the goal difference, weighting them equally.
   (a) For each fan, state the (weakly) preferred sets for:
      (i) a victory for the Reds, by one goal to nil;
      (ii) a draw in which each team scores two goals; and
      (iii) a victory for the Blues by two goals to one.
   (b) Show that Fan C is indifferent between any pair of scores (r_0, b_0) and (r_1, b_1), for which $2(r_1 - r_0) = (b_1 - b_0)$.
   (c) Hence or otherwise, draw a diagram indicating clearly Fan C's (weakly) preferred set for a defeat by three goals to four.

4.1.2 Illustrating a preference ordering

In Chapter 3 we introduced the budget set, arguing that every budget set is closed and convex, defining its boundary, the budget constraint, as the set of consumption bundles that have an acquisition cost no greater than the sum of money available to finance purchases, while all bundles in the interior of the set have a lower acquisition cost. That is, we could define the budget set in terms of a property of each element of the set.

By the end of this chapter we will be able to set out an equivalent statement for preferred sets. Using preference relations, the statement is not quite as easy to make as for budget sets, so we illustrate the point that we intend to make in Figure 4.1. We have moved from binary comparisons of pairs of consumption bundles to a *preference ordering*, using the diagram to summarize the preferences of one consumer, Daniel, defined for all possible consumption bundles, $N = \{(b, c): b, c \geq 0\}$. In the diagram, Daniel's (weakly) preferred set for consumption bundle Z: (b_z, c_z) is bounded by a curve: this passes through bundle Z, is everywhere downward-sloping, and becomes flatter as we move along it from left to right. The interior of the preferred set is the area above and to the right of the boundary. This preferred set is closed and convex: it has a well-defined boundary; and if we draw a line between any two points on the boundary, the line lies entirely within the preferred set. It is also *infinite*. Note, though, that while in Chapter 3 we would have illustrated Daniel's budget set by a triangle, whose edges were the axes and the budget constraint, in Figure 4.1, the preferred set in the diagram extends outwards without limit. For every bundle Y: (b_y, c_y): $b_y > b_z$ and $c_y > c_z$ so that bundle Y contains more bread and more cheese than bundle Z, $Y > Z$.

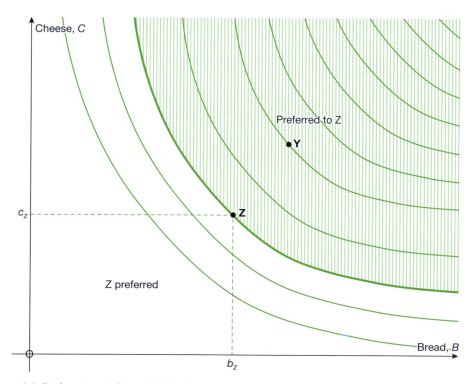

Figure 4.1 Preferred set of bundle Z in the context of a preference map

We show only Daniel's preferred set for bundle Z in Figure 4.1, but given the nature of the underlying preference ordering, we can in principle identify the preferred set for every consumption bundle. All of the curves in Figure 4.1 can be understood as representing the boundary of distinct preferred sets, just as different budget constraints represent the boundaries of distinct budget sets. All the curves shown have much the same shape as the curve that passes through Z, and curves never intersect each other. This is consistent with Daniel's preference ordering which reflects a unique ranking of preferences: specifically, we note that the preferred set for a more preferred bundle is contained entirely within the preferred set for a less preferred bundle.

Under these circumstances, we might usefully talk about the strength of preference for any particular bundle relative to Z, or any other bundle we might choose as a comparator. Bundles that are similar to Z, because they contain roughly as much of both goods, will be approximately as strongly preferred as Z; while bundles close to the origin, with much less of both goods, will be preferred much less strongly than Z; and bundles containing much more of both goods will be much more strongly preferred than Z. We must always remember that these statements about strength of preference require a comparison with strength of preference for a reference bundle – we cannot hope to define an absolute measure of something that is personal and essentially a matter of belief or judgement. But those are matters which we defer to Chapter 5.

Well-behaved preferences An ordering represented by infinite, convex, closed, nested preferred sets.

We have illustrated Daniel's preference ordering in Figure 4.1, so that the preferred set, P(X), for every consumption bundle, X, is closed, convex and infinite, and so that if for any two bundles Y and Z, $Y \succcurlyeq Z$, then the preferred set of Y nests or is contained within the preferred set of Z [or in symbols, $P(Y) \subseteq P(Z)$]. These properties of the diagram are consistent with Daniel having **well-behaved preferences** (or a well-behaved preference ordering).

We shall divide our remaining analysis in this chapter into two parts. Firstly, we shall define a set of assumptions that allow us to confirm that a consumer, such as Daniel, will be able to form a unique preference ordering over all consumption bundles; then we shall think about additional requirements that must be imposed for preferences to be well behaved, on the basis that while we might want to consider preference orderings that are not well behaved at certain points, they are assumed within the standard model of resource allocation. The term *well behaved* simply describes preferences that conform to the assumptions of economic theory, not preferences that are realistic, or desirable, or plausible.

4.2   Essential properties of preferences

The material of this section relies on quite complex concepts, and while it will repay close study, it is, in some ways, the most difficult part of the whole book, and we proceed carefully. Firstly, we reiterate an important difference between the analysis in Chapter 3 and what is set out here. In defining the budget set, we can rely on a measurable property of each consumption bundle, its acquisition cost, and then use that function to specify the nature of the boundary of the affordable set. With a preference relation, we are only able to compare pairs of bundles. Preferences are always relative, and we are unable to define any absolute, objective measure of strength of preference. Our objective is to define a unique preference ordering. As already noted, preferences emerge from pairwise comparisons of consumption bundles drawn from the set N = {(b, c): b, c ≥ 0}.

4.2.1 Completeness and reflexivity

By yourself

X4.3   Applying the strong preference operator, $>$, over the set of bundles C = {(b, c): b, c ≥ 0}, under what circumstances might the statements 'X $>$ Y' and 'Y $>$ X' both be false?

X4.4   Show that if 'X $>$ Y' is false, then 'X $\leqslant$ Y' is true; while if 'X $\geqslant$ Y' is true, then 'X $<$ Y' is false.

Consider some specific reference consumption bundle, Z: (b_z, c_z), as in Figure 4.1. To define Daniel's preferred set for Z, he has to be able to compare every consumption bundle in set C with bundle Z. In addition, since Z could be any bundle, we wish it to be possible to for Daniel to compare any pair of consumption bundles in the set N. The preference relation then has the property of **completeness**. By assuming completeness, we rule out the possibility of Daniel being unable to compare and rank any two consumption bundles: should neither seem better than the other, this results from indifference rather than from an inability to make the appropriate comparison.

Completeness A preference relation defined for every pair of consumption bundles.

An implication of completeness is that it is possible to compare bundle Z with itself. Since we are using the weak version of preference, 'Z $\geqslant$ Z', simply means, 'Z is at least as good as Z'.' While it might seem that it is quite obvious that this is true, applying the strong version of preference, the statement, 'Z $>$ Z', is false. Were that to be true, we would be claiming, 'Z is better than itself'. The property that Z lies in its own (weakly) preferred set means that weak preference has the property of **reflexivity**.

Reflexivity A preference relation that allows the bundle to be compared with itself.

Essential Maths 4.1: Definition of a binary relation

We define a binary relation b over some set of objects, S. The relation allows us to compare some qualitative characteristic of pairs of elements of the set where there is no quantitative measure.

For example, in an art gallery, the relation b: 'is more beautiful than' can be defined over S: the objects in the gallery's collection. Similarly, for a set, S, of film actors, we might define b: 'is more talented than'. For the set, S, of students in a class, we might have b: 'has darker hair than'.

Choosing any two elements, s and t, in S, either the relationship b holds between s and t, or else it does not hold. If it holds, then we denote it symbolically as s b t, and say that the statement is true; while if it does not hold, we say that the statement s b t is false.

The weak preference relation is binary. For X, Y members of the set of consumption bundles, N, we read X $\geqslant$ Y as meaning 'X is (weakly) preferred to Y'; and this statement can either be true or false.

Strict preference is not reflexive. It is perhaps not entirely obvious why reflexivity is important, but remember that our objective is to define the preferred set to Z. If Z is not in the preferred set, then the boundary must include the neighbouring bundles to Z. If we have a countable set of alternatives, as in the questions in Exercises X4.1 and X4.2, then we can define these neighbouring bundles. But here, the quantities of bread and cheese, b and c, can take any value. So, we are unable to define the bundles that are next to Z on Figure 4.1, and we are therefore unable to draw the boundary of the preferred set – instead of being closed, the preferred set is open.

We have defined the set of bundles preferred to Z as consisting of all bundles that are considered to be at least as good as Z. Z is on the boundary of the set because it is just as good as itself. So, if the boundary is well defined, all bundles on the boundary must be just as good as Z, and our consumer is indifferent between all bundles on the boundary. Given a choice among them, it does not matter which one is chosen. We therefore say that the boundary of the preferred set is the *indifference set* of Z, and the curve representing that boundary is known as an **indifference curve**. To summarize what we have shown, note that in Figure 4.2 we can identify three regions: the interior of the preferred set, consisting of all bundles that are (strictly) preferred to Z; the boundary of the (weakly) preferred set, which is the indifference curve showing all bundles that are ranked equally with Z; and the remaining consumption bundles – and bundle Z is (strictly) preferred to all of these.

Indifference curve
The representation of all equally preferred consumption bundles.

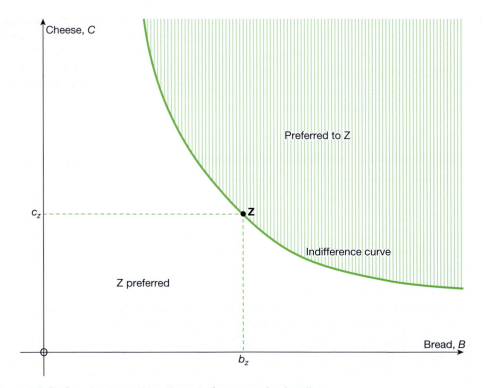

Figure 4.2 Preferred sets partition the set of consumption bundles

4.2.2 Transitivity

Looking at Figure 4.2, requiring completeness and reflexivity seem to be enough to ensure that we shall be able to define the preferred set for every consumption bundle. This is indeed the case, although we shall not seek to demonstrate the point formally. So far, though, all we have done is to show that it is possible to define a closed preferred set for a single bundle. We still need to make one further assumptions about preferences to ensure that we can generate a preference ordering, for an ordering requires that the boundaries of the preferred sets, the indifference curves, do not intersect.

To see why this property might be important, suppose that we define the preferred sets for bundles X and Y. The boundaries of the preferred sets – the indifference curves that pass through X and Y – intersect at Z, as in Figure 4.3. In the diagram, Y lies in the preferred set of X and X lies in the preferred set of Y. So, X is strictly preferred to Y, which is strictly preferred to X. This means that X is strictly preferred to itself, which is impossible.

Essential Maths 4.2: Conditions for an ordering under a relation (1)

For the binary relation b defined over set S, there is a unique ordering of the elements of S under the relation b if the relation is:

- complete, so that for every pair s and t in S, $s\ b\ t$ is either true or false, and never undefined;
- reflexive, so that for every s in S, $s\ b\ s$ is true;
- transitive, so that for every s, t and v in S, if $s\ b\ t$ and $t\ b\ v$, then $s\ b\ v$.

For some value s in set S, we can define the relationship set, B(s) = {t: $t\ b\ s$ (is true)}. For a complete, reflexive, and transitive binary relation, b, B(s) is closed, with boundary I(s) = {v: $v\ b\ s$ and $s\ b\ v$}. (The boundary is defined so that all elements are ranked equally.) Now, if t lies in the interior of the relationship set, B(s), its relationship set, B(t), is contained within B(s), and there is no element of S that lies in both I(s) and I(t); their intersection is the empty set. Under these conditions, the relationship sets are ordered.

Essential Maths 4.3: Conditions for an ordering under a relation (2)

We define a strong binary relation as follows: where s and t are ranked equally, $s\ b\ t$ is false; and we define a weak binary relation similarly: where s and t are ranked equally, $s\ b\ t$ is true. By the definition of reflexivity, for the relationship to be closed, the binary relation must be weak.

We can illustrate ordering graphically. Assuming that t is not in I(s), the relationship set B(t) lies wholly within B(s), and the boundaries of B(s) and B(t) never touch. A relationship map consists of the boundaries of the relationship sets of several elements of S.

For the (weak) preference relation, the boundary of the preferred set for any consumption bundle is the indifference curve that passes through the bundle. If bundle X is (strictly) preferred to bundle Y, then the indifference curve through X, I(X), lies wholly within the preferred set P(Y) and nowhere touches the boundary I(Y). The preference relation is ordered, and can be illustrated by a preference map consisting of indifference curves showing the boundaries of various preferred sets.

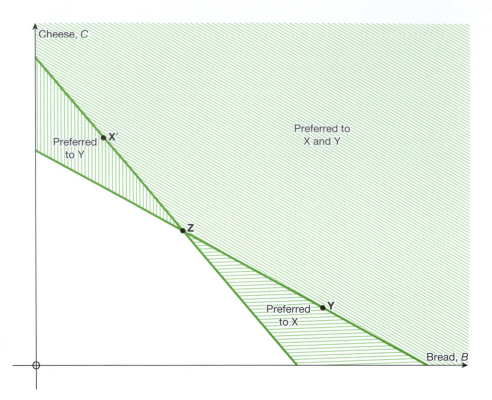

Figure 4.3 Intersecting indifference curves are not consistent with a preference ordering

Transitivity A prefer-ence relation that is consistent, and can therefore be applied successively.

In Exercise 4.5, it is impossible for the indifference curves through B and C to intersect in case (1), but essential that they do in case (2). Preferences are *transitive* in case (1), but *intransitive* in case (2). Formally, the property of **transitivity** applies to a preference relation

Essential Maths 4.4: Additional properties of binary relations

- A binary relation is convex if the relationship set, B(s), is convex for every s in set S. (We have defined the term 'convex set' in Chapter 3.)
- A binary relation is monotonic if every t (in S): t > s lies in the relationship set P(S). This means that t is defined so that in at least one dimension it takes a larger value than s, and in no dimension a smaller value.

If every preferred set, P(X), is convex, then the underlying preference relation is also convex.

Say that consumption bundle Y contains more of at least one good and no less of any good than consumption bundle X. Then Y > X. If X < Y, the preference relation is monotonic. Greater consumption is always preferred.

In our diagrams, the boundaries of preferred sets for a convex, monotonic preference relation slope downwards, and become flatter, moving from left to right, as in Figure 4.1. If Y > X and X < Y, then:
- Y lies further away from the origin than X, and Y is preferred to X.
- P(Y) ⊂ P(X), so that the preferred set of Y is a (proper) subset of the preferred set of X.

Convex preferences are therefore identical with well-behaved preferences.

if for any three consumption bundles, A, B, and C, chosen so that $A \succcurlyeq B$ and $B \succcurlyeq C$, then $A \succcurlyeq C$. This ensures that that there is consistency in rankings, which can then be applied consecutively (since knowing that A is weakly preferred to B, and B to C, we can infer the ranking of A and C). In diagrams, transitivity ensures that indifference curves never intersect.

By yourself

X4.5 Consider the three consumption bundles, A: (b_A, c_A), B: (b_B, c_B) and C: (b_C, c_C), for which $A \succcurlyeq B$ and $B \succcurlyeq C$.

(a) For there to be a unique ordering of the preferences, what must be true about the comparison of A and C?

(b) Sketch two diagrams, indicating the preferred sets of C and B, drawn in such a way that:

(1) in one A must lie in the preferred sets of both B and C; and

(2) in the other A lies in the preferred set of B, but not in the preferred set of C.

We stop short of saying that intransitivity is impossible, because it is in fact quite easy to find situations in which people seem to demonstrate such preferences. The usual way is to imagine a situation where the three alternatives each have three different properties. For example, suppose that someone is deciding which university to attend and that the three characteristics that matter to this person are the quality of the teaching programme, the location of the university, and the sports facilities on campus. Each of the three universities is highest ranked for one of these characteristics. From reading the universities' publicity material or from visiting the campus, the potential applicant is exposed to persuasively presented arguments about each, so that after visiting university X, the applicant ranks this above university Y because of its teaching programme, but then on visiting to university Y, ranks this above university Z because of its location. Deciding to visit university Z to confirm that X is preferable to Z, the applicant discovers that when comparing X to Z, Z is preferable because of its sports facilities. There is nothing to be done in such a situation except to consider the problem further, recognizing that no university is unambiguously the best.

Requiring the preference relation to be transitive has the happy effect of ruling out such cyclical preferences. Assuming transitivity ensures that we can concentrate on those situations where people have a unique ranking of outcomes, so that the preference relation supports an ordering.

By yourself

X4.6 Show that if for consumption bundles X, Y and Z, $X \succcurlyeq Y$, $Y \succcurlyeq Z$, and $Z \succcurlyeq X$, preferences can only be transitive if all three bundles lie on the same indifference curve.

X4.7 Elena strictly prefers consumption bundle A to bundle B, is indifferent between B and C, strictly prefers C to D, and is indifferent between A and D. Confirm that Elena's preferences violate transitivity; and that in a diagram the indifference curve passing through bundles A and D and the one passing through bundle B and C must intersect.

X4.8 Suppose Fedor claims that bundle X lies in the strictly preferred set of Y, but Y lies in the strictly preferred set of X. We persuade him firstly to exchange Y for X (and some money) and then X for Y (and some more money), so that he finishes with the original consumption bundle, but less money. What do you think would happen to someone with Fedor's preferences over time?

4.3   Well-behaved preferences

Monotonicity If bundle Y has no less of any good than bundle Z, then Y is (weakly) preferred to Z.

We return to discussion of Daniel's preferences over consumption bundles (b, c), made up of quantities, b, of bread, and c, of cheese. If we assume that the preference relation is complete, reflexive and transitive, there will be a preference ordering. The standard model of resource allocation assumes that the preference relation will conform to additional assumptions of **monotonicity** and *convexity*. We have already defined these formally in Essential Maths 4.4. Where the preference relation is monotonic, then starting from any reference bundle, Z, and adding any quantity of one or more of the goods available for consumption but not removing any goods, the new bundle, Y, will lie in the preferred set. A simple way of thinking about this is that goods are good. Goods, in being consumed, always provide some benefit to the consumer; more simply, more is always better. We show below that monotonicity rules out the possibility of satiation, which occurs when consumers prefer bundles with less of one or more goods.

Convexity Every preferred set is convex.

We have stated the last assumption, **convexity**, in terms of the convexity of all preferred sets. We have illustrated this property in Figure 4.4. The consumption bundles Y and Z lie on the same indifference curve, I(Z), so the preferred sets are identical: P(Y) = P(Z), and the sets have boundary I(Z). The line that passes through Y and Z in the diagram lies within P(Z) between Y and Z. In general, then, a preference relation is convex if, choosing

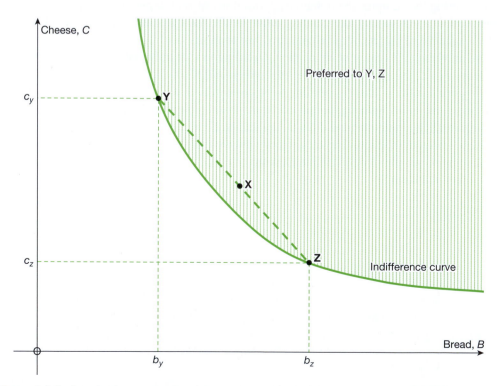

Figure 4.4 Preferred sets are convex

a pair of bundles, X and Y, in the preferred set of Z, P(Z), every bundle, which is a linear combination of X and Y (and which can therefore be depicted as a point on the line running between the bundles, X and Y), lies in the preferred set, P(Z).

Where these five assumptions – completeness, reflexivity, transitivity, monotonicity, and convexity, hold – there will be a preference ordering, which may be represented through a preference map, with indifference curves indicating the boundaries of preferred sets. Preferred sets of more preferred bundles nest within preferred sets of less strongly preferred bundles. All indifference curves are downward-sloping and become flatter when moving from left to right. Given such a 'well-behaved' preference relation, we can generally identify a unique consumption bundle Z, defined so that the intersection of the preferred set, P(Z), and the affordable set is simply Z – and this bundle, Z, is therefore the most-preferred, affordable consumption bundle.

4.3.1 The most-preferred, affordable bundle

We show this outcome in Figure 4.5, which is a slight adaptation of Figure 4.1. Consumption bundle, Z: (b_z, c_z) has preferred set, P(Z), which is the convex region bounded by the indifference curve through Z, I(Z), or I_3. The preference relation appears to be well behaved, supporting an ordering of bundles: the indifference curves I_1, I_2, I_3, I_4, and I_5 are associated with increasingly preferred bundles but never cross. So far, this is the content of Figure 4.1, described using the terminology developed in our discussion of preferences.

We now give our consumer a sum of money, m, which is just enough for bundle Z to be affordable. It follows that Z lies on the budget constraint, B(m), and that the affordable

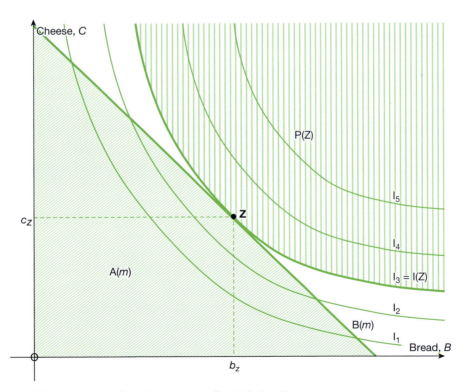

Figure 4.5 Z is the most preferred among the affordable bundles

set A(m) is the region bounded by the budget constraint and the two axes. Now, given that any consumption bundle that is preferred to Z lies in the set P(Z), the weakly preferred set of Z, and Z lies on the boundary of that preferred set, the only affordable consumption bundle in P(Z) is Z itself (and it lies on the boundary of the affordable set). The preferred set lies above and to the right of the affordable set, with a single point of intersection at Z.

Using slightly more formal language, the intersection of the affordable set, A(m) and the preferred set of Z, P(Z) is a set with only one element, Z. Using some mathematical notation, in the diagram, A(m) $\cap$ P(Z) = {Z}. Using geometry, we might note that the budget constraint, B(m), is the tangent to the boundary of the preferred set, which is the indifference curve I(Z). A tangent is a straight line that touches but does not intersect a curve. This is a very important result, and is the basis of the derivation of the equi-marginal principle, introduced in Chapter 1 as fundamental to the achievement of equilibrium resource allocations. It builds on the argument in Chapter 3 that in the face of scarcity, people will use all of their resources to finance consumption.

4.3.2   The marginal rate of substitution

In Chapter 3 we defined the opportunity cost as the quantity of one good that must be given up in order for a budget-constrained consumer to be able to afford another unit of some other good. In terms of Figure 4.5, the opportunity cost is the slope of the budget constraint, and is equal to the relative price of bread, p_b/p_c.

> **Marginal rate of substitution (MRS)**
> A rate of decline in consumption of the good which compensates for the rising consumption of an alternative good.

The marginal rate of substitution (MRS) is the equivalent of the opportunity cost, applied, in this case, to Daniel's preferred sets. It is the rate at which Daniel is willing to give up some cheese as consumption of bread increases, so that the resulting bundle will have the same preferred set as the old one. For example, starting from bundle Z, in Figure 4.6, if the consumption of bread increases but consumption of cheese remains the same, the new bundle will be to the right of Z, in the interior of the preferred set, P(Z). But if consumption of cheese then falls by just enough, the new bundle will be represented by a point such as Z' on the indifference curve I(Z), which lies to the right of Z and below it. In Figure 4.6, note that while Z' lies on the indifference curve I(Z), the curve diverges so slowly from the tangent of point Z that in that small interval, ZZ', it is difficult to confirm – just by looking at the diagram – that Z' does not lie on both the indifference curve and its tangent.

For our argument, we would ideally like to be able to draw the line joining Z and Z' as well as the indifference curve and tangent through Z. We have deliberately omitted this line from Figure 4.6 because the line ZZ' and the tangent through Z are so nearly coincident that even if both were extended to the edges of the diagram, they would be almost indistinguishable.

If Z and Z' are close enough, then the slope of the line joining them will be very close to the slope of the tangent through Z. The slope of the tangent through points Z represents the *marginal rate of substitution*. We might think of the marginal rate of substitution as a personal opportunity cost, showing the rate at which a consumer is willing to give up consumption of one good as consumption of the other good increases. Note that where the

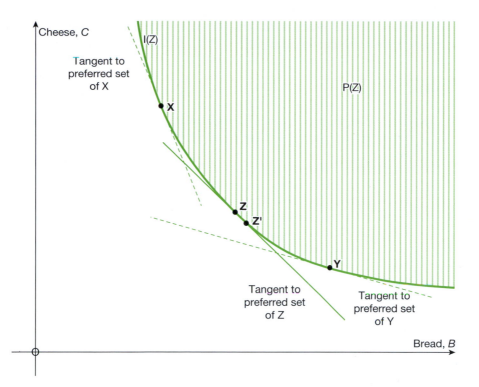

Figure 4.6 The marginal rate of substitution is the slope of the tangent at every point

relative price is the same for every consumption bundle, the marginal rate of substitution differs across consumption bundles. The tangents to points X and Y in Figure 4.6 clearly have different slopes from the tangent at Z. At all three points, the slope of the tangent, our measure of the marginal rate of substitution or MRS, is negative. Moving down the curve and to the right, we see that the MRS gradually approaches zero. As the quantity of bread

Essential Maths 4.5: **The slope of the tangent (1)**

What exactly does it mean to say that two points, Z and Z', in Figure 4.6 are close to each other? Suppose we cut out a square of paper, placing it under a microscope slide, and magnified the image fifty times. We would then see the indifference curve turning away from the tangent, and could easily distinguish the line passing through Z and Z' from the indifference curve and the tangent.

Now consider a further exercise. Choose point Z" that lies on the indifference curve somewhere between Z and Z' but much closer to Z than Z', say 1/50 of the distance from Z to Z'. On the original diagram, Z" would be so close to Z that we would not be able to distinguish it from Z. In the magnified version, Z and Z" are about the same distance apart as Z and Z' in Figure 4.6. Then, looking carefully at the region between Z and Z", we would see the indifference curve, I(Z), bending away very slightly from the tangent through Z, and that curvature would be just about enough for us to observe it by visual inspection. In this magnified section, the line joining Z and Z" would be almost completely indistinguishable both from the indifference curve and from the tangent at Z.

in the consumption bundle increases, the smaller the amount of cheese that Daniel will be willing to give up in return for an extra loaf.

By yourself

X4.9   Assume that Gabrielle faces much the same situation as Daniel, having a fixed amount of money, m, which she can use to buy a consumption bundle (b, c), consisting of quantities b of bread and c of cheese, with unit prices, p_b and p_c. Gabrielle's preferences are well behaved.
(a) On a diagram, sketch Gabrielle's affordable set.
(b) Assume that Gabrielle chooses a consumption bundle M: (b_M, c_M), which lies on her budget constraint, but for which the marginal rate of substitution is greater than the relative price. Illustrate such a point on your diagram as the intersection of the budget constraint and an indifference curve.
(c) Confirm that Gabrielle can afford to buy consumption bundles in the preferred set, P(M).
(d) Confirm that Gabrielle can also buy consumption bundles on the indifference curve, I(M), for which the acquisition cost $A(b, c) < A(b_M, c_M)$.
(e) Which do you think Gabrielle should do: maintain expenditure and buy a bundle that she prefers to M, as in (c); or reduce expenditure while buying a bundle in the set, I(M)?

X4.10   Suppose that Hanna faces an exactly similar problem to Gabrielle, except that she chooses a consumption bundle L: (b_L, c_L) that lies on an indifference curve for which the marginal rate of substitution is less than the relative price. Repeat X4.9.

Exercises X4.9 and X4.10 confirm that Gabrielle and Hanna cannot do better than select a consumption bundle for which the marginal rate of substitution equals the relative price, so that in effect their private opportunity costs equal the opportunity cost determined in the market. These exercises also raise further questions about the object of 'doing as well as possible'. It seems that they might either fix their expenditure, as considered in Chapter 3,

Essential Maths 4.6: **The slope of the tangent (2)**

We can apply the lessons from our thought experiment in Essential Maths 4.5 about the magnification of the area around Z in our diagram quite carefully.

- The slope of a straight line is the ratio of the vertical distance to the horizontal distance between any two points.
- The slope of the straight line joining two points on a smooth curve that are very close together is approximately the slope of the tangent to the curve at either point.
- If one brings the two points on the curve closer together, the approximation of the slope of the line joining them to the slope of the tangent improves.
- The slope of the tangent is the slope of the line passing through two points that are so close that they are indistinguishable.
- We define the slope of a curve at point Z as the slope of the tangent at Z.

We therefore define the marginal rate of substitution for some consumption bundle as the slope of the indifference curve that passes through that bundle.

or else fix their preferred set. If the only way of spending the money available for consumption is to purchase bread and cheese, then they should spend up to the limit of the money available to them. Since we assume that to be the case in the standard model, we will proceed on that basis.

4.4   Alternative preference orderings

In Figure 4.7, we show four indifference maps consistent with preference orderings that in some way violate the assumptions required in Section 4.3. We review the properties of the underlying preference relations briefly, exploring their characteristics, and, in the discussion following the exercises, we consider why such properties might problematic in terms of economic theory.

- In Figure 4.7a, the indifference curves are all closed loops; the preferred sets are all convex, with more preferred sets nesting within less preferred sets. Somewhere within the smallest loop, we should be able to find a consumption bundle, B, that is preferred to every other one. We call this consumption bundle the **bliss point**. Thinking about bread and cheese, there is presumably a physical limit to consumption. Too much of either would be unpleasant. The idea of the bliss point is that there is one bundle that constitutes the best possible combination – if we are thinking about consumption bundles as being the amounts consumed in a single sitting, then the bliss point is the best liked of all combinations.

  Bliss point The ideal consumption bundle.

- In Figure 4.7b, the indifference curves are all open loops; the preferred sets are again convex, with more preferred sets nesting within less preferred sets. Although such preferences are not well behaved according to our formal definition, it is still possible to identify a unique most-preferred, affordable bundle. Once again, there is an issue of satiation. Suppose that we start from a consumption bundle, such as A, where the indifference curve is upward-sloping. In the exercise, we shall see that it is possible for a consumer to give up both bread and cheese, and still to obtain a more preferred bundle. Economists tend to be uncomfortable about admitting such possibilities because these conflict very strongly with the underlying assumption that resources are scarce. Were someone able to consume less and be better off, then we would expect them to do so.
- The indifference curves in Figure 4.7c do not support convex preferred sets. If we choose any two points on a single indifference curve and draw a straight line between them, then that line passes through the region made up of less preferred, rather than more preferred, consumption bundles. Here, it is the behaviour of the marginal rate of substitution that is interesting. Since the slopes of the indifference curves increase, as we move along them from left to right the marginal rate of substitution becomes larger as consumption of bread increases. The more bread that there is in the consumption bundle, the more cheese the consumer is willing to give up as consumption of bread increases further.
- The last possibility, in Figure 4.7d, perhaps captures the situation in some modern diets in which carbohydrates ('carbs') are considered to be bad and protein good (although, to capture that effect fully, we should really replace cheese with steak).

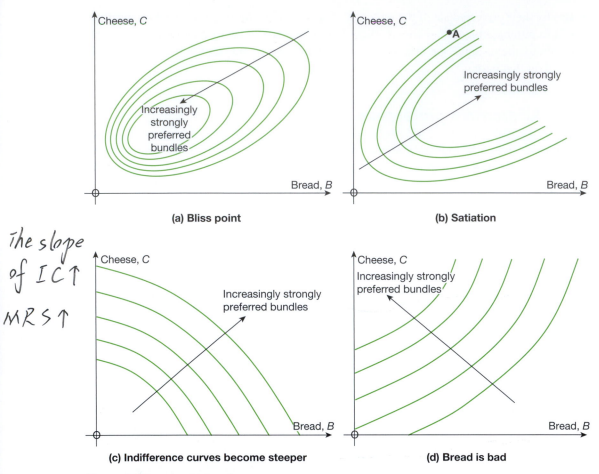

Figure 4.7 Non-standard preferences

The slope of IC↑ MRS↑

Once again, indifference curves bound convex preferred sets, and more strongly preferred sets nest within less strongly preferred sets. However, the indifference curves are upward-sloping, rather than downward-sloping. We can say quite simply that in this case 'bread is bad'.

By yourself

(It may be useful to draw sketches in these exercises using one colour of ink for indifference curves and another for budget constraints, and to shade preferred and affordable sets using pencil.)

X4.11 Sketch a diagram similar to Figure 4.7a, in which indifference curves take the form of nested closed loops. Choose a point within the most-preferred set (the smallest loop), and label it B. This is the bliss point.

(a) Draw a budget constraint that touches one of the closed loops at consumption bundle K between the origin and the bliss point, B. Shade the preferred set P(K) and the affordable set bounded by the budget constraint that passes through K.

  (i) Identify clearly the intersection of the budget set and the preferred set P(K).

  (ii) What is the most-preferred, affordable bundle in this case?

  (iii) Does this consumer spend all the money available?

(b) Repeat exercise (a), but this time drawing a second budget constraint that touches the preferred set, P(K), further away from the origin than the bliss point, B.

    (i) Explain why the preferred set is the same as before, and that the affordable set has become larger.

    (ii) Identify clearly the intersection of the new budget set and the preferred set P(K).

    (iii) What is the most-preferred, affordable bundle in this case?

(c) In this situation, does the consumer spend all the money available? Explain why this might occur, concentrating on any differences between parts (a) and (b).

X4.12 Sketch a diagram similar to Figure 4.7b, in which indifference curves take the form of nested open loops. From a point, A, on the upward-sloping segment of the outermost indifference curve, extend a straight line that intersects the indifference curves that bound the more preferred sets.

(a) Explain why consumption bundle A can never be the most-preferred, affordable set.

(b) Draw a budget constraint that just touches the innermost indifference curve at point M.

    (i) Sketch the affordable set and the preferred set.

    (ii) Identify the intersection of the preferred set and the affordable set, and hence the most-preferred affordable bundle.

    (iii) Why might we always expect the most-preferred, affordable bundle to be found on the downward-sloping section of an indifference curve?

(c) Why might we say that in the upper segment of these indifference curves, where the indifference curves are upward-sloping but flattening out, the consumer's appetite for cheese has been satiated?

X4.13 Sketch a diagram similar to Figure 4.7c, in which indifference curves take the form of nested curves that become increasingly steep.

(a) Draw a budget constraint that just touches the indifference curve closest to the origin at point T: (b_T, c_T): $b_T, c_T > 0$. Sketch the affordable set bounded by the budget constraint and the preferred set of T, indicating clearly the intersection of the affordable and preferred sets.

(b) Explain why T is not the most-preferred, affordable bundle in this situation.

(c) Indicate what you consider to be the most-preferred affordable bundle by the letter V, giving reasons for your choice.

(d) Draw another diagram with a set of indifference curves that have a similar shape to the ones that you have just used but that do not have such a steep slope at the intersection on the bread axis. Draw a budget constraint that intersects the indifference curve closest to the origin on the bread axis and that is steeper than the indifference curve.

    (i) At this intersection, which is larger: the marginal rate of substitution or the relative price?

    (ii) If your budget constraint intersects other indifference curves in your map, at each intersection which is larger: the marginal rate of substitution or the relative price?

    (iii) What do you expect will be the most-preferred affordable consumption bundle in this case?

    (iv) Suppose we consider a society in which cheese has recently been invented, so that until now only bread has been consumed. Predict consumer responses to this new good. What would have to happen for consumers to start buying cheese?

(Continued)

> **X4.14**   Sketch a diagram similar to Figure 4.7d, in which indifference curves take the form of upward-sloping, nested curves. Draw in a budget constraint, and indicate the affordable set.
>   (a) Label the intersection of the budget set with the cheese axis, R. Sketch the preferred set of R (it may be necessary to add to the diagram an indifference curve passing through R).
>   (b) Identify the intersection of the affordable set and the preferred set of R.
>   (c) Show that the consumer will always prefer a bundle with less bread if the quantity of cheese is held constant. Hence or otherwise, explain our claim that in this situation, 'Bread is bad.'

4.5   Conclusions

The examples in Exercises X4.11–X4.14 rely upon preference structures that might be problematic. Well-behaved preferences exclude the possibility of there being bliss points (Figure 4.7a), and indeed satiation (Figure 4.7b) – more of every good is definitely better. The marginal rate of substitution never increases as the quantity of any one good in the consumption bundle increases (Figure 4.7c), so we generally expect consumers to choose mixtures of goods, rather than just one of two. And, goods are never bad (Figure 4.7d), which is the point about satiation once again, but with satiation occurring with zero consumption of a good. In fact, all that we are able to rule out is (a) satiation, and (b) even a locally increasing marginal rate of substitution.

We have completed two tasks in this chapter. Firstly, we have defined a set of assumptions about preference relations that we shall use in subsequent analysis, confident that where they hold, the preference ordering will be 'well behaved'. Secondly, we have shown that with an appropriately defined set of preferences, we can obtain a unique, most-preferred, affordable consumption bundle. This will be the foundation of our further analysis.

That analysis will address the problem that we cannot simply write down a consumer's preference ordering of all consumption bundles. It will take advantage of the fact that complete, reflexive, and transitive preferences always support a preference ordering. This is enough for us to be able to create a numerical index of strength of preference, assigning a unique number to every indifference set. With well-behaved preferences, at least in principle, it should be possible to write down a rule that will assign every consumption bundle a number that reflects its position in the preference ordering, with more preferred bundles receiving higher numbers. In Chapter 5, we explore some rules of this type, which take the mathematical form of utility functions.

Summary

Consumers are able to compare pairs of consumption bundles and to decide which one they prefer. By means of such pairwise comparisons it is possible for a consumer to form a preference ordering, which is a ranking of all possible consumption bundles. For preferences over a set of consumption bundles to support a preference ordering, they must be complete, reflexive, and transitive; and since strong preferences do not satisfy reflexivity, we use weak preferences instead.

Weak preferences allow for the outcome that bundles A and B are equally strongly preferred – in this case, we say that the consumer is indifferent between the bundles. We show all bundles between which the consumer is indifferent on an indifference curve. If the preference relation satisfies the necessary assumptions, every bundle lies on an indifference curve, and indifference curves will never cross.

For our standard model of resource allocation, we require 'well-behaved' preferences, imposing two further assumptions: monotonicity (that increasing consumption of one good while holding consumption of the others constant must always increase the strength of preference); and convexity (that the preferred set is always convex). If these assumptions are satisfied, then indifference curves will be convex and downward-sloping and will curve away from the origin.

Defining the marginal rate of substitution as the slope of the indifference curve, we argued that the most-preferred, affordable bundle will be found where the budget constraint is the tangent to an indifference curve, with the marginal rate of substitution equal to the relative price of the goods.

Visit the companion website at **www.palgrave.com/mochrie** to access further teaching and learning materials, including lecturer slides and a testbank, as well as guideline answers and student MCQs.

Utility functions

What we do in this chapter

Everybody has preferences. We saw in Chapter 4 that, starting from a preference relation, defined over a set of consumption bundles, we can generate an ordering of the bundles. In this chapter, we shall assume that it is possible to represent the ordering through a *utility function*. The function takes as its inputs the quantities of each good in a given consumption bundle and generates a numerical value, the *utility* of the consumption bundle. The ordering of bundles by utility score is the same as the ordering by the preference relation, so the utility function represents the consumer's preferences.

In Chapter 4 we defined assumptions necessary for preferences to be well behaved;

and we extend that analysis, setting out the corresponding restrictions on the form of utility functions. To do this, we define marginal utility functions, which measure the rate at which utility changes as consumption of one good increases, while consumption of others remains constant; we then express the marginal rate of substitution between two goods as the ratio of marginal utilities.

We introduce the *Constant Elasticity of Substitution* (CES) form of utility function, concentrating in this chapter on the creation of preference maps for special cases, such as pairs of good that are *perfect substitutes*, pairs that are *perfect complements*, and the *Cobb–Douglas utility function*.

5.1　The concept of utility

In the second half of the 19th century, as economists started to explore the nature of preference relations, many believed that it would eventually be possible to develop some objective measure of the value, or *utility*, of a consumption bundle. It would then be possible to use this second property of consumption bundles in combination with their acquisition cost, as defined in Chapter 3, to identify the most-preferred, affordable consumption bundle in any situation.

Anyone reading this chapter very quickly might believe that it contains such an argument. But that would be to miss some important points about our understanding of the nature of utility. Suppose that we were to offer many people a choice between two pairs of shoes. The shoes are identical, except that one pair is black and the other pair is brown. Some people would prefer the black shoes, some the brown shoes, a few might be indifferent, and some might even claim to be unable to express a preference. Where the price of a pair of shoes, or the acquisition cost of a consumption bundle, is an objective, observable property, preference orderings, whether over pairs of shoes or a set of consumption bundles, are subjective and private. The efforts to find an objective interpretation of utility were unsuccessful, and economists gradually adopted the interpretation that we present here: a utility function is a numerical representation of an individual preference ordering.

Suppose that this were not so. We might expect advertisements, which are intended to persuade us to buy goods, to include statements such as, 'I like this bundle twice as much as my old one' or 'This new product has given me 15 extra units of value'. That such statements immediately seem contrived and unnatural should be enough to confirm that we have no language in which to describe preferences on a measurable, commonly understood scale.

By yourself

X5.1   Using the concept of utility, evaluate the claim that we can increase total utility by transferring wealth from rich people to poor people. (You may find it useful to think of a rich miser, such as Ebenezer Scrooge in Charles Dickens's *A Christmas Carol*, and someone who is voluntarily poor, such as St Francis of Assisi, who renounced his family's wealth.)

X5.2   Suppose that my boss calls me into his office and offers to double my salary. Giving reasons, explain whether or not you agree with these statements:
   (a) 'I prefer having the higher salary to my existing salary.'
   (b) 'My utility will double if I accept this offer.'
   (c) 'My utility will increase by at least 50 points if I accept this offer.'

To apply the concept of **utility**, we begin by considering the preferences of one person, Eva, over a set of consumption bundles. We assume that Eva's preferences are complete, reflexive, and transitive. As demonstrated in Chapter 4, these assumptions are sufficient to ensure that she can form a preference ordering over the set of consumption bundles. Eva now decides to represent the preference ordering by assigning a number, $U(Z)$, to every consumption bundle Z. The higher the ranking of bundle Z in the preference ordering, the larger the value of $U(Z)$ will be. Eva's utility function $U : Z \rightarrow U(Z)$ has the property that if, and only if, she (weakly) prefers bundle Z_1 to bundle Z_2, then she would report a utility score for bundle Z_1 that is no less than her utility score for bundle Z_2. In symbols

> **Utility** A measure of the strength of preference for a bundle, set by the preference ordering.

$$Z_1 \succcurlyeq Z_2 \Leftrightarrow U(Z_1) \geq U(Z_2) \tag{5.1}$$

The symbol '$\Leftrightarrow$' means that the statements 'Z_1 is weakly preferred to Z_2' and 'The utility of Z_1 is no less than the utility of Z_2' are equivalent. As well as being able to infer the ordering of the utility scores of specific bundles from the preference ordering, we can also infer the preference ordering from the utility scores assigned to bundles. Eva's utility function is simply a numerical representation of her preference ordering.

5.1.1   Uniqueness up to a monotonic transformation

Compare this interpretation of Eva's utility scores with the information that we might obtain from temperature measurements. In the 18th century, scientists realized that they needed some way of assigning numerical values to objects so that they might be ranked according to their thermal energy. While temperature is an observable property, it has no naturally defined scale. Even today, in the United States of America it is still usual to report temperatures using the Fahrenheit scale, while the rest of the world has adopted the Celsius scale. Temperature in the Fahrenheit scale, F, can be calculated from the temperature in Celsius, C, by the formula $F = 32 + 1.8C$. This tells us that 0 in the Celsius scale is 32 in the Fahrenheit scale, and that the unit of measurement – one degree – in Celsius is 1.8 degrees in Fahrenheit. These properties mean that the Fahrenheit scale is a linear transformation of the Celsius scale. In physical theory, it is not necessary for every temperature scale to be a linear transformation of any other, but both empirical and theoretical traditions in temperature measurement support this convention: Fahrenheit and Celsius both took advantage of various reproducible physical properties of water and saline solutions to create their temperature scales.

In contrast, all that we have required of Eva is that she reports a utility score for every consumption bundle, which is consistent with her preference ordering. Any transformation of her utility values that preserved their ordering would be admissible.

Suppose that we have Eva's utility scores, $U(Z)$, defined for every bundle. We now propose an alternative measure of utility, $V(Z)$, constructed according to some function, $v : U(Z) \rightarrow v[U(Z)]$, which allows us to generate V scores from the U scores. (This is, in effect, like the process of conversion from Celsius to Fahrenheit.) For any consumption bundle, Z:

$$V(Z) = v[U(Z)] \tag{5.2}$$

Monotonically increasing transformation A larger domain value leads to a larger image value.

There are in principle two ways of obtaining the value $V(Z)$. Either Eva could report it directly, rather than the U value; or else we can take the reported U value and transform it according to the function v. The only restriction that we can place on v is that it should be **monotonically increasing**, so that for any pair of consumption bundles Z_1 and Z_2:

$$U(Z_1) \geq U(Z_2) \Leftrightarrow V(Z_1) \geq V(Z_2) \tag{5.3}$$

If Eva reports a U value for bundle Z_1 that is no smaller than her V value for bundle Z_2, then her V value for Z_1 will be no smaller than her V value for Z_2, and *vice versa*. The transformation of the utility function does not alter the ordering of utility values, and so U and V both represent Eva's preference ordering over the set of consumption bundles.

By yourself

X5.3   Confirm that Expression 5.3 is true: that is, if $U(Z_1) = U(Z_2)$, $V(Z_1) = V(Z_2)$.

X5.4   Suppose that $v[U(Z)]$ is increasing in $U(Z)$, so that if $U(Z_1) \geq U(Z_2)$, $V(Z_1) \geq V(Z_2)$. Confirm that Expression 5.3 is true.

X5.5   Define three bundles: Z_1 : (6, 4); Z_2 : (3, 7); and Z_3 : (5, 5). Frances' preference ordering is: $Z_2 > Z_3 > Z_1$. She assigns the bundles utility scores: $U(6, 4) = 10$; $U(3, 7) = 15$; and $U(5, 5) = 12$. Confirm that her ranking of the bundles remains the same after the transformations: (1) $v[U(Z)] = 1 + U(Z) + [U(Z)]^2$; and (2) $w[U(Z)] = [1 + U(Z)]^{0.5}$. (You will need a calculator to obtain values in the second transformation.)

X5.6   Suppose that we obtain the following utility values for bundles A, B, C, D, and E:

Bundle Z	A	B	C	D	E
Utility, $U(Z)$	1	2	3	4	5

For each of the following rules:
(a) Calculate the utility values for each bundle under the new rule.
(b) Calculate the difference in the utility values between bundles A and B, B and C, C and D, and D and E.
(c) Decide whether or not the relation appears to be monotonically increasing:
   (i) $v(U) = 1 + U$ (ii) $v(U) = U^2$ (iii) $v(U) = U^2 + U$
   (iv) $v(U) = U^2 - 4U$ (v) $v(U) = U^{0.5}$ (vi) $v(U) = U^{-1}$
   (vii) $v(U) = \ln U$

Where temperature and most other physical scales of measurement are unique up to a linear transformation (as in the rule $F = 32 + 1.8C$), utility is unique only up to a monotonically increasing transformation. As we see in Exercise X5.5, there is no objective measure of a change in utility. Monotonically increasing transformations allow the utility scale to be stretched or compressed.[1]

5.2 Utility functions as preference orderings

In Chapter 4 we defined the set of bundles among which the consumer is indifferent as the *indifference set*. Such sets are shown on a preference map by an *indifference curve*, with each indifference curve forming the boundary of a weakly preferred set. Figure 5.1 is therefore largely a reproduction of Figure 4.1. Starting from the reference bundle Z (b_z, c_z), we have drawn the indifference curve through Z, labelling it I_3 as before, but showing that along this curve the utility of every bundle, $U(X) = 3$. The preferred set lies above and to the right of I_3, with indifference curves I_4 and I_5 associated with levels of utility 4 and 5 respectively.

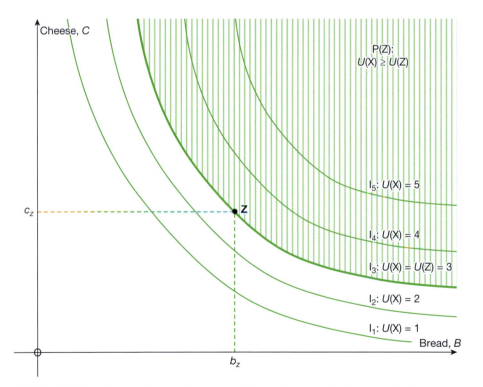

Figure 5.1 A utility function enables us to represent the preference ordering numerically

---

1 With utility is being treated as an ordinal concept, we argue that it is impossible to make inter-personal comparisons of utility, especially where these are based on transfers of wealth between people. In his essay, 'Giving to the homeless', Conor Morgan-Hughes has nonetheless argued that some forms of charitable giving are more easily understood by assuming that people believe a small donation is more valuable to a poor person than that money would be to them. To read Conor's essay, go to the online student essay bank on the companion website for this book, **www.palgrave.com/mochrie.**

We have redefined the preferred set as consisting of all consumption bundles to which we have assigned utility greater than or equal to the utility of the reference bundle Z.

For utility to be more useful than the general concept of a preference ordering, we work with functional forms that generate a utility value for each bundle using the quantity of each good in that consumption bundle. In effect, instead of $U(Z)$, the utility of bundle Z, we concentrate on calculating $U(b_z, c_z)$, the utility of a bundle consisting of quantities b_z of bread and c_z of cheese. Note that this is similar to our development of the acquisition cost function in Chapter 3, except that there the linear form of the function followed immediately from our assumptions about prices. With a utility function, we can impose no stronger requirements on its form than that the function should be consistent with the underlying preferences being complete, reflexive, transitive, monotonically increasing and convex, so that that the preference relation is well behaved.

- Completeness is not a particularly strong requirement. It means that the function, U, is defined for every possible combination of the values b and c. So, for every bundle, $Z : (b_z, c_z)$, we are able to calculate $U(b_z, c_z)$.
- The requirement of reflexivity is that a bundle lies in its own weakly preferred set. This will hold if $U(b_z, c_z) \geq U(b_z, c_z)$, which is certainly true.
- Transitivity effectively requires that the preference relation is consistent, in the sense that for bundles X, Y, and Z, if $X \succcurlyeq Y$ and $Y \succcurlyeq Z$, then $X \succcurlyeq Z$. Thinking of the utility function, then if $X \succcurlyeq Y$ and $Y \succcurlyeq Z$, $U(b_x, c_x) \geq U(b_y, c_y)$ and $U(b_y, c_y) \geq U(b_z, c_z)$. It then follows that $U(b_x, c_x) \geq U(b_z, c_z)$. Since the value of the utility function increases with the ranking of the bundle in the preference ordering, it is impossible that X should be preferred to Y or Y to Z, and the utility of bundle Z be greater than the utility of bundle X.

> **By yourself**
>
> **X5.7**   Being able to assign a larger utility number to a consumption bundle requires the underlying preferences to be transitive. Demonstrate that if for bundles A, B, and C, $U(A) \geq U(B)$ and $U(B) \geq U(C)$, then $A \succcurlyeq C$.

We claimed in Chapter 4 that these three assumptions are sufficient for a consumer to form a preference ordering, and these are also the minimum requirements for preferences to be represented by a utility function. In developing the standard model, we impose further assumptions, monotonicity and convexity, so that the preference relation is well behaved. To define these assumptions in terms of utility, we rely not on the underlying utility function but on the marginal utility functions, which measure how utility changes as consumption of one good increases.

5.2.1 Marginal utility

Marginal utility of a good The rate of change of utility as consumption of the good increases, consumption of other goods being held constant.

George's utility, $U(b, c)$, is a function of the quantities of bread and cheese that he consumes. We define his **marginal utility** of bread, $MU_B(b, c)$, as the rate at which his utility changes as he increases consumption of bread while holding consumption of cheese constant; and his marginal utility of cheese $MU_C(b, c)$, very similarly, as the rate at which his utility changes as he increases consumption of cheese while holding consumption of bread constant. More generally, the marginal utility of a good is a function that measures the rate of change of utility as consumption of that good increases while holding consumption of all others constant.

Like acquisition cost and utility, marginal utility functions are defined over all possible consumption bundles. However, the marginal utilities are derived from the total utility function, in a way that we shall define rather more fully in Chapter 6. Introducing the concept in this chapter, we use an intuitive and generally approximately correct measure, treating the marginal utility as the additional utility generated from consuming one more unit of a good while holding consumption of other goods constant. So for George, starting from the consumption bundle, $(b, c) = (5, 2)$, the marginal utility of bread, $MU_B(5, 2)$, is the value of a 6th loaf of bread (holding consumption of cheese at 2 kg); and the marginal utility of cheese, $MU_C(5, 2)$, is the value of another 1 kg of cheese (holding consumption of bread at 5 loaves).

Note that the marginal utilities of each good vary with the current consumption bundle. For George, it may be that for the current consumption bundle $(b, c) = (5, 4)$, $MU_B(5, 4) \neq MU_B(5, 2)$, even though the quantity of bread in each bundle is the same.

5.2.2 The marginal rate of substitution

In Figure 5.2 we show George as consuming consumption bundle Z_1, but considering the alternative bundle, Z_2. Bundles Z_1 and Z_2 are only a little different: Z_1 contains a little more cheese and a little less bread than Z_2. Both lie on indifference curve I_1, along which all consumption bundles have a total utility of one. George should therefore consider bundles Z_1 and Z_2 to be perfect substitutes.

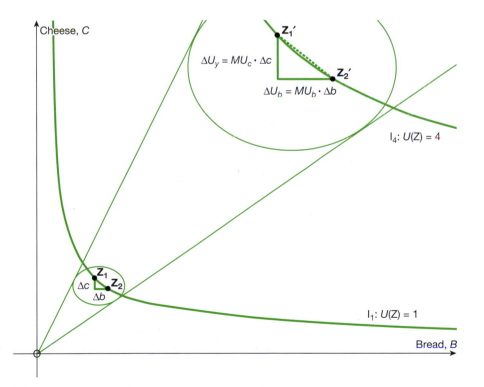

Figure 5.2 Offsetting changes in consumption can maintain utility level

Since the consumption bundles Z_1 and Z_2 lie on a single indifference curve, if George decides to consume Z_2 instead of Z_1, there will be no change in his utility. Using symbols, $\Delta U = 0$. (We read the 'Δ' symbol (the Greek upper-case letter, delta) as 'The change in', so the statement $\Delta U = 0$ means 'The change in utility is zero'.)

We have defined utility, $U = U(b, c)$, so that it is a function of the quantities of both goods in the consumption bundle (b, c). When George switches between bundle Z_1 and bundle Z_2 both b and c change, but $U\left(b_{Z_1}, c_{Z_1}\right) = U\left(b_{Z_2}, c_{Z_2}\right)$. We assert that there have been two offsetting changes. Firstly, increasing his consumption of bread increases George's utility by an amount ΔU_B. Secondly, reducing his consumption of cheese decreases his utility by an amount ΔU_C. For Z_1 and Z_2 to be on the same indifference curve, these two changes must cancel out, and

$$\Delta U = \Delta U_B + \Delta U_C = 0 \qquad [5.4]$$

Marginal utilities measure the rate of change of utility as the consumption of one particular good changes. We think of it (informally) as a measure of the change in utility per additional unit of consumption. Then the total change in utility resulting from a change in consumption of a good will be (approximately) equal to the marginal utility of that good multiplied by the total change in consumption. So, for the change in consumption of bread, Δb, we have $\Delta U_B \approx MU_B \cdot \Delta b$, while for the change in consumption of cheese, Δc, we have $\Delta U_C \approx MU_C \cdot \Delta c$. (The '$\cdot$' operator here indicates that we multiply together these two factors.) We can now write:

$$\Delta U = \Delta U_B + \Delta U_C = MU_B \cdot \Delta b + MU_C \cdot \Delta c = 0 \qquad [5.5]$$

This is illustrated in Figure 5.2. The diagram shows the effect of consuming bundle Z_2 instead of bundle Z_1, but it also shows another pair of bundles, Z_1' and Z_2', chosen so that the larger bundles, Z_1' and Z_2', contain four times as much bread and cheese as the smaller ones, Z_1 and Z_2, and so they are also four times as far apart. In thinking about illustrating our argument, these alternatives are intended to emphasize that while we need to be able to show points that are far enough apart to be easily distinguishable, when we do that the change in consumption may not be very small. Alternatively, we could argue that we are only really considering the switch from Z_1 to Z_2, and that we have increased the scale of the drawing so that we can see the effect of this small change more easily. On this reading, X' and Z' are simply proxies for X and Z and the area within the large ellipse is simply a magnification of the area within the small ellipse.

Rearranging the last equality in Expression 5.5, we obtain:

$$MU_B \cdot \Delta b = -MU_C \cdot \Delta c \qquad \boxed{\text{Subtract } MU_C \Delta c \text{ from both sides}}$$

$$\frac{\Delta c}{\Delta b} = -\frac{MU_B}{MU_C} \qquad \boxed{\text{Divide both sides by } MU_C \Delta b} \qquad [5.6]$$

The left-hand side of Expression 5.6 is the change in consumption of cheese divided by the change in consumption of bread. This is the slope of the line joining Z_1 and Z_2. In Chapter 4 we argued that as Δb becomes smaller and smaller, this line will approximate the tangent to the indifference curve at Z_1, whose slope is George's marginal rate of substitution.

We interpret Expression 5.6 as saying that the marginal rate of substitution, evaluated for bundle Z_1 is (minus one times) the ratio of marginal utilities.

$$MRS(b_{Z_1}, c_{Z_1}) = \left.\frac{\Delta c}{\Delta b}\right|_{(b_{Z_1}, c_{Z_1})} = -\frac{MU_B(b_{Z_1}, c_{Z_1})}{MU_C(b_{Z_1}, c_{Z_1})} \qquad [5.7]$$

We will return to Expression 5.7 in Chapter 6. It is important for the application of the equi-marginal principle and the identification of the most-preferred, affordable consumption bundle, which is the solution of the consumer's resource allocation problem in the standard model.

5.2.3 Well-behaved preferences

If the preference relation is monotonically increasing and convex, then in a diagram such as Figure 5.1 indifference curves are downward-sloping and convex and never cross, so that preferred sets are nested.

By yourself

X5.8 Heidi currently intends to purchase and consume bundle X : (b_x, c_x), where b_x is the quantity of bread and c_x the quantity of cheese in the bundle. She prefers bundle $X_1 : (b_x + \delta b, c_x)$. What do you conclude about Heidi's marginal utility of bread, MU_B? Why does she not intend to purchase bundle X_1?

X5.9 Explain why, if Heidi's preferences are monotonically increasing, she would report marginal utilities, MU_B and MU_C, that would always be greater than zero.

X5.10 Suppose that Heidi reports that her marginal utility of bread, MU_B is constant, but that her marginal utility of cheese, MU_C, decreases with consumption.
  (a) Draw a diagram to show Heidi's current consumption bundle, X : (6, 3), and her current marginal rate of substitution, $MRS(6, 3) = -1$.
  (b) Suppose that Heidi reduces her consumption of bread and increases her consumption of cheese, while maintaining her current level of utility. Confirm that her MRS will increase.
  (c) Repeat (b), but showing that MRS will decrease following an increase in bread consumption and a decrease in cheese consumption.
  (d) What do you conclude about the curvature of this indifference curve?

X5.11 Repeat X5.10, but for Isabel, who reports that her marginal utility of bread, MU_B, is decreasing, but that her marginal utility of cheese, MU_C, increases with consumption.

X5.12 Repeat X5.10, but for Jiang, who reports that both of her marginal utilities, MU_B and MU_C, decrease with consumption.

[handwritten annotations:] $b\downarrow\ MU_B\downarrow\ MU_{C_0}\ c\uparrow$
$c\uparrow\ MU_C\downarrow\ MU_{B_0}\ b\uparrow$

From the exercises, we find that if

- MU_B decreases as consumption of bread increases, while MU_C remains constant when consumption of cheese increases; or if
- MU_C decreases as consumption of cheese increases, while MU_B remains constant when consumption of bread increases; or if
- MU_B decreases as consumption of bread increases, and MU_C decreases when consumption of cheese increases

[handwritten annotations:] $MU_B\downarrow\ b\uparrow$ $MU_C\downarrow\ c\uparrow$

$b \to$ consumption of Bread
$c \to$ consumption of cheese

then we can be certain that the marginal rate of substitution will increase towards zero as we increase consumption of bread and reduce consumption of cheese to hold utility constant. The associated indifference curve will then be convex.

The assumption of diminishing marginal utility is a sufficient condition, and not a necessary one – in other words, it is stronger than we need. In Chapter 6 we will show that increasing marginal utilities can be consistent with a diminishing marginal rate of substitution.

Property	Set theory (Preferences)	Functional form (Utility)
Completeness	For every pair of bundles, either A and B A $\succcurlyeq$ B or B $\succcurlyeq$ A (or both).	$U(b_z, c_z)$ is defined for every bundle Z : (b_z, c_z)
Reflexivity	A $\succcurlyeq$ A, so that A lies in its own (weakly) preferred set	$U(b_z, c_z) \geq U(b_z, c_z)$
Transitivity	For every triple of bundles A, B and C, if A $\succcurlyeq$ B and B $\succcurlyeq$ C, then A $\succcurlyeq$ C	If $U(b_x, c_x) \geq U(b_y, c_y)$ and $U(b_y, c_y) \geq U(b_x, c_x)$, then $U(b_x, c_x) \geq U(b_z, c_z)$
Monotonically increasing	For every A, B : A $\geq$ B (if A contains more of at least one good and no less than B of any good), A $\succcurlyeq$ B	Marginal utilities, MU_b and $MU_c > 0$
Convexity	For every A : A $\succcurlyeq$ B, the line joining A and B lies in the preferred set of B	**A sufficient condition:** Marginal utilities MU_b and MU_c are decreasing

Table 5.1 The assumptions required for well-behaved preferences

We summarize the restrictions required for a utility function to represent well-behaved preferences. The first three are quite straightforward and ensure the existence of a preference ordering. The last two could be combined as a requirement that total utility is always increasing, but at a decreasing rate. Going back to our bundle X : (b_x, c_x), say that we fix the amount of cheese, but allow the quantity of bread to increase. Total utility will also increase, but the increase will be smaller and smaller as we add more bread to the consumption bundle. The same argument would hold if we fixed the quantity of bread, but allowed the amount of cheese to vary. Each time we add another kilogram of cheese, total utility will increase, but the successive increments will each be smaller than the previous one.

It follows that if a consumer, such as George, were to be given an endowment consisting of a large amount of cheese and a small amount of bread, and if he were to exchange some cheese for some bread, the quantity of bread that he would need in order to be as well off before and after the exchange will be small. On the other hand, if the quantity of cheese in the initial consumption bundle is large and the quantity of bread is small, George would assign another loaf of bread a comparatively high value, and so be willing to trade a relatively large amount of cheese for it.

Figure 5.3 shows how the marginal rate of substitution changes on a single indifference curve, passing through point Z. A movement to the right and down means that consumption of bread increases, while consumption of cheese falls. With diminishing marginal utilities, we would expect MRS to increase towards zero; and this is before recognizing that there will often be interactions terms in utility functions, meaning, for example, that MU_c will increase along with the consumption of bread.

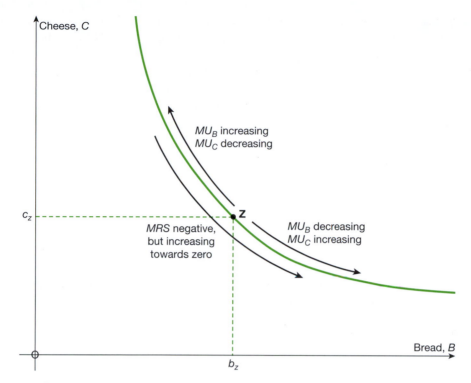

Figure 5.3 Decreasing marginal utility and diminishing MRS

5.3 An introduction to some important utility functions

It is helpful to use utility functions to represent preferences so that we can analyse resource allocation using mathematical tools and generate predictions about how the most-preferred, affordable consumption bundle will change as prices and the money available to finance consumption change. In this chapter we consider several utility functions, most of which are drawn from a single family whose properties we discuss in detail in Chapter 9.

5.3.1 The linear utility function: perfect substitutability

The acquisition cost function, which we introduced in Chapter 3, has the form $A(b, c) = p_b b + p_c c$. We said that it is linear because the graphs of every contour are straight lines. It is formed by multiplying the quantities of bread and cheese by their respective prices, and then summing them together.

A linear utility function is constructed in exactly the same way. For every consumption bundle, we can multiply the quantities of bread and cheese that they contain by constant weighting factors, and then sum them together. For bundle X (b, c) we now write:

$$U(b,c) = w_b b + w_c c \tag{5.8}$$

Interpreting the weighting parameters in economic terms turns out to be a quite straightforward exercise, for they are marginal utilities.

By yourself

X5.13   For the linear utility function given in Expression 5.8, assume that the quantity of cheese in the bundle remains constant.
   (a) Show that as b increases by one unit from 1 to 2, utility U increases by w_b units.
   (b) Show that as b increases by ten units from 20 to 30, utility U increases by $10\,w_b$ units.
   (c) Show that as b increases by k units, from b_0 to $b_1 = b_0 + k$, utility U increases by kw_b units.
   (d) Hence or otherwise, explain why the marginal utility of bread is w_b and the marginal utility of cheese is w_c.

X5.14   The marginal rate of substitution is the ratio of marginal utilities.
   (a) Find an expression for the marginal rate of substitution, and confirm that it is the same for all consumption bundles.
   (b) Show that all indifference curves are straight lines.
   (c) Sketch a preference map showing at least three distinct indifference curves.

The results of the exercises are illustrated in the left-hand panel of Figure 5.4. The indifference curves are straight, downward-sloping lines, whose slope, $MRS = -\frac{MU_B}{MU_C}$. Say Irina's marginal rate of substitution, $MRS = -\frac{1}{6}$. Irrespective of her current level of consumption, a loaf of bread is worth $\frac{1}{6}$ kg of cheese to her; and so she is willing to trade up to six loaves of bread for a kilogram of cheese. She would be entirely indifferent between the alternatives of receiving: (1) six more loaves; (2) one additional kilogram of cheese; and (3) three more loaves and a further 0.5 kg of cheese. Whenever she trades bread for cheese, it would be in the proportion 6 : 1. If we take a basket containing six loaves as our unit of bread, and a kilogram of cheese as our unit of cheese, then one unit of bread is as valuable to this consumer as a unit of cheese. Wherever someone appears to exhibit this constant proportional valuation of goods, we say that the goods are **perfect substitutes**.

> **Perfect substitutes** A pair of goods for which the marginal rate of substitution is constant.

Bread and cheese are not typical examples of a pair of perfect substitutes. In most cases, pairs of substitute goods are functionally identical, and so many people have no preference for one over the other. Think of the examples from Chapter 1 of the coffee served at two adjacent cafés or the fuel from competing petrol stations. Suppose that we each buy

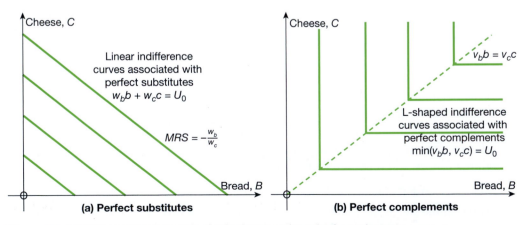

Figure 5.4 Preference maps for a pair of substitutes and a pair of complements

a cup of coffee but from different cafés. We should be willing to swap them. In the same way, we have argued that if people exhibit a preference for using one petrol station over another, this is simply a matter of habit, intended to reduce the cost of completing the transaction.

5.3.2 Perfect complements

Perfect complements are in many ways the exact opposite of perfect substitutes. Assume

> **Perfect complements** A pair of goods for which the marginal rate of substitution is zero.

that Irina considers tomatoes and onions to be perfect complements. She only uses them to make the base of a sauce for pasta, and she always combines them in the ratio, 2 : 1. If by mistake she were to add more tomatoes, she would obtain no additional value from consumption: the marginal utility obtained from the additional tomatoes would be zero. The same is true of the value derived from consumption of onions.

In such a case, assume that Irina starts from a bundle containing T tomatoes and O onions, and nothing else. From the preceding discussion, we suggest that Irina obtains no value from the T tomatoes in the bundle on their own, and none from the O onions on their own: these goods have to be consumed together. Irina's utility increases so long as it is possible to pair 2 kg of tomatoes with 1 kg of onions, so that as consumption of one increases, consumption of the other must also increase in the optimal proportion.

Continuing with our usual notation, we write the utility function for a pair of perfect complements in this way:

$$U(b,c) = \min(v_b b, v_c c) \qquad [5.9]$$

As in the previous discussion, v_b and v_c are related to the marginal utilities of bread and cheese. We read the operator, 'min', as, 'the minimum of the values, $v_b b$ and $v_c c$'. Expression 5.9 tells us that for any consumption bundle (b, c), Irina's utility is going to be the lesser of the utilities that might be derived from b loaves of bread and c kg of cheese.

To see that if the consumption bundle contains a greater proportion of one good than is optimal, the marginal utility of that good is zero, it may be easier to write the utility function as:

$$U(b, c) = \begin{cases} v_b b, \text{ if } v_b b < v_c c \\ v_c c, \text{ otherwise} \end{cases} \qquad [5.10]$$

This version demonstrates that the level of utility depends on the value that the consumer assigns to the amounts of bread and cheese separately, and not in combination, as was the case with the perfect substitutes.

By yourself

X5.15 Suppose that in Expression 5.10, $v_b = 2$ and $v_c = 9$.
  (a) Calculate the total utility obtained from the bundles X = (9, 2), Y = (18, 3), and Z = (45, 12).
  (b) For each of these three bundles, what would be the increase in utility from adding to the consumption bundle:
      (i) one loaf of bread?
      (ii) 1 kg of cheese? [*Note*: Adding cheese is separate from, not consecutive to, adding bread.]

(c) Beginning from bundle X, explain how utility changes as:
   (i) more and more bread is added to the consumption bundle (while the amount of cheese is held constant);
   (ii) more and more cheese is added to the consumption bundle (while the amount of bread is held constant).
(d) Using your answers to the previous questions:
   (i) Sketch the indifference curve passing through X.
   (ii) Sketch a preference map showing the indifference curves on which bundles X, Y and Z lie.

As we see from Exercise X5.15 and Figure 5.4, the indifference curves for perfect complements are L-shaped. The vertex of each curve lies on the line, $v_b b = v_c c$, where there is no excess of either good in the bundle. Were Irina to begin from a consumption bundle on this line and buy any quantity of only one good, the additional material would yield zero utility.

5.3.3   A diminishing marginal rate of substitution: Cobb–Douglas utility

Perfect substitutes and perfect complements are limiting cases of well-behaved utility functions. The linear function of perfect substitutes is associated with preferences that are weakly (or, only just) convex. The utility function for perfect complements is associated with preferences that barely satisfy the assumption of non-satiation. Ordinarily, we expect preferences and the associated utility function to meet both of these conditions, so that indifference curves are downward-sloping but flatten out as we move from left to right along them.

A very simple utility function exhibiting these properties is:

$$U(b, c) = bc \qquad [5.11]$$

In Expression 5.11, the utility of a consumption bundle is the product of the quantities of bread and cheese that it contains. This is an example of a Cobb–Douglas utility function. The Cobb–Douglas functions were the first utility functions to be used in applied economics. For consumption bundles consisting of quantities x and y of two goods, we write the Cobb–Douglas utility, V:

$$V(x, y) = x^\alpha y^\beta \qquad [5.12]$$

In our example, the values of the indices α and β are both set to 1.

We shall examine the properties of the functions defined in Expressions 5.11 and 5.12 in much more detail in subsequent chapters. Here, we introduce the preference map for our example, which is illustrated in Figure 5.5. The most straightforward way of obtaining the information that we need to sketch this preference map is to obtain an expression, in terms of the quantity of bread, b, for the quantity of cheese, c, in every consumption bundle in each indifference curve, defined so that utility $U = U_0$ and is constant. Each curve can then be formed by drawing each of these points and joining them carefully. We do this in Exercise X5.16.

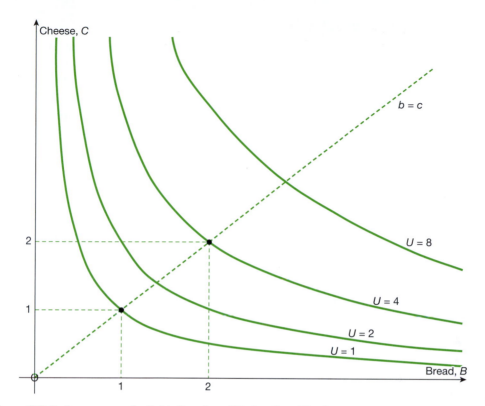

Figure 5.5 Preference map for Cobb–Douglas utility function, $U(b, c) = bc$

By yourself

X5.16 The goal is to replicate Figure 5.5. Given the utility function, $U = bc$, we shall sketch the indifference curves for which $U = 1$, $U = 2$, $U = 4$ and $U = 8$.
(a) Rearrange the expression $U = bc$, so that c is the subject.
(b) Complete the following table:

b	0.2	0.5	1	2	5	10
$c(b)\ [U = 1]$						
$c(b)\ [U = 2]$						
$c(b)\ [U = 4]$						
$c(b)\ [U = 8]$						

(c) Show each of these points on a diagram, only showing consumption bundles for which b and c are no more than 10.
(d) Sketch the indifference curves by joining together the points identified on each curve.

The preference map in Figure 5.5 appears to support well-behaved preferences. All four indifference curves are downward-sloping and convex, and never intersect. None of them appear to cross the axes.

5.3.4   A useful type of utility function

There are surprisingly few types of well-behaved utility function. The three examples that we have considered so far are special cases drawn from a single class of utility functions, all of which exhibit constant elasticity of substitution. In the context of utility functions, the elasticity of substitution, σ, is a mathematical property, fully defined in Chapter 9, which states how the composition of bundle Z : (b, c), defined as the ratio $\frac{c}{b}$, on any indifference curve changes with the MRS. Taking the example of Cobb–Douglas utility functions, the elasticity of substitution, $\sigma = 1$. Moving along an indifference curve, if the marginal rate of substitution, $MRS = -\frac{MU_B}{MU_C}$, increases by 1% then the ratio, $\frac{c}{b}$, will also increase by 1%.

For the utility function

$$U(b, c) = b^{\frac{1}{2}} + c^{\frac{1}{2}}$$ [5.13]

it turns out the elasticity of substitution $\sigma = 2$. Moving along an indifference curve, if the marginal rate of substitution, $MRS = -\frac{MU_B}{MU_C}$, increases by 1% then the ratio, $\frac{c}{b}$, will increase by 2%. That the elasticity of substitution is greater for the function in Expression 5.13 than for the Cobb–Douglas function means that the curvature of its indifference curve is less. in Figure 5.6, this is shown by the graph of the indifference curve, $b^{\frac{1}{2}} + c^{\frac{1}{2}} = 2$, passing through the point, Z : (1, 1), as do the indifference curves $b + c = 2$ and $bc + 1$. We see that the curve $b^{\frac{1}{2}} + c^{\frac{1}{2}} = 2$ is less curved than the indifference curve associated with the Cobb–Douglas utility function, $bc = 1$, but more curved than the line $b + c = 2$ along which the goods would be perfect substitutes.

By yourself

X5.17   We now replicate Figure 5.5, but for the utility function, $U = b^{\frac{1}{2}} + c^{\frac{1}{2}}$.
(a) Rearrange the expression, $U = b^{\frac{1}{2}} + c^{\frac{1}{2}}$, so that c is the subject.
(b) Complete the following table:

b	0	0.0625	0.25	1	4	9
$c(b)$ [$U = 0.5$]						
$c(b)$ [$U = 1$]						
$c(b)$ [$U = 2$]						
$c(b)$ [$U = 3$]						

(c) Show each of these points on a diagram.
(d) Sketch the indifference curves by joining together the points identified on each curve.

Once again, the exercise suggests that this utility function is associated with well-behaved preferences. All four indifference curves are downward-sloping and convex, and never cross. There are some properties of the indifference curves in Exercise X5.17 that we cannot obtain from this exercise. Concentrating on the graph of the curve $b^{\frac{1}{2}} + c^{\frac{1}{2}} = 2$, as illustrated in Figure 5.6, the indifference curve touches the bread axis at $b = 4$, where it is flat, and the cheese axis at $c = 4$, where it is vertical. For a bundle containing much more bread than cheese, represented by a point close to the horizontal axis, the indifference curve is quite flat and the MRS is small (and negative). For bundles containing much more cheese than bread, the indifference curve is steep, and the MRS is large.

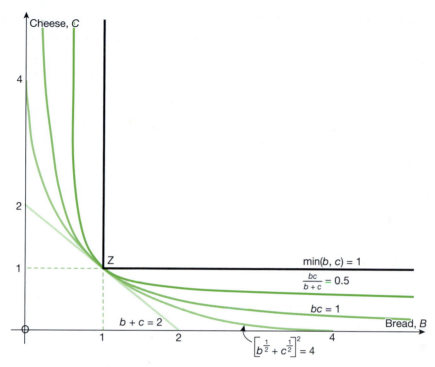

Figure 5.6 A variety of indifference curves

In Figure 5.6, the only curve whose properties we have not considered has the equation:

$$\frac{bc}{b + c} = 0.5 \qquad\qquad [5.14]$$

This is an indifference curve of the utility function, $U(b, c) = \left(\frac{1}{b} + \frac{1}{c} \right)^{-1}$. We note that the curvature of this indifference curve is greater than that of the indifference curve, $bc = 1$, associated with the Cobb–Douglas utility function.

By yourself

X5.18 For the utility function, $U(b,c) = \left(\frac{1}{b} + \frac{1}{c} \right)^{-1}$, confirm that:

(a) The utility function can be rewritten $U(b,c) = \frac{bc}{b+c}$.

(b) The consumption bundle, $(1, 1)$ lies on the indifference curve, $\frac{bc}{b+c} = 0.5$.

(c) The indifference curve can be expressed in explicit form, $c = \frac{b}{2b-1}$.

(d) If $b = 0.5$, then it is impossible to evaluate this expression for c.

(e) If $b < 0.5$, then $c < 0$; and we disregard the consumption bundle.

(f) As $b \to \infty$, $c \to 0.5$; which is to say, when b takes larger and larger values, c will become closer and closer to 0.5.

Exercise X5.18 helps to explain some of the properties of this indifference curve. Firstly, we note that it is necessary that $b, c > 0.5$. As the value of b approaches 0.5, c has to be very large; and *vice versa*. Parts (d) and (f) confirm that it is impossible to find a bundle on the indifference curve either when $b = 0.5$ or when $c = 0.5$. In addition, from part (e) we conclude that if either $b < 0.5$ or $c < 0.5$, while it is possible to evaluate the explicit form of the indifference bundle, we obtain a negative value. This is not possible, since the quantity of every good in the consumption bundle has to be at least zero.

5.4   Conclusions

We have seen that if we are able to define a utility function for which marginal utilities are always positive, then we exclude the possibility of satiation. In addition, if we assume that the marginal utilities are decreasing, then the underlying preferences will certainly be convex, and so insisting on positive but decreasing marginal utilities for each good is sufficient to ensure that a utility function is well behaved.

Throughout this book, we will frequently use examples in which the utility functions have a constant elasticity of substitution, a mathematical property, which relates to the responsiveness of the composition of consumption bundles to changes in the marginal rate of substitution on any indifference curve. The family of CES utility functions allow us to analyse resource allocation for pairs of goods that are perfect substitutes, for other pairs that are perfect complements, and also where the utility function takes a Cobb–Douglas form.

In terms of indifference curves, perfect substitutes form one limit of this family of functions since indifference curves are linear, meaning that the convexity property is only just satisfied. Perfect complements form another limit, in which monotonicity of preferences (that is, non-satiation) is only just satisfied. Between these two limits we find utility functions, represented graphically by indifference curves which vary by their curvature. It seems intuitively sensible that greater curvature should be associated with goods that form pairs of complements, while a low value of curvature should be associated with goods that form substitutes.

Figure 5.6 is valuable in showing us the range of shapes of indifference curve that we shall encounter. The next step in our analysis will be to develop the properties of these functions so that we can complete our discussion of the standard model of resource allocation for consumers.

By yourself

X5.19   Economists frequently refer to utility as being an *ordinal* rather than a *cardinal* concept because it is only possible to interpret the ranking of utility values, not their absolute value.

(a) Suppose that the amount of money that Arun has doubles. Would it be reasonable to suppose that his utility from consumption doubles?

(b) Would it be reasonable to suppose that his utility from consumption increases but does not double?

(c) Critically assess the statement, 'Money is more valuable to the poor than to the rich, so we should redistribute income from the rich to the poor.'

X5.20   We have said that sufficient conditions for a utility function to be well behaved are that the marginal utilities are positive but decreasing. We can show that for the function $U(x, y) = x^{0.5} + y^{0.5}$, the marginal utility $MU_x(x, y) = 0.5x^{-0.5}$ and the marginal utility $MU_y(x, y) = 0.5y^{-0.5}$.

(a) Confirm that the marginal rate of substitution $MRS = -(y/x)^{0.5}$.

(b) Confirm that the consumption bundles (4, 0), (1, 1), and (0, 4) all generate utility 2.

(c) Confirm that the marginal rate of substitution for the three bundles in part (b) takes the values 0, −1 and undefined.

(d) Repeat the exercise, sketching indifference curves that pass through the bundles (0.25, 0.25) and (4, 4).

(e) Confirm that the marginal rate of substitution on all three indifference curves that you have sketched have a slope of −0.5 where they meet the line $y = x/4$, but a slope of 2 where they meet the line $y = 4x$.

X5.21 The utility function $U(s, t) = s^2t^2$ has associated marginal utilities $MU_s(s, t) = 2t^2s$ and $MU_t(s, t) = 2s^2t$.

(a) Show that if $t = 1$, then MU_s is increasing in s; and if $s = 2$, MU_t is increasing in t.

(b) Find the marginal rate of substitution for this utility function.

(c) Confirm that the indifference curve associated with utility level 1 passes through the bundle (1, 1) and that there it has gradient $MRS = -1$.

(d) Which, if either, of the following statements is true?

  (i) The marginal utility of good S is always decreasing for utility functions that represent well-behaved preferences.

  (ii) The marginal rate of substitution is always decreasing for utility functions that represent well-behaved preferences.

X5.22 Consider a rather different utility function from the ones that we have seen already:

$$U(b,c) = b^{1/2} + c.$$

(a) Obtain expressions for the indifference curves $U = 4$, $U = 6$, and $U = 8$ in terms of the variable c.

(b) Complete the following table:

b	0	2	4	6	8	10
c(b) [U = 4]						
c(b) [U = 6]						
c(b) [U = 8]						

(c) Show these points on a diagram, and construct the indifference curves.

(d) Given that $MU_B = \frac{1}{2}b^{-1/2}$ and $MU_C = 1$, calculate MRS. What do you conclude about the slope of the indifference curves, $U = 4$, $U = 6$ and $U = 8$ when $b = 4$? Can you generalize your answer for the slopes of any pair of indifference curves and any level of consumption, b?

Summary

Preferences have limitations in helping us understand how people choose between alternatives. We therefore prefer to use the concept of a utility function as a representation of preferences. Such a function must satisfy certain conditions if it is to represent well-behaved preferences. We expect it to be increasing in the quantity of every good that might be consumed, but to increase at a decreasing rate.

In many economic applications, we are not interested in the total utility, but in the marginal utilities of alternative changes in resource allocations. We define the marginal utility of a good as the rate at which total utility increases as consumption of that good also increases, while holding consumption of all other goods constant. We find that the slope of an indifference curve, the marginal rate of substitution, is then the ratio of marginal utilities.

We shall concentrate our attention on one particular family of utility functions in our analysis, all of which have a constant elasticity of substitution. We have introduced three special cases of these functions: one that allows us to analyse the behaviour of perfect substitute goods, one that allows us to analyse the behaviour of perfect complements, and the Cobb–Douglas utility functions.

Visit the companion website at **www.palgrave.com/mochrie** to access further teaching and learning materials, including lecturer slides and a testbank, as well as guideline answers and student MCQs.

$m \uparrow$ $U \uparrow$ $G \uparrow$
(good)

6

The most-preferred, affordable bundle

What we do in this chapter

Chapters 3–5 have developed material that we can use to solve the consumer's problem of resource allocation. This argument will use the *equi-marginal principle*, introduced in Chapter 1 as one of two essential solution concepts, and used throughout microeconomic theory. It confirms that resource allocation is *efficient* in two senses: firstly in the technical sense that there is no way of generating a given level of outputs without increasing the inputs available; and secondly that there is no possibility of altering the pattern of use of the inputs in order to increase the achievable outputs.

The problem that we have set up involves a single person's decision about how to allocate a quantity of a resource, *m*, typically money, to purchase a consumption bundle (*b*, *c*) consisting of quantities of goods B and C. The consumption bundle is valued as a source of *utility*. In this context, the equi-marginal principle requires the purchase of a consumption bundle in which the input resource is used up entirely and where, at the margin, the output per unit of input (here the marginal utility per currency unit) is equal across the goods in the consumption bundle.

We approach this problem in two ways. The first should by now be familiar: finding the *utility-maximizing* consumption bundle given a budget constraint. The other will be to find the cheapest consumption bundle that allows someone to reach a *target utility*. We show that the problems are in fact closely related, and we discuss informally the circumstances under which the two problems have the same solution.

6.1 Application of the equi-marginal principle

We have now assembled all the ideas that we need in order to introduce the standard model of resource allocation for consumers, which is one of the most important building blocks in microeconomic theory. In Chapter 3 we defined the budget set, showing that the slope of its boundary represents the opportunity cost of one good, measured as the rate at which someone who is budget-constrained must give up consumption of one good in order to increase consumption of another one. In our example, the opportunity cost of bread is the quantity of cheese that a budget-constrained consumer, whom we now call Juliet, must forgo in order to buy one more loaf. This opportunity cost was the ratio of prices for the two goods: in our example, the price of bread divided by the price of cheese. We argued in Chapter 4 that it is reasonable to expect someone to be budget-constrained, spending all the money available at any time, arguing that this is a necessary consequence of the assumption that Juliet's preferences over all possible consumption bundles are well behaved, so that they are both monotonically increasing and convex.

We concluded Chapter 4 by arguing that that the most-preferred bundle could be identified as the point on a diagram at which an indifference curve (effectively the boundary of a preferred set) just touches the affordable set. Interpreting the slope of the indifference curve as the marginal rate of substitution, which we defined as a measure of personal opportunity cost, we were able to characterize the most-preferred, affordable bundle, given well-behaved preferences as the (unique) bundle for which the personal and market opportunity costs are identical. We illustrate this outcome in Figure 6.1. Juliet is restricted to choosing a consumption bundle within the affordable set, $A(m)$, with budget constraint $B(m) : p_b b + p_c c = m$. She is therefore just able to reach the preferred set $P(Z^*)$.

The preference relations of Chapter 4 give rise to a preference ordering of possible consumption bundles. We typically capture the ranking of bundles through the use of a utility function. Utility was defined in Chapter 5 simply as a measure of the strength of a consumer's preference for a particular bundle within that ordering. We shall see in this chapter that we do not need to know much about the total utility of a bundle: instead, we will concentrate upon its marginal utilities. We now define the marginal utility of a good

Essential Maths 6.1: The nature of the derivative function (1)

We want to understand how the value of some specific function $z = z(x)$ changes as the value of the argument, x, changes.

If z is linear, so that the rule governing $z(x)$ takes the form $tx + s$, where s and t are constant parameters, we can work out the rate of change very easily:

$$\frac{\Delta z}{\Delta x} = \frac{z(x_1) - z(x_0)}{x_1 - x_0} = \frac{tx_1 + s - (tx_0 + s)}{x_1 - x_0} = t \qquad \text{[M6.1]}$$

The rate of change of a linear function is constant, and is given by the slope parameter, t. What if the function is not linear? We can only obtain the general expression, $\frac{\Delta z}{\Delta x} = \frac{z(x_1) - z(x_0)}{x_1 - x_0}$, but cannot evaluate this ratio. But we can study the ratio if the interval Δx (or $x_1 - x_0$) is very small.

Essential Maths 6.2: The nature of the derivative function (2)

The smallest value that Δx might take is not zero, but immeasurably different from it: that is, so close to zero that we cannot distinguish it from zero, yet it is not zero. (We have already met the argument that in the set of all real numbers, there is no 'next largest' number.)

How do we work out the rate of change of z across the immeasurably small interval Δx? Instead of measuring it directly, we evaluate it as the limit of the rate of change across small finite intervals:

$$\lim_{\Delta x \to 0} \frac{\Delta Z}{\Delta X} = \lim_{x_1 \to x_0} \frac{Z(X_1) - Z(X_0)}{X_1 - X_0} \qquad \text{[M6.2]}$$

In a graph, the finite approximation to the rate of change is the slope of the straight line, or chord, joining the points $P_0 (x_0, z(x_0))$ and $P_1 (x_1, z(x_1))$. As the interval $\Delta x \to 0$, the chord $P_0 P_1$ becomes indistinguishable from the tangent at P_0. Expression M6.2 is the slope of the tangent when $x = x_0$.

as a measure of the rate of change of utility as consumption of one good increases while consumption of other goods remains constant. As in Chapter 5, the marginal rate of substitution is the ratio of marginal utilities, and so for Juliet, at consumption bundle Z, $MRS = -\frac{MU_B}{MU_C}$.

Looking at Figure 6.1, we see that for the most-preferred, affordable bundle, $Z^*(b^*, c^*)$, the marginal rate of substitution is equal to the price ratio, and also to the ratio of marginal utilities. It therefore follows that the price ratio and the ratio of marginal utilities are equal. Then, at Z^*:

$$-\frac{p_b}{p_c} = MRS\,(b^*, c^*) = -\frac{MU_b(b^*,c^*)}{MU_c(b^*,c^*)} \tag{6.1}$$

Expression 6.1 is an equilibrium condition, which holds only for the most-preferred, affordable bundle. That is why we specify the consumption bundle for which we are calculating the marginal utilities and the marginal rate of substitution. We do not need to do this for prices, since they are constant, no matter how much of either good is found in the consumption bundle. Expression 6.1 can be rearranged thus:

$$\frac{MU_b(b^*,c^*)}{p_b} = \frac{MU_c(b^*,c^*)}{p_c} \tag{6.2}$$

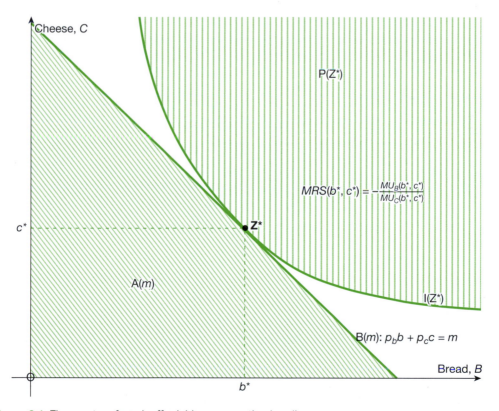

Figure 6.1 The most-preferred, affordable consumption bundle

Expressions 6.1 and 6.2 are both expressions of the equi-marginal principle, which applies whenever a consumer, like Juliet, makes the most efficient use of resources. To use this solution technique, we need to be able to derive the marginal utility functions from her total utility.

6.2   Marginal utility functions

When we drew preference maps in Chapters 4 and 5, we relied on preferred sets of specific bundles. We now wish to rely upon a utility function, U, defined for all consumption bundles, (b, c), to capture the information in the preference ordering. To draw the graph of a utility function, we need two dimensions for the inputs, and a third one for the level of utility. On paper, there are still only two dimensions, and while we will often use preference maps, interpreting indifference curves as contours of the utility function, there are other ways to represent a utility function. In Figure 6.2, we show the graph of what is perhaps the simplest example: the minimand function, $U = \min(b, c)$, in which we assume that the goods are perfect complements. In the diagram, we seem to be looking down on this three-dimensional shape. We can see through the graph of the function to the (b, c) plane, which has been rotated. The consumption bundle (3, 3) is illustrated on that plane, showing that the surface of the utility function is three units above the input bundle at that point.

Now imagine that we were to stand at the origin, looking up at the physical representation of the function. We would appear to be standing at a corner of the base of a pyramid, where two faces meet. From the ridge, we can trace out contours, with the ridge at the vertex of each. But unlike any pyramid that we might encounter while visiting Egypt, this one stretches on endlessly. It has no other corners, and no peak.

Essential Maths 6.3: The derivative function

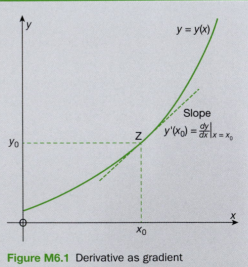

In Figure M6.1, which shows the curve that is the graph of the function, $y = y(x)$, passing through Z : (x_0, y_0), line ZT forms the tangent at $x = x_0$. The slope of ZT is the instantaneous rate of change of y when $x = x_0$, as defined in Expression M6.2.

We say that the derivative function, written as

$$y' : x \rightarrow y'(x) \text{ or } \frac{dy}{dx} \qquad \text{[M6.3]}$$

measures the instantaneous rate of change of y with respect to x.

To obtain the derivative functions, we apply some rules of differentiation.

Figure M6.1 Derivative as gradient

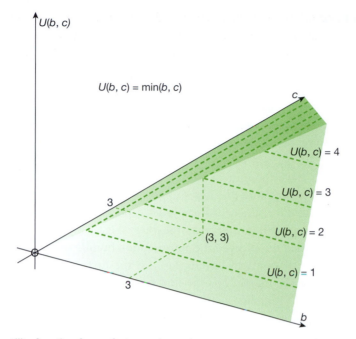

Figure 6.2 The utility function for perfect complements

More generally, we might think of a utility function representing well-behaved preferences as being like a smooth, concave hill that has no summit. If the zero consumption bundle is at the bottom of this hill, then increasing the value of b is like moving East, while increasing the value of c is like moving North. Going in either direction, or indeed on any bearing between East and North, we climb the hill. The total utility is then a measure of height climbed from the zero consumption bundle. We now think of the marginal utilities as the rate at which total utility increases, moving East (as we increase consumption, b) or North (as we increase consumption, c). In other words, we can think of the marginal utilities as the slope of the hill measured in an Easterly and a Northerly direction.

Essential Maths 6.4: **Rules of differentiation**

These rules are sufficient to differentiate all power functions of the form $y: y(x) = x^a$, and all polynomial functions of the form $y = a_n x^n + a_{n-1} x^{n-1} + a_{n-2} x^{n-2} + \dots + a_1 x + a_0$:

- Power rule: for $y(x) = x^a$, derivative $y'(x) = ax^{a-1}$
- Constant rule: for $y(x) = b$, derivative $y'(x) = 0$
- Scalar multiple rule: for $z(x) = ky(x)$, where k is constant, derivative $z'(x) = ky'(x)$
- Sum of functions rule: for $y(x) = y_1(x) + y_2(x)$, derivative $y'(x) = y_1'(x) + y_2'(x)$

These rules are sufficient to differentiate functions that can be formed by combining power and polynomial functions:

- Product rule: for $y(x) = y_1(x) \cdot y_2(x)$, derivative $y'(x) = y_1'(x) \cdot y_2(x) + y_1(x) \cdot y_2'(x)$
- Quotient rule: for $y(x) = \frac{y_1(x)}{y_2(x)}$, $y'(x) = \frac{y_1'(x)y_2(x) - y_1(x)y_2'(x)}{[y_2(x)]^2}$
- Chain rule, or function of a function rule: $y(x) = y_1[y_2(x)]$, derivative $y'(x) = y_1'[y_2(x)] \cdot y_2'(x)$

6.2.1 Derivation of the marginal utility functions

Marginal utility The rate of change of utility as the quantity available of one good increases.

The marginal utility of bread is the rate at which utility increases as consumption of bread increases, while consumption of cheese is held constant. We have already noted in Chapter 5 that there is a difference between the average rate of change of utility given a finite increase in the consumption of a good, and the instantaneous rate of change defined for some particular consumption bundle. The average rate of change is the total change divided by the number of additional units – that is, the change in utility per unit added.

For example, let us take the unit of consumption as a single slice of bread, already a small fraction of our usual unit of one loaf. Suppose that we add four slices of bread to the consumption bundle, and that the consumer, Juliet, reports an increase in utility score of 8. The average rate of change of her utility over the interval is then 1.25 per slice.

However, had we added the slices to the consumption bundle one at a time, Juliet's valuation of the additional slices might have been 3 for the first one, 2.5 for the second, 1.5 for the third and 1 for the fourth. For the first two slices, the average rate of change of utility would then be 2.75 per slice, while for the last two slices, it would be 1.25 per slice. Similarly, for the first three slices, the average rate of change of utility would be 2.33 per slice, but for the last three it would be 1.67 per slice. The calculations illustrate a problem with using an average rate of change: depending on the width of the interval, the average will change. We want a unique and unambiguous measure of the rate of change, and this means using the instantaneous rate of change.

Obtaining the instantaneous rate of change requires mathematical techniques of differential calculus, which are a little more complex than calculating a simple average. The necessary arguments are set out very briefly in Essential Maths 6.6, concentrating on arguments about the nature of derivative functions. Also stated are the rules of differentiation, which we have to use repeatedly to become proficient in solving optimization problems.

Essential Maths 6.5: Derivatives of some useful functions

- For $z = bx$, $z'(x) = b$, which we already know to be the slope the line $z = bx$ [Scalar multiple rule]
- For $z = a + bx$, $z'(x) = b$, which we already know to be the slope of the line
  $z = a + bx$ [Sum of functions rule]
- For $z = x^2$, $z'(x) = 2x$ [Power rule]
- For $z = x^{0.5}$, $z'(x) = 0.5x^{0.5}$ [Power rule]
- For $z = x^{-1}$, $z'(x) = -x^{-2}$ [Power rule]
- For $z = (1 + x^{0.5})^2$, $z_2(x) = 1 + x^{0.5}$, and $z_1[z_2(x)] = [z_2(x)]^2$
  - $z_2'(x) = 0.5x^{-0.5}$, and $z_1'[z_2(x)] = 2[z_2(x)] = 2(1 + x^{0.5})$;   [Chain rule]
  - so $z'(x) = z_1'[z_2(x)] \cdot z_2'(x) = x^{-0.5}(1 + x^{0.5}) = 1 + x^{-0.5}$

For $z = \frac{x}{1+x}$, we add 1 and subtract 1 in the numerator; $z = \frac{1+x}{1+x} - \frac{1}{1+x} = 1 - (1+x)^{-1}$
- Here $z(x) = 1 - z_1[z_2(x)]$, where $z_2(x) = 1 + x$ and $z_1[z_2(x)] = 1 - [z_2(x)]^{-1}$;   [Chain rule]
  - $z_2'(x) = 1$, and $z_1'[z_2(x)] = [z_2(x)]^{-2} = (1 + x)^{-2}$;
  - so $z'(x) = z_1'[z_2(x)] \cdot z_2'(x) = (1 + x)^{-2}$

Derivative functions effectively allow us to measure the rate of change of a variable over a finite interval that is immeasurably small. This eliminates the ambiguity over definition and measurement of the rate of change, and provides us with a measure of the instantaneous rate of change of a function, typically for any value for which the original, objective function might be defined. In graphical terms, instead of measuring the rate of change as the slope of the chord joining two points on a graph, we instead define it as the slope of the tangent that passes through a single point on the graph.

6.2.2 Example: marginal utility of Cobb–Douglas utility function $U : U(b, c) = bc$

Juliet reports that her preferences over bundles (b, c) can be represented by the utility function

$$U:U(b, c) = bc \qquad\qquad [6.3]$$

where, as usual, b is the quantity of bread and c the quantity of cheese in the consumption bundle. We now find the marginal utility function for bread, obtaining an expression, $MU_B(b, c)$. Given the definition of the marginal utility as the rate of change of utility with respect to the consumption of bread, just for now we fix the quantity of cheese at 3 kg. The utility function becomes:

$$U(b, 3) = 3b \qquad\qquad [6.4]$$

Note that, by making this assumption, c is fixed, while the quantity of bread is still variable. Instead of utility being a function of two variables, we momentarily treat it as a function of one variable, say:

$$U_3:U_3(b) = 3b \qquad\qquad [6.5]$$

Expression 6.5 defines U_3 as a linear function of b, so, applying the rules of differentiation for a linear function of one variable, we obtain the marginal utility, $MU_{B; 3} = \frac{dU_3}{db}$:

$$MU_{B;3}(b) = 3 \qquad\qquad [6.6]$$

Essential Maths 6.6: Functions of two variables

We define a function of two variables, $z = z(x, y)$. For any pair (x, y) in the domain set, there is a unique image $z(x, y)$. Where for functions of a single variable we have drawn the graph of $z(x)$ as a curve lying above the x-axis, we might draw the graph of a function of function of two variables as a sheet lying above the (x, y) plane, as in Figure 6.2.

Frequently, we depict the graph of a function by a contour map. This shows pairs (x, y) for which z takes particular values. Indifference maps are examples of contour maps.

We can also illustrate sections of a function. The most commonly used sections are chosen so that either x varies and y is held constant at some value y_0, or so that y varies and x is held constant at some value x_0. We are then able to define the functions $z_1 : x \rightarrow z(x; y_0)$, and $z_2 : y \rightarrow z(y; x_0)$. With one variable being held constant, these are functions of one variable. We define a continuum of functions, all having the form of z_1, one for every possible realization of y_0; and similarly there is a continuum of functions of the form of z_2.

Expression 6.6 says that if Juliet's consumption bundle contains 3 kg of cheese, then the marginal utility of bread, $MU_B = 3$. Every additional loaf of bread will increase the utility score by 3. The rate of change of U will simply be the number, 3, by which we multiply b in Expression 6.4. The same sort of argument will apply if we consider a bundle with 4 kg or 9 kg or 12.25 kg of cheese: we will find that the rate of change of U will simply be the quantity of cheese. Allowing the value of cheese in the consumption bundle to vary, it seems reasonable that we should obtain the marginal utility function for bread, MU_B:

$$MU_B(b, c) = c \qquad\qquad [6.7]$$

Expression 6.7 says that the marginal utility of bread is equal to the quantity of cheese in the consumption bundle. We can obtain the same results by applying the rules of differential calculus, as they apply to functions of two variables, and as they are set out in Essential Maths 6.7. For this first example, though, we set aside the rules, arguing instead from 'first principles' and showing how the rules of differentiation emerge.

By yourself

X6.1   Suppose that Juliet is currently planning to buy the bundle, $Z_0 : (b_0, c_0)$. She considers adding a quantity δb to the bundle, creating a new bundle, $Z_\delta : (b_0 + \delta b, c_0)$. Given her utility function $U : U(b, c) = bc$:
(a) Calculate the values of $U(b_0, c_0)$ and $U(b_0 + \delta b, c_0)$.
(b) Calculate the change in utility $\delta U = U(b_0 + \delta b, c_0) - U(b_0, c_0)$.
(c) Confirm that the rate of change of utility $MU_B(b_0, c_0) = c_0$.

X6.2   Repeat X6.1, but assume that Juliet is now planning to buy the bundle, $Z : (b, c)$, and thinking about the effect of increasing consumption of cheese by an amount δc.

X6.3   By applying the rules of (partial) differentiation, confirm that $MU_B(b, c) = U_b(b, c) = \frac{\partial U}{\partial b} = c$ and that $MU_c(b, c) = U_c(b, c) = \frac{\partial U}{\partial c} = b$.

X6.4   Sketch graphs showing the total utility, and the marginal utility, of cheese when there are 4, 9, and 16 loaves in the consumption bundle.

Essential Maths 6.7: Partial derivatives of functions of two variables

With a function of one variable, $z = z(x)$, there is only one argument in the function. We define the derivative function $z'(x)$ as the instantaneous rate of change of the function, and interpret its value for any choice of x as the slope of the gradient to the graph of z for that value of x.

With functions of two variables, $z = z(x, y)$, there are two arguments, x and y. We may define a rate of change of the function as x varies while y is held constant, and a separate rate of change as y varies while x is held constant. We represent these instantaneous rates of change by partial derivative functions, $z_x(x, y)$ and $z_y(x, y)$, or alternatively, $\frac{\partial z}{\partial x}$ and $\frac{\partial z}{\partial y}$.

For the section $z_1 : z_1 \to z(x, y_0)$, the partial derivative $z_x(x, y) = z'(x, y_0)$. The partial derivative, z_x, is an expression for the derivative, z', defined for all possible sections of the form $y = y_0$. We can apply the rules of differentiation, interpreting them in this way: in a partial derivative with respect to x, any term in y (and not x) is held constant; and any factor that is a function of y is also held constant.

The exercises demonstrate that the marginal utility functions can be obtained either by calculating the instantaneous rate of change, by taking the limit of an average rate of change as the interval over which the change is measured approaches zero; or else by applying the rules of (partial) differentiation, which are generalizations of the formal argument from first principles. As a matter of efficient resource use, after applying the formal argument in one further example we shall simply rely upon the rules to obtain derivative functions.

6.2.3 Example: marginal utility of Cobb–Douglas utility function, $V : V(b, c) = b^2c^2$

As in the previous function, the utility function, V, is a product of two functions of one variable, $V_1 : V_1(b) = b^2$, and $V_2 : V_2(c) = c^2$. It is therefore quite straightforward to apply the argument of differentiation from first principles.

By yourself

X6.5   Given his utility function, $V : V(b, c) = b^2c^2$, Karl is considering the value of the bundle, $Z_0 : (b_0, c_0)$. He considers adding a quantity δb to the bundle, which would create a new bundle, $Z_\delta : (b_0 + \delta b, c_0)$.
   (a) Calculate the values of $V(b_0, c_0)$ and $V(b_0 + \delta b, c_0)$.
   (b) Show that the change in utility $\delta V = V(b_0 + \delta b, c_0) - V(b_0, c_0) = [2b_0.\delta b + (\delta b)^2]c_0^2$.
   (c) Confirm that the rate of change of utility $MU_B(b_0, c_0) = \lim_{\delta b \to 0} \frac{\delta V}{\delta b} = 2c_0^2 b_0$.

X6.6   Repeat X6.5, but assume that Karl is now planning to buy the bundle $Z : (b, c)$ and thinking about the effect of increasing consumption of cheese by an amount δc.

X6.7   By applying the rules of (partial) differentiation, confirm that:
   $MV_B(b, c) = V_b(b, c) = \frac{\partial U}{\partial b} = 2c^2 b$ and that $MV_c(b, c) = V_c(b, c) = \frac{\partial U}{\partial b} = 2b^2 c$.

(Continued)

Essential Maths 6.8: Partial derivatives of some useful functions

- For $z = xy$, $z_x(x, y) = y$, which we already know to be the gradient of the line, $z = yx$

   [Product of variables rule]

- For $z = ax + by$, $z_x(x) = a$, which we already know to be the gradient of the line, $z = ax$

   [Sum of variables rule]

- For $z = x^{0.5}y^{0.5}$, $z_x(x, y) = 0.5y^{0.5}x^{-0.5}$ [Product of variables and power function rules]

- For $z = (x^{0.5} + y^{0.5})^2$, $z_1(x, y) = x^{0.5} + y^{0.5}$, and $z_2[z_1(x, y)] = [z_1(x, y)]^2$

   $z_2'(z_1) = 2z_1 = 2(x^{0.5} + y^{0.5})$, and $z_{1x}[x, y] = 0.5x^{-0.5}$;   [Chain rule]

   so $z_x(x, y) = x^{-0.5}(x^{0.5} + y^{0.5}) = 1 + (y/x)^{-0.5}$

- For $z = \dfrac{x}{x + y}$, we add y and subtract y in the numerator; $z = \dfrac{x + y}{x + y} - \dfrac{y}{x + y} = 1 - y(x + y)^{-1}$

   Define $z_1(x) = x + y$ and $z_2[z_1(x), y] = 1 - [z_1(x)]^{-1}y$;   [Chain rule]

   $z_1'(x) = 1$, and $z_{2x}[z_1(x), y] = [z_1(x)]^{-2}y = (x + y)^{-2}y$;

   so $z_x(x, y) = (x + y)^{-2}y$

- For $z = \frac{xy}{x + y}$, $z = y\left(\frac{x}{x + y}\right)$, so using the previous result, $z_x(x, y) = (x + y)^{-2}y^2$.

   [Product of variables]

X6.8   Sketch graphs showing the total utility, and the marginal utility, of cheese when there are 2, 3, and 4 loaves in the consumption bundle.

X6.9   Applying the rules of differentiation, obtain the marginal utilities of bread and cheese for the following utility functions, U:

(a) $U(b, c) = k_b b + k_c c$ (b) $U(b, c) = b^{0.5} c^{0.5}$ (c) $U(b, c) = b^{0.5} + c^{0.5}$

(d) $U(b, c) = (b^{0.5} + c^{0.5})^2$ (e) $U(b, c) = \dfrac{bc}{b + c}$

From the exercises, we see that for the function $V : V(b, c) = b^2 c^2$, as consumption of one good increases, while holding consumption of the other constant, total utility increases at an increasing rate, while marginal utility is linear and increasing. Specifically:

$$MU_B(b, c) = \frac{\partial V}{\partial b} = V_B(b, c) = 2c^2 b; \text{ and } MU_C(b, c) = \frac{\partial V}{\partial c} = V_C(b, c) = 2b^2 c \qquad [6.8]$$

6.3   The marginal rate of substitution function

We have defined the marginal rate of substitution (MRS) as the ratio of the marginal utilities. It is a measure of the rate at which someone will give up consumption of one good as consumption of a second good increases, on the basis that the utility of consumption will not change.

6.3.1   Uniqueness of utility up to a monotonic transformation

In Chapter 5 we argued that any monotonically increasing function of a utility function is itself a utility function, with both functions representing the same preference ordering. Consider Juliet's and Karl's utility functions:

$$U : U(b, c) = bc; \text{ and } V : V(b, c) = b^2 c^2 \qquad [6.9]$$

By yourself

X6.10   Confirm that $U(b, c) > 0$, if $b, c > 0$; and that $\frac{dV}{dU} = 2U > 0$ if $U > 0$. Defining the marginal rate of substitution, $MRS(b, c) = -\frac{MU_B(b,c)}{MU_C(b,c)}$, show that for the functions U and V:

$$MRS(b, c) = -\frac{c}{b} \qquad [6.10]$$

From Expressions 6.8 and 6.9, we see that $\frac{\partial V}{\partial b} = 2bc \frac{\partial U}{\partial b}$; and it is straightforward to confirm that $\frac{\partial V}{\partial c} = 2bc \frac{\partial U}{\partial c}$. This is simply an application of the chain rule of differentiation, defined in Essential Maths 6.4.

Since $V(b, c) = [U(b, c)]^2$, we can express V as a function of U, writing $V : V(U) = U^2$, where $U(b, c) = bc$. Applying the chain rule, the partial derivative of V with respect to b is then the derivative of V with respect to U, multiplied by the partial derivative of U with respect to b. That is:

$$V_b(b, c) = V'[U(b, c)] \cdot U_b(b, c) \qquad [6.11]$$

Applying a similar argument for the partial derivatives of cheese, we confirm by a rather different route from that applied in Exercise X6.10 that the marginal rates of substitution for both functions are identical:

$$MRS = -\frac{MU_B(b, c)}{MU_C(b, c)} = -\frac{V_b(b, c)}{V_c(b, c)} = -\frac{V'[U(b, c)] \cdot U_b(b, c)}{V'[U(b, c)] \cdot U_c(b, c)} = -\frac{U_b(b, c)}{U_c(b, c)} \quad [6.12]$$

This demonstrates what we mean in saying that a utility function is unique up to a monotonic transformation. It confirms that any preference ordering can be represented by many utility functions. With the functions, U and V, for any consumption bundle Z : (b, c), the values $U(b, c)$ and $V(b, c)$ will most likely be different, the marginal utility measures will be $U_b(b, c)$ and $V_b(b, c)$; and $U_c(b, c)$ and $V_c(b, c)$ will be different, but the marginal rate of substitution will be the same, irrespective of which utility function has been used.

Thinking in terms of an indifference map, we have confirmed that the slope of the indifference curve passing through any bundle will be the same for both functions. The indifference curves associated with both utility functions have the same shape, and so the preferred set of any bundle Z will be the same whichever utility function we use. As argued in Chapter 5, monotonically increasing transformations of a utility function preserve the underlying preference ordering.

6.3.2 Homogeneity

The marginal rate of substitution given in Expression 6.10 is a function of the ratio of the quantities in the consumption bundle, $\frac{c}{b}$. Most utility functions that we use have this property, and it has a nice graphical representation, illustrated in Figure 6.3. The linear relation

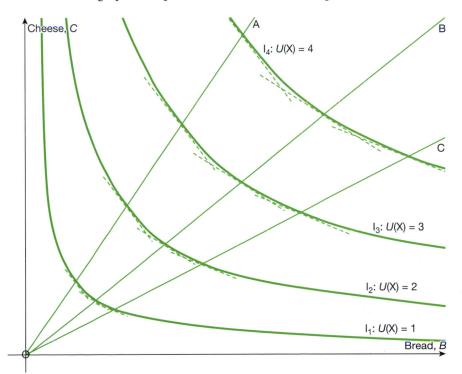

Figure 6.3 With homogeneous utility functions, indifference curves have the same shape

$c = rb$, where r is constant, can be represented graphically by a straight line passing through the origin. Along such a line, the ratio $c/b = r$, so the marginal rate of substitution will also be constant. The indifference curves on a preference map can then be formed through a process of radial expansion, each indifference curve having the same shape, but stretched or compressed to a different extent from every other one.

Homogeneity of degree t The responsiveness of a function to scalar changes in inputs.

Every utility function that possesses the property of **homogeneity**, as defined in Essential Maths 6.9, exhibits this property. It is quite straightforward to confirm that all Cobb–Douglas (and indeed all CES) utility functions are homogeneous. A utility function U has this property if, taking any consumption bundle Z : (b, c) and multiplying the quantity of goods in the bundle by some scalar factor, λ, to form the consumption bundle, $Z_\lambda : (\lambda b, \lambda c)$, then:

$$U(\lambda b, \lambda c) = \lambda^t U(b, c) \qquad [6.13]$$

Utility increases by a factor λ^t where t, the degree of homogeneity, measures the responsiveness of the function to changes in the scale of inputs. For a utility function that is homogeneous of degree $t = 1$, the increase in utility is directly proportional to the value of the scalar, λ. For a utility function that is homogeneous of degree $t < 1$, the increase in utility will be less than proportional to the value of the scalar, λ. For example, if a utility function, U, is homogeneous of degree $t = 0.5$, then $U(\lambda b, \lambda c) = \lambda^{0.5} U(b, c)$, so that if $\lambda = 2$, $\lambda^t = \sqrt{2}$. The quantities in the consumption bundle double, but utility increases by a factor of $\sqrt{2}$.

By yourself

X6.11   Calculate the degree of homogeneity of the utility functions, U:

(a) $U(b, c) = k_b b + k_c c$ (b) $U(b, c) = b^{0.5} c^{0.5}$ (c) $U(b, c) = b^{0.5} + c^{0.5}$

(d) $U(b, c) = (b^{0.5} + c^{0.5})^2$ (e) $U(b, c) = \dfrac{bc}{b + c}$.

X6.12   Obtain expressions for MRS in all five cases above, where possible writing each as a function of the ratio $\frac{b}{c}$.

Essential Maths 6.9: Homogeneity of functions

We say that the function $z(x, y)$ is homogeneous of degree r (HODr) if for every pair (x, y) in the domain and for every number $\lambda > 0$:

$$z(\lambda x, \lambda y) = \lambda^r \cdot z(x, y)$$

If we multiply the input pair, (x, y), by a scalar λ, then the image, z, increases by a factor λ^r.

- If $r = 1$, the increase in the image is proportional to the increase in the subject.
- If $r = 0$, the image does not change as the subject increases.

If $z(x, y)$ is HODr, then so are the partial derivatives $z_x(x, y)$ and $z_y(x, y)$.

For a contour $C : z(x, y) = z_0$, written explicitly as $y = y(x; z_0)$, the gradient of the contour, $y'(x) = -\frac{z_x(x,y)}{z_y(x,y)}$. It is possible to show that on any ray, $y = \kappa x$, $y'(x) = -\frac{z_x(x, \kappa x)}{z_y(x, \kappa x)} = y'(\kappa)$, so that the gradient of the contour is the same, whatever the value of x.

X6.13   We have confirmed that the functions $U : U(b, c) = bc$ and $V : V(b, c) = b^2c^2$ represent the same preferences.

(a) Confirm that the function $W : W(b, c) = b^{0.5}c^{0.5}$ also represents these preferences.

(b) Confirm that the partial derivative V_b is increasing in b while V_c is increasing in c, that U_b is independent of b and U_c independent of c, and that W_b is decreasing in b and W_c is decreasing in c.

X6.14   Even though it is often convenient to do so, why can we not simply assume that marginal utilities will always be decreasing?

The property of homogeneity will be quite important when we apply the standard model to analysis of businesses' profit maximization. For the moment, we are interested in the fact that for homogenous functions, the marginal rate of substitution for all bundles in which bread and cheese are in any fixed proportion is constant – whether that proportion be one loaf of bread to every 3 kg of cheese, or six loaves of bread to every 1 kg of cheese, or more generally b loaves to c kg of cheese. The exercises suggest that for utility functions the degree of homogeneity is associated with whether or not a utility function has decreasing marginal utility. Since there are monotonically increasing transformations that change a homogeneous utility function from having diminishing marginal utility to a form that has increasing marginal utility, while still representing the same preferences, the assumption of diminishing marginal utility, set out in Table 5.1, is useful but not essential.

6.4   The most-preferred, affordable consumption bundle

We have already demonstrated that at the most-preferred consumption bundle, the marginal rate of substitution is equal to the price ratio. As we shall see now, it is quite easy to find the equation of the line for which the marginal rate of substitution takes that value. This gives us the proportion of bread to cheese for all possible most-preferred consumption bundles, independent of the money that might be spent. We can then use the budget constraint to work out, given a specific amount of money to hand, which of these bundles is just affordable and so is most preferred.

6.4.1   Example: Cobb–Douglas preferences

We represent Leena's preferences using a utility function in Cobb–Douglas form, U:

$$U(b, c) = b^{0.25}c^{0.75} \tag{6.14}$$

By yourself

X6.15   Confirm that the utility function in Expression 6.14 is homogeneous of degree 1, and that the marginal utilities, MU_B and MU_C, are decreasing.

Leena is able to spend $m = 64$. She faces prices $p_b = 1.6$ and $p_c = 12$. So we can write her budget constraint as:

$$1.6b + 12c = 64 \tag{6.15}$$

From Expression 6.14, by partial differentiation, we obtain the marginal utility functions MU_B and MU_C:

$$MU_B(b,c) = 0.25b^{-0.75}c^{0.75}; \text{ and } MU_c(b,c) = 0.75b^{0.25}c^{-0.25} \qquad [6.16]$$

The marginal rate of substitution is then simply the ratio of the marginal utilities:

$$MRS = -\frac{MU_b}{MU_c} = -\frac{0.25b^{-0.75}c^{0.75}}{0.75b^{0.25}c^{-0.25}} = -\frac{c}{3b} \qquad \boxed{\text{Multiply numerator and denominator by } b^{0.75}c^{0.25}} \qquad [6.17]$$

The algebraic manipulations in Expression 6.17 require an understanding of the rules for manipulating indices (specifically, that a negative power of a variable in the numerator of a fraction can be written as a positive power in the denominator, and vice versa). We should also note that Expression 6.17 is simply minus one-third times (c/b), where c/b is the ratio of bread to cheese in the consumption bundle. As with all homogeneous functions, we find that Expression 6.17 may be stated in terms of the ratio in which the goods are consumed.

Going back to the budget constraint given in Expression 6.15, we write this in explicit form:

$$c = \frac{64 - 1.6b}{12} = \frac{80 - 2b}{15} \qquad \boxed{\text{Multiply numerator and denominator by } 1.25} \qquad [6.18]$$

From Expression 6.18, we see that the slope of the budget constraint is $-\frac{2}{15}$. This is the relative price of bread, expressed as the opportunity cost – the rate that a budget-constrained consumer must give up consumption of cheese in order to buy more loaves.

We can now find the most-preferred affordable bundle. We know that it can be found at a point such as Z in Figure 6.4, where the indifference curve through Z is tangent to the budget constraint. In terms of the underlying geometry of the diagram, we say that the slope of the budget constraint must be equal to the slope of the indifference curve, and that both are the marginal rate of substitution. From Expression 6.17, $MRS(b, c) = -\frac{c}{3b}$, and from Expression 6.18, the slope of the budget constraint, $-\frac{p_b}{p_c} = -\frac{2}{15}$. For these to be equal:

$$\boxed{\text{Multiply numerator and denominator by } 5b}$$

$$\boxed{\text{Remove common factor, 3, from denominator}} \quad \frac{c}{3b} = \frac{2}{15}, \text{ so } 5c = 2b \text{ and } c = 0.4b \qquad [6.19]$$

In Expression 6.19, the quantity of cheese is a constant fraction of the quantity of bread in the bundle. Its graph is a straight line, starting from the origin, with slope, $g = 0.4$. Perhaps surprisingly, the amount of money, m, that Leena is willing to spend does not appear in Expression 6.19. We therefore interpret Expression 6.19 as indicating that the product mix, $\frac{b}{c}$, in the most-preferred, affordable consumption bundle remains constant, irrespective of the amount of money, or income, available to finance consumption. All consumption bundles for which MRS equals the price ratio lie on the upward-sloping line in Figure 6.4, whose equation is Expression 6.19. We call this line the **income expansion path**. If the amount of money available to the consumer changes, but the prices of bread and cheese remain the same, the most-preferred, affordable bundles before and after the price change will lie on this straight line.

Income expansion path A curve showing the most-preferred affordable consumption bundles as income varies.

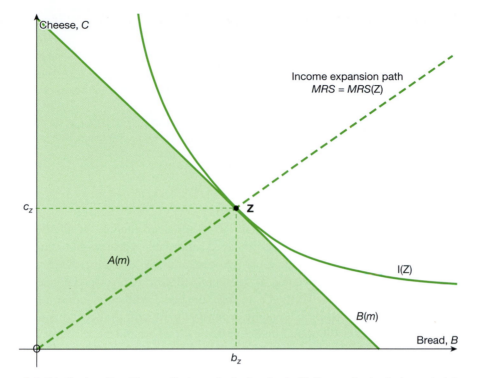

Figure 6.4 Z is the bundle with specified marginal rate of substitution on the budget constraint

In Figure 6.4, we have the upward-sloping income expansion path and the downward-sloping budget constraint. They meet at one point, Z, for which Expressions 6.15 and 6.19 hold.

[6.19]: $c = 0.4b$; so in [6.15], $12c = 4.8b$

Use '*' symbol to indicate solution of problem

$$1.6b^* + 4.8b^* = 64; \text{ so } 6.4b^* = 64, \text{ and } b^* = 10 \tag{6.20}$$

Then given that $c = 0.4b$, we see that $c^* = 4$. Leena's most-preferred, affordable consumption is, Z^*:

$$(b^*, c^*) = (10, 4) \tag{6.21}$$

We may check this by evaluating Expression 6.15 for the value $(b^*, c^*) = (10, 4)$, confirming that the acquisition cost of this bundle is indeed 64. Leena chooses the bundle lying on her income expansion path, which is just affordable.

By yourself

X6.16 Suppose that a consumer has utility $U = b^{0.5}c^{0.5}$. For each of the following situations:
(a) Obtain the marginal utilities MU_b and MU_c and the marginal rate of substitution.
(b) For each of the following situations:
    (i) Obtain the relative price of the goods.
    (ii) Find the income expansion path.

(Continued)

(iii) Find the most-preferred, affordable consumption bundle:

    (i)   a consumer has an income $m = 60$, and faces prices $p_b = 2$ and $p_c = 3$;

    (ii)   a consumer has an income $m = 84$ and faces prices $p_b = 6$ and $p_c = 7$;

    (iii)   a consumer has an income $m = 144$ and faces prices $p_b = 9$ and $p_c = 16$.

X6.17   Now suppose that the consumer has utility $U = b^{0.5} + b^{0.5}$. Repeat X6.16, but for the following situations:

(a) A consumer has an income $m = 60$, and faces prices $p_b = 2$ and $p_c = 3$;

(b) A consumer has an income $m = 100$ and faces prices $p_b = 4$ and $p_c = 6$;

(c) A consumer has an income $m = 144$ and faces prices $p_b = 3$ and $p_c = 9$.

Method of equal gradients A method of solving problems of choice that explicitly applies the equi-marginal principle and resource constraints.

We call this the **method of equal gradients**. Of all the ways of finding the most-preferred, affordable consumption bundle, this is probably the most intuitive, and also the most clearly grounded in the specifics of economic theory. It is essentially a two-step process. The first is to solve the equal gradient condition, $\frac{MU_B}{MU_C} = \frac{p_b}{p_c}$, to obtain the income expansion path, and the second is to find the consumption bundle on that path where the affordability constraint is binding. Assuming that preferences are well behaved, it will generally provide us with a unique solution to the problem of the consumer's problem of allocating their expenditure across the available goods.

6.5   The least expensive, acceptable consumption bundle

The standard model allows economists to analyse decision making. Through the last four chapters, we have set up a sequence of relatively straightforward problems of utility maximization, carefully designed so that we might explore them with only a little technical knowledge, our objective throughout having been to identify the most-preferred, affordable consumption bundle in situations where people face fixed prices, have a fixed amount of money to finance consumption, and have well-behaved principles. We have developed the method of equal gradients, which applies the equi-marginal principle. The method is simple and flexible, and we will use it in solving many other problems throughout this book. Some of these problems will be more complex and involve decisions that are obviously more important than being able to identify the optimal combination of bread and cheese for a single person. For example, in Part III we will apply the standard model to certain decisions that businesses make about hiring inputs for the production process. We shall see there that in thinking about such decisions it is sensible to set up the businesses' choices almost as the opposite of what we have seen so far. It turns out that efficient firms always minimize the cost of producing a given output. As there are some situations in which cost minimization is important for consumers as well, we conclude this chapter by setting out an example of this interpretation of the standard model.

Up to this point, we have fixed the amount of money, m, that is available to finance consumption. This has meant treating money as a constraint upon choice since the chosen bundle must lie in the budget, or affordable, set. We have turned the objective of finding the best, or most-preferred, bundle within the affordable set into a utility maximization problem, and in Figure 6.4 we have depicted the solution of the problem. The consumer's objective is to reach the indifference curve that just touches the affordable set. More generally, we might say that this is an example of a problem of **constrained maximization**, because we find the highest possible value of utility given the affordability constraint.

> **Constrained maximization**
> Methods for solving problems of choice whereby solutions are drawn from a restricted set.

The 'opposite' problem begins by assuming that the chosen consumption bundle must meet some standard of acceptability. An extreme case would be subsistence. If bread and cheese are the only (edible) goods available to a consumer, then some bundles will contain so little nutrition that the consumer would starve to death. We can reasonably argue that subsistence, or access to enough food to survive, is a binding constraint on our choices. We can extend this argument: few of us would be content with simple subsistence, and there are many benefits to long-term health from achieving nutrition levels well above the subsistence level. More generally, we might wish to argue that there are minimum levels of consumption that are socially acceptable. For example, in most countries, there are complex planning rules that stipulate the minimum quality of housing. Over time, as wealth increases, these will be revised upwards.

We represent this situation in Figure 6.5. Here, the indifference curve through Z represents a binding acceptability constraint. This consumer, Michael, believes that only consumption bundles within the preferred set P(Z), effectively the lightly shaded region in the diagram, are acceptable. Michael's objective is now to find the least expensive way of purchasing an acceptable bundle. We propose that Z^* is the cheapest, acceptable consumption bundle.

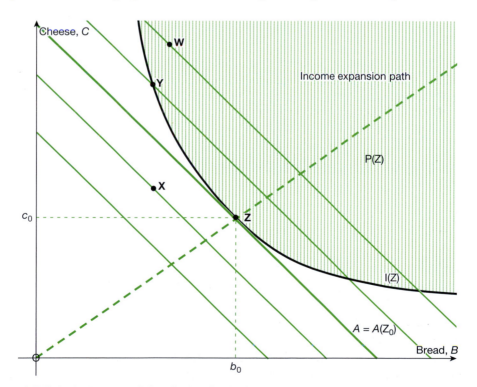

Figure 6.5 Z_0 is the least costly bundle that lies in the acceptable set

The geometry of the argument should already be broadly familiar. We show several downward-sloping lines in the diagram. The acquisition cost, $A(b, c)$, is the same for every bundle on a line. The lines all have the same slope, which is the relative price of the goods; once again, this represents the opportunity cost of bread (or more generally, the good whose consumption is measured on the horizontal axis). We now show that there is no acceptable bundle that has a lower acquisition cost than Z^*.

Let us first consider a consumption bundle, such as X, whose acquisition cost $A(X)$ is less than $A(Z^*)$. Bundle X must lie outside the preferred set, $P(Z^*)$, in Figure 6.5, and so it does not meet the acceptability criterion. It therefore cannot be the cheapest, acceptable consumption bundle.

Similarly, any bundle, W, whose acquisition cost $A(W)$ is greater than $A(Z)$, lies above the line $A = A(Z)$ in Figure 6.5. It is possible to reduce the quantity of both goods in the consumption bundle while remaining in the preferred set. This would happen if we replaced bundle W with bundle Y, for example. It is therefore not possible for the cheapest, acceptable bundle to lie in the interior of the preferred set $P(Z)$.

Lastly, if we consider a bundle, such as Y, that lies on the boundary of $P(Z)$, and so lies on the indifference curve through Z^*, then the constant acquisition cost line passing through Y must lie further out from the origin than the line passing through Z^*. It is therefore impossible to find an acceptable bundle whose acquisition cost is less than $A(Z^*)$; and Z is indeed the cheapest, acceptable bundle.

6.5.1   Solving the minimum expenditure problem

Here, we present our previous example, reworking it as required for this situation. Our objective is to minimize the acquisition cost, A:

$$A(b, c) = 1.6b + 12c \qquad [6.22]$$

As usual, the acquisition cost is a linear function. We write the minimum acquisition cost as A_0. Then, with $A(b, c) = A_0$, we rearrange Expression 6.22 in explicit form, with c the subject of the expression:

$$c = \frac{A_0 - 1.6b}{12} = \frac{1.25A_0 - 2b}{15} \qquad [6.23]$$

This is more or less same as the explicit form of the budget constraint in Expression 6.15. The relative price, or the opportunity cost, of bread is again $-\frac{p_b}{p_c} = -\frac{2}{15}$.

We now define the constraint for this problem:

$$V(b, c) = c^3 b = 640 \qquad [6.24]$$

By yourself

X6.18   Confirm that the utility functions, $U : U(b, c) = b^{0.25}c^{0.75}$ and $V : V(b, c) = c^3b$, represent the same preferences, by showing that: (1) V is a monotonically increasing transformation of U; and (2) $MRS(b, c)$ is the same when calculated using functions U and V.

Expression 6.24 defines an indifference curve of the utility function, V, in Exercise X6.18. Although the form of V is different from the form of U in the previous example, both functions represent the same preferences. By definition, on an indifference curve, utility is constant. Considering different consumption bundles on the curve, the change in utility between them is exactly zero. Keeping utility constant as we substitute bread for cheese means that the increase in utility from the higher consumption of bread must be equal and opposite to the reduction in utility from forgoing consumption of cheese. Remember that for vanishingly small changes in consumption, the change in utility resulting from a change in consumption of a good is the good's marginal utility times the change in consumption. We write the change in utility V as dV:

$$dV = V_b(b,c) \cdot db + V_c(b,c) \cdot dc \approx 0 \tag{6.25}$$

In Expression 6.25 we have used the partial derivatives of the utility function to represent the marginal utilities, so here:

Use power rule of differentiation

$$c^3 \cdot db + 3bc^2 \cdot dc \approx 0 \tag{6.26}$$

Divide all terms by c^2 $c \cdot db \approx -3b \cdot dc$ Subtract $3b \cdot dc$ from both sides $\tag{6.26a}$

As $db \to 0$, obtain derivative $\left. \dfrac{dc}{db} \right|_{V=V_0} = -\dfrac{c}{3b}$ Divide both sides by $-3b \cdot db$ $\tag{6.27}$

Expression 6.25 is approximately true for any pair of consumption bundles that lie close together on any indifference curve. Given the definition of the partial derivatives as instantaneous rates of change, it is not exactly true since average rates of change across a finite interval are unlikely to be the same as the instantaneous rates of change for some particular consumption bundle. In Expression 6.26, we obtain the partial derivatives of the specific function, V, and then rearrange them. In Expression 6.27, we argue in effect that as the interval over which we measure the change gets smaller and smaller, the average rate of change of c approaches the derivative, $\frac{dc}{db}$, which we can represent as the gradient of the indifference curve, or $MRS(b, c)$. Note that Expression 6.27 is exactly the same as Expression 6.17 in the previous example.

Introducing Figure 6.5, we argued that the cheapest, acceptable bundle is found at Z_0, where the constant expenditure line is tangent to the utility constraint. At bundle Z_0, the gradient of the line, $A(b, c) = A_0$ must equal $MRS(b_0, c_0)$, which is the gradient of the indifference curve, which bounds the acceptable set. Since Expressions 6.27 and 6.17 are identical, as are Expressions 6.23 and 6.18, the relationship between the quantities of bread and cheese in consumption bundle Z_0 will be given by Expression 6.19, which we write here as:

$$b = 2.5c \qquad \text{Inverse of [6.19]} \tag{6.28}$$

If we assume that the boundary of the acceptable set represents the minimum socially acceptable standard of consumption, Expression 6.28 suggests that as living standards increase, or if some people have higher minimum living standards than others, the minimum acceptable bundle will increase in size, but the proportions of bread and cheese that it contains will stay constant.

Before, we had the upward-sloping income expansion path, and a downward-sloping budget constraint. Here we have an upward-sloping living standards expansion path, and a downward-sloping acceptability constraint. As before, they meet at one point, Z, at which both expressions are true. Then:

> **Substitute for b from [6.28] into [6.24]**
>
> $2.5c^4 = 640$; so $c^4 = 256$, and $c = 4$ [6.29]

It follows that $b = 10$, and we have exactly the same solution as we had in our earlier example.

6.6   Conclusions

Economic efficiency
A state in which reallocation of resources cannot improve the outcome.

It is no mere coincidence that the solutions to the two problems that we have explored are the same. We have defined Leena as a budget-constrained, utility maximizer, and Michael as a preference-constrained, expenditure minimizer. They have the same underlying preferences, and face the same prices for goods. They both use their resources in a manner that is **economically efficient**. This means that it is impossible for either of them to use their resources in any other way and improve the outcome. Where Leena fixes the amount of money that she is able to spend, and effectively works out how much utility she can purchase, Michael sets the minimum acceptable level of utility, and effectively works out how to achieve this as cheaply as possible. Leena is unable to wring any more utility out of the money to hand; while Michael finds it impossible to generate any more than the minimum acceptable without spending at least the amount of money that is available to Leena.

We can see the equivalence of the utility maximization and expenditure minimization problems by concentrating on Leena's decision making only. She begins with a fixed amount of money, to be spent on purchasing the most-preferred, affordable bundle. Calculating the utility that she derives from consumption, we might instead solve the problem of reaching that level of utility as cheaply as possible. Leena will want to spend the same amount of money and purchase the same bundle as when maximizing her utility. More generally, a consumer who begins with a fixed sum of money, m, can find the maximum achievable utility, $V(m)$, and will then confirm that the expenditure, $E[V(m)]$, needed to obtain utility $V(m)$ is simply m. By going through the utility maximization process, then reversing through the expenditure minimization process, and finishing with the starting sum of money, we confirm that there is no cheaper way of buying the utility-maximizing bundle, and no way of deriving more utility from a given sum of money. Within the standard model, resource allocations that reflect the equi-marginal principle are always economically efficient.

This is perhaps the most important chapter in Part II. We therefore end with a varied set of examples. In some of these, the underlying preferences are not well behaved, while in others they are well behaved, but slightly unusual. Some use maths, some use logical argument, but a good way to approach all of them is to think in terms of the shape of the indifference curves: well-behaved curves are smooth, downward-sloping, and convex. Affordable sets are triangular. Then there is one, and only one, point on each indifference curve where a constant acquisition cost line touches it: at that point, the conditions for economic efficiency will be met.

By yourself

X6.19   We have stated that there are five assumptions necessary for preferences to be well-behaved: (i) completeness; (ii) reflexivity; (iii) transitivity; (iv) monotonicity; and (v) convexity. For each assumption, state why it is essential, and sketch a diagram showing indifference curves in which that assumption, and that assumption only, is violated.

X6.20   Consider the following situation. Geoff's utility function is $U : U(b, c) = b^2 + c^2$ and he tries to use the rules that we have set out in this chapter to confirm that the utility-maximizing choice is the one that is predicted by the process in this chapter. Geoff reports that he tried the consumption bundle predicted, but found it much less satisfying than the one he chose without trying to use the rules.

  (a) Write down the equation of the indifference curve, $U = 1$.
  (b) Show that the marginal rate of substitution $MRS = -b/c$.
  (c) Show that on the indifference curve, $\frac{d^2c}{db^2} < 0$, so that the indifference curve is concave.
  (d) Sketch the indifference curve and explain why it should be that if $p_B < p_C$ then Geoff will spend all his money on good B.
  (e) Of the assumptions about preferences introduced in this chapter, which do not apply to Geoff's preferences?

X6.21   Sketch the following diagram, which represents Helga's preferences over goods B and C. We measure the quantity of good B on the horizontal axis and the quantity of good C on the vertical axis. Now draw an upward-sloping straight line starting from the origin. Above the line, every indifference curve is vertical, while to the right of the line, every indifference curve is horizontal. (Every indifference curve is formed of two segments, one vertical, and one horizontal, which meet on the straight line that you have drawn.)

  (a) Choose a consumption bundle to the right of the upward-sloping straight line. Explain the effect on utility of increasing the quantity of increasing: (i) the quantity of good B in Helga's consumption bundle; and (ii) the quantity of good C.
  (b) Repeat part (a) for a consumption bundle that lies above the line.
  (c) Now sketch a downward-sloping line representing a constant acquisition cost given that Helga has an amount of money m to spend. Choose the line so that it just touches an indifference curve at its vertex. We have argued that where a constant acquisition cost line just touches an indifference curve, Helga cannot reallocate resources and increase the utility from consumption. Confirm that in an affordable consumption bundle it is impossible to increase either the quantity of good B or else the quantity of good C and increase utility.
  (d) Discuss whether or not the assumptions in X6.19 – (i) completeness; (ii) reflexivity; (iii) transitivity; (iv) monotonicity; and (v) convexity – are satisfied in your diagram. Hence explain whether or not you consider Helga's preference to be well behaved.
  (e) Explain why we consider that Helga considers goods B and C to be perfect complements.

X6.22   Ivan's preferences between goods B and C are such that they can be represented by the utility function $U(b, c) = 2b + c$.

  (a) Confirm that Ivan obtains the same level of utility from the consumption bundles $(b, c) = (10, 0)$, and $(b, c) = (0, 20)$.
  (b) Sketch a diagram showing these two bundles and the indifference curve that they lie on.
  (c) Discuss whether or not Ivan's preferences appear to satisfy the assumptions of (i) completeness; (ii) reflexivity; (iii) transitivity; (iv) monotonicity; and (v) convexity. Does it seem to you that Ivan's preferences are well behaved?

(Continued)

(d) Now suppose that Ivan can buy units of good B at price $p_b = 4$, and units of good C at price $p_c = 2$. Sketch Ivan's budget constraint, given that the amount of money available for consumption $m = 40$.

(e) From your diagram, what do you think is the best that we might say about Ivan's resource allocation?

(f) Now suppose that the price of good C increases slightly to 2.05. Sketch the new budget constraint, given that Ivan still has $m = 40$ to finance consumption. How does your answer to part (e) change?

(g) Repeat part (f), but now with the price of good B increasing to 4.005.

(h) If we know that Ivan chooses a mixture of goods B and C, what can we say about the price ratio p_b/p_c?

(i) Why do we consider that Ivan considers goods B and C to be perfect substitutes?

X6.23 X6.21 and X6.22 explore special cases of preferences.

(a) In X6.21, what assumption of 'good behaviour' is barely satisfied? In X6.22, which (different) assumption of 'good behaviour' is barely satisfied?

(b) In diagrammatic terms, what is ruled out as contrary to the assumptions of good behaviour?

X6.24 In some textbook diagrams, indifference curves are drawn so that they are convex, but become upward-sloping at high values of consumption of one good. Explain what the upward-sloping component of the indifference curve means in terms of the assumptions of good behaviour.

X6.25 Sometimes economists have argued for the existence of a bliss point, the most-preferred bundle. Sketch a diagram in which all the assumptions of good behaviour – except monotonicity – are satisfied, and there is still a bliss point. On your diagram, sketch a budget constraint that passes above and to the right of the bliss point. Explain how a consumer's behaviour will differ when there is a bliss point from the situation in which there are well-behaved preferences.

X6.26 We have generally talked in terms of the most-preferred consumption bundle involving the purchase of both goods B and C. Suppose that Kaila spends all her money on good B, and none on good C. How might we reconcile this outcome with the fact that she has well-behaved preferences? [*Hint:* Suppose that the condition that Kaila's marginal rate of substitution is equal to the price ratio is satisfied only when all her money is spent on good B; and then consider what Kaila would do if that condition were never satisfied, so that for any consumption bundle the marginal rate of substitution is greater than the price ratio.]

Summary

We start with the assumption of a utility-maximizing consumer, whose preferences are well behaved, and who has a fixed amount of money to spend on two goods whose prices are fixed. We then characterize the most preferred, affordable bundle for that consumer in diagrammatic terms as lying on the constant acquisition cost line that forms the budget constraint, typically at the point where an indifference curve touches, but does not intersect, the constraint. At this point, the slope of the indifference curve, the marginal rate of substitution, is equal to the ratio of the prices of the good. Given well-behaved preferences, there will be a unique most preferred, affordable bundle containing a mixture of the two goods.

For an expenditure-minimizing consumer, facing a similar problem but required to reach a fixed level of utility, we characterize the cheapest, acceptable bundle in diagrammatic terms as lying on the indifference curve that forms the preference constraint, typically at the point where a constant acquisition cost line touches, but does not intersect, the constraint. At this point, the same conditions hold as in the case of the utility-maximizing consumer, and there is again typically a uniquely defined solution to this problem.

The marginal rate of substitution of any pair of goods is the ratio of their marginal utilities. This means that for any solution to the resource allocation problems set out in this chapter:

$$\frac{MU_x}{MU_y} = \frac{p_x}{p_y} \text{ or } \frac{MU_x}{p_x} = \frac{MU_y}{p_y} \qquad [\text{S6.1}]$$

This important condition in Expression S6.1 is stated in two ways to demonstrate firstly the equality of gradients of the indifference curve and the acquisition cost line, and secondly the equi-marginal principle in the form that the ratio of marginal utility to the price of the good is the same for every good satisfied whenever there is an optimal choice. It will hold both for a utility-maximizing and an expenditure-minimizing consumer, and it means that the utility gained from the last cent spent on either good is the same. For a consumer with well-behaved preferences, it is sufficient to ensure that any reallocation of expenditure would reduce the total utility generated from consumption.

Our solution method for the resource allocation problem facing a consumer is to solve expression S6.1 for all possible constraining values. This gives the income expansion path. We then find the consumption bundle on the actual constraint for which S6.1 is satisfied.

Visit the companion website at **www.palgrave.com/mochrie** to access further teaching and learning materials, including lecturer slides and a testbank, as well as guideline answers and student MCQs.

7

Demand functions

What we do in this chapter

In Chapter 6 we developed two closely related methods for finding the quantities of bread and cheese that a consumer will demand. In both cases, we assumed that the prices of both goods were fixed.

- Method 1: As well as prices, we also set the amount of money that the consumer has to spend and found the most-preferred (utility-maximizing), but affordable, consumption bundle.
- Method 2: Instead of setting the money available, we set the minimum acceptable utility from consumption and found the cheapest, acceptable consumption bundle.

In this chapter, we ask what happens when income (in Method 1), the minimum acceptable utility (in Method 2), or the prices of goods change. The answer is that the quantities of the goods in the optimal consumption bundle change, so we say that the consumer's demands change.

To calculate how the quantities demanded alter, we could take the new parameters and apply the solution process again. This can get quite tedious. So instead we solve a more general

problem: finding the quantities demanded for any price of bread and any price of cheese, and any amount of money (or target utility).

We then find *demand functions* – rules that tell us how much bread and how much cheese there will be in the most-preferred consumption bundle. Given the demand functions, we can explore how the demand for bread will change as the price of cheese changes, or how the demand for bread will change as the amount of money available changes.

In the discussion, we shall use graphs frequently. The important graphs are:

- *Demand curve*: how the demand for a good changes as its price changes.
- *Engel curve*: how the demand for a good changes as the amount of money available changes.
- *Income offer curve*: how the demand for both goods changes as the amount of money available changes.
- *Price offer curve*: how the demand for both goods changes as the price of one good changes.

7.1 Maximizing utility with any level of income

We begin with an example that should largely be familiar:

The utility function takes the form

$$U = b^{0.25}c^{0.75} \qquad\qquad [6.14]$$

We shall assume that the price of a loaf of bread, $p_b = 1.6$, while cheese costs $p_c = 12$ per kg. The consumer has an amount, m, to spend. So, we can write the budget constraint:

| b and c are **variables** | $1.6b + 12c = m$ | m is a **parameter** | [6.15'] |

This is simply the example of Leena's decisions, used at the start of Section 6.4, with one small difference: now, we do not set the value of the amount m that she has to spend.

| **Variable** A value in a model that is obtained by solving the model. |

In this problem, b and c are the *variables*, because we shall obtain their value in terms of the *parameters*. Leena chooses her consumption bundle, Z: (b, c), given the parameter values. We treat the price of bread, $p_b = 1.6$, as a defined parameter, as is the price of cheese,

| **Parameter** A value in a model that is fixed but indeterminate. |

$p_c = 12$. We know their values (as does Leena). The amount of money available, m, is an undefined parameter – its true value is fixed, but unknown. Neither we, nor Leena, know what m will be. If Leena has to finance her expenditure from earned income, it may be that her wages vary from time to time. Parameters are different from variables in that we take their values as given and so seek to express the variables as functions of the parameters. The present example is different from the examples considered in Chapter 6, purely because of the introduction of the unknown parameter, m.

We note how little has changed in setting up the problem. Leena's utility function in Expression 6.14 is exactly the same as it was before; so if we were to sketch a preference map, it would be unchanged. The slope of the indifference curve, $MRS(b, c) = -\frac{c}{3b}$, which is Expression 6.17. The slope of the budget constraint, $-\frac{p_b}{p_c} = -\frac{2}{15}$, as in Expression 6.18. Leena's objective is still to choose the most-preferred, affordable bundle, and the income expansion path is still given by Expression 6.19: $c = 0.4b$.

We can use this example to see just why the income expansion path has that name. The value of the money available to finance consumption, m, has been left indeterminate. We wish to find the consumption bundle that lies on both Leena's income expansion path and her affordability constraint, Expression 6.15'. Substituting for c in Expression 6.15' from Expression 6.19, we obtain:

> [6.19]: $c = 0.4b$; so in [6.15'], $12c = 4.8b$

$$1.6b^* + 4.8b^* = 6.4b^* = m \qquad [7.1]$$

$$\text{So: } b^* : b^*(m) = \frac{m}{6.4}$$

> Demand for bread as a function of income

If we set $m = 64$, then $b^* = 10$, as in Expression 6.20. Expression 7.1 gives us Leena's demand for bread, given the amount of money that she has to finance consumption, m; or, slightly more generally, for any realization of the parameter m.

By yourself

X7.1 Calculate Leena's demand for cheese when she has an amount of money, m, to finance consumption. Check that your answer is correct by calculating her spending on bread and cheese, and checking that her total spending is m. What fraction of her total expenditure m is on bread?

7.1.1 Engel curves

If replacing fixed numerical values with indeterminate parameters only reduced the calculations necessary to calculate the quantities of goods demanded for different levels of income, we would have a useful tool but no more. In our example, we have shown that when the amount of money available is m, the consumption bundle chosen is Z^*:

$$Z^* : (b^*(m), c^*(m)) = \left(\frac{m}{6.4}, \frac{m}{16}\right) \quad \boxed{\text{The most-preferred consumption bundle as a function of income}} \quad [7.2]$$

There are two ways that we can present the information in Expression 7.2 graphically. Firstly, as in Figure 7.1, we can sketch two **Engel curves**, one for the amount of bread in the consumption bundle and the other for the amount of cheese. Engel curves show the relation between the consumer's income and the quantity chosen of one particular good. Secondly, we can sketch the income expansion path, which we met in Chapter 6.

Engel curve A graph of demand plotted against income.

In our example, the equations of the Engel curves are:

$$b(m) = \frac{m}{6.4}; \text{ and } c(m) = \frac{m}{16} \quad [7.3]$$

These define straight lines which pass through the origin. Without money, a consumer is unable to purchase anything; but as income increases, the quantity of both goods in the consumption bundle increases in proportion to the amount of money available, m.

Expenditure share The proportion of money spent on a specific good.

Remember that in the previous chapter the price of bread $p_b = 1.6$ and that the price of cheese $p_c = 12$. We define the **expenditure share** of a good as the amount of money spent on it divided by the total sum available for consumption. As we found in Exercise X7.1, the expenditure share of bread may be written as s_b, where

$$s_b = \frac{p_b \cdot b}{m} = \frac{1.6m}{6.4m} = 0.25 \quad \boxed{\text{A quarter of the money available is spent on bread}} \quad [7.4]$$

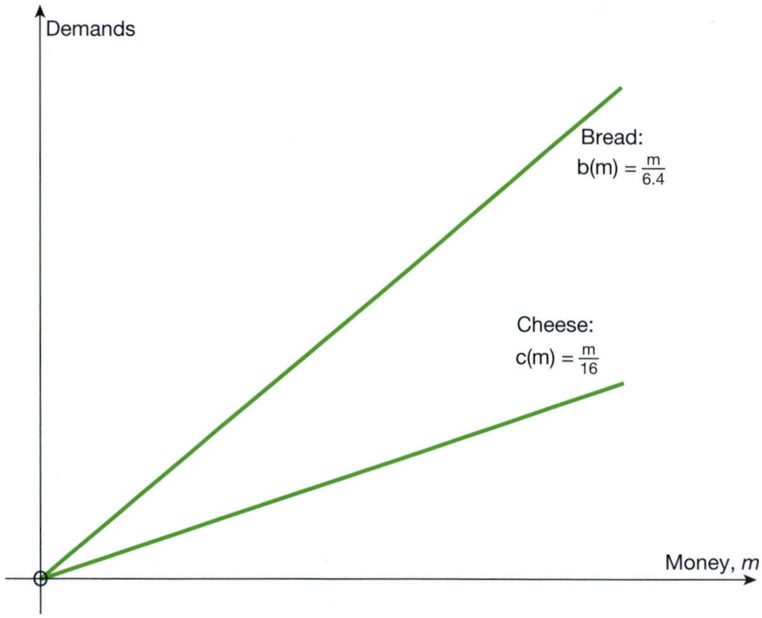

Figure 7.1 Engel curves for bread and cheese

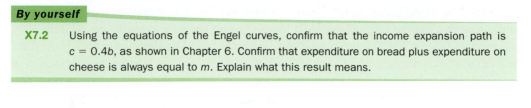

By yourself

X7.2 Using the equations of the Engel curves, confirm that the income expansion path is $c = 0.4b$, as shown in Chapter 6. Confirm that expenditure on bread plus expenditure on cheese is always equal to m. Explain what this result means.

So long as we restrict our attention to homogeneous utility functions, as defined in Chapter 6, the Engel curves will be straight lines. As income increases but prices remain the same, the consumption of all goods increases proportionately with income. Expenditure shares are constant, and both the Engel curves and the income expansion path are linear.

7.1.2 Normal and inferior goods

Working with other forms of utility function, we would not necessarily obtain this result. There are three situations that are worth distinguishing, all illustrated in Figure 7.2. Firstly, the Engel curve might become steadily steeper, indicating that as the amount of money available for consumption rises, expenditure on the good increases more quickly. For quite a broad range of incomes, the demand for petrol follows this. As people's disposable income increases, they typically drive larger, heavier cars for longer distances, and so the expenditure share of petrol will increase. We call such goods **superior**.

Superior good A good for which demand increases more rapidly than income.

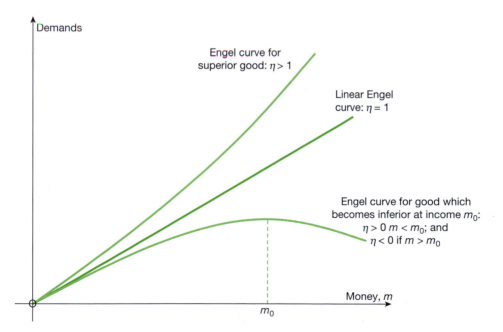

Figure 7.2 Engel curves for superior, normal, and inferior goods

Secondly, the Engel curve might slope upwards, but become flatter as income increases, indicating that expenditure on the good increases with the sum available for consumption, although not so quickly. This is typical of the demand for good-quality cuts of beef. Here, there is a range of incomes over which demand increases, as people switch from cheaper sources of protein. But there are naturally limits to the consumption of meat. We classify a good, X, as **normal** if the quantity demanded, x: $x = x(m)$, is a function of the amount of money available whose derivative $\frac{dx}{dm} > 0$. Superior goods are then a subset of normal goods.

> **Normal good** A good for which demand increases with income.

Lastly, it is possible that there is some range of incomes for which the Engel curve is downward-sloping. In this case, it is not important whether or not the curve becomes steeper or flatter as the money available increases. What matters is that as income increases, less of the good is demanded, so that the derivative of demand with respect to the money available is negative. Using the notation that we have already introduced, the derivative of demand with respect to the money available, $\frac{dx}{dm} < 0$. We say that such a good is **inferior**. Building on previous examples, bus travel and burgers seem likely to be examples of such goods.

> **Inferior good** A good for which demand decreases with income.

By yourself

X7.3 Explain why the following statements are false:
  (a) Where there are only two goods to consume, we expect both of them to be inferior.
  (b) Where there are only two goods to consume, we expect the demand for both to increase more rapidly than income.
  (c) With only two goods, if demand for one good increases more quickly than income, then the other good must be inferior.

To summarize:

- For a good to be normal, the quantity consumed must increase with the money available. The Engel curve is upward-sloping and the income elasticity of demand is greater than zero.

Essential Maths 7.1: Elasticity (1)

Elasticity measures the responsiveness of one variable to a change in the value of another one. For variables x and z, we define the x-elasticity of z as the percentage change in the value of z associated with a 1% change in the value of x. Often we calculate this elasticity as the proportional change in z divided by the proportional change in x.

As before, we define the change in x across the interval between x_0 and x_1 as $\Delta x = x_1 - x_0$. The proportional change in x is then:

$$\frac{\Delta x}{x_0} = \frac{x_1 - x_0}{x_0} \qquad \text{[M7.1]}$$

The associated values of z are $z_0 = z(x_0)$ and $z_1 = z(x_1)$, so that the change in z is $\Delta z = z_1 - z_0 = z(x_1) - z(x_0)$. Defining the proportional change in z in a similar way to the proportional change in x:

$$\frac{\Delta z}{z_0} = \frac{z(x_1) - z(x_0)}{z(x_0)} \qquad \text{[M7.2]}$$

- For a good to be inferior, the quantity consumed must decrease with the money available. The Engel curve is downward-sloping and the income elasticity of demand is less than zero.
- For a good to be superior, the quantity consumed must increase more rapidly than the money available. The Engel curve is upward-sloping and becomes steadily steeper and the income elasticity of demand is greater than one.

7.1.3 The income elasticity of demand

We have considered upward-sloping Engel curves for normal goods, and downward-sloping Engel curves for inferior goods, describing their characteristics in terms of the derivatives of demand. It turns out, however, that a derivative is not the best measure for calculating the strength of response of demand to a change in the amount of money available. If we change the units in which we measure quantities of goods, or the unit of money, then the derivatives will change. We would like a scale-free measure of responsiveness of demand, and for that we use the measure known as the income elasticity of demand. We shall denote this measure by the Greek letter η (eta).

> **Income elasticity of demand** The responsiveness of a consumer's demand to a change in income.

Suppose that Nadia starts off with an amount m_0 to spend on some good X. With this sum of money, she buys $x_0 = x(m_0)$ units of good X. When the amount of money available to finance consumption increases from m_0 to m_1, she buys $x_1 = x(m_1)$:

Income elasticity of demand

$$\eta = \frac{\left[\dfrac{x(m_1) - x(m_0)}{x(m_0)}\right]}{\left[\dfrac{m_1 - m_0}{m_0}\right]}$$

Numerator: Change in demand as a proportion of initial demand

Denominator: Change in money available as a proportion of initial money available

[7.5]

Essential Maths 7.2: Elasticity (2)

We can now define ε: the x-elasticity of z as: $\varepsilon = \dfrac{\Delta z / z_0}{\Delta x / x_0} = \dfrac{\Delta z}{\Delta x} \cdot \dfrac{x_0}{z_0} = \dfrac{\Delta z}{\Delta x} \Big/ \dfrac{z_0}{x_0}$ [M7.3]

The last expression has a useful graphical representation: in the graph of $z(x)$, it is the slope of the chord joining (x_0, z_0) and $(x_0 + \Delta x, z_0 + \Delta z)$, divided by the slope of the line starting from the origin, and passing through (x_0, z_0). (See Figure M7.1.)

In theoretical models, it is often useful to take the limit of the second expression as $\Delta x \to 0$:

$$\varepsilon = \frac{\Delta z}{\Delta x} \cdot \frac{x_0}{z_0} \to \frac{dz}{dx} \cdot \frac{x}{z} \qquad \text{[M7.4]}$$

This measures the responsiveness of z as x changes for any value of x. Large values of z mean that it is highly responsive to changes in x; positive and negative values reflect the sign of the derivative.

As noted in Essential Maths 6.1 and 6.2, it is possible to simplify Expression 7.5 by using the notation Δm for the change in income, and Δx for the change in demand. Upon rearranging the resulting expression, we obtain:

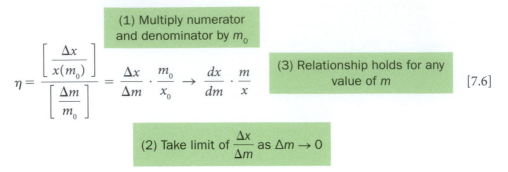

$$\eta = \frac{\left[\dfrac{\Delta x}{x(m_0)}\right]}{\left[\dfrac{\Delta m}{m_0}\right]} = \frac{\Delta x}{\Delta m} \cdot \frac{m_0}{x_0} \rightarrow \frac{dx}{dm} \cdot \frac{m}{x}$$ [7.6]

(1) Multiply numerator and denominator by m_0

(3) Relationship holds for any value of m

(2) Take limit of $\dfrac{\Delta x}{\Delta m}$ as $\Delta m \rightarrow 0$

Point elasticity The elasticity measure at a specific point on a curve.

Expression 7.6, the **point income elasticity** of demand, is the measure that we shall use in our discussion. For any amount of money, m, with associated demand, $x(m)$, the instantaneous rate of change of demand with income is the derivative, $\frac{dx}{dm}$. So, on the left-hand side of Expression 7.6, we start with the proportional change in demand, x, associated with the proportional change in the money available, m. This is simply the definition of elasticity in Expression 7.4, but referring to the change in the money available as Δm instead of $x_1 - x_0$. In step (1), we turn the elasticity into an expression consisting of a measure of the rate of change of demand, $\frac{\Delta x}{\Delta m}$, multiplied by the sum of money available and divided by the initial demand for the good. Step (2) is to allow the change in the amount of money available to become vanishingly small, so that we can use the derivative

Essential Maths 7.3: Elasticity (3)

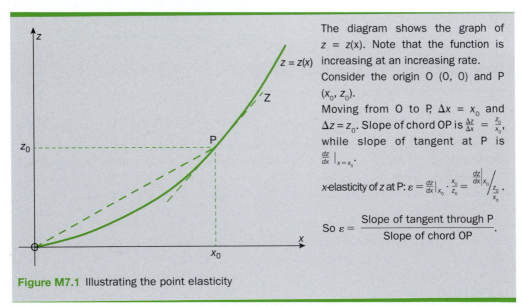

The diagram shows the graph of $z = z(x)$. Note that the function is increasing at an increasing rate.
Consider the origin O (0, 0) and P (x_0, z_0).
Moving from O to P, $\Delta x = x_0$ and $\Delta z = z_0$. Slope of chord OP is $\frac{\Delta z}{\Delta x} = \frac{z_0}{x_0}$, while slope of tangent at P is $\frac{dz}{dx}\big|_{x=x_0}$.

x-elasticity of z at P: $\varepsilon = \frac{dz}{dx}\big|_{x_0} \cdot \frac{x_0}{z_0} = \frac{dz}{dx}\big|_{x_0} / \frac{z_0}{x_0}$.

So $\varepsilon = \dfrac{\text{Slope of tangent through P}}{\text{Slope of chord OP}}$.

Figure M7.1 Illustrating the point elasticity

function as the rate of change. In step (3), then, we write down a formula for calculating point elasticities, which we shall use in many situations throughout the book.

Suppose that we have found that the demand for good $x(m) = km$, where k is a constant value. Then the first derivative of demand, $\frac{dx}{dm} = k$, and so Expression 7.6 becomes:

$$\eta = k \cdot \frac{m}{km} = 1 \qquad [7.7]$$

We have said that the income elasticity of demand measures the proportionate change in demand relative to a proportionate change in the money available to finance consumption. Expression 7.6 tells us that if money available increases by 10%, then demand increases by 10%; or that if money available falls by one-quarter, demand falls by one-quarter; or more generally, that if money m changes by some factor r, so that the consumer has rm to spend, then demand for this good will also change by a factor r, from $x(m)$ to $rx(m)$. This means that $x(rm) = r \cdot x(m)$, which is the requirement, introduced in Section 6.3, for a function to be homogeneous of degree 1.

By yourself

X7.4 Sketch a diagram showing an Engel curve that starts from the origin, but is upward-sloping and becomes steeper and steeper. Choose two or three points on the curve. Confirm that for each point, the slope of the tangent is greater than the slope of the line that joins the point to the origin. Using the definition of the income elasticity of demand, what do you conclude about its value for all points on the curve?

X7.5 Repeat X7.4, for a curve that is upward-sloping, but that becomes steadily flatter.

X7.6 When does an Engel curve have elasticity equal to zero? [*Hint:* Use Expression 7.6.] At such a point, is the good normal or inferior?

X7.7 Suppose that Omar reports that his utility, derived from consumption of a bundle of bread and cheese, is $U = b^{0.5}c^{0.5}$. For each of the following price pairs, (p_b, p_c):
(i) $p_b = 2$ and $p_c = 3$; (ii) $p_b = 6$ and $p_c = 7$; (iii) $p_b = 9$ and $p_c = 16$
(a) Obtain Omar's income expansion path, and his demands for bread and cheese.
(b) Illustrate his demands using Engel curves.
(c) Calculate the expenditure shares of bread and cheese, and his income elasticity of demand for both goods.

X7.8 Now suppose that Philippa has utility $U = b^{0.5} + c^{0.5}$. Repeat X7.7, but for prices:
(i) $p_b = 2$ and $p_c = 3$; (ii) $p_b = 4$ and $p_c = 6$; (iii) $p_b = 3$ and $p_c = 9$

7.1.4 Applying the elasticity concept: superior goods are not luxuries

Suppose that Rahima's income elasticity of demand for petrol is about 1.5. Following a 10% increase in the money that she has available to finance consumption, we expect her demand for petrol to increase by 15%. An income elasticity greater than one means that spending on the good increases more rapidly than money available for spending – we say that demand is *income elastic*.

In some textbooks, goods whose income elasticity of demand $\eta > 1$ are called *luxuries*. This terminology is not ideal because it is easy to imagine that spending on some quite mundane goods will increase more rapidly than income – if not fuel itself, perhaps total spending on car travel, given that people with higher incomes tend to drive larger, more expensive cars, may be willing to drive more often, and perhaps even tend to drive longer distances – with the result that their total spending on car travel will increase more rapidly than income.

We have defined such goods as being *superior*, and this fits more closely with the previous discussion. A good on which expenditure increases more rapidly than income, so that its income elasticity is greater than one, is, in some sense, the opposite of an inferior good, on which expenditure falls as income increases. Returning to our transport analogy, think about a city (for example, Amsterdam) where there are a great variety of ways of travelling. Were we to sit in a café on a busy street and watch how people are travelling, we might reach the conclusion that younger people are more likely to walk or cycle, while older people tend to drive cars or use public transport. We might also notice that people in business suits are more likely to drive than to use any other form of transport.

Car transport is the most expensive form of travel. HMRC, the tax authority in the UK, allows employers to pay employees £0.45 per mile driven on company business. This is an estimate of the typical full cost of car travel. HMRC allows £0.20 per mile for cycling, and nothing for walking. If we accept that walking is the cheapest form of transport, with cycling next (and also assume that in many cities the cost of public transport is approximately the £0.20 per mile allowed for cycling), then we may conclude that our time spent looking out of the café window has provided us with evidence that car travel is a *superior good* and walking and cycling are *inferior goods*.

By yourself

X7.9   Explain how reasonable you consider the HMRC allowance of £0.20 per mile cycled to be. [*Note:* 1 mile = 1.609 km.]

X7.10   What evidence have we collected of car travel being a superior good? How would you assess the claim that public transport within cities tends to be an inferior good? Do you think that the same could be said of long-distance travel (for example trans-Atlantic air travel to North America)?

X7.11   Other than differences in income, what factors might lead younger people to be more likely to use self-powered transport than older people? Why might the presence of such factors mean that we could easily overestimate the income elasticity of demand?

7.1.5 Income offer curves (income expansion paths, again)

Engel curves show how one person's demand for a single good changes as there is more money available to finance consumption. The income expansion path, introduced in

Income offer curve An alternative name for the income expansion path.

Chapter 6, shows how demand for two goods changes as the money available to finance consumption increases. The income expansion path is also called the **income offer curve**, and we shall use that name in this section.

By yourself

X7.12   Giving reasons, state whether you believe that air travel is a superior, a normal (but not superior), or an inferior good. Sketch an income offer curve showing how use of air and car travel might change as income increases.

X7.13   We observe some people who drive everywhere, and others who have no car and only use public transport (ignoring walking and cycling). Suppose that there is a threshold income at which someone will buy a car, switching from public transport only to car use only. Sketch the income offer curve that illustrates this situation. [*Hint:* The income offer curve will not be continuous, but will jump when the switch is made.]

X7.14   If bread and cheese are normal goods but neither is superior, sketch the income offer curve for Salma, who consumes 2 kg of cheese and 9 loaves. [*Hint:* What very simple shape is defined as soon as we know two points on it?]

In Figure 7.3, we have an income offer curve (an income expansion path) that captures something of the situation discussed in X7.13. We draw the income offer curve as starting from the origin. Someone who has no money to spend on transport cannot travel. Bus travel begins as a normal good, with consumption increasing with income. To demonstrate that the income offer curve is effectively the same as the income expansion path, we show it passing through three points where budget constraints are tangent to indifference curves. When m, the money available for consumption, is small, the expenditure share of bus use is high. As m increases, the expenditure share of car travel increases steadily. The income offer curve becomes steeper, indicating that car use is a superior good, with income elasticity of demand $\eta > 1$. Eventually, as the expenditure share of car use continues to increase, bus use begins to decline. Bus travel is an inferior good when m is large enough.

7.2   Maximizing utility as prices change

Now that we have considered how to treat the money available to finance consumption, m, as an indeterminate parameter within a consumer's resource allocation decision, we turn to the equivalent problem, in which the price of one good, p_b, is allowed to vary, while money, m,

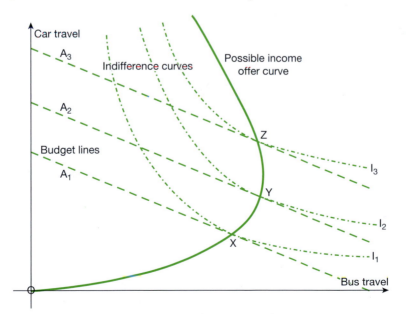

Figure 7.3 Income offer curve for bus and car travel

and other prices, p_c, are held constant. We introduce demand and price offer curves, which are the equivalent of Engel and income offer curves. We shall consider their properties in much more detail in Chapter 9, and then use them throughout the book. As in Section 7.1, we begin by adapting an example from Chapter 6 to obtain a simple demand function.

We once again consider the problem that we set out in Section 6.4, where Leena seeks to identify her most-preferred, affordable consumption bundle, subject to a fixed budget constraint. On this occasion, we fix the amount of money available to finance consumption, $m = 64$, but allow the price of bread p_b to vary, so that it becomes the indeterminate parameter in the model.

The utility function takes the form

$$U = b^{0.25}c^{0.75} \qquad\qquad [6.14]$$

We shall assume that the price of a loaf of bread, p_b is **indeterminate**, while cheese costs $p_c = 12$ per kg. The consumer has an amount, m, to spend. So, we can write the budget constraint:

$$p_b b + 12c = 64 \qquad\qquad [6.15'']$$

Our explanation of the solution is quite brief. The utility function, Expression 6.14, is unchanged. Leena's preferences are therefore the same as before, so that there is no change to their representation in a preference map. For any consumption bundle, (b, c), $MRS(b, c) = -\frac{c}{3b}$, as in Expression 6.18.

Since the price of bread, p_b, is not fixed, the price ratio is not fixed. We therefore write it as $\rho = \frac{p_b}{12}$ (ρ is the Greek letter 'rho'), emphasizing that the budget constraint becomes steeper as p_b changes. For Leena's most-preferred, affordable consumption bundle Z*: (b^*, c^*), the marginal rate of substitution, $MRS(b^*, c^*)$, equals (minus 1 times) the price ratio, ρ. So:

$$\frac{c}{3b} = \rho = \frac{p_b}{12}; \text{ and } c = \frac{p_b}{4} \cdot b \qquad\qquad [7.8]$$

As before, Expression 7.8 defines the income expansion path, identifying all the most-preferred, affordable consumption bundles when the price of cheese $p_c = 12$, whatever the price of bread, p_b, turns out to be. Once again, the most-preferred, affordable consumption bundle lies on both the income expansion path, in Expression 7.8, and the budget constraint, in Expression 6.15.

Substituting the right-hand side of Expression 7.8 for c in Expression 6.15, we obtain:

$$p_b.b^* + 3p_b.b^* = 64; \text{ so that } 4p_b.b^* = 64; \text{ and } b^* = \frac{16}{p_b} \qquad\qquad [7.9]$$

7.2.1 The demand curve

Expression 7.9 is Leena's demand for bread. It tells us how much bread she will buy, given her preference over consumption bundles, money, $m = 64$, with which to finance consumption, a fixed price of cheese, $p_c = 12$, and an indeterminate price, p_b, for a loaf of bread. The demand for bread is therefore a function of the price of bread, with the money available for consumption and the price of cheese fixed. We illustrate this relation between price and quantity, the **demand function**, in Figure 7.4.

> **Demand function** The relation between the price of a good and the quantity that a consumer buys.

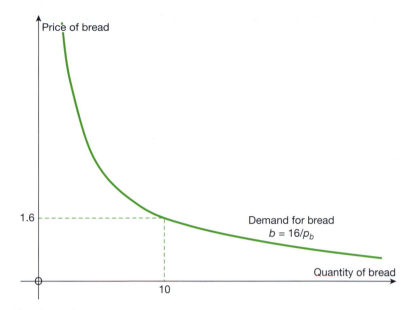

Figure 7.4 The demand curve

The demand curve in Figure 7.4, as argued originally in Chapter 2, is downward-sloping, meaning that as the price of bread increases, Leena will purchase less of it. There is one distinctive feature of Leena's demand curve, which is quite useful. We can rewrite Expression 7.9 as $p_b.b = 16$. The price of a loaf multiplied by the number bought is Leena's total expenditure on bread. In this case, it is constant. In the Figure 7.4, the total expenditure is represented by the area of the rectangle formed by the horizontal line, $b = 1.6$, and the vertical line, $p_b = 10$. As price p_b changes, demand, $b(p_b)$ will adjust so that Leena's total expenditure remains unchanged.

> **By yourself**
>
> **X7.15** Sketch the diagram that we have found, by using the following values of p_b and calculating the associated values of b : 0.4, 0.8, 1.2, 1.6, 2.4, 3.2, 4.8.
>
> **X7.16** We have said that spending on bread stays the same as its price changes. What does this imply about spending on cheese? Given that the price of cheese is constant, calculate the effect of a change in the price of bread on the demand for cheese.

7.3   The price elasticity of demand

The income elasticity of demand measures the responsiveness of a consumer's demand to changes in m, the amount of money available. The price elasticity of demand measures the responsiveness of a consumer's demand, x, to changes in the price, p_x.[1]

---

1   Tristan Blümli's essay in the online student essay bank demonstrates how mobile phone producers can exploit the willingness of some consumers to upgrade their handsets on a regular basis. This uses the fact that there will be differences in the elasticity of demand across consumers. While the essay concentrates on demand elasticities, the ideas are relevant to the practice of price discrimination through bundling (see Section 16.3). You can read Tristan's argument (and other students' essays) on the companion website for this book, at **www.palgrave.com/mochrie.**

Price elasticity of demand The responsiveness of a consumer's demand to changes in prices.

We use our definition of elasticity to define the **price elasticity of demand**, ε, as a point elasticity:

$$\varepsilon = \frac{\text{Proportional change in demand}}{\text{Proportional change in price}} = \frac{db}{dp_b} \cdot \frac{p_b}{b} \qquad [7.10]$$

Going back to the example of Leena's demand for bread in Expression 7.9, and differentiating, we obtain $\frac{db}{dp_b} = -\frac{16}{p_b^2}$. We now calculate the elasticity by substituting for b and its derivative:

$$\varepsilon = -\frac{16}{p_b^2} \cdot \frac{p_b}{\frac{16}{p_b}} = -\frac{1}{p_b^2} \cdot \frac{p_b}{p_b^{-1}} = -\frac{p_b}{p_b^{(2-1)}} = -\frac{p_b}{p_b} = -1 \qquad [7.11]$$

$\frac{db}{dp_b}$

Multiply fractions

b

Divide through by 16

Apply rules of indices

For this demand function, associated with a Cobb–Douglas utility function, the price elasticity of demand is constant. The value of elasticity, $\varepsilon = -1$, indicates that the proportionate change in the inverse of demand following some proportional change in price is equal and opposite to the proportionate change in price. For small changes in price, this means that the change in demand is approximately equal and opposite: for example, a 10% increase in price will lead to a reduction in demand of around 9%. This breaks down for larger price changes. A 20% price reduction would be followed by a 25% increase in demand.

By yourself

X7.17   Demonstrate that with unit price elasticity of demand for good X, so that $\varepsilon = -1$, the total amount of money that a consumer will spend on good X will remain constant as prices change.

7.3.1 Elastic and inelastic demands

With demand falling in response to price increases, the price **elasticity of demand**, ε, will generally be less than zero. It will be useful to distinguish between goods for which $0 > \varepsilon > -1$, whose demand is *inelastic*, and those for which $\varepsilon < -1$, whose demand is *elastic*.

Elastic (or inelastic) demand A proportionate reduction in demand following a price rise that is greater than (less than) the proportionate price rise.

Perfectly inelastic demand No change in demand after a price rise.

Making this distinction, we ignore the situation where $\varepsilon = -1$, which we encountered in our example. We sometimes describe this as the case of *unit elasticity*, one being the unit of measurement.

The price elasticity of demand, ε, is a measure of the responsiveness of demand to changes in price. For any good X, we can define it as the percentage change in demand, x, following a change in the good's price, p. We begin with the special cases of perfectly inelastic and perfectly elastic demand.

We say that a person's demand for a good is **perfectly inelastic** if $\varepsilon = 0$, so that following any proportional change in price this person's demand does not change at all. Following a price increase, this person will increase expenditure directly in proportion with the price increase.

> **Perfectly elastic demand** The demand falls to zero after any price rise.

In the same way, we say that a person's demand is **perfectly elastic** if the elasticity is so large that it cannot be defined. We write $\varepsilon \to -\infty$, which we usually read as meaning that the elasticity is infinite. If the price increases at all, demand and expenditure fall to zero; but if the price is reduced, the consumer will spend money only on this good.

We have confirmed that when the price elasticity of demand $\varepsilon = 0$, increasing price leads to increasing expenditure; that when $\varepsilon = -1$, increasing price does not change expenditure; and as $\varepsilon \to -\infty$, increasing price leads to falling expenditure. It seems reasonable to conjecture that if the demand function is inelastic, with $0 > \varepsilon > -1$, then a price increase will be associated with increasing expenditure; while if the demand function is elastic, with $\varepsilon < -1$, then a price increase will be associated with a reduction in expenditure.

By yourself

X7.18 For the demand function $x : x = 100p^{-0.5}$:
  (a) Calculate the quantity demanded for prices $p = 0.25, 1, 4, 9$, and 16, and sketch the demand curve.
  (b) Show that the elasticity of demand is -0.5. On your graph, show how the proportional change in price relates to the proportional change in demand.

X7.19 For the demand function $x : x = 100p^{-2}$:
  (a) Calculate the quantity demanded for prices $p = 0.5, 1, 2, 3$, and 4, and sketch the demand curve.
  (b) Show that the elasticity of demand is -2. On your graph, show how the proportional change in price relates to the proportional change in demand.

X7.20 Assume that a consumer's preferences are defined by the Cobb–Douglas utility function, $U : U(x, y) = x^\alpha y^{1-\alpha}$, that the consumer has $m = 60$ to spend, and that the price of good x, $p_x = 2$, while the price of y, p_y, might vary.
  (a) Show that the demand, $y = \frac{60(1-\alpha)}{p_y}$.
  (b) Confirm that the elasticity of demand $\varepsilon_p = -1$.

X7.21 Expenditure on a good is the product of demand and price. Demonstrate that expenditure on a good for which demand is inelastic increases with its price, while expenditure on a good for which demand is elastic falls with its price.

7.3.2 Elasticity of demand for power functions

In Exercises X7.18 and X7.19 we use examples for demand functions, which are power functions. For good X selling at price p_x, we define a single consumer's demand for the good, x:

$$x(p_x) = Ap_x^{-b} \qquad [7.12]$$

We have seen that a Cobb–Douglas utility function yields such a demand function, with $b = 1$, ensuring that expenditure on the good remains constant as its price changes. As shown in Figure 7.4, the graph of the demand function was then downward-sloping, and convex. It approached, but did not reach, either axis. All demand functions of the form of Expression 7.12 have this form.

We now apply the formula in Expression 5.10 to calculate the price elasticity of demand for a power function:

Power rule of differentiation

$p^{-1} = \frac{1}{p}$

$$\varepsilon = \frac{dQ}{dp} \cdot \frac{p}{Q} = (-bAp^{-1-b}) \cdot \frac{p}{(Ap^{-b})} = -b \cdot \left(\frac{Ap^{-b}}{p} \right) \cdot \left(\frac{p}{Ap^{-b}} \right) = -b \qquad [7.13]$$

Demand function

So, where demand can be represented by a power function, it always has a constant price elasticity of demand; the elasticity is the value of the index $-b$ in the demand function.

We have not tried to define a utility function that gives rise to a demand function with constant elasticity. Such demand functions are most useful in applied economics, where we have to estimate the responsiveness of demands to price changes, using observations of the quantity demanded of a good as its price changes. The estimate of the elasticity of demand, ε, allows us to predict the percentage change in demand that will follow a small (percentage) change in price. While we should strictly apply this to individual demands, we typically have to generate the estimate for the market demand.

For example, studies of the demand for rail travel provide estimates of the price elasticity of demand, ε, typically in the range $-0.6 > \varepsilon > -1$. We illustrate the basis of such estimates in Figure 7.5. We observe the actual demand of many people: ideally, we would want to know about the demands of several thousand passengers. We show people paying a variety of different prices, reflecting the fact that on a railway network there will be considerable variation in the price paid per kilometre travelled. In the diagram, people who face a relatively high price of rail travel tend to use trains less. The curve in Figure 7.5 is our best estimate, $\hat{X}$ of the 'true' demand function.

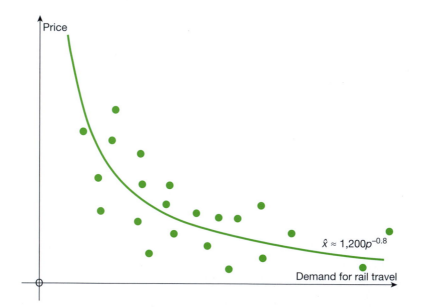

Figure 7.5 Estimating the price elasticity of demand

Asserting that:

$$\hat{x} = 1{,}200p^{-0.8} \qquad\qquad [7.14]$$

the estimate of the price elasticity $\hat{\varepsilon} = -0.8$, so we expect each 1% increase in price to be associated with a change in demand of -0.8%. Demand is inelastic, falling in response to a price increase, but by a slightly smaller proportion.

To generate this estimate, we firstly make many assumptions. Among the most important of these, we assume that every person in the sample has the same preferences, the same utility function, the same amount of money with which to finance consumption, and faces the same prices for all other goods. We would normally choose an appropriate statistical estimation technique to generate the curve, designed to fit the observations, Expression 7.14, which explains as much of the variation in the observed demand as possible.

7.3.3   Elasticity of demand for linear functions

In much the same way as we have just considered demand functions with constant price elasticity, we consider linear demand functions as providing us with an approximation of the effect of changes in price on the quantity demand. For the linear demand function, x:

$$x(p) = a - bp \qquad\qquad [7.15]$$

If we set p to zero, so that the good is free, the consumer's demand will be a. The price is zero on the horizontal (quantity) axis in Figure 7.6 and so we show that intercept at a. In addition, if the price of the good increases, the demand for the good falls by b for every unit increase in price. Setting x to zero, and rearranging Expression 7.15, we find that the price is then $\frac{a}{b}$, and this gives us the intercept on the vertical (price) axis. (We can quickly confirm that this is correct by substituting for p in Expression 7.15 and checking that for this price, $x = 0$.)

We apply the formula for the elasticity:

$$\varepsilon = \frac{dx}{dp} \cdot \frac{p}{x} = -b.\left(\frac{p}{a-bp}\right) = -\frac{bp}{a-bp} \qquad\qquad [7.16]$$

The mathematics is simpler than in the previous case, but the final expression needs a little bit more interpretation.

- When $p = 0$, so that the good is free (at the intercept on the quantity axis), $\varepsilon = 0$, and demand, $x = a$, is perfectly inelastic.
- As $p \to \frac{a}{b}$, and $x(p) \to 0, \varepsilon \to \infty$. Approaching the intercept on the vertical axis, demand becomes perfectly elastic.

- At the midpoint of the line (where $p = \frac{a}{2b}$ and $x(p) = \frac{a}{2}$),

$$\varepsilon = -\frac{b.\left(\frac{a}{2b}\right)}{a - b.\left(\frac{a}{2b}\right)} = -\frac{\left(\frac{a}{2}\right)}{a - \left(\frac{a}{2}\right)} = -\frac{\left(\frac{1}{2}\right)}{1 - \left(\frac{1}{2}\right)} = -1.$$

It is also possible to show that the derivative $\frac{d\varepsilon}{dp} < 0$. As price increases, the value of the elasticity falls. Since the elasticity of demand is negative, the largest possible value it can take is 0, and so it decreases from 0 to -1 in the lower half of the graph and from -1 without any limit in the upper half of the graph. Therefore, demand is price inelastic in the lower half of the graph and price elastic in the upper half. At the moment, this may simply seem interesting. However, when analysing the profit-maximizing behaviour of businesses in Part IV, we will often use

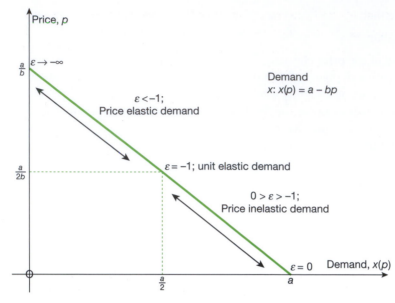

Figure 7.6 The elasticity of demand for a linear demand function

linear demand functions, and these features will be important. For example, we will demonstrate that, to maximize its profits, a business facing such a demand function will choose a combination of price and output where its demand is elastic. In Figure 7.6, this occurs in the upper half of the demand curve, so that the price $p > \frac{a}{2b}$ and the quantity demanded, $q < \frac{a}{2}$.

By yourself

X7.22 For the demand function $x : x(p) = 100 - 2p$:
  (a) Calculate demand when price is zero, and the price when demand is zero, and sketch the demand curve.
  (b) Obtain the formula for the price elasticity of demand in this case. Confirm that the price elasticity of demand is zero when the good is free, undefined if demand is choked off by a high price, and minus one at the mid-point of the demand curve.
  (c) Confirm that the derivative of the price elasticity of demand, $\frac{d\varepsilon_p}{dp} = -\frac{50}{(p-50)^2} < 0$. Explain what this means in terms of the relationship between the price of the good and its elasticity of demand.

X7.23 For the demand function $q = 400 - 8p$, repeat X7.22a and X7.22b, and then:
  (a) Show that when demand is elastic, this consumer reduces spending on the good if the price rises.
  (b) Show that when demand is inelastic, this consumer increases spending on the good if the price rises.
  (c) At what price do you consider that the consumer will spend the most money?

7.3.4 Elasticity of demand for petrol

Brons *et al.* (2008) undertook what is known as a meta-analysis of the market demand for petrol ('gasoline' in the US). They found that the short-run elasticity of demand for petrol, $\varepsilon_{SR} \approx -0.2$, with the long-run elasticity, ε_{LR}, being rather higher, with $\varepsilon_{LR} \approx -0.5$. (The elasticity of market demand differs from the elasticity of individual demand: it measures the overall responsiveness of buyers to changes in price.)

The short-run elasticity measures the immediate responsiveness of demand to a change in price. Were petrol prices to increase by 5p per litre, say from £1.22 to £1.27 per litre, so that there was a 4% increase in price, we would predict a change in demand equal to the price elasticity times the percentage change in price, which is here about $-0.2*4\% = -0.8\%$. But over the long run, the response may be rather larger, with demand falling by around 2%.

These conclusions seem intuitively sensible. When petrol prices go up, probably most people will complain. We have to buy petrol regularly, so we are likely to notice when the price increases; and there tends to be substantial media coverage of petrol price rises. But beyond complaining, particularly in the short run, people do not respond very much to the price changes. They have to travel to work, may use a car to go shopping, and like the flexibility in planning travel that a car provides.

In the longer run, however, there are more opportunities to substitute away from petrol consumption. Some people might decide to buy a smaller car that uses less fuel; others may switch from a car fuelled by petrol to one fuelled by diesel or LPG, or buy a hybrid or an electric car; some commuters might join a car pool; and some people might use different forms of transport for some (short) journeys. So, it seems reasonable that the long-run consumption of petrol should be substantially more elastic than the short-run elasticity. In Part IV, we shall see that inelastic market demand is associated with substantial monopoly power.

7.3.5 The price offer curve

To finish our discussion, we consider the behaviour of the price offer curve, which is the equivalent of the income offer curve. It illustrates how the most-preferred, affordable bundle changes as the price of one good, say p_b, changes, holding constant the price of the other good, p_c, and the money available for consumption, m.[2]

In Figure 7.7, consumption bundles are formed from a combination of bus travel, b, and car travel, c, We assume that the price of car travel $p_c = 0.5$, and that our consumer, Thomas, has an amount $m = 50$ to finance consumption. Increases in the price of bus travel are then shown by the budget constraint pivoting clockwise around their intersection with the car travel (vertical) axis. We therefore have the budget constraint:

$$p_b b + 0.5c = 50 \qquad [7.17]$$

Figure 7.7 shows a selection of indifference curves, each of which just touches a budget constraint. Each point of tangency represents the most-preferred, affordable bundle for a particular realization of the parameter p_b. The higher the value of p_b, the steeper the budget constraint will be. By analogy with the income offer path, the diagram shows a **price offer path**. This is the solid curve connecting all of the most-preferred, affordable bundles. It shows how demand for *both* goods will change as the price of bus travel changes. The curve is drawn so that it meets the vertical axis *below* the intersection of the budget constraints with the car travel axis.

> **Price offer path** The set of all the most-preferred, affordable consumption bundles that are formed when the price of one good varies.

---

2 An interesting example of a price increase has been the imposition in parts of the United Kingdom, of a mandatory donation to charity by someone making a purchase who also takes a new disposable bag. Calum MacPherson's essay in the online student essay bank demonstrates that in several experiments a relatively small fee has reduced demand by around 80%. You can read Calum's argument (and other students' essays) on the companion website for this book, at **www.palgrave.com/mochrie.**

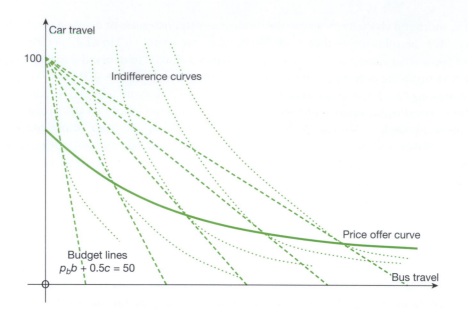

Figure 7.7 Price offer curve for bus and car travel

As the price of bus travel, p_b, increases without limit, the budget constraint becomes steeper and steeper. If bus travel were to be infinitely expensive, Thomas's budget constraint would be vertical. Showing the intercept of the price expansion path below the intercept of the budget constraint means that no matter how expensive bus travel becomes, Thomas will be satiated with car travel and will not spend all the money available to finance consumption. The diagram is therefore not consistent with the assumption of well-behaved preferences.

Let us now look more closely at the behaviour that Figure 7.7 suggests, trying to understand how Thomas might respond to government policy, which typically seeks to encourage the use of public transport by providing subsidies for its use and imposing taxes and other levies upon car use. We simply note here that as the relative price of public transport falls, Thomas appears willing to continue to substitute its use for car use.

By yourself

X7.24   Suppose that Thomas considers travel both by bus and by car simply to be necessary as he moves from one activity to another. Why might this suggest that bus and car travel will be close substitutes? Sketch a diagram showing the price expansion path. [*Hint:* Remember that if goods are perfect substitutes, there is only one price ratio at which both will be consumed.]

X7.25   What reasons can you give for supposing that following a reduction in the price of public transport, the increase in bus usage might be greater than the reduction in car usage?

X7.26   We have concentrated in this discussion on the price of travel. What other costs do you think we should also take into account? Suppose that instead of thinking about the prices in monetary terms, we concentrate on the time cost. How might we then interpret the price expansion path?

X7.27   Could we ever observe an upward-sloping price offer path? Explain your answer.

7.4   Conclusions

In Chapter 6, we solved the problem of finding the most-preferred, affordable consumption bundle for a set of fixed parameters (m, p_b, p_c). In this chapter, we have allowed either m, the money available to finance consumption, or else one of the prices, p_b and p_c, to be indeterminate. We started by allowing m to be indeterminate, since that allowed us to build very directly on the method of equal gradients, introduced in Chapter 6 to identify the most-preferred, affordable consumption bundle: that discussion involved little more than the introduction of some terminology.

The second part of the chapter was concerned with obtaining demand functions. Once again, this built on examples introduced in the previous chapter, and so we quickly introduced some applications of the theory, especially related to the price elasticity of demand. Perhaps the most important point here is that it is not always possible, especially in applied economics, to restrict ourselves to functional forms for demand, which are derived from theoretical considerations about well-behaved preferences. We shall not derive demand functions that are either linear functions or power functions from a standard utility function. But in economics, we often find ourselves having to come up with estimates of elasticities, or of the responsiveness of demand to price changes, where we need a local estimate, and in such cases modelling demand as a power function can be very useful. Similarly, when developing the theory of the firm, it will often be possible to illustrate certain arguments using simple functional forms, and for that, linear demand functions are sufficient. We need to understand the behaviour of a range of demand functions, because there will be situations where we use them all.

Summary

This chapter has involved the introduction of many definitions that are important as we analyse how to solve the problem of finding a consumer's most-preferred, affordable consumption bundle in situations where we allow one parameter to be indeterminate. Holding the other parameters in our model constant, we generate functional forms of individual demands, which we generally illustrate graphically.

- Engel curves show how a consumer's demand for a good changes with the amount of money available for consumption.
- Income offer curves, introduced previously as income expansion paths, show how the most-preferred, affordable bundle changes

as the amount of money available for consumption changes.

- Demand curves show how a consumer's demand for a good changes as the price of that good changes.
- The price offer curve shows how the most-preferred, affordable bundle changes as the price of one good changes.

We also defined the concept of elasticity, which is a measure of the responsiveness of one variable to changes in the value of another variable.

- The income elasticity of demand is a measure of the responsiveness of a consumer's demand for a good to a change in the amount of money available for consumption. For normal goods, demand increases with income, so the income elasticity is positive. For inferior goods, demand falls with income, so the income elasticity is negative.

- The price elasticity of demand is a measure of the responsiveness of a consumer's demand for a good to a change in the price of that good. We expect the price elasticity to be less than zero, with the effect of a price increase being a reduction in demand. If the price elasticity lies between zero and minus one, we say that the demand is price inelastic; while if the price elasticity is less than minus one, we say that demand is price elastic.

Engel curves and demand curves allow us to show the relation between demand for a good and (1) the money available to finance consumption, and (2) the price of a good. Income offer curves and price offer curves show how demands for several goods respond to changes in a single parameter. Similarly, elasticities are measures of the responsiveness of demand, which are scale-free.

Visit the companion website at **www.palgrave.com/mochrie** to access further teaching and learning materials, including lecturer slides and a testbank, as well as guideline answers and student MCQs.

8

Price changes

Back in Chapter 6, we set out the resource allocation problem both for a utility-maximizing consumer and for an expenditure-minimizing consumer. Then, in Chapter 7, we considered how to obtain the demand functions for a utility-maximizing consumer. In this chapter we study the choices of the expenditure-minimizing consumer, obtaining additional demand functions.

As in Chapter 6, these demand functions show how the demand for a good changes as its price changes. In the case of an expenditure-minimizing consumer, we do not obtain the same demand functions as we did in Chapter 7, because of the different effects of a price change on budget and preference constraints.

To explain this difference, we argue that if the price of a good changes, we would expect to observe the change in demand associated with utility maximization. We break that change in demand down into two components: an income and a substitution effect. We show that the *substitution effect* is the result of the relative price change, while the *income effect* is the result of the loss of ability to purchase previously affordable consumption bundles. We also show that change in demand for a cost-minimizing consumer is the substitution effect for a utility-maximizing consumer. We show that when prices change, and unlike the utility-maximizing consumer, the cost-minimizing consumer experiences a compensating change in the money available for consumption.

We then show how the effects of a price change can be understood through the income and substitution effects. We demonstrate that if the price of a normal good (as defined in Chapter 7) increases, the consumer will demand less of it.

8.1 The indirect or compensated demand for a good

Section 6.4 demonstrated that with the prices of all goods fixed, all possible least-cost, acceptable bundles, one of which will be chosen by an expenditure-minimizing consumer, lie on the income expansion path. We had already defined that as the set of utility-maximizing, affordable consumption bundles. The expenditure minimization and utility maximization problems were therefore in many ways mirror images. In Section 7.2, treating the price, p_c, as an indeterminate parameter, we showed how we might obtain individual demand functions, $c : c = c(p_c)$, for a utility-maximizing consumer. In this chapter it will be convenient to refer to these demand functions as the ordinary, or Marshallian, demand. We will also obtain an alternative demand function, the Hicksian, or compensated, demand, $c^H : c^H = c^H(p_c)$, for an expenditure-minimizing consumer.

To obtain these new demand functions, we use the utility function from the examples in Section 6.4, in which we analysed a single, expenditure-minimizing consumer's demand for bread and cheese. This consumer, Michael, will only consider consumption bundles that offer him some minimum utility.

Our objective is to minimize the acquisition cost, A:

$$A(b, c) = 1.6b + p_c c \qquad \text{[6.22']}$$

…

We now define the constraint for this problem:

$$V(b, c) = c^3 b = 640 \qquad \text{[6.24]}$$

Expression 6.22' is Michael's objective, which is now slightly more general than in the earlier examples because the price of cheese, p_c, is now an indeterminate parameter, rather than a fixed one. His acceptability constraint is unchanged from the earlier examples. We illustrate Michael's expenditure minimization in problem in Figure 8.1. Note how it differs from the problems introduced at the start of Section 7.2: as the price of a good changes, Leena, seeking to maximize her utility, faced a change in her affordability constraint, whereas here, Michael, seeking to minimize expenditure, will face a change in the acquisition cost, A, which is his objective. As the price changes, his cheapest, acceptable bundle switches from Z_0 to Z_1.

8.1.1   The cheapest, acceptable bundle

We want to find the cheapest bundle that satisfies Michael's acceptability constraint. That is to say, we identify the bundle $Z_0 : (b_0, c_0)$, which minimizes $A(b, c)$, with $V(b_0, c_0) \geq 640$. Given the similarity of this problem to previous ones, we only sketch out the solution.

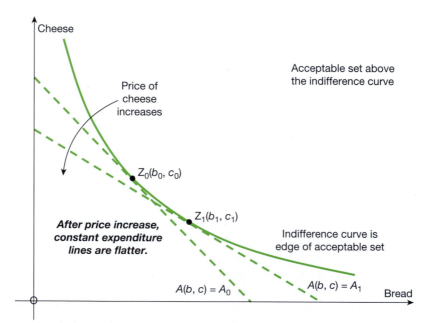

Figure 8.1 The effect of an increase in the price of cheese

We can be certain that for bundle Z_0, as for all consumption bundles, MRS is given by Expression 6.27, which we restate here:

$$\left.\frac{dc}{db}\right|_{V=V_0} = -\frac{c}{3b} \qquad [6.27]$$

Any line on which Michael would face a constant acquisition cost has gradient:

$$-\frac{p_b}{p_c} = -\frac{1.6}{p_c} = -\frac{8}{5p_c} \qquad [8.1]$$

For equality of the gradients of indifference curves and constant acquisition cost lines, $MRS = -\frac{p_b}{p_c}$

Two definitions of MRS	$\dfrac{c}{3b} = \dfrac{8}{5p_c}$; so $b = \dfrac{5}{24}p_c c$	Multiply both sides by $\frac{5b}{8p_c}$	[8.2]

By yourself

X8.1   Confirm that if $p_c = 12$, then Expression 8.2 may be written $b = 2.5c$. Show that for any value of p_c, Michael's expenditure on cheese will then always be three times his expenditure on bread.

Exercise X8.1 simply confirms that if we assume that $p_c = 12$, then Michael's income expansion path, Expression 8.2, is what we saw in earlier examples, both for Michael and for Leena, who we presented as seeking to maximize her utility. We will confirm in Chapter 9 that both Michael and Leena have the same income expansion path, $p_c c = 3p_b b$. Expenditure on cheese is three times as much as expenditure on bread for every consumption bundle on that expansion path. Differences in the outcomes of Michael's expenditure minimization problem and Leena's utility maximization problem therefore come down to the differences in their constraints: Leena's acquisition cost $A_L = 64$; and Michael's utility $U_M = 640$.

Using Expression 8.2, we now substitute for b in Expression 6.24, finding the intersection of the income expansion path and the indifference curve that forms the lower boundary of the acceptable set. The solution is Michael's expenditure-minimizing consumption, c_0, in terms of the price, p_c, or his Hicksian demand for cheese, $c_0 = c^H(p_c)$.

$$\left(\frac{5}{24}p_c \cdot c_0\right) \cdot c_0^3 = 640 \qquad [8.3]$$

By rules of indices, $c^3 \cdot c = c^4$	$c_0^4 = 640 \cdot \left(\dfrac{24}{5p_c}\right) = \dfrac{3{,}072}{p_c}$	
Also, $(c^4)^{0.25} = c^1 = c$	$c_0 = \left(\dfrac{3{,}072}{p_c}\right)^{0.25}$	[8.4]

8.1.2 The nature of the Hicksian solution

Just by looking at Expression 8.4, we can see that the function is not the same as Leena's demand function, found in Section 7.2, where there was an inverse relation between the quantity demanded and the price.

By yourself

X8.2 Using Expression 8.2, calculate the quantity of bread, b_0, in the cheapest, acceptable bundle, Z_0. [*Note*: This will be a function of p_c.]

X8.3 Given the Hicksian demands, $b^H(p_c)$ and $c^H(p_c)$, confirm that for any price, p_c:

(a) the marginal rate of substitution, MRS, is equal to the price ratio $\dfrac{p_b}{p_c} = \dfrac{1.6}{p_c}$; and

(b) the cheapest, acceptable bundle, Z_0, always lies on the indifference curve $c^3b = 640$, which is the boundary of the acceptable set.

X8.4 Calculate the acquisition cost, $A(b_0, c_0)$, of the cheapest, acceptable bundle, and show that it increases with the price of cheese, p_c.

X8.5 Confirm that for Leena, the price elasticity of demand $\varepsilon_{p_c} = \dfrac{dc^*}{dp_c} \cdot \dfrac{p_c}{c^*(p_c)} = -1$, but that for Michael, $\varepsilon_{p_c} = \dfrac{dc^H}{dp_c} \cdot \dfrac{p_c}{c^H(p_c)} = -0.25$.

X8.6 Suppose that the price of cheese increases from $p_{c0} = 12$ to $p_{c1} = 16$. Confirm that initially Leena and Michael would have chosen the same consumption bundles, but that after the price increase Leena reduces her consumption of cheese while maintaining her consumption of bread, whereas Michael increases his consumption of bread while reducing consumption of cheese, though by less than Leena.

While Michael has a fixed utility target, Leena's highest achievable utility is a decreasing function of the price, p_c. This reflects that fact that while Michael is able to increase the money available for consumption as p_c increases, Leena has to hold her expenditure constant.

8.2 Analysing the effects of a price change

We now illustrate Leena's and Michael's responses to a rise in the price of cheese from $p_{c0} = 12$ to $p_{c1} = 16$ in Figure 8.2. Before the price change, Leena's affordability constraint is tangent to Michael's acceptability constraint at $Z_0 : (10, 4)$. The initial *income expansion path* (IEP), $c = 0.4b$, also passes through Z_0, and so we are certain that both wish to buy the consumption bundle, $Z_0 : (10, 4)$. After the price change takes place, Leena's affordability constraint pivots anti-clockwise around its intersection with the 'Bread' axis (this intersection is not shown in the diagram, so that we can illustrate the changes in demand more clearly; however, Leena's new budget constraint is flatter, and given any level of consumption of bread, she can afford to buy less cheese). We show Leena as simply reducing her planned consumption of cheese, so that she now purchases bundle $Z_1^* : (10, 3)$, at the intersection of the new budget constraint and the new income expansion path, $c = 0.3b$. Her payoff $V(10, 3) = 270$, so she definitely prefers the original consumption bundle, Z_0, to the new one, Z_1^*.

Michael's acceptability constraint, $V(b, c) = 640$, is unaffected by the price change. He therefore responds to it by increasing the sum available for consumption, so that he is able to buy the consumption bundle, Z_1, which is the intersection of the affordability constraint and the new income expansion path. To buy this bundle he has to increase expenditure from $A_0 = 64$ to $A_1 \approx 79.4$. In switching from Z_0 to Z_1, Michael substitutes bread for cheese.

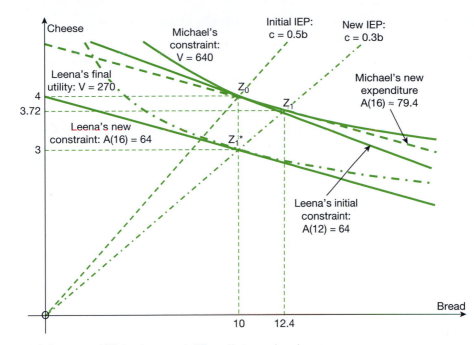

Figure 8.2 Leena and Michael respond differently to a price change

He is just as well off after the price change as he is before it, at least as measured by his utility. At the new prices, the consumption bundles Z_1 and Z_1^* are on the same income expansion path. Were Leena to have enough money, she would choose Z_1 rather than Z_1^*. Similarly, if Michael were to reduce his utility target, then he might decide to purchase bundle Z_1^*.

We might argue that Leena serves as a better model for consumer behaviour than Michael. In the face of the price change, Michael is suddenly able to produce more money with which to finance additional purchases. Within our model, we cannot explain where that money comes from, nor indeed why he would not choose to spend it so as to improve his payoff at the original prices. We shall therefore concentrate on Leena's utility-maximizing decisions, using Michael's expenditure minimization process to understand Leena's decisions more fully. We therefore refer to Leena's demand functions, obtained as the result of solving a utility maximization problem as **ordinary** or **Marshallian demand** functions.

> **Ordinary (Marshallian) demand** The demand of the utility-maximizing consumer.

If utility maximization is the 'ordinary' problem, then expenditure minimization, as developed by Hicks in the 1930s, is the dual of this problem. We set up the problem by effectively treating a fixed value of the original objective function (utility, in this case) as a constraint, and then seeking to minimize the value of the function that provided the original constraint (the acquisition cost, in this case). The outcome is the **compensated** (or **Hicksian**) **demand** function, based on the achievement of expenditure minimization. In assuming a utility constraint, it is probably best if we think in terms of the problem of achieving a given standard of living.

> **Compensated (Hicksian) demand** The demand of the expenditure-minimizing consumer.

8.2.1   Substitution, income, and total effects of a price change

On the basis that we should treat Leena's utility-maximizing problem as the usual one that consumers have to solve, we refer to the shift, from Z_0 to $Z_1{}^*$, in her most-preferred, affordable consumption bundle, as the **total effect** of the price change. We observe the total

Total effect The change in demand following a price increase for a consumer with a fixed amount of money to spend.

effect when a consumer continues to allocate the same amount of money to consumption after the price change as beforehand. In general, the total effect of the price change is therefore the change in a consumer's Marshallian, or ordinary, demands.

Since he is an expenditure-minimizing consumer, Michael's response to the price change reflects a pure **substitution effect**. In Figure 8.2, we show the substitution effect as the shift from Z_0 to Z_1. Given the increase in the price of cheese, the budget line through Z_1 is shallower than the budget line through Z_0, so that the substitution effect is the change in the Hicksian demands, $(b^H(p_c), c^H(p_c))$, associated with the shift from Z_0 to Z_1. This will be the only effect

Substitution effect The change in demand following a price increase for a consumer with a fixed utility target.

of the price change for a consumer who, like Michael, is able to allocate enough money to consumption to achieve the original level of utility from consumption.

The *income effect* is our measure of the divergence between Leena's and Michael's responses to the price change. With her fixed budget, after the price change, Leena will buy bundle $Z_1{}^*$. As we have noted, to be able to buy bundle Z_1, Michael has to obtain some more money from somewhere. Suppose that we were now to give Leena the same additional amount of money as Michael is willing to spend. We would expect them both to make the same decisions, since we know that they have the same income expansion path. Buying consumption bundle, Z_1, Leena will attain her original level of utility. The additional money compensates her for the effect of the change in prices. More generally, we can define

Income effect The change in demand following a price increase that is associated with a loss of purchasing power.

the income effect as the change in a consumer's demands given the change in purchasing power associated with the price change. As we will see below, we can measure the change in purchasing power by consideration of the change in the affordable set caused by the price change.

We illustrate the total effect, the substitution effect and the income effect in Figure 8.3. Point $Z_0 : (b_0, c_0)$ represents the consumer's initial most-preferred, affordable consumption bundle. Point $Z_1 : (b_1, c_1)$ represents the cheapest, consumption bundle that allows the consumer to maintain the original level of utility at the new prices. Point $Z_1{}^* : (b_1{}^*, c_1{}^*)$ represents the most-preferred, affordable consumption bundle after the price change.

We report the effects of the price change as:

- from Z_0 to $Z_1{}^*$: the change in ordinary (or Marshallian) demands for a utility-maximizing consumer, representing the total effect of the price change;
- from Z_0 to Z_1: the change in compensated (or Hicksian) demands for an expenditure-minimizing consumer, representing the substitution effect; and
- from Z_1 to $Z_1{}^*$: the effect of the change (here, the loss) of purchasing power resulting from the change in the affordable set, representing the income effect.

We have defined these effects so that the total effect is the sum of the income and substitution effects.

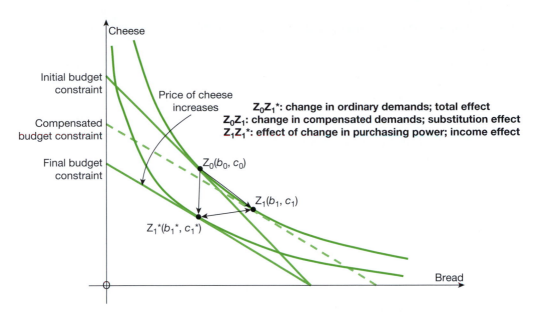

Figure 8.3 The relation of ordinary and compensated demands

By yourself

X8.7 Suppose that the least-cost, acceptable bundle changes from Z_0 to Z_1 after the price of cheese doubles. What other price change would lead to this change in compensated demands? What could you say about the acquisition cost of the new bundle in this case? Sketch a diagram showing the income and substitution effects for this alternative price change.

X8.8 Using diagrams, confirm that bundle Z_1 is not affordable at the original prices, and that bundle Z_0 is not affordable at the new prices.

X8.9 Sketch a diagram that shows a budget constraint reflecting the new prices through the original, most-preferred affordable bundle, Z_0. Show that after the price increase, the most-preferred, affordable bundle on this new budget constraint will be preferred to Z_1. Illustrate the substitution and income effects in this case.

X8.10 Consider the following problem. Uma has utility function $U(b, c) = (bc)^{0.5}$, where (just for a change), we define b as the number of books she purchases and c as the number of concerts she attends. Uma is willing to spend 200 on books and concerts. The prices of both books and concerts are initially 10.

(a) Find Uma's ordinary demands, given these prices.

(b) Show that Uma obtains a utility of 100; and that her compensated demands, given the constraint that she must achieve a utility of 100, are the same as her ordinary demands.

The price of concert tickets now increases to 12.5.

(c) Calculate Uma's ordinary demands after the price change. [*Note:* The demand for books should not change.]

(d) Calculate Uma's compensated demands after the price change. (Remember that we assume that utility from consumption will be 100.)

(Continued)

(e) Calculate the substitution and income effects of the price change for both books and concert tickets.

(f) Sketch a diagram showing these effects.

X8.11   Repeat X8.10 for Vishal, whose utility function $V = x^{0.5} + y^{0.5}$. [*Note:* In part (b), you will treat Vishal as a cost minimizer with a utility target of $2\sqrt{10}$.]

8.2.2   Nominal and real incomes

Real income The capacity to generate utility from consumption.

Nominal income The money that is available to purchase goods and services.

Turning back to the analysis of a price change, we should distinguish between the **real income** and the **nominal income** of a consumer. In our theory of resource allocation, rich and poor consumers differ in their capacity to command resources, and hence in the quantities of consumption goods they are able to obtain. By our assumption of monotonicity of preferences, the larger the budget set, the higher the level of utility that is obtained. We define real income in terms of the ability to command resources, and nominal income in terms of the amount of money available to fund consumption.

We relate the concept of real income to the effect on demands of a price increase on the Marshallian and Hicksian demands. An income-constrained, utility-maximizing consumer is characterized by having a constant sum of money available to finance consumption, whereas an expenditure-minimizing, preference-constrained consumer is characterized by having a constant utility target. We have seen in our example that as prices increase, the preference-constrained consumer spends more to maintain a given target utility. Rather than being constrained by a fixed money income, having the ability to adjust spending to achieve a constant level of satisfaction implies that the consumer has in some sense a constant real income.

We demonstrate the difference between nominal and real income in Figure 8.4. Here we are thinking of the problem that Uma faces in deciding which combination of books and concert tickets to buy. After an increase in the price of concert tickets, Uma's budget constraint rotates anti-clockwise around its intersection with the 'Books' (horizontal) axis. The shaded area shows consumption bundles that were affordable before the price increase but have now become unaffordable. While nominal income has remained unchanged, real income has fallen. Uma is worse off after the price rise than she was before it.

When we treated Uma as an expenditure minimizer solving the dual problem, the situation was different. Her increased expenditure after the price change allowed her to achieve the same utility as beforehand. We have already noted that she would not be able to afford Z_0, which she considered to be the cheapest, acceptable bundle before the price change. Instead, she buys bundle Z_1, which was unaffordable before the prices changed. It makes sense for us to say that having a constant real income means being able to generate a constant amount of utility.

When economists first started to think about how to measure the effects of changes in price consumption, Eugen Slutsky proposed decomposing the total effect into substitution and income effects, which involved defining constant real income on the basis that the consumer should be able to buy the initial bundle, Z_0, before and after the price change. Intuitively, this seems entirely reasonable. The definition that we have suggested in terms

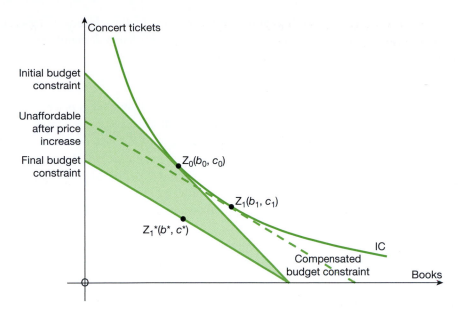

Figure 8.4 Nominal and real income with a price change

of the capacity to generate utility emerged from John Hicks' work some years later. In effect, Slutsky was thinking about income and substitution effects for a utility-maximizing consumer, whereas Hicks developed a much more complete theory that could accommodate both utility maximization and expenditure minimization, and this definition of constant real income emerged within it. The difference is important in theory, but in practice the two measures are very similar, unless the change in prices is large. In Exercise X8.9, we have considered Slutsky's measure. It leads to the consumer with constant real income being able to increase utility, which does not seem entirely satisfactory.

8.3 The Hicks decomposition of the total effect

As we develop this argument about how the total effect of a price change can be split into an income and a substitution effect, it will be useful to have an example in mind. We therefore continue to think about Uma and Vishal, as they decide how to allocate resources to the purchase of books and concert tickets.

Firstly, we set out our notation. We continue to think about the effects of a change (not necessarily an increase) in the price of concert tickets, Δp_c. We denote the total change in Uma's ordinary demand for concert tickets as Δc:

$$\Delta c = \Delta c^M(\Delta p_c; p_b, m) \qquad [8.5]$$

The Greek upper-case delta, 'Δ', is here our symbol for a finite change in value. The superscript M on the demand for concert tickets, c, indicates that we are considering a change in Uma's Marshallian (ordinary) demand. Note that we do not need to know Uma's total demand for concert tickets, but only the change in demand following the change in price, Δp_c. The other parameters $-p_b$, the price of books, and m, the money available to finance consumption – are shown as indeterminate but constant. In the same way, treating the substitution effect as the change in Uma's compensated, or Hicksian demand, we can adapt our notation, writing the substitution effect as Δc:

$$\Delta c = \Delta c(\Delta p_c, p_b, v_0) \tag{8.6}$$

where v_0 is Uma's utility from consumption before the price change takes place.

We show these effects in Figure 8.5. On the vertical axis, we show Uma's demands for concert tickets at the consumption bundles Z_0, Z_1 and $Z_1{}^*$. At Z_0, her Marshallian demand, given money to finance consumption m, is the same as her Hicksian demand, given utility target v_1. Moving between bundles Z_0 and $Z_1{}^*$, the Marshallian demands change following the increase in price p_1 (with other parameters remaining constant). Similarly, between bundles Z_0 and Z_1, the Hicksian demands change following the change in price, Δp_c.

We also need a measure of the income effect. In Figure 8.5, we have emphasized that bundle Z_1 can either represent Uma's Hicksian demands after the price change, or else her ordinary demands after the price change and compensation for her loss of real income.

- Before the price change, Uma buys bundle Z_0, which has acquisition cost $A(p_{c0}, p_b, v_0) = m$.
- To buy bundle Z_1 after the price change, she would pay an acquisition cost, $A(p_{c1}, p_b, v_0) = m_1$.
- Uma continues to have income m.
- We write the change in her real income, $\Delta m = m - m_1$:

$$\Delta m = \Delta m(\Delta p_c, p_b, v_0) = -\Delta A(\Delta p_c, p_b, v_0) \tag{8.7}$$

The change in real income is equal in size, but opposite in sign, to the change in acquisition cost necessary to maintain the original utility, v_0. Given this change in real income, Δm, the

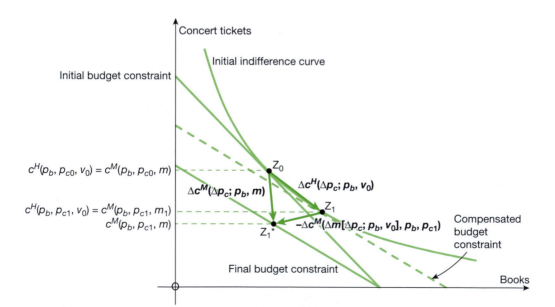

Figure 8.5 Slutsky decomposition of price effect, using functional forms

income effect, Δc^N, is the change in Uma's ordinary demand, c^M, resulting from the change in real income. Applying the same notation as before, we write Δc^N:

$$\Delta c = \Delta c(\Delta m, p_b, p_c) \qquad [8.8]$$

with Δm as defined in Expression 8.7. We might therefore write out the income effect a little more completely as:

$$\Delta c^N = \Delta c^M[-\Delta A(\Delta p_c, p_b, v_0), p_b, p_{c1}] \qquad [8.9]$$

The additional step here has been to replace the change in income with the reduction in expenditure that is effectively the measure of the loss of real income. We can now write out the Hicks decomposition in terms of changes in demands as $\Delta c = \Delta c^S + \Delta c^N$:

$$\underbrace{\Delta c^M(p_b, \Delta p_c, m)}_{\text{Total effect}} = \underbrace{\Delta c^H(p_b, \Delta p_c, v_0)}_{\text{Substitution effect}} + \underbrace{\Delta c^M(p_b, p_c, -\Delta A(p_b, \Delta p_c, v_0))}_{\text{Income effect}} \qquad [8.10]$$

8.3.1 Some applications

Complex as the notation in Expression 8.10 appears, it does little more than to state what we already know about the decomposition. The total effect and the substitution effect are movements along Marshallian and Hicksian price expansion paths. The income effect is the movement along the income expansion path associated with the new price, and is the difference between the total and the substitution effects. We apply these ideas in some straightforward examples.

By yourself

X8.12 Suppose that Wang's preferences are represented by utility function $U(b, c) = 2b + 3c$.
 (a) Initially prices are $p_b = 10$ and $p_c = 15$. Sketch indifference curves for $U = 20$, $U = 30$ and $U = 40$. Indicate on the diagram Wang's most preferred affordable consumption bundles, given that $m = 150$.
 (b) Show the change in demand that occurs if p_c increases to 16.
 (c) Explain why there is no change in utility. What do you conclude about the income effect in this case?

X8.13 Suppose that Xavier's preference can be represented by the utility function $U(b, c) = \min(2b, 3c)$.
 (a) Initially prices are $p_b = 10$ and $p_c = 15$. Sketch indifference curves for $U = 10$, $U = 15$ and $U = 20$. Indicate Xavier's most preferred, affordable consumption bundle given that $m = 150$.
 (b) Show the change in demand that occurs if p_c increases to 20.
 (c) Illustrate the income expansion path on this diagram and the total effect of the price change. What do you conclude about the income effect in this case?

X8.14 The only goods available to Zeki are biscuits and coffee, whose prices are p_b and p_c. Zeki has an amount of money m to finance purchases, and he chooses his most-preferred, affordable consumption bundle $Z^*(b^*, c^*)$. His preferences are well behaved.
 (a) Draw a diagram to show the shape of the indifference curve on which Zeki's most-preferred, affordable consumption bundle lies. Demonstrate that:
   (i) if the price of one good changes, then Zeki's demands will change; and

(Continued)

(ii) the substitution effect will increase his demand for the good that has become relatively cheaper, and decrease the demand for the good that has become relatively more expensive.

(b) Draw a separate diagram, with a single budget constraint. Choose a bundle on it, which will represent Zeki's initial most-preferred, affordable consumption bundle, Z_0. Add an indifference curve passing through that point. Zeki's favourite café now announces that it will reduce the price of coffee by 50% for the next month.

(i) On your diagram, indicate the substitution effect.

(ii) Show Zeki's income effect, for the three cases: (1) coffee and biscuits are normal goods; (2) coffee is a normal good, but biscuits are inferior; and (3) biscuits are normal, but coffee is inferior.

(iii) Explain why it must be that if coffee is a normal good, Zeki will drink more of it when the price falls.

From Exercise X8.12, we should conclude that if goods are perfect substitutes then, following a price change, there will be a substitution effect but there will be no income effect. Similarly, from X8.13, we should conclude that with perfect complements, there will be an income effect but no substitution effect, following a price change.

The result of Exercise X8.14 is important within economic theory. The substitution effect is always negative, so that as price increases, demand falls, and the derivative is certainly less than zero. However, the income effect can lead either to an increase or to a reduction in demand for a good. In Figure 8.6, we show the situation facing Zeki. A reduction in the price of coffee leads to him substituting coffee for biscuits, reflecting the change in the relative price. We have assumed that coffee and biscuits are both normal goods, so that both Marshallian demands are increasing functions of the money available

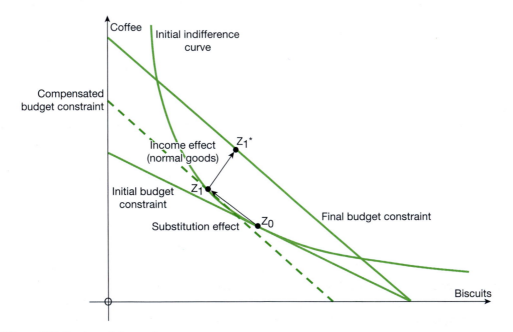

Figure 8.6 The law of demand

for consumption. Since the reduction in the price of coffee increases real income, the demand for coffee increases further. Generalizing, we obtain:

The law of demand: if a consumer's preferences are well behaved and a good is normal, so that the consumer's demand for the good increases when the money available to finance consumption increases, then if the price of the good increases, the consumer's ordinary demand for the good will fall.

Discussion. Any price increase reduces real income and demand for every normal good: the income effect is negative for a normal good. The substitution effect, or the pure price effect, results from the change in relative prices and is always negative. For a normal good, the income effect reinforces the substitution effect and the ordinary demand certainly decreases after a price increase.

By yourself

X8.15 We find that Zeki's preferences can be represented by the utility function, $U : U(b,c) = b^{\frac{1}{3}}c^{\frac{2}{3}}$. He is willing to spend $m = 30$, with the initial prices, $p_{c0} = 2.5$ and $p_b = 1$. During the coffee promotion, its price falls to $p_{c1} = 1.25$.
(a) Obtain Zeki's
    (i) most-preferred, affordable consumption bundle at the original prices;
    (ii) most-preferred, affordable consumption bundle after the reduction in the price of coffee;
    (iii) Hicksian demands based on the original utility achieved, and new prices.
(b) Calculate the substitution effects, the income effects and the total effects of this price change.
(c) Explain whether or not Zeki considers coffee and biscuits to be normal goods.

X8.16 Suppose that we have a situation where the price of biscuits $p_b = 1$, the money available for consumption $m = 30$, but the price of coffee p_c is not defined. Obtain Zeki's ordinary and compensated demand functions. Sketch their graphs, and explain why Zeki's ordinary demand curve is more elastic than his compensated demand curve.

X8.17 Suppose that Adele considers coffee to be an inferior good. Given the law of demand, why would you expect her compensated demand for coffee to be more elastic than her ordinary demand?

In Exercises X8.16 and X8.17 we introduce a useful implication of the law of demand. For a normal good, the ordinary demand curve will be flatter than the compensated demand curve, reflecting the fact that the income effect amplifies the substitution effect. Ordinary demands for normal goods are therefore more responsive to price than compensated demands. For inferior goods the opposite is true, and the compensated demand curve will be less elastic because the income effect works in the opposite direction to the substitution effect.

8.3.2 The decomposition defined in terms of rates of change

In the examples used in this chapter, we have considered measurable changes in prices, with the result that there are also measurable changes in demands. The notation of Expression 8.10, set out in terms of changes, suggests that it should be possible to restate the decomposition in terms of (instantaneous) rates of change, using the notation of differential calculus.

As in previous examples, we firstly define an average rate of change as the change in demand per unit change in price. For the ordinary demand, we obtain $\frac{\Delta c}{\Delta p_c} = \frac{\Delta c^M(p_b, p_c, m)}{\Delta p_c}$; then, allowing the change in price, Δp_c, to fall to zero, we obtain the partial derivative:

$$\frac{\partial c}{\partial p_c} = \frac{\partial c^M(p_b, p_c, m)}{\partial p_c} \qquad [8.11]$$

This is the total effect of the price change. In our example of Uma buying her most-preferred, affordable consumption bundle consisting of books and concert tickets, Expression 8.11 measures the rate of change of her ordinary demand for tickets as their price changes. Similarly, we can define the substitution effect as the rate of change of the Hicksian demands with respect to the change in price. We write:

$$\frac{\partial c^S}{\partial p_c} = \frac{\partial c^H(p_b, p_c, m)}{\partial p_c} \qquad [8.12]$$

For Uma, Expression 8.12 measures the rate of change of her compensated demand for tickets as their price changes. These partial derivatives are simply definitions, helping us to develop an alternative formulation of the decomposition, and we do not seek to develop them any further, or to evaluate them for particular demand functions.

To obtain a version of Expressions 8.11 and 8.12 for the income effect, we have to do a little more work. We want an expression for the rate of change of consumption resulting from the change in real income caused by the change in prices. We argued that a price increase forces a consumer to reduce expenditure below the level required to attain the original level of utility. Defining the income effect, in Expression 8.9, we identified a chain of relationships. We rewrite Expression 8.9 very compactly as:

$$\Delta c^N = \Delta c^M\{\Delta m[\Delta A(\Delta p_c)]\} \qquad [8.13]$$

The income effect is here a function of the change in the real income, Δm, which is a function of the change in the acquisition cost, ΔA, required to compensate the consumer for the price change, which is itself a function of the change in the price, Δp_c. Forming the derivative, we apply the chain, or function of a function, rule, so that there are three multiplicative factors in the derivative:

$$\frac{dc^M}{dm} = \frac{\partial c^M}{\partial m} \cdot \frac{dm}{dA} \cdot \frac{\partial A}{\partial p_c} \qquad [8.14]$$

We work from right to left to simplify Expression 8.14. The partial derivative, $\frac{\partial A}{\partial p_c}$ is the rate of change of the acquisition cost with the price of the good. For any bundle (b, c), its acquisition cost $A(b, c) = p_b b + p_c c$. If there is very small change in p_c, the price of concert tickets, there will be almost no change in the quantities of books and tickets in the consumption bundle. The change in the acquisition cost of the bundle will then result from the change in expenditure on tickets, and so will be approximately the product of the quantity of concert tickets in the bundle multiplied by the change in the price, or $\Delta x \approx c\Delta p_c$. The quality of this approximation will, as usual, improve as the change in price tends to zero, so that in the limit we have $\frac{\partial A(p_b, p_c, v_0)}{\partial p_c} = c$.

The second component in Expression 8.14, represents the effect, Δm, on real income of the change in the acquisition cost of the compensated demand, ΔA. This is an accounting identity, with the change in real income being equal and opposite to the additional cost of maintaining the original level of utility. Writing $\Delta m = -\Delta A$, we see that in Expression 8.14, the derivative $\frac{dm}{dA} = -1$.

Lastly, we have the rate of change of demand with respect to the sum spent. We can say no more about this than to note that in Expression 8.15 it is the partial derivative of the Marshallian demand with respect to the sum available, $\frac{\partial c^M(p_b, p_c, m)}{\partial m}$. Even so, we are able to simplify Expression 8.14 substantially:

$$\frac{dc^M}{dm} = \frac{\partial c^M(p_b, p_c, m)}{\partial m} \cdot (-1) \cdot (c) = -c \cdot \frac{\partial c^M(p_b, p_c, m)}{\partial m} \qquad [8.15]$$

We can now write down an expression for the Hicks decomposition, expressing the total effect, the substitution effect, and the income effect in terms of rates of change. Expression 8.15 becomes:

$$\underbrace{\frac{\partial c^M(p_b, p_c, m)}{\partial p_c}}_{\text{Total effect}} = \underbrace{\frac{\partial c^H(p_b, p_c, v_0)}{\partial p_c}}_{\text{Substitution effect}} - \underbrace{c^M(p_b, p_c, m) \cdot \frac{\partial c^M(p_b, p_c, m)}{\partial m}}_{\text{Income effect}} \qquad [8.16]$$

As with Expression 8.9, being able to express the decomposition in terms of rates of change does not substantially change the analysis. It is, however, quite straightforward to confirm that Expression 8.16 is consistent with the demonstration of the law of demand. It also suggests that the larger the expenditure share of good C, the larger the income effect will be, and so the larger the divergence between the ordinary and the compensated demands.

By yourself

X8.18 Bruno has a utility function, U: $U(b, c) = b^{1/2} c^{1/2}$, where b is the quantity of beef and c the quantity of chicken that he eats.

(a) Show that if Bruno has an amount $m = 64$ to spend, while facing prices $p_b = 2$ and $p_c = 8$, he will choose consumption bundle $(b^*, c^*) = (16, 4)$, and will generate utility $U(16, 4) = 8$.

(b) Repeat part (a), but assume that the price p_b is allowed to vary, so that we obtain the ordinary demands, $b^M(p_b)$ and $c^M(p_b)$, as functions of the price p_b.

(c) Obtain the compensated demands, $b^H(p_b)$ and $c^H(p_b)$.

(d) Confirm that the Hicks decomposition is valid for Bruno's demands for beef and chicken. Discuss how the income and substitution effects lead to changes in the ordinary demands as the price p_b increases.

8.4 The cost of a price change to the consumer

'Does money make us happy?' From within the standard model, we should give a qualified but negative answer. Utility might well reflect happiness. If we think of the utility derived from consumption as a measure of a sense of well-being, then happiness and utility seem likely to be closely related. We obtain utility, and tend to be happier, if we are warm, well fed, in love, and surrounded by friends and family. We may even obtain utility and feel happy when writing, or arguing about, microeconomics. Money is therefore not necessary for happiness.

Within the standard model, money is a resource, whose availability forms the constraint on consumption possibilities for a utility maximizer. Not being a good, it cannot appear in a consumer's utility function, but we shall treat it here as being a store of utility.

Suppose that we concluded that money is completely distinct from utility. Were we to go to a local bookstore and explain that even though we have no money, we would very much like to take a copy of Adam Smith's *Wealth of Nations* and read it because we cannot imagine anything that would make us happier, we could be accused of many things – lying and theft being among the most obvious. While possessing money does not in itself make us happier, it enables us to buy goods and services. Once again, it is not ownership that makes us happier. Just as it is not ownership, but careful perusal of a copy of *The Wealth of Nations*, that will help us to understand economics, utility is derived only from the consumption of goods and services. The standard theory of resource allocation involves the conversion of money, a fungible resource, into a variety of goods and services, and so, through consumption of the goods and services, the generation of utility. Money is therefore necessary to buy the direct sources of utility, and so we argue that money is its indirect source. Along with the prices of all goods, the total amount of money available for consumption is an argument of the Marshallian demands of a utility-maximizing consumer.

In Chapter 9, we will restate the standard model, defining what is known as the indirect utility function. For the utility function, $U: U = U(b, c)$, defined over consumption bundles containing quantities b and c of two goods, the indirect utility is the total utility that can be obtained given the consumer's budget constraint, $A(b, c) \leq A_0$. We may write the indirect utility function, V:

$$V(p_b, p_c, m) = U[b(p_b, p_c, m), c(p_b, p_c, m)] \qquad [8.17]$$

where $b(p_b, p_c, m)$ and $c(p_b, p_c, m)$ are the Marshallian demands. Therefore, while we cannot simply define the utility of money, we can talk about the capacity of money to generate utility.

8.4.1 Money as a measure of utility

Defining utility as a numerical index of a preference ordering, we argued that there is no objective scale of utility. Economists have attempted to find a way around that problem by saying that we can think of money as being in some sense the measure of utility. This is more complicated than simply saying that the amount of money that someone might allocate to consumption is also that person's utility.

To explain the concept of a money metric utility function, consider Figure 8.7. We would like to be able to compare bundles Y and Z, but they lie on different indifference curves. However, we know that for one particular consumer, Chloe, bundle Z lies on the same indifference curve as bundle Z_1, bundle Y lies on the same indifference curve as bundle Y_1, and bundle Y_1 and Z_1 lie on the same income expansion path. We therefore compare Y and Z by comparisons of Y_1 and Z_1.

We treat bundle Z_1 as Chloe's compensated demands, given that she has to be able to achieve the same level of utility, U_0, as at bundle Z. In order to purchase Z_1, Chloe therefore has to spend an amount, $A_0 = A^*(p_b, p_c, U_0)$, where p_b and p_c are the prices that she faces, U_0 is her minimum acceptable utility, and A^* is the minimum expenditure needed to achieve utility U_0. In the same way, we treat bundle Y as Chloe's compensated demands, where she has to achieve the level of utility, U_1, achieved by consuming bundle Y. She has to spend $A_1 = A^*(p_b, p_c, U_1)$.

Remember that utility is simply a way of indexing a preference ordering, so that any function that is an increasing function of some particular utility function is also a utility function. From the diagram, we see that that Chloe prefers bundle Z to bundle Y, and also that the acquisition cost of Z_1, which she considers to be just as good as Z, is greater than

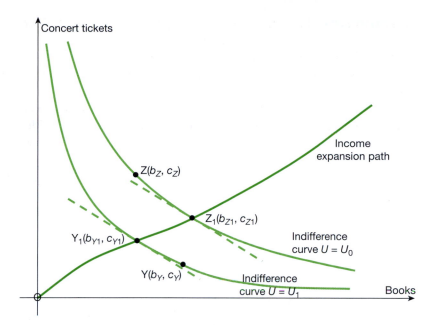

Figure 8.7 Ranking consumption bundles

the acquisition cost of Y. We will not prove the point formally, but there is nothing special about our bundles Y and Z. The higher the cost of the comparator bundle, the more highly Chloe will rank the original. This means that for any consumption bundle, Z (b, c), we can treat the function A^*:

$$A^* = A^*(U(b,c); p_b, p_c) \qquad [8.18]$$

as a measure of the expenditure necessary to generate the utility derived from consuming bundle Z, given particular prices, p_b and p_c. The function A^* is increasing in $U(b, c)$, and so is itself a utility function.

By yourself

X8.19 We represent Chloe's preferences by the utility function, $U : U(b, c) = b^{0.5} + c^{0.5}$. She faces prices $p_b = p_c = 10$.

(a) Obtain her Hicksian demand functions, and the amount, $A^*(U)$, that Chloe has to spend to obtain utility, U.

(b) Show that $\frac{dA^*}{dU} > 1$. What does this suggest about the marginal value of money for Chloe?

Money metric utility was perhaps a final attempt to provide the unique measure of utility that a cardinal interpretation of the concept would require. Effectively, it defines the marginal utility of money as a constant – there is no reason why we should not say that the basic unit of utility is a euro, or a dollar, or a krona, or a pound, or some standardized 'util'. We associate well-being with expenditure on some sort of standardized bundle, in which consumption of goods takes place in fixed proportions because prices are fixed. Nonetheless, exercise X8.19 suggests that there may not be a constant marginal utility of money, and we shall explore this point further in Chapter 9.

8.5   Conclusions

The standard model of resource allocation, as developed to this point, seems to involve nothing more complicated than a visit to a supermarket with a single aisle, the shelves on one side filled with a generic *b*-good, and the shelves on the other filled with a generic *c*-good. Each shopper decides how much of each good to put in their shopping trolley. We have shown that shoppers might approach this problem of filling the shopping basket in two ways: either by choosing the most-preferred, affordable consumption bundle, or by choosing the cheapest, acceptable bundle.

We have argued that if two people – one who chooses the most-preferred, affordable bundle, and the other who chooses the cheapest, acceptable one – were both to select the same bundle, and the relative prices of the goods were then to change, there would be different responses to these price changes. We can be certain that the consumer buying the cheapest, acceptable bundle will substitute the good that is now relatively less expensive for the one that is relatively more expensive. We can also be certain that were the price of a normal good to increase, then the consumer buying the most-preferred, affordable consumption bundle would demand less of it.

We say that for someone selecting the most-preferred, affordable bundle, demand functions have the ordinary, or Marshallian, form. Constrained by having a fixed amount of money to spend, this consumer's demands will change both as the prices of goods change and as the constraint changes. To call these the 'ordinary' demands seems quite reasonable, because in terms of our standard model with well-behaved preferences, we expect people to have a fixed amount of money and to spend it all. In the same way, we describe the demands of a person choosing the cheapest, acceptable bundle as compensated, or Hicksian. In this case, the constraint is the achievement of a set level of utility. Compensation refers to the possibility of people being able to offset the effects of a price change: if the price of a good falls, anyone trying to achieve a utility target can do so while spending less. Yet, in the standard model, that seems to involve giving up the possibility of additional utility. The divergence of ordinary and compensated demands reflects the income effect.

We have argued that there is a sense in which money, although never an argument of a utility function, can be argued to have utility. By acquiring goods with money, and consuming them, people generate utility. So, money is the means for acquiring the sources of utility. Our entire discussion up to this point has been about how to use money most effectively for this purpose. But money does more than this. It allows us to schedule consumption over time: to respond to unexpected events, such as an unforeseen price increase, so that we can alter our consumption plans. It is received from the sale of goods and services; and most people work (in effect, selling labour services) in order to exchange time and effort for money in the form of wages or a salary. This gives us three ways of applying or developing the standard theory, as it relates to the consumer: firstly, considering optimal consumption over time instead of at a single point in time; secondly, analysing how to plan consumption in the face of risk and uncertainty; and thirdly, examining how to allocate time to work as part of a utility maximization problem. We shall consider all three of these later in the book, largely developing and applying the standard model rather than trying to replace it.

Summary

In this chapter, we have first defined the Hicksian or compensated demand functions, which show how the demands of an expenditure-minimizing consumer vary as the price of a good changes, given a fixed utility target. We have treated this as an alternative to the utility maximization approach that gives rise to the Marshallian or ordinary demands.

We have defined the substitution and income effects associated with a price change that add together to give the total change in the Marshallian demands. The substitution effect results from the change in relative prices and is also the change in the Hicksian demands, while the income effect is the result of the change in purchasing power, or real income, and reflects the change in the budget set as a result of the price change.

We have defined the Slutsky decomposition of the change in ordinary demands resulting from the price change as the sum of the income and substitution effects, writing:

$$\frac{\partial x^M}{\partial p_x} = \frac{\partial x^H}{\partial p_x} - x^M \frac{\partial x^M}{\partial m}$$

In this expression, the left-hand side is the rate of change of the Marshallian demand for good X as the price of good X changes. The right-hand side consists of the substitution effect, the rate of change of the Hicksian demand as the price changes, and the income effect, the rate of change of demand as income changes multiplied by the ordinary demand.

Finally, we have considered limitations of our theory, noting that the utility maximization and expenditure minimization approaches result from very different assumptions about people's capacity to raise money for consumption purposes.

Visit the companion website at **www.palgrave.com/mochrie** to access further teaching and learning materials, including lecturer slides and a testbank, as well as guideline answers and student MCQs.

9

The CES utility function

We have already met the *Constant Elasticity of Substitution* (CES) family of utility functions in a few examples. These utility functions have very straightforward properties that make them useful in economic modelling. We now consider their properties rather more systematically, beginning with a definition of the functional form, confirming that all of these functions are homogeneous and that they represent well-behaved preferences.

We then obtain the *ordinary* and *compensated demand functions* and the *elasticities of demand*, confirming that the Hicks decomposition holds for these functions. Lastly, we define the *elasticity of substitution*, and confirm that this elasticity is constant for all CES functions. We conclude with some comments about the behaviour of people whose preferences can be represented by such utility functions.

9.1 CES functions

The *elasticity of substitution* is a mathematical property of a utility function. We shall define it properly at the end of the chapter. For now, we simply assert that all functions of the form of the function, U:

$$U(x,y) = \begin{cases} \left[\theta x^a + (1-\theta)y^a\right]^{\frac{\rho}{a}}, \text{if } a \leq 1, \text{and } a \neq 0 \\ x^{\rho\theta}y^{\rho(1-\theta)}, \text{if } a = 0 \end{cases} \qquad [9.1]$$

possess the characteristic of a constant elasticity of substitution. We shall see in this chapter that we can use the CES utility functions to represent preferences for goods that are pairs of perfect substitutes, and also for goods that are pairs of perfect complements. Cobb–Douglas utility functions turn out to be members of the family of CES utility functions for the parameter value $a = 0$. For this value, it is not possible to evaluate utilities using the other form of the function.

Note that in Expression 9.1, there are three parameters:

- a: related to the ease with which goods can be substituted for each other;
- θ: related to the expenditure share of the goods; and
- ρ: the degree of homogeneity of the function.

We summarize our results for the family of functions defined in Expression 9.1 at the end of the chapter. In the text of the chapter, we simplify the form of the functions to U:

$$U(x,y) = \begin{cases} \left[x^a + y^a\right]^{\frac{1}{a}}, \text{ if } a \leq 1, \text{ and } a \neq 0 \\ x^{0.5}y^{0.5}, \text{if } a = 0 \text{ (so that } \theta = 0.5) \end{cases} \qquad [9.2]$$

In Expression 9.2, the utility function always exhibits constant returns to scale. If the quantity of both goods in a consumption bundle increases by a set proportion, the value of the utility function increases by the same proportion. There is therefore a linear relationship between the sum of money required to finance consumption, m, and the level of utility that a consumer might achieve, $V(m)$. In addition, if $p_x = p_y$, then for every possible value of the parameter a, a consumer will divide expenditure equally between the two goods, purchasing the same quantity of each.

9.1.1 Homogeneity

Recall that a function $z : z = z(x, y)$ is homogeneous of degree r if for any pair (x, y), $z(\lambda x, \lambda y) = \lambda^r \cdot z(x, y)$. In the case of the family of utility functions defined in Expression 9.2, when we multiply the quantity of all goods in a consumption bundle, (x, y), by some number, λ, then we increase the utility, $U(x, y)$, by a factor, λ^r.

From Expression 9.2, and setting the restriction $a \neq 0$, we obtain:

Evaluate the function	Common factor $(\lambda^a)^{1/a} = \lambda$

$$U(\lambda x, \lambda y) = \left[(\lambda x)^a + (\lambda y)^a\right]^{\frac{1}{a}} = \left[\lambda^a x^a + \lambda^a y^a\right]^{\frac{1}{a}} = \lambda\left[x^a + y^a\right]^{\frac{1}{a}} = \lambda U(x, y) \qquad [9.3]$$

The new consumption bundle is λ times the scale of the original one, and the final utility is also λ times the original utility. Such a function is therefore homogeneous of degree 1 (HOD 1).

By yourself

X9.1 Confirm that the utility function, $U : U(x, y) = x^a y^{1-a}$, is HOD 1.

X9.2 Confirm that the members of the family of utility functions defined in Expression 9.1 are HOD ρ.

X9.3 Confirm that the utility function, $U : U(x, y) = \min[ax^\rho, by^\rho]$, is HOD ρ.

X9.4 Show that the utility function, $U : U(x, y) = x^{\frac{1}{3}} + y^{\frac{1}{3}}$, is a member of the family of functions in Expression 9.1, and that it is HOD $\frac{1}{3}$.

X9.5 Show that the utility functions, $U : U(x, y) = (x^{-1} + y^{-1})^{-1}$, and $V : V(x, y) = (x^{-2} + y^{-2})^{-0.5}$, can also be written as $U : U(x, y) = \frac{xy}{x+y}$, and $V : V(x, y) = \dfrac{xy}{(x^2 + y^2)^{\frac{1}{2}}}$. Confirm that both U and V are HOD 1.

9.1.2 Marginal utility and the marginal rate of substitution

The marginal utility of good X is the partial derivative of the utility function with respect to the quantity x in the consumption bundle (x, y). Partially differentiating the function in Expression 9.2 with respect to x, we obtain the partial derivative:

Apply chain rule of differentiation	$U = W^{1/a};\ W = x^a + y^a;$ $U_x = U'(W) \cdot W_x$	$z^{ab} = (z^a)^b$

$$MU_X(x, y) = \frac{\partial U}{\partial x} = \frac{1}{a}\left[x^a + y^a\right]^{\frac{1-a}{a}} \cdot (ax^{a-1}) = \frac{\left[x^a + y^a\right]^{\frac{1-a}{a}}}{x^{1-a}} = \left(\frac{\left[x^a + y^a\right]^{\frac{1}{a}}}{x}\right)^{1-a} = \left(\frac{U(x, y)}{x}\right)^{1-a} \qquad [9.4]$$

$$x^{a-1} = \left[x^{1-a}\right]^{-1} = \frac{1}{x^{1-a}}$$

The simplest form

We can apply exactly the same argument to obtain $MU_X(x, y)$, the marginal utility of good Y:

$$MU_Y(x,y) = \frac{\partial U}{\partial y} = \left(\frac{U(x,y)}{y} \right)^{1-a} \tag{9.5}$$

We have two marginal utilities, and so need both partial derivatives. As in previous examples, when taking the partial derivative with respect to x, we assume that y remains constant (and vice versa).

By yourself

X9.6   Without using Expressions 9.4 or 9.5 obtain the marginal utilities of goods X and Y for the utility functions, U:

(a) $U : U(x, y) = x^{\frac{1}{2}}y^{\frac{1}{2}}$ (b) $U : U(x, y) = x^{\frac{1}{3}} + y^{\frac{1}{3}}$ (c) $U : U(x,y) = \left(x^{\frac{1}{3}} + y^{\frac{1}{3}}\right)^3$

(d) $U : U(x, y) = \dfrac{xy}{x+y}$ (e) $V : V(x,y) = \dfrac{xy}{(x^2 + y^2)^{\frac{1}{2}}}$.

X9.7   Confirm that for the functions in X9.6c–e, we can rely on Expressions 9.4 and 9.5 to calculate the marginal utilities.

X9.8   Confirm that for the general form of CES utility functions in Expression 9.1:

$$MU_X(x,y) = \rho\theta \, \frac{U(x,y)^{\frac{\rho-a}{\rho}}}{x^{1-a}}, \text{ if } a \leq 1; \text{ and } MU_Y(x,y) = \rho(1-\theta) \, \frac{U(x,y)^{\frac{\rho-a}{\rho}}}{y^{1-a}}, \text{ if } a \leq 1$$

The marginal utilities are important only because we calculate the marginal rate of substitution, $MRS(x, y)$, for any bundle as their ratio. Using Expressions 9.4 and 9.5, we obtain:

$$MRS(x, y) = -\frac{\partial U}{\partial x} \bigg/ \frac{\partial U}{\partial y} = -\left[\frac{U(x, y)}{x} \right]^{1-a} \bigg/ \left[\frac{U(x, y)}{y} \right]^{1-a} = -\left(\frac{y}{x} \right)^{1-a} \begin{array}{l} \text{Common} \\ \text{factor} \\ U(x, y)^{1-a} \end{array} \tag{9.6}$$

In Expression 9.6, we are able to express the marginal rate of substitution as a function of the ratio in which the goods are consumed, $\frac{y}{x}$. This is consistent with the properties of a homogeneous utility function, introduced in Chapter 6. We note from Expression 9.6 that since x and $y > 0$, and since the marginal rate of substitution $MRS < 0$, the indifference curve is downward-sloping. This confirms that the underlying preferences are monotonically increasing.

By yourself

X9.9   Use Expression 9.6 to confirm that along any line passing through the origin that has the equation $y = kx$, the marginal rate of substitution, $MRS(x, y) = -k^{1-a}$.

X9.10   For the following utility functions, obtain the marginal utilities of x and y and calculate the marginal rate of substitution:

(a) $U : U(x, y) = 3x + 2y$ (b) $U : U(x, y) = x^a y^{(1-a)}$ (c) $U : U(x,y) = x^{\frac{1}{3}} + y^{\frac{1}{3}}$

(d) $U : U(x, y) = [x^{\frac{1}{2}} + y^{\frac{1}{2}}]^2$ (e) $U : U(x, y) = 5x^{\frac{1}{2}} + 3y^{\frac{1}{2}}$

X9.11   For the utility function $U : U(x, y) = \min(3x, 2y)$, show that:

(a) the only possible values of the marginal utility of good X are 0 and 3, while the only possible values of the marginal utility of good Y are 0 and 2;

(b) the marginal rate of substitution cannot be defined when $3x \leq 2y$; and

(c) $MRS(x, y) = 0$ if $3x > 2y$.

9.1.3 Convexity

For well-behaved preferences, we also require preferences to be convex, so that each indifference curve is convex. Continuing with the form of the CES utility function in Expression 9.2, we write the equation of a single indifference curve, $U = U_0$, in implicit form:

$$\begin{cases} [x^a + y^a]^{\frac{1}{a}} = U_0, \text{ if } a \leq 1, \text{ and } a \neq 0 \\ x^{0.5}y^{0.5} = U_0, \text{ if } a = 0 \end{cases} \qquad [9.7]$$

By yourself

X9.12   Show that it is possible to write:

(a) the equation of the indifference curve in explicit form as:

$$y = \begin{cases} \left[U_0^a - x^a \right]^{\frac{1}{a}}, \text{ if } a \leq 1, \text{ and } a \neq 0 \\ \dfrac{U_0^2}{x}, \text{ if } a = 0 \end{cases} \qquad [9.8]$$

(b) the derivative, $\dfrac{dy}{dx}$:

$$\left. \frac{dy}{dx} \right|_{U=U_0} = MRS(x, y, U_0) = -\left(\frac{y}{x} \right)^{(1-a)} \qquad [9.9]$$

If the indifference curve in Expression 9.7 is convex, by differentiating Expression 9.9 we find that:

$$\frac{d}{dx}[MRS\,(x, y, U_0)] \geq 0 \qquad [9.10]$$

We demonstrate the condition in Expression 9.10 by differentiating Expression 9.9:

$$\frac{dMRS}{dx} = -\frac{d}{dx}\left(\frac{y}{x} \right)^{1-a}$$

Apply chain rule and quotient rule, treating MRS and y as functions of x
$$= -(1-a) \cdot \left(\frac{y}{x} \right)^{-a} \cdot \left\{ \frac{MRS}{x} - \frac{y}{x^2} \right\}$$

Substitute for $\dfrac{dy}{dx}$ from [9.9]
$$= (1-a) \cdot \left(\frac{y}{x} \right)^{-a} \cdot \left\{ \frac{y^{1-a}}{x^{2-a}} + \frac{y}{x^2} \right\}$$

Extract factor y/x^2
$$= (1-a) \cdot \left(\frac{y^{1-a}}{x^{2-a}} \right) \cdot \left\{ \frac{x^a}{y^a} + 1 \right\} = (1-a) \cdot \left(\frac{y^{1-2a}}{x^{2-a}} \right) \cdot (x^a + y^a) \quad [9.11]$$

Remember $x^a = 1/x^{-a}$

Extract factor y^{-a} to eliminate fraction

Note that with the exception of the factor $(1 - a)$, all parts of Expression 9.11 are powers of x or y and so must be positive. The sign of Expression 9.11 is positive if $1 - a > 0$ or if $a < 1$. We conclude that every indifference curve that is the graph of Expression 9.7 is downward-sloping and convex, so that the underlying preferences are well behaved.

By yourself

X9.13   Use the argument above to confirm that for $a = \frac{1}{2}$, indifference curves are convex, but that for $a = 2$, indifference curves are concave.

X9.14   Confirm that the indifference curve, with equation, $x^{0.5}y^{0.5} = 1$, is convex.

X9.15   By evaluating Expression 9.11 or otherwise, confirm that indifference curves of the utility functions in X9.10 are all (weakly) convex.

9.2   Indifference curves for CES utility functions

We have established that all CES utility functions represent well-behaved preferences and are homogeneous. From here on, we shall only consider the set of functions specified by Expression 9.2, exploring how changing the value of the parameter a affects the underlying preferences, the demand functions, and changes in demand following changes in prices. We illustrate some of these effects graphically by illustrating how changing the value of a affects the shape of the indifference curve on which the consumption bundle $(x, y) = (4, 4)$ lies.

By yourself

X9.16   For the utility function, $U : U(x, y) = x + y$:
(a) Confirm that the indifference curve that passes through $(x, y) = (4, 4)$ also passes through the consumption bundles $(8, 0)$ and $(0, 8)$; and that $MRS = -1$.
(b) Show this indifference curve on a diagram. [*Note:* It will be useful to draw the diagram at least approximately to scale, and to extend the x- and y-axes to 16.]

X9.17   For the utility function, $U : U(x, y) = x^{\frac{1}{2}} + y^{\frac{1}{2}}$:
(a) Confirm that the indifference curve that passes through $(x, y) = (4, 4)$ also passes through the consumption bundles $(16, 0)$ and $(0, 16)$.
(b) Confirm that $MRS = -\left(\frac{y}{x}\right)^{\frac{1}{2}}$, so that $MRS(16, 0) = 0$; $MRS(4, 4) = -1$; and $MRS(0, 16)$ is not defined. What do you conclude about the slope of the indifference curve at each of these three consumption bundles?
(c) Remembering that the indifference curve is convex and downward-sloping, sketch it on the diagram used in X9.16.

X9.18   Repeat X9.17 for the utility function, $U : U(x, y) = x^{\frac{1}{3}} + y^{\frac{1}{3}}$, but showing that:
(a) The indifference curve passing through $(x, y) = (4, 4)$ also passes through the consumption bundles $(32, 0)$ and $(0, 32)$.
(b) $MRS = -\left(\frac{y}{x}\right)^{\frac{2}{3}}$, so that the indifference curve is flat where it meets the horizontal axis, vertical where it meets the vertical axis, and just touches the line $y = 8 - x$ at $(x, y) = (4, 4)$.
(c) The indifference curve passes close to the points $(16, 0.28)$ and $(0.28, 16)$. Hence, add this indifference curve to the diagram used in X9.16.

X9.19   For the utility function, $U : U(x, y) = (xy)^{\frac{1}{2}}$:
(a) Confirm that the indifference curve that passes through $(x, y) = (4, 4)$ also passes through the consumption bundles $(16, 1)$, $(8, 2)$, $(2, 8)$ and $(1, 16)$. Drawing a new diagram, to the same scale as the diagram for X9.16, sketch this indifference curve.
(b) Confirm that for this indifference curve, as $x \to \infty, y \to 0$; and that as $x \to 0, y \to \infty$.
(c) Confirm that $MRS = -\left(\frac{y}{x}\right)$, so that $MRS(16, 1) = -16$; $MRS(4, 4) = -1$; and $MRS(1, 16) = -0.0625$.

X9.20 Repeat X9.19 for the utility function, $U : U(x,y) = \frac{xy}{x+y} = \left(\frac{1}{x} + \frac{1}{y}\right)^{-1}$, showing that:

(a) The indifference curve that passes through $(x, y) = (4, 4)$ also passes through the consumption bundles $(18, 2.25)$, $(10, 2.5)$, $(6, 3)$, $(3, 6)$, $(2.5, 10)$, and $(2.25, 18)$. Hence sketch its graph on the diagram used for X9.19.

(b) Confirm that $MRS = -\left(\frac{y}{x}\right)^2$, so that $MRS(18, 2.25) = -\frac{1}{64}$; $MRS(10, 2.5) = -\frac{1}{16}$; $MRS(6, 3) = -\frac{1}{4}$; $MRS(4, 4) = -1$; $MRS(6, 3) = -4$; $MRS(2.5, 10) = -16$; and $MRS(2.25, 18) = -64$.

(c) Confirm that if $x \to \infty$, then $y \to 2$, but that if $x \to 2$, $y \to \infty$. On the diagram, draw in these two lines, which the indifference curve approaches but does not cross.

X9.21 Using the same diagram as in X9.19 and X9.20, and for the utility function $U : U(x, y) = \min(x, y)$, draw the indifference curve that passes through the bundle $(x, y) = (4, 4)$. Discuss the behaviour of the MRS function.

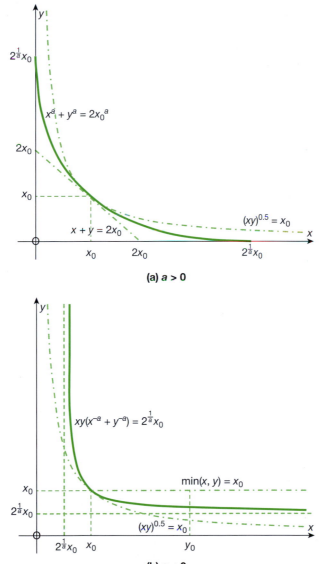

(a) $a > 0$

(b) $a < 0$

Figure 9.1 Indifference curves of CES utility

The diagrams in Exercises X9.16–X9.21 demonstrate that the indifference curves for CES utility functions have shapes similar to the curves shown in Figure 9.1 (which is adapted from Figure 5.6). Considering Figure 9.1a, with $a > 0$, the indifference curve of the function, $U : U(x,y) = [x^a + y^a]^{\frac{1}{a}}$, which passes through point $Z_0(x_0, x_0)$:

- has tangent $x + y = 2x_0$, so that $MRS(x_0, x_0) = -1$;
- meets the horizontal axis at point $(2^{\frac{1}{a}}x_0, 0)$, for which $MRS(2^{\frac{1}{a}}x_0, 0) = 0$, so that the indifference curve is then flat; and
- meets the vertical axis at point $(0, 2^{\frac{1}{a}}x_0)$, for which $MRS(0, 2^{\frac{1}{a}}x_0)$ is not defined, so that the indifference curve is then vertical.

By yourself

X9.22   Confirm that all indifference curves of the utility function, $U : U(x,y) = [x^a + y^a]^{\frac{1}{a}}$, for which $0 < a < 1$, have the properties stated above.

Starting from the value $a = 1$, for which the goods are perfect substitutes and the indifference curve has the equation $x + y = 2x_0$, and then allowing the value of a to fall towards zero, the indifference curve becomes more curved, with the point of intersection with the axes moving away from the origin. If $0 < a < 1$, the axes are tangent to the indifference curve. It is possible for us to find a consumption bundle $(x, y): MRS(x, y) = -r$, so long as $r \geq 0$. As we shall see in Section 9.3, whatever the relative prices of the goods, a consumer with preferences in this form will buy a consumption bundle $(x^*, y^*): x^*, y^* > 0$, so that the consumption bundle contains some of both goods.

Turning to Figure 9.1b, with $a < 0$, the indifference curve passing through point $Z_0(x_0, x_0)$:

- has tangent $x + y = 2x_0$, so that $MRS(x_0, x_0) = -1$ (not shown in the diagram);
- is bounded by the line, $x = 2^{\frac{1}{a}}x_0$, since otherwise the consumption bundle will not generate sufficient utility (and so all consumption bundles must contain more than $2^{\frac{1}{a}}x_0$ of both goods);
- approaches, but does not cross, the horizontal line $y = 2^{\frac{1}{a}}x_0$; and as $y \to 2^{\frac{1}{a}}x_0$, $x \to \infty$, and $MRS(x,y) \to 0$, so that the indifference curve is flat; and
- approaches, but does not cross, the vertical line, $x = 2^{\frac{1}{a}}x_0$; and as $x \to 2^{\frac{1}{a}}x_0$, $y \to \infty$, and $MRS(x,y) \to -\infty$, so that the indifference curve is vertical.

By yourself

X9.23   Confirm that all indifference curves of the utility function, $U : U(x,y) = [x^a + y^a]^{\frac{1}{a}}$, for which $a < 0$, have the properties stated above.

If we start from the value $a = 0$, for which the indifference curve has the form $(xy)^{0.5} = x_0$, represent Cobb–Douglas preferences, and then allow the value of a to become negative, the indifference curve becomes still more curved. Indifference curves for the Cobb–Douglas preferences never cross the axes. The axes are instead asymptotes, lines that the indifference curves approach but never touch. For values of the parameter $a < 0$, asymptotes are parallel to, but distinct from, the axes. Once again, it is possible to find a consumption bundle $(x, y): MRS(x, y) = -r$ on every indifference curve, so that whatever the relative prices of the goods, a consumer with preferences in this form will buy a consumption bundle that contains some of both goods.

9.3 Demand functions for a CES utility function

We begin with the ordinary demand functions for a consumer with a CES utility function. Such a consumer maximizes utility by allocating money to the purchase of consumption bundle (x^*, y^*):

$$\max_{(x,y)} \left[x^a + y^a \right]^{\frac{1}{a}} : p_x x + p_y y = m \qquad [9.12]$$

We apply the equality of gradients conditions so that the marginal rate of substitution, $MRS(x, y)$, will be equal to the price ratio, $-\frac{p_x}{p_y}$. Using the definition of MRS in Expression 9.6:

$$\left(\frac{y}{x} \right)^{1-a} = \frac{p_x}{p_y} \qquad [9.13]$$

we obtain the income expansion path:

$$y = \left(\frac{p_x}{p_y} \right)^{\frac{1}{1-a}} x \quad \boxed{\text{Raise both sides to the power of } 1/(1-a)} \qquad [9.14]$$

We now find the consumption bundle that lies at the intersection of the budget constraint and the income expansion path, which we do by substituting the income expansion path in Expression 9.14 into the budget constraint from Expression 9.12:

$$m = p_x x + p_y \left(\frac{p_x}{p_y} \right)^{\frac{1}{1-a}} x = p_x x \left\{ 1 + \left(\frac{p_x}{p_y} \right)^{\frac{a}{1-a}} \right\} = p_x x \left\{ \frac{p_x^{\frac{a}{1-a}} + p_y^{\frac{a}{1-a}}}{p_y^{\frac{a}{1-a}}} \right\}$$

$\boxed{\text{Substitute for } y}$ $\boxed{\text{Extract common factor } p_x x}$ $\boxed{\text{Write expression as fraction}}$

Then we rearrange to solve for x:

$$x^M(p_x, p_y, m) = \frac{m}{p_x} \left\{ \frac{p_x^{\frac{a}{1-a}}}{p_x^{\frac{a}{1-a}} + p_y^{\frac{a}{1-a}}} \right\} \quad \boxed{\text{Divide both sides by } p_x \text{ and multiply by the inverse of the fraction in braces}} \qquad [9.15a]$$

It is quite straightforward to confirm that:

$$y^M(p_x, p_y, m) = \frac{m}{p_y} \left\{ \frac{p_y^{\frac{a}{1-a}}}{p_x^{\frac{a}{1-a}} + p_y^{\frac{a}{1-a}}} \right\} \qquad [9.15b]$$

It is probably more usual to rewrite the demands in Expression 9.15 as:

$$x^M(p_x, p_y, m) = m \left\{ \frac{p_x^{-\frac{1}{1-a}}}{p_x^{-\frac{a}{1-a}} + p_y^{-\frac{a}{1-a}}} \right\} \qquad [9.16a]$$

$$y^M(p_x, p_y, m) = m \left\{ \frac{p_y^{-\frac{1}{1-a}}}{p_x^{-\frac{a}{1-a}} + p_y^{-\frac{a}{1-a}}} \right\} \qquad [9.16b]$$

To obtain the ordinary demand functions in the form of Expression 9.16, we apply the algebraic identity: $\frac{s}{s+t} \equiv \frac{t^{-1}}{s^{-1} + t^{-1}}$, rearranging the resulting expression. Since these steps simply involve algebraic manipulation, they are not written out here.

By yourself

X9.24 For the following utility functions – and except for functions (a) and (b), for which you may find graphical analysis more straightforward – use Expression 9.16 to obtain the Marshallian or ordinary demands for a consumer, for whom $m = 200$, $p_y = 5$ and p_x is allowed to vary:

(a) $U : U(x, y) = 3x + 2y$; (b) $U : U(x, y) = \min(2x, 3y)$; (c) $U : U(x, y) = x^{0.5}y^{0.5}$;

(d) $U : U(x,y) = x^{\frac{1}{3}} + y^{\frac{1}{3}}$; (e) $U : U(x, y) = [x^{\frac{1}{2}} + y^{\frac{1}{2}}]^2$; (f) $U : U(x, y) = (x^{-1} + y^{-1})^{-1}$;

(g) $U : U(x,y) = \frac{xy}{(x^2 + y^2)^{0.5}}$.

X9.25 By obtaining the partial derivative, $\frac{\partial x^M}{\partial p_x}$, or otherwise, confirm that for the utility functions in X9.24c, X9.24e and X9.24f, the demand, $x^M(p_x; 5, 200)$, decreases as the price, p_x, increases.

X9.26 By obtaining the partial derivative, $\frac{\partial y^M}{\partial p_x}$, or otherwise, confirm that:

(a) for the utility function in X9.24e, the demand, $y^M(p_x; 5, 200)$, is an increasing function of the price, p_x;

(b) for the utility function in X9.24c, the demand, $y^M(p_x; 5, 200)$, remains constant as the price, p_x, changes; and

(c) for the utility function in X9.24f, the demand, $y^M(p_x; 5, 200)$, is a decreasing function of the price, p_x.

9.3.1 Hicksian demands

We have found the Marshallian, or ordinary, demands, for a utility-maximizing consumer, who has a fixed sum, m, to finance consumption, and who faces fixed unit prices, p_x and p_y. We now turn to the alternative problem, that of finding the Hicksian, or compensated, demands. These represent the allocation of resources made by someone seeking to achieve a target utility level, U_0, when the prices of goods X and Y are p_x and p_y respectively.

We now state the consumer's objective as being to minimize expenditure by allocating money to the purchase of consumption bundle (x, y) while achieving a given target utility.

$$\min_{(x, y)} p_x x + p_y y : [x^a + y^a]^{\frac{1}{a}} = U_0 \tag{9.17a}$$

From the previous discussion, we know that the equilibrium condition – that the marginal rate of substitution is equal to the price ratio – will be satisfied at all points on the income expansion path found in the utility maximization problem, Expression 9.14, which is repeated here:

$$y = \left(\frac{p_x}{p_y}\right)^{\frac{1}{1-a}} x \tag{9.17b}$$

We now find the consumption bundle that lies at the intersection of the indifference curve forming the utility constraint and the income expansion path. Substituting Expression 9.17b into the utility constraint in Expression 9.17a:

$$U_0 = \left[x^a + \left\{\left(\frac{p_x}{p_y}\right)^{\frac{1}{1-a}} x\right\}^a\right]^{\frac{1}{a}} = x \cdot \left[1 + \left(\frac{p_x}{p_y}\right)^{\frac{a}{1-a}}\right]^{\frac{1}{a}} = x \cdot \left[\frac{p_x^{\frac{a}{1-a}} + p_y^{\frac{a}{1-a}}}{p_y^{\frac{a}{1-a}}}\right]^{\frac{1}{a}}$$

Write expression as fraction

Substituting for y

Common factor x: raised to power of a then $1/a$

Then rearranging to solve for x:

$$x^H(p_x, p_y, U_0) = U_0 \left[\frac{p_y^{\frac{a}{1-a}}}{p_x^{\frac{a}{1-a}} + p_y^{\frac{a}{1-a}}} \right]^{\frac{1}{a}}$$

[9.18a]

Expression 9.18a is the Hicksian demand for good X. We obtain the Hicksian demand for good Y:

$$y^H(p_x, p_y, U_0) = U_0 \left[\frac{p_x^{\frac{a}{1-a}}}{p_x^{\frac{a}{1-a}} + p_y^{\frac{a}{1-a}}} \right]^{\frac{1}{a}}$$

[9.18b]

As with the Marshallian or ordinary demands in Expression 9.16, we rewrite the Hicksian demands:

$$x^H(p_x, p_y, U_0) = U_0 \left[\frac{p_x^{-\frac{a}{1-a}}}{p_x^{-\frac{a}{1-a}} + p_y^{-\frac{a}{1-a}}} \right]^{\frac{1}{a}}$$

[9.19a]

$$y^H(p_x, p_y, U_0) = U_0 \left\{ \frac{p_y^{-\frac{a}{1-a}}}{p_x^{-\frac{a}{1-a}} + p_y^{-\frac{a}{1-a}}} \right\}^{\frac{1}{a}}$$

[9.19b]

The Hicksian or compensated demands form the expenditure-minimizing bundle for a consumer with a fixed acceptability constraint.

By yourself

X9.27 Repeat X9.24, but obtaining the Hicksian demands, x^H and y^H, for the following cases, with $p_x = p_y = 5$ and with the minimum acceptable utility, U_0, is allowed to vary:
(a) $U : U(x, y) = 3x + 2y$;   (b) $U : U(x, y) = \min(2x, 3y)$;   (c) $U : U(x, y) = x^{0.5} y^{0.5}$;
(d) $U : U(x, y) = x^{\frac{1}{3}} + y^{\frac{1}{3}}$;   (e) $U : U(x, y) = [x^{\frac{1}{2}} + y^{\frac{1}{2}}]^2$;   (f) $U : U(x, y) = (x^{-1} + y^{-1})^{-1}$;
(g) $U : U(x, y) = \frac{xy}{(x^2 + y^2)^{0.5}}$.

X9.28 For the utility function in X9.27c, obtain the Hicksian demands, x^H and y^H, when the price $p_y = 5$, the minimum acceptable utility $U_0 = 20$, and the price, p_x, is allowed to vary.

X9.29 Repeat X9.28 for the utility function in X9.27e, with $U_0 = 80$.

X9.30 Repeat X9.28 for the utility function in X9.27f, with $U_0 = 10$.

9.3.2 The indirect utility function

The Marshallian or ordinary demands in Expression 9.16 specify the utility-maximizing bundle for a consumer with a fixed sum to finance consumption, m, and facing fixed prices, p_x and p_y. We now define the level of utility that such a person can generate given these parameter values as the **indirect utility**, V:

Indirect utility The greatest utility possible given prices and the money available to finance consumption.

$$V(p_x, p_y, m) = U(x^M, y^M)$$

[9.20]

In Expression 9.20, we note that while utility, U, is derived from the consumption of goods, the level of utility that people can actually achieve depends both on the underlying utility function and the values of the parameters, which define the affordable set.

Evaluating Expression 9.20 by substituting the solution to the utility maximization problem from Expression 9.16 into the utility function, we obtain:

This is the substitution

$$U(x^M, y^M) = \left\{ \left[m\left(\frac{p_x^{-\frac{1}{1-a}}}{p_x^{-\frac{a}{1-a}} + p_y^{-\frac{a}{1-a}}} \right) \right]^a + \left[m\left(\frac{p_y^{-\frac{1}{1-a}}}{p_x^{-\frac{a}{1-a}} + p_y^{-\frac{a}{1-a}}} \right) \right]^a \right\}^{\frac{1}{a}}$$

Extract common factors: these are raised to power of a, then $1/a$; so to power of $a^*(a^{-1}) = 1$

$$= \frac{m}{p_x^{-\frac{a}{1-a}} + p_y^{-\frac{a}{1-a}}} \left[p_x^{-\frac{a}{1-a}} + p_y^{-\frac{a}{1-a}} \right]^{\frac{1}{a}}$$

Terms in bracket are numerators of the fractions in demand function raised to power a

$$= m \left[p_x^{-\frac{a}{1-a}} + p_y^{-\frac{a}{1-a}} \right]^{(\frac{1}{a}-1)}$$

Gather together powers of $p_x^{-\frac{a}{1-a}} + p_y^{-\frac{a}{1-a}}$

Simplify indices

$$= m \left[p_x^{-\frac{a}{1-a}} + p_y^{-\frac{a}{1-a}} \right]^{(\frac{1-a}{a})} = V(p_x, p_y, m)$$

V is the indirect utility   [9.21]

For our argument, perhaps the most important point to note from Expression 9.21 is that the indirect utility is a linear function of m, the amount of money available, which is consistent with the utility function being homogeneous of degree 1.

By yourself

X9.31   Confirm that the indirect utility function is:
(a) homogeneous of degree -1 in prices (so that if both prices, p_x and p_y, increase by $k\%$, but m, the money available to finance consumption, remains constant, the indirect utility, V, decreases by $k\%$);
(b) homogeneous of degree 0 in prices and the sum available to finance consumption.

X9.32   Explain why it is sensible that the indirect utility should not change as m, p_x and p_y increase by the same proportion.

9.3.3   The expenditure function

Expenditure function The least money required to reach an acceptable utility, given the prices of goods.

The expenditure function is the equivalent for an expenditure-minimizing consumer of the indirect utility function for a consumer who maximizes utility. It is therefore the expenditure needed to reach the minimum acceptable utility. We obtain the expenditure function by evaluating the acquisition cost in Expression 9.17, for the Hicksian demands from Expression 9.19:

$$A(x^H, y^H) = p_x \cdot U_0 \left(\frac{p_x^{-\frac{a}{1-a}}}{p_x^{-\frac{a}{1-a}} + p_y^{-\frac{a}{1-a}}} \right)^{\frac{1}{a}} + p_y \cdot U_0 \left(\frac{p_y^{-\frac{a}{1-a}}}{p_x^{-\frac{a}{1-a}} + p_y^{-\frac{a}{1-a}}} \right)^{\frac{1}{a}}$$

Acquisition cost of optimal bundle

Extract common factors, applying laws of indices as before

$$= \frac{U_0}{\left(p_x^{-\frac{a}{1-a}} + p_y^{-\frac{a}{1-a}} \right)^{\frac{1}{a}}} \left[p_x \cdot p_x^{-\frac{1}{1-a}} + p_y \cdot p_y^{-\frac{1}{1-a}} \right]$$

Terms in bracket are numerators of the fractions in demand function raised to power $1/a$

$$= \frac{U_0}{\left(p_x^{-\frac{a}{1-a}} + p_y^{-\frac{a}{1-a}}\right)^{\frac{1}{a}}} \left[p_x^{-\frac{a}{1-a}} + p_y^{-\frac{a}{1-a}}\right] \quad \boxed{\text{Collect powers of } p_x, p_y}$$

$$\boxed{\substack{\text{Gather together} \\ \text{powers of } p_x^{-\frac{a}{1-a}} + p_y^{-\frac{a}{1-a}}}} = U_0 \left[p_x^{-\frac{a}{1-a}} + p_y^{-\frac{a}{1-a}}\right]^{-\frac{1-a}{a}} = E(p_x, p_y, U_0) \quad \boxed{\substack{E \text{ is the total} \\ \text{expenditure}}} \quad [9.22]$$

By yourself

X9.33 Suppose that $U_0 = m\left[p_x^{-\frac{a}{1-a}} + p_y^{-\frac{a}{1-a}}\right]^{\left(\frac{1-a}{a}\right)}$, the indirect utility achievable when there is an amount m to finance consumption. Show that $E(p_x, p_y, U_0) = m$.

X9.34 For the utility function, $U : U(x, y) = [x^{\frac{1}{2}} + y^{\frac{1}{2}}]^2$, with prices initially set at $p_x = 2$ and $p_y = 3$, a utility-maximizing consumer has $m = 30$ to spend. Confirm each of the following statements.

(a) The marginal utilities of goods X and Y are $MU_x = x^{-\frac{1}{2}}[x^{\frac{1}{2}} + y^{\frac{1}{2}}]$ and $MU_y = y^{-\frac{1}{2}}[x^{\frac{1}{2}} + y^{\frac{1}{2}}]$.

(b) The marginal rate of substitution, $MRS = \left(\frac{y}{x}\right)^{\frac{1}{2}}$.

(c) The income expansion path may be written $y = \frac{4}{9}x$.

(d) The utility-maximizing consumption bundle $(x^*, y^*) = (9, 4)$, and the consumer derives a utility of 25 from consuming it.

(e) A cost-minimizing consumer who purchases the bundle $(x^*, y^*) = (9, 4)$ must have a minimum acceptable utility, $V = 25$.

Exercise X9.33 shows that the expenditure function and indirect utility functions are inversely related. If we take an amount of money, m, and calculate the maximum possible utility, $V = V(m)$, that someone might generate from it, and then require that person to spend the least amount of money possible, E, while achieving the original level of utility, $V(m)$, then $E[V(m)] = m$, and the expenditure will be the original sum of money.

This is a rather technical implication of the argument that resource allocation is efficient, in two senses, which we first met in Chapter 6. Firstly, resource allocation is *technically* efficient. Taking the input resource to be money, it is impossible to generate more utility without having more money available. We can be certain that the constraint – whether the utility constraint for an expenditure-minimizing consumer, or the budget constraint for a utility-maximizing consumer – will be binding. Secondly, it is *economically* efficient. It is impossible to reallocate expenditure, buying an alternative consumption bundle that costs as much as the chosen bundle, and thereby to increase the level of utility. The condition that the marginal rate of substitution is equal to the price ratio for this pair of goods must be satisfied.

9.4 The Hicks decomposition for a CES utility function

We showed in Chapter 8 that the effect of a price change on the Marshallian, or ordinary, demands can be split into two components: a substitution effect, which is the change in Hicksian, or compensated, demands; and an income effect, which reflects the change in the affordability of goods. We now analyse this decomposition for CES utility functions, as defined in Expression 9.2. We firstly rewrite Expression 8.16 as:

$$\frac{\partial x^M(p_x, p_y, m)}{\partial p_x} = \frac{\partial x^H(p_x, p_y, U_0)}{\partial p_x} - x^M(p_x, p_y, m) \cdot \frac{\partial x^M(p_x, p_y, m)}{\partial m} \quad [9.23]$$

$\boxed{\text{Total effect}} \qquad \boxed{\text{Substitution effect}} \qquad \boxed{\text{Income effect}}$

9.4.1 The total effect

We stated the Marshallian demand, $x^M : x^M(p_x, p_y, m) = m\left\{ \dfrac{p_x^{-\frac{1}{1-a}}}{p_x^{-\frac{a}{1-a}} + p_y^{-\frac{a}{1-a}}} \right\}$, in Expression 9.16a. To obtain the derivative, $\frac{\partial x^M}{\partial p_x}$, it will be helpful to rewrite x^M as a product of two functions, f and g:

$$x^M(p_x, p_y, m) = f(p_x) \cdot g(p_x) : f(p_x) = m\left(p_x^{-\frac{1}{1-a}}\right); g(p_x) = \left(p_x^{-\frac{a}{1-a}} + p_y^{-\frac{a}{1-a}}\right)^{-1} \qquad [9.24]$$

Expression 9.24 indicates how we might apply the product and chain rules of differentiation:

Power rule

Chain rule: power rule applied to expression in brackets

Chain rule: differentiate content of bracket *wrt* p_x

$$\frac{df}{dp_x} = -\frac{m}{1-a}\left(p_x^{-\frac{1}{1-a}-1}\right); \quad \frac{dg}{dp_x} = -\left(p_x^{-\frac{a}{1-a}} + p_y^{-\frac{a}{1-a}}\right)^{-2} \cdot \left(-\frac{a}{1-a}p_x^{-\frac{a}{1-a}-1}\right)$$

Definition of product rule

$$\frac{dx^M}{dp_x} = \frac{df}{dp_x} \cdot g(p_x) + f(p_x) \cdot \frac{dg}{dp_x}$$

Substitute from definitions

'+' sign since product of two negative factors

$$= -\frac{m}{1-a}\left(p_x^{-\frac{1}{1-a}-1}\right)\left(p_x^{-\frac{a}{1-a}} + p_y^{-\frac{a}{1-a}}\right)^{-1} + m\left(p_x^{-\frac{1}{1-a}}\right)\left(p_x^{-\frac{a}{1-a}} + p_y^{-\frac{a}{1-a}}\right)^{-2} \cdot \left(\frac{a}{1-a}p_x^{-\frac{a}{1-a}-1}\right)$$

Extract common factor

What is left after common factor removed

$$= \frac{m}{1-a}\left(p_x^{-\frac{1}{1-a}-1}\right)\left(p_x^{-\frac{a}{1-a}} + p_y^{-\frac{a}{1-a}}\right)^{-1}\left\{-1 + ap_x^{-\frac{a}{1-a}}\left(p_x^{-\frac{a}{1-a}} + p_y^{-\frac{a}{1-a}}\right)^{-1}\right\}$$

Simplify index

Extract factor $\left(p_x^{-\frac{a}{1-a}} + p_y^{-\frac{a}{1-a}}\right)^{-1}$ from braces

$$= \frac{m}{1-a}\left(p_x^{-\frac{2-a}{1-a}}\right)\left(p_x^{-\frac{a}{1-a}} + p_y^{-\frac{a}{1-a}}\right)^{-2}\left\{-\left(p_x^{-\frac{a}{1-a}} + p_y^{-\frac{a}{1-a}}\right) + ap_x^{-\frac{a}{1-a}}\right\}$$

Collect terms

$$= \frac{m}{1-a}\left(p_x^{-\frac{2-a}{1-a}}\right)\left(p_x^{-\frac{a}{1-a}} + p_y^{-\frac{a}{1-a}}\right)^{-2}\left\{-(1-a)p_x^{-\frac{a}{1-a}} - p_y^{-\frac{a}{1-a}}\right\}$$

Extract factor $-(1-a)$ from braces

$$= -m\left(p_x^{-\frac{2-a}{1-a}}\right)\left(p_x^{-\frac{a}{1-a}} + p_y^{-\frac{a}{1-a}}\right)^{-2}\left\{p_x^{-\frac{a}{1-a}} + \left(\frac{1}{1-a}\right)p_y^{-\frac{a}{1-a}}\right\} \qquad [9.25]$$

Expression 9.25 is the rate of change of the ordinary demand, x^M, as the price, p_x, changes while the other parameters are held constant. This is the total effect of a price change, and we see that it has a negative sign: any increase in price causes a decrease in demand. This is consistent with all goods being normal when there is a CES utility function.

9.4.2 The substitution effect

The substitution effect is here the partial derivative, $\frac{\partial x^H}{\partial p_x}$. We stated the Hicksian demand,

$$x^H : x^H(p_x, p_y, U_0) = U_0 \left\{ \frac{p_x^{-\frac{a}{1-a}}}{p_x^{-\frac{a}{1-a}} + p_y^{-\frac{a}{1-a}}} \right\}^{\frac{1}{a}}$$ in Expression 9.19. Note that the forms of the

Hicksian and the Marshallian demand functions are very similar. Our calculations are therefore much the same as when calculating the substitution effect.

By yourself

X9.35 Confirm that:

(a) $x^H = f(p_x) \cdot g(p_x)$, where $f(p_x) = U_0 \left(p_x^{-\frac{1}{1-a}} \right)$ and $g(p_x) = \left(p_x^{-\frac{a}{1-a}} + p_y^{-\frac{a}{1-a}} \right)^{-\frac{1}{a}}$.

(b) $\frac{df}{dp_x} = -\frac{U_0}{1-a} \left(p_x^{-\frac{2-a}{1-a}} \right)$ and $\frac{dg}{dp_x} = \frac{1}{1-a} p_x^{-\frac{1}{1-a}} \left(p_x^{-\frac{a}{1-a}} + p_y^{-\frac{a}{1-a}} \right)^{-\frac{1+a}{a}}$.

(c) $\frac{\partial x^H}{\partial p_x} = -\frac{U_0}{1-a} \left(p_x^{-\frac{2-a}{1-a}} \right) \cdot \left(p_y^{-\frac{a}{1-a}} \right) \cdot \left(p_x^{-\frac{a}{1-a}} + p_y^{-\frac{a}{1-a}} \right)^{-\frac{1+a}{a}}$. [*Note:* You will need to apply the product rule, and then to simplify the expression.]

(d) If $U_0 = m \left(p_x^{-\frac{a}{1-a}} + p_y^{-\frac{a}{1-a}} \right)^{\frac{1-a}{a}}$, then:

$$\frac{\partial x^H}{\partial p_x} = -\frac{m}{1-a} \left(p_x^{-\frac{2-a}{1-a}} \right) \cdot \left(p_y^{-\frac{a}{1-a}} \right) \cdot \left(p_x^{-\frac{a}{1-a}} + p_y^{-\frac{a}{1-a}} \right)^{-2}. \qquad [9.26]$$

(e) $\frac{\partial x^H}{\partial p_x} < 0$.

(f) Subtracting Expression 9.26 from Expression 9.25:

$$\frac{\partial x^M}{\partial p_x} - \frac{\partial x^H}{\partial p_x} = -m \left(p_x^{-\frac{2}{1-a}} \right) \cdot \left(p_x^{-\frac{a}{1-a}} + p_y^{-\frac{a}{1-a}} \right)^{-2}. \qquad [9.27]$$

With the forms of the Marshallian and Hicksian demand functions being similar, it is perhaps not surprising that the form of their derivatives should also be very similar. Indeed, in Exercise X9.35f we show that they are identical apart from one term, which, if the Hicks decomposition holds, will be the income effect. The negative value of the derivative confirms that, as expected, the change in demand, x^H, resulting from the substitution effect, which reflects a change in relative prices, is always in the opposite direction to the change in the price, p_x.

9.4.3 The income effect and the decomposition

We have predicted that Expression 9.27 represents the income effect. We define the income effect as the rate of change in consumption resulting from the change in real income associated with a price change. In Expression 9.23, we write it as $-x^M(p_x, p_y, m) \cdot \frac{\partial x^M}{\partial m}$.

By yourself

X9.36   Confirm that:

(a) $\dfrac{\partial x^M}{\partial m} = \left(p_x^{-\frac{1}{1-a}} \right) \cdot \left(p_x^{-\frac{a}{1-a}} + p_y^{-\frac{a}{1-a}} \right)^{-1}$;

(b) $-x^M \cdot \dfrac{\partial x^M}{\partial m} = -m\left(p_x^{-\frac{2}{1-a}} \right) \cdot \left(p_x^{-\frac{a}{1-a}} + p_y^{-\frac{a}{1-a}} \right)^{-2}$;   [9.28]

(c) and $\dfrac{\partial x^H}{\partial p_x} - x^M \cdot \dfrac{\partial x^M}{\partial m} = \dfrac{\partial x^M}{\partial p_x}$.

The actual decomposition, given the preliminary work, turns out to be quite trivial We concentrate on interpretation of the factor $\left\{ p_x^{-\frac{a}{1-a}} + \left(\frac{1}{1-a} \right) p_y^{-\frac{a}{1-a}} \right\}$, which we placed in braces in Expression 9.25, and which demonstrates the decomposition of the total effect. The term $p_x^{-\frac{a}{1-a}}$ comes from the income effect as set out in Expression 9.27, while the $\left(\frac{1}{1-a} \right) p_y^{-\frac{a}{1-a}}$ comes in the substitution effect, as set out in Expression 9.26. Otherwise, these expressions are identical.

The size of the substitution effect relative to the income effect is therefore given by the ratio:

$$\left(\frac{1}{1-a} \right)\left(\frac{p_x}{p_y} \right)^{\frac{a}{1-a}}$$ [9.29]

It follows that there is a large substitution effect relative to the income effect if the relative price $\frac{p_x}{p_y}$ is large, in which case the consumer purchases a bundle with more of good Y than of good X. In this case, increasing the price, p_x, leads to a relatively large change in the expenditure share of good X through substitution. The substitution effect will also be relatively large when $1 - a$ is close to zero, so that a is close to 1. We have seen that as a increases, the curvature of indifference decreases, so a small change in relative price leads to a larger movement along the indifference curve.

By yourself

X9.37   For each of the following utility functions, obtain the income and substitution effects. [*Note:* You can treat all of these as CES utility functions, with the last three being special cases.] The value of parameter a in each is: (a) 0.5; (b) -1; (c) 0; (d) 1; and (e) undefined ($-\infty$).

(a) $U(x, y) = [x^{\frac{1}{2}} + y^{\frac{1}{2}}]^2$;   (b) $U(x, y) = [x^{-1} + y^{-1}]^{-1}$;   (c) $U(x, y) = x^{0.5} y^{0.5}$;

(d) $U(x, y) = x + y$;   (e) $U(x, y) = \min[x, y]$.

X9.38   We define the Hicks decomposition of the change in the ordinary demand, x^M, following a change in price p_y as:

$$\frac{\partial x^M(p_x, p_y, m)}{\partial p_y} = \frac{\partial x^H(p_x, p_y, U_0)}{\partial p_y} - y^M(p_x, p_y, m) \cdot \frac{\partial x^M(p_x, p_y, m)}{\partial m}$$ [9.30]

For a consumer with a CES utility function, maximizing utility in the usual way, show that:

(a) The total effect, $\dfrac{\partial x^M(p_x, p_y, m)}{\partial p_y} = \frac{a}{1-a} m\left(p_x p_y \right)^{-\frac{1}{1-a}} \left(p_x^{-\frac{a}{1-a}} + p_y^{-\frac{a}{1-a}} \right)^{-2}$.   [9.31]

(b) The substitution effect, $\dfrac{\partial x^H(p_x,p_y,m)}{\partial p_y} = \frac{1}{1-a}\, m\Big(p_x p_y\Big)^{-\frac{1}{1-a}}\Big(p_x^{-\frac{a}{1-a}}+p_y^{-\frac{a}{1-a}}\Big)^{-2}.$ [9.32]

(c) The income effect, $-y^M(p_x,p_y,m)\dfrac{\partial x^M(p_x,p_y,m)}{\partial m} = -m\Big(p_x p_y\Big)^{-\frac{1}{1-a}}\Big(p_x^{-\frac{a}{1-a}}+p_y^{-\frac{a}{1-a}}\Big)^{-2}.$ [9.33]

(d) The substitution effect is always positive, and the income effect is always negative.

(e) The total effect is always less than the substitution effect.

(f) The total effect is positive if $a > 0$, and negative if $a < 0$.

In Expression 9.30, we differentiate demands with respect to the price p_y, which changes, holding price p_x constant. We also rely on the argument in Section 8.3.2 that the rate of change of necessary expenditure, $\frac{\partial E}{\partial p_y} = y^M(p_x, p_y, m)$.

We already know that both goods are normal. As the amount of money to finance consumption, m, increases, demand for both goods increases, in proportion to the increase in m. We also know that the substitution effect always leads to a reduction in the Hicksian demand for the good that has become relatively more expensive and an increase in the Hicksian demand for the good that has become less expensive. So, if the price p_y increases, we expect the demand $x^H(p_x, p_y, U_0)$ to increase, but demand $y^H(p_x, p_y, U_0)$ to decrease.

The nature of the total effects of a price change depend on the value of parameter a. In Exercise X9.34, we confirmed that when $a > 0$, so that the substitution effect is relatively large, if price p_y increases, then the Marshallian demand, $x^M(p_x, p_y, m)$ increases, while $y^M(p_x, p_y, m)$ decreases. However, if $a < 0$, then the substitution effect is relatively small, and the relatively large income effect means that the Marshallian demand for both goods falls.

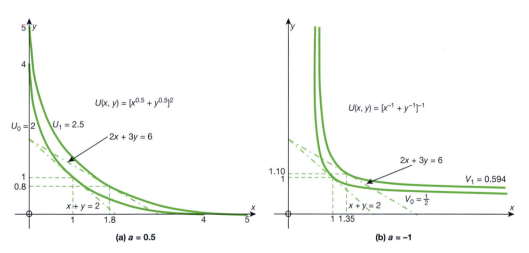

Figure 9.2 Effects of price changes

By yourself

X9.39   In Figure 9.2, we illustrate the effect of a price change on the Marshallian demands, $x^M(p_x, p_y, m)$. In both panels, $m = 2$, and initially $p_x = p_y = 1$, with p_x falling to $\frac{2}{3}$. In Figure 9.2a, the utility function is $U : U(x, y) = [x^{0.5} + y^{0.5}]^2$; while in Figure 9.2b, the utility function is $V : V(x, y) = [x^{-1} + y^{-1}]^{-1}$.

(a) Confirm that the budget constraint is initially $x + y = 2$, but that after the price change it may be written $2x + 3y = 6$.

(b) Use Expression 9.16 to calculate the ordinary demands before and after the price change.

(c) Confirm that when $a = 0.5$, the consumer's indirect utility increases from 2 to 2.5, while when $a = -1$, indirect utility increases from 0.5 to 0.606 (approximately).

A consumer for whom $a = 0.5$ is much more able to substitute one good for another after a price change. We expect the change in the composition of the most affordable consumption bundle following a price change to be greater when $a > 0$ than when $a < 0$. We have already said that for values of a close to 1, the goods are very good substitutes; and that when a is large but negative, the goods are complements. We can now classify all pairs of goods according to the value of the parameter a:

- For $a < 0$, we find $\frac{\partial x^M}{\partial p_x}, \frac{\partial y^M}{\partial p_x} < 0$; and $\frac{\partial x^M}{\partial p_y}, \frac{\partial y^M}{\partial p_y} < 0$. The demand for both goods decreases when the price of either good increases, and so the goods are a pair of *gross complements*.

- For $a > 0$, we find $\frac{\partial x^M}{\partial p_x} < 0, \frac{\partial y^M}{\partial p_x} > 0$; and $\frac{\partial x^M}{\partial p_y} > 0, \frac{\partial y^M}{\partial p_y} < 0$. As the price of one good increases, demand for it falls, but demand for the other good increases. The goods form a pair of *gross substitutes*.

By yourself

X9.40   For Cobb–Douglas preferences, we write the utility function, $U : U = x^{0.5} y^{0.5}$. Confirm that $\frac{\partial y^M}{\partial p_x} = 0 = \frac{\partial x^M}{\partial p_y}$, so that the goods lie on the boundary between gross complements and gross substitutes.

X9.41   For a pair of *net complements*, $\frac{\partial x^H}{\partial p_x}, \frac{\partial y^H}{\partial p_x} < 0$; and $\frac{\partial x^H}{\partial p_y}, \frac{\partial y^H}{\partial p_y} < 0$, so that as the price of one good increases, the Hicksian demands for both goods decrease. Assuming that there are only two goods in the consumption bundle, explain why it is impossible for them to form a pair of net complements.

9.5   The elasticity of substitution

We define the composition, g_S, of consumption bundle, S, as $g_S = \frac{y_S}{x_S}$, so that g is simply the ratio of the goods in the bundle. In Figure 9.3, we illustrate the values of g for consumption bundles S and T, which lie on the same indifference curve, as the slopes of the lines OS and OT. With bundle S containing less of good X and more of good Y than bundle T, $g_S > g_T$.

As before, we define the marginal rates of substitution as the gradient of a tangent to the indifference curve. The indifference curve is steeper at S than at T, so $MRS_S < MRS_T$ (remembering that indifference curves are downward-sloping).

We see in Figure 9.3 that as we move along an indifference curve, the change in the marginal rate of substitution, MRS, is associated with a change in the composition of the

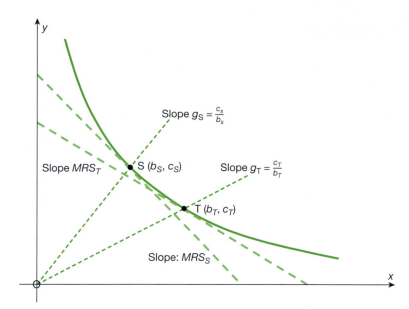

Figure 9.3 The elasticity of substitution

consumption bundle, g. Following the definition in Chapter 5, the elasticity of substitution, σ, is a measure of responsiveness of the composition, g, to a change in MRS, the marginal rate of substitution of the consumption bundle, while holding utility constant. Using the point elasticity definition, we write:

> **Elasticity of substitution** The proportional change in the composition of a bundle that results from a small proportional change in the marginal rate of substitution.

$$\sigma = \frac{dG}{dMRS} \cdot \frac{MRS}{G} \qquad [9.34]$$

With well-behaved preferences, the elasticity of substitution will always be greater than zero. In Figure 9.3, we have assumed that the indifference curve will be downward-sloping and convex, $MRS_S < MRS_T < 0$. The total change, $\Delta MRS = MRS_T - MRS_S > 0$. The proportionate change, $\frac{\Delta MRS}{MRS_S} = \frac{MRS_T - MRS_S}{MRS_S} < 0$. In the same way, $g_S > g_T > 0$. So the change, $\Delta g = g_T - g_S < 0$, and the proportionate change, $\frac{\Delta g}{g_S} = \frac{g_T - g_S}{g_S} < 0$. Writing the elasticity of substitution, σ, as the ratio of these proportionate changes:

$$\sigma = \frac{\Delta g}{g_s} \bigg/ \frac{\Delta MRS}{MRS_s} \qquad [9.35]$$

Expression 9.35 is the measure of arc elasticity, which converges to the point elasticity in Expression 9.34 as $\Delta MRS \to 0$. We have written it as a ratio of two negative numbers, and so $\sigma > 0$.

By yourself

X9.42 Consider the Cobb–Douglas utility function, $U(x, y) = x^{\frac{1}{2}} y^{\frac{1}{2}}$. Calculate the MRS in terms of the ratio, $\frac{y}{x}$, and hence obtain an expression for $g\left(\frac{y}{x}\right)$. Show that the elasticity of substitution $\sigma = 1$.

X9.43 Suppose that the elasticity of substitution $\sigma = 0$. What do you infer about the effect of a change in MRS on the composition, g, of the consumption bundle? What can you say about goods for which $\sigma = 0$?

(Continued)

X9.44   Suppose that the elasticity of substitution $\sigma \rightarrow \infty$. What do you infer about the effect of a change in *MRS* on the composition, *g*, of the consumption bundle? What can you say about goods for which $\sigma \rightarrow \infty$?

X9.45   Consider the general CES utility function, $U : U(x, y) = [x^a + y^a]^{1/a}$. By calculating *MRS* in terms of the ratio, $\frac{y}{x}$, show that the elasticity of substitution, $\sigma = \frac{1}{1-a}$. Obtain the value of σ when $a = 1$ and as $a \rightarrow -\infty$. Explain why these calculations are consistent with the arguments that you developed in Exercises X9.43 and X9.44.

X9.46   Using the definition of the Hicksian demands in Expression 9.19, show that $g^H = \frac{y^H}{x^H} = [\frac{p_x}{p_y}]^{\frac{1}{1-a}} = -MRS^{\frac{1}{1-a}}$. Confirm that for the Hicksian demands, the elasticity of substitution, $\sigma = \frac{1}{1-a}$.

X9.47   Given that in X9.46 the income expansion path is linear, explain why the effect of a price change on both the Hicksian and the Marshallian demands across a group of consumers will depend on the total sum of money used to finance consumption, and not on its distribution.

Given the restriction $a \leq 1$, the elasticity of substitution for a CES utility function will never be negative, which is consistent with preferences being well behaved. If the value of *a* is close to 1, then the elasticity of substitution will be very large, which is consistent with the goods being close substitutes; but if *a* is negative and large, the value of the elasticity will be close to zero, which is consistent with the goods being close complements. The elasticity of substitution is therefore an index of the ease with which one good can be substituted for another.

9.6   Conclusions

All of the members of the family of CES utility functions represent well-behaved preferences, and we have been able to describe their properties in some detail. While the analysis in this chapter has been more reliant on mathematical tools than that in earlier chapters, we have been able to explain our formal results using methods that are largely intuitive. For example, the elasticity of substitution determines the shape of indifference curves. The indifference curves determine both the Marshallian and Hicksian demand functions, and also the strength of the substitution and income effects, and therefore enable us to classify goods as pairs of substitutes or pairs of complements.

Having acknowledged that our analysis in this case has been much more dependent on the use of mathematics than before, it is reasonable to point out that we have nevertheless been able to derive all of these technical results using a very limited range of mathematical tools. More advanced mathematical techniques would enable us to derive rather more general, but also rather more abstract, results. By concentrating on the behaviour of a single family of utility functions, which is used very widely within economic theory, we have been able to apply the standard theory of resource allocation for a consumer who chooses either the most-preferred, affordable consumption bundle or else the cheapest, acceptable bundle. We have taken our analysis beyond the simple derivation of demand functions, identifying how this consumer will respond to changes in prices and incomes.

This is as much as we need to do in developing the standard theory for consumers' resource allocation. However, it is not the end of our use of the techniques that we have developed here. We shall next apply them in Part III to the resource allocation decisions of businesses, and we shall also use them in Parts V and VI. Now that we have derived all of the standard results – especially the Marshallian and Hicksian demand functions, the indirect utility function and the expenditure function – we shall not need to derive them again in future. Instead, we can simply quote these results, reducing the volume of calculation that is required and concentrating on the development of economic analysis.

Summary

We have derived the algebraic properties of the CES family of functions, confirming that they are all homogeneous of degree 1, so that the level of utility that a consumer generates is a linear function of the amount of money available to finance consumption. We have shown that the underlying preferences are well behaved, and so have been able to calculate the income expansion path, from which we have been able to derive both the Marshallian and Hicksian demand functions for these utility functions. From these, we have been able to confirm that goods are normal, so that all demands increase with income. We have completed the Slutsky decomposition, demonstrating the relative importance of the income and substitution effects in price changes; and we have finished by thinking about how to interpret the curvature parameter, a, and its implication for the relationship between changes in demand with price changes for the two goods. For values of $a < 0$, the goods are complements, with their demands responding to a price change by moving in the same direction; while for values of $a > 0$, the good are substitutes, with their demands responding to a price change by moving in opposite directions.

Here are some important results for the utility function $U = [x^a + y^a]^{1/a}$:

- Marginal utility: $MU_x = \left(\dfrac{U(x,y)}{x}\right)^{1-a}$; $MU_y = \left(\dfrac{U(x,y)}{y}\right)^{1-a}$

- Marginal rate of substitution: $MRS = -\left(\dfrac{y}{x}\right)^{1-a}$

- Elasticity of substitution: $\sigma = \dfrac{1}{1-a}$

- Marshallian demands: $x^M = m\left\{\dfrac{p_x^{-\frac{1}{1-a}}}{p_x^{-\frac{a}{1-a}} + p_y^{-\frac{a}{1-a}}}\right\}$ and $y^M = m\left\{\dfrac{p_y^{-\frac{1}{1-a}}}{p_x^{\frac{a}{1-a}} + p_y^{\frac{a}{1-a}}}\right\}$

- Hicksian demands: $x^H = U_0\left\{\dfrac{p_x^{-\frac{a}{1-a}}}{p_x^{\frac{a}{1-a}} + p_y^{\frac{a}{1-a}}}\right\}^{\frac{1}{a}}$ and $y^H = U_0\left\{\dfrac{p_y^{-\frac{a}{1-a}}}{p_x^{\frac{a}{1-a}} + p_y^{\frac{a}{1-a}}}\right\}^{\frac{1}{a}}$

- Indirect utility: $V(p_x, p_y, m) = m\left[p_x^{-\frac{a}{1-a}} + p_y^{-\frac{a}{1-a}}\right]^{\left(\frac{1-a}{a}\right)}$

- Expenditure function: $E(p_x, p_y, U_0) = U_0\left[p_x^{-\frac{a}{1-a}} + p_y^{-\frac{a}{1-a}}\right]^{-\frac{1-a}{a}}$

- Hicks decomposition (for own price effect): $\dfrac{\partial x^M}{\partial p_x} = -\dfrac{m \cdot p_y^{\frac{a}{1-a}}}{p_x^2\left(p_x^{\frac{a}{1-a}} + p_y^{\frac{a}{1-a}}\right)^2}\left(\dfrac{p_y^{\frac{a}{1-a}}}{1-a} + p_x^{\frac{a}{1-a}}\right)$ (the first

  term in the final bracket represents the substitution effect, and the second term represents the income effect.)

Having demonstrated these standard results, we shall use them without proof in future examples.

Visit the companion website at **www.palgrave.com/mochrie** to access further teaching and learning materials, including lecturer slides and testbank, as well as guideline answers and student MCQs.

Resource allocation for firms

We now turn to the resource allocation decisions of firms as they undertake production, and as they compete with one another to make sales. Just as we developed an account of resource allocation for consumers in Part II, we shall now set out principles that should guide the behaviour of all firms. They should hold for the simple businesses considered in Part I – the market stalls, the cafés and the bakeries – but also for giant corporations, such as Google, Facebook, and Microsoft. Our analysis again involves the assumption that firms seek to maximize an objective, although with profit replacing utility, while imposing constraints on the extent to which this is possible.

We begin our account, in Chapter 10, by treating businesses as if their objective were simply to minimize the cost of producing any particular level of output. We develop the concept of a production function, which has similarities with the utility function of Chapter 5. Chapter 11 is devoted to developing solution techniques for firms' cost-minimizing problems. We use techniques developed in Chapter 8, setting a firm a fixed output target and then finding the levels of all inputs that the firm needs to hire. Given the price of hiring inputs, we obtain the necessary cost of producing a given output;

and allowing output to vary, we may define total cost as a function of output. In Chapter 12, we consider firms' ability to respond to changes in demand in both the 'long run' and the 'short run'. We distinguish these by assuming that in the long run businesses can alter the level of all inputs in the production process, while the short run is the time period in which use of some inputs is fixed. Throughout Chapters 10–12, we argue that businesses should use resources efficiently, in two senses:

- *technical efficiency*: no firm should be able to reduce its input use and maintain its output;
- *economic efficiency*: in the long run, when usage of all inputs can be varied, no firm should be able to change its input use *and* maintain its output *and* reduce its costs of production.

Efficiency and cost minimization form the support act in our analysis. They are important, but only in preparing for our discussion of *profit maximization*. Unless a firm is able to generate profits for its owners on a regular basis, it will cease to exist. In Chapter 13, we define profit as the difference between the revenue, which a firm earns from selling output, and its costs of production. For businesses, profit is good, more profit is better, and the largest possible profit is best.

It turns out that we cannot examine profit maximization without also knowing something about the structure of the market in which the firm operates. In Chapters 13 and 14, we concentrate on the example of market stalls, introduced in Chapter 1, for which the market environment matches the assumptions of *perfect competition* very closely. Chapter 13 examines the profit-maximizing behaviour of a single market stall. Chapter 14 ends our initial statement of the standard model, bringing together the behaviour of people and businesses. We calculate market supply and demand as functions of price for some special cases. On this basis, we are able to identify the equilibrium price and the quantity. But where in Chapter 2 we took potential buyers' *WTP* and potential sellers' *WTA* measures as given, in Chapter 14 we analyse what happens when profit-maximizing firms meet utility-maximizing people.

10

Production

We define the process of production in terms of microeconomic theory, emphasizing parallels between the generation of utility (in Part II) and the production of output (this chapter). Production uses inputs, which have to be combined to generate outputs; in this chapter, we set out principles that it would desirable for *production* processes to follow. We think about how to combine *technologies* – that is, different combinations of inputs – and identify those which are efficient relative to a given production target. As we did in the discussion of consumer's resource allocation, we derive conditions under which production is 'well behaved'. Where these conditions are met, we can identify a unique combination of inputs for which a firm can produce a target output at the lowest possible cost.

We then introduce the concept of the *production function*, which measures the maximum output achievable with any set of inputs. We define the *marginal product* of an input as the rate of change of output as use of that input increases. We then show that if the marginal products of all inputs are positive but decreasing, so that increasing use of a single input leads to higher output but at a decreasing rate, then the production function will be well behaved. We argue that these conditions are perfectly reasonable and should apply to every business.

Throughout the chapter, we emphasize similarities with the resource allocation problem facing people as consumers, especially as set out in Chapters 3–6. We move quickly through the discussion because so much of it describes in a new way material that is already familiar.

10.1 The terminology of production

At the beginning of Part II, we examined resource allocation in the context of individual decision making. We now turn to decision making by businesses. A certain amount of repetition seems inevitable. We are still dealing with the branch of economics traditionally called *price theory*, and our underlying objective is to understand the effects of changes in prices on behaviour. All that has altered is that our emphasis has shifted from people to businesses. Businesses choose freely both how much output they will produce and how they will use inputs to produce it. We simply assume in this chapter that there is a finite, maximum output that a business can produce, given its chosen production inputs.

Our first step is to set out what is generally meant in economic theory by a process of **production**. Just as we reduced people to consumers, interested only in purchasing a consumption bundle so as to maximize their utility, we now reduce businesses to **firms**, economic entities that hire inputs to produce a target output as cheaply as possible.

The only part of consumption that we can observe is the purchase of goods in the market. Acts of consumption, and the generation

Production The process by which a firm takes factor inputs and turns them into goods and services.

Firm A business entity; often a limited company.

of utility, are private. In contrast, firms use resources to hire production inputs in order to produce outputs, which they then bring to the market. We might say that consumers use goods as *inputs* into their own, private *production process*, with utility as the *output*. Knowing the inputs to the production process, either for a consumer or for a firm, we can calculate the achievable output.

Although there are parallels in the formal theories of resource allocation for consumers and firms, we have to make some important distinctions. For example, we defined consumption as involving the use of the goods and services after they are purchased. In our theory, there is nothing left, not even waste for recycling. In discussing production, we shall instead talk about **factors of production**, which firms have to hire. If we hire a car, at the end of the rental agreement we have to return the car, in good condition, to its owner. For the owner,

> **Factor of production**
> An asset hired by a firm in its production process.

the car is an asset; the rental agreement simply allows someone else to use it. Renting an asset is therefore different from buying a good, because there is not even a temporary transfer of ownership and the user's rights in terms of the agreement are strictly limited.

We shall say more about the nature of factors of production as we develop the theory. Here, we emphasize the nature of the most obvious factor input: the labour used in production processes. In most jurisdictions, no one has a right of property in another person. Slavery is illegal. A firm can hire workers to provide services, but it never owns them. Even in advanced economics, a very simple version of this hiring process can be seen in large cities. Every morning casual workers who are looking for a job will congregate in specified places. Potential employers, such as building contractors, will appear, announcing how many labourers they require. The workers may be hired for a day, for a week, even for a month. The deal is struck there and then. The contract may be informal, with no health insurance, no pension rights and no taxes being paid: just cash in hand at the end of the day. Even in this informal contract, the underlying asset – the person – is not being bought or sold, and the employer only benefits from that person's time and effort expended in work.[1]

Of course, most professionals have formal contracts that make it unnecessary to go through such a process. My own university does not wait to see how many students have turned up for an intermediate microeconomics lecture before deciding whether or not it is worthwhile hiring me for that day! At the end of the academic year, my contract does not terminate, requiring me to agree a new one with my employer. Throughout Part III, though, we will in effect assume that employment is casual, so that there is no ongoing contract of employment, but also no mutuality of obligation. Either the business or the worker can end the relationship at any time; moreover, just as the business is not obliged to assign work when none is required, so the worker is not required to take on any particular piece of work.

---

1   While such labour markets seem likely to clear, or indeed may often be characterized by excess supply, this may occur at a wage that is not socially acceptable. Many countries have defined minimum wage levels to prevent the exploitation of workers. As Anne-Marie Gardner explains in her essay in the online student essay bank, these remain controversial, in spite of substantial evidence that they have been beneficial for many recipients. Read Anne-Marie's essay on the companion website for this book, at **www.palgrave.com/mochrie.**

10.2 The process of production

We wish to develop a structure for firms' resource allocation decisions. Following the argument that led to the derivation of the most-preferred, affordable consumption bundle in Part II, we now emphasize the firm's cost of hiring the bundle of factor inputs used in production rather than in the composition of the bundle itself. We therefore define the firm's problem as being that of minimizing the cost of producing a target output, and so firstly we need to find the Hicksian, or compensated, demands for an expenditure-minimizing firm, and then, having solved that problem, we find the costs that the firm must pay.

In analysing resource allocation decisions in Chapters 6–9, where we treated the consumer as an expenditure minimizer, we needed to know the cost of buying different consumption bundles and the utility that the consumer could generate from them. This suggests that if we are able to identify how much it costs a firm to hire different input bundles, and provided we know how much output the firm can produce with each bundle, then it should be possible to identify the cheapest acceptable input bundle, whose cost will then be the amount that the firm must spend in order to reach a production target. Remember, though, that we required consumers' utility function to be well behaved. We shall argue that it is desirable for us to place similar restrictions on a firm's **production function**.

> **Production function** The relationship between inputs used and output.

For a consumer to solve the expenditure minimization problem, subject to an acceptability constraint, we needed:

- two goods, units of which could be purchased at fixed prices, and a fixed income, giving the acquisition cost;
- a preference relation over combinations of goods, or consumption bundles, that was well behaved; and
- a minimum acceptable value of utility, associated with a weakly preferred set, which formed a constraint on the resource allocation.

Given those assumptions, we were able to identify the cheapest, acceptable consumption bundle. We argued that for this consumption bundle, the acceptability constraint was just binding, and that for each good the ratio of marginal utility to price would be the same. Allowing for changing prices, we obtained the Hicksian demand functions.

10.2.1 The cost of production

We expect our model of production to have the same structure as our model of consumption. We have already introduced labour as a factor input in production, noting that firms have to hire it rather than to buy it. In the same way, we introduce a second factor input, capital input. For now, we shall simply assume that capital consists of financial assets that are lent to a firm so that it can engage in production, rather than materials that are used up in it, or even physical assets. If we think of a firm being set up for a particular purpose, perhaps running a major sporting event like the Olympic Games, then that firm will be dissolved after it has served its purpose. The owners of the capital will require its return, plus a fee for having advanced it.

> **Capital input** The monetary value of assets used in business.

Following the usual practice in economics, set in the 18th century, we shall call the hiring cost of labour its 'wage'. In the same way, we refer to the 'interest on capital'. The wage will simply be the payment made to a worker who provides an hour's labour. Interest will likewise be a payment to the owners of capital for its use in the business.

> **Labour input** The number of hours of effort directed to production activity.

We denote the total number of labour hours that the firm purchases, the **labour input**, as L, and the total financial value of its assets as K. The wage, w, is the price of labour; while the interest rate, r, represents the costs that the firm would have to pay to a bank to finance its ongoing activities. We then define an input bundle (K, L) and its associated acquisition cost:

$$C(K, L) = rK + wL \qquad\qquad [10.1]$$

While the symbols have changed, this is almost the same as the acquisition cost of a consumption bundle, as discussed in Chapter 3. If we fix the acquisition cost at C_0, then we can write the quantity of labour that the firm can hire as:

$$L = \frac{C_0 - rK}{w} \qquad\qquad [10.2]$$

This is a straight line with slope $-\frac{r}{w}$, the relative price of the two factor inputs. Again, this result should be familiar from Chapter 3. There we argued that any line with this expression had a constant acquisition cost. Following standard practice, we shall refer to the set of input bundles that has a constant acquisition cost as an **isocost line**. In Figure 10.1, we show some

> **Isocost line** All of the input combinations that can be hired for a set price.

isocost lines. Given that the hiring cost of every bundle on a line is the same, the higher the total acquisition cost, the further away from the origin the line will be, so that $C_5 > C_4 > C_3 > C_2 > C_1$. *The acquisition cost is the objective that the firm seeks to minimize.*

By yourself

X10.1   Confirm that, given input prices w for labour and r for capital, the acquisition cost A: $A(L, K) = wL + rK$ is weakly convex.

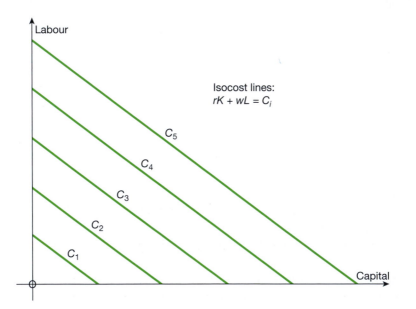

Figure 10.1 Isocost lines

10.2.2   Technologies

Having defined the hiring cost of any combination of input factors, and the isocost sets, we turn to the output that firms can produce. We assume that the maximum output, B, achievable using input combination (K, L) can be represented by means of a *production function*, so that $B = B(K, L)$. We would like the production function to have the same mathematical properties as the utility function, so that its contour map consists of downward-sloping, convex curves that never intersect or touch. The argument that we shall use to demonstrate this will be rather different from the argument about the form of preferences: while preferences give rise to nothing stronger than an ordering of consumption bundles, the output of a production process is a measurable quantity.

The concept of technology, as it is used in the analysis of the production function, is important here. We define the technology, τ, as the ratio of factor inputs, so that for input quantities (K, L), $\tau = \frac{K}{L}$. This is an old, but also rather abstract, use of the term. It captures the intensity of capital usage relative to labour usage, taking productive capacity of the factors as given, and is therefore the essence of the resource allocation decision of a firm, given that its objective is to reach some particular level of output. (During this piece of analysis, we should put to one side the meaning of 'technology' in everyday language.)

> **Technology** The relative intensity of use of input factors in production.

As defined here, the technology, τ, is a measure of the capital hired per worker employed by the firm. For high values of τ, technology is *capital intensive*; for low value, it is *labour intensive*. We can write:

$$K = \tau L \qquad\qquad [10.3]$$

This, as indicated in Figure 10.2, is the equation of a straight line that passes through the origin and has gradient τ. The more capital intensive the technology, the steeper the line representing it will be.

We assume that the firm has exactly two technologies available to it, τ_1 and τ_2, where $\tau_2 > \tau_1$, so that technology τ_2 is more capital intensive than technology τ_1. There is more capital employed per worker in τ_2 than in τ_1. Where these constant technology lines meet any isocost line, the total interest paid to the owners of the capital is a higher proportion of the total costs of production when a firm uses technology τ_2. Technology τ_1 is of course the more labour intensive one. In Figure 10.2, we show technology τ_1 as the line OA and technology τ_2 as the line OB.

We now assume that the technology is perfectly divisible. Firms can vary their usage of capital and labour by infinitesimally small amounts. The assumption is designed to rule out 'lumpiness' in the production process, such as we would find if the firm had to hire an integer number of workers or purchase a small number of relatively large machines. With perfectly divisible technologies, firms can vary usage of inputs by a very small proportion, so long as they maintain the required factor input ratio.

> **Perfect divisibility** Technology that allows infinitesimally small increments in factor use.

So long as technologies remain productive at the margin, so that by hiring more factors one always increases output, perfect divisibility ensures that firms can reach any level of output using any given technology. Slightly more formally, we can say that for any fixed

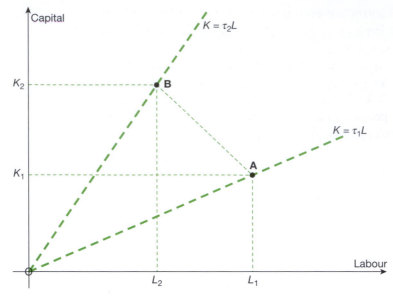

Figure 10.2 A choice of two technologies

technology, the production function is continuous. Small changes in factor usage lead to small changes in output, so that there are no jumps or discontinuities in production.

By yourself

X10.2   A firm has to choose between using technology 1, for which $K/L = \tau_1 = 0.5$, or technology 2, for which $K/L = \tau_2 = \frac{4}{3}$. The firm can produce output $B = 2L$ using the technology 1 and $B = 4L$ using technology 2. Both technologies are perfectly divisible.

(a) Sketch a diagram showing the input combinations associated with technologies 1 and 2. Indicate on the diagram which is the more capital intensive.

(b) Now indicate on the diagram the input combinations for which the firm might be able to produce its target output, $B = 1,200$. (Remember to calculate the firm's capital usage.)

(c) Suppose that the firm decides to hire the input combination $(K, L) = (350, 450)$. It then allocates 150 units of capital and 300 units of labour to production using technology 1, and uses the remaining 200 units of capital and 150 units of labour to produce output using technology 2. Calculate the quantity of output produced using each technology, and the firm's total output.

(d) Repeat the exercise in part (c) using these total input combinations:
   (i) $(K, L) = (375, 375)$, with 25% of output produced using technology 1; and
   (ii) $(K, L) = (325, 525)$, with 75% of output produced using technology 1.

(e) On your diagram, indicate the input combinations obtained in parts (c) and (d). Hence sketch the isoquant $X = 1,200$. [*Note*: An isoquant is a curve on which output stays constant as inputs vary. The isoquant connects the five output combinations that you have found in parts (b), (c) and (d).]

(f) Recalling our discussion of the properties of utility functions (in Section 5.2.1), what do you conclude from the shape of the isoquant about labour and capital?

In Exercise X10.2, it is easy to jump to the conclusion that since we have found five input combinations, all of which lie on the line with equation $3K + L = 1,500$, the whole of the line forms the **isoquant**, or constant output curve, for which output $B = 1,200$. This is not quite true, though. Remember that the firm has only two technologies available to it. In the exercise, the firm takes advantage of the perfect divisibility of the technologies to produce its target output, allocating a fraction of input factors to produce output using technology τ_1 and the remainder using technology τ_2. We call such combinations *hybrid technologies*.

> **Isoquant** A curve that shows input combinations for which output is constant.

The situation in Exercise X10.2 is similar to that shown in constructing point **C** in Figure 10.3. The firm produces $\frac{3}{5}$ of its target output using technology, τ_1, and resources **OG**, and $\frac{2}{5}$ using technology, τ_2, and resources **GB**. Without demonstrating the result, it should be clear that the line **OC** will lie between lines **OA** and **OB**, so that any hybrid technology will be at least as capital intensive as technology, τ_1, but no more capital intensive than technology τ_2. Then, for every hybrid technology, $\tau = f\tau_1 + (1 - f)\tau_2$, it must be that $K = \tau L$: $\tau_1 < \tau < \tau_2$. As in Figure 10.3, the firm can achieve its target output not just by choosing the input combinations **A** and **B**, but also by using any hybrid technology, such as **C**, which can be represented by a point on the line **AB**.

By yourself

X10.3 Suppose that the firm hires more labour than it uses at **A** or more capital than it uses at **B**. What would happen to production? Complete the isoquant passing through **A** and **B**.

The additional resources that the firm hires are redundant. At **A**, the firm is already using the most labour intensive technology. Hiring more labour does not allow the firm to increase its output. The same holds when hiring more capital than at **B**. The available technologies limit the firm's capacity to substitute one factor of production for another.

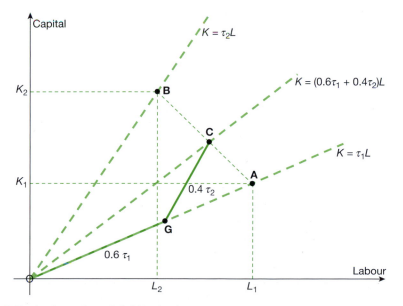

Figure 10.3 Production using a hybrid technology

You should be able to satisfy yourself that at point **A** there would be a corner in the isoquant, so that it becomes horizontal. Similarly, above **B**, the isoquant will be vertical. Although not smooth, the isoquant is (weakly) convex, and so we might expect the underlying production function to be well behaved.

10.2.3 Introducing new technologies

Assume that in the bakery industry there are two technologies, as discussed above. (In terms of Figure 10.3, a firm using the labour intensive technology, τ_1, will choose an input combination represented by a point on the flatter line; while a firm using the capital intensive technology, τ_2, will choose an input combination represented by a point on the steeper line.)

We suppose that technology **A** represents the inputs used by Handmade Bakers, an artisan bakery, whose production techniques require a relatively large proportion of manual handling. In Figure 10.4, the input combination that allows the artisan bakery to meet a particular production target, B_0, is shown at **A** (K_1, L_1). Its competitor, Batch Bakeries – which uses the most capital intensive technology, with most processes entirely mechanized – needs to hire the input combination **B** (K_2, L_2) to produce the same output, B_0.

These two firms have adopted the most extreme possible technologies. Now suppose that a new bakery, City Bakers, plans to enter the industry using a new technology, τ_3, rather than a hybrid combination of the existing technologies, τ_1 and τ_2. The new technology is more capital intensive than τ_1, and also more labour intensive than technology τ_2. We show it in Figure 10.4 as the line on which input bundles **C**, **D**, and **E** lie. We have already shown, though, that it might be possible to produce the same output as at **A** and **B** at any other point on the line **AB**.

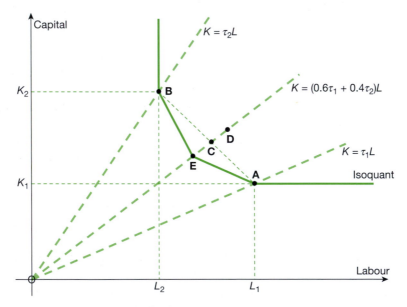

Figure 10.4 Production using a new technology

By yourself

X10.4   We have already confirmed that City Bakers might use the hybrid technology to produce its target output using input bundle **C**. Using this, explain why City might prefer to use the hybrid technology if the new technology would require the input bundle **D** to meet the production target. Similarly, explain why City might use the new technology if it could meet the production target using input bundle **E**.

We conclude that a new technology will be introduced only if it enables a firm to utilize resources more efficiently. If it is already possible for a bakery to produce output B_0 using the factor input combination at **C**, then it will be cheaper for the firm to use the existing technology given that to use the new technology would require the input combination at **D**, which uses more capital and labour. Firms use technologies so as to utilize resources efficiently. Given any particular input combination, it will not be possible to allocate their use across alternative technologies and increase output. This contributes further to the argument that isoquants will not be concave. In Figure 10.4, we see that the bakeries now have a choice between the three technologies, and so might achieve the production target, B_0, using one of the input combinations, **A**, **B** or **E**, or indeed some combination of them. The most technically efficient combinations then lie on the isoquant. If it hired more of any input, we would expect the firm to be able to meet its production target; but if between points **A** and **B** if it hired less, the firm would fail to meet its production target.

> **Technical efficiency** Production using an input combination such that using less of any input produces a fall in output.

10.3   Production functions and isoquants

We have introduced the production function and isoquants in Section 10.2, but now define them a little more carefully. We draw on the discussion in Section 5.3, where we showed that preferences are well behaved if they can be represented by a utility function for which all marginal utilities are everywhere decreasing. There we argued that if utility increases, but at a decreasing rate, as consumption of one good increases (while consumption of all other goods remains constant), then the utility function has a diminishing marginal rate of substitution. Given that we have defined the production function in this resource allocation problem as being analogous to the utility function in the consumer's problem, we might reasonably expect that if the rate of change of output with respect to output is positive, but decreasing, so that the partial derivatives $\frac{\partial B}{\partial K}$ and $\frac{\partial B}{\partial L} > 0$, but $\frac{\partial^2 B}{\partial K^2}$ and $\frac{\partial^2 B}{\partial L^2} < 0$, then the isoquants representing the production function will be downward-sloping and convex. That is, in mathematical notation: on the isoquant, $B = B_0$, $\frac{dK}{dL}\big|_{B=B_0} < 0$ and $\frac{d^2K}{dL^2}\big|_{B=B_0} > 0$. In Figure 10.5, we show this ideal form of isoquant: smooth, downward-sloping, and convex. We consider first the nature of the first and second partial derivatives of production functions, arguing that it is reasonable to expect the function to be concave. We then allow for firms to have access to a continuum of technologies rather than to a finite number. This ensures that isoquants are smooth.

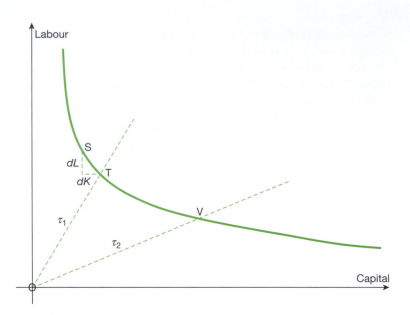

Figure 10.5 A smooth, downward-sloping isoquant

10.3.1   Marginal product functions

By yourself

X10.5   Suppose that a firm is in an industry where it needs no capital. Its production function can be written as $B = 20L^{0.5}$, where B is output and L is the firm's labour usage.
(a) Show that if the use of labour doubles, output increases by a factor of $\sqrt{2}$.
(b) Find the first and second derivatives, $\frac{dB}{dL}$ and $\frac{d^2B}{dL^2}$.
(c) Sketch graphs showing B and $\frac{dB}{dL}$ as a function of L and K.

X10.6   How realistic is it to suppose that a firm can undertake production without any capital? [*Note:* You may want to consider the examples of simple businesses that we introduced in Chapter 1.]

Total product The output that a firm can produce when use of only one input varies.

Marginal product The rate of change of output as usage of one input varies.

In some economics textbooks, where a firm has only one (variable) factor of production, as with labour in Exercise X10.5, the production function is called the **total product** *of the factor*. As in the theory of resource allocation for the consumer, our interest is less in the total product than in the *marginal product*, which we measure as the rate at which total product changes as factor usage changes.

In Exercise 10.5, the derivative $\frac{dB}{dL}$ is the **marginal product** of labour. Since that marginal product is positive, but decreasing, whenever the firm hires more labour, it does increase output, but the increase in output for a given increase in labour use becomes smaller and smaller as the firm hires more labour.

By yourself

X10.7   Suppose that a firm requires an input bundle of labour and capital (L, K), with its output given by the production function, $B = 20L^{0.5}K^{0.5}$.

(a) Show that if the use of labour, L, doubles, while the use of capital, K, remains constant, output increases by a factor of $\sqrt{2}$.

(b) Show that if the use of capital, K, doubles, while the use of labour, L, remains constant, output increases by a factor of $\sqrt{2}$.

(c) Using partial differentiation, find the marginal products of labour and capital, MP_L and MP_K.

(d) Confirm that the marginal product of labour is a decreasing function of labour usage, but an increasing function of capital usage; and that the marginal product of capital is a decreasing function of capital usage, but an increasing function of labour usage.

(e) Suppose that both capital and labour usage double. What is the effect on the firm's output, and on the marginal products of labour and capital?

Exercise X10.7 introduces the Cobb–Douglas production function; many of its mathematical properties should already be familiar from the discussion of the utility function that has the same form. We see that in this case the marginal products of labour and capital are both positive but decreasing. Were a firm to increase use of either factor, while leaving use of the other factor constant, its output would increase, but at a decreasing rate. This is very similar to the result we obtained in X10.5.

On the other hand, if we doubled the use of capital and labour so that the input bundle that the firm uses was twice the size that it was originally, then the firm would double its output, while continuing to produce output using the same technology as before, while the marginal products of capital and labour remained unchanged. At the margin, capital and labour remain equally productive. Looking at the production function, we can see that there is an interaction between capital and labour, and so as the usage of one factor increases, the marginal product of the other increases. With the Cobb–Douglas production function, the effects of proportionate changes in factor usage have exactly offsetting effects on the marginal products.

By yourself

X10.8   Consider the production functions:

(1) $X = K^{0.5} + L^{0.5}$;   (2) $Z = [K^{0.5} + L^{0.5}]^2$

(a) For each of these functions, obtain the marginal products of labour and capital.

(b) Using partial differentiation, confirm that for both functions the marginal product of labour is decreasing in labour usage; and that the marginal product of capital is decreasing in capital.

(c) Confirm that for function (1) the marginal product of labour remains constant as capital usage increases, but that for function (2) the marginal product of labour increases as capital usage increases.

(d) Suppose that usage of capital and labour doubled. For each production function, explain what would happen to output, to the marginal product of labour, and to the marginal product of capital.

We know from Chapter 9 that the production functions in Exercises X10.7 and X10.8 all have a constant elasticity of substitution, so that they are all homogeneous. The Cobb–Douglas form in Exercise X10.7 and the CES form in Example (2) in Exercise X10.8 are homogeneous of degree 1. Increasing labour and capital usage by the same proportion ϕ, the firm also increases its output by the proportion ϕ. The CES form in Example (1) of Exercise X10.8 is homogeneous of degree 0.5. If this firm increases capital and labour usage by the same proportion ϕ, then it will increase its output, but only by a proportion $\phi^{0.5}$. We now show that all three functions display diminishing marginal product, and that because of the effect on the marginal product of one factor of increasing usage of the other, it is possible for a production function both to display diminishing marginal product and to be linearly homogeneous.

10.3.2   Diminishing marginal product

In the two cases where the production functions are homogeneous of degree 1, the reduction in the marginal product of one factor resulting from a proportionate increase in the use of that factor is exactly offset by the increase in marginal product resulting from the same proportionate increase in the use of the other factor. In the case in which the function is homogeneous of degree 0.5, marginal product declines, because increasing the use of one factor has no effect on the marginal product of the other factor. In all three cases, the marginal products are decreasing functions of the variable factors.

By yourself

X10.9   Why might it be reasonable to expect the marginal product of both factors to be decreasing? [*Hint:* Remember that usage of the other factor is held constant, and that 'Too many cooks spoil the broth.']

X10.10   Suppose that a firm whose output, X, can be modelled using the Cobb–Douglas production function, $X : X(K, L) = AK^aL^{1-a}$, expands its activities while maintaining its technology. The parameter $a < 1$.

(a) Show that the marginal product of capital, $MP_K = \dfrac{\partial X}{\partial K} = \dfrac{aAL^{1-a}}{K^{1-a}} = \dfrac{aX}{K}$, and that the marginal product of labour, $MP_L = \dfrac{\partial X}{\partial L} = \dfrac{(1-a)AK^a}{L^a} = \dfrac{(1-a)X}{L}$.

(b) Confirm that both marginal products are decreasing functions of the variable factor.

X10.11   Suppose that with the CES production functions in X10.8, a firm hires only labour. How much output can it produce? How reasonable do you consider this to be?

X10.12   In terms of the discussion of substitutes and complements in Chapter 9, how would you define capital and labour in X10.8? What conclusions might we draw about desirable values of the elasticity of substitution?

Diminishing marginal product, unlike diminishing marginal utility, is an essential property of any production process. Exercise X10.9 suggests the following exercise. Suppose that the marginal product of labour in a bakery is increasing. Doubling the workforce, while holding the capital constant – and thus presumably keeping the bakery in the same building – more than doubles output. In a very large bakery, this may be perfectly reasonable as we increase the number of workers from one to two, or even from 100 to 200. But let us suppose that with 200 workers, every function in the bakery is being undertaken by its staff perfectly efficiently. If the number of workers is doubled again, to 400, there are now two people to do every job. The additional workers seem likely to be underemployed. Yet, for the marginal product of labour to increase (as we have assumed), these additional workers will cause output to increase more rapidly than employment. At this point, the assumption of constant, or indeed increasing, marginal product would be troubling. But let us press on with the assumption. Were there to be no restriction on the extent of increasing marginal product, a single, small bakery could carry on hiring more and more staff until it was able to supply the demand for bread for the whole world. To avoid this, we must insist for every production function that no marginal product can increase for all possible values of any input.

10.3.3   The marginal rate of technical substitution

Having established the rule of the diminishing marginal product, we replicate the argument of Chapter 5, where we introduced the marginal rate of substitution. We begin by noting that as we move from one input combination to another on a given isoquant, the change in output will be zero. For input combinations S and T in Figure 10.5, the bakery produces B_0, so the change in output $dB = 0$. As a result of this change in input usage, the firm hires more capital and less labour, so the change in capital usage $dK > 0$, while the change in labour usage $dL < 0$. The increase in capital leads to an increase in output, while the reduction in labour usage reduces output. For total output to remain constant, these two effects just balance.

In Chapter 5, we argued that the change in utility from a small change in consumption of that good is approximately equal to the product of the marginal utility and the change in consumption. Here we argue that the change in output resulting from a change in factor usage is the product of the change in usage of factor F, where $F = K, L$, and the marginal product, MP_F. Then the change in output B may be written:

$$dB = MP_K(K, L).dK + MP_L(K, L).dL = 0 \qquad [10.4]$$

In Expression 10.4, we evaluate the marginal products for a specific input bundle, (K, L). We can now rearrange the expression, obtaining:

$$MRTS_{KL} = \left.\frac{dL}{dK}\right|_{X=X_0} = -\frac{MP_K}{MP_L} \qquad [10.5]$$

This is almost the same as Expression 5.7, in which the marginal rate of substitution, *MRS*, is equal to the ratio of marginal utilities. Expression 10.5 is therefore the slope of the isoquant. We shall call it the marginal rate of technical substitution, because it relates to changes in the technology of production; in diagrams, we shall represent it as the slope of the isoquant. The minus sign in Expression 10.5 reminds us that the isoquant will slope downwards: since both marginal products are greater than zero, increasing factor usage leads to an increase in output.

> **Marginal rate of technical substitution** The rate at which one factor input must be substituted for another in order to maintain output.

10.3.4   A continuum of technologies

We shall demonstrate the desirability of assuming that firms are able to choose from an infinite variety of technologies by extending the argument of Section 10.2.3. We had developed the argument so that there were three technologies, τ_A, τ_B, and τ_C, available to a bakery wishing to produce output B_0. These were the (labour intensive) Artisan technology, the (capital intensive) Batch technology, and the (intermediate) Composite technology. A bakery would be able to choose input combinations A, B, or C, using only one of the

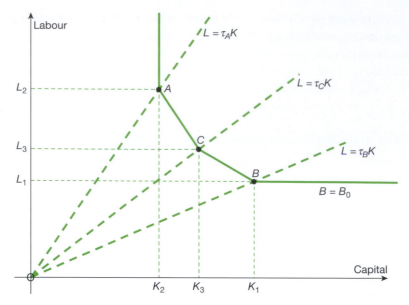

Figure 10.6 A finite range of technologies

technologies or some combination of them. In Figure 10.6, we have drawn in a convex shape joining these three input bundles. This shape will form the boundary of the feasible set, consisting of all input combinations that allow the firm to reach its target output, B_0.

> **By yourself**
>
> **X10.13** Explain why the straight-line segments are consistent with production for any given technology being homogeneous of degree 1.
>
> **X10.14** The convex shape has a vertical segment above point A and a horizontal segment to the right of point B. Explain briefly why this might occur. [*Hint:* Think about the range of technologies available to the firm.]

From Exercises X10.13 and X10.14, we conclude that:

- No firm will hire more than K_1 units of capital or L_2 units of labour.
- Any firm using an input combination that lies above or to the right of the convex shape to produce output B_0 could reduce inputs of either or both factor inputs without reducing output.
- Any firm that uses an input combination represented by a point below or to the left of the convex shape cannot produce output X_0 and so must increase input usage to meet its production targets.
- Production using some combination of factor inputs that lies on the convex shape between points A and B is technically efficient in the sense that the firm can only just meet its production target, B_0. We assume that the firm will restrict its choice to this set, given target output B_0.

Note that in Exercises X10.13 and X10.14 we have defined the isoquant passing through **A**, **B**, and **C** as the boundary of the feasible set. On this boundary, output is equal to the firm's target, so that production is technically efficient. We can define the set of inputs, S, for which production will reach its target:

$$S = \{(K, L): B(K, L) \geq B_0\} \tag{10.6}$$

The argument to this point assumes that each bakery has to choose from among a finite set of technologies. Just as we have assumed that each technology is perfectly divisible, we now suppose that there is a continuum of technologies, each imperceptibly different from the most similar alternatives, but that each is efficient in the sense that it cannot be synthesized more efficiently by a mixture of other technologies.

By yourself

X10.15 Suppose that bakeries can choose from a continuum of technologies, with each technology defined by a unique capital: labour ratio, $\tau : \tau_1 \leq \tau \leq \tau_2$. As in X10.2 and X10.3, bakeries can combine inputs using different technologies, with output, B, linear in capital usage, K, for all technologies.

(a) Using diagrams, demonstrate that it is impossible that firms might choose to use every available technology when there is a concave segment of an isoquant. Discuss why we should now expect isoquants to be smooth curves.

(b) Discuss how the technology index, τ, and the marginal rate of technical substitution change as production becomes more capital intensive.

Exercise 10.15 explores assumptions that are sufficient for the firm's feasible set to be well behaved. We have relied upon the assumptions that technology is perfectly divisible, and that there is a continuum of technologies, with the marginal product of all inputs positive, but decreasing, in which case all isoquants will be downward-sloping, smooth, and convex.

We illustrate this situation in Figure 10.7, which is very similar to Figure 6.5, in which we first presented the expenditure minimization problem for the consumer. There, we found

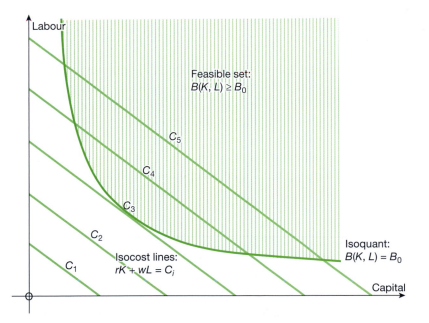

Figure 10.7 The cheapest feasible input combination

that the cheapest, acceptable consumption bundle was located at the point on the indifference curve associated with the minimum acceptable utility at which a constant expenditure line just touched the curve. Once again, we have an exactly analogous result. The isoquant that forms the boundary of the feasible set is the firm's production constraint: it must produce at least this output. By inspection, it appears that it is impossible for the firm to spend less than it would at point C_3, where the constant expenditure line just touches the constraining isoquant.

The remainder of this argument should be familiar. The slope of the constant expenditure line is the price ratio (from Expression 10.3), while the slope of the isoquant, the marginal rate of technical substitution, is the ratio of the marginal products (from Expression 10.5). We can write this as:

$$MRTS_{K,L} = -\frac{MP_K}{MP_L} = -\frac{r}{w} \qquad [10.7]$$

Rearranging Expression 10.7 slightly, we obtain the very useful variant of this equilibrium condition:

$$\frac{MP_K}{r} = \frac{MP_L}{w} \qquad [10.8]$$

Expression 10.8, tells us that, for both factors, as usage increases, the rate of increase of output divided by the cost of hiring additional factors is the same. In equilibrium, the firm should be indifferent about increasing spending on either factor by a small amount, because allocating money to purchase either resource would generate the same increase in output. This is very similar to the argument in Section 6.5, where we considered the expenditure-minimizing problem for a typical consumer.

10.4   Returns to scale

In effect, we introduced the concept of **returns to scale** in production when discussing the properties of Cobb–Douglas and constant elasticity of substitution production functions in Section 10.3. We noted that they are homogeneous: where the technology of production is held constant, so that $K = \tau L$, then, as a business expands or contracts its usage of inputs, there is a simple functional relationship between the size of the input bundle and the output. In general, if a production function $B = B(K, L)$ is homogeneous of degree r, then starting from a specific input bundle (K_0, L_0):

> **Returns to scale** A measure of the responsiveness of output to the scale of inputs.

$$B(\lambda K_0, \lambda L_0) = B(\lambda \tau L_0, \lambda L_0) = \lambda^r B(\tau L_0, L_0) \qquad [10.9]$$

We can relate the **scale of production** to the value of λ. We can think of the firm using a composite input consisting of a single unit of labour, and τ units of capital. We call this the standardized bundle **S**: $(\tau, 1)$. The scale of production is then the number of **S**-bundles that the firm hires. Initially, the firm hires L_0, but then changes the scale of production by a factor λ, so that it hires λL_0 instead. Doubling the scale of production would mean setting $\lambda = 2$, and so doubling the use of both labour and capital

> **Scale of production** Given constant technology, a measure of the extent of use of all input factors.

while reducing scale by 10% would mean setting $\lambda = 0.9$, and reducing use of labour and capital by 10%. In such changes, technology, expressed as the ratio of capital to labour usage, remains constant.

The returns to scale measure the responsiveness of output to changes in the scale of inputs. By assuming that technology remains constant, we have effectively made output a function of a single variable. In Section 10.3, we argued that each factor should have a diminishing marginal product, so that as usage of one factor increases while holding usage of all others constant, production would increase, but at a decreasing rate. For composite factors, this need not be the case. In considering examples of Cobb–Douglas and constant elasticity of substitution production functions in Exercises X10.7 and X10.8, we looked at two cases where the production functions were homogeneous of degree 1, so that the increase in output was always proportional to the increase in the scale of production. When the change in output is always proportional to the change in inputs, we say that returns to scale are constant.

To be slightly more formal in our definition, given technology, τ, so that $K_0 = \tau L_0$, the firm initially employs L_0 units of the standardized input, **S**, producing output $B(L_0) = B_0$. Increasing inputs by a factor λ, the firm hires $L_1 = \lambda L_0$ units of the standardized input, producing output, $B(L_1) = B_1 = \lambda^\rho B_0$, where ρ is the returns to scale of production. Where there is a linear relationship between inputs and outputs, $\lambda = \mu$ and $\rho = 1$. This is what we have assumed in much of our discussion. Note that in Exercise X10.8, case (1), the production function was homogeneous of degree 0.5. Output increases more slowly than inputs, and we say that the firm faces decreasing (or diminishing) returns to scale in production. Similarly if output increases more quickly than inputs, we say that the firm faces increasing returns to scale.

By yourself

X10.16 Show that if a production function is homogeneous of degree r, then the firm faces diminishing returns to scale if $r < 1$, constant returns to scale if $r = 1$, and increasing returns to scale if $r > 1$.

X10.17 Discuss the effect on our arguments about the creation of a hybrid technology if returns to scale were always decreasing.

10.5   Conclusions

This chapter has introduced the concepts necessary for us to be able to analyse the management of the production process of a firm. Firms hire inputs in order to undertake production, and we have argued that the rules that apply to consumers' resource allocation decisions also apply to firms. This is a very simple account. Given the very general nature of factors of production, which we shall discuss further in the next chapter, our assumptions have disregarded almost all of the problems that a business might face in reality. In particular, it might seem that we have introduced the concept of technology and then discarded it almost immediately. However, giving firms the ability to use hybrid technologies is sufficient to ensure that the production function is well behaved. The additional assumption of a continuum of technologies allows us to represent the production function using mathematical forms of the sort that we have used in solving constrained optimization problems for consumption. To that extent, it is a convenience, rather than being essential.

We assume in our modelling that businesses are able to allocate resources entirely costlessly. In reality, businesses spend considerable time and effort managing these decisions. Some economists argue that as well as labour and capital, businesses need to hire a third essential input: entrepreneurship. This additional factor enables businesses to solve resourcing problems more efficiently than competitors. Our discussion of new technologies has suggested that firms might seek to engage in process innovation by reducing the inputs of labour and capital required to produce additional output. One of the roles of the entrepreneurship input is to manage process innovation: it is probably more usual nowadays to think of entrepreneurship in terms of business formation and the development of entirely novel products. As we develop our argument, it will become clear that there is little role for such activity in the standard model, because of our assumption of perfect information.

Summary

We define a factor input combination used by a firm to produce output by an ordered list consisting of the quantities of the various factors that a firm might hire. Each factor input may be hired at a fixed price, so that the cost of any input bundle can be obtained by multiplying the quantity of each good by its price, and summing together these products.

The firm knows the maximum quantity of input that can be produced from any given input bundle. A firm with a fixed production target must hire an input bundle for which that level of production is feasible.

Where there are only two goods, it is possible to depict the feasible set by the area bounded from below by an isoquant, a curve showing all input combinations at which the firm can just meet its production target. The shape of the isoquant depends on the variety of technologies available for production, and the efficiency of hybrid technologies that can be created from them.

If we assume that there is a continuum of technologies and that there are no increasing returns to any factor of production, then every isoquant will be smooth, downward-sloping and convex. In such cases, the production function is well behaved.

The slope of an isocost line, on which the hiring cost of all input combinations is equal, is the relative factor input price.

We define the marginal product of a factor input as the rate of change of output when its usage increases (and use of all other factors remains constant). The marginal rate of technical substitution for any consumption bundle is then the ratio of marginal products and represents the slope of the isoquant passing through that bundle.

The firm minimizes the cost of producing its target output by choosing a factor input combination for which the relative factor input price equals the marginal rate of technical substitution.

Visit the companion website at **www.palgrave.com/mochrie** to access further teaching and learning materials, including lecturer slides and a testbank, as well as guideline answers and student MCQs.

Extension exercises

In Chapter 10, we have discussed the cost minimization problem facing a firm seeking to achieve a set production target. This is formally identical to the resource allocation problem for an expenditure-minimizing consumer. We now use CES production functions, obtaining factor demand and cost functions. In solving examples and problems, we can therefore use the results reported at the end of Chapter 9, reducing the volume of calculation that we need to perform.

By yourself

X10.18   Use the definition of homogeneity to confirm which of these productions function are homogeneous, stating the degree of homogeneity.
(a) $X = \min[cK, d(L - L_0)]$ (b) $X = sK + tL$ (c) $X = 50.\ln(K + L)$
(d) $X = K^a L^{1-a}$

X10.19   Sketch an isoquant map for the production function in X11.4a, and illustrate the output expansion path. Discuss how the technology of production changes as output increases. [*Hint:* Start by sketching the isoquants for the function $X = \min(cK, dL)$.]

X10.20   Define the marginal products of capital and labour for each of the production functions in X10.18, and – except for part (a) – the marginal rate of technical substitution.

X10.21   Suppose that production becomes more capital intensive as output increases. Draw a curve on a diagram that could represent the output expansion path, which illustrates the combination of factor inputs that the firm uses at different production levels. Show the marginal rate of substitution for at least three points on this path, and sketch possible indifference curves passing through them.

From our experience of using utility functions, we expect that a CES production function will be homogeneous, so that all indifference curves will have the same shape, each one mapping onto the others by a process of radial expansion. This means that where isoquants intercept a given line passing through the origin, the marginal rate of technical substitution will be the same for all isoquants. In Chapter 11, we use this result to show that if we find the cost-minimizing input combination for a given output, then we will have found the unique cost-minimizing technology for all firms that face those input prices.

We defined the conditions for a solution of this cost minimization problem in Section 10.3.4, summarizing them in Expression 10.7: that the marginal rate of technical substitution, or the ratio of marginal products, equals the ratio of factor input prices. When minimizing costs, the ratio of marginal products to input prices is the same for all factors.

11

Cost functions

In Chapter 10, we set out an economic model in which a firm might identify the least costly combination of factor inputs that enables it to meet a fixed production target. We now consider the minimum cost of production for any level of output. This gives us a function, the *total cost function*, whose value is the amount that a firm must spend, assuming that its use of factor inputs is both technically and economically efficient and that it can hire any quantity of factor inputs at a constant unit cost.

From the total cost of production, we obtain the *average cost function* (the cost per unit of output) and the *marginal cost function* (the

rate of change of total cost with respect to output). Average cost is useful in thinking about whether or not the firm is breaking even or making profit; marginal cost is important in determining whether the level of production should be changed to increase the firm's profitability. We shall examine how these are related to each other and also to the returns to scale in the production function, as defined in Chapter 10. We shall discuss the behaviour of cost functions for CES production functions. We shall finally observe that the presence of diseconomies of scale in production lead to eventually increasing average costs.

11.1 The cost of production

In this chapter, we develop the concept of the necessary costs of production, obtaining a firm's **cost function** in the context of the standard model of resource allocation. We

Cost function The least possible expenditure required to produce any level of output, given input prices.

continue to assume that firms, if they are to produce any output, have to hire two factor inputs, labour and capital, whose prices are wages and interest. The assumption of two factors of production allows us to present our analysis using diagrams: nonetheless, nothing within the structure of the argument compels us to limit our analysis to these two-factor inputs.

Recall our preliminary discussion in Chapter 10. We defined labour and capital as the inputs that a firm has to hire from people. Labour is perhaps the easier factor to understand, since it is the amount of time that people spend working. But even here, there is a considerable simplification. In effect, we assume that all workers are identical. In our bakery example, we consider the labour services provided by a master baker with 25 years of experience as comparable with those of an apprentice who has been employed for only a few weeks. We should note that, at the very least, we need to distinguish between skilled and unskilled labour; nevertheless, in this chapter we set all such distinctions aside.

Turning to the nature of capital, in the same way we pay no attention to the many subtleties that characterize the discussion of capital. We would normally expect a statement of the assets and liabilities of a business to include:

- fixed assets, such as buildings and machinery used in production;
- current assets, such as cash at the bank, payments due from trade debtors, and stocks of goods held for sale;
- current liabilities, such as overdraft financing, accrued charges for services already consumed (such as heat and light), and payments due to trade creditors;
- long-term debt finance, such as term loans drawn down on a bank, secured by a charge over heritable assets, such as land and buildings; and
- the share capital of the business, loosely defined as the amount invested in the firm by its founders, plus profits retained within the business.

Under this definition, capital is a liability within the firm's financing structure. Were the firm to cease trading, this would be the amount of money available to the owners after all other obligations have been met. In terms of our analysis, however, we should consider capital to be the amount of money needed to finance the business. Consider the example of trade credit. Many large businesses settle their bills to suppliers after 60 days. In effect, they expect suppliers to provide them with trade finance. Many firms often pay their taxes substantially in arrears, using tax authorities in a very similar way as another source of (short-term) funding. We shall therefore treat capital not just as the residual funds left after the sale of assets and the settlement of all debts but as the finance used to purchase company assets – both fixed assets, such as land and buildings, and the wide variety of raw materials, goods and services that are used up in production.

By yourself

X11.1   Using the definition above, why might we argue that workers who supply labour services also provide a business with short-term financing?

X11.2   If a firm becomes insolvent, it is unable to repay all of its debts. Given the accounting definition of equity capital as the residue returned to the owners after payment of debts, what is the capital of an insolvent business?

X11.3   In a legal definition, we might consider the owners of a business to be the people who have an entitlement to some share of the money left after the payment of all liabilities.
(1) If a business is structured as a *partnership*, then the partners are the owners, but have unlimited liability for the debts of the business.
(2) If a business is structured as a *limited company*, then the shareholders are the owners, but have limited liability for the debts of the business.
Discuss the different ways in which the owners of these businesses will be affected if an insolvency event occurs.

For an accountant or a lawyer, capital has a relatively complex definition. In our analysis it remains a simple but general concept. We simply acknowledge that it might take many forms, and be provided in many different ways. We shall also simplify the process of production, concentrating on the requirement that it involves the hiring of labour and capital inputs. In reality, production involves the purchase and processing of raw materials, the use of utilities (such as electricity and water), a range of administrative activities, and the purchase of services (such as property insurance and audit fees); for our analysis, though, these are simply intermediate inputs: goods that are purchased in order to produce the final output. This intermediate resource allocation problem, which relates to the efficient use of capital within the firm, will also be put aside as we simplify our analysis as much as possible.

We also do not consider activities that are designed to increase the value of the firm's output, such as marketing, advertising, and research and development. Later in the book, when we relax our assumptions about the nature of competition, we shall provide a rationale for producers' willingness to incur such costs. Our immediate task, though, is to complete the development of the standard model, returning to the assumptions of perfect competition introduced in Part I: specifically that the size of the firm is small, that products are uniform, and that decisions are taken with perfect information. Wherever these hold, there can be no role for marketing activity, for consumers know that every firm is producing goods of exactly the same quality. Nor can there be any role for product and process development activities, since a firm's many competitors will copy innovations immediately, and all firms will share equally in any revenue increase or cost reduction that might result.

11.1.1 Homogeneity and the output expansion path

Where the production function is homogeneous as the output varies, the firm will not change the technology that it uses. We demonstrate this in Figure 11.1, with the gradients of every isoquant being the same where they intersect any given straight line. Returning to the bakery example introduced in Chapter 10, we also illustrate in Figure 11.2 isoquants for a specific constant elasticity of substitution production function:

$$B_0 = \left[K^{0.5} + L^{0.5}\right]^2 \tag{11.1}$$

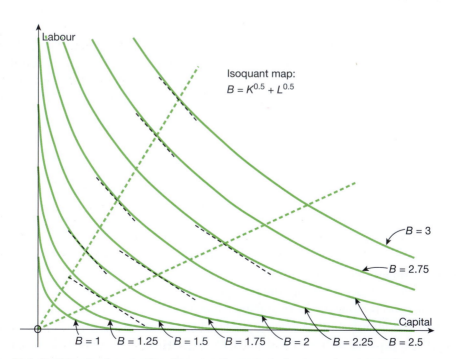

Figure 11.1 At all levels of production, firms use the same technology, given input prices

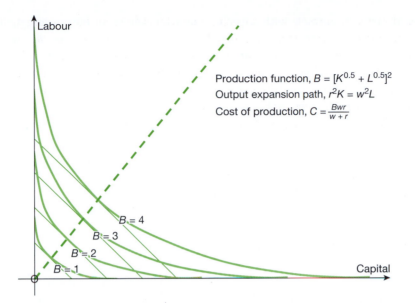

Figure 11.2 illustration showing Labour on the vertical axis and Capital on the horizontal axis, with the production function and output expansion path:

Production function, $B = [K^{0.5} + L^{0.5}]^2$
Output expansion path, $r^2K = w^2L$
Cost of production, $C = \frac{Bwr}{w + r}$

$B = 4$
$B = 3$
$B = 2$
$B = 1$

Figure 11.2 The output expansion path

This is homogeneous of degree 1. We also illustrate the nature of the solution to the constrained optimization problem where the firm meets a production target, B_0, by spending the smallest possible amount of money when hiring labour input, L, and capital input, K, when wage, w, is paid to labour, and interest rate, r, is paid to capital. We can write the equation of any isocost line as:

$$C_0 = wL + rK \qquad [11.2]$$

In Figure 11.2, we show four isocost lines, each of which is the tangent to a different isoquant. At each of these points of tangency, the marginal rate of technical substitution is equal to the factor price ratio. As we expect for a homogeneous production function, all four points of tangency lie on the same straight line, whose equation we shall confirm below is:

$$L = \left(\frac{r}{w}\right)^2 K \qquad [11.3]$$

Expression 11.3 defines the output expansion path on which the bakery's choice of inputs will lie, whatever its output might be. All that we have assumed is that the bakery's production function is homogeneous, and that it faces fixed factor input prices. These assumptions are sufficient for us to conclude that the ratio of capital to labour inputs will be the same across bakeries, and they will all use the same technology. A large bakery is simply a multiplication of a smaller one.

11.1.2 Calculation of minimum cost

When we developed our model of resource allocation for consumers, we concentrated on finding the most-preferred affordable bundle of goods. Here, in order to find the least-cost input combination, we need to take an extra step and find the cost of hiring those inputs.

We begin with an example with specific parameter values: an output target, $B_0 = 400$, wage $w = 20$, and interest rate $r = 5$. Considering Figure 11.2, we already know that feasible factor input combinations lie on or above the isoquant $B_0 = 4(00)$. We also know that there is some point P on the isoquant at which the output expansion path and the isoquant intersect and at which the conditions for minimum achievable cost are satisfied. To solve this problem, we write our example compactly:

$$\min_{K,L} 20L + 5K : \left[K^{0.5} + L^{0.5} \right]^2 = 400 \qquad [11.4]$$

We apply the solution method set out in Chapter 9, but using the condition from Expression 10.7: that the marginal rate of technical substitution equals the ratio of input prices:

$$MRTS = -\frac{MP_K}{MP_L} = -\left(\frac{L}{K} \right)^{0.5} = -\frac{r}{w} = -0.25 \qquad [11.5]$$

Solving Expression 11.5, we find that $K = 16L$. Then, substituting for K in the production target in Expression 11.4, we have $25L = 400$; so that the cost-minimizing input combination $(K^*, L^*) = 256,16$. We can usefully confirm this result by comparing it with the Hicksian demand function obtained for an expenditure-minimizing consumer in Expression 9.19, which we write here as:

$$K^H = B_0 \left\{ \frac{r^{-\frac{a}{1-a}}}{r^{-\frac{a}{1-a}} + w^{-\frac{a}{1-a}}} \right\}^{\frac{1}{a}} ; \; L^H = B_0 \left\{ \frac{w^{-\frac{a}{1-a}}}{r^{-\frac{a}{1-a}} + w^{-\frac{a}{1-a}}} \right\}^{\frac{1}{a}} \qquad [11.6]$$

Evaluating Expression 11.6 for the parameter value $a = 0.5$, and for the case where $B_0 = 400$, $r = 5$ and $w = 20$, we confirm our solution.

Then, obtaining the cost of production $C(K^*, L^*) = 1,600$, we can confirm that it is correct by comparing the calculation with the formula for the expenditure function for a consumer. Here, we adapt Expression 9.22, writing it as:

$$C(w, r, B_0) = B_0 \left(w^{-\frac{a}{1-a}} + r^{-\frac{a}{1-a}} \right)^{-\frac{1-a}{a}} \qquad [11.7]$$

Again, we can easily verify that for the parameter values in this example Expression 11.7 takes the value $C = 1,600$. This demonstrates that the problems of resource allocation for consumer and producer are formally identical; we have relied on the results that obtained in studying the theory of the consumer to reduce the quantity of calculation in solving these problems.

11.1.3 The cost function

The solution of the example and Exercises 11.4–11.6 lead naturally to Proposition 11.1, for which the proof is Exercise 11.7. The proposition confirms that, for this class of production functions, we are able to define a cost of production for a firm that depends only upon its output target, B, and the factor prices that it faces, w and r. We can see from Expression 11.7 that the cost function is linear in output, B, and also in the prices, w and r. That means that costs will increase proportionately with output, and also with both factor prices: if all prices increase by the same proportion, firms will not wish to change their technology, so that the cost of reaching any particular target output will change proportionately with the input price level.

We have assumed that while the bakery is able to choose its output target freely, it will take factor prices as given. This assumption is an extension of the assumption that the bakery is small relative to the whole product market, for we now also assume that all firms are small relative to factor markets. Each firm's share of the demand for capital and labour is very small. Under this assumption, every firm is like the bakery and so can hire any quantity of factor inputs at a given price. So long as all firms are small relative to the economy as a whole, they will have no market power and will not be able to affect either the wage paid to labour or the interest paid on capital.

By yourself

X11.4 In the example, we have found the bakery's cost of producing a fixed quantity of baked goods. Assume that the bakery's production target, B, is variable, but that factor input prices remain the same. Confirm that Expression 11.5 is the condition for cost minimization, and that the cost function is C: $C(B) = 4B$.

X11.5 Assume that a chemical company can produce a volume D of detergent, and that the production function takes the form $D = 98\,[K^{-1} + L^{-1}]^{-1}$, where K and L are the quantities of factor inputs, hired at prices $w_K = 4$ and $w_L = 25$.
  (a) Obtain the marginal products and the marginal rates of technical substitution.
  (b) Confirm that the first-order condition for cost minimization may be written as $K = 2.5L$.
  (c) By substituting for K in the production function or otherwise, obtain the cost-minimizing factor input combination and the total cost of production.
  (d) Confirm that for the input combination $(K, L) = (100, 250)$, output $D = 7,000$, and that the first-order condition for cost minimization is satisfied.
  (e) Obtain the equation of the isoquant that passes through the input combination given in part (d).
  (f) Sketch a graph showing this isoquant, the output expansion path, and the isocost line that is tangent to the isoquant.

X11.6 Assume that a creamery's output of cheese is F. We may write $F = 8K^{1/3}L^{2/3}$, where K and L are the quantities of factor inputs, hired at prices r and w.
  (a) Obtain the marginal products and the marginal rates of technical substitution.
  (b) Confirm that the first-order condition for cost minimization may be written as $2rK = wL$.
  (c) By substituting for K in the production function or otherwise, obtain the cost-minimizing factor input combination and the total cost of production when $r = 4w$. [*Note:* This will be a function of w.]
  (d) On a diagram, sketch the isoquant that passes through the input combination $(K, L) = (5, 40)$. Confirm that the first-order condition is satisfied at this point and add to the diagram the isocost line that is tangent to the isoquant.

Exercises X11.4–X11.6 demonstrate that when firms choose to solve this cost minimization problem, the isocost line forms the tangent to the isoquant that is the boundary of the acceptable set at the point where the output expansion path intersects the isoquant. The firm just meets its production target. This confirms that production is technically efficient, as defined in Chapter 10. We can also define production as being *economically efficient* – were a firm to hire any other input combination that allowed it to achieve its target output, its costs would increase.

Proposition 11.1

The cost function of a firm facing production function $B = \left[K^a + L^a\right]^{\frac{1}{a}}$, where:

(1) K and L are the quantities of factor inputs that the firm chooses to hire;

(2) a is a measure of their substitutability; and

(3) factor prices, w and r, are fixed and constant:

$$C(B,w,r) = B\left(w^{-\frac{a}{1-a}} + r^{-\frac{a}{1-a}}\right)^{-\frac{1-a}{a}}$$ [11.8]

(The proof of this statement is X11.7, whose argument follows directly from Chapter 9.)

By yourself

X11.7   [*Hard*] Assume that a firm produces output B, and that it faces a CES production function with elasticity of substitution $\sigma = (1 - a)^{-1}$. Then using quantity K of capital and quantity L of labour, the firm is able to produce:

$$B = \left[K^a + L^a\right]^{1/a}$$

We also assume that the firm is able to hire any quantity of capital at interest rate r and any quantity of labour at wage w.

(a) Obtain the marginal product functions and the marginal rate of technical substitution for this production function.

(b) Confirm that the first-order condition for cost minimization, which is also the equation of the income expansion path, may be written: $\frac{L}{K} = \left(\frac{r}{w}\right)^{\frac{1}{1-a}}$.

(c) Confirm that the indirect demands for capital and labour may be written:

$$K = B\left[\frac{r^{-\frac{a}{1-a}}}{r^{-\frac{a}{1-a}} + w^{-\frac{a}{1-a}}}\right]^{\frac{1}{a}} \quad \text{and} \quad L = B\left[\frac{w^{-\frac{a}{1-a}}}{r^{-\frac{a}{1-a}} + w^{-\frac{a}{1-a}}}\right]^{\frac{1}{a}}$$

(d) Hence or otherwise, confirm that the total cost of producing output B is as given in Expression 11.7.

With factor prices treated as fixed, we treat the firm's cost of production as a function of output, B. For given factor prices (w_0, r_0), we write $C = C(B; w_0, r_0) = C(B)$, which is the technically and economically efficient cost of production, and so represents the necessary costs of reaching output, B. (This point is demonstrated in Figure 11.3.) The bakery has a production target, B_0. The set of feasible input combinations lies on or above the isoquant B_0. When production is technically efficient, it takes places on the isoquant, since any reduction in factor usage will stop the firm achieving its output target. On the isoquant, it is possible to vary usage of one factor as long as usage of the other factor changes so that the firm can maintain its output. For example, we can see in Figure 11.3 that for firms using input bundles Q_0 and Q_1 to produce output X_0, production is technically efficient. Both lie on the isocost line C_3. From Q_0, it is possible for the firm to increase the use of capital (and decrease the use of labour) so that it continues to produce output X_0. Similarly, starting from input bundle Q_1, the firm can increase its usage of labour and reduce its usage of capital, while maintaining output X_0.

By yourself

X11.8   Complete the argument relating to economic efficiency, explaining why the bakery achieves both technical and economic efficiency when using input bundle P.

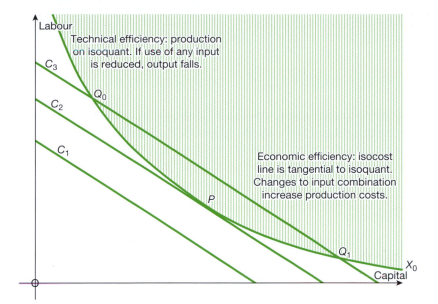

Figure 11.3 Technical and economic efficiency

> **Economic efficiency**
> A property of the cost-minimizing input bundle: changing inputs while holding expenditure constant causes costs to increase.

We confirmed in Chapter 10 that where production is technically and **economically efficient**, so that the firm minimizes the cost of production, then for all factors of production that the firm hires, the ratio of marginal product to price will be the same. We interpreted this condition as meaning that for very small changes in factor inputs, the rate at which output will increase as expenditure on one factor increases will be identical across factors of production. Our concern here is with the expenditure on hiring factors of production, rather than with their level of use.

It may be useful to rewrite the condition for economic efficiency derived in Chapter 10:

$$\frac{w}{MP_L} = \frac{r}{MP_K} \qquad [11.9]$$

This inversion of Expression 10.7 has a simple purpose when thinking about cost minimization. Remember that any firm whose production is technically and economically efficient will only be able to cut costs by cutting factor usage and thus output. Expression 11.9 tells us the rate at which a firm can cut costs if it reduces its output target. When production is both technically and economically efficient, this rate of reduction in costs (for infinitesimally small changes in production) can be achieved through reduction of the use of either factor or both factors.

We have now defined the total cost function and derived it for some important examples of production functions. From here on, we shall typically assign a cost function to a firm without going through the process of cost minimization. We shall typically be interested in properties that it might be reasonable for cost functions to possess, such as convexity. Generally, we shall use quite intuitive techniques of graphical analysis. As in our discussion of consumer choice and demand in Chapters 4 and 5, where we concentrated on the effects of changes at the margin, our attention will be focused less on the total cost of production for a firm and more on measures of average and marginal costs.

11.2   Average and marginal cost functions

The *marginal cost function* measures the rate of change of total costs with output, while the *average cost function* measures the total cost per unit of output. Average cost is useful in thinking about whether or not the firm is breaking even or making profit, while marginal cost is important in determining whether the level of production should be changed to increase the firm's profitability. We shall now discuss the properties of these functions.

11.2.1   Definitions

Average cost The production cost per unit of output.

Let us say that firm D, a dressmaker, produces output D at total cost $C = C(D)$. We expect costs to be increasing in output, D, and never to be less than zero. We first define the average cost of production, $AC(D)$, as the total cost divided by output, so that:

$$AC(D) = \frac{C(D)}{D} \qquad [11.10]$$

In this case, the average cost measures the firm's cost per dress made. In Chapter 12 we shall discuss in more detail the fact that we can think of a part of the total cost of production, F, as being fixed, in the sense that the dressmaker has to pay these costs irrespective of the volume of production. As production increases, the share of these fixed costs attributable to each unit of output will fall. As an example, suppose the dressmaker has entered into a long-term lease of its factory. Irrespective of the number of dresses it makes, it will still have to pay the rent. The larger the number of dresses made, however, the smaller the fraction of the rent that has to be absorbed by each unit of production.

Marginal cost The rate at which costs change as output changes.

The **marginal cost** function, $MC(D)$, measures the rate at which total cost changes as output changes. From Chapter 3 onwards we have had considerable experience of expressing rates of change in terms of the derivative function, so here we simply define the marginal cost as the derivative of total cost with respect to output:

$$MC(D) = C'(D) \qquad [11.11]$$

For example, suppose that, like many manufacturers in developing countries, the dressmaker pays its workers *piece rates*, or a fixed sum for each unit produced: in that case, as production increases, wage payments will increase in proportion to output. If all other costs are fixed, the marginal cost will simply be the piece rate. Given payment w per unit produced, the total cost of producing output D is then:

$$C = C(D) = F + wD \qquad [11.12]$$

The average cost or cost per unit is:

$$AC(D) = \frac{F}{D} + w \qquad [11.13]$$

The marginal cost is:

$$MC(D) = C'(D) = w \qquad [11.14]$$

By yourself

X11.9   For the following total cost functions, calculate the average and marginal cost functions, sketching graphs of each as output, X, varies between 1 and 5 units.

(a) $C = kX$ (b) $C = 1 + x$ (c) $C = 9 + x$ (d) $C = rX^2$ (e) $C = 1 + x + x^2$

X11.10   Given $AC(X) = \frac{C(X)}{X}$, show that the derivative function, $\frac{dAC}{dX} = \frac{MC(X) - AC(X)}{X}$. Hence confirm that if marginal cost is greater than average cost, average cost is increasing, and that if average cost is greater than marginal cost, average cost is decreasing.

X11.11   Using the results of Exercise 11.10, differentiate the average cost function twice to obtain the conditions that must be satisfied for there to be a minimum value of average cost. Confirm that for the function used in X11.9e, these conditions are satisfied when output $x = 1$.

This set of exercises leads us through some useful relationships between average and marginal cost.

- Firstly, we see in X11.9a that when total costs are proportionate to output, average and marginal costs are equal and constant. This is consistent with the results of the later exercises, for in this case average cost is constant, so marginal cost is also constant.
- Then, allowing for an element of fixed costs but keeping marginal costs constant, as in X11.9b and X11.9c, we see that average cost is greater than marginal cost, but is decreasing. This result is also confirmed in the later exercises. In defining average cost, we noted that as output increases, a smaller fraction of the fixed costs should be attributed to each unit.
- Lastly, if we allow for costs increasing at an increasing rate, which is the situation in X11.9d and X11.9e, marginal cost is an increasing function. In the first of these exercises, we find that average cost is also increasing, but more slowly than marginal cost; and that marginal cost is never less than average cost. This is the situation illustrated in Figure 11.4. There, we measure the average cost at point Z on the cost curve as the slope of the chord, OZ,

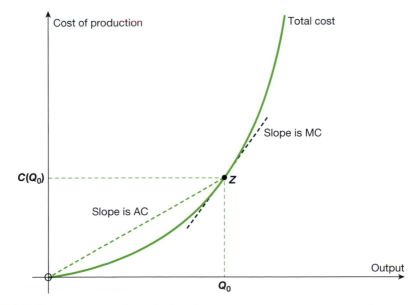

Figure 11.4 Defining average and marginal costs

and the marginal cost as the slope of the tangent at Z. In the last example, we see that marginal cost equals average cost when output $X = 1$. For higher levels of output, marginal cost is greater than average cost, and both average and marginal cost increase.

- It is always true that when marginal cost is greater than average cost, average cost is increasing. For example, suppose that the cost increments associated with successive one-unit increases in output are 5, 6, 8, 11, and 14. Total costs are then 5, (5 + 6 or) 11, 19, 30, and 44, while average costs are 5, 5.5, 6.33, 7.5, and 8.8.

Since cost increments are defined over discrete units, it is not strictly correct to describe them as marginal costs, as the marginal function is a derivative and therefore a measure of the instantaneous rate of change of total costs as output increases. In practice, a single unit is usually a very small proportion of output, and so the additional cost associated with an increase in output of one unit is a very good approximation to the true marginal cost. It is therefore normal practice to refer to such cost increments as marginal cost. The *total costs* of production are simply the sum of the successive cost increments, while the *average cost* is the total cost divided by the number of units.

The cost increment and the average cost measures are the same for the first unit, because they are identical measures. But the increase in costs of 6 in the second unit is spread across both the first and the second unit. For the cost increment, we allocate all the additional costs to one unit; while for the average costs, we spread it evenly across all units of output. Average cost increases with production, but not by the total cost increment.

Think about the example of a café, introduced in Chapter 1. The marginal cost of making a cup of coffee is the labour time required and the cost of the raw materials. The average cost already includes all of the set-up costs of the café (such as the rent and decoration of the building, and the purchase of machinery) and the indirect costs (such as heating and lighting). In this case, we expect the marginal cost to be small, relative to the price paid, which will include a contribution to all of these other costs.

- The more formal argument in Exercises X11.14 and X11.15 builds quite naturally on these insights. In X11.14, we confirm in effect that the first-order condition for a minimum value of average costs will be satisfied when average cost equals marginal cost; while in X11.15, we find that the second-order condition is satisfied if the total cost function is convex, so that it increases at an increasing rate. The following exercises lead us to the same conclusions, but using a geometric rather than an analytical argument.

By yourself

X11.12 In Figure 11.4, we show the marginal and average costs for output Q_0.
  (a) Explain this geometric representation of these cost measures.
  (b) Demonstrate that the result obtained in X11.10 (when $MC > AC$, AC is increasing) holds in this case.

X11.13 Adapt Figure 11.4, so that the firm has fixed costs (or so that total cost $C(0) > 0$), with total costs increasing at an increasing rate.
  (a) Confirm that when output is zero, the average cost, $AC(0)$, is undefined.
  (b) On your diagram, indicate clearly the output, Q_0, for which average costs are equal to marginal costs.
  (c) Demonstrate that for output $Q < Q_0$, average cost is higher than marginal cost; while for output $Q > Q_0$, marginal cost is greater than average cost.
  (d) Hence or otherwise, confirm that at output $Q = Q_0$, average cost is minimized.

11.2.2 Returns to scale

In Chapter 10, we linked the degree of homogeneity to the nature of a production function's returns to scale. We summarize that discussion in Table 11.1.

Degree of homogeneity	Returns to scale
Less than one	Decreasing
One	Constant
More than one	Increasing

Table 11.1 Homogeneity and returns to scale

A change in the scale of production occurs when the use of all factors changes by the same proportion. For example, in our two-factor model of production, the scale of production doubles when both labour and capital inputs double. Similarly, the scale of production increases by 1% when usage of both factors increases by 1%. There is no possibility of a firm substituting one factor for another as it changes its output.

We have assumed that firms are able to hire any quantity of factor inputs at fixed prices. When varying the scale of production, firms are not able to obtain any bulk discount, but nor does higher demand for inputs (at firm level) lead to price increases. Let us begin with the case that returns to scale are constant, so that a 1% increase in scale of production leads to a 1% increase in output. The 1% increase in scale means that there is a 1% increase in the quantities of capital and labour that the firm hires. For initial factor inputs K and L, changes in factor usage may be written as $\Delta K = 0.01K$, and $\Delta L = 0.01L$. Initially, firm costs $C = wL + rK$, but they increase to $C + \Delta C = w(L + \Delta L) + r(K + \Delta K) = 1.01(wL + rK)$, so that $\Delta C = 0.01C$. By definition of constant returns to scale, $\Delta B = 0.01B$. The proportionate increase in costs, $\frac{\Delta C}{C}$, equals the proportionate increase in output, $\frac{\Delta B}{B}$.

By yourself

X11.14 Extend the argument begun in the previous paragraph to show that, given the assumption of constant returns to scale:
(a) Factor demands L and K are linear in output X.
(b) Total costs are linear in output X.
(c) Average cost, AC, equals marginal cost, MC.

X11.15 Now extend the argument to show that if there are increasing returns to scale:
(a) Factor demands L and K are increasing, but concave, in output X. (That is, as output increases, labour and capital usage will increase; but the proportionate increase in use is less than the proportionate increase in output.)
(b) Total costs are increasing, but concave, in output X.
(c) Average cost, AC, decreases in output.
(d) Average cost, AC, is greater than marginal cost, MC.

X11.16 Repeat the argument of X11.14 to show that if there are diminishing returns to scale:
(a) Factor demands L and K are increasing, but convex, in output X. (That is, as output increases, labour and capital usage will increase; but the proportionate increase in use is greater than the proportionate increase in output.)
(b) Total costs are increasing, but convex, in output X.
(c) Average cost, AC, increases in output.
(d) Average cost, AC, is less than marginal cost, MC.

(Continued)

X11.17   A production function is homogeneous of degree r if $X(tK, tL) = t^r X(K, L)$ for all values of t, K and L. Confirm that the results of X11.14–X11.16 hold in the case of functions that are respectively homogeneous of degrees one, greater than one and less than one; and that where a production function is homogeneous of degree r, the factor demand and total cost functions are homogeneous of degree $1/r$ in output.

We can summarize the most important outcomes of these exercises in Figure 11.5. Panel (a) illustrates how, with increasing returns to scale, average costs fall with output but are higher than marginal costs; while in panel (b), with diminishing returns to scale, average costs rise with output but are less than marginal costs. It would have been possible to draw a third panel showing the situation with constant returns to scale: average costs would be constant, and equal to marginal costs.

X11.17 below requires us to show the exact relationship between the degree of homogeneity of a production function and the associated total cost function. Homogeneity is quite a strong restriction to place on a production function. It ensures that returns to scale do not vary with the level of output. In Figure 11.5, we show average and marginal costs without requiring the underlying production function to be homogeneous.

11.2.3   Average and marginal costs for CES production functions

In Chapter 10, we introduced the family of constant elasticity of substitution production functions:

$$Q = \left[K^a + L^a\right]^{1/a} \tag{11.15}$$

As written in Expression 11.15 the function exhibits constant returns to scale and is homogeneous of degree 1. Applying the standard condition for cost minimization derived in X11.7b, we can confirm that any firm facing this production function will use the same input ratio, irrespective of the level of output:

$$\frac{L}{K} = \left(\frac{r}{w}\right)^{\frac{1}{1-a}} \tag{11.16}$$

Given such a fixed input ratio, we might continue to say that firms in effect hire a composite unit of 'labour + capital'. This unit A: $(1, \tau)$ consists of one additional worker and the

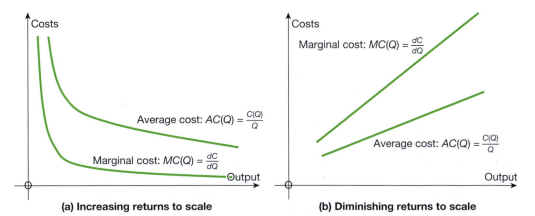

(a) **Increasing returns to scale**   (b) **Diminishing returns to scale**

Figure 11.5 Average and marginal costs and returns to scale

capital needed to support that worker. With constant returns to scale, the additional output produced by successive additions of this composite input unit would always be the same.

Applying Proposition 11.1, we can write the cost function:

$$C(B,r,w) = B \cdot (r^{-\frac{a}{1-a}} + w^{-\frac{a}{1-a}})^{-\frac{1-a}{a}} \qquad [11.17]$$

Differentiating Expression 11.17 with respect to output, we obtain marginal cost; whereas dividing total costs by output, we obtain average costs. Here, $MC = AC = c$, where

$$c = (r^{-\frac{a}{1-a}} + w^{-\frac{a}{1-a}})^{-\frac{1-a}{a}} \qquad [11.18]$$

is a function of the factor input prices.

It is quite simple to adapt the CES production function with constant returns to scale so that it is homogeneous of degree ρ. The transformed function exhibits increasing returns (if $\rho > 1$) or else decreasing returns (if $\rho < 1$). All that is necessary is to raise the production function to the power ρ, so that:

$$B = [K^a + L^a]^{\rho/a} \qquad [11.19]$$

By yourself

X11.18   A cost-minimizing firm faces the production function in Expression 11.19, and fixed factor costs w and r. Using the arguments developed in Section 9.2.1, where we found the Hicksian demands when a consumer's utility takes the form of a CES function, and also from X11.11, where we found the total cost function a CES production function, confirm that:

(a) The first-order condition for cost minimization is still given by Expression 11.16.

(b) The total cost function is:

$$C(B,r,w) = B^{\frac{1}{\rho}} \cdot (r^{-\frac{a}{1-a}} + w^{-\frac{a}{1-a}})^{-\frac{1-a}{a}} \qquad [11.20]$$

(c) The average cost function is:

$$AC(B,r,w) = B^{\frac{1-\rho}{\rho}} \cdot (r^{-\frac{a}{1-a}} + w^{-\frac{a}{1-a}})^{-\frac{1-a}{a}} \qquad [11.21]$$

(d) The marginal cost function is:

$$MC(B,r,w) = \frac{B^{\frac{1-\rho}{\rho}}}{\rho} \cdot (r^{-\frac{a}{1-a}} + w^{-\frac{a}{1-a}})^{-\frac{1-a}{a}} \qquad [11.22]$$

(Continued)

Essential Maths 11.1: **Optimization of functions of one variable**

In our calculations so far, we have simply needed to obtain the derivatives of objective functions. We now use derivatives to solve optimization problems, using the first- and second-order optimization conditions for functions of one variable.

Define a function of one variable, $z : z = z(x)$. Its first derivative, $z' = z'(x)$, and its second derivative, $z'' = z''(x)$. Both derivative functions are themselves functions of x. Evaluating the functions, if $z'(x) > 0$, the function is increasing; and if $z'(x) < 0$, the function is decreasing. But if $z'(x) = 0$, the function is neither increasing nor decreasing. For every value $x_0 : z'(x_0) = 0$, function z is stationary at $x = x_0$.

Now think of how we might illustrate a stationary value of a function. In a graph of a function, the slope at any point is the gradient of the tangent to the graph. For an increasing function the tangent is upward-sloping; while for a decreasing function, the tangent will be downward-sloping. A line that is neither upward nor downward-sloping is horizontal. It is flat.

(e) The total cost function is homogeneous of degree $1/\rho$.

(f) The average and marginal cost functions are homogeneous of degree $(1 - \rho)/\rho$.

(g) If $\rho < 1$, total costs are increasing and convex, average costs are increasing, and $MC > AC$; but if $\rho > 1$, then total costs are increasing and concave, average costs are decreasing, and $MC < AC$.

11.2.4   Eventually diminishing returns to scale

With the examples in Section 11.2.3, returns to scale for any function are always increasing, always constant, or always decreasing. However, when we come to think about the profit-maximizing decisions of firms that face perfectly competitive markets in Chapter 14, the analysis will be simplified considerably if we assume that returns to scale are **eventually diminishing**. If a production function possesses this property, then a firm that chooses a low enough level of output will face increasing returns to scale. There will be some level of output, though, for which returns to scale are constant; and at any higher level of output, there will be diminishing returns to scale. We might justify this assumption on the basis that as production increases, there are diseconomies of scale, for example the complexity of coordinating and managing activities, which eventually over-whelm any possible efficiency gains from continued expansion of the business.

> **Eventually diminishing returns to scale** Returns to scale that diminish only when output is high.

In discussing the degree of homogeneity of production and cost functions in Section 11.2.3, we argued that these are inversely related. When the production function is homogeneous of degree ρ, the cost function is homogeneous of degree $1/\rho$. We have also argued that for a firm whose output is Q, increasing returns to scale are associated with

Essential Maths 11.2: **The zero derivative**

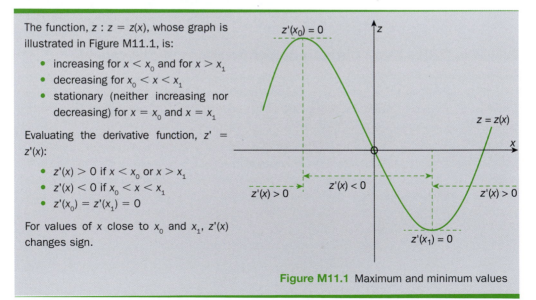

The function, $z : z = z(x)$, whose graph is illustrated in Figure M11.1, is:

- increasing for $x < x_0$ and for $x > x_1$
- decreasing for $x_0 < x < x_1$
- stationary (neither increasing nor decreasing) for $x = x_0$ and $x = x_1$

Evaluating the derivative function, $z' = z'(x)$:

- $z'(x) > 0$ if $x < x_0$ or $x > x_1$
- $z'(x) < 0$ if $x_0 < x < x_1$
- $z'(x_0) = z'(x_1) = 0$

For values of x close to x_0 and x_1, $z'(x)$ changes sign.

Figure M11.1 Maximum and minimum values

concave total costs, $C(Q)$, and with decreasing average costs, $AC(Q)$, which are greater than marginal costs, $MC(Q)$; and that diminishing returns to scale are associated with convex total costs, $C(Q)$, and increasing average costs, $AC(Q)$, which are less than marginal costs, $MC(Q)$. In Figure 11.6, we show how these properties can all be seen in the graph of total costs when the function exhibits eventually diminishing returns to scale.

Looking at this diagram closely, we see that we have to change our explanation of the relationship between the cost functions slightly. There is no difficulty when output is less than Q_1. The total cost function is concave, average costs are decreasing, and marginal costs are less than average costs. This is exactly our description of the properties of the cost functions when the underlying production function exhibits increasing returns to scale. There is also no problem when output is greater than Q_0. The total cost function is convex, average costs are increasing, and marginal costs are greater than average costs. This is exactly our description of the properties of the cost functions when the underlying production function exhibits diminishing returns to scale.

The change in our explanation involved outputs between Q_0 and Q_1. In Figure 11.6a, total costs are convex, which is consistent with production exhibiting decreasing returns

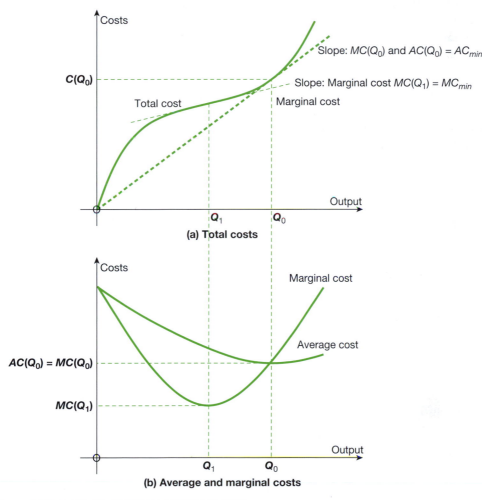

Figure 11.6 Eventually diminishing returns to scale

to scale. In Figure 11.6b, average costs are decreasing, and average costs are higher than marginal costs. In our previous discussion, we have claimed that this property is associated with increasing returns to scale. We therefore need to change the definition of returns to scale very slightly. In Figure 11.6b, output Q_0 minimizes average costs, while output Q_1 minimizes marginal costs. For output in excess of Q_0, average cost, or cost per unit, is increasing; while for output in excess of Q_1, marginal cost, or cost of incremental units, is increasing. In both cases, it seems reasonable to argue that we have an indication of diminishing returns to scale in production. In the former case, we have diminishing *total* returns, but in the latter one we have diminishing *marginal* returns to scale.

Essential Maths 11.3: Local maximum of functions of one variable

Suppose that we evaluate the derivative for a value of x that is close to, but just a little less than, x_0, say $x = x_0 - \delta x$. For all values of x between $x_0 - \delta x$ and x_0, $z'(x) > 0$. The objective function, z, is increasing as x approaches x_0 from below. Similarly, for some value of x that is close to, but just a little greater than, x_0, say $x = x_0 + \delta x$, then for all values of x between $x_0 - \delta x$ and x_0, $z'(x) < 0$. Starting from x_0, if x either increases or decreases, $z(x)$ decreases, and so in the interval $[z - \delta x, z + \delta x]$, the maximum value of z is found at $x = x_0$. When $z = z_0$, the function is stationary, and has a local maximum.

Now, for $x = x_0 - \delta x$, the derivative $z'(x - \delta x) > 0$; while for $x = x_0 + \delta x$, the derivative $z'(x + \delta x) < 0$ (and for $x = x_0$, $z'(x_0) = 0$. Around x_0, the derivative is decreasing. The second derivative measures the rate of change of the derivative, so we expect that $z''(x_0) < 0$. Therefore for any function $z = z(x)$, and for any value x_0 for which $z'(x_0) = 0$ and $z''(x_0) < 0$, z has a local maximum at $x = x_0$.

Given that a function for which the second derivative $z''(x) < 0$ is concave, it follows that if z is locally concave around $x = x_0$, then if $z'(x_0) = 0$, z has a maximum when $x = x_0$.

Essential Maths 11.4: Local minimum of functions of one variable

Not all stationary points are maxima. The zero derivative condition holds for local minima as well. In Figure M11.1, the function has a minimum at $x = x_1$. For values of $x : x = x_1 - \delta x$, $z(x) > z(x_1)$ so that z is decreasing as x approaches x_1 from below, and $z'(x) < 0$.

Similarly, for $x : x = x_1 + \delta x$, $z'(x) > 0$, so that z decreases as x approaches x_1 from above.

Starting from $x = x_0$, if both increases and decreases in x will lead to $z(x)$ increasing, then in the interval $[z - \delta x, z + \delta x]$, the function z is stationary when $x = x_1$ at a local minimum of z.

For $x = x_1 - \delta x$, $z'(x_1 - \delta x) < 0$, but for $x > x_1 + \delta x$, $z'(x_1 + \delta x) > 0$; and $z'(x_1) = 0$. Across the interval, $[x_1 - \delta x, x_1 + \delta x]$, the derivative is increasing, so we expect that the second derivative $z''(x_1) > 0$. For the function $z : z = z(x)$, if for some value x_1, $z'(x_1) = 0$ and $z''(x_1) > 0$, z has a local minimum at $x = x_1$.

Remember that a function whose second derivative $z''(x) > 0$ is convex. Sufficient conditions for a local minimum are that $z'(x_0) = 0$ and $z''(x_0) > 0$.

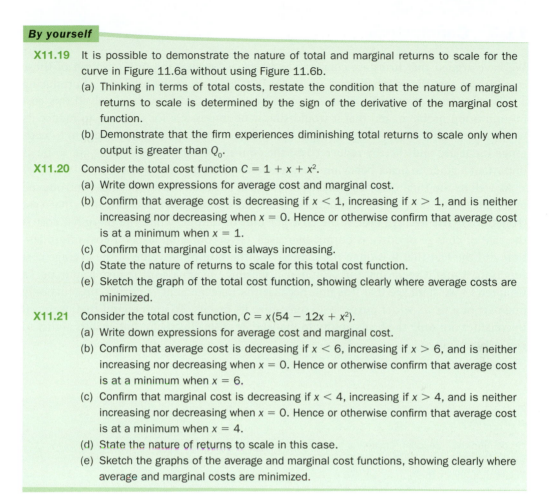

By yourself

X11.19 It is possible to demonstrate the nature of total and marginal returns to scale for the curve in Figure 11.6a without using Figure 11.6b.
(a) Thinking in terms of total costs, restate the condition that the nature of marginal returns to scale is determined by the sign of the derivative of the marginal cost function.
(b) Demonstrate that the firm experiences diminishing total returns to scale only when output is greater than Q_0.

X11.20 Consider the total cost function $C = 1 + x + x^2$.
(a) Write down expressions for average cost and marginal cost.
(b) Confirm that average cost is decreasing if $x < 1$, increasing if $x > 1$, and is neither increasing nor decreasing when $x = 0$. Hence or otherwise confirm that average cost is at a minimum when $x = 1$.
(c) Confirm that marginal cost is always increasing.
(d) State the nature of returns to scale for this total cost function.
(e) Sketch the graph of the total cost function, showing clearly where average costs are minimized.

X11.21 Consider the total cost function, $C = x(54 - 12x + x^2)$.
(a) Write down expressions for average cost and marginal cost.
(b) Confirm that average cost is decreasing if $x < 6$, increasing if $x > 6$, and is neither increasing nor decreasing when $x = 0$. Hence or otherwise confirm that average cost is at a minimum when $x = 6$.
(c) Confirm that marginal cost is decreasing if $x < 4$, increasing if $x > 4$, and is neither increasing nor decreasing when $x = 0$. Hence or otherwise confirm that average cost is at a minimum when $x = 4$.
(d) State the nature of returns to scale in this case.
(e) Sketch the graphs of the average and marginal cost functions, showing clearly where average and marginal costs are minimized.

The production functions in X11.20 and X11.21 have slightly different characteristics. In X11.20 there is a constant term, which represents a fixed element of costs. We have already noted that as output increases, the share of fixed costs absorbed in any unit of output decreases; and for low levels of output, this is enough for average costs to fall, even though marginal costs are increasing. We conclude that the underlying production function must exhibit increasing total returns at low levels of output, diminishing total returns at higher levels of output, and diminishing marginal returns at all levels of output. Turning to X11.21, we see that the firm produces at minimum marginal cost when output $x = 4$, and at minimum average cost when output $x = 6$. In this case, the underlying production function exhibits both eventually increasing total and marginal returns to scale.

In Chapter 12, when we consider the differences between firms' short-run and long-run decision making, we shall refer to production functions like the one in X11.20. In Chapters 13 and 14, when we examine the behaviour of a firm that faces a perfectly competitive market, we will allow for the more general form of eventually diminishing returns to scale found in functions such as the one examined in X11.21.

11.3   Conclusions

We have argued that firms are concerned with costs because the minimization of those costs means that they are behaving efficiently. In talking about the total cost of producing a particular level of output, we have assumed implicitly that firms have solved this cost minimization problem, and that it would simply be impossible for any firm to reduce its use of inputs without reducing its output. It would also be impossible for the firm to rearrange input use and thereby reduce costs: the equi-marginal principle turns out to be as important a guide to firms' behaviour as it was for consumers' behaviour.

As well as the total cost of production, or the cost function, we have also introduced other measures of a firm's production costs: the average cost and the marginal cost (functions). The average cost is the cost per unit of output, while the marginal cost is the rate of change of costs as output increases. Given our emphasis on cost minimization and the fact that it is often possible to find the minimum value of the average cost function, it might seem that this would be a sensible objective for the firm to pursue. In Chapter 13 we shall see that it is not, because the management of costs represents only one part of a firm's wider purpose: to maximize its profits. To understand that, we need to consider not only the firm's ability to manage its costs effectively, but also its ability to generate revenues.

Summary

We defined the total cost function of a firm as expressing the minimum expenditure on factor inputs that allows the firm to achieve a given production target. We defined the nature of the two most commonly used factors, labour and capital. We argued that firms can only achieve the minimum expenditure given by the cost function if they use inputs so that production is technically and economically efficient. We saw that this can only happen if, for all factors of production, the ratio of marginal product to price is identical.

We demonstrated that if the production function is homogeneous, then – assuming that all firms face the same factor prices – firms will adopt the same technology (factor input ratio); subsequently, there will be no qualitative differences in the structures of small and large firms.

We obtained the total cost function for some standard production functions by obtaining the Hicksian demands (given output target and factor input prices). In Proposition 11.1, we stated the total cost function for members of the family of CES production function.

We defined the average cost function as a measure of the cost per unit of output; and the marginal cost function as a measure of the rate of change of costs with respect to output, representing it as the first derivative of total costs with respect to output.

We examined the relationships between average and marginal cost functions.

We showed that where a firm experiences increasing (marginal) returns to scale, total cost is an increasing, concave function; marginal cost is a positive-valued, decreasing function; and average cost is less than marginal cost.

We showed that where a firm experiences diminishing (total) returns to scale, total cost is an increasing, convex function; marginal cost is a positive-valued, increasing function; and average cost is less than marginal cost.

We showed that a firm experiences eventually diminishing returns to scale, such that the firm faces increasing returns to scale in production until output exceeds a certain threshold; marginal cost will be less than average cost at low enough levels of output, but will increase more rapidly than average cost. Where the firm faces diminishing returns to scale, marginal costs are increasing and become greater than average costs.

Visit the companion website at **www.palgrave.com/mochrie** to access further teaching and learning materials, including lecturer slides and a testbank, as well as guideline answers and student MCQs.

Costs and planning

What we do in this chapter

We have defined a firm's *cost function* as a measure of the total payments that it must make to hire factor inputs to reach all possible production targets. We have assumed that the firm's resource allocation is always economically efficient. In this chapter, we assume that capital usage is much more difficult to vary than labour usage because of the time that it takes to construct buildings, plant and machinery. In the short run, capital usage is fixed and firms vary production by changing labour usage. Production is *technically efficient*, but not *economically efficient*.

With this restriction in place, we derive the short-run total costs of production, incorporating the distinction between fixed costs and variable costs. With usage of capital fixed, the firm is committed to paying its hiring cost, but the cost of hiring labour remains variable. We obtain measures of the *(total short-run) cost*, $C_{SR}(Q)$, the *total fixed cost*, $TFC(Q)$, and the *total variable cost*, $TVC(Q)$, all of which we write as functions of output, Q, and from which we derive average and marginal functions.

We develop the relationship between the short-run and the long-run cost function by thinking of the planning process for a firm. In any given time period, the firm wishes to achieve economic efficiency, and so in planning production it will decide on its capital usage. If the firm plans to sell more output than it is able, it hires more capital than it actually needs. It responds, in the short run, by hiring less labour than if it were still able to vary capital usage. Short-run costs can therefore never be less than long-run costs, and will generally be greater.

Fungible assets
Assets such that individual units are perfect substitutes.

In Chapter 11, we defined capital as the funding used to purchase the assets which businesses use when producing output. Defined in this way, capital is fungible. It can be applied to any purpose within the firm: the purchase of raw materials or machinery, the hire of business premises and machinery, or the development of new goods and services. Once used for a given purpose, the liquid capital becomes fixed in physical assets. Fixed assets, such as land and buildings, are held by the firm, so they are not used up in production processes. In contrast, current assets are needed for production and are rapidly recycled within the business. For example, using cash held at the bank, a business might purchase raw materials, work them into goods for sale or hold them as stock items before selling them on credit, with the cycle being completed when the purchaser pays for the goods and the producer is able to deposit funds with the bank.

In this chapter, we simplify the discussion by assuming that all assets are fixed. We can then treat capital as the assets held by a business that are not used up in the production process (rather than treating it as all financial claims of other parties on the business). We shall argue that businesses cannot change their use of capital (assets) quickly, because such changes take time. In Section 12.1, we present several examples making this point.

12.1   The non-fungibility of capital assets

London won the right to host the Olympic Games of 2012 in July 2005, just over seven years before they took place. Several new buildings had to be built on the chosen site in the East of London: not just the main stadium, but also the aquatic centre, the velodrome, and several smaller sporting arenas, as well as an athletes' village, capable of accommodating just under 20,000 people. In addition, substantial improvements to public transport were needed, as was a media centre to host global broadcasts. The scale of this project was very large indeed. In bidding to host this event, and using costs from the previous three Olympic Games (in Sydney, Athens, and Beijing), it was reasonable to plan for capital costs of €15bn, or approximately €250 per person in the UK. The then Prime Minister, Mr Blair, joined the bid team in order to emphasize that for the UK government this was to be a national project, which, although being delivered by private organizations, would have the strongest possible government support.

Before almost every such large sporting event, stories appear in the media about the cost over-runs and the lack of preparedness of the organizers. Montreal, which held the Olympics in 1976, perhaps holds a record of sorts: after enormous cost over-runs, labour disputes, and a boycott by African countries (which objected to competing with countries that maintained sporting links with the apartheid regime in South Africa), the Games ran relatively smoothly; even so, the provincial government was left with a debt that had to be repaid over more than 20 years, while the original design concept for the stadium, which had a movable roof, was not completed until 1987. Los Angeles, which hosted the Olympic Games in 1984, learned the lessons from Montreal; rather than looking to taxpayers for finance, the organizers turned to private business. Sponsorship burgeoned, with licences to supply almost every service being sold off, as businesses exploited fully the marketing advantages that they hoped would accrue to them from being associated with the world's largest sporting event. The organizers of the London Games took into account the experience of previous host cities. In the weeks leading up to the event, the most publicized story of project failure concerned the security firm G4S, which was not able to provide enough trained staff for stewarding the event, leading to the deployment of soldiers instead.

The need to hold the bidding process so far in advance demonstrates that such a large project cannot be completed overnight. To concentrate on the most obvious, physical aspect, once the organizers have decided upon a design for the main stadium and started building, they can vary some of the details of its construction but they cannot easily dismantle the stadium and rebuild it. For these large sporting events, huge structures are created in cities – structures that will have limited alternative uses afterwards.[1] For example, a part of Qatar's successful bid to host the World Cup for football in 2022 is a most unusual plan to disassemble parts of the five stadia currently being built, and to ship them to countries that do not have good sports facilities.[2] In these cases, once construction contracts have been signed and physical structures have emerged out of the ground, the project capital will have been transformed from fungible money, which could be applied to any purpose, into buildings, which has few alternative uses and which cannot be adapted or redeveloped easily. The capital inputs used in such projects are largely determined years in advance.

In contrast, as the stories about the difficulties in recruiting security staff at the Olympic Games remind us, labour is a much more variable factor input. It appears that G4S calculated correctly how many staff it needed to train and had a programme in place to do this.

Its miscalculation was to underestimate the proportion of the trained staff who would later quit, preferring instead to take on other jobs. It was at this point that the army stepped in and offered to provide soldiers: the soldiers possessed many of the necessary skills and were less likely to terminate their contracts. The assumption that businesses will find it easier to vary the labour input into their operations than to vary the capital input seems quite reasonable. For all these reasons, we treat capital as the fixed asset in the short run, and labour as the variable asset.

12.1.1 Distinguishing between the short run and the long run

Short run A period in which the use of one factor is fixed.

Up to this point, we have assumed that firms, like consumers, can make any resource allocation decision with no costs, other than those of hiring the factors of production. Here we make a strong assumption, that it is impossible in the period that we call the **short run** for a firm to change usage of one or more factors.

By yourself

X12.1 Compare a bridge and a tunnel as examples of fixed investments. [*Note:* To start your argument, consider the old London Bridge, which was reconstructed in Lake Havasu, Arizona, between 1968 and 1970. Could anything similar be done with a tunnel?] For each, what do you consider to be 'the long run' and 'the short run'?

X12.2 Hospitals are large complex projects. In recent years, it has become increasingly common for health service providers to commission specialist companies to 'build, own, operate and transfer' new medical facilities. As the name suggests, the management company agrees to provide all services in the facility for a period of 25–30 years, at the end of which it transfers ownership to the health service provider.
(a) Discuss possible advantages and disadvantages of this approach.
(b) Why would each party want to tie the other into a long-run contract?
(c) What do you consider to be 'the long run' in this case?

X12.3 Many developed countries have substantially reduced their coal-mining industries in recent years, in many cases without extracting all recoverable reserves. What are the fixed assets associated with a mine? Why might it be desirable for a mining company to enter into a long-run contract with an electricity-generation company? How should we define 'the long run' in this case?

The exercises confirm that there are many projects where the development phase might run for several years. The presence of fixed assets can also affect project financing. In Exercise X12.1, we do not discuss financing because road bridges and tunnels will often be financed through general taxation, and charges for access to rail networks are very complex. A mine is in some ways like a tunnel, and a mine operator will typically wish to enter into a contract with a buyer of its output that will allow the operator to recover its costs. Once sunk, the pit is a fixed asset that has to be maintained, at considerable expense. Such a contract enables the mine owner to raise external finance, secured against the likely income streams from the mine's activities.

In the same way, the operator of a hospital facility will wish the contract to be long enough for the rental received from the healthcare provider – which is the contractor's tenant – to repay the costs of construction and operation (and to make profits). At the end of that period, the operator will in effect have bought the hospital and ownership will transfer from the operator to the provider. This is a sufficiently long time that there may be advances in medical technology or changes in demand for services, possibly because of population change, that might necessitate the construction of a replacement hospital in the last years of the existing contract.

It is very unlikely that the contract in such cases would permit either side simply to quit. It would be designed so that neither side could easily break it, although there might be scope for variation in its terms over its lifetime. For example, the contract would typically include requirements for maintenance and upgrading throughout the period of the contract, and these might have to be specified separately when they were required. Here, though, we simply note that the capital embodied in the hospital is most certainly not fungible for the whole period; and that once the hospital has been built, the underlying assets have few alternative uses.

When we treat capital as perfectly fungible, we risk falling into what the great historian of economics, Joseph Schumpeter, called the Ricardian vice: that is, thinking purely in terms of the long run. We therefore ignore the fact that firms have to adjust their planning to the long run over many years and that implementing plans can be very costly. In our examples, we have concentrated on physical assets, partly because it is very easy to see that it is impossible to build a hospital or to sink a mine overnight.

> **Long run** A period in which the use of all factors can be varied.

We have already defined capital as the amount of money needed to acquire the assets used in the firm. In these exercises, we have discussed assets in terms of their ability to generate a stream of income over time, which gives their financial value. We can think of the capital in a business as being invested so that it generates a flow of income. In effect, investors supply the capital, which is just a sum of money available at the present time, in order to receive a flow of future income. Thinking about the healthcare example again, we have two businesses: one specializes in the treatment of patients, while the other specializes in facilities management. The facilities manager might raise the finance to build the hospital, but it secures its ability to make regular payments to investors by entering into a service supply contract with the healthcare provider. Treated purely as a financial transaction, building a hospital involves the commitments of funds now in order to receive a stream of income in the future.

12.2   The short run in production

We define the *short run* as the period during which the capital assets of a business cannot be altered, but in which it can vary the quantity of labour inputs, as discussed in the examples in Section 12.1. The firm's short-run problem is therefore rather simpler than the long-run problem. Instead of a large project requiring substantial capital, we return to the bakery example from Chapter 1. If its capital stock is fixed, then it cannot change its premises, it cannot buy and install new equipment, and it cannot adopt new production techniques. We should rule out even quite simple changes, such as buying new delivery vans, or installing new display cases in its shops. There will, though, be no restrictions at all on the use of labour inputs. The bakery management can change the number of hours of work that it requires its staff to provide, managing the labour input by such means as changing the working pattern or the duties of employees, hiring additional staff, and also laying off existing ones. While simple in theory, the design and management of labour contracts has some very interesting features.

By yourself

X12.4 In managing labour inputs during a recession, firms sometimes ask workers to take extended holidays. Why would a firm not use its right to terminate contracts and hire new workers? [*Hint:* Think about the transactions costs involved in hiring new workers, and the nature of the employment contract.]

X12.5 It is common for firms to enter into 'rolling contracts' with senior managers. These have a fixed termination date, but can be renewed for a fixed period before termination. Why might a firm choose to hire most workers using an open-ended contract, but to hire senior managers using a sequence of rolling contracts?

12.2.1 Using labour as the variable input

We write the bakery's short-run production function in terms of the number of loaves, B, produced using fixed capital, K_0, and variable labour input, L, as:

$$B = B(L; K_0) \qquad [12.1]$$

We have adapted our notation from that used in Chapters 10 and 11 to emphasize the point that the capital input, K_0, is constant. For the purposes of the short run, the capital input is no longer a variable, under the firm's control, but a part of the choice environment around which the firm must work. In effect, K_0 is a parameter in the firm's short-run decision making, so that the labour input, L, is the only variable.

In discussing resource allocation decisions in Chapter 11, we noted that the bakery might choose any feasible combination of inputs that enabled it to meet its production target, but we concluded that it would always hire the cheapest one possible so that production was both economically and technically efficient. In the short run, output is a function of (variable) labour and (fixed) capital, and the firm simply has to hire the quantity of labour needed to meet its production target. This suggests that in the short run the bakery will seek only to achieve technical efficiency. We expect the bakery to choose the quantity of labour, L_{SR}, that just allows it to meet its production target, B_0, so that L_{SR} satisfies the condition:

$$B = (L_{SR}; K_0) = B_0 \qquad [12.2]$$

In Expression 12.2, we have the implicit solution of the bakery's short-run problem. For a given production function, output target and capital stock, L_{SR} is the minimum, feasible level of labour usage.

12.2.2 Deviation from plans

As defined in Section 12.1.1, the long run is the planning period, with the short run being the period in which operational decisions are made. During the planning period, the bakery will have set out its production plans: both its planned output in the current short run, and the quantities of capital and labour inputs to be used in the business. From the standpoint of the planning period, the bakery's plans should ensure that it will be able to produce its target output at the lowest possible cost, achieving economic efficiency. If the forecasts of future activity in the business plan were perfectly accurate, then the bakery would implement the plan exactly.

Suppose that in its planning, the bakery sets an output target, $B = B^*$. To achieve this, it hires capital, K_0, in the planning period, which is the fixed capital in the next period in which the plan is implemented and in which production takes place. Since the bakery would use a long-run approach in the planning period, this is the capital that it would hire to produce the output, B^*, at minimum cost, so we can write:

$$K_0 = K_0(B^*) \qquad\qquad [12.3]$$

We say that the bakery implements its production plan in the *current period*. It may hire labour inputs according to the plan, but more typically it will need to adjust its labour hiring decision to the actual market conditions.

We begin by assuming that that the plan is completely accurate. In the current period, the firm produces output, $B = B^*$, using the capital K_0 and labour input L_0, chosen so that:

$$L_0 = L_0(B^*) \qquad\qquad [12.4]$$

The input combination (K_0, L_0), chosen during the planning period, minimizes the cost of producing output, B^*. Unsurprisingly, given that it is the economically efficient choice, the bakery would stick to its plan, were it completely accurate. Its short-run and long-run factor demands and output would be identical, producing B^* with inputs (K_0, L_0).

Yet plans are rarely fulfilled in this way. We should expect to see deviations (hopefully small ones) between the market conditions assumed in planning and the real conditions that the bakery actually faces. For example, the bakery might not have taken account of new house building close to its shops, with the increased population resulting in higher than predicted demand. Alternatively, the town might be affected by an economic downturn as a large employer closes a factory, causing some people to move away from the town. Under these circumstances, we might expect demand for bread to be lower than planned. These are examples of *demand shocks*, because their effect on the market emerges from changes in the market demand function. We can also identify shocks to the supply side, which affect the market through the market supply function: for example, the effect of higher world grain prices, which leads to higher production costs and which the bakery will try to pass on to the consumer. For now we simply note that shocks such as these affect the market outcome: we will consider the interaction between demand and supply in more detail in Chapter 14.

We might easily continue the list of reasons for expecting variation between the plan and the actual market conditions almost indefinitely; in general, positive shocks, such as an increase in the local population or a reduction in sales taxes will lead to an increase in sales, while negative shocks, such as higher wages or additional regulations, will lead to a reduction in sales. Since we do not expect any plan to be perfectly accurate, we concentrate on how the firm responds to such changes in market conditions. We denote the current period production target as B_0, noting only that we do not expect it to be equal to the planned production target B^*. Where the bakery would have planned to hire $L_0(B_0)$, it actually hires the quantity $L_{SR}(K_0)$, chosen, as in Expression 12.2 to allow the firm to meet the new target output, B_0. The short-run demand for labour therefore emerges as a response to unforeseen changes in market conditions.

12.2.3   Differences between the long-run and short-run optimum

In the short run – or, from the perspective of planning output, in the production period – the quantity of capital that the bakery hires is fixed at K_0. Since the capital stock is fixed before the start of the current period analysis, we have shown it as a parameter in the problems of choosing the short-run labour input. In Figure 12.1, we show the capital stock, K_0, as a vertical line, and note that it acts as the short-run output expansion path, which emphasizes that the only way for the firm to alter its output is to vary the amount of labour that it hires. In the diagram, we have assumed that the bakery's production function is $B = K^{1/2} + L^{1/2}$, and have sketched isoquants showing the possible range of outputs that the bakery might achieve.

Figure 12.1 illustrates a situation in which the bakery has planned to produce 2.5 m loaves per year, but has also considered the effects on the demand for labour of having to increase output to as much as 3 m loaves or to reduce it to 2 m loaves. Hence, we show isoquants representing these three levels of output. (Given that the bakery industry is very mature, with supply and demand conditions in most markets well defined, a 20% variation on plan in any year would be extreme, but this scenario allows us to illustrate the short-run deviation from the long run very clearly in our diagram.)

Prior to the start of the trading period, during which its capital is fixed, the bakery plans for output of 2.5 m loaves, obtaining its cost-minimizing factor input allocation at the point of tangency between the isoquant and the isocost line. We know from discussion in Chapter 11 that this point of tangency lies on the output expansion path, indicated by the upward-sloping straight line passing through the origin. We have also shown how the firm would in the long run respond to any change in demand by changing the scale of production, reducing factor inputs together to cut output from 2.5 m to 2 m loaves, or increasing inputs together in order to increase production to 3 m loaves.

In the short run, however, the bakery is constrained to choose an input combination that lies on the vertical line $K = K_0$, which is its short-run expansion path. If its planned output

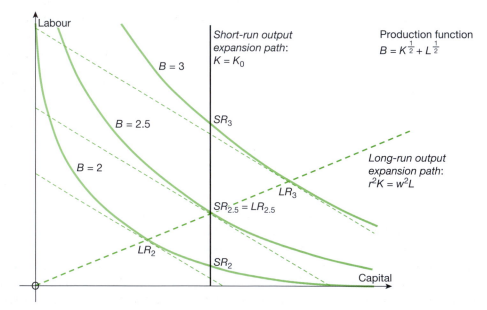

Figure 12.1 Short-run divergences from long-run equilibrium

turns out to be its actual output then, even in the short run, the bakery simply chooses the long-run optimal input combination at the intersection of the short-run and the long-run expansion paths. In Figure 12.1, we see that where the plan is fulfilled, the expansion paths intersect. If the bakery wants to reduce production, it is unable to reduce the capital inputs in the short run, and so must reduce the labour inputs more than it would choose in the long run, choosing the point on the isoquant $B = 2$ where it meets the short-run output expansion path, $K = K_0$, the point SR_2 in the diagram. Note firstly that this point lies to the right and below the long-run least-cost input combination, confirming that the bakery will shed the excess labour inputs, but also note that the isocost line through LR_2 passes below SR_2, confirming that the cost to the bakery of producing 2 m loaves is higher in the short run when it has over-invested in capital than it would be in the long run.

The analysis of the case where the bakery needs to produce 3 m loaves is almost identical, and so we simply state the results. The bakery will need to hire more labour in the short run than it would wish to hire in the long run so that it compensates for under-investment in capital, and this will increase the costs of production in the short run above what they would be when reaching this production level in the long run. Our conclusion should be unsurprising. Since the bakery is unable to alter its use of capital, and so cannot achieve economic efficiency when there is any deviation from plan, its short-run total costs cannot be less than its long-run total costs.

12.3 Analysis of short-run costs

We do not say that short-run costs are necessarily greater than long-run costs, since they would be equal were the firm's plan to be fulfilled perfectly. We illustrate the implied relationship between these two cost curves in Figure 12.2. In the diagram, the short-run total cost curve touches, but does not intersect, the long-run total cost function at the planned output: therefore, the total cost curves share a common tangent at this level of output. For any other level of output, the short-run total cost curve will lie above the long-run cost curve. In the long run, the total cost of achieving zero output will be zero: the firm can produce output $B = 0$ by refusing to hire any inputs, and so its cost of production $C(0) = 0$.

In the short run, though, the firm must pay the costs of the capital that it has already hired for the whole of the short-run period, a total of rK_0. We call costs that must be incurred, irrespective of the level of production, *fixed costs*, distinguishing them from the labour costs, $wL(B)$, which vary with the quantity of loaves that the bakery ends up producing. Since the labour costs are determined in the short-run period in which production takes place, and depend upon the level of production, we refer to them as *variable costs*.

12.3.1 Marginal costs in the short run

Since the short-run total cost is higher than the long-run total cost except where actual output is equal to planned output, it follows that the short-run and long-run marginal cost will also be equal at planned output. We shall not prove this result, or any others about the relationship between short-run and long-run marginal costs, because they are a little tricky; instead we concentrate on relatively intuitive demonstrations. If short-run total costs are never less than long-run total costs, the graphical relationship between their curves must be as shown in Figure 12.2 with the short-run total cost curve lying above the long-run

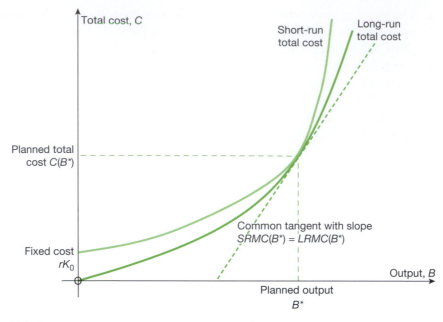

Figure 12.2 Short-run and long-run total costs

total cost curve, except at the planned level of output, B^*, where the curves touch but do not cross. For this to happen, they must have the same gradient at the planned output, B^*, and we have illustrated this point in the diagram by showing a common tangent. Since the slope of a tangent to a curve is its derivative, and marginal cost is also defined as the derivative of total cost, we have the result that for output B^*, $MC_{SR}(B^*) = MC_{LR}(B^*)$.

We now demonstrate that it is reasonable to suppose that when output is below the planned level the short-run marginal cost will be less than the long-run marginal cost. Intuitively this is reasonable, since the bakery would then hire more than the optimal quantity of capital given actual output. It therefore reduces output by reducing labour usage, but has to reduce labour usage more rapidly than it would in the long run because capital usage is fixed, and the variable part of costs therefore falls more quickly as output contracts.

We can divide short-run total costs into fixed and variable costs, so that:

$$TC_{SR}(B) = TFC + TVC(B) \qquad [12.5]$$

Here we do not describe the constant fixed costs as a function of output B. In addition, to simplify notation slightly, we do not use the subscript 'SR' for fixed and variable costs because these measures of costs arise only in the short run. Then, differentiating Expression 12.5 with respect to B, we obtain the marginal costs:

$$MC_{SR}(B) = \frac{dTC_{SR}}{dB} = \frac{dTVC}{dB} \qquad [12.6]$$

Expression 12.6 simply reflects the fact that fixed costs do not vary with output.

We now know the following:

- The long-run total cost of producing zero output is zero [$TC_{LR}(0) = 0$], since if the bakery shuts down production then in the long run it will require neither capital nor labour inputs.

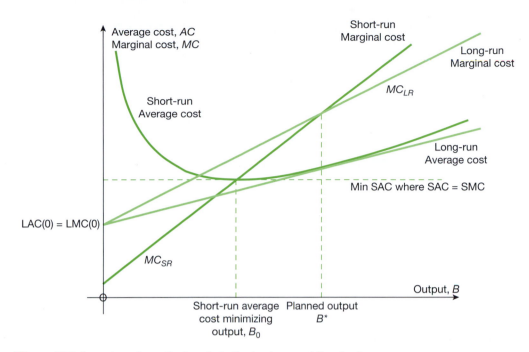

Figure 12.3 Average and marginal costs in the long run and the short run

- The short-run total cost of producing zero output is the fixed cost $[TC_{SR}(0) = TFC]$, since if the bakery shuts down production then in the short run it still has to pay the cost of hiring its capital.
- From the preceding two points, the short-run total variable cost of producing zero output is zero.
- From the earlier discussion, $TC_{LR}(B^*) = TC_{SR}(B^*)$.

In Figure 12.3 we use these observations to argue for the relationships between long-run and short-run average costs and long-run and short-run marginal costs. Firstly, as output, B, increases from zero to B^*, the increase in short-run total costs is less than the increase in long-run total costs, since $TVC(B^*) < TC_{SR}(B^*) = TC_{LR}(B^*)$. This follows from our previous analysis. When the firm produces less than was planned, it hires more (fixed) capital, and less (variable) labour than it would in the long run. The total cost of production is higher in the short run because of high fixed costs. Marginal costs, measuring the rate of change of costs as output expands, will be lower in the short run than in the long run, because only labour usage can change with output in the short run. For the range of outputs $0 \leq B < B^*$, therefore, we expect that $MC_{SR}(B) < MC_{LR}(B)$. Similarly, without trying to prove the point formally, it will certainly be true that if $MC_{SR}(B) > MC_{LR}(B)$ for all values of output $B > B^*$, the planned output $TC_{SR}(B) > TC_{LR}(B)$. Thus in Figure 12.3, the short-run marginal cost curve, MC_{SR}, intersects the long-run curve, MC_{LR}, from below at the planned output, B^*.

We can also analyse the relation between the short-run marginal cost and the marginal product of labour. In Expression 12.6, we define the short-run marginal cost as the derivative of short-run total costs with respect to output. Recall from Section 12.3 that the marginal product of labour, MP_L, is the rate of change of output with respect to the labour input (given that the capital input is constant at $K = K_0$), so that $MP_L = \frac{dB}{dL}\big|_{K = K_0}$. The inverse of this rate of change, $\frac{dL}{dB}\big|_{K = K_0} = \left(\frac{dB}{dL}\right)^{-1}$, is the rate of change of the labour input required as the production target increases. Using some algebraic notation, we can define the marginal cost $MC(B)$:

$$MC_{SR}(B) = \frac{dTC_{SR}}{dB} = \frac{dTVC}{dB} = w \cdot \frac{dL(B)}{dB} = w \Big/ \frac{dB}{dL} = \frac{w}{MP_L} \qquad [12.7]$$

The first thing to say about Expression 12.7 is that dimensionally it is quite sensible. We can think of marginal cost, MC_{SR}, as a money value divided by an output value. The wage rate, w, is simply a money value, and the marginal product, MP_L is measured in terms of output. We can also think of the wage as the rate at which costs increase with labour usage, and, very similarly, we can think of the marginal product as the rate at which output increases with labour usage. Their ratio is then the rate at which costs change as output increases, which is the definition of marginal cost.

Thinking about this in a slightly more intuitive way, consider finite approximations to the instantaneous rates of change. Treating the marginal product of labour for a bakery as the increase in the number of loaves caused by increasing the labour input by a very small amount, say one hour per year, and the wage rate as the payment made to a worker for that extra hour's work, then this ratio (the wage payment divided by the increase in the number of loaves produced) is the additional cost per loaf. We shall next meet Expression 12.7 in Chapter 14 when examining the profit-maximizing behaviour of the bakery.

12.3.2   Average costs in the short run

We begin with the distinction between short-run average fixed costs and short-run average variable costs. Adapting Expression 12.5:

$$AC_{SR}(B) = \frac{TC_{SR}(B)}{B} = \frac{TFC}{B} + \frac{TVC(B)}{B} = AFC + AVC(B) \qquad [12.8]$$

As production increases, the fixed cost per unit falls. In addition, though, it is impossible to define the average fixed cost for an output of zero. This means that as production falls towards zero, the short-run average cost will increase without limit. Similarly, as output increases without limit, the short-run average cost will approach the average variable cost.

Recall the discussion of diminishing marginal product in Section 10.3.2. Given our definition of short-run marginal cost in Expression 12.7, short-run marginal costs must eventually increase, and short-run average costs will eventually follow. We can now safely make the following predictions:

- when short-run output is at the planned level B^*, short-run and long-run average costs will be the same;
- at all other levels of output, short-run average costs will be higher than long-run average costs;
- average cost will be a decreasing function for very low levels of output, as average fixed costs fall;
- since average costs initially fall, and eventually increase, there will be some level of output, B_0, for which average costs will be at a minimum; and
- at that level of output, short-run average costs will be equal to short-run marginal costs.

All of these claims are illustrated in Figure 12.3. If the bakery's plan is fulfilled perfectly, it will hire the planned labour input, L_0, and produce planned output, B^*. Long-run and short-run total costs are then equal, and long-run and short-run average costs will be also equal. Given that short-run total costs, $TC_{SR}(B)$, are greater than long-run total costs, $TC_{LR}(B)$, for any other level of output, B, it must be that the short-run average cost, $AC_{SR}(B) \geq AC_{LR}(B)$ for every output, B, with equality when $B = B^*$, so that actual output equals planned output. Applying the argument used in Section 12.3.1 for total costs, it follows that short-run and long-run average costs share a common tangent when $B = B^*$. We show this in Figure 12.3, where on the line $B = B^*$, as well as the common tangency of short-run and long-run average cost curves, the short-run and long-run marginal cost curves intersect, with the short-run marginal cost curve steeper than the long-run marginal cost curve. Around the output, B^*, for which the plan is fulfilled perfectly, the cost of adjusting output is greater in the short run, when only the labour input is variable, than it would be in the long run, when all inputs are variable.

Although it is possible to define the average cost of zero production in the long run (because as output falls towards zero, costs fall towards zero), it is impossible to do this in the short run, since the fixed costs of hiring capital have to be absorbed over a very small amount of output. Hence the short-run average cost curve is initially very steep and downward-sloping, and close to the cost axis but never intersecting it. As output increases, the average fixed cost falls, but the average variable cost is increasing, reflecting the gradually increasing marginal cost. It follows that the short-run average cost has a minimum: we have shown this at the output B_0, where short-run average and marginal costs are equal. We have to see this configuration given that whenever marginal cost is greater than average cost, average cost will increase with output; while whenever marginal cost is less than average cost, average cost will fall with output. At the minimum, marginal cost is neither increasing nor decreasing, and so marginal and average costs must be equal.

12.4 Conclusions

Note in Figure 12.3 that the firm does not minimize average cost at its planned output. It is important that we do not typically assign a firm the objective of minimizing average costs (or indeed any other measure of costs). Instead, the proper objective for the firm is always to maximize profits; but since we have not thought about the demand for the firm's output or its revenue, we cannot yet solve that problem. There is a minimum of short-run average costs, because the average fixed cost declines with output while the average variable cost increases. This result simply reflects our definition of short-run costs, and does not guide a firm's resource allocation.

We have treated the short run in terms of the need for firms to deviate from their plans. Production takes place on the short-run expansion path, which permits technical efficiency but not economic efficiency. If the bakery wishes to increase its production in the short run, it will increase its labour usage in the short run by more than it would wish in the long run; long-run adjustment to the new market environment will involve reducing labour inputs and increasing capital inputs, so that the firm chooses an economically efficient input combination, which lies on the long-run output expansion path in Figure 12.1. In both the short run and the long run, we assume that every firm will allocate its resources as efficiently as possible. The firm's capacity to vary usage of capital in the long run ensures that it is able to produce any output at a cost that is no higher than the cost it would face in the short run. It is for this reason that we treat economic efficiency as part of the long-run outcome for firms, but rely on technical efficiency alone in the short run.

Summary

We defined the capital employed in a business in terms of the assets purchased in order to produce outputs. We argued that while financial capital is entirely fungible, the assets purchased with it are often fixed, both for the time that it takes to ready them for producing output, and also for the length of any contracts for which their use is required.

We noted that it is likely that a firm will find it much easier to vary its labour usage than its capital usage.

We distinguished between the long run, in which the use of all factors is variable, and the short run, in which only labour usage is variable. We considered a slightly different definition, in which the long run formed the firm's planning horizon, with operational activities taking place in the short run. The firm therefore chose its capital assets during the (long-run) planning period, deciding on how to manage labour inputs in the (short-run) operational framework, where the capital assets are fixed.

Short-run production and cost functions then emerge from consideration of deviation from the planned output. Given that capital usage is fixed, the firm can only achieve economic efficiency in production if it is able to implement its plan perfectly. Otherwise, in the short run, although it may achieve technical efficiency, the firm will incur higher total costs than in the long run.

We saw that where the firm exceeds its planned output, it will use a more labour intensive technology than would be optimal, and where output falls short of planned levels, it will use a more capital intensive technology.

In the short run, it is possible to divide costs into fixed costs (here, the costs of the use of capital) and variable costs (here, the costs of the wages due to labour). In the long run, there are no fixed costs.

Since total costs cannot be less in the short run than in the long run, equality requires the firm's plan to be fulfilled perfectly. In addition, since fixed costs are zero in the long run, and greater than zero in the short run, it follows that:

- the short-run marginal cost curve intersects the long-run marginal cost curve from below at planned output;
- average fixed costs are infinite when output is zero;
- short-run average total costs approach average variable costs at very high levels of output;
- average variable costs eventually increase, given the diminishing marginal product of labour; and
- at the planned output, short-run and long-run average costs are equal; while otherwise, short-run average costs are greater than long-run average costs.

Visit the companion website at **www.palgrave.com/mochrie** to access further teaching and learning materials, including lecturer slides and a testbank, as well as guideline answers and student MCQs.

13

Firm supply in perfect competition

What we do in this chapter

Across Chapters 13 and 14, we examine the profit-maximizing behaviour of a firm in the context of a *perfectly competitive market*. In this chapter, we derive the relationship between the market price and the firm supply. The market price is exogenous, so that firms treat it as given.

Building on our discussion of the cost-minimizing behaviour of businesses, we introduce the concepts of firm *revenue* and *profits*, and derive conditions that must be satisfied for a firm to maximize its profits. These conditions are the equality of marginal revenue and marginal costs at the profit-maximizing output, together with restrictions on their derivatives.

Turning to analysis of perfect competition, we rule out all sources of *market power*. Assuming that all firms produce identical outputs and that consumers are fully informed about the market, we argue that firms will be able to sell any quantity of output up to the market demand at the common *market price*, which all firms will adopt. This gives us an individual firm's *(total) revenue function*.

We then apply conditions for profit maximization, assuming that firms face eventually diminishing returns to scale in production. We show that the firm's *supply function* is the inverse of its marginal cost function.

Firms make goods in order to sell them. Discussing firms' engagement with markets in Chapter 1, we argued that when a firm faces increasing demand, then it will be able to sell more output, or raise its selling price; or indeed do both. We now try to explain this behaviour in the context of firms that always seek to maximize their profit. In Section 1.3, we defined a seller's willingness to accept, $WTA(q_F)$, as the minimum price at which firm F would be willing to sell more output, given that it had already produced output q_F. There is no maximum price that the firm would be willing to accept. Any price higher than $WTA(q_F)$ is always acceptable to a firm.

In Chapters 10–12, we have argued that firms always minimize the cost of producing any target output, with the production process being technically (and, in the long run, economically) efficient. We developed total, average and marginal cost functions to capture important characteristics of firms' internal operations. We could ignore these in our initial discussion of market behaviour in Chapter 1, but now we tie together the firm's cost minimization processes with its market interaction, through analysis of profit maximization. As a first step, we define measures of firm revenue, in much the same way as we have introduced measures of cost.

13.1 Profits, costs, and revenues

Profits are simply the difference between a firm's total revenues and its total costs; a firm's total revenues, $R(X)$, are the income that it generates from sales of goods, X. We shall see in this chapter and the

Profit A firm's revenues from sales, less the costs of production.

next one how the exact form of a firm's total revenue function depends upon the structure of the market in which it operates. In this introduction, we set out some general principles that hold for all market structures, and so for any form of revenue function.

If a firm sells all its output at one price, its **total revenue** will be the product of the price and the quantity demanded. We shall assume that the firm accepts the market price, and can sell any quantity of output at this price. The firm then chooses the profit-maximizing output. Implicitly, we treat sales revenue as being determined by the strength of demand for output, while costs vary with the input prices and the state of technology, as captured in the production function. Profit links demand and supply conditions, providing us with another form of efficiency in production: the firm should not make more output than it can sell.

> **Revenue** (total revenue) A firm's income from selling output.

By yourself

X13.1   Explain why the assumption that firms only produce the quantity of output that they can sell ensures market clearing.

13.1.1 The profit function

We now write a firm's profit, Π, as the difference between revenue, R, and cost, C, all of which are functions of output, Q:

$$\Pi(Q) = R(Q) - C(Q) \qquad [13.1]$$

We want to find the output Q^* that maximizes profit, so that $\Pi^* = \Pi(Q^*)$. Looking at Expression 13.1, for profit to be increasing in output, total revenues must increase more rapidly than total costs. In the same way, profits will fall as output rises if costs increase more quickly than revenues. The rate of change of costs is then greater than the rate of change of revenues.

We show these relationships in Figure 13.1. It may be useful to think of this as being the situation facing a petrol station in the discussion in Chapter 1. As the petrol station sells more output, its costs seem likely to increase proportionately, at least approximately. Larger petrol stations have very much the same structure as smaller ones. We also argued in Chapter 1 that as a petrol station increases the price that it charges for fuel, we would expect it to lose some customers, but not all of them, suggesting that the demand function will be a decreasing function of its price.

In Figure 13.1, when output is zero, total costs and total revenues are both zero. By shutting down production the petrol station breaks even. There cannot be any fixed costs, so that this is long-run analysis, with the firm able to vary the use of all input factors. As well as shutting down, the petrol station could achieve zero revenue if it simply gave petrol away, with price $p = 0$. Although we might usually think of the petrol station as setting price, and selling as much as it can at that price, to be consistent with our analysis in Chapters 10–12, we shall assume that it has an output target, and that it adjusts its price to achieve this. Rather than thinking in terms of a demand function, with the quantity sold determined in terms of the price, we instead think in terms of the **inverse demand function**, with the price at which transactions take place being determined by the firm's output. The inverse demand is then the market *WTP*.

> **Inverse demand function** The price a firm can set as a function of the quantity consumers demand.

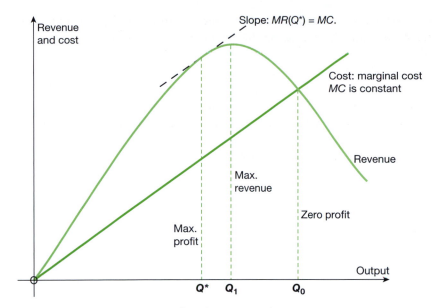

Figure 13.1 Profit maximization in terms of total revenue and costs

Looking at the total revenue curve in Figure 13.1, we see that it increases in output until the output Q_1, and then starts to fall. At output Q_0, increasing costs meet falling revenues, and, as at zero output, the petrol station would only just break even, making zero profit. For any output greater than Q_0, it would make a loss, which we simply report as a negative profit.[1]

By yourself

X13.2   Why should we never expect to see a firm making losses in the long run? [*Hint:* Think about what it means when a firm produces zero output.]

X13.3   Sketch a diagram in which a firm never makes profits, but minimizes losses at some output Q_0. Why might such a firm choose to produce output Q_0 rather than stopping production? [*Hint:* Suppose that there is a fixed element in total costs, so that $TC(0) > 0$, and that total costs increase at an increasing rate, while total revenues are linear.]

13.1.2   Profit maximization

We have already introduced the first- and second-order conditions associated with a local maximum of a function in Essential Maths 11.1. We applied these conditions to find the minimum value of average cost in Section 11.2. The (necessary) first-order condition for maximum profit is that the first derivative of Expression 13.1 is zero. Then, differentiating both sides of Expression 13.1, and evaluating it for the profit-maximizing output, Q^*:

$$\Pi'(Q^*) = R'(Q^*) - C'(Q^*) = 0 \qquad\qquad [13.2]$$

---

1   In this analysis, we assume that the nature of the good is fixed. Andrew Turton asks a simple question in his essay on the online student essay bank: why do restaurants in the US offer larger serving sizes than their UK counterparts? He argues that the differences can be understood in terms of the much lower share of ingredients (and labour time) in input costs. You can read Andrew's essay (and those of other students) on the companion website for this book, at **www.palgrave.com/mochrie.**

When Expression 13.2 is satisfied, total revenue and total costs increase at the same rate. This happens in Figure 13.1 for output Q^*, where the tangent to the total revenue is parallel to the total costs line. In Section 11.2, we defined the *marginal cost function* as the derivative of total costs with respect to output. In the same way, we define *marginal revenue* as the derivative of total revenue with respect to output. We then understand Expression 13.2 as saying that when marginal revenue equals marginal cost, profits do not change quickly when there is a change in output. It is often more convenient to express this necessary condition for profit maximization in terms of the equality of marginal revenue and marginal costs:

$$MR(Q^*) = MC(Q^*) \qquad\qquad [13.3]$$

Expression 13.3 is a necessary condition for profit maximization. While it must be satisfied, it is not enough by itself to ensure that Q^* is the firm's profit-maximizing output. It could, for example, be satisfied at a firm's profit minimizing output, were one to exist. To be certain that Q^* maximizes profits, we need to confirm that the profit function is concave around Q^*, so that the second derivative of the profit function is less than zero at Q^*. For many, but not all functions, it is sufficient to check that the second derivative is less than zero, or that:

$$\Pi''(Q^*) = R''(Q^*) - C''(Q^*) = MR'(Q^*) - MC'(Q^*) < 0 \qquad\qquad [13.4]$$

In the graphical illustration in Figure 13.1, Expression 13.4 certainly holds when $Q = Q^*$. Since costs increase at a constant rate, $C''(Q^*) = 0$; and with revenue increasing at a decreasing rate, $R''(Q^*) < 0$. In Figure 13.2 (and also in Exercise X13.7 below), we have a similar situation, which we describe by using measures of average and marginal revenues and costs, rather than their totals. In the diagram, separate lines indicate how average and marginal revenues vary with output, but a single line is sufficient for both average and marginal costs. We confirmed that when total costs are linear, as in Figure 13.1,

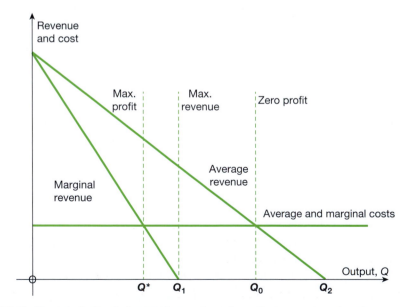

Figure 13.2 Profit maximization in terms of average and marginal revenue and costs

average and marginal costs are constant, as shown in Figure 13.2. (In X13.5 below, we argue that if total revenue is linear, then average and marginal revenue will both be constant and equal.)

By yourself

X13.4   Confirm that $AR(Q) = p$, so that the average revenue and the inverse demand functions are identical.

X13.5   Define the average revenues of a firm as total revenues per unit sold, so that $AR(Q) = TR(Q)/Q$. Confirm that if the market price, p_0, does not change as the firm increases its output, then its total revenue function is linear, while its average revenue, $AR(Q)$, and marginal revenue, $MR(Q)$, are constant and equal to the price, p_0.

X13.6   Given the definition of average revenues as revenue per unit sold:
(a) Differentiate the function with respect to output Q, confirming that $AR'(Q) = [MR(Q) - AR(Q)]/Q$.
(b) Show that if average revenues are constant, $AR(Q) = MR(Q)$; but that if average revenues are decreasing, $AR(Q) > MR(Q)$.

X13.7   Given a linear cost function, $C(Q) = cQ$ and a linear inverse demand function $p(Q) = a - bQ$.
(a) Write down the firm's total revenue function, and obtain its average and marginal revenue functions.
(b) Obtain the firm's average and marginal cost functions.
(c) Show that the firm generates zero revenue if it stops production or else if it produces $Q_1 = b/a$.
(d) Show that the firm maximizes revenues by producing output $Q^M = a/2b$.
(e) Show that the firm breaks even by stopping production, or else by producing $Q_0 = (a - c)/b$.
(f) Show that the firm maximizes profits by producing output $Q^* = (a - c)/2b$.
(g) Sketch two diagrams, one showing the outputs Q^*, Q^M, Q_0 and Q_1 on total revenue and cost curves; the other showing these outputs in relation to average and marginal revenues, and average and marginal costs.

In Figure 13.2, we capture the relationships between average and marginal revenues, and average and marginal costs, implied in Figure 13.1. The average revenue curve is a downward-sloping straight line, with the marginal revenue curve also downward-sloping and always below the average curve. In Exercise X13.7, we explore the relationship between the average and marginal revenue curves for this special case. The most important features are that the curves intersect on the vertical axis (when the firm has zero output), and that the marginal revenue line is twice as steep as the average revenue line. Marginal revenue is zero at the total revenue-maximizing output, Q_1, in Figure 13.2, while the price or average revenue falls to zero at output Q_2. From Exercise X13.7, we see that $Q_2 = 2Q_1$.

The last, and most important, point that we check in Figure 13.2 is that profits are maximized at the intersection of the marginal revenue and marginal cost curves, when output $Q = Q^*$. We can quickly conclude that Expression 13.4 is satisfied. The marginal cost line is flat, so its gradient is zero. The marginal revenue line is downward-sloping, so its gradient is less than zero. Another way of putting this is to say that decreasing marginal revenue and constant marginal cost ensure that the profit function is concave around Q^*, so that there is then a profit maximum. We summarize these results in Proposition 13.1.

Proposition 13.1

A firm using economically efficient technology produces output, $Q \geq 0$, at total cost, $C = C(Q)$. It sells that output at price $p = p(Q)$. We assume that C is an increasing function of Q, and that p never increases in Q. We define the total revenue of the firm, $R = R(Q) = p(Q).Q$, and the total profit, $\Pi = \Pi(Q) = R(Q) - C(Q)$. For output, Q^*, for which $\Pi'(Q^*) = R'(Q^*) - C'(Q^*) = 0$ and $\Pi'(Q^*) = R''(Q^*) - C''(Q^*) < 0$, the firm maximizes profits.

Proof: This follows directly from the definitions of profit and the necessary and sufficient conditions for the maximum of a function.

By yourself

X13.8   Confirm that for the linear cost function, $C = cQ$, and the linear inverse demand function, $p = a - bQ$, the conditions for a profit maximum are satisfied for output $Q^* = \frac{a-c}{2b}$, so that price $p^* = \frac{a+c}{2}$ and the maximum profit $\Pi^* = \frac{(a-c)^2}{4b}$. Sketch a diagram showing the average and marginal revenue curves, the average and marginal cost curves, the profit-maximizing output, Q^*, the price, p^*, and the total profit.

X13.9   Confirm that for the quadratic cost function $C = cQ^2$ and the linear inverse demand function $p = p_0$, so that the market price does not change with the level of output, the conditions for a profit maximum are satisfied for output $Q^* = p_0/(2c)$, so that the maximum profit $\Pi^* = \frac{p_0^2}{4c}$. Sketch a diagram showing the average and marginal revenue curves, the average and marginal cost curves, the profit-maximizing output, Q^*, the price, p_0, and the total profit.

Price taker A firm that accepts the market price as given.

We have characterized the situation facing the firm in Exercise X13.8 as being similar to that facing a petrol station. It has some relatively loyal customers, who would continue to use it after it increases its price (and also some potential customers who would switch to it if it reduces its price). The petrol station does not simply have to accept the market price. In contrast, though, in Exercise X13.9, the business is a **price taker**. This is a situation of considerable interest to us, for this is typical of the firm in perfect competition, which is the benchmark market environment in the standard model. In terms of the examples of market structure from Chapter 1, we should relate this situation to the market stall example, the very simplest business that we could imagine. With stallholders simply accepting the market price, their marginal revenue is constant. We can only obtain the conditions for profit maximization if, at output, Q^*, the marginal cost function is increasing, which is consistent with production having diminishing returns to scale. This suggests that in perfect competition, the technology of production is not easily scalable, so that firms, as in the market stall example, are necessarily small.

13.2   Perfectly competitive markets

The fruit market example from Chapter 1 now becomes central to our thinking. We restate the set of Assumptions A2 which defined the market environment of perfect competition, and the Propositions P2, which we believe characterize market equilibrium. Remember that we consider markets to be highly competitive when many buyers and sellers, none of

---

Assumptions *A2*

Perfect competition

A2.1   All firms are small relative to the size of the market.

A2.2   All firms produce a single good or service, and there are no differences in quality between firms' product.

A2.3   For every firm, the cost of production increases more quickly than production, so that if output repeatedly increases by a set amount, the additional cost of production becomes steadily larger.

A2.4   There is perfect freedom of entry and exit into the market, so that a new firm can set up operations, an existing one can shut down operations, and any firm can change its output.

A2.5   All customers are small relative to the size of the market.

A2.6   The cost of acquiring information is zero.

---

whom has a large market share, know everything about market conditions, and so buy and sell units of a good whose quality is known always to be uniform, with the only possible difference across transactions being the price reached. These propositions formalize our belief that all transactions should take place at a unique market price, set so that the market clears, with the quantity of the good that firms produce and bring to the market just equal to the quantity that people demand, and the market price and trading volume dependent upon supply and demand conditions.

By yourself

X13.10   Confirm the following statements:

(a) If a firm is a price taker, selling the output, Q, at a fixed price, p_0, which does not change as Q changes, then the firm's total revenues are $R = p_0 Q$; its average revenue is $AR = p_0$; and its marginal revenue is $MR = p_0$.

(b) For such a firm, the profit-maximizing conditions stated in Proposition 13.1 will hold at an output Q^*, defined so that $MC(Q^*) = MR(Q^*)$ and $MC'(Q^*) \geq 0$.

(c) For a price taker that maximizes at output Q^*, the firm cannot face increasing returns to scale in production at Q^*.

X13.11   Suppose that a firm is a price taker, but that it faces increasing *marginal* returns to scale. Sketch a diagram showing the relationship between average and marginal revenues and average and marginal costs. Indicate on your diagram the output Q_0 for which $MC = MR$. Confirm that $MR'(Q_0) > MC'(Q_0)$, and that the firm makes a loss when output is Q_0. Confirm that by producing at Q_0 the firm maximizes its loss, rather than its profit.

We did not fully justify the Propositions, P2, when we first met them because our measures of willingness to pay, *WTP*, for people, and willingness to accept, *WTA*, for firms, appeared without justification. Through our analysis of the consumer's resource allocation problem, we understand consumers' demands in terms of prices and the amount of money available to finance consumption. We still have to complete the derivation of firms' supply, though. Exercise X13.10 is an important step towards doing this. It builds on the rule that must hold in all markets – that for profit maximization, marginal revenue equals marginal cost – and adds conditions that are consistent with the market being perfectly competitive. Whereas consumers are always price takers, firms are only price takers when they face perfect competition.

Proposition **P2**

Market clearing with perfect competition

P2.1   All transactions in the market take place at a single price, the market price, p^M.

P2.2   The total demand for the good or service (the market demand, Q^D) depends on the market price, p^M. If the market price, p^M, increases, then the market demand, Q^D, will decrease.

P2.3   The total supply of the good or service (the market supply, Q^S) depends on the market price, p^M. If the market price, p^M, increases, then the market supply, Q^S, will increase.

P2.4   The market price $p^M = p^*$, for which $Q^D(p^*) = Q^S(p^*)$, so that market demand equals market supply, clears the market, ensures that all feasible exchanges take place, and maximizes the total surplus from market exchange. The price, p^*, and the quantity traded, $Q^* = Q^D(p^*) = Q^S(p^*)$, form the market equilibrium.

P2.5   Since the market demand, Q^D, is decreasing in the market price, p^M, and the market supply, Q^S, is increasing in the market price, p^M, the market equilibrium is stable.

13.2.1   Returns to scale and profit maximization

In conditions of perfect competition, no firm will want to charge more than the market price because it will be unable to sell any output. But charging less than the market price might seem to be attractive. We need to confirm that firms will not cut prices all the way to zero, and Exercise X13.10 helps to explain this point. When firms commit resources to production, the total cost is the absolute minimum cost of achieving its output. Firms will only produce output to the extent that this will lead to profits: and for profit maximization, marginal revenues equal marginal costs. From X13.10, we see that a firm in a perfectly competitive market, which is therefore a price taker, will not wish to expand beyond the level of output, Q^*, for which marginal cost, $MC(Q^*) = p_0$, the market price, and $MC'(Q^*) \leq 0$. Exercise X13.11 confirms that it is impossible for a firm in a perfectly competitive market to maximize profits when facing increasing returns to scale.

At this point, it is convenient to assume that firms face eventually diminishing returns to scale, a concept we introduced in Chapter 10. In Figure 13.3, we show total costs and revenues in panel (a); and average and marginal revenues, and average and marginal costs, in panel (b), thereby highlighting profit-maximizing behaviour. At low levels of output, below Q_1, the firm faces diminishing returns to scale. The total cost function is concave, and the marginal and average costs functions are decreasing. For higher levels of output, above Q_0 in Figure 13.3, total costs are convex, and the marginal and average cost functions are increasing.

In panel (b), since the firm is a price taker, average and marginal revenues will always be equal to the market price. In symbols, $p_0 = MR(Q) = AR(Q)$. These two measures of revenue are identical, and their value is independent of output. In the diagram, then, we show them by the same flat line. Marginal costs, though, increase if output $Q > Q_1$, while average costs increase if output $Q > Q_0$. We show marginal costs as a curve that has a minimum at $Q = Q_1$, and which meets the average cost curve at $Q = Q_0$, the output that minimizes average costs.

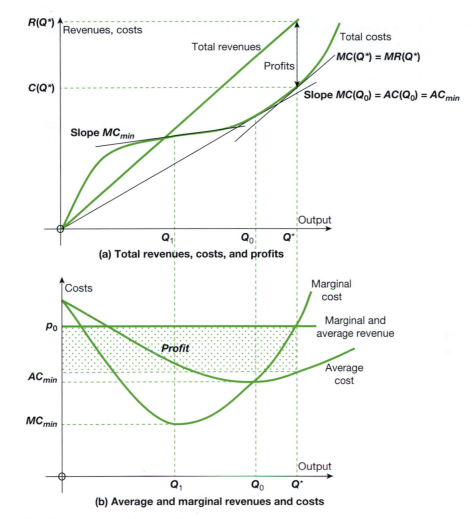

Figure 13.3 Eventually diminishing returns to scale

By yourself

X13.12 By referring to Figure 13.3 or otherwise, confirm the following:
  (a) There are two values of output at which the first-order condition for a profit maximum, $MC(Q) = MR(Q)$, is satisfied.
  (b) If $Q \geq Q_1$, then the second-order condition, $MC'(Q) \geq MR'(Q)$, is satisfied.
  (c) The unique profit-maximizing output is Q^*.
  (d) When output is Q^*, total profit $\Pi(Q^*) = [p_0 - AC(Q^*)].Q^*$.

X13.13 Adapting Figure 13.3, sketch diagrams to show how this firm would respond as the market price falls from p_0:
  (a) to a level above AC_{min};
  (b) to a level between AC_{min} and MC_{min};
  (c) to a level below MC_{min}.
  In each case, identify the firm's profit-maximizing level of output, its average cost of production, and its total profit.

(Continued)

X13.14   A firm's total cost function, $C = C(Q) = 15Q - 6Q^2 + Q^3$. It can sell any amount of output it wishes at a price $p_0 = 15$. Write down the firm's total revenue, average revenue, and marginal revenue functions; and also the firm's total profit function.

(a) Confirm that the firm breaks even, so that its profit $\Pi(Q) = 0$, if output $Q = 0$ or $Q = 6$.

(b) Obtain the firm's average cost and marginal cost functions.

(c) Confirm that $MC(0) = AC(0) = 15$; and marginal cost, MC, is minimized when $Q = 2$, while average cost, AC, is minimized when $Q = 3$. Calculate the minimum values, $MC(2)$ and $AC(3)$.

(d) State the range of outputs Q for which the firm faces: (1) increasing total returns to scale; and (2) diminishing marginal returns to scale.

(e) Confirm that the first-order condition for profit maximization, $p = MC$, is satisfied if the firm chooses output $Q = 0$ or $Q = 4$. Confirm that the second-order condition is also satisfied if $Q = 4$.

(f) Confirm that the profit function has a minimum at $Q = 0$ and a point of inflexion at $Q = 2$.

(g) For values of output, Q, between 0 and 6, sketch: (1) the revenue, cost and profit functions (all on one diagram); and (2) the average and marginal revenue and average and marginal cost functions (all on a second diagram). Clearly mark on your diagrams the key characteristics of these functions, obtained in parts (a)–(g).

(h) Suppose that the market price falls to p_1. How should the firm react: (1) if $p_1 > 6$; and (2) if $p_1 < 6$?

Suppose that Figure 13.3 and Exercises X13.12–X13.14 capture the essence of the market environment facing the owner of a market stall. The stall owner, like the owner of any firm, chooses the output at which conditions for profit maximization in Proposition 13.1 are satisfied. The business's marginal cost is then increasing, but equal to the market price. With average cost above its minimum at the profit-maximizing output, Q^*, average cost will be less than marginal cost, and the stall will make profits, with profit per unit sold being simply the difference between the market price and the firm's average cost given output, $Q = Q^*$. Given that it sells Q^* units of output, we can write the stall's profit per unit as $p_0 - AC(Q^*)$. The stall's total profit is the shaded area in Figure 13.3b. In X13.14, we specify a total cost function, C, and the market price, p_0, confirming the level of output, Q^*, at which profit maximization takes place. A stallholder who knows the costs of production and the market price can work out the business's profit-maximizing output.

Even if the first- and second-order conditions for profit maximization are satisfied, they do not guarantee that a firm will make a profit; from X13.13, we can see that if the market price, p_0, falls below AC_{min}, the lowest possible value of average cost, then the firm necessarily makes a loss. Remember that the firm's average revenue $AR = AR(Q) = p_0$. No matter how much the firm decides to produce, the cost per unit, measured by the average cost, AC, is then greater than the average revenue, AR. The market stall makes a loss on every unit of output that it sells.

Suppose though, that $C(0) = 0$. There are then no fixed costs to running the business, and facing such a low price its owner can just decide to close it down. We might say that this business has left the market; but it might just be that the owner has decided to suspend production, waiting to see whether the market environment changes, and intending to start up production again. In X13.14, this would occur if the market price were to fall so that $p_0 < 6$. Then we would have $p_0 < AC_{min}$. Unable to avoid losses at any level of output, the firm would decide to stop production.

13.2.2 The supply function

We can now summarize this argument as Proposition 13.2.

Proposition 13.2

A firm facing a perfectly competitive market uses economically efficient technology to produce output $Q \geq 0$, at total cost, $C = C(Q) \geq 0$, with $C(0) = 0$. It sells all of that output at market price, $p = p_0$. The firm's production function exhibits (eventually) diminishing returns to scale, so that the firm's average cost function has a minimum value, $AC(Q_0) = AC_{min} > 0$.

If $p_0 \geq AC_{min}$, we define the firm's profit-maximizing output implicitly as $Q*: MC(Q*) = p_0$, so that marginal cost at the profit-maximizing output equals the market price.

If $p_0 < AC_{min}$, $Q* = 0$.

Define the firm's supply function, $Q^S = Q^S(p)$. Then:

$$Q^S(p_0) = \begin{cases} MC^{-1}(p_0), & \text{if } p_0 \geq AC_{min} \\ 0, & \text{if } p_0 < AC_{min} \end{cases}, \qquad [13.5]$$

where the function MC^{-1} is the inverse of the marginal cost function.

Discussion: The conditions for profit maximization when $p_0 \geq AC_{min}$ follow by application of Proposition 13.1. When $p_0 < AC_{min}$, the firm makes losses in producing any level of output. These can avoided by ending production, given $C(0) = 0$. The supply function is the quantity, $Q^S = Q^S(p)$, that the firm will produce given the market price. Where $p_0 \geq AC_{min}$, we invert the relationship between price and output obtained by applying the profit maximization conditions, defining the supply function in explicit form.

With eventually diminishing returns to scale, the firm makes its supply decision based on whether or not it is better to be in the market or to remain out of it. For prices below the minimum value of the firm's average costs, AC_{min}, the firm cannot make a profit, and so it produces no output, quitting the market. If the market price, p_0, equals AC_{min}, then the firm will produce the average cost-minimizing output, Q_0: $AC(Q_0) = AC_{min} = p_0$. At this output, average and marginal costs are equal. At higher prices, we apply the solution to the profit-maximizing problem, which we have just found. The firm increases its output, Q^S, so that the firm's marginal cost, $MC(Q^S)$ is the market price, p_0.

This gives us an implicit definition of the supply function. In Expression 13.5, we assume that it is possible for us to invert the marginal cost function, so that we can state the supply function explicitly. Increasing marginal costs, resulting from the diminishing returns to scale in production needed for profit maximization, are sufficient to ensure that the supply function is increasing in price. For every price, p_0, we can then define a single level of output, $Q^S(p_0)$, for which the profit-maximizing conditions are satisfied. We see in Figure 13.4 the two segments of the supply function: the vertical line extending from the origin for low prices where there is no output; and the upward-sloping segment for higher prices.

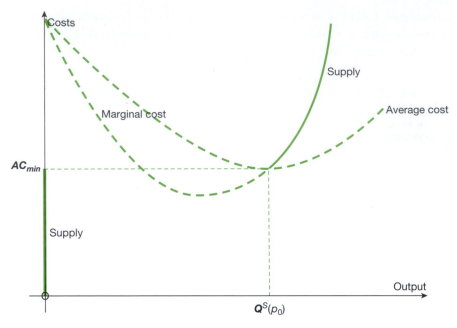

Figure 13.4 Firm supply

By yourself

X13.15   For each of the following cost functions, $C = C(Q)$, obtain the average and marginal cost functions, and sketch them. In each case, show that the cost functions exhibit (eventually) diminishing returns to scale. Indicate clearly the firm's supply on your sketches.

(a) $C(Q) = 0.5Q^2$ (b) $C(Q) = 4Q^{1.5}$ (c) $C(Q) = Q + Q^3/3$

(d) $C(Q) = 8Q + Q^2$ (e) $C(Q) = 30Q - 9Q^2 + Q^3$ (f) $C(Q) = 12 + 8Q + Q^2$

We have expressed firm supply in Proposition 13.2 for cost functions with eventually diminishing returns to scale, so that average costs eventually increase. For the first four functions in Exercise X13.15, firms face diminishing returns to scale and increasing average costs at every level of output. This means that the average cost-minimizing level of output, $Q_0 = 0$, and $AC(0) = MC(0)$. In drawing the average and marginal cost curves we find that they start from the same point on the vertical axis, and that the marginal cost curve is always steeper than (and so lies above) the average cost curve. It follows immediately that if the market price, $p > AC(0)$, then there will be some level of output, $Q^* > 0$, for which $MC(Q^*) = p > AC(Q^*)$. Choosing output Q^*, the firm will make positive profits, and it is easy to check that the second-order conditions for a maximum are satisfied.

We have illustrated three possible outcomes in Figure 13.5. Panel (a) captures firm behaviour when the cost function has the form in Exercise X13.15d. The upward-sloping segment of the supply function is the whole of the marginal cost curve, and begins from its intersection with the price axis. Panel (b) shows the situation facing a firm whose total cost function has the form in Exercise X13.15b. Average and marginal cost curves are increasing, but concave. The marginal cost is always greater than the average cost, and this means that the upward-sloping segment of the supply function begins at the origin. For any market price

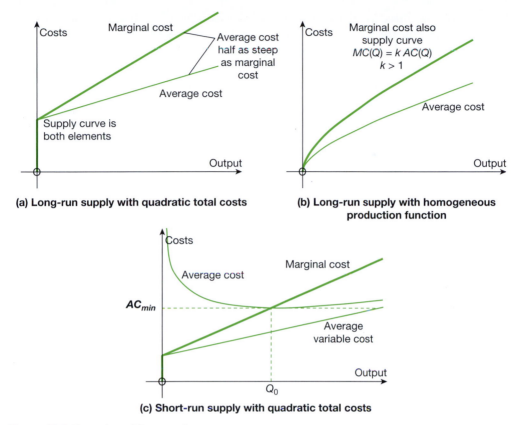

(a) Long-run supply with quadratic total costs

(b) Long-run supply with homogeneous production function

(c) Short-run supply with quadratic total costs

Figure 13.5 Examples of firm supply curves

$p_0 > 0$, the condition $MC(Q^\star) = p_0$ will be satisfied for some value, $Q^\star > 0$. As the market price falls to zero, firms will reduce output, but they will not quit the market. In terms of the theory which we have developed, this is an interesting example. It is consistent with the underlying production function being homogeneous of degree r in the scale of input use, where $0.5 < r < 1$. If a firm increases production and hence the demand for inputs, costs will increase more quickly than output, and we can show that the (total) cost function is homogeneous of degree $\rho = r^{-1}$ in the output Q, so that $1 < \rho < 2$. The average and marginal cost functions are then homogeneous of degree $\rho - 1$. Given that $0 < \rho - 1 < 1$, the average and marginal cost curves start at the origin, slope upwards, and are concave. If we were to follow through the analysis of production and costs in Chapters 10 and 11, we should expect to find that firm supply would be the inverse of marginal cost for all prices, with the firm never wishing to quit the market.

13.2.3   Fixed costs in the short run

Exercise X13.15f differs from the other examples because there are fixed costs. We have discussed the properties of similar short-run cost functions in Section 12.3, so we review them briefly here. With fixed costs, the average cost of production cannot be defined when output $Q = 0$. The firm is committed to paying fixed costs, whether or not it remains in the market. In terms of our previous discussion, we think of this as meaning that the firm has hired capital and converted this into fixed assets that it cannot easily liquidate again. But the fact that these costs are fixed means that they should not affect the firm's short-run decision making. In the short run, the firm's output choice affects revenues and variable costs only. While it is true that marginal cost is the rate of change of total cost with respect to output, it is important to treat it as the rate of change of total *variable* cost.

We have to alter slightly the claim in Proposition 13.2 that the firm will set its long-run profit-maximizing output, Q^*, so that $MC(Q^*) = p_0$, the market price. Suppose we simply noted that in Figure 13.5c the average cost function is convex and has a minimum value at $Q = Q_0$. It might seem that at a price less than AC_{min} the firm should quit the market, setting $Q = 0$, to avoid making losses. But were the firm to follow that course of action, it would in fact make a loss equal to the fixed costs. Instead of trying to avoid all losses, the firm's decision to continue production will be based on making sufficient revenue from selling output to meet all fixed costs (and to offset at least some of the variable costs).[2]

For total costs, $C = C(Q) = C_0 + C_v(Q)$, where fixed costs are C_0 and $C_v(Q)$ is the variable component of total costs, defined so that $C_v(0) = 0$ and $C_v'(Q) > 0$. We write the firm's profit, net of fixed costs, Π_v, as:

$$\Pi_v = \Pi + C_0 = R - C_v \qquad\qquad [13.6]$$

This is the difference between revenue and variable costs.

By yourself

X13.16   Using Expression 13.6, or otherwise:

    (a) Confirm that when output is zero, the firm makes a loss, $\Pi(0) = -C_0$.

    (b) Differentiating twice, confirm that the conditions for profit maximization in Proposition 13.2 will be satisfied, so long we define the firm's objective as being to maximize the profit net of fixed costs, Π_v.

    (c) Show that a firm facing short-run cost function, $C(Q) = 12 + 8Q + Q^2$, and market price $p_0 = 14$, will maximize its short-run profits by choosing an output, $Q^* = 3$, at which it makes a loss, $\Pi(3) = -3$.

In Exercise X13.16c we obtain exactly the outcome indicated in Figure 13.5c. The marginal cost and average cost curves are upward-sloping lines, meeting the origin at the same point on the vertical axis. The marginal cost curve is twice as steep as the average variable cost curve, and so, irrespective of the level of output, Q, $MC(Q) > AC(Q)$. Then, if the market price $p_0 > MC(0)$, the firm will choose to produce output Q^*: $MC(Q^*) = p_0$, even if it makes a loss. The revenue earned will be greater than the firm's variable costs, and the total loss will be less than the fixed costs. We summarize this outcome in Proposition 13.3.

---

2   We conduct this analysis assuming that there is no uncertainty and that firms have no financing constraints. Stephen Ricca's essay in the online student essay bank suggests that governments will often intervene in businesses that have run into trading difficulties. The best argument that can be made for such action is that the government is better able to bear the risks associated with waiting for an improvement in business conditions. You can read Stephen's essay (and those of other students) on the companion website for this book, at **www.palgrave.com/mochrie.**

Proposition 13.3

Profit maximization in the short run

A firm facing a perfectly competitive market has already hired fixed factor inputs at cost C_0. It hires variable factor inputs to produce output $Q \geq 0$, at total variable cost, C_v, so that total cost $C = C(Q) = C_0 + C_v(Q) \geq 0$, with $C_v(0) = 0$. It sells its output Q, at constant market price, $p = p_0$. Production exhibits (eventually) diminishing returns to the variable inputs. The firm's short-run average (total) cost function has a minimum value, $AC(Q_0) = AC_{min} > 0$, and the average variable cost function has a minimum value $AVC(Q_1) = AVC_{min} > 0$.

(1) If $p_0 \geq AVC_{min}$, we define the firm's profit-maximizing output implicitly as Q^*: $MC(Q^*) = p_0$.
(2) If $AVC_{min} \leq p_0 \leq AC_{min}$, the firm will make a loss, $\Pi(Q^*) \leq C_0$, and revenues $R(Q^*) \geq C_v(Q^*)$.
(3) If $p_0 < AVC_{min}$, $Q^* = 0$.
For a firm with supply function, $Q^S = Q^S(p)$. Then:

$$Q^S(p_0) = \begin{cases} MC^{-1}(p_0), & \text{if } p_0 \geq AVC_{min} \\ 0, & \text{if } p_0 < AVC_{min} \end{cases}, \tag{13.7}$$

where the function MC^{-1} is the inverse of the marginal cost function.

Discussion: As with Proposition 13.2, the conditions for profit maximization when $p_0 \geq AVC_{min}$ follow by application of Proposition 13.1. When $p_0 < AVC_{min}$, the firm shuts down production, since for any output $Q > 0$, the loss $\Pi(Q) > C_0$.

13.3 Conclusions

Firms have the objective of maximizing profits, or the difference between sales revenue and costs of production. We have restricted our attention in this chapter to the behaviour of firms that face the market conditions of perfect competition, first introduced in Chapter 2. These very restrictive assumptions make the problem that firms face much easier, and we have been able to solve the profit-maximizing problem, showing that as the market price (which firms take as being beyond their influence) increases, output will also increase so that the marginal cost of the firm's output equals the market price. It follows that profit-maximizing firms in perfect competition face diminishing returns to scale in production.

We have presented a discussion of firm behaviour in both the short run and the long run. With fixed costs in the short run, it is very easy to argue that marginal costs will eventually increase, if a firm increases its output enough. It is perhaps more difficult to argue that marginal costs will eventually increase in the long run, but we find it convenient to make that assumption here since it will allow us to analyse the behaviour of the industry, and not just the firm, in the long run, when we allow new firms to enter the market to exploit profit opportunities – or indeed for existing firms to exit the market or to merge with competitors.

Summary

A firm selling output Q at price $p(Q)$ generates total revenue $R = R(Q) = p(Q).Q$. Its marginal revenue $MR = MR(Q) = R'(Q)$, the rate of change of revenue as output increases.

Its average revenue $AR = AR(Q) = R(Q)/Q$, the revenue per unit sold. If all units of the good are sold at the same price, then $AR(Q) = p(Q)$.

The firm maximizes its profits by producing and selling output $Q*$: $MR(Q*) = MC(Q*)$ and $MR'(Q*) \leq MC'(Q*)$.

If the firm participates in a perfectly competitive market, there will be many buyers and sellers, none of whom has a large market share, and all of whom know everything about market conditions, and so buy and sell units of a good whose quality is known never to vary across sellers. All firms set the same price, the market price, chosen so that no other firm can undercut them.

In perfect competition, firms can sell any quantity of the good for the market price, p_0. Firm revenue $R = p_0 Q$, so $MR = AR = p_0$. For profit maximization at output $Q*$, $p_0 = MR = MC(Q*)$ and $MC'(Q*) \geq 0$.

These conditions could be satisfied by a firm making a loss. To avoid this, we require $p_0 \geq AC_{min}$, the minimum value of average cost. In economic terms, this is equivalent to insisting that firms experience diminishing returns to scale in production when profits are maximized.

Firm supply, Q^S is a function of market price, p_0:

$$Q^S(p_0) = \begin{cases} MC^{-1}(p_0), & \text{if } p_0 \geq AC_{min} \\ 0, & \text{if } p_0 < AC_{min} \end{cases}$$

. If the market price is below minimum average cost, the firm does not produce any output. If the market price is at least as much as minimum average cost, supply is the inverse of the firm's marginal cost.

If $AC(0) = MC(0)$ and both are increasing, then no matter how low the market price, the firm will always produce some output.

The preceding discussion holds for firms making decisions in the long run. In the short run, firms face fixed costs, C_0. Profit in the short run continues to be maximized at an output $Q*$, for which marginal revenue and costs are equal, and marginal costs are increasing, but the firm will continue to produce output so long as any loss that it makes is less than the fixed costs of production.

Visit the companion website at **www.palgrave.com/mochrie** to access further teaching and learning materials, including lecturer slides and a testbank, as well as guideline answers and student MCQs.

Equilibrium in perfect competition

We bring together the analysis of firm supply and consumer demand, aggregating across all firms to obtain market supply, and aggregating across all consumers to obtain market demand. We return to the argument of Chapter 2, that all sales take place at the market price, the price at which the total quantity supplied by firms equals the total quantity sought by all consumers and there is market clearing.

We concentrate on firms' behaviour, identifying conditions under which new firms enter the market and existing firms change the scale of their production. We show that for a market in long-run equilibrium, all firms produce the same output, achieving the minimum average

cost, which is also the market price. Profits are eliminated entirely, so no firms wish to enter or exit the industry. Profits appear only in the short run, acting as a signal for further entry or for the expansion of the scale of production in existing businesses. Losses, as the mirror image of profits, signal the need for firms' exit from the market or for contraction in the scale of production.

We confirm that the equilibrium is stable. Shocks that cause changes in either market supply or market demand will eventually lead to a new equilibrium in which market supply and demand are again equal, but with a different combination of market price and quantity traded.

Market equilibrium occurs in a perfectly competitive market when the total quantity that potential buyers of a good wish to purchase at a given price equals the total quantity that potential buyers are willing to sell into the market. Until now, we have only considered individual decision making by firms and people. We now consider how the market environment affects the choices of individual firms.

Market equilibrium
The market price and the quantity traded such that the market supply equals the market demand.

While it is relatively straightforward to aggregate individual demands to obtain the market demand as a function of the market price, it may seem a little odd to argue that market supply is the sum of individual firms' supply at that price. If market supply depends upon individual supply decisions, which in turn depend upon the market price, which is itself related to market supply, we appear to be in danger of developing a circular argument in which market supply is determined by market supply.

We resolve this problem by applying the assumptions of perfect competitions, in particular that individual consumers and firms are 'small' relative to the market. *Smallness* relates to their effect on market supply and demand. If the amount that one firm produces is removed from the market supply, the change in market supply is so small that the equilibrium price does not change at all. (We shall also assume that the market demand at any price would not be affected by the removal of any one consumer from the market.) This is sufficient to ensure that firms do act as price takers, with no one firm having the ability to affect the market equilibrium.

We assume that the market demand, Q^D, and the market supply, Q^S, are functions of the market price, p, and that the market demand will not increase and the market supply will not decrease following an increase in market price:

$$\frac{\partial Q^D}{\partial p} \leq 0, \text{ and } \frac{\partial Q^S}{\partial p} \geq 0 \qquad\qquad [14.1]$$

In diagrams, the demand curve is typically downward-sloping, while the supply curve will slope upwards. At any market (clearing) price, market supply equals the market demand. There is neither excess supply, nor excess demand. Throughout our analysis, we shall consider problems in which the market equilibrium is unique.

By yourself

X14.1   Suppose that the market demand curve is decreasing in price, and that the market supply curve is increasing in price. Define the excess market supply as the difference between market supply and market demand at any price. Show that the excess market supply is itself increasing in price, and that there can only be a single value of price and output at which the two curves intersect.

X14.2   We assume that market price cannot fall below zero. Suppose that there is excess market supply at any price greater than zero. Sketch a diagram showing this situation. Characterize your solution in terms of the concept of scarcity.

X14.3   Suppose that the graph of market supply is a flat line and that the graph of market demand is a downward-sloping line. Sketch the graphs of market supply, market demand, and excess supply.

14.1   Firms' adjustments to market conditions

In Figure 14.1, which we read from right to left, we show the interaction between an individual firm's supply and demand functions and the market supply and demand functions. This market clears at a price p_0, for which the market supply, $Q^S(p_0) = Q^M$, as does the market demand, so that $Q^D(p_0) = Q^M$. For every firm, f, the market price, p_0, is taken as given. Each firm supplies the profit-maximizing quantity, $q_f^* = q_f(p_0)$, according to the

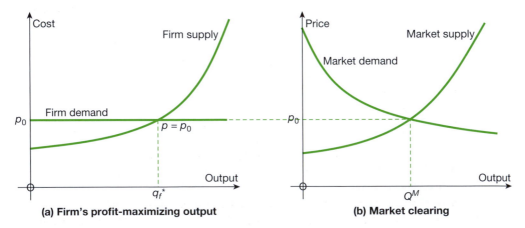

(a) Firm's profit-maximizing output   **(b) Market clearing**

Figure 14.1 Market clearing and firm profit maximization

profit-maximizing conditions set out in Chapter 13. While the diagram is new, the argument to this point should already be familiar.

Looking at panel (a) in Figure 14.1, we note that it is drawn so that the firm faces diminishing returns to scale. Remembering the relationship between firm supply and marginal costs, set out in Section 13.2, it appears that marginal costs are increasing at an increasing rate. The technology of production facing this firm is very difficult to scale up. Given that we also require the firm to be small relative to the total market, it will be useful to have in mind the market stall example. We shall continue to assume that each stall is separately owned. Our interest here is in understanding how such businesses respond to changing market conditions over time.

The shortest time period in which a trader might make decisions is a single day. Assume that all traders have to buy produce early in the morning from a wholesale market, and cannot replenish stock or return it unsold. Think in particular about soft fruit, such as raspberries or strawberries. Any produce that cannot be sold on the day will have to be destroyed. Say that the market closes at 17:00. Five minutes beforehand, the trader is likely to be willing to accept any offer for the goods. As we argued in Chapter 2, in this very short run the only flexibility open to the trader is in the price. The quantity brought to market is already fixed. Production has already taken place, and all costs have already been incurred.

> **By yourself**
>
> **X14.4**   Adapt Figure 14.1 to show the firm and market supply curves in the very short run.

14.1.1 Short-run adjustments

As discussed in Chapter 12, we define the short run as the period in which it is possible to vary use of one factor input, typically labour, but not the other. Capital usage, K_0, is therefore fixed, while labour usage, L, is variable. For example, let us assume that a market stall requires two people to work in it. The exact pattern of hours worked is likely to vary through the year, responding to seasonal variation in demand.

> **By yourself**
>
> **X14.5**   Adapt Figure 14.1 to show the firm and market supply curves in the short run, with the firm making a loss in the short run but continuing production. Show that this is consistent with profit maximization.
>
> **X14.6**   Consider a firm that has a production function $Q(K, L) = 9K^{1/3}L^{2/3}$. The firm has already acquired the capital stock $K_0 = 1,000$, which it will not be able to vary in the short run. It plans to hire $L_0 = 8$ staff.
>
> (a) Confirm that the firm will be able to produce $Q_0 = 360$ units of output when its plan has been met.
>
> (b) Applying the usual cost-minimizing condition, calculate the factor input price ratio, w_K/w_L.
>
> (c) Calculate the cost of producing output Q_0 given the planned factor usage, when $w_L = 1,000$. How much profit does the firm make if the market price $p_0 = 50$?
>
> (d) Write down the firm's short-run production function, and hence the firm's short-run total cost function.
>
> (e) Obtain the short-run average total cost, the short-run average variable cost, and the short-run marginal cost. Sketch these functions, and indicate the firm's short-run supply function.

Production in the short run involves adjustment of labour usage, so that $L = L_{SR}(Q, K_0)$. Each stall in the market is able to adjust how much labour it hires, but cannot vary its use of capital. From the point of market analysis, this gives us a useful way of thinking of the short run: it is the length of time that a potential entrant needs to raise and apply its capital, given the likely market conditions. Using our distinction from Chapter 12 between decision making in the planning period and production control in the current period, we treat the short run as the production period. All market stalls have the same (complete) information about market demand and market supply in the production period. With access to the same technology, they share a common (long-run) production function. We therefore expect every stall to have hired the same quantity of capital, and this allows us to analyse short-run behaviour by concentrating on the behaviour of a 'representative' firm. After solving one firm's profit maximization problem, we can simply apply that decision across all firms, adding up their outputs to obtain the market supply.

For the stall owners in a fruit market, this all seems reasonable. Whereas a large retail business may have spent millions of pounds over the last twenty years introducing point-of-sale technology that allows it to manage stock levels throughout the business much more efficiently, stall owners are still probably quicker at counting up the number of boxes left at the end of a day's trading. They might now keep their records in spreadsheets and place orders with a wholesaler electronically, but many remain largely cash businesses, lagging other businesses even in the introduction of payment card readers for non-cash transactions. But in an industry in which almost nothing can be hidden from competitors, any innovation that is profitable for one business would be profitable for all businesses, and would be adopted almost simultaneously across the industry. We should be very confident that all of the market stalls will behave identically.

14.1.2   The profit-maximizing condition in perfect competition

This example builds on the arguments introduced in Chapter 12. As before, we write a firm's short-run production function as:

$$Q = Q(K_0, L) \qquad [14.2]$$

This indicates that the firm can hire any quantity of labour, L, but has already hired capital, K_0. We now invert the production function so that the firm's labour usage is a function of the target output and its capital usage:

$$L = L(Q, K_0) \qquad [14.3]$$

We can now write the firm's profits as:

$$\Pi(Q, K_0) = p_0 Q - wL(Q, K_0) - rK_0 \qquad [14.4]$$

with the market price, p_0, fixed by the interaction between market demand and market supply. Note that this is a function with only one choice variable for the firm, the output, Q. The firm has already chosen K_0. Prices, of both the product and of the factor inputs, are fixed parameters. In Expression 14.4, the firm's simply has to choose the profit-maximizing level of output, Q, given that capital is fixed. By writing the profit function in this way, we emphasize that the firm's objective is to make profits from selling output. Its variable costs depend on its use of labour, and that depends upon the firm's production choice.

We shall assume that if the firm hires no labour, it is unable to produce any output. As we saw in Chapter 13, the firm will pay fixed costs, $C_0 = rK_0$, the cost of hiring capital. To find the profit-maximizing output, we differentiate Expression 14.4, setting the derivative to zero:

$$\Pi'(Q, K_0) = p_0 - wL'(Q, K_0) = 0 \qquad [14.5]$$

We can interpret Expression 14.5 in terms of economic concepts we have already met. The function $L = L(Q, K_0)$ defines the quantity of labour that the firm will hire in order to produce output, Q. Since it is the inverse of the short-run production, $Q = Q(K_0, L)$, its derivative, $L'(Q, K_0)$ is the inverse of the derivative of the short-run production function, $Q' = Q'(K_0, L)$. We have already introduced this relationship in Section 12.3.1, showing in Expression 12.7 that the short-run marginal cost equals the wage divided by the marginal product of labour. Remembering from Proposition 13.2 that in perfect competition a firm maximizes profits by choosing output so that price equals marginal cost, we can also see that Expression 12.7 simplifies to Expression 14.5 in the case of perfect competition.

Another way of approaching this point is to remember that the derivative of the inverse function is the inverse of the original derivative. In this case, since the labour usage function, L, is the inverse of the short-run production function, Q, its derivative, L', is the multiplicative inverse of the derivative of the production function, Q'. Then:

$$L'(Q, K_0) = [Q'(K_0, L)]^{-1} = \frac{1}{MP_L} \qquad [14.6]$$

We can now rewrite Expression 14.5 as:

$$\Pi'(Q, K_0) = p_0 - \frac{w}{MP_L} = 0 \qquad [14.7]$$

The first term in the derivative in Expression 14.7 is the firm's marginal revenue, and the second one is its marginal cost. We can obtain a more useful interpretation of Expression 14.7 by rearranging the equation as:

$$w = p_0 \cdot MP_L(K_0, L^*) = VMP_L(K_0, L^*) \qquad [14.8]$$

where VMP_L is the 'value of the marginal product' function, a measure of the rate at which revenue increases with labour usage. (The marginal product measures the rate at which output increases as labour usage increases. By multiplying marginal product by the market price, we obtain the rate at which revenue increases.) We summarize the condition as saying that the firm maximizes its profits by choosing the labour input for which the wage equals the value of the marginal product, so that revenues and costs increase at the same rate as labour usage varies. Once again, we have a situation in which profit maximization occurs when marginal revenues and costs are equal.

By yourself

X14.7 Show that, in the short run, we can write the firm's profit maximization condition as $MC = w/MP_L$.

X14.8 Suppose that it is possible to write a firm's short-run production function, $Q = AL^b$, where parameters $A > 0$, and $b < 1$ are fixed. Obtain the firm's (total) cost function, given that it has already committed itself to paying fixed costs, F. Obtain the supply function, showing output, Q, as a function of price, p, for a given wage, w.

(Continued)

X14.9   For the following (long-run) production functions, $Q = Q(K, L)$, write down expressions for:

  (i)   the short-run production function, $Q^S = Q^S(K_0, L)$;
  (ii)   the marginal product of labour, $MP_L = Q^{S'}(K_0, L)$;
  (iii)   the short-run demand for labour, $L^S = L(Q^S, K_0)$;
  (iv)   the short-run total cost function, $C^S = C(Q^S, K_0)$;
  (v)   the short-run marginal cost function, $MC^S = C^{S'}(Q^S, K_0)$;
  (vi)   the short-run supply function, $Q^S = Q^S(p, w, K_0)$.

You may assume that the firm has a capital stock, $K_0 = 10,000$, that the cost of a unit of capital $r = 5$, and that the cost of a unit of labour $w = 4$.

  (a) $Q(K, L) = K^{½}L^{½}$;   (b) $Q(K, L) = 20[K^{½} + L^{½}]$;   (c) $100(L + K)^{½}$

X14.10   Sketch the isoquant map for the production function in X14.9c, and discuss whether or not you believe that the firm would behave as suggested in the question.

X14.11   Repeat X14.9a for any wage, w, and any interest rate, r, obtaining the short-run supply as a function of the market price, p, the wage, w, and the capital stock, K_0.

We argued in Chapter 12 that in the short run firms will adapt to unexpected changes in the underlying market conditions, such as a shift in demand or a change in the input prices in production, by changing their production plan. We expect a shift in demand to affect the firm's decisions through the interaction of the market supply and market demand functions, changing the market price. Note, though, that a change in the interest rate will have no effect on the firm's short-run decisions, given that the capital stock is fixed, so that there will be no change in the profit-maximizing condition. However, it may affect the decision to remain in the market, since the firm must cover its fixed costs. A change in wages, on the other hand, *would* have an effect on firm behaviour. In all three cases in Exercise X14.9, firm supply is a decreasing function of the wage rate. As the price of hiring labour increases, firms' marginal costs increase, and so the profit-maximizing condition (price equals marginal cost) is satisfied for a lower output.

14.1.3   Market equilibrium in the short run

We now bring together the short-run market supply and the market demand for a perfectly competitive market. With market demand, Q^D, defined as the sum of individual demands, q_c, we simplify our analysis by assuming that all consumers have the same preferences, represented by a homogeneous utility function, so that the share of expenditure devoted to any good is independent of individual income. Given the (relative) price of the good, each consumer will spend the same proportion of the money available for consumption on it. Then, adding together across the consumers the amount of money that each has available to finance consumption, for given prices, market demand for the good is obtained through knowing the proportion of money available for consumption.

Assume that consumers consider good Q and some composite good, X, made up from the consumer's preferred combination of other goods, to be perfect complements, with $U_c = \min(4q_c, x_c)$. For preferences of this form, the income expansion path has the equation $x_c = 4q_c$, irrespective of the prices charged. It follows that, as prices change, there is no substitution effect. The proportions of the two goods in the consumption bundle remain constant. We also define the composite good X in such a way that the price of a single unit $p_X = 1$, but we allow p, the price of a unit of good Q, to vary. We can now write the utility maximization problem for a consumer able to spend m_c as:

$$\max\{\min(4q_c, x_c)\} : x_c + p \cdot q_c = m_c \qquad [14.9]$$

Substituting from the equation of the income expansion path, we can easily obtain the demand function for the consumer: $q_c = \frac{m_c}{p+4}$. Given the homogeneity of preferences, this expression is linear in the money available for consumption. Every consumer's demand for good Q is proportional to the total amount that the consumer will spend, m_c. Doubling the money that a consumer can spend would have the same effect on market demand as adding another consumer to the market with the same amount of money to spend. Then, aggregating from individual demand, q_c, to the market demand, Q^M, the market demand function turns out to be exactly the same as the demand of a single consumer, who can spend as much as all the consumers who are actually in the market. For consumers able to spend amounts, $\mathbf{m} = (m_1, m_2, \ldots, m_C)$, we obtain market demand, Q^D:

$$Q^D(\mathbf{m}, p) = \sum_{i=1}^{C} \frac{m_i}{p+4} = \frac{M}{p+4} \qquad [14.10]$$

where $M = \sum_{c=1}^{C} m_c$ is the total amount of money that consumers spend. The market demand, Q^M, is then decreasing and convex in the market price, p. We show its graph in Figure 14.2, with $M = 1{,}250{,}000$. The curve approaches but does not intersect the price axis, and cuts through the output axis.

For the supply side of this market, we assume that there are $F = 200$ firms in the market, all with the Cobb–Douglas production function, $q_f = q(K_0, L) = 2K_0^{\frac{1}{2}}L^{\frac{1}{2}}$, and with the cost of production $C = 5K_0 + 10L$. This is very similar to the situation in Exercise X14.9a. The firm's demand for labour depends on both its output target, q_f, and the volume of capital that has already hired, $K_0 = 5{,}000$; so here we can write $L = q_f^2/20{,}000$. Substituting into

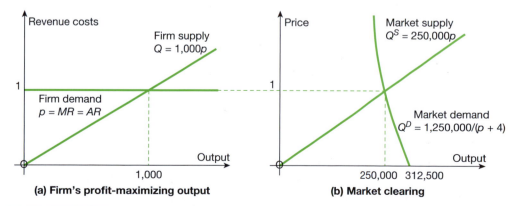

(a) Firm's profit-maximizing output   **(b) Market clearing**

Figure 14.2 Example with goods perfect complements and production Cobb–Douglas

the expression for the firm's costs, and differentiating, we find the marginal cost function, $MC(q_f) = 0.001q_f$. For profit maximization, $MC = p$, the market price, and so we can write the firm's supply function, $q_f = q_f(p) = 1{,}000p$. Aggregating across the 250 firms in the market, we can write the market supply:

$$Q^S = Q^S(p) = 200{,}000p$$

As shown in Figure 14.2, market supply is a linear, increasing function of the market price. We obtain the market price from the intersection of the upward-sloping market supply, Q^S, and the downward-sloping market demand, Q_D. Note that we can be quite certain that there will be some price, $p^M: p^M > 0$, for which the market clears, since the market supply curve starts at the origin. Even when the market price is very low, firms choose to produce some output.

For the market to be in equilibrium at the market price, p, the market supply, $Q^S(p)$, equals the market demand, $Q^D(p)$. As illustrated in Figure 12.2, in this case, when market supply and market demand are equal, the equilibrium price $p = 1$, the quantity traded $Q^D = Q^S = 250{,}000$, and each of the $F = 250$ firms produces $q_f = 1{,}000$.

By yourself

X14.12 Consider the case where there are 200 firms in the market, each with production function $Q_f = 20K_0{}^{1/2}L^{1/2}$. The price of a unit of capital $r = 3$, and the cost of a unit of labour $w = 12$.

(a) Write down the quantity of labour that the firm hires as a function of its short-run output, $L = L(Q_f, K_0)$.

(b) Write down the firm's short-run cost function, $C = C(Q_f)$, and hence obtain its marginal and average cost functions.

(c) Show that firms minimize their average costs by producing output $Q_f = 10K_0$.

(d) Confirm that for output $Q_f = 10K_0$, firms' marginal and average costs are equal, with $MC(10K_0) = AC(10K_0) = 0.6$.

(e) Confirm that the market supply function, $Q^S = Q^S(p^M) = 10{,}000K_0p/3$.

X14.13 Now suppose that all 200 firms have already hired capital, $K_0 = 10{,}000$, so that the market supply, $Q^S = 100{,}000{,}000p/3$. Sketch a diagram showing the relationship between firm supply and market supply.

X14.14 Sketch graphs of the short-run marginal cost, the short-run average (total) cost and the short-run average variable cost functions for the firm in X14.9b, and explain the relationship between these curves and firm's short-run supply function.

X14.15 Continuing to work with the production function in X14.9b, suppose that there are F firms in the market, all of them identical. Write down an expression for the market supply, $Q^S = Q^S(p)$.

X14.16 Now suppose that there are C consumers in the market, each of whom has a sum of money m_i to finance consumption of goods. We shall assume that there are two goods available for consumption, the good of interest, and a composite that represents all other goods. We assume that all consumers have the same utility function, $U_i = U(q_i, x_i)$, where q_i is the quantity of the good of interest, and x_i is the quantity of the composite good. For Cobb–Douglas preferences, so that $U(q_i, x_i) = q_i{}^{0.5} x_i{}^{0.5}$:

(a) Calculate each consumer's demand, q_i, and hence the market demand, $Q^D = Q^D(p)$.

(b) Sketch the market supply and market demand functions for this good.

(c) Show that if there is market clearing, then $p = \sqrt{\frac{M}{2.5F}}$.

14.2 The long run

In the short run, the size of the industry is largely fixed. There cannot be entry of new firms, and the firms in the market are unable to change capital usage. In the long run, both of these restrictions vanish. We have seen that, in the short run, firms choose the level of labour input (and hence output) for which the value of the marginal product of labour equals the market price of the good. So long as the marginal product of labour is a decreasing function of output, this ensures that firms maximize their profits. Decreasing MP_L also rules out the possibility of firms trying to undercut their competitors and secure the whole market. Firms can make either profits or losses in the short run, since firms will carry on production so long as their revenues are greater than their variable (labour) costs, even if they are nonetheless less than the total costs.

We know from the discussion in Chapter 13 that firms behave differently in the long run, shutting down production if there is any loss. But the possibility of firm entry, or of adjustment of the scale of production by existing firms, also eliminates profits. To see why this must be the case, let us consider a simple diagrammatic analysis, which adopts the standard textbook assumption of eventually diminishing returns to scale.

For this, we use Figure 14.3, in which we show the short-run and long-run average and marginal cost curves, with the firm's (long-run) capital usage set so that if its plan were realized perfectly it would undertake production at minimum average cost. That is, following the approach of Chapter 12, we envisage the firm as making plans for a market environment in which the market price $p^* = \min(AC_{LR})$. The firm's planned output is therefore Q_0.

The relationship with the other cost curves follows from the arguments of Chapter 13. The short-run average cost touches, but does not intersect, the long-run average cost at the planned output; so the minimum short-run average cost is also achieved at the expected

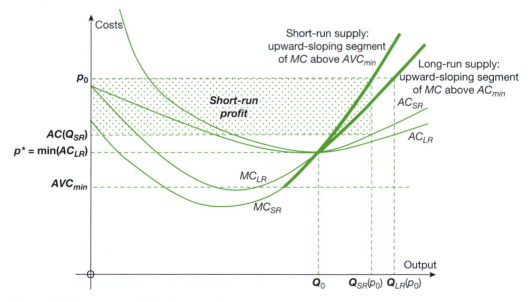

Figure 14.3 Long-run and short-run supply

price, p^*. Except at the planned output, Q_0, the short-run average cost is greater than the long-run average cost. From Chapter 11, we know that at the minimum average cost, the marginal cost intersects the average cost function from below; while from Chapter 12, we know that the short-run marginal cost curve intersects the long-run marginal cost curve from below at the planned output, Q_0. As a result, all four measures of cost take the value p^* at output Q_0, as shown in Figure 14.3. The long-run supply curve appears as the upward-sloping segment of the long-run marginal cost curve above its intersection with the long-run average cost curve, while the short-run supply curve is the upward-sloping segment of the short-run marginal cost curve, above minimum average variable cost.

We assert that p^* is the long-run market price. Since the firm makes no profits at this price, it is indifferent between continuing production and quitting the market. This is a desirable condition for a long-run equilibrium, since no firms will want to enter the market (and reduce the market price) and no firms will want to leave the market (and allow other firms to make profits).

By yourself

X14.17 Explain why the long-run average cost curve always lies below the short-run average (total) cost curve.

X14.18 Explain why the long-run marginal cost curve can lie above the short-run marginal cost curve.

X14.19 Suppose that Figure 14.3 is best interpreted as showing how output in the production period deviates from the plans laid earlier.
(a) Explain how changes in demand conditions might lead to the market price increasing to p_0 in the short run.
(b) Discuss how firms within the industry might respond to such a change in market conditions in the (new) short run.

In Figure 14.3, we show the situation that a firm faces after a (demand) shock that leads to an increase in the market price, but with no changes to costs and thus supply. In the short run, the market price rises to p_0 and the conditions for short-run profit maximization are satisfied when the firm produces output $Q_{SR}(p_0)$. This firm, and presumably all of the other small, identical, price-taking firms in the market, are making unexpected profits. Firms that decided to stay out of the market are presumably regretting the missed profit opportunity.

Now, let us consider the long run in this market. We assume that there are many businesses that could enter the market, all of which would have access to the same production techniques as the existing ones. This means that there are two possible long-run effects of the change in demand and the increase in the market price:

- existing firms consolidate the expansion of output in the short run by hiring more capital and increasing the scale of production;
- new firms enter the market, copying the behaviour of the firms that are already in the market.

By yourself

X14.20 Characterize the long-run equilibrium for this market, based on the discussion above, and emphasizing the role of entrant firms.

Using the representative firm argument, if one firm believes that it can increase profits by behaving in a particular way, then all firms should believe that they can increase profits by behaving in the same way. At first sight, it might seem reasonable for a price-taking firm to plan to expand its output in the long run to $Q_{LR}(p_0)$ and so make larger profits in the long run than in the short run. But this argument cannot be right.

Firstly, remember that we are discussing a *representative* firm. Were the owner of *that* business to identify an opportunity for profit, then the owners of *all* businesses should recognize it. All would seek to expand output. Not only firm supply but also market supply would increase, reducing the market price and hence profits.

Secondly, this firm is representative not only of the firms that are already in the market but also of all firms that might choose to enter the market. The presence of profits leads to entry. Until all profit opportunities are exhausted, firms will continue to enter. In equilibrium, the standard profit-maximizing condition, $p = MC(Q_f)$ has to be satisfied, but we also require firms to make zero profits, so that $p = AC(Q_f)$.

We can now summarize our discussion in a concluding proposition, Proposition 14.1.

---

*Proposition **14.1***

In a perfectly competitive market, in which all agents are perfectly informed and in which both individual firm supply and consumer demands are small relative to market supply and demand, we define the market supply, $Q^S = Q^S(p)$ and the market demand, $Q^D = Q^D(p)$, as functions of the market price p, where $Q^S = \sum_{f=1}^{F} q_f(p)$, as defined in Propositions 13.2 for the market in the long run.

(1) There is a unique market price p^* for which $Q^S = Q^D$, so that the market clears.
(2) If, in addition, the conditions for long-run profit maximization required for Proposition 13.2 are satisfied, firms enter the market, all choosing the level of output for which $p = LAC_{min}$, the minimum long-run average cost. In equilibrium, the market-clearing price, $p^* = LAC_{min}$; and profits are eliminated in the industry.

Discussion: This is the argument of Exercises X14.19 and X14.20. Note that whereas in the short run, given the fixed number of firms in the market, firms adjust their output to maximize profits, in the long run all firms produce a fixed output, so market supply adjusts through the entry of additional firms.

14.2.1 The relationship between the short run and the long run

In Figure 14.4 we show the relationship between a representative firm's decision making and the market outcome. Panel (a) should be familiar, since it is essentially Figure 14.3, with the firm facing eventually diminishing returns to scale. Panel (b) demonstrates how the short-run and the long-run market equilibria will be different if the market demand increases. We assume that firms make their plans – both whether to enter, and how much capital to hire should they do so – on the basis of the *expected market demand*. Were that expected outcome to occur, then long-run equilibrium would emerge at E* in panel (b), with the F_0 firms in the market producing output Q_0, and the market clearing at price p^*. In the short run, we allow for firms being unable to respond fully to changes in market conditions. Facing the higher level of *actual market demand*, those firms that have entered the market hire more labour than planned in order to expand their output and to take advantage of this profit opportunity. Since it is impossible for other firms to enter the

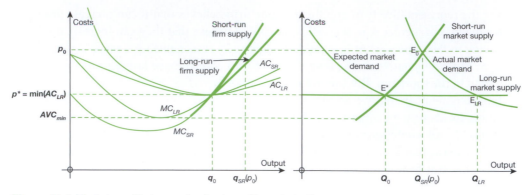

Figure 14.4 Market equilibrium and a firm's profit maximization

market, short-run market clearing occurs at E_0 in panel (b), with the price increasing to p_0, each firm producing output $q_{SR}(p_0)$, and quantity $Q_{SR}(p_0)$ being traded.

In the long run, firms can increase their use of capital and, in addition, other firms can enter the market. We might expect to see a process of adjustment during which existing firms take advantage of the continuing profit opportunities to hire more capital and to expand their output further, as entrants prepare their production plans. But with firms continuing to make profits and to set prices above minimum average costs, the only possible long-run equilibrium is at point E_{LR} in panel (b), at which the market price, p^*, has been re-established at the minimum long-run average cost. All firms then produce the original planned output, q_0; but with entry occurring, there are now F_1 firms in the market, so that the market-clearing output increases to Q_{LR}.

By yourself

X14.21 Using graphical analysis, explain how the market will respond to a negative demand shock, so that the *actual market demand* is less than the *expected market demand* at any price.

Figure 14.4b exhibits a rather striking outcome: the long-run market supply curve is a flat line. This follows naturally from the preceding argument. In the long run, allowing both entry and exit, the number of firms in the market will adjust to demand conditions. The only possible long-run equilibrium involves the elimination of profit opportunities and situations where firms make losses. Given that we have argued that, in perfect competition, the industry should consist of a large number of very small firms, in the long run market clearing is driven by the entry and exit of businesses.

By yourself

X14.22 In our discussion in this section, we have assumed eventually decreasing returns to scale, so that the minimum average cost occurs at output $q_0 > 0$. Suppose instead that the average cost-minimizing firm output $q_0 = 0$. Discuss how this would affect the predictions of our model.

X14.23 We argued in Section 13.2 that where the production function is homogeneous of degree less than 1, $AC(0) > 0$, and $MC(q_f) > 0$ for all values of output. Discuss the predictions of the model in this case.

> **X14.24**   In Section 13.2, we also argued that increasing returns to scale are inconsistent with profit maximization. Suppose that the firms in a perfectly competitive market face constant returns to scale in production. Adapt Figure 14.4 so that in the short run the market price is (1) above and (2) below the long-run average cost. Explain why in this case it is not possible to make any prediction about the size of firms in the long run.

In discussing profit maximization, we have argued that only diminishing returns to scale are consistent with perfect competition; X14.23, however, suggests that assuming homogeneity of degree less than 1 leads to the prediction that in the long run firm size falls to zero, and the market price too. Firms become vanishingly small. In X14.24, we see that where firms have constant returns to scale, they can be of any size within a perfectly competitive market. We are unable to make a prediction about optimal firm size in the way that would be possible if there were eventually diminishing returns to scale in production.

14.3   Conclusions

The argument of this chapter may seem to depend to some extent on sleight of hand. We want firms to be price takers, and so we assume that they are unable to affect the market price at all – not just that their effect on the market price is very small, but that it is actually non-existent. We will give a justification for this claim when we examine what might determine firms' behaviour under conditions of imperfect competition. The argument is perhaps easiest to understand in the context of the long run, in which firms are able to enter and exit the market. Firm size in the long-run equilibrium for the industry turns out to be determined by average cost minimization. If the market price is above that level, then firms will make profits, and there will firm entry to eliminate profits. It is clearly impossible for the market price to be below the minimum average cost, since then every firm would exit the industry. We are then left with the situation in which no firm can reduce its production costs, and all profits are eliminated. It is perhaps unsurprising, given these observations, that the perfectly competitive industry of our theory turns out to be a benchmark, compared with which all actual, existing industries exhibit some degree of inefficiency and misallocation of resources.

There are some important limits to our analysis. We have only been able to derive cost functions given a production function and an output target for homogeneous production functions. Yet, homogeneity is inconsistent with eventually diminishing returns to scale. One way of sidestepping this particular problem is to define the long run as a very long period of time indeed, one that we never expect to reach because it is always in the future. This is consistent with our definition of the long run as a planning horizon, with production taking place immediately. Then, we do not need to worry about the nature of returns to scale in production, since the marginal product of variable factors will definitely be (eventually) diminishing. It will certainly be possible to find an output with minimum average cost, but at any point in time the number of firms in the market is fixed. The long-run equilibrium then becomes the state towards which the market tends, but with successive shocks, both to demand and supply, it is never quite reached.

Summary

For there to be equilibrium in a perfectly competitive market, all sales take place at a single market price, $p* > 0$, at which market supply, $Q^S(p)$, equals market demand, $Q^D(p)$.

Firms respond to the presence of profits by adjusting output. In the short run, this will involve changes in the use of variable factors of production, with firms choosing a level of output at which the price of the variable factor, w_F, is equal to the value of its marginal product, VMP_F. At the margin, the income generated from extra sales is just offset by the costs of hiring the additional resources required to produce them.

In the short run, unless firms' plans are fully implemented, the market price will be different from the planned price, and so firms may make either profit or losses.

In the long run, all factors of production are variable. It is therefore possible for existing firms to vary the scale of production, but also for new firms to enter the market and for existing ones to exit.

We concentrate upon a situation in which firms experience eventually diminishing returns to scale. This ensures that the long-run average cost function has a well-defined minimum value, $\min(AC_{LR})$.

It is then possible that firms will make profits (or losses) in the short run. In the long run, we argue that we need to consider the behaviour of all potential businesses, whether or not they are already active in the market. All businesses that are active in the market during the long run will adopt the scale of production at which average costs are minimized, so that when profits are minimized, the market price $p*$ equals the long-run average and marginal costs.

Adjustment to the long run is then achieved by the entry and exit of firms, and we expect the long-run market supply to be perfectly elastic, so that the market price will always be $p*$.

In the absence of eventually diminishing returns to scale, it is difficult to generate useful predictions from the model.

Visit the companion website at **www.palgrave.com/mochrie** to access further teaching and learning materials, including lecturer slides and a testbank, as well as guideline answers and student MCQs.

---

[1] www.businessinsider.com/2004-athens-olympics-venues-abandoned-today-photos-2012-8?op51

[2] www.archdaily.com/449922/zaha-hadid-s-2022-qatar-world-cup-stadium-unveiled

part IV

Market power

The standard model of the economy, developed for a single market in Parts I–III, presents the ideal arrangements for buying and selling goods or services. There are no market participants large enough to be able to affect market prices through their choices. All participants are perfectly informed. The assumption that the product traded in each market is uniform, and ruling out physical product differentiation, advertising or branding as mechanisms to increase the value of sales, are almost deductions from the assumption of perfect information.

An economy consisting solely of perfect markets would be rather dull. It would be rather like Orson Welles' depiction of Switzerland in the film *The Third Man* – 'They had brotherly love, they had five hundred years of democracy and peace – and what did that produce? The cuckoo clock.' For economic activity that is a little more like Welles' characterization of Italy – 'for thirty years under the Borgias, they had warfare, terror, murder and bloodshed, but they produced Michelangelo, Leonardo da Vinci and the Renaissance' – we have to allow markets to be imperfect. The first way in which we shall do this is to allow for *market power*.

We have described firms in perfectly competitive markets as *price takers* because of their inability to influence the prices that are charged in the market, so that in the long run they make zero profits. Now we shall treat market power as emerging from violation of the assumptions of the standard model. Granting firms market power means that they do not have to behave as price takers; it is then possible that they will have the capacity to make profits in the long run. In the first half of Part IV, we shall concentrate on *size* as the source of market power. Producing a large share of the total market output, such firms' production decisions have substantial effects on the market supply and market price, and hence on their own profits.

As far back as Chapter 2, we argued that it is impossible to improve on the outcome of the standard model. At the market price, there is no willing buyer or willing seller who is unable to trade. In terms of the profit-maximizing behaviour of firms, studied in Part III, the general condition that marginal revenue and costs are equal implies that price equals marginal cost. Every firm expands its output until it can no longer find any willing buyers.

In Chapters 15–17, we shall assume that large firms are able to *restrict their output* so that the market supply is limited and the market price forced up; it follows that when marginal revenues and costs are equal for these firms, the market price is greater than the marginal cost. The firms could then expand their output, selling the additional units at a price lower than the market price, but still covering the additional costs of production. Market power, in this form, is not economically efficient. We have assumed that firms are only interested in maximizing profit, and if this can be achieved by limiting output in the face of limited competition, firms will do that. From Chapter 15 onwards, we therefore argue that society has an interest in managing market power in order to promote more efficient outcomes.

There is an important difference between managing and eradicating market power. In Chapters 15–17, we shall consider examples such as *natural monopoly*, in which allowing a single firm to undertake some specific kind of activity is the most efficient arrangement. We shall show that allowing firms with market power to use *price discrimination*, so that there is no longer a single market price, can also be socially beneficial. And we shall also argue that *restricting entry* into a market can be beneficial if that encourages innovation, and more efficient use of factor inputs over time.

In Chapter 17, we introduce standard models of *oligopoly*: markets in which only a few firms participate. These are named after the economists who first defined them: Cournot (in which firms choose output levels), Bertrand (in which firms choose price levels), and Stackelberg (in which one firm chooses its output, and others respond). In Chapter 18, we show that such models can be represented by mathematical games. The application of *game theory* to economic analysis is one of the most important developments in microeconomic theory in the last fifty years, and it is now the subject of many textbooks. The central concept is *strategic interdependence.* Where market supply is undertaken by only a few businesses, it seems reasonable that each firm's decision should affect the payoffs – the profits – of the others. It follows that the choice that each firm should make depends on the choices being made by its competitors. In the simplest games, introduced in Chapter 18, all choices have to be made at the same time. We solve such games by using the concept of the *Nash equilibrium.* Every firm chooses its action based on correct beliefs about how the other firms will behave. If every firm predicts its competitors' behaviour correctly, it follows that none of them would wish to change their behaviour once they can actually see what the others have chosen to do.

15

Monopoly

We define market power as the ability of a single market participant, here a firm choosing a level of output, to affect prices. We move from a situation in which all agents are *price takers* to one in which firms are *price makers*. In diagrams, we can represent this as moving from horizontal lines to downward-sloping demand curves.

Market power can take many forms. In this chapter we examine a straightforward example, *monopoly*. In this market structure, there is only one firm. This can be the result of a production function with increasing returns to scale, which we define as a *natural monopoly*. It can be the result of some form of *restriction on entry* into the market, such as where a single firm controls access to a natural resource, or where there is a *statutory monopoly*, such that entry is prevented by law.

We examine the profit-maximizing conditions for a monopolist firm by applying the general conditions for profit maximization derived in Chapter 13. We show that this kind of firm tends both to produce less output than a perfectly competitive firm and to charge a higher price. Compared with perfect competition, monopoly typically leads to worse outcomes for consumers, while enabling the monopolist to make supernormal profits. The extent of these profits depends upon the elasticity of demand. With highly elastic demand, the monopoly's ability to set prices above its marginal costs, and thereby to earn monopoly profits, is very limited. With less elastic demand, profit can be a large proportion of revenue.

15.1 Market power and monopoly

In the standard model, we eliminate all sources of market power. Firms face a production function that exhibits eventually diminishing returns to scale when output is still only a small fraction of the total volume traded in the market. Consumers always buy from the firm that sets the lowest price. In Chapters 13 and 14, we have argued that all firms will be equally efficient, setting their output so that the market price is also their average and marginal cost. All (economic) profits are then eliminated.

In these circumstances, every firm's demand function is perfectly elastic. Suppose that the market price is p^M. Any firm that tried to increase its price above the market price on its own would risk losing all of its sales. Equally, were a firm to cut its price, it would gain the whole market. Desirable as that might sound, as marginal costs increase with output, and as we have assumed that the marginal cost equals the market price when the firm has a low share of the market, such an increase in sales would cause the firm huge losses.

Formalizing the argument, we can say that for a small firm in a perfectly competitive market that faces market price p^M and sets price, p_f, the firm demand, q_f, is:

$$q_f = \begin{cases} 0, \text{if } p_f > p^M \\ q : 0 \leq q \leq Q^M, \text{if } p_f = p^M \\ Q^M(p_f), \text{if } p_f < p^M \end{cases} \qquad [15.1]$$

where Q^M, the market demand function, decreases in the price that the firm sets, p_f.

We show the graph of this demand relation in Figure 15.1. (Strictly, we should not call the relation in Expression 15.1 a 'function' because $q_f(p^M)$ is not uniquely defined.) The vertical segment shows that the firm cannot sell any output at any price above the market price, p^M. The downward-sloping segment shows that if the firm sets a price $p_f < p^M$, it gains the whole market. It would then obtain a **monopoly** position, acting as the sole supplier in the market, even though, as we have argued, it would make a loss. Only on the horizontal segment, in which it sets the market price, is it possible that the firm will share the market with other firms.

> **Monopoly** The firm is the only supplier in a market.

We can see from this discussion that the assumptions of perfect competition require adaptation for monopoly to emerge. We shall first introduce a model of monopoly that illustrates how the decisions made by a monopolist lead to a reduction in welfare relative to the outcome in a perfectly competitive market. After that, we shall examine natural monopoly, and discuss the extent to which it is reasonable for society to tolerate monopoly power.

With a single firm providing the whole market supply, and no possibility of entry or exit, monopoly is in many ways the antithesis of perfect competition. Under monopoly, in Figure 15.1, firm demand and market demand would be identical, and so we show the

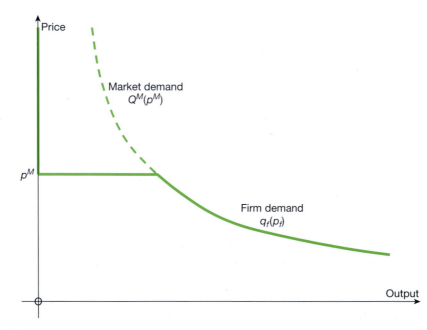

Figure 15.1 Firm demand in perfect competition

whole of the market demand curve. With no competitors, there will be no highest price that the firm can set. We can simplify the demand function slightly from Expression 15.1, writing:

$$q_f = \max(0, Q^M(p_f)) \qquad\qquad [15.2]$$

Expression 15.2 suggests that it is still possible that there will be a price high enough to choke off demand. In perfect competition, firm demand increases from zero to the whole market demand as the firm's price falls below the market price. For the monopoly, however, and indeed for any firm with market power, as the price at which the firm sells output changes by a small amount, the demand, q_f, also tends to change by a small amount. It may then be possible to find the derivative of the demand function, $q_f'(p_f)$; so long as its graph is smooth and continuous, and can be drawn without any gaps or corners, we can be certain that the response of demand to a small change in price will also be small. We see from Figure 15.1 that with perfect competition, this is not always the case. A very small increase in price, from just below to just above the market price, would lead to the loss of all sales.

15.1.1 Pricing and output in monopoly

With a monopoly, there can only be one seller in the market and there is no possibility of any entry. For example, a firm might have a monopoly of certain services on an isolated island with a small population. Suppose that there is only one garage: everyone who needs to buy fuel must go to that garage. The position of the garage on the island is entirely secure: not only is it the only current supplier, but the costs of entry will be high enough to deter anyone else from attempting to compete with it. The garage does not have to accept the market price. Instead, we expect it to set a price, on a 'take it or leave it' basis, with demand adjusting according to that price.

By yourself

X15.1   Suppose that we are considering the monopoly enjoyed by the only bakery on an island. Discuss its decision making process, explaining why we consider that it will be a price maker, rather than a price taker.

We expect a monopolist firm, such as the bakery in Exercise X15.1, to choose its output, with demand conditions determining the price in the market. Throughout this chapter, we shall generally assume that a monopolist sets output, q_f, achieving a sales price, $p_f = p(q_f)$, given by the inverse demand function. As seen already in Section 13.1, the inverse demand is the firm's average revenue, given that all units of the good are sold at the same price, p_f.

For the purposes of analysis, as shown in Figure 15.2, the substantial difference between monopoly and perfect competition is that the demand curve for a monopolist is downward-sloping, while the demand curve for a firm facing a perfectly competitive market is flat. We assume that the monopolist firm faces constant returns to scale in production, so that the average and marginal cost curves are simply a horizontal line. In Figure 15.2, then, as well as allowing price to vary with output, we have dropped the assumption from Chapter 14 of (eventually) diminishing returns to scale.

By definition (in Section 13.1), we know that if marginal revenue is decreasing then average revenue must also be decreasing, but still greater than marginal revenue. We show these relationships in Figure 15.2 for the average and marginal revenue curves, $AR(q_f)$ and

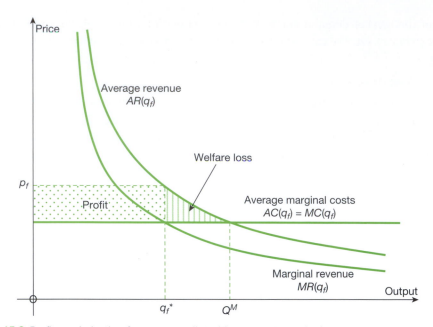

Figure 15.2 Profit maximization for a monopolist with constant marginal costs

$MR(q_f)$. Applying the standard profit-maximizing conditions, then at the profit-maximizing output, the first-order condition

$$MR(q_f^*) = MC(q_f^*) = c_0 \qquad\qquad [15.3]$$

is satisfied. The second-order condition

$$MR'(q_f^*) < MC'(q_f^*) \qquad\qquad [15.4]$$

is also satisfied. In Figure 15.2, the marginal cost curve is flat, so $MC'(q_f) = 0$, while the marginal revenue curve is downward-sloping, meaning that $MR'(q_f) < 0$. When the first-order condition is satisfied, the second-order condition certainly will be. The

Essential Maths 15.1: A function as a sum of increments

For the function $Z = Z(x)$, we have defined the marginal function $MZ = MZ(x) = z'(x)$, the derivative of Z. In diagrams, we represent $MZ(z_0)$ by the gradient of the tangent to the graph of Z, passing through $(z_0, M(z_0))$. We now seek set out a method for obtaining Z given MZ.

Consider a finite approximation to the marginal function, the average rate of change of Z over an increment Δx, evaluated between x_0 and $x_0 + \delta x$. Denote the change in Z by ΔZ. Then the marginal function $MZ(x_0) \approx \frac{\Delta Z}{\Delta x} = \frac{Z(x_0 + \delta x) - Z(x_0)}{\delta x}$, so that it is approximately the rate of change of Z over a small, finite interval.

We now divide the interval $0 \leq x \leq x_0$ into N increments, each of width δx. Then by the definition above, $Z(x_0) = Z(0) + \sum_{n=1}^{N} \left\{ Z(\frac{nx_0}{N}) - Z\left(\frac{(n-1)x_0}{N}\right) \right\}$. The value $Z(x_0)$ is the value of $Z(0)$ plus the sum of the N increments of Z as x increases from 0 to x_0.

assumptions that average revenue is a decreasing function of output, and that there are constant returns to scale in production, are enough to ensure that the firm makes profits. Then $AC(q_f^*) = MC(q_f^*) < AR(q_f^*)$ and the monopoly makes profits, shown as the shaded rectangle in Figure 15.2. We discuss below the nature of the area called the 'welfare loss'.

> **By yourself**
>
> **X15.2** Suppose that a monopoly faces inverse demand, $p = p(q_f) = p_0 - p_1 q_f$, and total costs, $C_f = c_0 q_f$.
>   (a) Obtain the firm's marginal and average costs, MC_f and AC_f, and its total, marginal, and average revenues, TR_f, MR_f, and AR_f.
>   (b) Calculate the profit-maximizing level of output, the price that the firm will then charge, and the profits that it will make.
>   (c) Sketch a diagram showing MC_f, AC_f, MR_f, and AR_f. Indicate clearly the profit-maximizing output, and the resulting price and profits.
>
> **X15.3** Repeat X15.2 for the inverse demand $p = p_0 - p_1 q_f$, and the total costs $C_f = c_0 + c_1 q_f + c_2 q_f^2$.
>
> **X15.4** Repeat Exercise X15.2 for the inverse demand $p = A q_f^{-1}$, with these total costs: (a) $C_f = c_0 q_f$; (b) $C_f = c_0 q_f^{2/3}$.
>
> **X15.5** Repeat Exercise X15.2 for the inverse demand $p = p(q_f) = p_0 - p_1 q_f$, with these total costs: (a) $C_f = c_0 q_f^2$;   (b) $C_f = c_0 q_f^{3/2}$.

In all of the exercises, we find that the inverse demand (or average revenue) is a decreasing function of output q_f, so that marginal revenue is less than average revenue. With constant returns to scale in production, this guarantees that the monopoly will be profitable. In Exercises X15.4b and X15.5b, though, the cost function is increasing, but concave. This is consistent with the monopoly's production function having increasing returns to scale. In such a situation, average costs will be decreasing, and will be greater than marginal costs. We shall come back to this possibility in Section 15.2, arguing that with increasing returns to scale, the industry is a natural monopoly because it will be served most efficiently served by a single firm.

15.1.2   The welfare loss in monopoly

To finish off discussion of Figure 15.2, we need to explain the approximately triangular shape labelled 'Welfare loss'. The monopoly maximizes its profits by choosing the output for which the marginal revenue and the marginal cost are equal, with demand conditions determining the price at which the good will sell. If we consider increasing output from q_f^* to Q^M, we can see that right up to output Q^M the price that the monopolist could obtain from sales – its average revenue – would be greater than the marginal cost, which is the rate at which total costs increase with sales. When output is Q^M, $p^M = AR(Q^M) = MC(Q^M)$. At output Q^M, the marginal consumer's willingness to pay (WTP) equals the rate of increase of the monopolist's costs of production, which, by the definition in Chapter 1, is the seller's willingness to accept (WTA). Applying the argument about voluntary exchange in Section 1.1, were this to be the only transaction in the market, the monopolist and the marginal consumer should then be willing to enter into an exchange at price p^M.

But, of course, this marginal transaction is not the only one that takes place. When the monopolist increases output, it is bound by the law of one price. Not only the additional units but *all* of its output must now be sold at the lower (market-clearing) price. For this reason, when output is at its profit-maximizing level, q_f^*, marginal costs and revenues are equal, and for greater output, marginal cost exceeds marginal revenue. The monopolist restricts its output to q_f^*. The area denoted welfare loss then represents the value that consumers would be willing to pay above the costs of production for output between q_f^* and Q^M. In this case, we can think of the welfare loss as the cost to society of there being a monopoly rather than perfect competition.

> **Welfare loss of monopoly** The cost to society of a good being produced by a monopoly rather than by a perfectly competitive industry.

By yourself

X15.6   Confirm that in Figure 15.2: (a) there is no producer surplus; and (b) the maximum consumer surplus is equivalent to the area enclosed by the marginal cost and average revenue curves.

X15.7   Suppose that the market demand of a monopoly is linear (and decreasing in price), while the average cost is linear (and increasing in output). Sketch a diagram to show the average and marginal revenues and the average and marginal costs. Indicate the profit-maximizing and the welfare-maximizing levels of output; and label the areas on your diagram that represent the firm's profits, its producer surplus, the consumers' surplus, and the welfare loss from the monopoly.

X15.8   Why might it be reasonable to conclude that in Exercises X15.1–X15.6 we are considering the long run? How reasonable is it to expect there to be a monopoly in these circumstances?

Essential Maths 15.2: The summation of incremental areas in a graph

We represent this summation in a graph. As usual, the horizontal axis measures the value of x. The vertical axis will measure the incremental rate of change $\frac{\Delta Z(x)}{\Delta x}$. Multiplying this rate of change by the increment, δx, we obtain the product $\Delta Z(x)$. In a graph, this is the area of a box, of width δx and height $\frac{\Delta Z(x)}{\Delta x}$, the incremental rate of change. From the previous discussion, the sum of the area of all of these narrow strips represents the change in the value of Z, $Z(x_0) - Z(0)$.

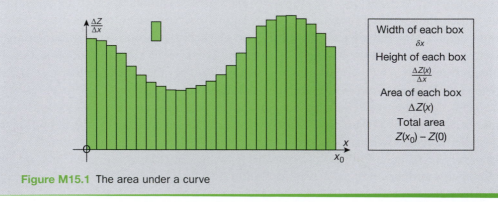

Width of each box
δx
Height of each box
$\frac{\Delta Z(x)}{\Delta x}$
Area of each box
$\Delta Z(x)$
Total area
$Z(x_0) - Z(0)$

Figure M15.1 The area under a curve

We found in Chapter 13 that it is possible for firms to make profits in perfectly competitive markets in the short run, but have also argued in Chapter 14 that competition leads to the elimination of profits in the long run. The short run and the long run differ, since firm entry is possible only in the long run. Associating (economic) profits with market power, the fixed number of firms in the short run is a (transient) source of market power. Even for perfect competition fully to dissipate market power, we have to be considering the long run. Since there are no fixed costs in the monopolist's cost function in Exercises X15.1–X15.6, we seem to be considering long-run costs. Somehow the monopolist makes profits, but entry does not occur. In Section 15.2 we shall consider two explanations for this: firstly, other firms may not wish to enter the market because they believe they would not be able to make profits; and secondly, it may not be possible for other firms to enter the market, typically because there is some legal restriction that prevents entry.

15.1.3   Relating costs, welfare, and profit

We summarize this introductory discussion of monopoly in Figure 15.3. Market supply is undertaken by a single firm, so that the market demand curve is also the firm's average revenue curve. Since average revenue is a decreasing function of output, marginal revenue is also decreasing and less than average revenue. The firm's production function exhibits eventually diminishing returns to scale. There is a minimum value of average costs; at that output, marginal and average costs are equal, with marginal costs increasing. At output, q_f^*, the increasing marginal cost curve cuts through the decreasing marginal revenue curve. The monopoly therefore maximizes profits by setting output q_f^*, with the market clearing at price p_f^*. There are then people willing to pay a price above the marginal cost of production,

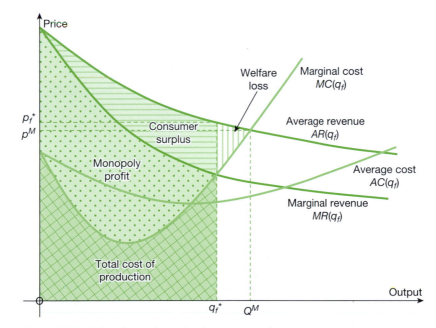

Figure 15.3 General case of profit maximization for a monopolist

but who are not willing to buy the good at that price. If the monopoly were instead to produce output Q^M, accepting the price p^M, then the WTP of the marginal consumer would be equal to the monopoly's WTA. Compared with the socially optimal outcome, the monopoly restricts output, with the market clearing at a higher price.

In Figure 15.3, we continue to show production in the long run. There are no fixed costs, and the total costs incurred when producing zero output, $C(0) = 0$. The average cost intersects the vertical axis, so that $AC(0)$ is defined.

> **By yourself**
>
> **X15.9**   Adapt Figure 15.3 to represent the monopoly making short-run decisions. Illustrate two distinct cases: (1) the monopoly makes profits in the short run; and (2) the monopoly makes losses, but wishes to continue production.

While the relationships between the curves in Figure 15.3 are already familiar, those between areas representing financial quantities are not. We have shown the total cost of production as the area underneath the marginal cost curve, rather than as a rectangle whose width is the firm's output and whose height is its average cost of production.

In Section 11.2, we defined the average cost or cost per unit, $AC(Q) = \frac{C(Q)}{Q}$, and the marginal cost, or rate of change of costs, $MC(Q) = C'(Q)$. It follows that the total cost is the product of average cost and output. Defining total cost in terms of the marginal cost requires the definition of the integral function in Essential Maths 15.1–15.3. In effect, we argue that the total cost, $C(q_f)$ can be calculated when marginal cost is defined in the range $0 \le q \le q_f$. To solve such problems, we can use the mathematical tools of integral calculus, which in many ways is the opposite of the differential calculus that we have been using up

Essential Maths 15.3: Graphical depiction of the definite integral

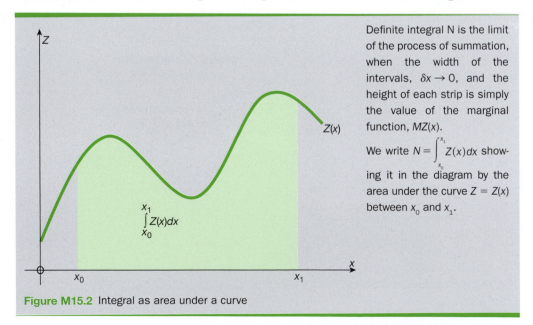

Definite integral N is the limit of the process of summation, when the width of the intervals, $\delta x \to 0$, and the height of each strip is simply the value of the marginal function, $MZ(x)$.

We write $N = \int_{x_0}^{x_1} Z(x)dx$ showing it in the diagram by the area under the curve $Z = Z(x)$ between x_0 and x_1.

Figure M15.2 Integral as area under a curve

until now. However, integral calculus is much more of an art than differential calculus. Its application can quickly become complicated, and so we do not examine its rules in any detail, concentrating instead on graphical arguments.

Applying the argument in Essential Maths 15.1–15.4 to the cost function, we can approximate the marginal costs across any one unit interval by the additional (total) cost of producing that unit. In a diagram, we might measure output on the horizontal axis and the value of such cost increments on the vertical axis. We can then show each increment by the area of a box that is one unit wide and whose height is the cost increment. The total cost of output, q_f, is then the total area of these boxes.

In introducing the concept of the derivative, we argued that we need to measure rates of change over an infinitesimally small interval, so that the derivative is truly the rate of change. Going through a similar process here, we allow the change in output in each of the boxes to fall to zero, so that they multiply in number, while also becoming vanishingly narrow. The height of each box will tend toward the marginal cost. Using symbols, we measure the total cost of output Q by *integrating* the marginal cost function, $MC(q)$, across the interval from 0 to Q. We might write:

$$C(Q) = \lim_{\delta q \to 0} \sum_{n=1}^{Q/\delta q} \frac{C(n.\delta q) - C((n-1)\delta q)}{\delta q} = \int_0^Q MC(q)\,dq \qquad [15.5]$$

Expression 15.5 defines the integral as the limit of the sum of cost increments across the interval $0 \leq q \leq Q$. By its definition, it is natural to represent it as the area underneath the marginal cost curve, and to interpret it as the total cost of production, as in Figure 15.3.

Essential Maths 15.4: The definite integral as the limit of a summation process

In the expression, $Z(x_0) - Z(0) = \lim_{N \to \infty} \sum_{n=1}^{N} \frac{Z\left(\frac{nx_0}{N}\right) - Z\left(\frac{(n-1)x_0}{N}\right)}{\Delta x} \cdot \delta x = \int_0^{x_0} MZ(x).dx$, we start by summing finite rates of change across N finite intervals, each of width δx, and effectively sum across

marginal values in the interval for which $0 \leq x \leq x_0$.

We use the name integration for this limit of the process of summation. In many ways, it is technically the opposite of differentiation; given a marginal function, it is possible to obtain the original function by identifying the function whose derivative is that marginal function. Since the rules of integration are rather more complex than the rules of differentiation, we do not consider them here.

In this chapter, it is enough to note that integrating the marginal function MZ across the interval $x_0 \leq x \leq x_1$, we obtain the change in the value of Z, so that $Z(x_1) - Z(x_0) = \int_{x_0}^{x_1} MZ(x)dx$.

By yourself

X15.10   Applying the same argument to marginal revenue as to marginal costs (in Figure 15.3), interpret the area between the output axis and the marginal revenue curve.

X15.11   Explain why the area between the marginal revenue and marginal cost curves yields the firm's profit.

X15.12   Interpret the area in Figure 15.3 between the inverse demand (average revenue) curve and the marginal cost curve in terms of consumers' *WTP* and the monopoly's *WTA*. Hence justify the argument that the area labelled 'Welfare loss' represents the cost to society of production being undertaken by a monopoly.

X15.13   Suppose that it is proposed that the monopolist should be required to produce output Q^M, the welfare-maximizing output. Write down an expression for the loss incurred by the monopolist in terms of the marginal revenue and cost functions, illustrating this area on a diagram. How might it be possible to compensate the monopolist for this loss?

From the Exercises X15.10–X15.13, we see that we can interpret changes in monetary stocks – cost, revenue, and profit – in terms of the area underneath their marginal value curves. For example, the loss that the firm would make, increasing output from q_f to Q^M, is the area between the marginal revenue and marginal cost curves. Since marginal cost is greater than marginal revenue, total costs increase more quickly than total revenue.

By yourself

X15.14   Given the marginal revenue and marginal cost curves in each of these three cases:
   (a) Find the output for which marginal revenue equals marginal cost.
   (b) Obtain the following functions of output: (i) total revenue; (ii) average revenue; (iii) total cost; (iv) profit; and (v) consumer surplus.
   (c) Sketch diagrams showing the marginal and average revenue curves and the marginal cost curve, indicating the total cost of the profit-maximizing output, the firm's profit, and the consumer surplus.
   (d) Estimate the welfare loss from monopoly:
      (i) $MC(q) = 2 + 0.2q$; $MR(q) = 4$;
      (ii) $MC(q) = 3$; $MR(q) = 6 - 0.15q$;
      (iii) $MC(q) = 2 + 0.3q$; $MR(q) = 8 - 0.9q$.

In Exercise X15.14, given marginal cost and marginal revenue, we obtain the total cost and total revenue for the monopoly by integrating the marginal functions over the interval between 0 and q, where q is the firm's output. From total revenue and cost, we can easily obtain the average revenue. Interpreting this as the willingness to pay (*WTP*) function, it is then possible to work out the total value of output to consumers. Subtracting the payments made to purchase the goods – the total revenue – we obtain a measure of consumer surplus, equal to the total amount that consumers would have been willing to pay to obtain the good, less the amount that they had to pay given the market-clearing price.

15.1.4   Elasticity of demand and the price–cost margin

We have identified a loss of welfare when production is undertaken by a monopoly, rather than in perfect competition. In the examples we have used, the assumption of diminishing returns to scale from low output, adopted throughout the discussion of perfect competition in Chapters 13 and 14, has been set aside, so that it is more efficient for a single firm to supply the market than for competition to emerge.

The welfare loss is one measure of the impact of monopoly. The price–cost margin is an alternative. We can derive it by relating the price elasticity of demand to the market price and the monopoly's marginal revenue, and hence to its marginal cost.

The price elasticity of demand, ε – defined in Chapter 7 as the proportional change in demand caused by a proportional change in the price of the good – measures the responsiveness of demand, q_f, to changes in the price at which the good sells, p_f.

$$\varepsilon = \frac{p_f}{q_f(p_f)} \cdot \frac{dq_f}{dp_f} \tag{15.6}$$

We can relate the marginal revenue of the firm, the price that it can charge, and the price elasticity of demand.

Defining marginal revenue as the derivative of total revenue, $MR(q_f) = \frac{d}{dq_f}(p(q_f) \cdot q_f)$. Then:

Apply the product rule of differentiation

$$MR(q_f) = p(q_f) + q_f \cdot \frac{dp_f}{dq_f} \tag{15.7}$$

Remember $\frac{dq}{dq} = 1$

Have to introduce factor $[p(q)]^{-1}$ to maintain the value of this expression

Extract the common factor, $p(q_f)$

$$MR(q_f) = p(q_f) \cdot \left[1 + \frac{q_f}{p(q_f)} \cdot \frac{dp_f}{dq_f} \right] \tag{15.8}$$

The derivative of the inverse function is the inverse of the derivative of the original function: $\frac{dq_f}{dp_f} = \left[\frac{dp_f}{dq_f} \right]^{-1}$

Invert the second term in the square bracket

$$MR(q_f) = p(q_f) \cdot \left[1 + \left(\frac{p(q_f)}{q_f} \cdot \frac{dq_f}{dp_f} \right)^{-1} \right] = p(q_f) \cdot [1 + \varepsilon^{-1}] \tag{15.9}$$

The expression in brackets is the inverse of Expression 15.6

Expression 15.9 links some important functional relationships. In reading it, remember that the price elasticity of demand $\varepsilon < 0$, since demand is a decreasing function of the market price. We can immediately say something about the value of ε. Since we are interested in the marginal revenue at the profit-maximizing output, where $MR = MC > 0$, then in Expression 15.9, $1 + \varepsilon^{-1} > 0$. It follows that $\varepsilon < -1$. But that means that when the monopoly maximizes profit, demand will be elastic. In perfect competition, demand is perfectly elastic, so that the elasticity, ε, is not defined. Expression 15.9 suggests that a profit-maximizing monopoly will not want demand to be too inelastic, and we explore the reasons for this in the following exercises.

By yourself

X15.15 For a monopoly facing the inverse demand function, $p = 100 - q_f$.
  (a) Obtain:
    (i) the total revenue and marginal revenue functions;
    (ii) the demand function and the price elasticity of demand (as a function of price).
  (b) Sketch the inverse demand curve and the marginal revenue curve.
  (c) Indicate on your diagram the range of outputs for which demand is elastic. Confirm that this is also the range of outputs for which $MR > 0$.

X15.16 Suppose that a firm faces inelastic demand at output q_f. By considering the effect on its revenue and costs of reducing its output, show that this firm will increase profits by reducing output.

X15.17 Using Expression 15.9, and the first-order condition for profit maximization, show that the price–cost margin

$$\frac{p_f - MC(q_f{}^*)}{MC(q_f{}^*)} = -\frac{1}{1 + \varepsilon} \qquad [15.10]$$

Confirm that in Figure 15.4 the price cost margin is also the ratio of profits to total costs.

X15.18 Using Expression 15.10, confirm that at the profit-maximizing output, $q_f{}^*$, the monopoly's demand function must be elastic, or that the price elasticity of demand, $\varepsilon_p < -1$. Show that as $\varepsilon_p \to -1$, the price–cost margin increases without limit; and that as $\varepsilon_p \to -\infty$, the price–cost margin approaches zero.

Price–cost margin (1)
A measure of mono-poly power: the ratio of price to marginal cost minus one.

The measure of the **price–cost margin** we obtain in Exercise X15.17 holds because we expect the monopoly to maximize its profits. The result of Exercises X15.15 and X15.16 are useful in explaining why profit maximization requires elastic demand. A monopolist facing inelastic demand can always reduce output, increase revenue and reduce costs, and hence increase profits.

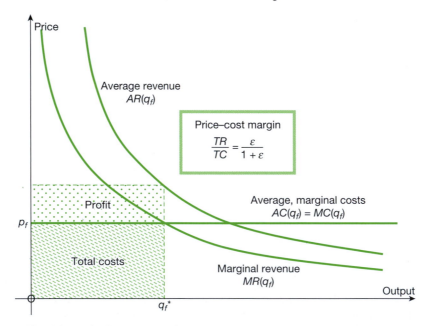

Figure 15.4 Elasticity and price–cost margins

Demand is unit elastic on the boundary between inelastic and elastic demand, where $\varepsilon = -1$. Considering Expression 15.9, we note that when elasticity, $\varepsilon = -1$, then $AR > MR = 0$. For profit maximization in this situation, $p > MC = 0$, and the mark-up is undefined. In contrast, when the firm faces perfect competition, as we know from Section 15.2.1, price equals marginal cost in equilibrium, so firms' mark-up is zero.

By yourself

X15.19 Given the demand function $q_f = Ap_f^{-b}$:
  (a) Confirm that the price elasticity of demand, $\varepsilon_p = -b$.
  (b) Obtain the inverse demand function: and show that when $b = 1$, total revenue $TR(q_f) = A$, so that marginal revenue $MR(q_f) = 0$. Confirm that the monopoly then maximizes profits by setting output to zero.
  (c) Assume that $b > 1$ and that the firm has total cost function $C = cq_f$. Calculate the profit-maximizing output and price, and illustrate these in a diagram showing both the average and marginal revenue curves and the average and marginal cost curves.

X15.20 Given the demand function $q_f = a - bp$:
  (a) Confirm that the price elasticity of demand, $\varepsilon_p = -bp/(a - bp)$.
  (b) Obtain the inverse demand function, the average revenue function, and the marginal revenue function. Sketch a diagram showing all of these.
  (c) Confirm that if the marginal revenue, $MR(q_f) > 0$, then the price elasticity of demand, $\varepsilon_p < -1$.
  (d) Using the result from part (c), confirm that if the firm maximizes profits, price $p_f > a/2b$.

From these exercises, we see that a monopolist's demand function has to be elastic where it maximizes profits. Otherwise, it would be possible for the monopolist to reduce sales and increase profits. We also see how elasticity of demand at the profit-maximizing output determines the size of the price–cost margin. Where demand is strongly price-elastic, so that market conditions are close to being perfectly competitive, the price–cost margin is low. Relatively inelastic demand (so that the price elasticity of demand is close to minus one) is associated with a very large price–cost margin.

We will not always have enough information about a monopoly's costs to be able to calculate the price–cost margin directly; in that case, it may be necessary to estimate it by considering how demand changes with the price of the monopoly's output, using the price elasticity of demand. It is sensible to treat the price–cost margin of zero that emerges in perfect competition in the long run as indicating the complete absence of market power; subsequently, the **price–cost margin** is a measure of the extent of monopoly power (or, more generally, market power). The larger its value, the greater the divergence between the firm's marginal cost and the price that it charges.

Price–cost margin (2) A monopoly's ability to make profits from a marginal transaction.

15.2 Natural and artificial monopoly

Firms like to have market power in order to make profits. Such a situation is difficult to maintain: for firms facing perfect competition, market power is entirely transitory. As time passes, new firms enter the market and existing firms adjust their scale of production. If this does not happen, there must be some force limiting the extent of competition. It is useful here to make a distinction between natural and artificial monopolies.

Natural monopoly A firm's monopoly power if derived from increasing returns in production.

Artificial monopoly A firm's monopoly power if derived from legal restrictions that prevent entry.

A **natural monopoly** is a situation in which other firms *choose* not to enter the market, whereas an **artificial monopoly** is one in which some sort of legal restrictions *prevent* entry. The definition of a legal restriction here is very broad, and includes attempts by a monopolist (or a firm with substantial market power) to establish contracts with suppliers and customers that prevent other businesses from entering the market. Such contracts can be reviewed by the civil courts and may be held to be illegal. Probably the best-known such ruling is the decision of the US Supreme Court in the case of Standard Oil of New Jersey *versus* the United States, 1911. The Court held that Standard Oil had for many years used its substantial share of production, refining and distribution of oil in the USA (approximately 90% of the total market) to write contracts that were so favourable to the company as to prevent other firms from entering the market. It therefore required that Standard Oil be divided into several smaller companies to increase competition. The Court applied a test of *restraint of trade*, which derived from the arguments we have considered in Section 15.1: that there should be evidence of higher prices, lower output or reduced product quality resulting from the exercise of market power. Effectively, the Supreme Court had to decide whether the monopoly was natural or artificial.

By yourself

X15.21   Accepting the argument that Standard Oil was able to extract better terms from its suppliers than could its potential competitors, explain how this might have affected its production function, giving the appearance of increasing returns to scale in production. How might Standard Oil also have increased prices to its customers above the level that competitors might be able to charge?

15.2.1   Natural monopoly

Increasing returns to scale in production imply that the monopoly's average and marginal costs decrease with output. We saw in Chapter 13 that increasing returns are not consistent with profit maximization in perfect competition. In Figure 15.5, we analyse this case for a monopoly. The marginal revenue curve is downward-sloping, and it intersects the marginal cost curve at two points. At the lower level of output, the marginal cost curve is steeper than the marginal revenue curve. The second-order condition for profit maximization therefore fails. At the higher level of output, q_f^*, the marginal revenue curve is steeper than the marginal cost curve, and the second-order condition is satisfied. For output, q_f^*, we see from the diagram that $p_f(q_f) = AR_f(q_f) > AC_f(q_f)$. The firm makes positive profits.

By yourself

X15.22   Suppose that a second firm plans to enter the market. It is able to produce a good of exactly the same quality, and faces exactly the same production (and cost) functions. The monopolist has already announced that if any other firm enters the market, it will increase its output so that it just breaks even. Why would it be difficult for entry to occur under such circumstances? Do you think that such a policy should be considered as 'restraint of trade'?

X15.23   Suppose that a firm does enter the market, producing an output q_1. Sketch a diagram showing the output of the monopolist, which now sets output so as just to break even.

> **X15.24** We show the firm as being able to sell an output Q^M at price p^M. Applying the argument used in X15.12, show that this is the welfare-maximizing output. Confirm that when producing output, Q^M, the monopoly makes a loss. How might government induce the monopolist to produce output, Q^M?

Figure 15.5, together with its interpretation in Exercises X15.22–X15.24, indicates the extent to which the market outcome changes as we move from perfect competition to natural monopoly. Firstly, note that the monopoly is 'natural' in the sense that no other firm will *wish* to enter the market. We have simplified the argument slightly by thinking of the monopolist forestalling entry by threatening to expand production, but a variant of the argument in X15.22 rules out small-scale entry because a small firm's average costs are higher than those of the monopolist. The impossibility of making profits given the costs of production is sufficient to ensure that entry will not occur. The continuing monopoly is natural in the sense that the monopolist's low marginal costs result from the nature of the production function. In contrast, in the Standard Oil case the Courts ultimately concluded that low costs resulted from the ability to depress input prices, and thus from an unfair advantage over potential competitors.[1]

The preceding argument suggests that a natural monopoly might be the best outcome that can be achieved in such a market. The firm is more or less immune from the effects of competition because of its cost advantages. In Figure 15.5, however, we show very

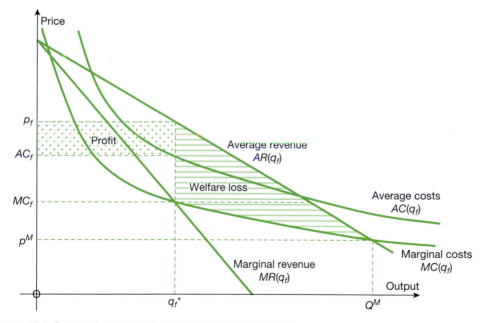

Figure 15.5 Decreasing marginal costs and natural monopoly

---

1   We often associate natural monopoly with network industries, such as telephony services. In the online student essay bank, Vivian Wanjiku explains that in much of Africa mobile phone technology has allowed the creation of money-transfer services for the first time. Here we see the power of a natural monopoly, able to provide novel services and thereby to improve consumer welfare. You will find Vivian's essay on the companion website for this book, at **www.palgrave.com/mochrie**.

considerable welfare costs of monopoly. One possible response is for public authorities to subject the monopoly to regulation. Instead of the monopoly being able to set its price freely, a public authority may give instructions to the monopoly, compelling it to behave in certain ways. For example, such a regulatory authority might require the monopoly to set its price to the welfare-maximizing price, p^M, so that, in Figure 15.5, the monopoly would produce output, $Q^M : MC(Q^M) = p^M$. The firm would then make losses, since $p^M < AC(Q^M)$. Such losses would only be sustainable if the regulator (the government) were to subsidize production. Subsidies would come from government tax revenue; however, as we shall see later, many methods of raising taxes also cause inefficiencies. As a result, governments have to balance the inefficiencies caused by the presence of a monopoly with the inefficiencies associated with distortions of market prices caused by regulation and taxation.

By yourself

X15.25   Suppose that the government does decide to set up a system of regulation of a market such as energy distribution, sometimes argued to be a natural monopoly. Explain why it might be difficult for the regulator to set the price p^M, which maximizes welfare. [*Hint:* Think about how easy it would be in reality to define that price, and also about the impact that this form of regulation would have upon the behaviour of the monopoly.]

The standard examples of natural monopolies are physical networks, such as fixed-line telecommunications. There is no advantage to owning a telephone if it cannot be connected to a network, and there is little point in having competing networks. It is more than a century since this principle was recognized in the United States,[2] with the government permitting AT&T to operate the only national long-distance telephone service. The agreement lasted for almost seventy years, only ending in 1982; at that point, technological advances, including the development of forerunners to mobile telephone networks, meant that the integration of local service providers with the national network was no longer essential. (In Europe, telephone networks were typically managed by national post offices, which were granted a statutory monopoly of service provision. Deregulation of service provision in Europe, including the privatization of publicly owned telecoms businesses, also began in the 1980s.)

Network externality
A benefit accruing to the user of a good or a service from its use by others.

We expect substantial market power to emerge where there are **network externalities**. Benefits accrue to members of networks from the size of the network. Fixed-line telephony is one such industry, but the emergence of Microsoft's Windows operating system or Facebook's social network as market-leading products also reflect such externalities. The higher the proportion of PCs that are shipped with Windows software installed, the more likely it is that software developers will want to have a Windows-compatible version of their products. Microsoft has faced several investigations over claims of abuse of its monopoly position. For example, in 2007 the European Court of Justice found that the company had restricted competition by bundling proprietary software with its operating systems, in particular Windows Media Player.[3] This program, along with several others, was installed on PCs along with the Windows

2   www.corp.att.com/history/history3.html
3   http://fsfe.org/activities/ms-vs-eu/timeline.en.html; http://news.bbc.co.uk/1/hi/business/6998272.stm

operating systems as part of a package prior to final sale. The Court concluded that such bundling of different services limited the opportunities for consumers to choose the software that they would use.

15.2.2 Artificial monopoly

All of these examples remind us that it is very easy to encroach upon a natural monopoly. By attaching to a firm's production services other than the one in which there is a natural monopoly, a firm may well be able to extend its market power, and thus its profits. This is an important cause of complaints about abuse of market power. This was the case for the court-mandated break-up of the AT&T's Bell System, which combined the natural monopoly of long-distance fixed-line telephony, essentially data transmission, with the business of managing local connections to the network. We are now used to being able to purchase telephone services from many providers, largely because of the development of mobile telephony, but it took many years to find effective ways of splitting service provision from data transmission.

We have an important problem here. Firms exist to make profits. They might make (economic) profits by producing a good more cheaply than competitors, by developing new products, or by finding new markets. Yet in our model of perfect competition, we make the strong assumption that every firm can obtain all the information it needs without paying any costs, which ensures that economic profits are transient.

By yourself

X15.26 In our example of the fruit market in Chapter 1, how likely it is that any firm would be able to sustain a competitive advantage over periods of: (a) a day; (b) a month; or (c) a year? How do you think this affects the behaviour of the firms in the market?

X15.27 Why might we argue that it is essential to tolerate some degree of market power if there is to be innovation and invention in the economy?

X15.28 What justification, if any, would you give for each of the following measures?
  (a) *Patents* – these prevent any business other than the one holding the patent from producing a specified output or using a specified technique of production.
  (b) *Copyright* – this prohibits the copying of a particular expression of an idea in text or music.
  (c) *Trademarks and registered designs* – these restrict the freedom of other producers to copy the appearance of goods.

As the author of this textbook, copyright seems to me a necessary intellectual property right. I have to confirm that the expression of ideas contained in this text is original. My publisher will then, as far as possible, seek to ensure that no one else is able to reproduce my text. Were this not possible, then anyone might copy my work and publish their own version. Copyright is intended to ensure that the creators of the original expression of ideas are compensated fairly for their work. While not ignoring the range of motivations that impel people to engage in acts of creativity – such as writing poetry and songs, for which the (financial) reward is typically very small – we might argue that a reasonable prospect of payment will encourage, rather than discourage, such creative efforts. Note, however, that it will typically be the publisher, rather than the author, that seeks to ensure that the expression of the idea is protected. (There are exceptions, of course: with copyright lasting for up to seventy years after the author's death, the estate of a best-selling author – for example Agatha Christie, a prolific author of detective fiction – may be ferociously protective of the author's reputation, as it manages the value of the author's overall body of work.)[4, 5]

We can think of a publisher as being a specialist in the large-scale production and distribution of original material. We can then argue that a publisher, just as much as the author, has an interest in asserting ownership of the expression of ideas and the rights to control the dissemination of this expression. The emergence of electronic media, and the associated reductions in publishing costs, mean that there is perhaps less reason for authors to work with traditional publishers: a few successful authors have switched to electronic self-publishing. While reducing the costs of publishing very considerably, such authors lose the support of editors, design specialists and marketing departments. While we might argue that in book publishing the product is relatively difficult to copy, this does not apply to the music industry.

By yourself

X15.29   What might be the effects on the music industry of the abolition of copyright? Consider in particular the impact on the distribution of recordings and the decision to create and perform new material.

Suppose we agreed that there was no reason why anyone should be made to purchase a recording generated from the original source, should it be possible to download, or stream, a cheaper version. A free version, of similar quality to the licensed one, is a cheaper way of obtaining utility, and so it is economically rational to choose it. We could easily imagine a situation in which musicians typically became part of a community, relying on recommendations and being paid only for live performances. Small-scale, intimate performances might become entirely normal, with the layers of management between performers and audience being stripped away, and with reputations being built online. But that in turn would allow for the manipulation of reputation, creating a role for managers.[6]

15.3   Conclusions

Monopoly is simply one form of market structure. It differs from perfect competition in many ways. While we have talked about a welfare loss if a monopoly is allowed to choose its own output, we have also noted that in the presence of increasing returns to

---

4   Distribution channels within the music industry have also changed very substantially, with the emergence of streaming technologies (and other, illegal alternatives). In the online student essay bank, James Murray argues that this is leading to performing artists depending much more upon live performance and merchandise sales for the bulk of their income, and also to their taking much greater control of their performance. You can read James's essay on the companion website for the book, at **www.palgrave.com/mochrie.**

5   www.theguardian.com/media/2012/feb/29/acorn-media-bys-stake-agatha-christie; http://www.agathachristie.com/terms-and-conditions

6   www.economist.com/news/obituary/21602979-prince-rupert-zu-loewenstein-financial-adviser-rolling-stones-died-may-20th-aged

scale it may well be the most efficient outcome. We have suggested that monopoly, and more generally market power, is likely to be transitory. Sustained profits will encourage the entry of new businesses into the market, possibly using innovative production techniques to erode the original source of market power. So, while the language of efficiency suggests that perfect competition is preferable to monopoly, the matter is rather more complicated.

Perhaps the best argument for monopoly is that it allows firms making innovations the opportunity to make profits. Invention and innovation generally require considerable expenditure. Granting inventors and innovators the ability to control the dissemination of their ideas and techniques restricts competition in the market. An inventor may grant an exclusive licence to a company in return for a royalty payment on each unit sold. The producer is then able to use its monopoly to make economic profits lasting for the full period of the licence. Once again, the originators of ideas are able to obtain a return on their investment, and this encourages innovation. As with copyright, legal protections such as patent rights allow the creation of statutory monopolies, protected (at least for a period of time) by legal systems and courts.

Where the civil courts tend to oppose the use of market power is where firms are exploiting contracts to make monopoly profits, whether (as in the Standard Oil case) by obtaining lower prices from suppliers, or (as in the Microsoft case) by bundling services to expand their monopoly. Simplifying somewhat, we might conclude that monopoly power should be tolerated where it is a mechanism for rewarding risk, but be overturned where it is used to defeat welfare-enhancing competition.

Summary

A monopoly arises when a single firm supplies the whole of a market. The firm's demand and the market demand functions are then identical. The monopoly's inverse demand defines the price at which any given output might be sold.

Inverse demand is also the monopoly's average revenue. Since it is a decreasing function of output, we expect the monopoly's marginal revenue also to be a decreasing function, with average revenue greater than marginal revenue.

The monopoly maximizes its profits by choosing the level of output for which its marginal cost and marginal revenue are equal, with the marginal cost curve intersecting the marginal revenue curve from below. These conditions will certainly be met if production exhibits diminishing returns to scale at this level of output.

Under these circumstances, average revenue is greater than average cost, and the monopoly makes positive profits.

Since marginal revenue is less than average revenue when profits are maximized, the output under monopoly is less than the output under perfect competition. We define the area between the average revenue and marginal cost curves as the welfare loss caused by monopoly.

As well as the welfare loss, we can use the price–cost margin to indicate the extent of monopoly power.

We define a natural monopoly as a situation in which there are increasing returns to scale at all levels of output. The monopoly then has a cost advantage over all potential competitors.

We define a statutory monopoly as one that is created by law. We noted that statutory monopolies have often emerged during the formation of communications networks.

Firms may be granted some market power as a result of making an innovation or invention in order that they may more easily obtain a reasonable return to their efforts. Such intellectual property rights are also present in creative industries.

The judicial systems of most countries are able to review the practices of businesses that appear to have market power and to require these to be changed if the businesses are using market power to restrain competition.

Visit the companion website at **www.palgrave.com/mochrie** to access further teaching and learning materials, including lecturer slides and a testbank, as well as guideline answers and student MCQs.

chapter 16

Price discrimination

What we do in this chapter

A monopoly is able to influence the market price, and hence its revenue and profits, by choosing its output. The ability to influence market price is a result of market power. We shall examine several ways in which firms can use this power to their own advantage. Until now, we have assumed that all firms have to sell all of their output at a single price. In a situation where there is a monopoly, this will not necessarily be the case, and we define *price discrimination* as the practice of charging different prices for different units of output.

We identify three classes of price discrimination. *First-degree*, or *perfect*, *price discrimination* occurs when the monopoly is able to sell every unit of output for the full value of the willingness to pay. The mechanism that most readily accommodates perfect price discrimination is sale by auction. *Second-degree price discrimination* occurs where a firm with market power is able to charge different prices depending on the quantity of the good sold. Two mechanisms

are widely used. In a two-part tariff, firms charge an entry (or registration) fee and then additional user fees. This is often the practice with contracts for the supply of utilities, for example. Alternatively, businesses might sell bundles of goods and services. Everyone purchasing the same bundle pays the same price. *Third-degree price discrimination* requires firms to charge different prices to different classes of consumer, with student discounts being a typical example. In all three cases, we concentrate on how firms might use price discrimination to increase their profits.

Price discrimination allows firms to make larger profits than uniform pricing. Nonetheless, it can benefit society since it may lead to more rapid innovation. If the right to practise price discrimination has to be purchased, or if the firm's profits are taxed, then in principle it is possible to reverse the change in income distribution. We shall argue that price discrimination can then lead to an increase in welfare.

16.1   Price discrimination

Both perfect competition and monopoly are theoretical constructs, allowing us to explore how businesses would behave under certain, quite extreme, assumptions. In this chapter, we shall extend our understanding of markets by considering how firms can use market power to increase their profits using the technique of price discrimination.

Market power requires a demand function $q_f = q_f(p)$ for which the derivative $q_f'(p) < 0$. The graph of the demand curve (or more precisely, the inverse demand) is then downward-sloping. When this condition is satisfied, as we saw in Chapter 15, the firm is able to affect the price at which its output is sold, and thus its revenues and profits. Profit maximization then occurs at the output for which marginal revenue equals marginal cost. In a monopoly, we expect the firm to make positive profits, even in the long run.

In Chapter 15, we measured the consumer's surplus as the difference between average and marginal revenue integrated over the firm's output; or, in diagrammatic terms, as the area

> **Price discrimination** Selling units of a good at different prices.

bounded by the average and marginal revenue curves. By using **price discrimination**, or charging a variety of prices instead of a uniform price, a firm with market power can acquire some of what would otherwise be the consumer surplus. This plainly benefits the firm, but (as we shall see below) if it leads to increased sales it may also be beneficial to society as a whole.

Typically, we identify three forms of price discrimination. The *degree* of price discrimination refers to the pricing structure that the firm uses. In *first-degree price discrimination*, every unit of output is sold at a different price, which we expect to be the highest value that can be obtained. In *second-degree price discrimination*, the firm sets a different price for every customer, depending on the quantity of output being purchased. And in *third-degree price discrimination*, the firm sets different prices across different classes of consumers. Price discrimination of the first degree is most precise, and is sometimes known as *perfect price discrimination*. But, depending on the circumstances that the firm faces, all can be used effectively.

16.2   Price discrimination of the first degree

> **First-degree price discrimination** Selling each unit of a good at a different price.

First-degree price discrimination occurs when the firm is able to sell every unit of output at a different price, presumably the highest that it can achieve for each unit. We should expect each unit to be sold to the person with the highest *WTP*, with the price paid for each unit increasing in the *WTP*. In Figure 16.1, we show how a firm facing constant returns to scale in production, and so constant average and marginal costs but decreasing inverse demand and marginal revenue, might implement this form of price discrimination.

Given that the firm is to sell all its output at a constant price, then in Figure 16.1, to maximize its profits, it should set its output, q_f^*, so that the marginal revenue, at output

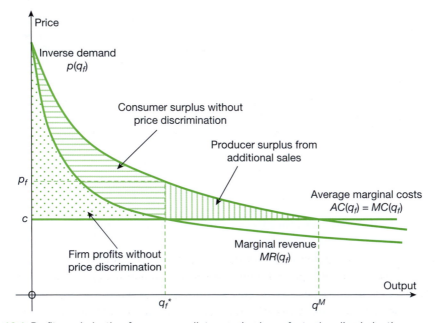

Figure 16.1 Profit maximization for a monopolist engaging in perfect price discrimination

q_f^*, equals the marginal cost. It then charges the price p_f. The profit is the area enclosed by the marginal revenue and marginal cost curves, while the consumer surplus is the area between the inverse demand and the marginal cost curve. (All this should be familiar from Section 15.1.)

Suppose instead that the firm engages in first-degree price discrimination, setting a different price for each unit of output. We have already asserted that prices should increase with the *WTP* of the buyer, and, using arguments about market efficiency, the firm should sell every unit to the person with the highest *WTP*. We simplify our analysis by assuming that for every unit sold, the price $p_i = WTP_i$, so price equals the value in consumption. In these circumstances, the firm engages in **perfect price discrimination**. Under uniform pricing, as the firm increases output it must accept a lower price on every transaction, which is why we have concluded that marginal revenue is less than average revenue for a monopoly. Under perfect price discrimination, though, the firm effectively banks the revenue from each sale; as output increases, the marginal revenue will be the transaction price – in effect, the willingness to pay, or the inverse demand. Going back to Figure 16.1, we can rewrite the firm's profit-maximizing condition as:

> **Perfect price discrimination**
> Selling each unit of a good at the buyer's *WTP*.

$$MR(q^M) = WTP(q^M) = p(q^M) = MC(q^M) \qquad [16.1]$$

This is satisfied at output Q^M, at which the inverse demand curve intersects the marginal cost curve. Note that the firm sets the same output as under perfect competition (as in Section 12.2), but that it appropriates both what had previously been the consumer surplus and also what we identified in Section 15.1.2 as the welfare loss under monopoly.

By yourself

X16.1 For price discrimination to take place, there must be no possibility of resale among consumers. Explain why this condition is necessary.

X16.2 Explain why a firm supplying personal services, such as a hairdressing salon or a beauty therapist, might find it relatively straightforward to engage in price discrimination compared with a firm selling an easily divisible but durable physical product, such as screws and nails.

X16.3 Suppose that the willingness to pay for a product $WTP(q) = 200 - 3q$, while the marginal cost of production $MC(q) = 20$. Draw a diagram showing the average and marginal revenue curves when there is no price discrimination, and the marginal cost curve. From the diagram calculate: (1) the firm's profit-maximizing output in the absence of price discrimination, and the price that the firm then charges; (2) the firm's profit, and the consumer surplus without price discrimination; and (3) the welfare loss when there is price discrimination. Explain how the outcome changes when price discrimination is permitted.

Compared with perfect competition, the firm does better under perfect price discrimination and consumers do worse. But perfect price discrimination eliminates the welfare loss from monopoly. It is therefore arguable that perfect price discrimination is (socially) beneficial. From our model, we know the firm's sales revenue. We know its costs. We can even calculate the share of its revenue that would be consumer surplus were it to sell all its output at price p^M.

Given these considerations, we might allow the government to levy a tax on the firm's profits, or to set a licence fee for the monopoly, conditional on it engaging in perfect price discrimination. Suppose that the government receives total payments that are greater than the appropriated consumer surplus, but less than the monopoly's profits. In addition, let us say that the government uses this revenue to reduce the taxes that consumers would otherwise pay. Lastly, suppose that the cost of managing the monopoly in this way is less than the recovered welfare loss. If all of these conditions are satisfied, then the reduction in taxes is large enough to compensate people fully for the loss of surplus associated with the monopoly. And since the surplus from the additional sales, which price discrimination enables, is greater than the administrative costs of administering the new taxes, social welfare increases. Allowing price discrimination in this form may have substantial social benefits.

By yourself

X16.4   Consider the situation of the firm in Exercise X16.3. The government has calculated that allowing perfect price discrimination and then collecting the tax from the firm will cost $W = 400$. Should the government permit price discrimination in these circumstances?

X16.5   Why might it be particularly difficult to engage in price discrimination in sales of music downloads? A few musicians have experimented with allowing people to download music in return for a donation, rather than by setting a fixed price. Explain why these experiments do not involve the practice of price discrimination.

16.2.1   Perfect price discrimination through auction sales

For price discrimination to occur, it is necessary to prevent resale among consumers: otherwise, the firm might sell some of the good to a person whose *WTP* is low, but who then sold it on to someone else whose *WTP* was rather higher. Exercise X16.5 suggests an even more fundamental problem: for price discrimination to be successful, we have to induce potential purchasers to reveal their *WTP*. Simply asking people to state their *WTP* might not be enough, because there is nothing to prevent someone from declaring a value that is much lower than the true one, ensuring that price discrimination is not perfect.

Suppose, though, that the firm uses the method of sale by auction (and suppose that the firm can carry out a sequence of auctions with one unit of the good being sold in each). We shall also assume that the cost of running an auction is very close to zero. While auction sales are the subject of Chapter 30, there are well-known forms of auction. For example, even if you have not participated in one, you will probably have seen an English auction (or ascending auction) take place. Potential bidders gather together in a room where they can all see each other, and, more importantly, where the auctioneer can see all of them. The auctioneer will call out a sequence of increasing prices. To bid, it is necessary to be the first to indicate willingness to pay each price. As the price rises, some people will drop out. Other bidders, willing to pay much more than the initial asking price, might now enter. Eventually, someone responds to a price that the auctioneer announces, but no one offers to pay a higher price. The good is sold to the last person to enter a bid.

We show in Chapter 30 that such an auction is efficient in the sense that the highest bid will be made by the person who has the highest *WTP*. Here, an intuitive argument is sufficient. Suppose that there are only two potential bidders, both of whom know their own *WTP*, but not the other potential bidder's *WTP*. The auctioneer does not know either *WTP*. Suppose that the auctioneer therefore deliberately calls out a price believed to be below both bidders' *WTP*. Say that bidder A responds first. Then when the auctioneer calls out a higher price that is still below bidder B's *WTP*, it is rational for bidder B to respond.

By yourself

X16.6 Explain why it is rational for bidder B to respond.

X16.7 Suppose that $WTP_A = 100$ and $WTP_B = 120$. Suppose that bidder A responds to price $p_n = 97.5$. How should bidder B respond to price $p_{n+1} = 100$? How does the auction end?

X16.8 In a situation where there are 100 bidders, suppose that the highest valuation $v_{(100)} = 150$ and the second highest valuation $v_{(99)} = 148$. How would you expect this auction to end? Suggest a general rule for ending the auction if it is run as a *clock auction*, in which some mechanism raises the price continuously, with bidders choosing the time when they withdraw from the auction.

X16.9 Consider a slightly different bidding process:
(1) Each bidder writes down a bid, places it in a sealed envelope, and delivers it to the auctioneer.
(2) When the auction closes to further bids, the auctioneer opens the envelopes.
(3) The auctioneer gives the good to the highest bidder.
(4) The highest bidder pays the auctioneer the second-highest bid.

Suppose that one bidder still has to decide what bid to make. Why might the bidder regret making a bid greater than *WTP*? [*Hint*: Think what happens if the bidder wins.] Why might the bidder regret making a bid less than *WTP*? [*Hint*: Think what happens if another bidder with a lower *WTP* wins.] What conclusions do you draw about this form of auction compared with the traditional one with verbal bids?

These exercises anticipate our analysis of the sale of a single item, where people place different, unobservable values on it. With ascending bids, bidders cannot do better than to follow a rule of stopping bidding when the price reaches their willingness to pay. With the sealed-bid auction, in which the winner pays the second-highest bid, we have a different structure but the same outcome. The important point is that these sale mechanisms are efficient. They encourage the truthful revelation of bidders' valuations of the item. This ensures that the good is allocated to the person with the highest *WTP*, and also ensures that the seller will receive at least the second-highest valuation.

The auction mechanisms outlined here are designed for the sale of a single item. A firm with market power, seeking to implement perfect price discrimination, could in principle use a series of auctions. Each lot sold by auction would consist of a single unit; given the success of eBay, we know that it is, in principle, possible to run many such auctions simultaneously. It is not immediately obvious that it will be efficient for the firm to run a sequence of auctions until the winning bidder is just willing to pay the marginal cost of production. For example, suppose that bidders plan to purchase many units. They might all plan to bid less than their *WTP* on the first units. Winning these auctions, they pay less than *WTP*, but more than marginal cost, and so retain some surplus. The firm would have to decide whether the additional revenue obtained from adopting this selling mechanism justified its use.

We have previously noted that perfect competition and perfect monopoly are useful theoretical cases that we do not expect to observe in practice. The same can be said for perfect price discrimination. If a costless, efficient mechanism to reveal the true willingness to pay of purchasers were available, firms would use it. The fact that the existence of such a mechanism is extremely improbable in reality does not invalidate the thought experiment; this ideal situation allows us to estimate the maximum effect of price discrimination on market outcomes.

16.3   Price discrimination of the second degree

A favourite ploy of retailers is in effect to charge their customers different amounts depending on the quantity of the good purchased. The 'BOGOF' offer (buy one, get one free) is a well-known example. It costs as much for the consumer to buy two units of the good as it does to buy one unit. If we apply the usual profit-maximizing condition, that the firm should expand output until marginal revenues and costs are equal, in this case the condition can only be satisfied if $MC = 0$ — a happy, but very unlikely, state of affairs for the retailer.

By yourself

X16.10   Suppose that a customer buys only one unit of the good when the second unit is offered for free. What might we reasonably assume about the value of the second unit to this customer?

X16.11   What justifications might we give for a retailer choosing to use this form of promotional pricing? Think in particular about the possible effects on its revenues, but also consider the implications for its costs.

Second-degree price discrimination
Setting a different price for each buyer of the good.

The decision to make such offers can be justified in terms of the firm's marketing strategy. The important point here is the firm's pricing behaviour: the price per unit is a function of the number of units being purchased; this is our general definition of **second-degree price discrimination**. Then we have a situation where the price paid by consumer c may be written, p_c:

$$p_c = p(q_c) \qquad\qquad [16.2]$$

The BOGOF offer is a special case of a system of quantity discounts, with the price per unit falling as the quantity purchased increases.

By yourself

X16.12   Consider the situation facing a consumer who chooses among consumption bundles consisting of coffee and doughnuts. The price charged for a cup of coffee falls from £2.50 to £2.00 on the fifth cup of coffee. The price of a doughnut remains constant at £1.20, with no quantity discount being offered. Sketch the affordability (budget) constraint for a consumer willing to spend £24.00. Discuss the difficulties that such a constraint might cause in trying to solve the standard optimization problems.

In introducing the standard theory, we have emphasized the importance of the affordable set being convex. Exercise X16.12 shows that with price discounts, this condition will be violated. Depending on the form of individual preferences, some consumers will take advantage of the price discount and others will not. That in itself is unremarkable, but it has to be noted that in each of these groups, the marginal members will respond to small price changes by changing group, which leads to relatively large changes in consumption.

By yourself

X16.13 For the marginal consumer, suppose that the highest attainable indifference curve touches both segments of the affordability constraint. Sketch a diagram showing this situation for a consumer choosing among bundles of coffee and doughnuts. Indicate on your diagram the effect of a small increase in the relative price of coffee.

Suppose that the marginal consumer in Exercise X16.13 were to be indifferent between consumption bundles containing four and seven cups of coffee, but chooses the bundle with seven cups. With the relative price of coffee increasing, we would expect the consumer to substitute doughnuts for coffee, but where we normally think of the substitution effect as being small, in this situation the consumer might decide to stop taking advantage of the quantity discount, reducing consumption from seven to (slightly less than) four cups of coffee. A small change in price leads to a large change in the quantity consumed. In Figure 16.2, we show the (inverse) demand curves for two consumers. The curve $p_1(q)$ is much less elastic than the curve $p_2(q)$, with the two curves intersecting at quantity, q_0. By conditioning the price on whether the consumer buys more or less than some quantity, Q^*, the monopolist might be able to acquire more consumer surplus than with uniform pricing.

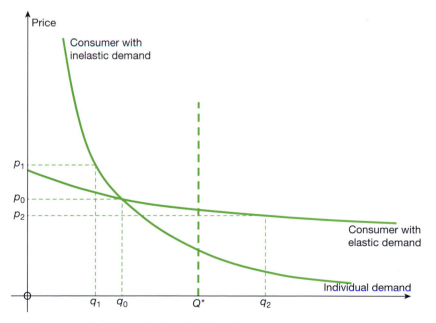

Figure 16.2 Consumer elasticity and price discrimination

By yourself

X16.14   Figure 16.2 is incomplete. It shows that price discrimination is possible, but does not show that it is desirable.

(a) Sketch a diagram with two linear individual (inverse) demand curves, D_1 and D_2, which have different slopes and different intercepts on the vertical (value) axis, and which intersect. Label them so that the price elasticity of demand of D_1 is less than for D_2 where they intersect. [Hint: To make your diagram consistent with Figure 16.2, make sure that you have chosen a level of marginal cost for which consumer 2 would demand none of the good at price p_1, so that $q_2 (p_1) = 0$; and also so that at the minimum quantity at which a quantity discount will be offered, Q^*, $WTP_1(Q^*) < p_2$.]

(b) Add the marginal revenue curves, MR_1 and MR_2, to this diagram.

(c) Assume that the firm faces constant returns to scale in production. Show its marginal cost curve; and hence identify the profit-maximizing outputs, q_1^* and q_2^*, and the prices, p_1 and p_2, that the firm should charge each customer.

(d) Identify areas on the diagram that represent the profit per customer. How might the use of quantity discounts increase the firm's profits?

In analysing market demand in Chapter 14, we assigned all consumers identical preferences, so that differences in individual demands simply reflected differences in income. Here, though, we assume that the preferences of two consumers, Maryam and Nia, differ. Say that Maryam's demand is represented by the less elastic demand curve, D_1, and Norma's by D_2. In Exercise X16.14, we have shown that using the quantity discount, the monopoly can charge Maryam price p_1 and Nia price $p_2 < p_1$, maximizing profits from sales to each of them.

Quantity discounts separate consumers in a very crude way. They provide potential purchasers with a menu, designed to elicit different responses from different people. Like the auction method considered in Section 16.2.1, they are a mechanism, but an inefficient one, because they do not lead to the exact revelation of preferences. However, quantity discounts are very simple and almost costless to implement, compared with auction sales.

16.3.1   Two-part tariffs

Two-part tariff
A charging structure based on an access fee plus usage fees.

In Figure 16.2, both Maryam and Nia have been able to keep some consumer surplus, even with quantity discounts leading to price discrimination. One way in which the firm could appropriate at least some of this surplus would be to set an access (registration) fee as well as a unit price for use of the product: a two-part tariff. This is a common practice in golf clubs: there is usually a membership fee that has to be paid every year, and in addition members have to pay a 'green fee' every time they play the course. We can also see this structure in utilities contracts, where there is a standing charge levied for access to the network and there are separate charges for every unit of the service that is consumed. Note that since access fees are paid before any of the product is purchased, they might affect decisions about whether to buy the good or not, but they cannot affect the decision about the quantity that will be purchased.

In terms of our theory of resource allocation, in section 6.4, we defined a utility-maximizing consumer's demand for a good in terms of the prices of goods and the amount of money available to finance consumption. Charging an access fee does not affect unit prices, but instead reduces the amount of money that is available after it has been paid. The choice that a consumer faces is then whether to pay the access fee or to forgo consumption of the good entirely.

By yourself

X16.15   On a diagram showing consumption bundles consisting of quantities of goods *A* and *B*, indicate the effect of the imposition of an access fee for good *B*. Sketch in an indifference curve demonstrating that the consumer would prefer to pay the user fee and buy a consumption bundle consisting of a mixture of goods, rather than simply spending the whole amount of money on good *A*.

X16.16   Explain why it is more likely that consumers will choose to pay the access fee for good *B* when the goods are complements, rather than substitutes.

In Figure 16.3, we show the demand curves for two consumers, Omar, with (inverse) demand, $p_1(q)$, and Paul, with inverse demand, $p_2(q)$. We note that Omar's demand is less elastic than Paul's. In the diagram, the monopoly sets prices, p_1 and p_2. Paying the higher price, p_1, Omar and Paul obtain surplus A_1 and A_2 respectively, where $A_1 > A_2$. Suppose that the monopoly introduces access fees, f_1 and f_2, with these prices. For fee, f_1:

$$A_1 > f_1 > A_2 \qquad\qquad [16.3]$$

Omar might agree to the contract (f_1, p_1), but Paul would not. This is a simple example of what we call a **participation constraint**. Consumer 1 is willing to pay the user fee f_1 and to buy a quantity q_1 at price p_1. We can compare this with the discussion in X16.15. There, the consumer had a choice between paying the user fee and being able to consume a mixture of goods *A* and *B*, or consuming good *A* only. For the participation constraint to be satisfied, the utility derived from the mixture of goods was greater than the utility obtained from consuming good *A* only. From Expression 16.3, the participation constraint is satisfied only for Omar.

Participation constraint Faced with a discrete choice, participation does not make the agent worse off.

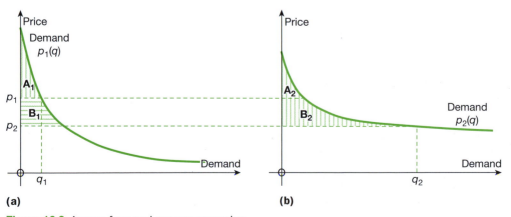

(a)   **(b)**

Figure 16.3 Access fees and consumer surplus

Now consider the consumers' response to the lower price, p_2. They obtain surplus $A_1 + B_1$ and $A_2 + B_2$ respectively, where $A_2 + B_2 > A_1 + B_1$. So, if the firm now sets an access fee f_2: $A_2 + B_2 > f_2 > A_1 + B_1$, then Paul's participation constraint is satisfied, but Omar's is not. Given the choice between two contracts, C_1: (f_1, p_1) and C_2: (f_2, p_2), Omar prefers C_1 and Paul prefers C_2, with their participation constraints being satisfied for their preferred contracts. The firm has successfully created a mechanism that enables it to capture some of Omar's and Paul's consumer surplus. It takes account of the differences in the price elasticity of demand, setting a low usage fee, f_1, but a high unit price, p_1, to create an attractive package for Omar; and a high usage fee, f_2, but a low unit price, p_2, to create an attractive package for Paul.

By yourself

X16.17   Write down the precise conditions that must be satisfied in order for the two consumers to choose the different supply contracts.

Incentive compatibility
A property of a mechanism such that participants reveal their true type.

In Exercise X16.17, as well requiring the participation constraint to be satisfied for each consumer for at least one contract specifying usage fee and unit price, we require the contracts to be **incentive compatible**. That is, the contracts have to be designed in such a way that at least one meets the participation constraint for each consumer; where both meet the participation constraint, then the consumers do not both choose the same contract, in effect revealing their preferences through their choices. Rather than the firm having to identify consumers by their characteristics, this mechanism offers consumers a menu of contracts, with consumers separating themselves into groups according to their preferences over the contracts on the menu. Once again, compared with auction mechanisms this is very simple, but it can be quite effective. This mechanism does not try to appropriate the surplus from each transaction, but rather tries to appropriate the surplus from each consumer.

16.3.2   Bundling

Bundling is a rather different form of price discrimination in which the monopoly packages together a variety of goods that could in principle be sold separately, and sells the package. The consumer is no longer free to choose any consumption bundle, but must choose from among the set of packages that the firm has selected in advance.

By yourself

X16.18   Consider the situation facing a car manufacturer. It believes that its customers consider cars to be a bundle of characteristics, which we summarize as speed and comfort. Assume that the firm has to trade off these characteristics, so that each model of car is located at a particular point on a production possibility frontier, which shows feasible combinations of speed and comfort.
   (a) Sketch a diagram with a concave production possibility frontier.
   (b) Suppose that the firm produces four models. Explain how doing so would allow the firm to meet the desires of consumers with different preferences.

In this case, bundling takes the form of product differentiation. The product is the same, but differences in the specification of models ensure allow the manufacturer to exploit differences in the distribution of consumers' *WTP*.

Another example draws on air travel. Airlines bundle services together differently for each of several classes of passenger – some long-distance flights have five separate cabins, in each of which the range of services provided to customers is different. Some of the most obvious differences are in the quality of the accommodation offered. Where seats in the economy cabin are approximately 0.78 m apart, 0.29 m wide, and recline approximately 10°, first-class seats are set nearly 2 m apart – long enough to fold them out into a flat bed, which is about 0.53 m wide. The effect is that passengers in the economy cabin are packed at least three times as densely as those in the business and first-class cabins. Even without considering the other services offered in these cabins – which may include almost unlimited free food and drink, beginning in the customer lounges and almost from the time passengers arrive at the airport, as well as greater baggage allowances and a much wider range of entertainment – the difference in seating density alone means that fares for travel in the premium cabins are typically a rather large multiple of the fares for travel in the economy cabin. The basic service, travel between two airports, is the same for all passengers, but the consumption bundles offered are very different, as are the profit margins that the airline is able to extract.[1]

In Figure 16.4 we illustrate the way in which an airline bundles these services. We abstract from all the components of the service offered, again defining two characteristics only, speed and comfort. In every cabin, the speed of travel is the same. The degree of

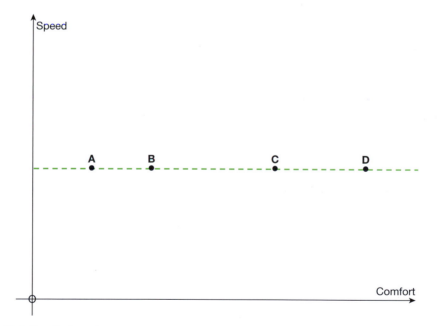

Figure 16.4 Bundling services

---

1 Even budget airlines, such as EasyJet, have increasingly started to use bundling, with an important element of their strategy now being to attract regular travellers, including business travellers. Charlotte Lovell's essay, in the online student essay bank, explores the reasons why customers like the possibility of a loyalty card, and the reasons why firms are willing to offer them only to regular customers. You can read Charlotte's essay (and those of other students) on the companion website for this book, at **www.palgrave.com/mochrie**.

comfort differs substantially. With four cabins, A, B, C, and D, and assuming that travellers have monotonic preferences, all would prefer to have the most comfortable service. There are good reasons to suppose that customers will differ very substantially in terms of their willingness to pay. For example, if we think of travel from London to a large Asian city, such as Delhi, Mumbai, or Kuala Lumpur, there will be some passengers going on vacation and others travelling on business. Travelling quickly to start a vacation is valuable, but travelling in great comfort is probably not essential. When travelling on business speed is important, but there is substantial value to comfort as well, because it reduces the time required for recovery. Imagine a senior executive travelling to a meeting which, if brought to a successful conclusion, would lead to the signing of a contract worth several million pounds: a price of several thousand pounds which secured a flat bed and constant service might then seem very reasonable. Bundling therefore allows the firm to extract some of the surplus from high-value passengers. Indeed, many airlines, particularly in highly competitive US markets, plan to break even on their economy cabin, but to make their profits from the fares they charge passengers in the premium cabins.

By yourself

X16.19   In previous examples, we have emphasized that a firm can exploit market power where customers respond differently to changes in prices. Apply these arguments to the case of bundling. Explain how the provision of a small set of bundles of different quality might enable the airline to extract additional surplus from consumers whose demand for services is inelastic.

X16.20   Criticize the argument that price discrimination is possible because travellers differ in their elasticity of demand for travel.

16.4   Price discrimination of the third degree

Third-degree price discrimination
Setting a different price for each class of buyer.

With second-degree price discrimination, a firm sets up a mechanism that compels consumers to reveal their willingness to pay for units of a specific good. With third-degree price discrimination, firms do not have such a technology, but can introduce price discrimination based on some characteristic of consumers. For example, most readers of this book will, at some stage, have benefited from discounts offered to students. To be eligible for the discount, it is typically necessary to provide proof of status. So, where with both first and second-degree price discrimination customers reveal something about their WTP through their choices, with third-degree price discrimination the firm makes assumptions about variation in its customers' willingness to pay – or, more precisely, the elasticity of their demand – given variation in the observable characteristics of consumers.

We have already examined the use of second-degree price discrimination in the context of air travel, discussing how airlines are able to bundle services in different ways. Within the economy cabin, airlines typically make extensive use of *yield management*. Suppose that two passengers sitting next to each other booked their tickets in one case three months and in the other case three days in advance of the flight. The basis of yield management is that someone who makes a booking three months in advance of the flight is likely to have substantial flexibility in their travel plans, and so will have a low willingness to pay for the flight. Someone who books a seat only three days in advance is considered to have much less flexibility in their plans, and so will have a high willingness to pay. Yield management software is designed to set prices according to individual *WTP*, so that the firm maximizes the revenue per seat, increasing the fare charged as time passes and seats are sold. At any point in time, potential passengers are offered a single price, but (typically) the more seats that have been sold on the flight, and the shorter the time until the flight departs, the higher the price will be. Note that airlines typically only use yield management in the economy cabin: space in premium cabins will usually be sold at a fixed price.[2]

16.4.1 Profit maximization

Let us now consider a situation in which there are two types of consumer. We can think of them as students and full-price customers; for simplicity, we shall assume that demand is linear in both market segments. We may then write the quantity that students will buy, q_S, and the quantity that full-price customers demand, q_F:

$$q_S = a_S - b_S p_S \qquad [16.4a]$$
$$q_F = a_F - b_F p_F \qquad [16.4b]$$

Note that the firm is able to set a different price in the two market segments. The firm has to be able to distinguish students from its other customers and to be able to prevent resale. Given the security requirements of air travel, this will generally be the case. We also suppose that the firm faces constant marginal costs, *c*.

We shall consider what happens when the firm uses third-degree price discrimination, comparing the outcome with uniform pricing. We shall see that differences in the price elasticity of demand across the sectors drive much of the behaviour. From Expression 16.4, we can calculate the price elasticity in the two market segments as:

$$\varepsilon_S = -\frac{b_S p_S}{a_S - b_S p_S}; \qquad \varepsilon_F = -\frac{b_F p_F}{a_F - b_F p_F} \qquad [16.5]$$

By yourself

X16.21 Confirm that if we restrict the value of the parameters, a_S, b_S, a_F and b_F so that $\frac{a_F}{b_F} > \frac{a_S}{b_S}$ and the firm adopts uniform pricing, so that $p_S = p_F = p$, then $\varepsilon_F > \varepsilon_S$.

X16.22 Using the demand function in X16.21:
(a) Sketch a diagram showing the demand curves in the two sectors. [*Hint:* Remember that we usually show the inverse demand or average revenue curve, so measure price on the vertical axis and quantity on the horizontal axis.]
(b) Use the diagram to explain the effect of a price increase on demand in each sector. In which sector is demand more elastic?

2 Pricing of train tickets follows very similar principles to the pricing of air fares, but with possibly even more emphasis on yield management. Jeremy Cottingham has written about his experiences of travelling to Edinburgh, calculating the breakeven cost of travel, and noting that many of the most widely advertised fares are so heavily discounted that they cannot meet the average cost per passenger. You can read Jeremy's essay on the companion website for this book, at **www.palgrave.com/mochrie.**

The restriction on parameters' values in Exercise X16.21 may seem complicated, but has quite a natural intuitive explanation. In each sector the ratio $\frac{a}{b}$ is the solution of the equation $a - bp = 0$, and so this is the price that just chokes off demand. We can then interpret the restriction as meaning there are some full-price passengers whose *WTP* is higher than the highest student *WTP*. In terms of the diagram in Exercise X16.22 and also Figure 16.5, this restriction is shown by drawing the vertical intercept of the (inverse) demand curve for the full-price customers higher than the intercept of demand for students.

In Figure 16.5, the demand curve for the full-price market segment is steeper than the demand curve for the student market segment. We have therefore assumed that $b_F < b_S$, so that as prices increase, demand falls more rapidly in the student market segment than in the full-price market segment. With the intercept of the demand curve for the full-price market segment on the quantity axis to the left of the intercept of the curve for the student segment, we have also assumed that $a_F < b_F$, so that if the good were to be free, demand in the student segment would be greater than that in the full-price segment. Demand among students is clearly more elastic than in the full-price market segment.

By yourself

X16.23   Given the assumption that the firm faces constant marginal costs, c, obtain the condition for profit maximization in each sector, $MR = MC$, and hence the profit-maximizing outputs and prices. Interpret the prices that the firm sets in each sector in terms of the marginal cost and the price that chokes off demand. Show that the total profit in each sector, $\Pi = \frac{1}{4b}(a - bc)^2 = \frac{1}{b}.(q*)^2$, where $q*$ is the profit-maximizing output for the sector.

X16.24   Confirm that the firm produces output $Q* = \frac{1}{2}(a_S + a_F - (b_S + b_F)c)$, and that it makes profits $\Pi* = \frac{1}{4}\left[\frac{a_S^2}{b_S} + \frac{a_F^2}{b_F} - 2(a_S + a_F)c + (b_F + b_S)c^2\right]$.

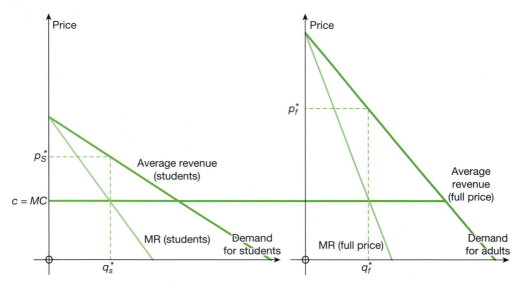

Figure 16.5 Implementing third-degree price discrimination

Exercises X16.23 and X16.24 involve the derivation of the profit-maximizing outcome for the firm. In Figure 16.5, we see the profit-maximizing conditions. Undertaking third-degree price discrimination, the firm sets the price for the full-price sector and a discounted student price. They are both chosen so that students and full-price customers will buy the output for which the standard profit-maximizing condition, $MR = MC$ is satisfied. So, when the firm maximizes its profits:

$$MR_F[q_F(p_F{}^*)] = MR_S[q_S(p_S{}^*)] = c \qquad [16.6]$$

Expression 16.6 says that in both sectors of the market the firm sets its price, which determines the demand in that sector, while in turn demand determines marginal revenue. We illustrate this point in Figure 16.5, although it is probably easier to reverse the argument. Starting from the intersections of the marginal revenue and marginal cost lines, we see the profit-maximizing outputs, $q_F{}^*$ and $q_S{}^*$; and then from the inverse demand, or average revenue lines, we see the prices, $p_F{}^*$ and $p_S{}^*$, which the firm sets.

With linear functions, as in Exercise X16.23, the profit-maximizing price for each market sector lies halfway between the constant marginal cost and the price that chokes off demand. The monopoly sells exactly half of the output that it would produce were it to meet the welfare-maximizing condition, $p = MC$, in both market segments. In effect, the monopoly makes separate profit-maximizing decisions in each market segment, treating them as separate markets.

16.4.2 Comparison with uniform pricing

We still need to show that this form of price discrimination is effective in enabling the monopoly to appropriate consumer surplus. Let us imagine that for some reason the firm does not engage in price discrimination, and so sells its output at a uniform price, p. It can then sell output, $q = q(p)$:

$$q(p) = q_F(p) + q_S(p) = a_F + a_S - (b_F + b_S)p \qquad [16.7]$$

Rearranging Expression 16.7, we obtain the inverse demand (or average revenue) function:

$$p(q) = \frac{a_F + a_S - q}{b_F + b_S} \qquad [16.8]$$

From Expression 16.8, we can obtain the marginal revenue, setting it equal to the marginal cost to find the profit-maximizing output. Noting that we again have a linear demand function, we can use the results in Exercises X16.23 and X16.24 to confirm that the firm maximizes profits by producing output q^*:

$$q^* = \tfrac{1}{2}[a_S + a_F - (b_S + b_F)c] \qquad [16.9]$$

It then makes profits:

$$\Pi^* = \frac{(q^*)^2}{b_S + b_F} \qquad [16.10]$$

By yourself

X16.25 Confirm that Expressions 16.9 and 16.10 define the profit-maximizing output and the profit maximum.

X16.26 Show that the firm sells the same output when engaging in price discrimination as when it sets a uniform price for all customers.

X16.27 Write an expression for the difference in the profits made with price discrimination, given in X16.24, and the profits made with uniform pricing, given in Expression 16.10. Show that the assumption $\frac{a_F}{b_F} > \frac{a_S}{b_S}$, introduced in X16.21, is sufficient to ensure that the firm makes more profit when using price discrimination.

The algebra in Exercises X16.25–X16.27 is a little tricky, but once again the underlying intuition is quite straightforward, and can be illustrated in Figure 16.6. Figure 16.6a should be familiar from Figure 16.5. It represents the outcome in each sector, with the firm setting a higher price in the full-price market segment than in the student segment. Figure 16.6b shows the situation in which the firm is unable to engage in price discrimination. We note that the inverse demand (average revenue) function kinks at output q_0, when the price is p_0. Going back to Figure 16.6a, at price p_0, demand in the student sector is choked off. If the firm sets a higher price, then it will make sales only in the full-price sector. The kink in the demand curve therefore reflects the entry of students into the market as the price falls below p_0. The market demand is the aggregate demand across the two sectors; thus, it is more responsive to price changes than the demand in either sector. The lower segment of the average revenue curve in Figure 16.6b is therefore flatter than the equivalent ones in the Figure 16.6a.

Notice that in Figure 16.6b the marginal revenue curve is discontinuous where students enter the market. Nonetheless, there is still only one price at which the standard profit-maximizing conditions are satisfied, which is shown as q^* in the diagram. From Exercises X16.25–X16.27, we can confirm that $q^* = q_F^* + q_S^*$, so that the monopoly produces the same output, whether or not it engaging in third-degree price discrimination. From Figure 16.6a we see that when it uses price discrimination the monopoly increases the price in the full-price sector, but reduces it in the student sector. Since demand in the full-price market

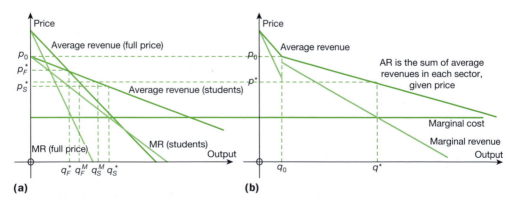

(a)   **(b)**

Figure 16.6 The outcome of third-degree price discrimination

segment is less elastic than demand in the student segment, the price changes are chosen so that the changes in quantity sold across the segments are equal in size (but opposite in sign). The price increase in the full-price sector must then be greater than the price reduction in the student sector; the increase in revenue from the student sector will then be less than the fall in revenue in the full-price sector, and the firm will increase its profits.[3]

By yourself

X16.28   Explain why one effect of price discrimination is that the firm increases revenue from students, while reducing it in the full-price sector.

X16.29   Relate the operation of third-degree price discrimination to the differences in the price elasticity of demand in the two sectors.

16.5   Conclusions

When we introduced monopoly in Chapter 15, we discussed whether or not the welfare costs resulting from the reduction in sales might be justified. Here we have considered some ways in which firms with market power might appropriate a greater proportion of the surplus created from the exchange. In discussing perfect price discrimination, we argued that it will be welfare increasing, but also that the increase in welfare will accrue entirely to the firm. Indeed, the firm is able to appropriate the entire surplus created in the market. This is a matter relating to the distribution of income. Using licensing, or taxes, it is in principle possible to transfer surplus back from the firm to consumers.

We have seen that first- and second-degree price discrimination depend upon mechanisms that cause consumers to reveal their underlying valuation of the good. Such mechanisms – auctions, quantity discounts, two-part tariffs and bundling – do not require the firm to know individual consumers' valuations of the good. We saw that in ascending auctions, no one can do better than bid until the price reaches their *WTP*. In second-degree price discrimination, we have argued that the monopoly offers a variety of contracts to consumers, effectively creating a choice environment in which the people with the highest willingness to pay also pay the most.

Third-degree price discrimination will be used in situations in which firms do not have the ability to develop such mechanisms. Instead, they must believe that there are systematic differences in the market demand across classes of consumer. Using examples with only two classes of consumer, we have argued that firms can resort to a pricing strategy that uses differences in the price elasticity of demand across market segments. The firm sets different prices for different consumer classes, charging lower prices where it believes demand to be more elastic. Of course, it is important that consumers cannot manipulate the characteristics that the monopoly uses to classify them.

---

3 Ben Wyer notes that while students obtain discounts when paying for admission to a cinema, they do not obtain further discounts after that. He argues that this is based on the fact that once they are in the cinema, they do not have much freedom to choose from competing suppliers. Any loss made on the discount can then be recouped by higher prices on food and drink. You will find Ben's essay on the companion website for this book, at **www.palgrave.com/mochrie.**

Summary

If a firm has market power, then its demand is a decreasing function of the market price, and the inverse demand (which is also the willingness to pay and average revenue functions) expresses price as a decreasing function of output. If, in addition, a firm can identify the willingness to pay of individual consumers, and consumers cannot undertake resale of the good or service, then the firm can practise price discrimination, selling different units of the same good at different prices.

We identify three degrees of price discrimination:

- First-degree (perfect) price discrimination: each unit is sold at a unique price. (In the special case of perfect price discrimination, this will be equal to the maximum willingness to pay given the quantity already sold.)
- Second-degree price discrimination (non-linear pricing): the unit price that a consumer pays depends upon the quantity purchased.
- Third-degree price discrimination: the firm charges the same price to all consumers of a particular type.

Under first-degree price discrimination, a firm maximizes profit by setting output so that the marginal willingness to pay equals the marginal cost. With perfect price discrimination, the firm appropriates the entire surplus generated in the market, but output reaches the level that it would in perfect competition. If it is possible to redistribute income from the firm to consumers, then perfect price discrimination can substantially reduce the welfare loss from monopoly with uniform pricing.

Proposals for the implementation of perfect price discrimination tend to be based around auction mechanisms.

Under second-degree price discrimination, the firm uses a mechanism that leads to different types of consumers choosing different quantities of the good. Examples include:

- two-part pricing, with the firm charging an access fee as well as user fees;
- bundling, with the firm combining a variety of goods and services into a single package, and consumers being required to select from the menu of packages.

In third-degree price discrimination, firms believe that the price elasticity of demand across market sectors differs. They can increase profit by charging higher prices in sectors where demand is inelastic and lowering prices in sectors where demand is elastic. In this case, instead of relying on a mechanism to induce consumers to reveal their type, firms must rely on externally verifiable characteristics of consumers to divide the market into sectors.

Visit the companion website at **www.palgrave.com/mochrie** to access further teaching and learning materials, including lecturer slides and a testbank, as well as guideline answers and student MCQs.

17

Oligopoly

In this chapter, we consider the situation where the few firms in the market constitute a so-called *oligopoly*, so that there is imperfect competition.

We approach imperfect competition in two ways. We have already argued that where firms have market power, it is possible for them to choose either the quantity that they sell or the price that they charge. We consider imperfect competition firstly in quantities (*Cournot competition*), and then in prices (*Bertrand competition*).

We shall see that competition in quantities is in many ways similar to monopoly, with firms enjoying limited monopoly power. In this form of imperfect competition, total market output is greater than with monopoly and the market price

is less; nonetheless, firms continue to make profit. We show that it is important that firms compete with each other, and that they avoid cooperation with other firms to limit output, raise prices and increase output, thereby behaving more like a monopoly.

We shall also introduce the concept of *strategic dependence*, whereby the decisions of one firm affect the profits made by others. We then extend analysis to competition in prices, showing that in certain circumstances the presence of even one other firm is enough to eliminate all profits in the industry. We conclude that where competition in quantities means that firms have market power, competition in prices effectively eliminates this.

17.1   Imperfect competition

Perfect competition and monopoly are the two extremes in the analysis of market behaviour. Many industries are dominated by a small number of firms, a situation called an oligopoly. The analysis of the standard model cannot be applied in such cases, since that

Oligopoly A market structure in which a few firms supply a good or service.

would mean modelling firms as if they were price takers, and so unable to affect the market equilibrium through their actions. Nor can we argue that because firms have market power they should all be treated as if they are monopolies, as this would require that there be only one firm in the market and no possibility of entry. Importantly, where monopoly eliminates interaction with other firms, with imperfect competition we expect the decisions of any one firm to affect the profits of all other firms in the industry. We shall assume that in oligopolistic markets there are many buyers, all small relative to the market, and that there is perfect information, so that the only deviation from the assumptions of the standard model relates to the industry structure. With perfect information, all firms produce identical goods, and if any firm tries to set a price different from that set by others, all consumers will know this. Firms that make sales must set the same price, the market price, so we exclude consideration of price discrimination.

We can usefully go back to examples introduced in Chapter 1.

- *Bakeries on an island:* Two bakeries have to decide how much bread to make (to sell the following day), each without knowing how much the other has decided to produce. For our analysis, the bakeries fix their output, bring it to the market, and must then accept the market-clearing price. Since the market-clearing price will depend on both bakeries' production decisions, we expect each bakery's profit-maximizing output also to depend on the other bakery's output. Our model therefore has to allow each bakery to form beliefs about its competitor's behaviour, with output being chosen to maximize profits given those beliefs.

- *Cafés in a village*: We argued in Chapter 1 that a café buys the raw materials needed to produce its output, but undertakes production only in response to actual demand. Facing limited competition, but with their output not fixed, the cafés must fix the prices that they will charge. It seems likely that there will be substantial differences in the interactions between the firms. For both cafés to make sales, given perfect information, they have to set the same price. But if one café knows the price that the other will set, we might then expect it to set a slightly lower price, and thereby capture the whole market. The only possible reason for not doing that would be if charging a lower price would mean making a loss. This suggests that, as with perfect competition, in the long run all profits would be eliminated.

> **Strategic interdependence** A situation in which the decisions of each participant affect all other participants' payoffs.

From these two examples, we see that where the market supply is oligopolistic, there is no single, standard theory; and indeed, there can be a variety of market outcomes. We shall see that for the bakeries, which we model as setting quantities, the market outcome is similar to monopoly. For the cafés, though, which we model as price setters, the outcome is much closer to perfect competition. In this chapter, then, we begin an exploration of the very large class of models in which strategic interdependence has an important role. In these models there will typically be a few entities, not necessarily firms, and the decisions that each makes will affect the payoffs that others receive.

This approach is not restricted to the examples of small firms, which we have already introduced. Coca Cola and Pepsi Cola are perhaps the best known duopoly in the world; while Proctor & Gamble and Unilever engage with each other across a wide range of fast-moving consumer goods. The supply of (liquid) gases in Europe is similarly dominated by Linde Group (of Germany) and Air Liquide (of France). Accountancy services for multinational corporations are concentrated in the 'Big Four': Price Waterhouse Coopers, Deloitte, KPMG, and Ernst & Young. We might easily multiply these examples.

17.2   Quantity-setting firms

We begin with a simple model with two bakeries, Thomas Auld and Sons Ltd (*Aulds*) and Black of Dunoon Ltd (*Blacks*), producing outputs q_A and q_B. The total market supply, Q^S, is simply the total amount that the two firms produce, so $Q^S = q_A + q_B$. The inverse market demand is linear, so that we write $p = a - bQ^D$, where p is the market price and Q^D is the total quantity demanded. For the market to be in equilibrium, demand and supply must be equal, so that:

$$p = a - b(q_A + q_B) \qquad\qquad [17.1]$$

Expression 17.1 confirms that while the bakeries choose their output, the market price will be determined by market clearing. Each firm's revenue is the product of the market price and its output, and so:

$$R_f = pq_f = [a - b(q_A + q_B)]q_f \qquad [17.2]$$

where $f = A, B$. Defining the market price in terms of industry output, we see immediately that each bakery's revenues will depend upon the other's output.

> **By yourself**
>
> **X17.1** How does an increase in *Aulds'* output affect *Blacks'* total revenue and profit, assuming that *Blacks* does not change its output? *[Hint: Use partial differentiation.]*

Given that the bakeries have perfect information, we assume that they use the same technology and use resources efficiently. We also assume that there are constant returns to scale in production, so that total costs are linear and marginal costs are constant. We have:

$$C(q_f) = cq_f \qquad [17.3]$$

We now examine what might happen when the bakeries choose their output separately, at the same time and without any discussion between them – that is to say, if they continue to compete rather than attempting to collude in any way to increase their profits by reducing their output.

17.2.1 Cournot's conjecture

The bakeries have perfect information about everything except their competitor's output. Economists starting to analyse such problems quickly realized that when making their decisions each bakery would have to rely on beliefs about the other's output. Such beliefs are called **conjectures**. The first suggestion about the form of such conjectures was made by the French economist, Antoine Augustin Cournot, in 1838. He proposed that we should treat each firm in a market by assuming that the other will fix its output. More generally, we can define the **Cournot conjecture** as the belief that competitor firms will produce a constant output irrespective of the output decision of the firm deciding its own output.

> **Conjecture** A belief about actions that competitors will choose.
>
> **Cournot conjecture** The belief that a competitor's output will not vary with own output.

In our example, then, we think of *Aulds* forming a conjecture about *Blacks'* output q_B, which we write as q_B^c. Using this conjecture, *Aulds* might consider its profit function to be the difference between conjectured revenues and costs:

$$\Pi_A^c = [a - b(q_A + q_B^c)]q_A - cq_A \qquad [17.4]$$

Aulds' profit in Expression 17.4 is shown as a conjecture, since it is based on the conjecture of *Blacks'* output, q_B^c. From the perspective of *Aulds'* profit-maximization decision, we can treat the conjecture, q_B^c, as a parameter. *Aulds* chooses the value of output, and so, differentiating the profit function in Expression 17.4, and setting the derivative to zero:

$$\frac{\partial \Pi_A^c}{\partial q_A} = a - 2bq_A - bq_B^c - c = 0 \qquad [17.5]$$

In Expression 17.5, the partial derivative depends upon both the firm's output and its conjecture of the other firm's output. The partial derivative sets out, in implicit form, a relationship between *Aulds'* own output and its conjecture of *Blacks'* output, which we have still to define. Given our assumptions that the two firms make their decisions entirely independently of each other and at exactly the same time, the Cournot conjecture – that competitors' output will not depend upon a firm's own output – seems reasonable.

We can solve Expression 17.5, obtaining the profit-maximizing output q_A^* as an explicit function of the conjecture q_B^c:

$$q_A^*(q_B^c) = \frac{a - c - bq_B^c}{2b} \tag{17.6}$$

Reaction function
The optimal choice as a function of conjectures about competitors' behaviour.

We shall call Expression 17.6 the **reaction function** for firm A. It tells us the profit-maximizing output for firm A, given its conjecture about firm B's output. Using the term *reaction* in these circumstances may sound odd, because firm A makes a decision before firm B sets its output, and thus what we are calling a 'reaction' actually anticipates the other firm's action.

Going back to Expression 17.6, we see that given our assumptions about the inverse market demand and total cost functions, the reaction function is a decreasing, linear function. The higher the conjectured value of firm B's output, the lower the output that firm A will produce. We might note that if firm A conjectures that firm B will not produce any output,

then it will produce output $q_A(0) = \frac{a - c}{2b}$. This is simply the output that we would expect firm A to produce were it to have a monopoly. Similarly, for the conjecture, $q_B^c = \frac{a - c}{b}$, firm A would choose to produce no output. Lastly, suppose that firm A changes its beliefs about firm B's output, so that the conjecture, q_B^c, increases by one unit. Firm A would then reduce its output by ½ unit.

By yourself

X17.2   Sketch a diagram with firm A's output on the horizontal axis, and the conjecture q_B^c on the vertical axis. In your diagram, sketch the reaction function for firm A, as given in Expression 17.6.

X17.3   Obtain the firm revenue and profit functions, and hence the reaction function for firm A, given:
(a) inverse market demand $p = 120 - Q^D$ with firm costs $C_A = 30q_A$;
(b) inverse market demand $p = 500 - 2Q_D$, with firm costs $C_A = 20q_A$;
(c) inverse market demand $p = 200 - 0.5Q^D$, with firm costs $C_A = 8q_A$.
In each case, sketch the reaction function.

X17.4   Confirm that if firm B exits the market, so that firm A has a monopoly, then the profit-maximizing output $q_A = \frac{a - c}{2b}$.

X17.5   Substitute the reaction function given in Expression 17.6 into the profit function given in Expression 17.4, writing firm A's profits, Π_A, as a function of the conjecture, q_B^c. Show that Π_A is a decreasing function of q_B^c.

To obtain *Aulds'* output in terms of its conjecture of *Blacks'* output, two simple steps suggest themselves. Firstly, we treat *Blacks* as having to solve a more or less identical problem to that faced by *Aulds*. In Exercise X17.6, we confirm that its reaction function is:

$$q_B^*(q_A^c) = \frac{a - c - bq_A^c}{2b} \qquad [17.7]$$

By yourself

X17.6   Replicate the argument by which we obtained the reaction function for firm *A* and confirm that firm *B*'s reaction function is given by Expression 17.7. Without further calculations, sketch the reaction function for firm *B* in each of the cases in Exercise X17.2.

The second step is to insist that in any equilibrium, both firms' conjectures will be correct. When firms bring their output to market, it turns out that each has produced the quantity that the other one expected. Neither firm is surprised by the behaviour of the other firm. We then say that these firms have **consistent conjectures**, so that $q_i^c = q_i^*$, for $i = A, B$. Then, since the reaction function is the profit-maximizing output given the conjecture of the other firm's output, with consistent conjectures, each firm maximizes its profits given the other firm's output.

Consistent conjectures All firms' beliefs about competitors' actions are correct.

Another way of thinking about this point is to note that if conjectures are consistent, then once each firm knows how much the other one actually produces, it would not want to change its own output. In our example, neither bakery could do better by changing its output (at least so long as the other one does not change its output either). It seems sensible that in this situation, in which there is strategic interdependence, if there is to a market equilibrium then conjectures should be consistent.

We illustrate the consistent conjecture equilibrium in Figure 17.1, describing the reaction functions for the two firms. Note that we show the bakeries' outputs on the axes, but the reaction functions still continue to be functions of their conjectures. Since we are interested in the market equilibrium, we focus on the only case where there are consistent conjectures. This is shown at the intersection of the two reaction functions. We simply do not expect the firms to set their outputs at any other level of output.

Simplifying the reaction functions in Expressions 17.6 and 17.7 by using the fact that in equilibrium both bakeries maximize profits given the other's output:

$$q_A^*(q_B) = \frac{a - c - bq_B^*}{2b} \qquad \boxed{\text{For equilibrium, conjecture } q_B^c = q_B^*(q_A)} \qquad [17.8a]$$

$$q_B^*(q_A) = \frac{a - c - bq_A^*}{2b} \qquad \boxed{\text{For equilibrium, conjecture } q_A^c = q_A^*(q_B)} \qquad [17.8b]$$

Then

$$\boxed{\text{Multiply through by factor } 2b} \quad 2bq_A^* = a - c - \tfrac{1}{2}(a - c - bq_A) \quad \boxed{\text{Substitute for } bq_B^*} \qquad [17.9]$$

$$\boxed{\text{Subtract } \tfrac{1}{2} bq_A \text{ from both sides}} \quad 3bq_A^* = a - c \quad \boxed{\text{Multiply through by factor } 2} \qquad [17.10]$$

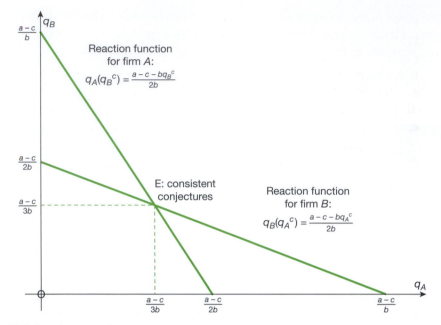

Figure 17.1 Consistent conjectures

Dividing through Expression 17.10 by $3b$, and evaluating Expression 17.8b using Expression 17.10 to substitute for $q_A{}^*$, we see that the consistent conjectures and profit-maximizing outputs are:

$$(q_A{}^c, q_B{}^c) = (q_A{}^*,\ q_B{}^*) = \left(\frac{a-c}{3b},\ \frac{a-c}{3b}\right)$$ [17.11]

as shown at point E in Figure 17.1.

Given the consistent conjectures in Expression 17.8, we can easily work out the market price by substituting back into Expression 17.1. We obtain $p = \frac{a+2c}{3}$. Then, substituting for price and output in Expression 17.4, we have:

$$\Pi_f{}^* = b\left(\frac{a-c}{3b}\right)^2 = b(q_f{}^*)^2$$ [17.12]

By yourself

X17.7 Without using Expression 17.10, confirm that in the three examples used in Exercise X17.3, there are consistent conjectures for outputs $q_A = q_B =$ (a) 30; (b) 80; (c) 128. In each case find the market price and the profit that each firm makes.

X17.8 For each case in X17.7, find the firms' maximum profits.

X17.9 Suppose that firm A's conjecture $q_B{}^c < q_B{}^*$. Show on a sketch that firm A will then produce output $q_A{}^*(q_B{}^c) > q_A{}^*$. Illustrate this situation in a diagram and show:
(a) This situation will not be an equilibrium. [*Hint*: Assume that firm B's conjecture $q_A{}^c = q_A{}^*(q_B{}^c)$.]
(b) If the firms are allowed to take turns in changing their conjectures according to the output that the other one last proposed, the equilibrium will be reached.

17.2.2 Stability of equilibrium

Exercise X17.9 demonstrates that the equilibrium is not only unique, but also stable. If one firm makes an error in its conjecture, we expect that error to be eliminated, so that equilibrium will be the eventual outcome of the interaction between firms. There are at least two ways in which this might happen. If firms engage with each other repeatedly, they may learn from their mistakes. Alternatively, we can assume that firms have perfect knowledge. In that case, each can carry out a thought experiment. When firm A forms its erroneous conjecture, $q_B^c \neq q_B^*$, it can work out its own best reply, $q_A^*(q_B^c)$. Next, it can work out firm B's best reply to its own best reply, in effect forming a new, and different, conjecture about firm B's output:

$$q_B^{c_1} = q_B^*\left[q_A^*(q_B^c)\right] \qquad\qquad [17.13]$$

By yourself

X17.10   Adapt Figure 17.1 to demonstrate that firm A's conjecture is consistent, then $q_B^{c_1} = q_B^c$.
In addition, show that if $q_B^c > q_B^*$, $q_B^c > q_B^{c_1} > q_B^*$

From X17.10 we see that, strictly speaking, errors in conjectures are *not* eliminated; instead, through this process they become vanishingly small. Taking $q_B^{c_1}$ as a new conjecture, firm A can further improve the accuracy of its conjecture, calculating $q_B^{c_2} = q_B^*\left[q_A^*(q_B^{c_1})\right]$. Repeating these calculations again and again, the firm's estimated conjecture approaches, but never quite reaches, the consistent conjecture. We can therefore think of the consistent conjecture as the limit of the adjustment process for any arbitrarily chosen initial conjecture.

We can also think of stability as being an important property of the equilibrium if there is a change in market demand. Suppose that the market is initially in equilibrium, but that an unexpected change in demand affects the firms' reaction functions and the market equilibrium. Firms will not respond immediately, given that the shift in demand is unexpected. With their output at the original, rather than the new, equilibrium output, each firm will realize that it should change its own output, while believing that its competitor will not change its output. In this case, both firms will gradually adapt their output, approaching ever closer to the new equilibrium, but not quite reaching it.

By yourself

X17.11   Given the examples in Exercise X17.3, sketch the original reaction functions, indicating the equilibrium outputs for the firms. Then sketch the new reaction functions after the following changes to the market environment:
(a) Inverse market demand is initially $p = 120 - Q^D$, but becomes $p = 240 - Q^D$, with firm costs $C_A = 30q_A$.
(b) Inverse market demand is initially $p = 500 - 2Q^D$, but becomes $p = 500 - 4Q^D$, with firm costs $C_A = 20q_A$.
(c) Inverse market demand $p = 200 - 0.5Q^D$, with firm costs initially $C_A = 8q_A$, becoming $C_A = 16q_A$.

17.2.3   Profit maximization given a production constraint

We can also solve the problem of profit maximization using the method of constrained optimization. Once again, we think of the example of the two bakeries, but concentrating on *Aulds'* production choice, assuming that *Blacks* produces some output, q_B. Note that this is *Blacks'* actual output, rather than a conjecture, because we will now concentrate on the bakeries' profits after they have both decided how much bread to bake.

The first point to note is that since *Blacks'* output, q_B, is fixed, $\frac{dq_B}{dq_A} = 0$. In Figure 17.2, we show two different output choices. Both appear as horizontal lines. The lower one, $q_B = \frac{a-c}{3b}$, would apply if *Blacks* were to choose the output in the Cournot equilibrium. The higher one, simply marked q_B^{0}, would apply were it to produce a higher level of output. It seems reasonable to argue that this choice constrains *Aulds'* ability to generate profits, since the range of possible outcomes now lies on the fixed output line, $q_B = q_B^{0}$. Effectively, the reaction function in Expression 17.8, illustrated graphically in Figure 17.2, is the solution of this constrained optimization problem when we assume that the constraint is always binding.

We now apply the method of equal gradients. For this, we begin by setting out *Aulds'* profits, which is the objective function, defined over all values (q_A, q_B):

$$\Pi_A = [a - c - bq_B]q_A - bq_A^2 \tag{17.14}$$

We see that the first term of the profit function is linear, and increasing, in output, q_A, while the second is quadratic, but decreasing. We also see that the function is linear, but decreasing, in output, q_B. We can write the total differential of the profit function as:

$$d\Pi_A = \frac{\partial \Pi_A}{\partial q_A} \cdot dq_A + \frac{\partial \Pi_A}{\partial q_B} \cdot dq_B = [a - c - bq_B - 2bq_A] \cdot dq_A - b \cdot q_A \cdot dq_B \tag{17.15}$$

> **Isoprofit curve**
> A contour of profit function, showing combinations of firm outputs for which one firm achieves a target profit.

Suppose that *Blacks* is already in the market, and that *Aulds* is deciding whether or not to enter it. With $q_A = 0$, the partial derivative $\frac{\partial \Pi_A}{\partial q_A} = [a - c - bq_B]$. So long as $q_B < \frac{a-c}{b}$, the partial derivative is greater than zero. Small-scale entry will definitely be profitable for *Aulds*, but since $\frac{\partial \Pi_A}{\partial q_B} < 0$, the profits that it makes at any level of output, q_A will decrease if *Blacks* increases its output.

In Figure 17.2, we show two contours of *Aulds'* profit function, also known as **isoprofit curves**. For every output pair (q_A, q_B) on an isoprofit curve, *Aulds* achieves a set level of profit. Just as isoquants show input combinations generating constant output, and indifference curves show consumption bundles that generate constant utility, each isoprofit curve represents the output combinations for which the firm makes a given level of profit. From the previous paragraph, we have confirmed that if both bakeries were to set low outputs, then *Aulds'* profits would be increasing in its own output, q_A, but decreasing in *Blacks'* output, q_B. This suggests that if q_A and q_B both increase by just the right amount, *Aulds'* profits will remain the same. The isoprofit curve is then upward-sloping.

It is impossible to keep on increasing both firms' outputs while maintaining the profit level, since the market price falls. Moving along the isoprofit curve, the differential in Expression 17.15 takes the value zero, so that:

$$\frac{dq_B}{dq_A} = -\frac{\frac{d\Pi_A}{dq_A}}{\frac{d\Pi_A}{dq_B}} = \frac{a - c - bq_B - 2bq_A}{bq_A} \tag{17.16}$$

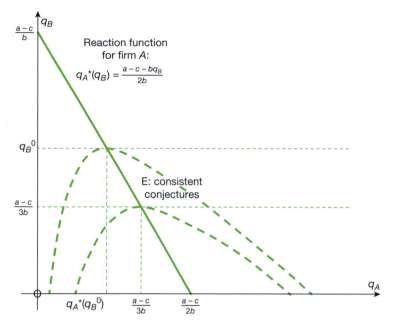

Figure 17.2 Isoprofit

By yourself

X17.12   Confirm the following:

(a) *Aulds'* profit function is concave in its own output, q_A, and has a maximum when the value of q_B is held constant.

(b) On the reaction function, $\frac{dq_B}{dq_A} = 0$. Explain what this means.

(c) In the area enclosed by the isoprofit curve, $\Pi_A = \Pi_A^0$, and the q_A-axis, the firm's profits are at least as great as Π_A^0, so that $\Pi_A \geq \Pi_A^0$.

In Figure 17.2, the isoprofit curves are concave, and their maxima lie on the best-reply line. We know that if *Blacks* were to reduce its output while *Aulds* were to hold its output constant, then *Aulds'* profits would increase. It therefore follows that in the area enclosed by an isoprofit curve and the horizontal axis, *Aulds'* profits are higher than on the isoprofit curve.

We conclude our argument by defining *Blacks* as having a minimum acceptable output level, $q_B = q_B^0$. In Figure 17.3, we have shown the (convex) constraint set for *Aulds*, $C = \{(q_A, q_B): q_B \geq q_B^0\}$ as the upper shaded area. All output combinations that satisfy the constraint lie in that area, while constraint $q_B = q_B^0$ is binding on its boundary. Then, given that isoprofit curves bound a convex set in which profit is no less than on the curve, *Aulds* maximizes its profits by choosing the output $q_A^*(q_B^0)$, so that the isoprofit curve at $(q_A^*(q_B^0), q_B^0)$ just touches the constraint, $q_B = q_B^0$. As with previous examples, there is a point of tangency between the constraint set and the objective set.

Writing *Aulds'* maximum profit, $\Pi_A^0 = \Pi_A(q_A^*(q_B^0), q_B^0)$, every output combination for which *Aulds* achieves or exceeds that profit level lies in the set of output combinations, $S = \{(q_A, q_B): \Pi_A(q_A, q_B) \geq \Pi_A^0\}$, which is bounded above by the isoprofit curve $\Pi_A = \Pi_A^0$. The profit-maximizing output, as in Figure 17.3, is the intersection between the

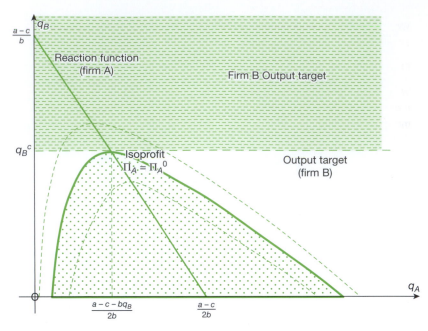

Figure 17.3 The constrained optimization solution

objective set and the constraint set. By definition, this output combination also lies on *Aulds'* reaction function. It is useful to note here that wherever one of *Aulds'* isoprofit curves meets the best-reply curve, the isoprofit curve has gradient, $\frac{dq_B}{dq_A}\big|_{\Pi_A = \Pi_A^0} = 0$.

17.2.4   Market power in quantity setting

The constrained optimization approach allows us to understand more precisely the mechanism of profit maximization in a duopoly with Cournot conjectures. It also emphasizes the extent to which quantity setting firms still have some market power. We rewrite the inverse market demand in Expression 17.1 as:

$$p = (a - bq_B) - bq_A \qquad\qquad [17.17]$$

Once again, we have replaced the conjecture, q_B^c, with a fixed output target, q_B, which we imagine that firm *B* is known to be committed to achieving. In Expression 17.17, parameter *a* represents the maximum *WTP* across all consumers. We imagine that firm *B* sells to all of the consumers who have the highest willingness to pay for the good. Firm *A* is then left with a monopoly of the remainder of the market. The maximum *WTP* among these consumers is $a - bq_B$, which, as far as firm *A* is concerned, is constant, so that Expression 17.17 represents the residual market demand after firm *B* has made its sales.

By yourself

X17.13   Confirm that firm *A* maximizes monopoly profits on the segment of the market left by firm *B* by choosing output combinations that lie on the best-reply line $q_A^*(q_B) = \dfrac{a - c - bq_B}{2b}$. Discuss briefly how we have dealt with the constraint in this case.

X17.14 Write down the residual demand that faces firm B when firm A is committed to producing an amount q_A. Hence confirm that firm B will maximize profits in the residual market segment by setting output $q_B*(q_A) = \dfrac{a - c - bq_A}{2b}$.

X17.15 What can we say about the residual profit-maximizing outputs and the planned outputs if the market is in equilibrium? Calculate the output that the two firms will produce when maximizing profits.

With each firm assuming that the other will attain a given output constraint, they each choose an output for which the isoprofit curve meets the constraint. In Figure 17.4, if *Aulds* believes that *Blacks* will produce output $q_B = \frac{a-c}{3b}$, so that the output combination (q_A, q_B) lies on the horizontal line, then by producing output $q_A = \frac{a-c}{3b}$, *Aulds* maximizes its profit given this constraint. Following on from the argument above, the isoprofit curve for *Aulds* then just touches the constraint. Applying the same argument for *Blacks*, should it assume that *Aulds* will produce output $q_A = \frac{a-c}{3b}$, *Blacks* will seek to maximize profits, knowing that the output combination will lie on the vertical line in Figure 17.4. We find that at output $q_B = \frac{a-c}{3b}$, the isoprofit curve just touches the line. Each acting as if it had a monopoly in the segment of the market left to it after the other has chosen its output, the two bakeries each exploit their market power to the greatest possible extent.

We have described the behaviour of the bakeries in three different ways, arguing that all lead to the same outcome. Firms have market power, and so, in maximizing profit, they produce a lower quantity, sold at a price higher than marginal cost, with a loss of welfare when compared with the standard model in which markets are perfectly competitive. Comparing competition in the quantities with the outcome of monopoly, output is higher,

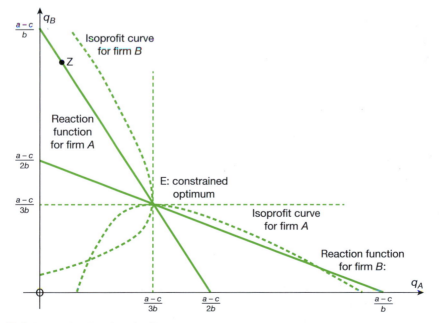

Figure 17.4 Constrained optima for firms

the market price is lower, and firm profits are lower. If we think of consumer surplus as the area enclosed by the market demand curve and the market price in a supply-and-demand diagram, it becomes clear that consumers generate greater surplus in this duopoly than they would under a monopoly, but less than under perfect competition.

There are many ways in which we could expand this discussion, for example giving one firm a cost advantage, or introducing fixed costs of production, so that we might consider short-run as well as long-run market behaviour. In Exercise X17.16, we consider changes in market conduct when the number of firms in the market increases. We noted that firms have a monopoly over the segment of the market left after every other firm has chosen its output; as more firms enter the market, that segment becomes progressively smaller as entry occurs, suggesting that market power erodes steadily as the market becomes more competitive.

By yourself

X17.16 We consider a situation in which there are n firms in the market. We identify these firms as $f = 1, 2, ..., n$. (Until now, we have assumed that $n = 2$.) We write the inverse demand function for the market as $p = 150 - Q$, where p is the market-clearing price, and the n firms' total output $Q = \sum_{f=1}^{n} q_f$. Each firm can produce any amount of output, q_f, at constant marginal cost, 30. We write each firm's total cost function as $C_f = 30q_f$.
  (a) Suppose that firms 2, 3, ... , n have chosen their outputs. Write down an expression for firm 1's profits in terms of the output of all n firms.
  (b) Partially differentiate firm 1's profit function with respect to output q_1.
  (c) Setting this derivative to zero, obtain firm 1's best-reply function.
  (d) Discuss how firm 1's output changes as the total output of every other firm increases.

In Exercise X17.16, we see that firm 1's profit-maximizing output depends on the total output that the other $n - 1$ firms decide to produce. When solving the problem for the case of two firms, A and B, we treated each firm as maximizing profits given the other's output decision, finding that both firms produced the same quantity. When $n > 2$, as in Exercise 17.16, there is also an outcome in which every firm produces the same output, and in so doing maximizes profits given the output of the other firms. Such an outcome is *symmetric*. The problem that each firm faces is the same, and so all, including firm 1, produce the same output.

By yourself

X17.17 Write firm 1's best-reply function as $q_1{}^*(q_2, q_3, ... , q_n)$. Suppose that all firms except firm 1 have chosen to produce output, $q_1{}^*$. Rewrite the expression for firm 1's best reply in X17.13. Find firm 1's profit-maximizing output when there are 2, 3, 4, 5, and 6 firms in the market. Discuss how the total output Q and the market price p change as firms enter the market. Show that consumer surplus therefore increases with more firms in the market.

X17.18 What do you think the long-run equilibrium will be in this market? [*Hint:* Remember that to explain the rise of monopoly, we argued that entry must either be prevented or be unprofitable.]

In perfect competition, entry leads to the elimination of profits. In the model that we have been discussing, the firms in the market have no power to prevent entry, and so we expect this market to become perfectly competitive. As noted in our introductory comments, there are many markets, such as those for branded consumer goods, in which the number of producers is small and the market is highly concentrated. This suggests that there must be some sort of barrier to entry, such as the economies of scale, which we argued in Chapter 16 might lead to the emergence of natural monopolies.

17.3   Leadership in competition in quantities

We consider a very early attempt to explain differences in behaviour among companies, assuming that firms make their decisions at different times. We shall see that the **quantity leader**, the firm that is able to make its output decision first, has greater market power than the other firm in the market, the *follower*. Restricting our attention to duopoly, we carry on with the nomenclature of the bakery example, with *Aulds* behaving as the leader, and *Blacks* as the follower. We shall not discuss the origin of leadership in detail – it might result from *Aulds* having entered the market first, or from its having a reputation for producing goods of higher quality, or having a cost advantage in production, or even having greater production capacity. All we need at present is for *Blacks* to permit *Aulds* to choose its output first.

Quantity leader The firm in an oligopoly that chooses its output level first.

> **By yourself**
>
> **X17.19**   The follower in this situation, *Blacks*, is able to choose its profit-maximizing output after the leader, *Aulds*. Criticize the argument that this is preferable to being the leader, because it is possible to verify the leader's output and so choose the profit-maximizing output.

We have argued that firms behave as if they have a monopoly over the segment of the market left after other firms have chosen their output. On this basis, we can be quite certain that *Blacks'* output will lie on its best-reply function. This is genuinely a response, set after *Blacks* has observed *Aulds'* output. Such an ordering of actions changes *Aulds'* profit-maximization problem substantially. As the quantity leader, *Aulds* can anticipate *Blacks'* response to its output choice, q_A. It now chooses the level of output that, anticipating that *Blacks* will choose the level of output, $q_B*(q_A)$, to maximize its profits, will maximize *Aulds'* own profits.

We proceed using a numerical example. Suppose that the inverse market demand, p, can be written:

$$p = 150 - Q^D \qquad [17.18]$$

As before, $Q^D = q_A + q_B$ is the total quantity produced, with firm f producing quantity q_f. We also assume that there are constant returns to scale in production, with both firms facing a constant marginal cost of 30.

> **By yourself**
>
> **X17.20**   Confirm that where the two firms set their outputs, q_A and q_B, simultaneously, $q_A = q_B = 40$. Calculate the market price and firm profits.

In Exercise X17.20, we find that we can write *Blacks'* reaction function, $q_B{}^*(q_A)$ as:

$$q_B{}^*(q_A) = \tfrac{1}{2}(120 - q_A) \qquad [17.19]$$

We now see the value of leadership. Expression 17.19 shows us *Blacks'* profit-maximizing output as a function of *Aulds'* output. When choosing its output, *Aulds* should use this function as its conjecture, $q_B{}^c$, of *Blacks'* output. (Note that *Blacks* does not form a conjecture, because it observes *Aulds'* output, q_A, before setting its own output, q_B.) Substituting *Aulds'* conjecture, $q_B{}^c$, in Expression 17.19 into the profit function, this becomes:

$$\Pi_A{}^c = (120 - \tfrac{1}{2}(120 - q_A) - q_A)q_A \qquad [17.20]$$

Aulds' profit here is only a function of its own output. Simplifying it, we write:

$$\Pi_A{}^c = \tfrac{1}{2}(120 - q_A)q_A \qquad [17.20a]$$

Differentiating Expression 17.20a and setting the derivative to zero, we find the profit-maximizing output to be $q_A = 60$.

By yourself

X17.21   Calculate the profit-maximizing output for firm *B*, and hence the market-clearing price. Find the profits that each firm makes. Compare the outcome with the outcome of simultaneous quantity setting in Exercise X17.20.

X17.22   Sketch a diagram showing the firm's reaction functions, obtained in Exercise X17.20. Show the profit-maximizing outputs from Exercises X17.20 and X17.21. What do you notice about firm *A*'s decision in X17.21?

X17.23   Show that in this situation with quantity leadership, firm *A* chooses the same output that it would choose if it were to have a monopoly, but that it makes less profit than in a monopoly because firm *B* does not quit the market.

X17.24   Explain why firm *A* cannot do worse in the sequential problem than in the simultaneous problem. [*Hint:* Remember that its objective is to maximize profits.]

In this case, the effect on firm output of *Blacks* allowing *Aulds* to engage in quantity leadership is that *Aulds* set its output to $q_A{}^* = 60$, the same output it would have set had it had a monopoly of production. *Blacks* sets output, $q_B{}^* = 30$. We explain this outcome in Figure 17.5. Recall that the profit maximization given the Cournot conjectures occurs at the intersection of the reaction functions. Acting as the quantity leader, *Aulds* will not maximize its profits if it seeks to achieve an outcome on its reaction function. Under the Cournot conjecture, *Blacks'* output will not change as *Aulds* increases its own; but with quantity leadership, *Blacks'* output, q_B, is a decreasing function of its own output, q_A. In Figure 17.5, then, we show *Aulds* maximizing its profits, with *Blacks'* reaction function acting as a constraint. The profit-maximizing outcome, F, is then the point of tangency between *Aulds'* highest achievable isoprofit curve and *Blacks'* reaction function. *Aulds'* isoprofit curve through point F lies within the isoprofit curve when the firms adopt the Cournot conjecture and choose their outputs simultaneously. We can therefore be certain that firm *A*'s profits increase when firm *A* sets output before firm *B*.

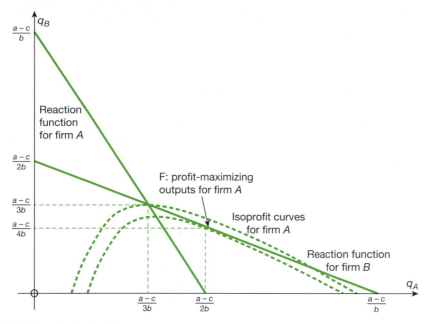

Figure 17.5 Quantity leadership

17.4 Simultaneous price setting

Simultaneous price setting leads to a pattern of behaviour that is quite different from that of simultaneous quantity setting. We adopt the usual implications of the assumption of perfect information, with all firms producing output of the same quality, all consumers being aware of this, and every firm that makes sales setting the lowest price in the market. We now assume that if two or more firms charge the same price, then consumers will choose among those firms at random, so that (in a large market) all firms making sales have an equal share of the market.

In Chapter 1, we suggested that cafés would compete through price, rather than quantity setting, suggesting that this would eliminate profits. Remember we argued that cafés undertake production in response to consumers' requests. Continuing to assume that the market demand is linear:

$$Q^D = \alpha - \beta p_{min} \qquad [17.21]$$

The market demand, Q^D, depends upon p_{min}, the lower of the prices p_A and p_B, which the firms set. Note too that Expression 17.21 specified the demand function, rather than the inverse demand. Consistent with the cafés responding flexibly to demand, the price at which they make sales determines the quantity traded. In the analysis of the market for bread, the bakeries fixed their output and let the price be determined by market conditions.

17.4.1 The best-reply function

We consider the behaviour of the *Artful Roast* café and the *Brewed Gold* café, setting prices p_A and p_B. For the *Artful Roast*, we can write demand, q_A:

$$q_A = \begin{cases} \alpha - \beta p_A, \text{ if } p_A < p_B \\ 0.5(\alpha - \beta p_A), \text{ if } p_A = p_B \\ 0, \text{ if } p_A > p_B \end{cases} \qquad [17.22]$$

We start by studying the situation when *Artful Roast* is able to observe *Brewed Gold*'s price, p_B, before setting its own price, p_A, so that we have sequential price setting. Expression 17.22 tells us that *Artful Roast* obtains the whole market if it sets a lower price than *Brewed Gold*, half of the market if it sets the same price as *Brewed Gold*, and none of the market if its price is higher than *Brewed Gold*'s.

By yourself

X17.25   Sketch a diagram showing the three segments of the firm's demand function. [*Hint:* You might find it useful to think about the relation between firm and market demand, as discussed in Chapter 12.]

X17.26   Using your diagram, confirm that: (a) after beginning with the situation where *Artful Roast* set a higher price than *Brewed Gold*, sales (and revenues) jump when p_A falls so that $p_A = p_B$; and (b) sales and revenues both jump again when p_A falls below p_B.

We now consider *Artful Roast*'s profits, Π_A, defined in terms of the price that it charges rather than the output that it sells:

$$\Pi_A = \begin{cases} (p_A - c)(\alpha - \beta p_A), \text{ if } p_A < p_B \\ 0.5(p_A - c)(\alpha - \beta p_A), \text{ if } p_A = p_B \\ 0, \text{ if } p_A > p_B \end{cases} \qquad [17.23]$$

If $p_A \leq p_B$, so that the firm makes sales, its profit per unit is the difference between the price, p_A, and the constant marginal cost, c. We now obtain *Artful Roast*'s reaction function through a series of exercises.

By yourself

X17.27   Confirm that *Artful Roast* cannot do better than choose p_A: $p_A > p_B$, if $p_B < c$. Briefly describe the outcome in this case.

X17.28   Define p_M as the price that *Artful Roast* would charge if it had a monopoly. By differentiating the expression for profit in Expression 17.23 and setting it to zero, find the profit-maximizing price for the monopoly, and discuss when *Artful Roast* might choose this price.

X17.29   Suppose that *Brewed Gold* chooses price p_B: $c < p_B \leq p_M$. Explain why *Artful Roast* can do no better than just to undercut *Brewed Gold*. [*Hint:* Confirm that *Artful Roast*'s profits increase the closer it can set its price to p_B.]

X17.30   Suppose that *Brewed Gold* chooses price $p_B = c$. Confirm that *Artful Roast* will not try to undercut *Brewed Gold*, and that it is impossible for *Artful Roast* to make profits. Does it matter to *Artful Roast* whether or not it matches price p_B?

Exercises X17.27–X17.30 indicate that *Artful Roast*'s reaction function is quite complex. We can see that if *Brewed Gold* sets p_B low enough, then *Artful Roast* cannot make a profit. We distinguish between the cases where $p_B < c$ and $p_B = c$, because in the latter case *Artful Roast* avoids making a loss when price matching. But unless $p_B > c$, *Artful Roast* cannot make a profit: it will generally set a price above p_B. On the other hand, if $p_B > c$, it is always possible for *Artful Roast* to undercut *Brewed Gold*. If p_B is above *Artful Roast*'s monopoly price, p_M, then *Artful Roast* will set that price. So, were Brewed Gold to set a high enough price, Artful Roast would undercut it substantially, take the whole market, and act as if it had no competitor. But, if *Brewed Gold* set a price between *Artful Roast*'s monopoly price and the marginal cost, *Artful Roast* would make the largest possible profit by just undercutting *Brewed Gold*. We summarize this discussion in Table 17.1.

Price p_B	Best reply $p_A(p_B)$
$0 \leq p_B < c$	$\{p_A : p_A > p_B\}$
$p_B = c$	$\{p_A : p_A \geq p_B\}$
$c < p_B \leq p_M$	$p_A = \max\{p : p < p_B\}$
$p_M < p_B$	p_M

Table 17.1 Best replies in price setting

In Table 17.1, we show the first two components of the best reply not as a single value, but rather as a set of values. This is where *Artful Roast* cannot do any better than avoid losses, and setting any price above p_B guarantees this because it will make no sales. While the function is complex, our conclusion can be expressed quite simply: whenever *Artful Roast* can make profits by undercutting *Brewed Gold*, it will do so; but when its objective is to avoid losses, it will never undercut the other firm.

17.4.2 Equilibrium outcomes

Note an important difference in the discussion of price setting here and the discussion of sequential quantity setting in Section 17.2. There, leadership was beneficial. Here, price leadership does not seem to have any benefit. Knowing p_B, *Artful Roast* can exploit profit opportunities, or else avoid making a loss. However, it may seem more sensible to argue that there should be simultaneous, rather than sequential, price setting since the cafés can change prices so quickly: should *Artful Roast* undercut *Brewed Gold*'s price, there is nothing to stop *Brewed Gold* responding quickly.

Suppose that there is no cost to announcing prices (repeatedly). If *Brewed Gold* announces a price, $p_B > c$, then *Artful Roast* will certainly undercut it. But unless *Artful Roast* announces price $p_A = c$, then *Brewed Gold* can in turn set a new price to undercut *Artful Roast*. And we can repeat these iterations in price cutting until one café announces $p_f = c$. The only way that the other one can then make any sales is by matching that price. Then $p_A = p_B = c$, and neither café makes any profits.

By yourself

X17.31 Confirm each of the following statements:
  (a) There is no equilibrium outcome in which a café sets a price $p_f < c$.
  (b) There is no equilibrium outcome in which $p = \min(p_A, p_B) > c$.
  (c) For an equilibrium, at least one café has to set a price $p_f = c$.
  (d) There is only one equilibrium outcome in which both firms make sales, and that is when both firms set price $p = c$, and so make zero profits.

We conclude that the presence of even one other firm is enough to eliminate all market power when firms compete in prices. Indeed, given that all that is required for equilibrium is that neither firm can reduce its price and make profits, it is possible that this outcome will emerge even when only one firm is active in the market. The capacity of the other firm to enter the market is enough to discipline the producer and to ensure that it sets its price equal to its marginal cost, so that the profit-maximizing condition for perfectly competitive firms is satisfied. We can be certain that firms competing in prices will undertake production until $WTP = WTA$, with consumer surplus being maximized.

17.5 Conclusions

This chapter demonstrates the sensitivity of the standard model to small changes in its specification. We have been careful to keep all of the assumptions, except the requirement that all firms are small relative to the market. When we have Cournot competition, with firms choosing their output, then we see the predictions of perfect competition emerging as a limit to increasing competition. But when we have Bertrand competition, with firms deciding the price that they will charge and adjusting supply to meet demand, we obtain very different results. The presence of any competitor is enough to ensure that the welfare-maximizing outcome emerges.

Going back to the bakery example, however, remember that we justified the Cournot assumption, that firms fix their output, by thinking about production taking place one day before sales occur. In other words, our simple example involved the analysis of the very short run. That means that the market supply curve is vertical, and so price has to adjust to clear the market. But the complete analysis of supply in the long run for a firm facing perfect competition will involve decisions about hiring capital and labour. Given the assumption that the firm faces eventually diminishing returns to scale in production when it is still small relative to the market, the long-run market supply will be perfectly elastic, as more and more firms, all of the same scale, enter in response to demand. In our example, the cafés, which have very elastic supply in the short run, can perhaps be understood as exhibiting elements of long-run competition in their behaviour; and indeed when Bertrand criticized Cournot's model he raised similar points, arguing that Cournot had given no reason to suppose that one firm could not undercut another, especially since it requires no effort for a firm to cut its price. Bertrand's argument suggests that for a duopoly to persist, there must be something in the technology of production, such as eventually diminishing returns to scale, so that no one firm would try to secure the market.

Summary

Oligopoly is a market structure in which a small number of firms provide all of the output in the market. Their decision making is characterized by strategic interdependence, since the decisions made by each firm affect the profits of all its competitors.

We distinguish between models of competition, in which firms compete by setting output, while prices are determined by demand conditions, and models of competition, in which firms compete by setting prices, responding to demand for their product.

Where firms compete in output, all choosing their output simultaneously, we adopted Cournot's conjecture: that a firm will assume that its competitors will not vary their output as it does. That is, firms assume that their competitors' outputs are constant.

We defined profit-maximizing output for a Cournot competitor, showing that this reaction function is a decreasing function of its competitors' output. We defined the reaction function as the outcome of a constrained optimization problem in which the firm seeks to maximize its output given the production decisions of the firm's competitors.

We argued that for equilibrium, conjectures must be consistent. This means that no firm wishes to change its output given the production decisions of its competitors.

The equilibrium in this model is stable. If market conditions change, firms might adapt to the new conditions through a process of gradual adjustment, rather than moving instantaneously to the new equilibrium.

With quantity setting, each firm behaves as if it has a monopoly over the segment of the market left to it after the other firms have taken their share of the market. As the number of firms in the market increases, the degree of market power falls, with perfect competition resulting as the number of firms increases without limit.

Sequential quantity setting is an alternative to simultaneous quantity setting. When this occurs, the first firm to set its output (the leader) will anticipate fully the response of the followers, choosing its output so that it increases its own profits.

Allowing competition in prices, only the firms that set the lowest price are able to set any output. Firms then respond to demand from consumers at the price that they set.

If the lowest price in the market is above the marginal cost, some firm might reduce its price and take the whole market. This process can only end when prices are equal to marginal cost. Even with two firms in the market, the market price, the quantity traded and the consumer surplus reach the levels that they would in a perfectly competitive market.

Visit the companion website at **www.palgrave.com/mochrie** to access further teaching and learning materials, including lecturer slides and a testbank, as well as guideline answers and student MCQs.

18

Game theory: concepts

We introduce *game theory* to analyse situations in which there is strategic interaction between the *players* in a *game.* Games describe the (market) environment facing players, including all of the actions that each of them might choose, and the payoffs to each combination of actions.

We first define several concepts and explore them in the context of a simple class of games, with two players, each of whom chooses between two actions at the same time. We define the concept of the *best reply* to every action of each player, and then the concept of a *strategy*; we then show that in equilibrium, both players' strategies are best replies to *conjectures* about the other player's actions. This is an informal definition of the *Nash equilibria* of the game. We note that every Nash equilibrium is stable against deviations by one player, so that no player will change strategy given the strategy of the other player. We also show that if the two players

are able to communicate with each other, it is possible to improve outcomes (for both players).

Game theory requires calculus to solve many maximization problems. The context within which these tools are used is very different from what we have seen before. The Essential Maths commentary is reasonably extensive, serving as a brief introduction to the analysis of two-player, two-action games. The text includes some quite fully worked examples that demonstrate how even these very simple games allow us to explore a wide range of situations of interest to economists and other social scientists. Our last two examples are very important, having many applications: the Prisoners' Dilemma, in which players benefit from being able to cooperate; and the Stag Hunt, in which players need to find ways of coordinating their actions to ensure that they achieve the highest possible payoffs.

18.1   The nature of a strategic game

Game theory is a very large area of economic theory. It takes us beyond the standard model, and we use it here to study certain forms of strategic interdependence among firms,

Game A mathematical model of interactions between decision makers.

Player A participant in a game.

which we introduced in Chapter 17, emphasizing that the profits made by each firm in an oligopoly depend upon the behaviour of all of the firms in the market. In contrast with the standard model, where we studied the behaviour of each decision maker in isolation, in games we have to analyse the behaviour of every **player**. Players receive *payoffs* at the game's conclusion, which depend on the actions of all players.

In Essential Maths 18.1, we set out all of the elements of a **strategic game of complete information**. Note that the models of oligopoly introduced in Chapter 17 can be characterized as games. In both the Cournot (quantity setting) and Bertrand (price setting) models there were a well-defined number of firms, or players. For each firm, we defined a set of *actions*, either the level of output or else the price charged. To determine the profit, or the *payoff*, that each firm received, we had to know the actions that all the firms chose. We shall call such a listing an **action profile** or an **outcome**. We modelled each firm as following the **strategy** of choosing the profit-maximizing action given its conjecture.

In Chapter 17, we did not use the term 'strategy', but instead talked in terms of finding the best response, the profit-maximizing action for each firm given its beliefs. For equilibrium, these conjectures were consistent. Each firm then chose the action that its competitor believed it would, and so maximized its profits given the actual behaviour of its competitor. From this discussion, we drew the important conclusion that neither firm would want to change its action unless its competitor changed *its* action. This idea, that no player in a strategic game will unilaterally change its strategy when conjectures are consistent, is the basis of the concept of **Nash equilibrium**.

Strategic game of complete information A game in which a fixed group of players choose their actions at the same time, anticipating others' behaviour. → 投;24

Action profile (outcome) Combinations of actions that might be chosen by players.

Strategy (1) Actions that a player chooses, given that player's beliefs (about other players' actions).

Nash equilibrium An outcome in which all strategies are the best replies to other players' actions.

We shall see below that it is possible in some circumstances that if the players could agree their strategies with each other before the start of the game, and commit to playing out the agreed strategies, then they could both do better than in the Nash equilibrium. We shall also see, even in very simple games, that there might be no Nash equilibrium or there might be more than one. Where we find more than one Nash equilibrium, players

Essential Maths 18.1: Defining a strategic game with complete information

We define a strategic game with complete information in terms of the number of players, the set of actions available to them, the action profiles or combinations of actions that the players might choose, and each player's payoff given the action profile.

- While we can set up a game with any number of players, P, we restrict our attention to two-player games, and label them, $p = A, B$.
- In general, players might choose from some range of actions. Action sets need not be finite, but we shall concentrate on games where players choose between two actions, $n = 1, 2$, which they perform at the same time. Action sets are $S_A = \{a_1, a_2\}$ and $S_B = \{b_1, b_2\}$.
- With two players choosing between two actions, the action profiles or outcomes of the game may be written $O = \{(a_1, b_1), (a_1, b_2), (a_2, b_1), (a_2, b_2)\}$.
- Payoffs $[v_A(a_{Ai}, a_{Bj}), v_B(a_{Ai}, a_{Bj})]$ are associated with each action profile.
- Players are fully informed about the structure of the game, but do not know the action that the other player will choose.

may seek to coordinate their actions so that one equilibrium emerges. Being able to apply the Nash equilibrium concept is only the very first step in developing an understanding of game theory.

So long as we know how many players there are, the action set from which each player might choose, and the payoffs that every player will receive in every action profile or outcome, we have fully described the choice environment facing the players in a strategic game of complete information. Except for knowing the other players' choices, all players are fully informed, and so know the structure of the game, including other players' payoffs in all action profiles. We assume that players understand that they are all solving essentially the same type of problem, trying to work out which action to choose given the options available to their opponents, but without knowing their actual choices, and so having to rely on *conjectures* about the other players' actions. Every Nash equilibrium of such a game is an action profile in which each player's strategy is a *best reply* to the other players' actions: in equilibrium, no player would wish to deviate unilaterally from the action profile. Given that players make their decisions simultaneously, this condition is essentially the same as our definition of consistent conjectures in Section 17.1.

18.1.1   A game of technology choice

In this chapter, we concentrate on two-player, two-action games. Before considering some standard examples, we consider a simplified version of competition in quantities, of the sort considered in Chapter 17. Now, though, our bakeries, *Aulds* and *Blacks*, are restricted to choosing between two levels of output, which we might call *High* and *Low*. We might think of the bakeries as having two technologies available to them: one that will allow them to produce a low output, and another that will allow them to produce a high output. Both know that there are two technologies. They will also each know that their competitor knows about the technologies, and that it has to choose which one to adopt. Each will realize that profits are strategically interdependent in this setting; and each can calculate how much profit its own firm will make, and how much the competitor firm will make, given both choices. We simply assume the level of profits shown in the Table 18.1, rather than deriving them from other analysis.

Essential Maths 18.2: Games in normal form

The normal form of a two-player, two-action strategic game is shown in the payoff (bi-matrix) table, Table M18.1. In each row, player X's action is held constant. In each column, player Y's action is held constant. Each cell then represents one of the four possible action profiles of the game, with the value of the players' payoffs, (v_x, v_y), shown in the appropriate cells.

Strategic game		Player B	
		Action b_1	Action b_2
Player A	Action a_1	$v_1(a_1, b_1), v_2(a_1, b_1)$	$v_1(a_1, b_2), v_2(a_1, b_2)$
	Action a_2	$v_1(a_2, b_1), v_2(a_2, b_1)$	$v_1(a_2, b_2), v_2(a_2, b_2)$

Table M18.1 Strategic game in normal form

		Blacks	
		High	Low
Aulds	High	(50, 50)	(120, 30)
	Low	(30, 120)	(80, 80)

Table 18.1 Strategic game played by two bakeries

In such a game, there will be four action profiles, and we can illustrate the form of the game in normal form, using the payoff table in Table 18.1. This shows the payoff pairs for *Aulds* and *Blacks* for each of the four possible action profiles, (*High, High*), (*High, Low*), (*Low, High*), and (*Low, Low*). Note that the first entry is *Aulds'* payoff, while the second one is *Blacks'* payoff. From this payoff table, we see how much profit each firm makes given its own and its competitor's output choice. We can now consider how each player will behave. We first consider *Aulds'* behaviour, considering a simplified version of the payoff table in which only its profits appear (Table 18.2).

		Blacks	
		High	Low
Aulds	High	**50**	120
	Low	**30**	80

Table 18.2 Payoff table for *Aulds*

To *Aulds*, *Blacks* is purely a competitor. *Aulds* has no interest in *Blacks'* performance or profitability, except insofar as that might affect its own profits. When *Aulds* considers how it should behave if *Blacks* chooses a high output, it will conclude (as in Table 18.2) that it can make more profit by producing a high output as well, and so we say that *High* is the *Aulds'* best reply to *High*.

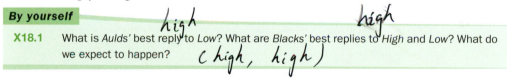

> **By yourself**
>
> **X18.1** What is *Aulds'* best reply to *Low*? What are *Blacks'* best replies to *High* and *Low*? What do we expect to happen?

Essential Maths 18.3: **Best replies**

In two-player, two-action games, we obtain player *P*'s best replies by comparing the payoffs, v_p, across the two actions, p_1 and p_2, holding the action chosen by the other player constant. The best reply will be the higher payoff in this comparison.

For example, in Table M18.1, facing action b_1, player *A*'s best reply, $a*(b_1)$ maximizes the payoff v_A. (The arrows show all the comparisons of payoffs that *A* and *B* might make.) Then:

$$a*(b_1) = \begin{cases} a_1, \text{if } v_A(a_1, b_1) \geq v_A(a_2, b_1) \\ a_2, \text{if } v_A(a_2, b_1) \geq v_A(a_1, b_1) \end{cases}$$ [M18.1]

Note that where the payoffs are equal, the player has two best replies. In Table M18.1, best replies are shown in green. We have:

$$a*(b_1) = a_1; \, a*(b_2) = a_1, a_2; \, b*(a_1) = b_2; \, b*(a_2) = b_1$$

Dominant strategy The action that is the best reply to all actions other players might choose.

Dominant strategy equilibrium The Nash equilibrium in which every player's strategy is dominant.

In Exercise X18.1, we find that for both firms, *High* is always the best reply: we say that *High* is a **dominant strategy**, the best reply to every action that the other bakery might choose, and so there is a single pair of consistent conjectures: (*High*, *High*). This action profile (*High*, *High*) forms the Nash equilibrium of the game. We note an interesting characteristic of this **dominant strategy equilibrium**: it is not the outcome that is best for the bakeries.

By yourself   *increase profit relatively compare with high,*

X18.2   Suppose that *Aulds* and *Blacks* agreed to build small bakeries. What would happen to their profits? Why might such an outcome not occur?   *suggest have difficulty coordinating behaviour*

We shall return to this problem in much more detail at the end of the chapter, when we show that this game has the structure of the *Prisoners' Dilemma*, a very widely studied two-player, two-action game. In this type of game, we assume that it is not possible for either player to communicate its intentions to the other in any credible way. Therefore, there is nothing to stop *Aulds* and *Blacks* reaching agreement that they should both remain small. But even while concluding their discussion, both will know that there is no benefit to keeping to the agreement, and so they both break it.

If this seems unconvincing, here is the same model demonstrated with a different motivation. Suppose that both bakeries have to choose between their existing means of production, and a new, innovative, technology that will allow them to produce more output at lower cost. In Table 18.3, all we have done is to change the names of the actions: whether to continue to use the old technology, or to adopt the new one.

		Blacks	
		New	*Old*
Aulds	*New*	(50, 50)	(120, 30)
	Old	(30, 120)	(80, 80)

Table 18.3 Technology adoption by the firms

Essential Maths 18.4: **Nash equilibrium**

We define a Nash equilibrium as an outcome profile from which neither player would wish to deviate unilaterally. In the context of two-player, two-action games, a Nash equilibrium profile

$$(a^*, b^*) : v_A[a^*, b^*] \geq v_A[a_i, b^*] \text{ and } v_B[a^*, b^*] \geq v_A[a^*, b_j] \qquad [\text{M18.2}]$$

Facing action b^*, player A cannot do better than choose action a^*. Likewise, facing action a^*, player B cannot do better than choose action b^*. Not knowing the action that the other player will choose, players form beliefs about the other player's choice of action. The Nash equilibrium action profile is then a set of consistent conjectures.

In Table M18.1, anticipating action b_1, player A chooses action $a^*(b_1) = a_1$; but anticipating action b_2, player A chooses either action, so that $a^*(b_2) = a_1 = a_2$. Similarly, anticipating action a_1, player B chooses $b^*(a_1) = b_2$; but anticipating action a_2, player B chooses $b^*(a_2) = b_1$. Action profile $[a_1, b_2]$ is then the only pair of consistent conjectures, so that $a^*[b^*(a_1)] = a_1$, and is the only Nash equilibrium.

By yourself

X18.3 Describe the game fully, listing: (1) the players; (2) the action set of each player; (3) the set of action profiles (outcomes); and (4) each player's payoffs in terms of the outcomes.
(a) Explain why *New* is a dominant strategy; and why the action profile (*New, New*) is the Nash equilibrium of the game.
(b) Confirm that both bakeries would be better off in the action profile (*Old, Old*).

Our explanation of the Nash equilibrium is now rather more satisfactory. Switching to the new technology is better for both players than continuing to use the existing one, irrespective of the decision that the other firm makes, and so both switch to the new technology. We see that when the bakeries adopt the new technology, their combined profits fall. This outcome is consistent with competition through innovation reducing the market power in an oligopoly over time.

18.1.2 Applying the Nash equilibrium concept

Now that we have shown that it is possible to treat the conduct of a duopoly as a two-player, two-action game, we shall consider some simple two-player, two-action strategic games of complete information, the first of which is shown in Table 18.4. We use numerical examples, but it is important for us to be aware of the rules that underlie the analysis of game. In this case, player A chooses between the actions *Up* and *Down*, while player B chooses between *Left* and *Right*. There are four action profiles: (*Up, Left*), (*Up, Right*), (*Down, Left*), and (*Down, Right*).

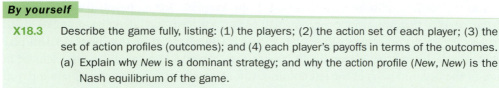

		Player *B*	
		Left	*Right*
Player *A*	*Up*	(3, 3)	(1, 2)
	Down	(2, 1)	(0, 0)

Table 18.4 A two-player, two-action strategic game

Essential Maths 18.5: **Dominance and iterative dominance**

Consider a game in which player $P = X, Y$ chooses from action set $A_P = \{p_1, p_2\}$.

Action x_1 is *dominant* if $x_1 = x^*(y_1) = x^*(y_2)$, so that x_1 is always the best reply for player X, generating a higher payoff than action x_1. Similarly, action y_2 is dominant if $y_2 = y^*(x_1) = y^*(x_2)$, so that y_2 is always the best reply for player Y. Where there is a dominant strategy for both players, we identify a dominant strategy equilibrium, here the action set $(x^*, y^*) = (x_1, y_2)$.

A *dominant strategy equilibrium* is a special case of a Nash equilibrium. It emerges in the Prisoners' Dilemma game.

If one player has a dominant strategy, and the other player does not, the equilibrium has the property of *iterative dominance*. Say that action y_2 is dominant. Since player X knows the structure of the game, including player Y's payoffs, X expects Y to follow the dominant strategy, y_2, and so chooses the best reply to action y_2.

The Nash equilibrium, $(x^*, y^*) = (x^*(y_2), y_2)$ is then iteratively dominant.

To find the Nash equilibrium, we first find the best replies. To emphasize the comparisons of the payoffs that we assume players will make, we have included the double-headed arrows. Player *A* conjectures either that player *B* will play *Left* or that player *B* will play Right. Conjecturing that player *B* will choose *Left*, player *A* compares the first element in each of the ordered pairs in the left column. Choosing *Up*, player *A* would obtain a payoff of 3, but choosing *Down*, player *A*'s payoff would be 2. Assuming that players wish to maximize their payoffs, player *A*'s best reply to *Left* is *Up*.

By yourself

X18.4   Confirm that player *A*'s best reply to the conjecture *Right* is *Up*; and that player *B*'s best reply to the two conjectures *Up* and *Down* is *Left*.

X18.5   Confirm that (*Up*, *Left*) is the only action profile for which both players form consistent conjectures.

X18.6   Show that neither player will wish to deviate from the profile (*Up*, *Left*).

This is a particularly simple example. The best reply for player *A* is always *Up*, and the best reply for player *B* is always *Left*. We describe such strategies, which are always chosen, irrespective of the actions that the other player might choose, as dominant, and thus obtain a dominant strategy equilibrium.

18.1.3   Strategic dominance

We say that a player has a dominant strategy if there is a single action that is that player's best reply to *all* actions that the other player in the game might choose. Strategic dominance emerges in the examples in Tables 18.1 and 18.4. We see that each player has a dominant strategy, and so we obtain the dominant strategy equilibrium of these games, as defined in Essential Maths 18.5.

In two-player, two-action games, there will generally be a unique Nash equilibrium if even one player has a dominant strategy. Consider the situation in Table 18.5. Player *Y* will always choose *Right*. Player *X* only has to consider the best reply to *Right*, and so long as the payoffs to *Up* and *Down* are not the same, Player *X* will have a unique best reply, here *Up*, so that (*Up*, *Right*) is the Nash equilibrium.

Essential Maths 18.6: Symmetric games

A two-player, two-action game is symmetric if players *X* and *Y* choose from a single action set, $A = \{a_1, a_2\}$, and payoffs satisfy the condition $v_X(a_X, a_Y) = v_Y(a_Y, a_X) = v_{XY}$.

Symmetric game		Player *Y*	
		Action a_1	Action a_2
Player *X*	Action a_1	(v_{11}, v_{11})	(v_{12}, v_{21})
	Action a_2	(v_{21}, v_{12})	(v_{22}, v_{22})

Table M18.2 Symmetric game

If both players choose the same action, they obtain the same payoffs. Choosing different actions initially, were both to change actions, each player would receive the payoff that the other did originally.

Iterative dominance		Player Y	
		Left	*Right*
Player X	*Up*	(2, 2)	(1, 3)
	Down	(3, 0)	(0, 1)

Table 18.5 Iteratively dominant equilibrium

By yourself

X18.7 Confirm that in the example in Table 18.5, player Y will always choose *Right*, and that player X will then choose *Up*. Confirm that if player Y were to choose *Left*, then player X would choose *Down*.

Strategic dominance is sufficient for us to solve games such as these. Note from Exercise X18.7 that player X does not have a dominant strategy. We therefore use player Y's dominant strategy to reduce the outcomes that player X must consider, identifying the one from which player X will obtain the highest payoff, given that player Y follows the dominant strategy. The equilibrium in this case results from the iterative elimination of dominant strategies.

18.1.4 Coordination

We will assume that the games in this section are *symmetric*. Then, assigning each player's actions in each action profile to the other player, in the new outcome, we also reverse each player's payoffs.

By yourself *payoff not depends on order → symmetric.*

X18.8 Confirm that the game shown in normal form in Table 18.3 is symmetric. Suppose that we reversed the order of the actions: would the game still be symmetric?

$A_A = A_B = \{N, 0\}$ *payoff pairs satisfy the rule* $V_A(a_1, a_2) = V_B(a_2, a_1)$

Essential Maths 18.7: **Equilibria in symmetric games**

Dominance: This arises (1) if $a_{11} > a_{12}$ and $a_{21} > a_{22}$, so that action a_1 is dominant; (2) if $a_{11} < a_{12}$ and $a_{21} < a_{22}$, so that action a_2 is dominant. In the important case of the Prisoners' Dilemma, $a_{22} > a_{11}$.

Coordination: This arises if $a_{11} > a_{12}$ and $a_{22} > a_{21}$, so that there are two Nash equilibria, (a_{11}, a_{11}) and (a_{22}, a_{22}), seen in the upper left and lower right cells of Table M18.2. Assume that $a_{11} > a_{22}$. Both players prefer the outcome (a_{11}, a_{11}) to (a_{22}, a_{22}), but this is not enough to ensure that it emerges. Important cases are the *Stag Hunt* and *Arm or Trade* games.

Asymmetric outcome: This arises if $a_{12} > a_{11}$ and $a_{21} > a_{22}$. There are two Nash equilibria, (a_{21}, a_{12}) and (a_{12}, a_{21}), seen in the lower left and upper right cells of Table M18.2. Assume that $a_{21} > a_{12}$. Then players prefer the outcome in which they obtain payoff a_{21}. If they choose their actions simultaneously, coordination of actions, as it arose in the Stackelberg model of sequential output setting, is impossible. Important cases are *Chicken* and *Hawk-Dove*.

By yourself

X18.9 Assume, as in Table 18.6, that players X and Y choose from the action set A = {*Left*, *Right*}, and that the game is symmetric.
(a) What can you say about the payoffs in the top left and bottom right cells of the game?
(b) What can you say about the payoffs in the bottom left and top right cells?

As shown in Essential Maths 18.7, where the game is symmetric, players will have the same payoffs when they choose the same actions. But if they choose different actions, they may receive different payoffs. If one chooses *Left* and the other *Right*, then the payoff to the player choosing *Left*, and the payoff to the one choosing *Right*, does not depend on the identity of the players choosing these actions, but instead is determined purely by the pattern of the actions.

There is no requirement that a game, even in the class of two-player, two-action games, should have a unique Nash equilibrium. In Table 18.6, we illustrate two situations in symmetric games to emphasize that there can be two Nash equilibria. In one, the equilibria are found in the upper left and lower right cells of the payoff table, so that the players choose the same actions. In the other, the equilibria are found in the bottom left and top right cells, so that the players choose different actions.

Coordination (1)		Player Y	
		Left	Right
Player X	Left	NE	
	Right		NE

Coordination (2)		Player Y	
		Left	Right
Player X	Left		NE
	Right	NE	

Table 18.6 *Symmetric payoffs with two Nash equilibria*

With the games being symmetric, the players must obtain the same payoff for the outcome {*Left*, *Left*}. Both also receive the same payoff when the outcome is {*Right*, *Right*}; but we expect the players' payoffs to be different in the outcomes {*Left*, *Right*} and {*Right*, *Left*}.

Essential Maths 18.8: A game without consistent conjectures

With both players choosing their actions at the same time, each has to anticipate the other player's action. In Table M18.3, player X's best reply, $x^*(y) = \begin{cases} x_1, \text{ if } y = y_1 \\ x_2, \text{ if } y = y_2 \end{cases}$, and $y^*(x) = \begin{cases} y_1, \text{ if } x = x_2 \\ y_2, \text{ if } x = x_1 \end{cases}$.

No action profile forms a set of consistent conjectures. In every outcome, one player would prefer to change action. Given the action sets, there can be no Nash equilibrium.

Strategic game without consistent conjectures		Player Y	
		Action y_1	Action y_2
Player X	Action x_1	$(v_X[\mathbf{x_1}, \mathbf{y_1}], v_Y[x_1, y_1])$	$(v_X[\mathbf{x_1}, y_2], v_Y[\mathbf{x_1}, \mathbf{y_2}])$
	Action x_2	$(v_X[x_2, y_1], v_Y[\mathbf{x_2}, \mathbf{y_1}])$	$(v_X[\mathbf{x_2}, \mathbf{y_2}], v_Y[x_2, y_2])$

Table M18.3 *Strategic game with no consistent conjectures*

By yourself

X18.10 Suppose that in the game, Coordination (1), for both players, the payoff to actions that form part of a Nash equilibrium is 2, and the payoff to the alternative action is 1. Complete the payoff table for Coordination (1), identify the best replies, and confirm that there are two Nash equilibria.

X18.11 Suppose that in a coordination (1) game with symmetric payoffs, players receive different payoffs in each action profile, say 3, 2, 1, and 0. Construct two different payoff tables in which the Nash equilibrium payoff pairs are (a) (3, 3) and (2, 2); and (b) (3, 3) and (1, 1).

X18.12 Repeat X18.11, but for a coordination (2) game with symmetric payoffs, with payoffs to the action profiles 10, 7, 5, and 2. Construct two different payoff tables in which the Nash equilibrium payoff values are (a) 10 and 7; and (b) 10 and 5. 注意 顺序

(10, 10) [7, 7)   (10, 10) (5, 5)

Games such as those in Exercises X18.11 and X18.12 tend to require **coordination** of actions since the Nash equilibrium does not help us identify the strategy that players will choose. In Exercise X18.11, it may be that both players will choose the action giving them the higher payoff. But we shall see in Section 18.3 how early applications of game theory to political science showed that, should they lack confidence that the other player's choices will be consistent with the achievement of the superior outcome, players might lock into a sequence of actions that seems sub-optimal. Using the Nash equilibrium principle, all we can say is that there are two equilibria, either of which might emerge.

Coordination game A game with several equilibria, in which players realize gains by coordinating their actions.

The coordination (2) game is more obviously problematic. As set out in Exercise X18.12, the players receive different payoffs in the two Nash equilibria, with the result that they rank the payoffs in the two equilibria differently. While in coordination (1) the problem is simply to find a way of ensuring that the players choose the action that supports the better outcome, in game (2) players disagree about their preferred outcome.

Quantity setting contest		Firm **B**	
		Lead	Follow
Firm **A**	Lead	(−100, −150)	(250, 100)
	Follow	(50, 200)	(150, 150)

Table 18.7 Competition in outputs

By yourself

X18.13 Confirm that in Table 18.7 there are two Nash equilibria: (*Lead, Follow*) and (*Follow, Lead*). Discuss how the Stackelberg approach might enable firms to avoid problems in such a situation.

X18.14 Suppose that firm *A* offers to make a payment to firm *B* of 50 after the game has been played, but conditional on firm *B* choosing *Follow*. Assuming that both firms make their decisions simultaneously, how might this help to resolve the coordination problem?

Remember that in this chapter we are considering strategic games, so that all decisions are made simultaneously. In the Stackelberg model, we assume that the firms make their decisions sequentially, with the follower able to observe the leader's output decision.

In using the terms *leader* and *follower*, we are here referring to roles that the firms assume voluntarily, and in Table 18.7 the willingness of the follower to cede leadership reflects both the asymmetric payoffs facing firms and the very high costs of the outcome in which both behave as leaders, inadvertently flooding the market. In this outcome, the firms' aggressive behaviour will push the price down (and possibly their marginal cost up), so that they will both make large losses. Thinking of the total profits that the firms make, we can see that the outcome (*Lead*, *Follow*) is best overall, with total profits of 350. While firm *B* would prefer (*Follow*, *Lead*), it has no reason to suppose that firm *A* would be willing to agree to this.

Exercise X18.14 suggests that (*Lead*, *Follow*) will be the most likely outcome if firm *A* can make a side payment to firm *B*. With the proposed payment, firm *B* continues to prefer the outcome (*Lead*, *Follow*) to (*Lead*, *Lead*). Unsurprisingly, firm *B* continues to want to avoid aggressive competition, so that *Follow* is still a best reply to *Lead*. But firm *B* is now indifferent between the outcomes (*Follow*, *Lead*) and (*Follow*, *Follow*). There is no longer a strategy for which *Lead* is the unique best reply. This means that *Follow* is (weakly) dominant for firm *B*. For firm *A*, it is now rational for firm *B* to choose *Follow*, and so it chooses *Lead*. This side payment changes the payoff structure of the game, and hence the equilibrium outcomes. Note though that there are still two Nash equilibria in both versions of this model, and that all we are doing is developing reasons why we should not expect to see one of them emerge.

18.1.5 Competitive games

Competitive game
A game in which increasing payoffs for one player require a reduction in others' payoffs.

The term **competitive game** is used to describe games such that if one player's payoff were to increase, the other player's would have to decrease. Imagine a simple example of splitting a cake, with the default share for both players exactly half of it. The cake is of fixed size, so for one player to obtain a greater share, and so a greater payoff, the other player must take a smaller share, and so a smaller payoff. We shall use an example of a cake division game in the next chapter, but here we introduce the simplest possible zero-sum game, the matching game. Imagine that Claudia and Dayna are sitting opposite each other. Firstly, they pay a stake of £100 each to play the game, which consists of them each raising either their left hand or their right hand at the same time. If both raise the same hand (either both choose *Left* or both choose *Right*), then Dayna pays Claudia £100, while if they raise different hands, Claudia pays Dayna £100. (Penalty shootouts in football offer another version of this game. The penalty taker and the goalkeeper have to decide whether to move to the right or to the left; except, of course, that penalty takers and goalkeepers are not allowed to gamble on the outcome of the shootout, but have other payoffs.)

By yourself

X18.15 Set out two payoff tables for this matching game, one showing the payments that Claudia and Dayna receive at the end of the game, and the other showing the payments net of the stake contributed. Confirm that in both payoff tables, there is no action profile that forms a Nash equilibrium. Using the concept of the best reply, explain why this should be.

We show the payoffs for the matching game in Table 18.8. Irrespective of the outcome, the payoffs sum to zero, so that this is an example of a purely competitive, **zero-sum game**. One player always receives some amount c, while the other loses c. In Exercise X18.15, $c = 100$. For Claudia and Dayna, considering participation in the game, it does not matter that they might receive a payment of £200 after taking part in the

> **Zero-sum game** A game in which payoffs in all outcomes sum to zero: a purely competitive game.

game. The relevant payoffs are that they will either be £100 better off or else £100 worse off when the game finishes.

The matching game		Dayna	
		Left	Right
Claudia	Left	$(c, -c)$	$(-c, c)$
	Right	$(-c, c)$	$(c, -c)$

Table 18.8 A competitive game

Both Claudia and Dayna wish to choose their payoff-maximizing action, conditional on their beliefs about the action that their competitor will choose. For Claudia, this means choosing the same action as Dayna; while for Dayna, it means choosing the alternative to Claudia's action. So if Claudia believes that Dayna will choose *Left*, she will choose *Left*. But if Dayna believes that Claudia will choose *Left*, she will choose *Right*. But in that case Claudia should choose *Right*. Then, Dayna will choose *Left*. We are back at the initial presumption, and can continue cycling around the action profiles without ever reaching equilibrium. Given this description, it seems to be a game of chance. We shall explain how we can analyse such games in Chapter 19.

18.2 The Prisoners' Dilemma

Possibly the best-known problem in game theory, the Prisoners' Dilemma has many important applications in economics. We have already met a version of it in our model of technology adoption, but here we set out its standard form and consider its application in other settings.

   Suppose that detectives have identified two people whom they suspect of colluding in a criminal enterprise. They have arrested both suspects, and are interrogating them separately. The suspects are unable to communicate in any way. The detectives will need a confession from one or other of the suspects to be able to secure a conviction on the major crime. The most powerful tool available to the detectives is that they have sufficient evidence to convict both of their suspects of a relatively minor crime. They therefore tell each suspect that if they cooperate with the investigation and provide the evidence needed to incriminate the other suspect, then their cooperation will be taken into account at any trial and they will receive only the (shorter) sentence for committing the minor crime. However, if they do not confess but their accomplice does, then they will receive a *longer* sentence than they would otherwise. In making these offers, the detectives might claim that, given the progress they are making in interrogating the other prisoner, they expect that the other suspect will confess. They might also make light of the fact that if *both* suspects confess, then both will go to trial and on conviction both will receive longer sentences than if they were both to remain silent.

18.2.1   Nash equilibrium in the Prisoners' Dilemma

We illustrate the Prisoners' Dilemma in normal form in Table 18.9.

- There are *two players*, *A* and *B*.
- The action set for both players, $a_i = \{Confess, Silent\}$.
- We define payoffs as costs related to the amount of time that prisoners would spend in jail, if convicted, and we assume that both prisoners wish to minimize these costs.

Prisoners' Dilemma		Prisoner *B*	
		Confess	*Silent*
Prisoner *A*	*Confess*	(−8, −6)	(−1, −9)
	Silent	(−12, −1)	(−2, −2)

Table 18.9 The Prisoners' Dilemma

By yourself

X18.16   Confirm that, for both players, Confess dominates Silent, and that the action profile (*Confess, Confess*) is the only Nash equilibrium.

In Table 18.9, outcomes are not symmetric. It may be that the costs that *A* and *B* face are different because *A* would be punished more heavily than *B*, or because time in jail is more costly to *A* than to *B*. The absolute size of individual payoffs is less important than their size relative to a player's other payoffs. As shown in Table 18.10, irrespective of the action that the other player chooses, the action *Confess* earns a shorter jail sentence than remaining *Silent*; it follows that *Confess* is always the best reply. For both players, *Confess* is a dominant strategy, and there is a unique Nash equilibrium outcome, $O^* = (Confess, Confess)$.

Prisoners' Dilemma		Prisoner *B*	
		Confess	*Silent*
Prisoner *A*	*Confess*	(**−8***, **−6***)	(**−1***, −9)
	Silent	(−12, **−1***)	(−2, −2)

Table 18.10 Nash equilibrium in the Prisoners' Dilemma

We have summarized these claims in Table 18.10, where the best replies to all actions are starred and printed in bold. As argued already, the only outcome with consistent conjectures is (*Confess, Confess*), and so this is the Nash equilibrium.

18.2.2   The nature of the dilemma

The 'dilemma' is that both prisoners know that for both of them the outcome (*Silent, Silent*) is preferable to the Nash equilibrium. Suppose that before the interrogations begin they agree to be silent. Irrespective of what they have agreed in advance, when they are made separate offers, they see advantages in breaking the prior agreement and confessing.

We can easily compare this with the choice of technology facing the firms in the introductory example in Section 18.1. There we saw that the firms would do better (together) if both were to stick with the original technology, rather than adopting the new one; but that each (individually) would do better adopting the new one, provided its competitor sticks with the existing one. For that reason, even if the firms were to agree beforehand that it would be in their interest to stick with the existing technology, there is no good reason for them actually to do this once production starts. Even though it is a different setting, the game has the structure of a Prisoners' Dilemma.[1]

By yourself

X18.17 Were the prisoners able to talk to each other during a break in interrogation, how likely is it that this Nash equilibrium would arise? Would your answer change if the prisoners were then returned to separate interview rooms, and the offer of sentence reduction only made at that point?

X18.18 If the suspects were members of a criminal gang, how likely is it that the only concern of the suspects would be the length of time that they would spend in jail? [*Hint:* Might the reduction in time spent in jail from confessing be offset by sanctions imposed by the criminal organization?] Illustrate your answer by showing how the payoff matrix changes. Does *Confess* still dominate *Silent*?

X18.19 Suppose that the criminal enterprise has produced considerable income, which the partners have yet to divide up between them. Can you suggest any type of agreement that the suspects might have reached to ensure that they remain silent? Show how the payoff matrix changes under these circumstances, and explain how such changes might have similar effects on the equilibrium outcome as those found in Exercise X18.18.

X18.20 Suppose that the police did not have the evidence necessary to secure the minor conviction if both suspects chose *Silent*. How would this change the payoffs in Table 18.10? What difficulties would this cause the police?

X18.21 Should the police be allowed to reward a suspect for providing information that leads to the conviction of an accomplice, where there is no other evidence that is admissible in court against either the suspect or the accomplice? Discuss this in the context of your answer to Exercise X18.20.

X18.22 Should the police be allowed to tell each suspect (separately) that it is likely that the other will confess?

X18.23 Consider a symmetric game in which both players, *X* and *Y*, choose between the actions *Left* and *Right*. If both choose *Left*, both obtain payoff *a*. If both choose *Right*, both obtain payoff *d*. If one chooses *Left* and the other chooses *Right*, the player choosing *Left* obtains payoff *b* while the player choosing *Right* obtains payoff *c*.
(a) Sketch the payoff table in this case.
(b) Write down conditions that must hold in order for *Left* to be a dominant strategy.
(c) Write down a further condition that must hold for the dominant strategy to have the characteristics of a Prisoners' Dilemma.

We can imagine the suspects planning how they will behave under interrogation. Suppose that they were not aware of the evidence of a minor offence. They might then believe that they were in the situation outlined in Exercise X18.20, and the police would have very limited capacity to make an offer. Indeed, Exercise X18.21 suggests that allowing the police

---

1 A situation similar to the Prisoners' Dilemma emerges whenever the participants in a game cannot easily commit to achieving an agreed outcome: in this case there is the opportunity of 'free riding'. In the online student essay bank, Andreea Piriu discusses how for students working together in a group there will often be a Prisoners' Dilemma type of problem. You will find Andreea's essay on the companion website for this book, at **www.palgrave.com/mochrie**.

to offer inducements to suspects may actually serve the interests of justice. In this situation, the choices are not obviously economic in nature, even though they have substantial effects on payoffs. For this reason, legal systems typically have rules about the conditions under which police officers (and other interested parties, including journalists) can provide inducements to reveal information, and also rules about the disclosure of those payments. For example, evidence that has been obtained through the offer of inducements might reasonably be given less weight. We have emphasized the role of confession, but in some situations courts may choose to disregard these statements, should there be insufficient corroboration or where there is doubt about their validity, perhaps in case they had been obtained under duress.

In the original Prisoners' Dilemma, the police use the minor offence to ensure that *Confess* is the dominant strategy. We have just considered the possibility of their using inducements to achieve that end. In both cases, the police are able to change the costs and benefits facing the prisoners, to make *Confess* dominant. In contrast, in Exercises X18.17 and X18.18, we examine ways in which the partners in the criminal enterprise can change the payoffs to the actions. It is often claimed that in organized criminal enterprises the threat of violent reprisal substantially reduces defection from an agreement to remain silent. Similarly, requiring the agreement of both partners to the division of the proceeds of crime means that they are much more likely to remain silent, since if only one defects, the other will certainly refuse that partner access to their gains.

We might think of silence as continuing cooperation with the other prisoner, while confession is defection from the agreement. The police wish to construct a situation in which the suspects know that although continuing to cooperate with each other is better than both of them defecting, for each of them individually being the only one to defect is even better. The criminals' objective is to ensure that they are in a situation where remaining silent is better than being the only one to confess. In Exercises X18.17–X18.21, note that the structure of the game does not change at all – just the payoffs. More precisely, all that we change is the relative size of the payoffs given beliefs about the other player's behaviour. As that happens, the Nash equilibrium of the game changes.

18.3   Cooperation and defection

The cause of the Prisoners' Dilemma is simple. It is impossible for the prisoners to communicate with each other; when they find themselves in a situation in which breaking their agreement is privately beneficial, they therefore have no incentive to continue cooperation. The Prisoners' Dilemma is indeed more than simply an introductory teaching example; it is a memorable way of setting out a problem that arises frequently in which people need to find ways of cooperating. We might argue, using either ethics or economics, or both, that it is undesirable for criminals, or indeed businesses, to work together, where that leads to the criminals evading justice or the businesses profiting at the expense of society.

Now, consider this thought experiment. You are a member of a large class. You are told that you have to complete an assignment with a partner drawn at random from the other students in the class. It turns out that you have never previously met your partner: indeed, you were not aware of your partner being a student in this class. You meet with your partner, who explains that because of work commitments it will not be possible to work together, and so you both agree to answer half of the questions, and to hand in your work separately. It is impossible for either of you to verify before undertaking your share that the other one has completed the agreed work.

18.3.1 Prisoners' Dilemma and coordination outcomes

We simplify the analysis by allowing you and your partner to choose between two actions, cooperation and defection. Cooperation means completing your half of the exercises, which will require working for several hours and exerting substantial effort. You and your partner will then both get the same mark for any material that is submitted, irrespective of who bore the effort. Defection means submitting no work. This has no cost (in terms of effort), but also no benefits. When you met with your partner to divide the work, you agreed in effect that cooperation is better than defection. But when the time comes to do the work, just as in the Prisoners' Dilemma, you have to decide whether this is indeed the case. Suppose that you receive an invitation to a party held on the night that you were planning to complete the assignment. Your payoff to defection increases. Should it be high enough, it will become dominant, as was the case in the Prisoners' Dilemma.

We have now created a problem, which can be represented by a strategic game in normal form.

- There are *two students*, *You* and your *Partner*.
- You each have *two actions* available, so that your action set $a_i = \{Defect, Cooperate\}$.
- We define payoffs as benefits accruing from completing the work net of costs, indicating these in Table 18.11 simply by a letter for each player, and for each outcome. To simplify analysis slightly, we assume that the situation is entirely symmetric:
  - the payoff to (*Cooperate, Cooperate*) for both of you is *b*;
  - the payoff to (*Defect, Defect*) for both is *c*;
  - the payoff received by a student who cooperates when the other one defects is *d*;
  - the payoff received by a student who defects when the other one cooperates is *a*.

Shared Assignment		Partner	
		Defect	Cooperate
You	Defect	(c, c)	(a, d)
	Cooperate	(d, a)	(b, b)

Table 18.11 The Shared Assignment problem

By yourself

X18.24 Using the payoff matrix:

(a) If *You* and your *Partner* agree that cooperation is better than defection, what can we conclude about the value of *b* relative to the value of *c*?

(b) If *You* believe that your *Partner* will cooperate, but nonetheless you decide to defect, what can we conclude about the value of *b* relative to *a*?

(c) What do you expect your *Partner* to do, even when believing that *You* will cooperate?

(d) If your *Partner* believes that *You* will defect, and *also* defects, what can we conclude about the value of *c* relative to *d*?

(e) What do you expect *You* to do, believing that your *Partner* will defect?

(f) Summarize the conditions required in this case for *Defect* to be a dominant strategy. Compare your answer with the conclusions of X18.21.

(Continued)

X18.25   Suppose that the payoff values $a > b > d > c$.

(a) Confirm that the students will agree to cooperate.

(b) Confirm that if *You* believe that your *Partner* will defect, *You* will cooperate.

(c) What will your *Partner* do, believing that *You* will defect?

(d) Show that the two action profiles in which one student cooperates and the other defects are both Nash equilibria.

(e) Compare the relationship between the payoff values given here and those found for the Prisoners' Dilemma in X18.23 and X18.24. Explain how they differ.

In Exercises X18.24 and X18.25, *Defect* is the best reply to *Cooperate* if $a > b$. *Defect* is also the best reply to *defect* when $c > d$, as in X18.24, and is then a dominant strategy. But if *Cooperate* is optimal, then $b > c$, and we have a complete ranking of the payoff values for X18.24:

$$a > b > c > d \qquad\qquad [18.1]$$

This is the relationship between payoffs that we have found in the Prisoners' Dilemma. In X18.25, though, we assume that $a > b > d > c$, reversing the ordering of the payoffs for a student who faces a defecting partner. As before, with $a > b$, both students are willing to benefit from the other's efforts, rather than to exert effort on their own. But in this situation, they would choose to carry on working if they believe that their partner will defect. We have a slightly odd outcome. If *You* believe that your *Partner* will choose *Defect*, *You* should then choose *Cooperate*. But since $a > b$, you *Partner* will choose *Defect* in response to *Cooperate*, so the outcome (*Cooperate*, *Defect*) satisfies the requirements of a Nash equilibrium.

We can also adapt the argument, so that your *Partner* will choose *Cooperate* believing that *You* will choose *Defect*, while *You* will choose *Defect* when expecting your *Partner* to choose *Cooperate*, so that (*Defect*, *Cooperate*) form a second Nash equilibrium. By making the payoff, $d > c$, *Defect* is no longer a dominant strategy, but the players in the game still do not reach the initially agreed cooperative outcome. In the two equilibria, only one student will complete the work already agreed, while the other one will not, but we cannot say whether it will be *You* or your *Partner* who sticks to the agreement. Note that in moving between Exercises X18.22 and X18.23, all that we have done is make a small change to the payoff structure of the game. This has quite substantial effects on the subsequent analysis.

By yourself

X18.26   Suppose that you find yourself in the situation described in the coordination game described in X18.25. How might you persuade your partner to choose *Cooperate*? [*Hint*: You may wish to encourage your partner to form beliefs about you that do not reflect your intentions!]

X18.27   The situation described here might seem entirely artificial. Nonetheless, students often have to work together with colleagues, and there will be occasions in which cooperation has to be based on trust because students have to work separately. What actions might students take to make an agreed, cooperative, outcome more likely?

Working on Exercises X18.26 and X18.27, we can see that behaviour in even a relatively simple situation can have complex motivations. There are two Nash equilibria, either of which might occur. Outsiders will not be able to predict what will happen with certainty. Exercise X18.26 suggests the possibility of disingenuous behaviour. A student who wishes to ensure cooperation should appear uncooperative. If persuaded by this appearance, the other student will choose *Cooperate*. The deception complete, will both then cooperate? Within this form of game, it is possible that the 'deceiver' will only succeed in self-deception. *Defect* is the best reply to *Cooperate*, and the Nash equilibrium should continue to be sustained, with the student indicating an intention to choose *Defect* putting that into practice.

As with the Prisoners' Dilemma, in this form of game, students cannot communicate in order to ensure cooperation. Given the ubiquity of social media, however, in reality the two students can easily keep in touch with each other, sharing progress on their work. We might imagine them agreeing at their initial meeting to complete the work sequentially. Rather than one student submitting a complete answer to one half of the questions, they might take turns in working on the problem set. Should one choose *Defect* while the process is still incomplete, the other student can credibly threaten to suspend cooperation. As we shall see in Chapter 19, such a structure implies a sequence of choices, with each student observing the choices that the other makes. Monitoring behaviour in this way, both students are able to punish deviation from the agreed strategy. Of course, such punishments need not take the form of suspension of cooperation. In the previous section we discussed some possible sanctions in the context of the standard Prisoners' Dilemma. With students, there may be a substantial risk to reputation if the cooperative student is able to tell other students that defection has taken place.

18.4 Coordination games

Consider the following problem.

> In a village where the men hunt for game, it is possible for any two to catch a large animal, such as a stag, sharing the meat between them. No hunter can catch a stag on his own. While a pair are hunting for a stag, each will have the opportunity to catch a smaller animal, a hare. Should one hunter do this, he is certain to catch the hare, but his partner will lose the stag. If both decide to hunt hares, they are both certain to catch them.

By yourself

X18.28 Suppose that both hunters value a share of the stag at 3 and a hare at 1, while returning home empty-handed has value 0.
(a) Defining the actions available to the hunters as *Stag* and *Hare*, set out the game in normal form.
(b) Identify the best reply to *Stag* and to *Hare*.
(c) Identify action profiles that form pairs of consistent conjectures.
(d) Discuss what you consider to be the most likely outcome in this case.

The *Stag Hunt* is a simple example of the game introduced as coordination (1) above. It presents us with a slightly different situation from the Prisoners' Dilemma. Instead of each player having a dominant strategy, leading to a sub-optimal outcome, we find that there are two Nash equilibria, one of which is better for both players than the other. So, it might seem straightforward to argue that both players will simply choose the better option for them both, *Stag*, and stick to that plan. There is no need for the sort of subterfuge that we considered in the cooperation problem in Section 18.3, where one player might try to persuade the other to cooperate by seemingly intending to defect.

We come back then to the question of whether or not players in such a game should trust earnest declarations by the other players. Suppose that one hunter does not believe that the other one is committed to completing the stag hunt. Such a hunter expects either to return empty-handed, or – doing the best possible in the circumstances – to catch a hare. Belief that the other player will not coordinate his actions leads to the breakdown of coordination.

By yourself

X18.29   We assume that the hunters live in the same (small) village.
   (a) If one player hunts a hare, how might the other player impose social costs that reduce the benefits from deviation?
   (b) Suppose that there is a kinship relation between the hunters. How might this affect their payoffs? Do you think that this would make cooperation more likely?
   (c) Suppose that each hunter has a sister, married to the other hunter. How might this affect the payoff to breaching cooperation?

The issue of trust is important in game theory, since it means believing that other players will perform certain actions in the future. Trust is necessary for coordination of actions. Where players have a dominant strategy, trust is trivial. Each player can be certain that the other will behave according to that strategy, even, as in the Prisoners' Dilemma, when they agree that there is a better alternative available. The *Stag Hunt* is the simplest example of a game in which trust is required to ensure coordination, since there is a 'no trust' equilibrium. Trust should emerge from the structure of the game, and from the belief that other players will recognize that coordination of actions is in their best interest.

We have suggested a slightly different mechanism in Exercise X18.29, which is to concentrate on kinship relations between the hunters. We might imagine someone being shunned by relations for failing to cooperate, so that substantial social costs can be imposed. The closer the familial ties, the more likely coordination will be. We might think of this as being a way of changing the payoffs to the game. The difficulty in this case is that we would like to devise a payoff structure in which *Stag* is the best reply to *Hare*, so that *Stag* becomes a dominant strategy.

By yourself

X18.30   If players believe that the other players in a game will behave in a certain way because that maximizes their payoff, is it reasonable to claim that they trust one another?

18.5   Conclusions

This chapter has been an introduction to some of the important concepts of game theory. We set out the simplest possible game structures: two-player, two-action strategic games of complete information. That characterization is very complete. It tells us the number of players, and the number of options open to each of them before the start of the game. The game itself effectively lasts an instant, as players decide upon their actions at the same time, carrying them out immediately.

These games are based on the rule *two is just enough*, on which we relied heavily in our discussion of the standard model as well. Games with two players, each choosing from two actions, while possessing perfect information about the economic environment, are the very simplest setting in which we can apply the Nash equilibrium concept.

We have also applied our rule that players seek to maximize their payoffs. In the game that we have analysed, payoffs result from both players' actions, so each player tries to anticipate the other's choice, choosing what they believe will be the payoff-maximizing actions. From such considerations we developed the concepts of the *best response* and the *Nash equilibrium*, showing that neither player would deviate unilaterally from such an equilibrium outcome.

Even limiting our consideration to two-player, two-action games, it is possible to find games that represent quite a rich structure of economic behaviour. Games in which both players have a dominant strategy might seem to be tediously simple; nonetheless, choosing the pattern of payoffs carefully, they include the Prisoners' Dilemma, a game in which the players should not reach the best possible outcome. We have seen that there might be more than one equilibrium, and that it is not a simple matter to see how players might coordinate their actions to ensure that a single outcome emerges, even in a game like the *Stag Hunt*, where one equilibrium should be preferred by all participants. We have also seen that there are some competitive games that can be represented as games of chance, and whose proper solution will be discussed in Chapter 19. And we have seen that game theory can prompt deep reflection on the nature of economic behaviour, such as our discussion of what it means to say that some particular outcome is likely to emerge so long as the players trust each other. While this is only a very preliminary discussion of game theory, it has already expanded and enriched both our economic vocabulary and our toolbox, providing us with a new way of defining and analysing problems.

Summary

A two-player, two-action strategic game of complete information is fully specified when we state the identities of the players, the actions that each might choose and the payoffs to each of the four possible action profiles or combinations of actions. The assumption of complete information means that both players know the structure of the game, including the other player's payoffs. In a strategic game, both players choose (and carry out) their chosen actions at the same time. A strategy in such a game is the action that a player will choose.

A Nash equilibrium is an action profile in a game from which neither player would wish to deviate without colluding with the other players. This is because each player's action completes an action profile that maximizes their payoff. In effect, given the other players' actions, no player can do better than to choose the action in the Nash equilibrium.

A player has a dominant strategy if the strategic action offers the highest payoff, irrespective of the actions chosen by the other player. Where both players have a dominant strategy, the game has a single dominant strategy equilibrium. This is a special case of a Nash equilibrium.

Where one player has a dominant strategy, then the other player can be certain that this action will be chosen, and so will choose the best reply to that action; this generally ensures that there is a single Nash equilibrium.

A game is symmetric if both players have the same action set, and, both choosing the action chosen by the other player, they each receive the payoff that the other player would have received from the original choices.

In a symmetric two-player, two-action game, there may be two Nash equilibria. If these equilibria involve the players choosing the same action and receiving the same payoff, one will be preferred to the other. However, we have not been able to provide a compelling reason for there being coordination on the preferred outcome, although we have argued that it will occur if both players trust each other enough.

If the two Nash equilibria involve players choosing different actions and so receiving different payoffs, there is no agreed ranking of the equilibria. This increases the coordination problem associated with multiple equilibria, which can most easily be resolved if there is some sort of asymmetry within the set-up, as in the *Leader–Follower* structure in the Stackelberg quantity leadership game.

A game is competitive if any action that increases one player's payoff will lead to a reduction in the other player's payoff. In a two-player, two-action competitive game, there is no action profile that forms a Nash equilibrium.

Visit the companion website at **www.palgrave.com/mochrie** to access further teaching and learning materials, including lecturer slides and a testbank, as well as guideline answers and student MCQs.

chapter 19

Game theory: applications

What we do in this chapter

We extend our analysis of firms' behaviour, applying principles of game theory. Firstly, we allow the two players in the game to choose from a continuum of actions. Developing the quantity setting model introduced in Chapter 17, we obtain the *Cournot–Nash equilibrium.* We also examine competition in prices, again developing the previous analysis to obtain the *Bertrand–Nash equilibrium.*

To analyse the model of quantity leadership from Chapter 17, we define the class of extensive games, in which there is a sequence of choices over time, with players being able to observe earlier actions before making decisions. In this structure, we develop the concept of *sub-game perfect equilibrium*, in which every action is a player's optimal choice when anticipating the outcome of the game. We find *sub-game perfect equilibria* by using the solution techniques of

backward induction, and show that the sub-game perfect equilibria are drawn from the Nash equilibria of extensive games.

As well as considering quantity leadership, we analyse the emergence of *punishment strategies* in quantity setting models, where there are repeated interactions between firms. These can resolve the problem of stability in a cartel. We then turn to other applications of extensive games, including *entry deterrence* and *contract design* to elicit effort from workers.

Lastly, we turn to *coordination games*, defining players' strategies as probability distributions across the actions available to them. In such models, we say that players adopt a *mixed strategy* over the actions. We conclude by defining the Nash equilibria in mixed strategies for such games.

19.1 Oligopoly models as games

In Chapter 17, we introduced models of oligopoly involving quantity setting, price setting and quantity leadership; and in Chapter 18, we introduced two-player, two-action strategic games of complete information. Our first examples of such games were simplifications of the quantity setting model of oligopoly. We begin here by bringing together the quantity setting model and the Nash equilibrium concept, treating the model as a game.

To find the Nash equilibria of a strategic game of complete information, we need to know the identity of the players, the set of actions open to them, and the payoffs to every action profile. Here:

- *Players:* Firms A and B.
- *Actions*: Firms $F = A, B$ choose output q_F, where $q_F \geq 0$.
- *Action profiles (outcomes)*: $O = \{(q_A, q_B) : q_A, q_B \geq 0\}$.
- *Payoffs*: Firm F makes profits $\Pi_F = \Pi_F(q_A, q_B)$.

To find the outcomes that are Nash equilibria, each firm chooses output q_F to maximize their payoff, given the other firm's output, q_G.

- Firm F forms conjecture $q_G = q_G^c$, and then chooses best reply $q_F^* = q_F^*(q_G)$, to maximize its profit.
- For a Nash equilibrium (q_A^*, q_B^*), $q_F^* = q_F^*(q_G^*)$, so that both firms correctly anticipate their competitor's output choice.

Both firms have all the information required to choose their profit-maximizing output, except that they have to anticipate the other firm's output. Neither firm can make any credible claim about their output plans, but can predict the effect of their own and their competitor's choice on payoffs. For a Nash equilibrium, when outputs are revealed, neither wishes to change their output given its competitor's output.

19.1.1   The Cournot–Nash equilibrium

In Figure 19.1, we illustrate the Cournot–Nash equilibrium for this very general game. For each firm, the best-reply curve, $q_F^*(q_G)$, is downward-sloping. At the endpoints of the reaction functions, one firm has the whole market. If firm B quits the market, so that $q_B = 0$, then firm A sets output, $q_F^*(0) = q_F^M$; while firm B will choose to quit the market when firm A sets output $q_A = q_A^0$, since $q_B^*(q_A^0) = 0$. We note that if firm B were to quit the market, firm A could set the profit-maximizing output for a monopoly. If firm A sets a high enough level of output, then firm B will choose to leave the market.

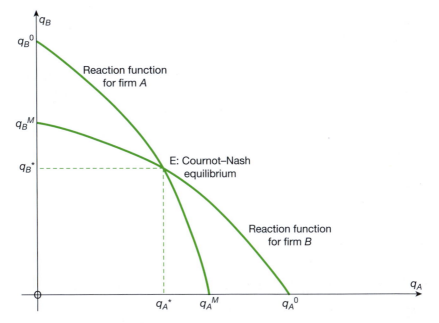

Figure 19.1 Cournot–Nash equilibrium

By yourself

X19.1   Given inverse market demand, $p = p(Q)$, where $Q = q_A + q_B$, and firm costs $c_F = c(q_F)$, where $F = A, B$, write down expressions for each firm's profits, and hence obtain their reaction functions in implicit form. (Remember to allow for the possibility that $q_G > q_G^0$.) Given that the inverse demand decreases as output q_B increases, demonstrate that so long as its marginal costs are not decreasing its output, the best reply $q_A{}^*(q_B)$ will be decreasing in q_B.

In Chapter 17.1, we argued that each firm in a Cournot game behaves as if it has a monopoly over the residue of the market left after its competitors have chosen their output. As the other firms' output increases, this residue decreases, and so the profit-maximizing output also decreases. The downward-sloping curves in the diagram reflect this. For a Cournot–Nash equilibrium both firms have to choose the best reply to their competitor's output. This can only happen where the best-reply curves intersect.

The graphs of the reaction functions shown in Figure 19.1 are concave, while in the examples in Chapter 17 they were linear. The important point is not their shape but that they are single-valued functions, so that irrespective of the amount that a firm produces, its competitor has a uniquely defined profit-maximizing output. The graphs are also smooth and continuous: if one firm's output increases very slightly, the decrease in the other firm's profit-maximizing output should also be very slight. All this reflects the fact that the effect of each firm's output on the other's profits comes through the impact of changes in the industry supply on price.

19.1.2   The Bertrand–Nash equilibrium

We now convert the model of competition in prices in Section 17.4 into a game, deriving the Bertrand–Nash equilibrium rather more formally than we did there. We continue to assume that there is complete information. Firms therefore have access to the same methods of production; when setting prices, they know that since all consumers are fully informed, only the firm setting the lowest price can sell any output. They are both aware that they face this market structure, and they both know that their competitor and all consumers are equally well informed. We can summarize the game as follows:

- There are two firms in the market. We denote the firm $F : F = A, B$.
- Each firm sets price p_F, which is the same for all buyers, so that there cannot be any price discrimination.
- Total market demand $Q = Q(\min[p_A, p_B])$, where $Q'(p) < 0$.
- Firm demand $q_F = \begin{cases} 0, \text{if } p_F > p_G \\ 0.5Q, \text{if } p_F = p_G \\ Q, \text{if } p_F < p_G \end{cases}$.
- Firms face costs $C_F = c \cdot q_F$, so that there is a constant marginal cost, $C_F' = c$.

The assumption of constant marginal costs is made simply for convenience in our discussion.

By yourself

X19.2   Confirm that a firm, *F*, will be able to make a profit if $p_F = \min(p_A, p_B) > c$.

X19.3   Suppose that there is some price p^M that firm *F* would set to maximize its profits if it had a monopoly. Describe firm *F*'s best replies in each of the following situations:
(a) Its competitor sets a price $p_G > p^M$.
(b) Its competitor sets a price $p_G : c < p_G \leq p^M$.
(c) Its competitor sets a price $p_G = c$.
(d) Its competitor sets a price $p_G < c$.

We show the best-reply function for firm *A* in Figure 19.2. It is more complex than the best-reply function in the Cournot game. Starting from a situation where both firms share the market because they set the same price, firm *A* can either cede the market to firm *B*, or else acquire the whole of it, just by raising, or cutting, its price, p_A, very slightly. When competition is in quantities, a small change in the amount produced always leads to a small change in the market price, and so a small change in firm revenues, costs, and profits. But with competition in prices, a small change can instead lead to large changes in sales, and so also large differences in profits.

As suggested in Exercise X19.3, firm *A* might react to firm *B*'s price in one of four different ways, depending on the price, p_B. If firm *A* matches or undercuts that price, so that $p_A \leq p_B$, it will make sales. It will obtain the whole market if $p_A < p_B$, so that it undercuts firm *B*, but will share the market if $p_A = p_B$. However, setting a price $p_A : p_A > p_B$, it surrenders the market to firm *B*. Firm *A* wants to make profits. We see in region IV in Figure 19.2 that firm *A* cannot do better than set the profit-maximizing price for a monopoly, and it will do this if $p_B > p^M$, the monopoly price. In region III, it will want to undercut firm *B*, since $p_B > c$ and it can obtain the whole market and make profits. In fact, firm *A* will want

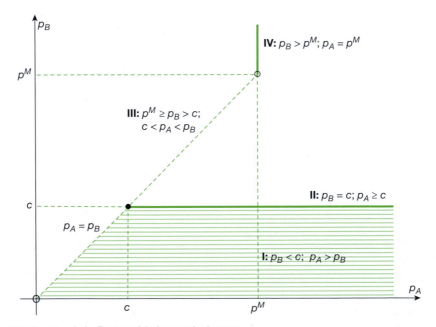

Figure 19.2 Best reply in Bertrand (price-setting) game

to undercut firm B very slightly. We cannot really show this in the diagram because we cannot define a price p_A that is the closest to any price p_B. For this reason, we don't actually show the best reply for firm A clearly in the diagram.

Suppose, though, that if firm A obtained any market share, it would make a loss. This would occur if $p_B < c$, and is indicated in Region I of the diagram. There, by setting a price $p_A > p_B$, firm A cedes the market, and avoids both profits and losses.

This leaves us with the case in region II, where $p_B = c$, where firm B sets a price at which firm A will only just break even if it shares the market. Firm A will not want to undercut firm B, since it would then acquire the whole market but make a loss. It can avoid this either by matching firm B's price (so that $p_A = p_B = c$), so that it makes sales but just breaks even; or else by setting a higher price, in which case it makes no sales, generates no revenues, but, as it incurs no costs, still breaks even.

By yourself

X19.4   Sketch a graph of the reaction function for firm B.

X19.5   Add to your graph the graph of the reaction function for firm A, depicted in Figure 19.2. [*Note:* It may be useful to use different colours for the two reaction functions.]

X19.6   Confirm that there cannot be a Nash equilibrium in regions I, III, and IV. Confirm that there is a Nash equilibrium in region II, where $p_A = p_B = c$.

X19.7   What would you expect to happen in the market if the firms both faced constant marginal cost, c_F, lower for firm A than for firm B, so that $c_A < c_B$? Show that in the equilibrium, firm A will set a price so that it is able to obtain the whole market and still make profits.

We obtained the result of Exercise X19.6 in Section 17.4, using a rather more informal argument. In the Bertrand–Nash equilibrium, one firm sets its price to the marginal cost, eliminating all profits. So long as the other firm does not set a price lower than the marginal cost, it will also break even. Neither firm can make profits. Exercise X19.7 confirms that this result depends upon the symmetry of the market environment in which the firms operate. If firm A has a cost advantage, it can both exclude firm B from the market and continue to generate profits.

19.2   Extensive form games and sub-game perfection

In a *strategic* game, all decisions are made before the start of the game, with players then following through with these decisions. In the extensive form of such a game, we allow for a sequence of actions, some of which might be observed by other players before they act. We see below that this gives rise to a rather more satisfactory definition of a player's strategy, making clear that a strategy is not simply the action that a player chooses. Strategies will continue to be set at the beginning of a game, but will cover all of the possible situations in the course of the game in which a player might have to make a choice.

Extensive form of game A representation of a strategic game in which decisions can be made sequentially.

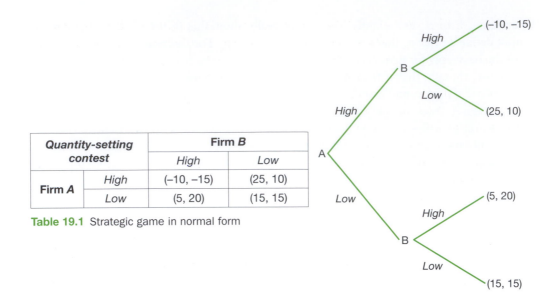

Quantity-setting contest		Firm **B**	
		High	Low
Firm **A**	High	(−10, −15)	(25, 10)
	Low	(5, 20)	(15, 15)

Table 19.1 Strategic game in normal form

Figure 19.3 Strategic game in extensive form

In Figure 19.3, we show an example of the two-player, two-action *coordination (2)* game, first introduced in Section 18.1. There we noted that there are two Nash equilibria, (*High*, *Low*) and (*Low*, *High*). We now offer a different explanation of the emergence of coordination by depicting the game in extensive form, using a game tree. Both firms still choose a level of output, but we now allow firm *A* a first-mover advantage, with firm *B* observing its competitor's decision before deciding upon its own output.

> **Strategy (2)** A listing of the actions that a player chooses (given previous actions) whenever called on to make a choice.

Given our proposed definition of a **strategy** as a listing of actions that a player might choose, conditional upon the actions that have already

Essential Maths 19.1: A strategic game with complete information in extensive form

A strategic game with complete information is defined in extensive form in terms of: the number of players; a player function determining which player makes a choice at each point in the game; the set of actions available to each player; the outcomes, or sequences of actions that might be chosen during the game; and each player's payoff given the outcome of the game.

- As in Chapter 18, while in principle we can set up a game with any number of players, P, we restrict our attention to two-player games, labelling them $p = A, B$.
- Although a game can continue indefinitely, we concentrate on games in which each player chooses one action, with player A choosing before player B.
- We concentrate on games where players choose between two actions, $n = 1, 2$. We define action sets $S_A = \{a_1, a_2\}$ and $S_B = \{b_{11}, b_{12}, b_{21}, b_{22}\}$. Player B has two actions, b_{n1} and b_{n2}, when player A chooses action a_n.
- The outcomes are all pairs of actions that might be chosen. With two players choosing between two actions, the outcome set, $O = \{(a_1, b_{11}), (a_1, b_{12}), (a_2, b_{21}), (a_2, b_{22})\}$.
- The payoffs, $[v_A(a_i, b_{ij}), v_B(a_i, b_{ij})]$, are defined for the action profiles listed above.

been chosen, firm *A*'s strategy is the choice that it makes between *High* and *Low* at the start of the game. Firm *B*'s strategy, on the other hand, will be the choice that it makes given that firm *A* has chosen *High*, as well as the choice that it makes given that firm *A* has chosen *Low*.

By yourself

X19.8   Confirm that firm *B*'s strategy is to choose the opposite action from firm *A*, so that if firm *A* has chosen *High*, firm *B* will choose *Low*; but that if firm *A* has chosen *Low*, firm *B* will choose *High*.

X19.9   Given firm *B*'s strategy in X19.8, find firm *A*'s strategy, and state the action profile that emerges in the equilibrium of this game.

In Exercise X19.9, we find that there is only one equilibrium outcome. Firm *A* chooses *High*, anticipating that firm *B* will choose *Low* when it sets its output. But we write the equilibrium as (*High*, [*Low*, *High*]), emphasizing the fact that firm *B* must have a plan in place just in case firm *A* were to choose *Low*. This is consistent with our definition of a strategy as an action plan allowing a player to respond optimally to previous actions in the game. Where strategies have this property, the equilibrium will have the property of *sub-game perfection*.

19.2.1   Sub-game perfection

Knowing the number of players, the action sets available to each player and the payoffs to all possible action profiles in a strategic game with complete information is enough to enable us to find all of the Nash equilibria. As noted in Essential Maths 19.1, to describe

Essential Maths 19.2: Depiction of an extensive form game in a tree

We use a game tree to show the sequential decision making structure for an extensive form game, and (later) to illustrate its sub-game perfect equilibria.

Players choose actions at nodes. In Figure M19.1, player *A* makes a choice at the initial node; and player *B* at the subsequent node. The game then reaches a terminal node, revealing players' payoffs, v_A and v_B.

Depending on the choice that a player makes, the choice set available to a player making a choice at a subsequent node may vary. In the diagram, when player *A* chooses action a_i, player 2 has choice set $B_i = \{b_{i1}, b_{i2}\}$.

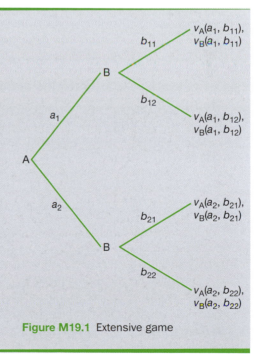

Figure M19.1 Extensive game

a game in extensive form we also need a player function, which indicates the *sequence* of the actions in the game – that is, the player who will make a decision at each point in the game, given the actions that have already taken place. In our simple example of quantity setting, firm A chooses output first, and firm B second.

> **History** The path through a decision tree, from the initial node to the payoffs.
>
> **Sub-history** The initial part of the history.
>
> **Sub-game** The part of game that begins at the end of a sub-history, whose length is the number of decisions made in it.

In deriving the sub-game perfect equilibria of such games, it will be helpful to define some terminology. Firstly, we define a complete **history** as a path threading its way through a game tree from the initial decision node to a terminal node, at which the game ends and the players receive their payoffs. This definition of a *history* is also the definition of an *outcome*. Instead, we define a *sub-history* of a game as the initial part of a complete history. We can think of the end of a sub-history as a **sub-game** of the full game, or the start of a new strategic game in extensive form. We also define the *length* of a (sub-)game as the number of choices that are made in any history.

The shortest possible sub-game has length 1. After a single decision, the sub-game reaches a terminal node, where the players receive their payoffs. In Exercise X19.8 and X19.9, we started by considering behaviour in these sub-games, identifying the payoff-maximizing choice in each one. Since the complete game was of length 2, we then considered the decision being made at the initial node, treating player A as being able to work out the choices that player B would make at both of the subsequent nodes. Player A's choice completes an equilibrium history, in which no player regrets the decisions that they made at the start of any sub-game. We call the process *backward induction*, with the equilibrium that emerges having the characteristic of **sub-game perfection**. We can see from Exercises X19.8 and X19.9 that the sub-game perfect equilibrium of the game is also a Nash equilibrium; not all Nash equilibria, however, are also sub-game perfect. We therefore say that sub-game perfection is a *refinement* of the Nash equilibrium concept.

> **Sub-game perfection** An outcome where choice made at end of every sub-history is optimal within subsequent sub-game.

Essential Maths 19.3: **Histories and sub-games in an extensive form game**

- A history is a sequence of choices that begins from the initial node and ends at one of the terminal nodes, so that it represents the whole of a path through the game tree from start to finish.
- A sub-history, *h*, is a sequence of choices beginning from the initial node and stopping at some intermediate node. It is the start of a complete history.
- A sub-game, *g*, is the part of the game that follows on from the end of a sub-history. A sub-game of a strategic game in extensive form is itself a strategic game in extensive form.
- At the end of any sub-history, the player function indicates which player has to make a choice at its terminal node. This is also the initial node of the sub-game that follows from the end of that sub-history.
- The length of a sub-game is the number of choices made in it. In a sub-game of length 1, after the first choice, the sub-game concludes at a terminal node.
- In Figure M19.1, there are two sub-histories: $h_1 = a_1$; and $h_2 = a_2$.
- There are two sub-games of length 1 : B chooses between $B_i = \{b_{i1}, b_{i2}\}$.

19.2.2 The Stackelberg (sequential output-setting) game

Once again, we go back to Chapter 17, considering the (Stackelberg) model of quantity leadership as a game. We shall build on that structure, with firm A taking on the role of leader. It decides its output, announces it, and commits itself to fulfilling its plans before firm B (the follower) decides how much it will produce. As noted in Section 17.3, it is entirely appropriate to style the follower's output decision a *best reply* because the firm is responding to the leader's output decision. The Stackelberg game differs from the output setting example earlier in this Section because we allow firms to choose any level of output, not just *High* or *Low*.

By yourself

X19.10 Consider the example used in Section 17.2, where firms A and B face inverse market demand $p = 150 - q_A - q_B$ and marginal cost $c = 30$.
  (a) Assume that firm A has chosen output q_A. Write down an expression for the profit that firm B makes, and calculate its profit-maximizing choice as a function of the output of firm A, q_A.
  (b) Assume that firm A is able to predict how firm B will respond to its choice. Obtain an expression for the profit of firm A that does not involve firm B's output. Hence, calculate firm A's profit-maximizing choice.

The analysis in Exercise X19.10 is very straightforward. Firm A knows that firm B will choose an output on its best-reply function, and so can use its first-mover advantage. We illustrate this point in Figure 19.4. We show the game in extensive form, with firm A choosing its output, q_A, at the initial node. This can be any value up to the maximum of 150, above which level the firm would not be able to dispose of all of its output, even giving it away for free. We show the choice set as the solid triangle, with the actual output that the firm chooses appearing as a line within the triangle. At the subsequent node, we show firm

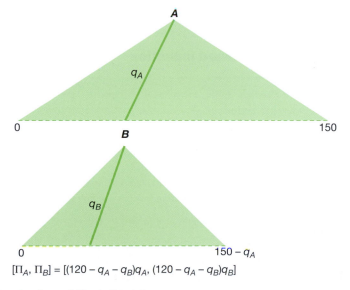

$$[\Pi_A, \Pi_B] = [(120 - q_A - q_B)q_A, (120 - q_A - q_B)q_B]$$

Figure 19.4 Extensive form of Stackelberg game

B's output choice. Remember that we think of firms competing in quantities as having a monopoly over the residue of the market left after the other firms have chosen their output. As a result, firm *B* chooses output q_B: $0 \leq q_B \leq 150 - q_A$. In Exercise X19.10, we confirm that the sub-game perfect equilibrium, $(q_A^*, q_B^*) = (60, 30)$.

By yourself

X19.11   Consider a more general form of the model used in X19.10. Firm *A* is the leader, and firm *B* the follower. Firms compete in quantities, with firm *F* producing output q_F, with inverse market demand, $p = a - b(q_A + q_B)$. There is a constant marginal cost, *c*.
(a) Write down expressions for each firm's profits.
(b) Express the profit-maximizing output of firm *B* as a function of q_A, the output of firm *A*.
(c) Similarly, express the profit-maximizing output of firm *A*, q_A^*, in terms of the parameters in this model, given your answer in part (b).
(d) Hence calculate the profit-maximizing output, q_B^* and the firms' equilibrium profits.
(e) Sketch a game tree similar to Figure 19.4 for this model, showing clearly the sub-game perfect equilibrium.

The game is already familiar from Section 17.2; and so we have illustrated it in Figure 19.5 not in a game tree but instead in an adaptation of Figure 17.5. This illustrates the difference between the outcome that emerges in the sub-game perfect equilibrium and the equilibrium itself. Once firm *A* has chosen its output, q_A, firm *B* has to choose its best reply. From Figure 19.4, and Exercise 19.11, we know that the best reply, $q_B^*(q_A)$, is a function of output, q_A. In Figure 19.5, we illustrate each of these choices in the best-reply line. The whole of that line appears in the sub-game perfect equilibrium, since each point shows an optimal choice for firm *B* for every one of the actions available to firm *A*. In terms of the game tree, analysis of the sub-games of length 1 shows just how firm *A* can use the fact that the outcome of the game will lie on firm *B*'s best-reply function.

Essential Maths 19.4: Backward induction

In a Nash equilibrium of a strategic game, every action is a best reply to the actions that other players choose. In a sub-game perfect equilibrium, every action anticipates perfectly the payoff-maximizing choices made in the sub-games contained within the game.

Beginning with all sub-games of length 1, the player making the final choice chooses the payoff maximizing choice in each one. Then considering a sub-game of length 2, the player making the initial choice in those sub-games can work out the choices of the player making the final choice in each of the possible sub-games of length 1 contained within the sub-game of length 2.

So, in Figure M19.1, there is a single (sub-)game of length 2. The choice of player *A* determines which of the sub-games of length 1 will be played, and player *A* is able to anticipate the choices that player *B* would make in each case.

Using backward induction, we find the optimal choices in sub-games and so in the game as a whole.

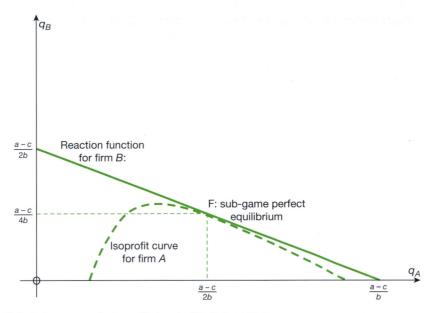

Figure 19.5 Sub-game perfect equilibrium in Stackelberg game

We can now demonstrate the output at which firm A maximizes its output given this restriction on the outcomes of the games, by finding the output at which an isoprofit curve just touches firm B's best-reply function. In Figure 19.5, we illustrate the sub-game perfect action profile of the game $(q_A^*, q_B^*) = \left(\frac{a-c}{2b}, \frac{a-c}{4b}\right)$. This, though, is not the sub-game perfect equilibrium, which we may write as:

$$(q_A^*, q_B^*(q_A)) = \left(\frac{a-c}{2b}, \left\{\frac{a-c-bq_A}{2b} : 0 \leq q_A \leq \frac{a-c}{b}\right\}\right) \qquad [19.1]$$

To reiterate, Expression 19.1 defines the sub-game perfect equilibrium as one choice for firm B for every output choice that firm A might make, plus the optimal output choice for firm A, anticipating the choices of firm B.

19.3 Cartel behaviour

In Cournot, Bertrand, and Stackelberg games, businesses seek to maximize profits, given beliefs about competitors' behaviour. We assume that all firms make their choices separately, so that there is no possibility of consulting or agreeing upon actions with competitors. Where firm **collude**, they reach an agreement to act as a cartel, which then restricts competition between them, so that typically the quantity traded falls, market-clearing price increases, and firm profits also increase. In many countries, collusion is illegal since it benefits firms at the expense of consumers.

> **Collusion** Agreement between firms regarding their behaviour in order to increase their profits.

Collusion turns out to be difficult to achieve because firms face a problem very similar to the Prisoners' Dilemma, introduced Section 18.1, in which the Nash equilibrium involves players breaking the plan that they agreed with their partner in crime. We might argue that in the opening examples in Chapter 18, the same problem bedevils any attempt at collusion, since the bakeries, *Aulds* and *Blacks*, would do better by avoiding competition, whether by building a small, rather than a large, factory, or by continuing to use the old, rather than the new, technology. Collusion would involve agreements to behave in the way that is jointly beneficial. But in these examples, the bakeries' dominant strategy was to break the agreement, and so we would predict that collusion would fail.

If collusion was bound to fail, this would be the end of the matter, and there would be no need for it to be made illegal. Making collusion illegal adds force to the argument that collusion is difficult to maintain. Firms cannot draw up contracts setting out their agreement, so they have no recourse in law for alleged breaches of contract. Nor might firms easily devise a system for verifying that they are all keeping to the agreement without alerting the competition authorities, who would break up the cartel. Irrespective of their (informal) agreement, when firm owners have to make decisions, they will maximize profits; and in the context of the game which we have already studied, this will prevent cartels forming, and disrupt attempts at collusion.

The situation facing the firms is shown in Figure 19.6, which is again based on the Cournot competition model. We expect both firms to choose an output on their best-reply lines, with the Cournot–Nash equilibrium emerging at their intersection, point E. Recall that in Section 17.2.4 we demonstrated that the firms' isoprofit curves passing through point E are perpendicular. We also saw that any action profiles of the Cournot game in which a firm's profits were greater than at the Nash equilibrium E must lie in the region enclosed by the isoprofit curve and the firm's output axis. Within the shaded lens, whose edges are the isoprofit curves through E, both firms make greater profits than at the Nash equilibrium. A collusive agreement might then stipulate the action profile, F: (q_A^M, q_B^M): both firms restrict their output, compared with E, so that the market price increases, and both firms increase their profits.

Figure 19.6 also demonstrates the problem of maintaining a cartel. If we suppose that firm *A* believes that firm *B* will keep the agreement, it will maximize its profits by setting

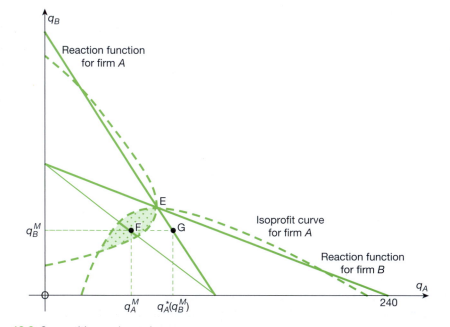

Figure 19.6 Competition and cartel outcomes

output according to its best-reply function. Then $q_A = q_A{}^*(q_B{}^M)$. Remember that the cartel agreement involves the firms reducing their output from the profit-maximizing output under competition, in order to force the market price up. In the diagram, we see that firm A's best reply is a level of output higher than when there is competition. Given that firm B keeps to the cartel agreement, firm A will do better by breaking it than by keeping to it.

By yourself

X19.12 Sketch a diagram based on Figure 19.6 showing best-reply functions for two firms, and an agreed action profile for a cartel. Show the outcomes where: (a) the cartel is maintained; (b) firm A deviates; (c) firm B deviates; and (d) both firms deviate. Discuss the level of each firm's profits in these outcomes, compared with the competitive Nash equilibrium.

X19.13 Demonstrate that there is a single weakly dominant equilibrium in the two-player, two-action game illustrated in Table 19.2.

X19.14 Explain why the situation is similar, but not identical, to the Prisoners' Dilemma discussed in Section 18.2.

X19.15 Consider the following argument. Both firms understand the decisions that the other firm is making. Firm B knows that firm A's best reply is to increase output.
(a) On your diagram, show firm B's best reply to firm A's best reply, $q_A(q_B{}^M)$.
(b) Using a similar argument, show how firm A might anticipate B's choice by changing its output choice, so that its output still lies on its best-reply line.
(c) On your diagram, show that the agreement will collapse, with firms producing at the Cournot–Nash equilibrium.

We can summarize the argument of Exercise X19.13 in a two-player, two-action strategic game in normal form, as illustrated in Table 19.2. Firms have a choice of cooperating in the cartel, which means that they produce the agreed output in terms of the cartel agreement; or of defecting from the cartel, in which case they will produce their best reply, assuming that the other firm still cooperates. Although firms do better in this situation by cooperating and keeping to the agreement than by both defecting, defecting offers both firms a higher payoff when the other firm cooperates, and the same payoff (as cooperating) when the other firm defects. *Defect* is then a weakly dominant strategy, and the outcome (*Defect*, *Defect*) is the only Nash equilibrium.

Cartel		Firm *B*	
		Defect $q_A(q_B{}^M)$	Cooperate $q_A{}^M$
Firm *A*	Defect $q_A(q_B{}^M)$	(1, 2)	(5, 2)
	Cooperate $q_A{}^M$	(1, 5)	(4, 4)

Table 19.2 The cartel problem

Exercise X19.15 invites us to criticize this argument. Instead of the firms simply assuming that the other firm will cooperate or defect, they anticipate defection and continue to adjust their outputs accordingly. Firms will repeatedly adjust their production plans, finally choosing the Nash equilibrium output in the non-cooperative game. The difference between the two cases is simple. In X19.13, both firms assume that the other will respect the agreement, while deciding that it is better that they themselves break it. Such behaviour seems rather myopic. It seems much better to argue, as in X19.15, that if firm A works out that it is in firm B's best interest to break the agreement, then firm A will do what is best for itself given firm B's expected behaviour. But then we enter into a recursive argument, because firm B will also anticipate that change in firm A's output. This means that firms will keep adapting their plans until best replies are consistent, and the (non-collusive) Nash equilibrium emerges.

19.3.1   A simple example

We consider cartel behaviour in a simple Cournot model. The inverse market demand, p, is a function of the quantity traded, Q:

$$p = 270 - Q \qquad [19.2]$$

where Q is the sum of quantities produced by firms A and B, so that $Q = q_A + q_B$. Both firms face a constant marginal cost of production, $c_i = 30$, and total costs, $C_i = 30q_i$. Acting as a cartel, instead of trying to maximize their profits individually, the firms seek to maximize their joint outputs. We can write the optimization problem as:

$$\max_{q_A, q_B} (270 - q_A - q_B)(q_A + q_B) - 30(q_A + q_B) \qquad [19.3]$$

In this situation, with linear demand and total cost functions, when we differentiate the objective function, Expression 19.3, we obtain:

$$\frac{\partial \Pi}{\partial q_A} = \frac{\partial \Pi}{\partial q_B} = 240 - 2(q_A + q_B) \qquad [19.4]$$

Setting these partial derivatives to zero, we find that this will occur for any combination of outputs for which $Q = q_A + q_B = 120$. For profit maximization, any combination of outputs for which total output is equal to 120 will generate the same industry profits. If we allow firms to make cash transfers after production has taken place, the firm producing more can ensure that the firm producing less obtains an equal share of the profits.

By yourself

X19.16   Suppose that there is no cartel agreement. Obtain the Cournot–Nash equilibrium, calculating the profits that the firms make.

X19.17   With the cartel agreement in place, calculate the profit-maximizing output, assuming that the firms produce equal quantities; and the increase in their profits compared with the situation where there is no cartel.

X19.18   Suppose that there is a cartel, but that the agreement specifies that the two firms produce different quantities, and that there is no profit sharing after sales have been made. Assume that $q_A < q_B$. Calculate the minimum value of q_A consistent with the firm entering into a cartel agreement.

From Exercises 19.16–19.18, we conclude that when the firms are able to mimic the behaviour of a monopolist by colluding, they will increase their total profits by 1,600, from 12,800 to 15,400, compared with the profits when there is no cartel. They need not share that increase in profits equally. From Exercise X19.18, we see that both firms are better off in the cartel when their joint output is at the profit-maximizing level, so long as the lower output is no less than $53\frac{1}{3}$. In Figure 19.7, we show the best-reply lines for the two firms, and also the line on which the joint output $q_A + q_B = 120$. We also show the isoprofit curves consisting of action profiles for which one or other firm would achieve its Nash equilibrium profits. Within the lens formed by the two isoprofit curves, we have highlighted the profit-maximizing output combinations. We do not know which one will occur, because once we have reached this line it is no longer possible to increase one firm's profits without reducing the profits of the other firm.

19.3.2 Making cooperation work

Collusion fails because firms have no way of ensuring that their supposed partners will stick to the agreement. Once again, we find ourselves addressing questions of trust, as in the discussion of coordination games in Section 18.4. Here, we only sketch out a solution. Suppose that there are repeated interactions between the firms. Rather than a cartel, suppose that there is a formal joint venture, governed by a formal agreement between the businesses. The parties to the venture either keep to the agreement, and *Cooperate*, or else they *Defect* by 'free-riding', exerting minimal effort. The venture runs for several periods, with the firms only receiving their payout at its end. Each firm decides chooses between *Cooperate* (*C*) and *Defect* (*D*) in each period. However, we suppose that after the firms make their choices, their partner can infer the action that they have taken, even without being able to observe it. To simplify the analysis, we

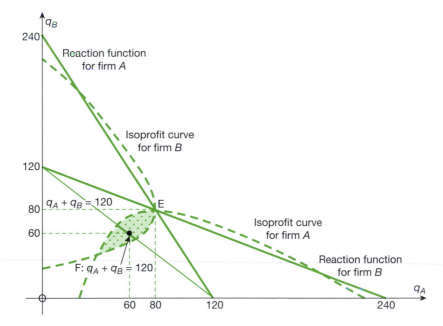

Figure 19.7 A cartel example

assume that if either firm concludes that its partner has defected, it will choose *Defect* from then on, and the project will collapse: we call this a *trigger strategy* because any firm choosing *Defect*, even once, is punished by the permanent removal of cooperation. Every firm participating in the joint venture believes that any attempt to *Defect* will be revealed and that it will cause the catastrophic failure of the project. (We could make the situation even less appealing if aggrieved partners then pursued the firm, which has abandoned the joint venture, for breach of contract.) Under these circumstances, no firm will defect. Since it is quite difficult to do so, we do not demonstrate the operation of such threats in a formal model here.

19.4   Mixed strategies in competitive games and games of coordination

When we introduced competitive games in Section 18.1, we saw that there are no outcomes in which both players' actions are best replies to the other player's actions; and so we concluded that there are no Nash equilibria. The structure of these games suggested that they would naturally be treated as games of chance. For example, we could replace the conscious decision making of the matching game illustrated in Table 18.8 with a simple randomization process, in which each player tosses a coin, with player A taking both of them if the upturned faces match, and player B taking both of them if they differ. The resulting strategic game of complete information is summarized in Table 19.3.

Heads or Tails?		**Player B**	
		Heads ($p_H = \frac{1}{2}$)	Tails ($p_T = \frac{1}{2}$)
Player A	Heads ($p_H = \frac{1}{2}$)	$(1, -1)$	$(-1, 1)$
	Tails ($p_T = \frac{1}{2}$)	$(-1, 1)$	$(1, -1)$

Table 19.3 Random outcome game

By yourself

X19.19   Confirm that in Table 19.3 there is no Nash equilibrium in which players' strategies are defined by the actions available to them.

X19.20   Explain why it would be very unusual for this game to have an extensive form in which player B could observe player A's coin before simply choosing between *Heads* and *Tails*.

X19.21   Which concept of probability would you use in (a) matching pennies (Table 19.3) and (b) the matching game (Table 18.8)?

The payoff structure in Table 19.3 is exactly the same as in Table 18.8. Player A would like the pennies to match, while player B would like them not to match. Note that whereas in developing the concept of the extensive form, we changed the decision making structure by allowing for decisions to be made at different times, here we allow the way in which decisions are made to be different. Tossing a coin in the air and reporting the outcome, neither player makes a conscious decision. Instead, they simply report what happens in a *trial*. In the examples of competitive games in Chapter 18 we assumed that the players did make a conscious choice. We now want to argue that their choices in that game have the same properties as a coin toss. We do this by arguing that their strategies will not be a single action, but rather a probability distribution across the actions available to them.

We have not previously met random outcomes and the concept of *probability*, and so we discuss it briefly in Essential Maths 19.6, explaining both how it emerges within statistical experiments and also three different interpretations of the concept.

We might think that probabilities will generally be defined by the relative frequency of events, with objective measures of probability being a formalization of such measures. This suits us in the situation of matching pennies. We might reasonably assume that both players will be using a *fair* coin to guide their decisions. With only two possible outcomes to any trial, or coin toss, *Heads* and *Tails*, the coin will be fair if the probability of each outcome is equal. We show this in Table 19.3, where we have indicated the probabilities, $p_H = p_T = \frac{1}{2}$. The probabilities of the two outcomes, *Heads* and *Tails*, are equal.

By yourself

X19.22   Suppose that there are *n* outcomes to a trial. Defining the probability of an outcome as being the relative frequency with which it occurs, explain why the sum of probabilities must equal one. Explain also why, if the outcome of a trial is truly random, then, when there are *n* outcomes, the probability of any single outcome $Pr_i = \frac{1}{n}$.

X19.23   Suppose that there 12 outcomes to a trial. What is the probability of outcomes 3, 5, 7, and 11 occurring? What is the probability of an even-numbered outcome?

Essential Maths 19.5: **Statistical experiments**

The subject in a simple experiment is given a bag that contains several balls, some of which are black and some of which are white. The experiment consists of the subject repeatedly taking a single ball out of the bag, noting down its colour, and replacing it. We assume that the subject never looks into the bag, and that the experimenter shakes the bag vigorously between draws.

These conditions are designed to ensure that successive *events* (or *trials*) in the experiment are random, and so unaffected by the choices or preferences of the experimenter or of the subject. They also ensure that successive events are *independent*, in the sense that it is not possible to make any inferences about the outcome of future trials from the outcome of the current or previous ones.

Defining the outcome of any single trial or event as the colour of the ball that the subject chooses, we argue that the outcome is not certain. Instead, we assert that we can associate a *probability* with each outcome, with probabilities capturing how likely it is that a given outcome will occur in any trial.

In game theory, though, players try to anticipate the behaviour of other players. In a strategic game, with choices made at the same time, all players try to achieve the highest possible value of their objective function, given their beliefs about how the other players will behave. In the version of the matching game set out in Table 18.8, the players had to decide for themselves which action from their action set to choose. But until they had made that decision, they might have chosen any action. We have assumed up to this point that players will choose a single action, on the basis that it will maximize their payoff. In this section, we treat them as randomizing: still choosing a single action, but using some probability distribution over the action set to choose it, just as if they had tossed a coin or rolled dice. In analysing such games, we rely on a subjective account of the probability distributions used by players to model the behaviour of other players. Even more importantly, we redefine players' strategies. They are no longer single actions chosen from the action set. Instead, strategies become probability distributions defined over a player's action set. We refer to these as **mixed strategies**.

Mixed strategy A probability distribution over actions, used to choose a player's action.

As an example of a mixed strategy, consider the situation facing 'floating voters' in an election. Some voters always vote for one political party. Others have no strong affiliation with any party, and so make their decision for whom to vote during the election campaign. We can imagine truly undecided voters who only make a final decision once in the polling booth, when faced with a ballot paper. Such voters tend to be the target of extensive political marketing during an election campaign. At any point during the election campaign, each candidate's campaign manager might be able to describe such a voter's intentions in terms of a probability distribution over the various actions; this, however, is a subjective distribution, based on experience of similar decisions made in other elections and knowledge of similar voters' declared intentions.

19.4.1 Example: the matching game

In the game of matching pennies, set out in Table 19.3, we have indicated the probabilities of the coins turning up *Heads* and *Tails* as $p_H = p_T = \frac{1}{2}$. Let us consider the position of

Essential Maths 19.6: Probability

There are three ways of understanding the probabilities of an outcome in an experiment:

Relative frequency: Drawing balls, we note how often a black ball and how often a white ball is drawn. Assume that in n trials, n_B black and n_W white balls are drawn. The probability of drawing a black ball is the relative frequency of this outcome, so $p_B = \frac{n_B}{n}$. The relative frequency is simply the fraction of trials in which a black ball appears. Note that the sum of probabilities always equals one, since some outcome must occur: here $p_B + p_W = 1$.

Objective: The experimenter knows that of n balls in the bag, n_B are black and n_W are white. Of n possible outcomes, all equally likely, the probability of a black ball, $p_B = \frac{n_B}{n}$. Using a model of the experiment, the probabilities of each outcome may be calculated in advance.

Subjective: The subject in the experiment does not know the relative frequency of black and white balls in this bag. From prior experience of drawing balls from bags, the subject has formed beliefs about these relative frequencies. Such probabilities are more properly inferences based on the information available to the subject.

player *A* in the few seconds after tossing the coin, but before knowing the outcome of player *B*'s coin toss. In this situation, player *A* has in effect chosen either *Heads* or *Tails*, but still only knows player *B*'s probability distribution over these actions.

By yourself

X19.24 Calculate player *A*'s expected payoff to (a) *Heads* and (b) *Tails*. What do you conclude about player *A*'s preference between *Heads* and *Tails*, given player *B*'s strategy? How will this change once player *B*'s choice is confirmed?

X19.25 What do you conclude about player *B*'s preferences between *Heads* and *Tails*?

X19.26 Calculate the expected payoffs for players *A* and *B* from the strategy of choosing each action with probability $Pr = \frac{1}{2}$, given that the other player is choosing the same strategy.

By our definition of a best reply, whenever a player obtains the same payoff from two actions, the player will be indifferent between those actions. We can now adapt that definition slightly. In Exercise X19.24, we see that player *A* can never obtain the same payoff from *Heads* and *Tails*, but with player *B* choosing *Heads* and *Tails* with equal probability, then, in considering which action to choose, player *A* considers that they offer the same expected payoff. In Exercises X19.25 and X19.26, applying the same argument, we see that the outcome is symmetric. Player *B* also expects to do as well choosing either *Heads* or *Tails*, and both players also obtain the same expected payoff by following the mixed strategy, $Pr_H = Pr_T = \frac{1}{2}$.

We now turn to the matching game of Section 18.1, and so reproduce Table 18.8 as Table 19.4, allowing for players' use of mixed strategies to guide our discussion. Once again, Claudia and Dayna choose between the actions *Left* and *Right*. We do this by allowing them to adopt any mixed strategy, $(Pr_L, Pr_R) = (\pi, 1 - \pi)$, with $0 \leq \pi \leq 1$. This is different from *matching pennies*, where players are assigned the strategy $Pr_L = Pr_R = \frac{1}{2}$.

Essential Maths 19.7: **Random variables and expected values**

Suppose that the experimenter pays the subject £1 for each black ball drawn from the bag, but makes no payment when a white ball is drawn. The payment, P_t, from any trial is a random variable:
$P_t = \begin{cases} 1, \text{ if Black} \\ 0, \text{ if White} \end{cases}$. The value taken by a random variable depends on the specific state of the world – given, in this case, by the colour of the ball drawn in this trial.

The *expected value*, *E*, of a random variable is the *probability-weighted* sum of its possible values. In this case, $E[P_t] = 1*Pr(Black) + 0*Pr(White) = Pr(Black)$.

In general, a random variable, *V*, which may take any one of *n* values, $v_1, v_2, v_3, \ldots, v_n$, each occurring with probability $p_1, p_2, p_3, \ldots, p_n$, has expected value:

$$E[V] = \sum_{i=1}^{n} p_i v_i = p_1 v_1 + p_2 v_2 + p_3 v_3 + \ldots + p_n v_n \qquad \text{[M19.1]}$$

The matching game		Dayna	
		Left $(Pr_L = \pi_D)$	Right $(Pr_R = 1 - \pi_D)$
Claudia	Left $(Pr_L = \pi_C)$	$(c, -c)$	$(-c, c)$
	Right $(Pr_R = 1 - \pi_C)$	$(-c, c)$	$(c, -c)$

Table 19.4 Mixed strategies in a competitive game

In this game, there is no Nash equilibrium in *pure strategies*, where the players choose an action with certainty, so that $\pi = 0$ (when choosing *Right*), or $\pi = 1$ (when choosing *Left*). Turning our attention to mixed strategies, in which $0 < \pi < 1$, both Claudia and Dayna might choose either action, with some positive probability. In making a choice between two actions, once Claudia and Dayna choose their own probabilities of choosing *Left*, they have also chosen their probabilities of choosing *Right*, since the sum of these two probabilities is one. In Table 19.4, for player X, $\Pr(Left) = \pi_X$ and $\Pr(Right) = 1 - \pi_X$.

We now consider Dayna's expected payoffs from each action, given that Claudia is following such a mixed strategy. Choosing *Left*, Dayna will receive $-c$ with probability π_C, and c with probability $1 - \pi_C$, so her expected payoff to *Left*, $E[V_D(L)]$, may be written:

$$E[V_D(L)] = \pi_C \cdot (-c) + (1 - \pi_C) \cdot (c) = (1 - 2\pi_C) \cdot c \quad [19.5]$$

By yourself

X19.27   Confirm that in choosing *Right*, Dayna has expected payoff $E[V_D(R)] = (2\pi_C - 1) \cdot c$.

X19.28   Show that:
(a) if $\pi_C > \frac{1}{2}$, $E[V_D(R)] > 0 > E[V_D(L)]$;
(b) if $\pi_C < \frac{1}{2}$, $E[V_D(R)] < 0 < E[V_D(L)]$; and
(c) if $\pi_C = \frac{1}{2}$, $E[V_D(R)] = E[V_D(L)] = 0$.

Exercise X19.28 tells us:
(a) that if $\pi_C > \frac{1}{2}$, the pure strategy, $\pi_D = 0$ (or *Right*) yields a higher expected payoff than the pure strategy, $\pi_D = 1$ (or *Left*), and so Dayna prefers *Right* to *Left* and every mixed strategy;
(b) that if $\pi_C = \frac{1}{2}$, the pure strategy, $\pi_D = 0$ (or *Right*) yields the same expected payoff as the pure strategy, $\pi_D = 1$ (or *Left*); and Dayna is indifferent between *Right* and *Left*, and every mixed strategy; and
(c) that if $\pi_C < \frac{1}{2}$, the pure strategy, $\pi_D = 0$ (or *Right*) yields a lower expected payoff than the pure strategy, $\pi_D = 1$ (or *Left*), and so Dayna prefers *Left* to *Right*, and every mixed strategy.

We concentrate on the interesting case $\pi_C = \frac{1}{2}$, so that Claudia chooses completely randomly between the outcomes, as if using a fair coin to determine her decisions. Dayna's expected payoffs from choosing *Left* and *Right* are then exactly equal, and so she is indifferent between those actions. She is also indifferent between these pure strategies and any mixed strategy. For any other value of π_C, Dayna will have a preferred action, or a *pure strategy*, which she will always choose. It is important that all of the actions chosen with non-zero probability in a Nash equilibrium in mixed strategies have the same expected payoffs.

By yourself

X19.29   Using the expected payoffs to the actions *Left* and *Right*, write down an expression for
Claudia's expected payoff when Dayna has decided to follow the mixed strategy, π_D.
By partial differentiation with respect to π_c, or otherwise, show that Claudia's expected
payoff will be increasing (in π_c) if $\pi_D < \frac{1}{2}$, decreasing if $\pi_D > \frac{1}{2}$, and constant if
$\pi_D = \frac{1}{2}$. Interpret these results.

Perhaps the easiest way to explain the argument of Exercise X19.29 is through a diagram. In
Figure 19.8, we show Claudia's and Dayna's best-reply functions. Remember that although
we see each of them choosing one action, either *Left* or *Right*, their underlying strategies
are a probability distribution over these actions. On the horizontal axis, then, we measure
the probability of Claudia choosing *Left*, and on the vertical axis, the probability of Dayna
choosing *Left*. Repeating the argument of Exercise X19.27, if Claudia believes that Dayna
is more likely to choose *Right* than *Left*, so that $\pi_D < \frac{1}{2}$, then Claudia will expect a higher
payoff from choosing *Right* than from choosing *Left*, and so will always choose *Right*. Similarly, if Claudia's best reply $\pi_c^*(\pi_D) = 1$. If $\pi_D > \frac{1}{2}$, then $\pi_c^*(\pi_D) = 0$, and Claudia always
chooses *Left*.

   We are left with the case where $\pi_D = \frac{1}{2}$, with Claudia believing that Dayna will choose
both *Left* and *Right* with equal probabilities. Only in this case do we expect Claudia to
choose a mixed strategy. In Exercise X19.28, we have seen that Claudia obtains an expected
payoff, $V_c(\pi_c, \frac{1}{2}) = 0$, not only to the pure strategies $\pi_c = 1$ (or *Left*) and $\pi_c = 0$ (or
Right), but also to every mixed strategy. We can write:

$$V_c(\pi_c, \frac{1}{2}) = 0, \text{ if } 0 \leq \pi_D \leq 1 \qquad\qquad [19.6]$$

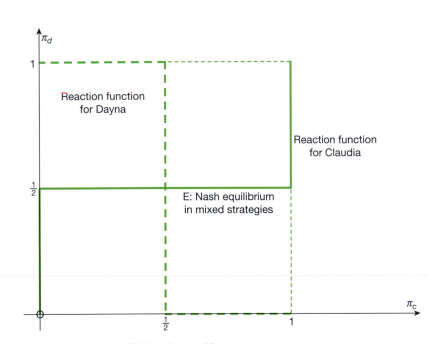

Figure 19.8 Mixed strategy equilibrium in matching game

Claudia is indifferent between strategies when Dayna's decision is random. Similarly, for Dayna, we can confirm that:

$$\pi_D{}^*(\pi_C) = \begin{cases} 0, \text{ if } 0.5 < \pi_C \leq 1 \\ [0,1], \text{ if } \pi_C = 0.5 \\ 1, \text{ if } 0 \leq \pi_C < 0.5 \end{cases} \qquad [19.7]$$

We illustrate these best-reply curves in Figure 19.8. Claudia follows the rule, 'Choose the action that Dayna is more likely to play; or any mixed strategy if Dayna is equally likely to choose *Head* or *Tails*.' Dayna in effect follows the opposite rule, choosing the action that Claudia is less likely to choose, but mixing when facing complete randomization.

By yourself

X19.30   Complete the analysis of the game, showing that there can only be consistent conjectures in this game, with neither player wishing to change their choice, at the Nash equilibrium in mixed strategies: $(\pi_C{}^*, \pi_D{}^*) = (\frac{1}{2}, \frac{1}{2})$.

X19.31   Confirm that if either Claudia or Dayna deviates from this equilibrium, then the other player's best reply will offer a higher expected payoff than in the equilibrium found in X19.30. Explain this result.

We have argued that both players must make their choices completely randomly. The argument of X19.31 is that if Claudia is able to identify anything to suggest that Dayna is more likely to choose *Left* than *Right*, then she should exploit this information by always choosing *Left*, and a positive expected payoff. But of course, if she anticipates this, Dayna can avoid this outcome by always choosing *Right*. Through randomization, then, the game is *fair*. Neither player expects to gain or lose from taking part in it; whatever the outcome, however, one player will gain, and the other will lose. It is truly a game of chance.

19.4.2   Coordination in the *Stag Hunt*

We now apply the concept of a mixed strategy to the *Stag Hunt*. In this two-player, two-action strategic game, illustrated in Table 19.5, there are two Nash equilibria in pure strategies, with players agreeing upon their ranking of these outcomes. With one outcome being better than the other for both players, we might expect that the better one would emerge. In Chapter 18, we argued that application of the Nash equilibrium concept is not enough by itself to ensure this outcome.

Stag Hunt		Player *B*	
		Stag	Hare
Player *A*	Stag	(5, 5)	(0, 2)
	Hare	(2, 0)	(2, 2)

Table 19.5 The *Stag Hunt* game

By yourself

X19.32 Confirm that (*Stag, Stag*) and (*Hare, Hare*) are Nash equilibria in pure strategies.

X19.33 Assume that player A believes player B follows the strategy: $\Pr(Stag) = p_B$. Confirm that for player A:

(a) the expected payoff to *Stag*, $v_A(Stag) = 5p_B$;

(b) the expected payoff to *Hare*, $v_A(Hare) = 2$;

(c) player A is indifferent between choosing *Hare* and *Stag* if $p_B = 0.4$.

X19.34 Confirm that there is a Nash equilibrium in mixed strategies $(p_A{}^*, p_B{}^*) = (0.4, 0.4)$. Calculate the probability of each outcome occurring, and hence confirm the expected payoffs, $v_A(p_A{}^*, p_B{}^*) = v_B(p_A{}^*, p_B{}^*) = 2$.

X19.35 Show that player A's best-reply function may be written $p_A{}^*(p_B) = \begin{cases} 1, \text{if } p_B > 0.4 \\ [0,1], \text{if } p_B = 0.4. \\ 0, \text{if } p_B < 0.4 \end{cases}$ Sketch

this best-reply function, the equivalent for player B, and confirm that there are three Nash equilibria in this strategic game, two in pure strategies, and one in mixed strategies. How might we define trust between the players in this context?

X19.36 We define the *minimax strategy* as choosing the action that maximizes the minimum possible payoff. Confirm that the minimax strategy here does not support the optimal level of cooperation.

Underlying this discussion is the fact that each player faces some uncertainty over the other's behaviour. The **minimax strategy** of Exercise X19.36 can be understood as a way of avoiding losing out from the failure of others to cooperate. A trusting person might end up with nothing; a mistrustful person, who always hunts a hare, will always catch one. But if everyone chooses *Hare*, no one does as well as they might.

> **Minimax strategy**
> The strategy of choosing the action that has the highest minimum payoff.

It might seem natural to argue that players need to trust each other in such a situation. We might think of trust as the willingness of a player to believe that other players will adopt the pure strategy of always playing the welfare-maximizing action, even though they the game has multiple Nash equilibria. With players able to choose a mixed strategy, the probability of player i hunting the stag is $p_i : 0 \leq p_i \leq 1$. In Exercise X19.35, we see that where both players believe that the other player is sufficiently likely to choose *Stag*, then cooperation will occur: both players should decide to hunt the stag so long as they believe that the probability, p, of their partner doing likewise is at least 0.4. Confidence that the other player will cooperate is enough to ensure that the preferred equilibrium emerges.

19.5 Conclusions

This has been a very rapid, and rather brief, introduction to elements of game theory, which have some application to the behaviour of firms. Whereas there is a single market structure, perfect competition, that is entirely consistent with the standard model of choice, there is no single model of imperfect competition, and market structures can vary considerably. We first saw this in Chapter 17, in which we examined cases of limited market power associated with lack of competition. By setting limited competition in the context of game theoretic models, we have seen that the techniques do not simply apply to models of interaction within an oligopoly. We shall study more complex games later in the book, as we consider how decisions can be made when people do not have access to all of the information that might be considered relevant to making decisions. Before that, in Part V, we shall conclude our discussion of the standard model, examining decision making and equilibrium in interlocking markets, and developing further the concept of economic welfare.

Summary

We can treat models of output choice in oligopoly (Cournot and Stackelberg) or price setting (Bertrand) as strategic games of complete information, so that each player chooses one action from a range of values. In the Cournot–Nash equilibrium firms retain some monopoly power, while in the Bertrand-Nash equilibrium they do not.

The Stackelberg game is best represented in extensive form, with choices illustrated in a game tree. The leader chooses its output first, with the follower replying, knowing the leader's choice. The leader can then anticipate the follower's action, increasing output and profits at the follower's expense.

For strategic games in extensive form, in addition to listing the players, their actions, and the payoffs to action profiles, it is also necessary to identify the player function. This identifies which player makes a choice at each decision node in the game, from the initial node at the start of the game through to the terminal nodes, after which players obtain their payoffs.

In analysing the extensive form of a game, it is useful to define histories, each of which is a complete sequence of choices made during the game; sub-histories, each one a sequence of choices running from the initial decision node through to some intermediate node; and sub-games, the part of the game that begins at the end of some sub-history.

Choices in the extensive form of a game should have the characteristic of sub-game perfection,

so that players anticipate the future history of the game at every node where they are called on to make a choice. This is a refinement of the Nash equilibrium concept; only a subset of Nash equilibria are sub-game perfect.

For certain strategic games, it is useful to allow players to adopt mixed strategies, which are probability distributions over the actions chosen. Players do not seek to form conjectures about the actions that other players might choose, but instead about the probability distributions that they might choose. They therefore concentrate on calculating the expected payoff-maximizing probability distribution that they should choose for themselves.

A Nash equilibrium in mixed strategies emerges where no player could change the probability distribution that they use and increase their expected payoffs.

We may apply mixed strategies to competitive games and coordination games. In competitive games, the mixed strategy ensures that players choose from the available actions according to some random process. In such a game of chance, players are indifferent among actions before the outcome is revealed.

In coordination games, we can use the mixed strategy concept to understand more clearly how a particular Nash equilibrium might emerge. To do so, every player must believe that other players are sufficiently likely to choose actions that will support the optimal outcome. It is then optimal for each player to choose such actions, and so complete the Nash equilibrium.

Visit the companion website at **www.palgrave.com/mochrie** to access further teaching and learning materials, including lecturer slides and testbank, as well as guideline answers and student MCQs.

part V

Welfare

The standard model enables us to explain how people and businesses, whose objectives are simple and well defined, interact in the market for a single good or service. This model cannot be complete. It assumes that people have an expenditure constraint, which is exogenous, and so determined outside the model. Firms make payments to hire factor inputs, but the model does not specify to whom these payments are made. In principle, filling in those two gaps is simple. The money that people use to purchase goods and services is ultimately derived from their ownership of the factors of production used in producing those goods and services. The standard model ignores this, relying upon the concept of *partial equilibrium*, so that market clearing occurs in only one market, while conditions in all other markets are held constant. We now wish to replace this with the concept of *general equilibrium*, in which we reach equilibrium simultaneously in all markets. Rather than a market price for a single good, we find a set of market prices, one for each good or service, with the supply just meeting the demand for each. It is no longer one market but, in principle, the whole economy that is in equilibrium.

The leap from the analysis of a single market to the analysis of a whole economy is large, so we shall break it down into a series of rather more manageable steps. We begin by exploring the exchange of two goods between two people, imposing the standard participation constraint: that for an exchange to take place, neither will be worse off after trade than they were before it. If we consider there to be a *process* of trade, rather than it all occurring at one time, we would expect it to stop when further trading would lead to at least one person being worse off. In other words, trade will continue until all potential gains, given prices, are exhausted.

After considering exchange in multiple markets, we turn our attention to the production of multiple goods. In an exchange economy, the quantities of all goods, and their distribution across people, are determined exogenously. It seems preferable to assume instead that it is the quantity of factors of production that is fixed. The combination of final goods and services available for consumption then depends upon the division of factor inputs across productive activities. Initially, we consider the requirements for efficiency in the use of factors of production, linking these to the conditions for efficiency in the exchange process.

We shall find out that there will generally be not just one efficient outcome but rather a continuum of efficient outcomes, some of which may seem to have very undesirable characteristics: for example, production and exchange might operate efficiently, but with one person consuming nearly all of the goods. Our economic models do not easily allow us to comment upon preferences over outcomes. Nevertheless, it is easy to find evidence of people objecting when they consider outcomes to be inequitable: Occupy Wall Street, Podemos (in Spain) and Syriza (in Greece) are just some, recent examples. We are able, though, to criticize arguments about the distribution of income on the basis that while redistribution of endowments does not affect the efficient operation of the economy, other policies, such as taxation of income, which change relative prices, are likely to be less effective.

An alternative approach to the problem of identifying an optimal distribution is to extend our definition of preferences over consumption bundles to the final distribution of goods and services. Here, we need some sort of social welfare function, ideally reflecting the preferences of society as a whole. Defining a function with reasonable properties is very difficult. It is possible to show that simple sets of assumptions about the form of the social welfare function, all of which seem entirely reasonable, are actually contradictory, and so cannot all hold at the same time. We therefore have to concentrate on simple cases in which

we can be certain of reaching outcomes that are acceptable.

In a partial equilibrium approach, we have assumed that people's preferences depend solely upon their own consumption. There are many situations in which someone might also take into account the choices of other people. In this part of the book we interpret such effects as externalities, showing how failure to take account of them will typically lead to inefficient outcomes in which prices no longer reflect the full costs or benefits of actions. There are several ways to address these issues.

Although not strictly a question of externalities, our discussion concludes by considering the characteristics of public goods. It is possible for the owner of a private good to stop someone else consuming it; for a private good, consumption by one person involves their using up the good, so that it is no longer available to anyone else. Public goods have very different characteristics. The classic example is the signal from a lighthouse (a more up-to-date example would be GPS technology). Use by one person does not prevent use by anyone else; nor indeed does it use up the resource, so that in principle there is no capacity limit. It is therefore not possible to use the market mechanism to manage the pricing and trade in public goods. We shall therefore discuss the design of efficient mechanisms that induce potential users of the goods to reveal their true valuations.

Exchange

What we do in this chapter

We have developed the standard theory to analyse resource allocation decisions for people making consumption decisions, and, across a variety of market environments, the profit-maximizing decisions of firms engaged in production activities. We now discuss how people, the ultimate owners of factors of production, will hire them out so that production, distribution, and exchange yield efficient outcomes. In this chapter, we only consider exchange, examining situations in which two people reach an agreement about how to divide a shared endowment. We introduce the *Edgeworth box* as a tool for understanding the properties of the optimal divisions of the endowment.

We next define the property of *Pareto efficiency*, arguing that this is consistent with there being an optimal division of the available goods. We show that any division of goods represented in an Edgeworth box for which the (weakly) preferred sets of the participants touch is Pareto-efficient. We then demonstrate that Pareto efficiency requires the two participants to have a common marginal rate of substitution. Thinking of exchange as occurring through

trade, we define this common marginal rate of substitution as being equal to the agreed relative price used in the exchange. Even with two people, it is possible for trade to lead to an optimal outcome.

Developing the discussion, we see that with well-behaved preferences (and so convex preferred sets) there will be a continuum of Pareto-efficient outcomes. In the Edgeworth–Bowley box, we represent all of these outcomes by a contract curve. We argue, without any formal proof, that for each point on the contract curve, it is possible to identify a set of initial endowments and a relative price for which a given point represents the efficient division of the endowment reached by trade. We therefore predict that the outcome of exchange will be efficient, with the participants choosing relative prices that ensure they reach an efficient outcome and secure all the possible gains from trade. We conclude that with the market mechanism providing such an outcome, there is no obvious advantage gained by giving the participants the freedom to negotiate the division of their endowments.

20.1 The exchange economy

Up to this point, we have used **partial equilibrium** analysis, explaining the effects of price changes in a single market. We have implicitly assumed that all markets, both for goods and services and for factors of production, clear independently, so that a change in the market conditions in one market does not affect conditions in

Partial equilibrium A market outcome that is determined by conditions in that market only.

another one. Our analysis of substitute and complement goods in Section 9.4 demonstrates that this cannot be the case. Changes in the price of one good led to changes in the demand for other goods. To understand simultaneous market clearing across an economy, we turn

General equilibrium
All market prices are determined at the same time, with simultaneous market clearing.

Exchange economy
A model in which endowments take the form of bundles of goods, which are then traded.

to the methods of general equilibrium analysis. In this chapter, as a first step, we consider models of market clearing in an exchange economy.

In an exchange economy, we dispense with production. People have to decide how best to divide an endowment of goods. We should think of the economy as having a large population, n; for the purposes of exposition, it turns out to be possible to concentrate on the smallest number needed for exchange, $n = 2$. As before, this enables us to present our analysis using diagrams. The equilibrium conditions that we obtain then carry through to larger values of n. If n were to be very large, we could think of every person in the economy as being small relative to the markets. Every individual's endowments and demands are then too small to have any effect on the price at which trade takes place, so we can treat all markets as perfectly competitive.

20.1.1   Securing the gains from exchange

We begin with a simple example. Liling and Maya have allotments on which they grow vegetables. They have just harvested crops of broad beans and carrots. We assume that initially they do not know each other, and so each eats what they themselves produce. We illustrate the situation in Figure 20.1, where we have turned the diagram for Maya (on the right) through 180°. The origin (zero consumption) point is at the top right-hand of the quadrant, with an increasing quantity of broad bean consumption shown by a movement to the left, and an increasing quantity of carrot consumption as a movement down. The initial division of the endowment, E, consists of the quantities that each has grown, so that it is divided with Liling having $E_L : (b_L, c_L)$, and Maya having $E_M : (b_M, c_M)$.

If we allow Liling and Maya to meet, there is the possibility of trade, as shown in Figure 20.2. There are divisions of the endowment that lie in both Maya's and Liling's preferred sets. In the usual way, the preferred sets consist of all consumption bundles

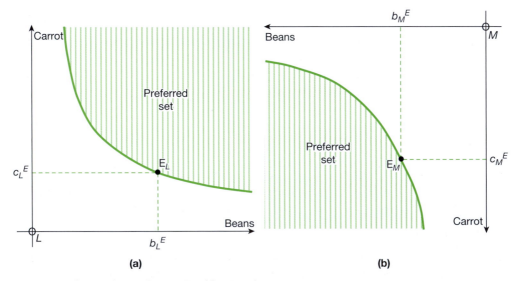

Figure 20.1 Consuming endowments without trade

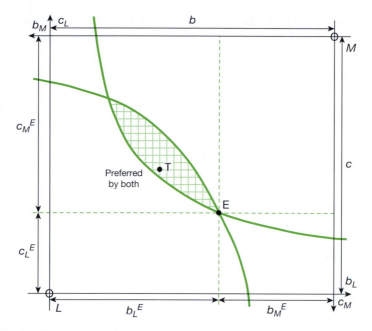

Figure 20.2 The feasible set for exchange outcomes

further away from the origins than the indifference curves passing through the endowment points. For Liling, this is the area above the indifference curve through E; while for Maya, it is the area below the indifference curve through E.

In effect, trade involves them agreeing to pool their endowments and then to divide them in a new way, so that they are both better off (or, at the very least, so that neither is worse off). Defining the consumption bundles after trade, $T_L : (b_L^T, c_L^T)$ and $T_M : (b_M^T, c_M^T)$, we can be certain that:

$$b_L^T + b_M^T = b = b_L^E + b_M^E \qquad\qquad [20.1a]$$

$$c_L^T + c_M^T = c = c_L^E + c_M^E \qquad\qquad [20.1b]$$

In Expression 20.1, the total endowment is $E : (b, c)$. In exchange, then, the quantities of the two goods are fixed, and it is only their division among the participants that changes. So, comparing the quantities that Liling and Maya consume with their original endowments, we find that:

$$b_L^T - b_L^E = -\left(b_M^T - b_M^E\right) \qquad\qquad [20.2a]$$

$$c_L^T - c_L^E = -\left(c_M^T - c_M^E\right) \qquad\qquad [20.2b]$$

In trade, each participant gives some of their endowment to the other one. If Liling gives Maya some broad beans and receives some carrots, then the terms in Expression 20.2a will have negative values, while those in Expression 20.2b will have positive values.

By yourself

X20.1 Given that the endowments represent Liling's and Maya's total wealth, explain why the expressions on the left-hand side of Expression 20.2 cannot both be positive.

In Figure 20.2, we amalgamate the two panels from Figure 20.1. The total endowment, E, and its division between Liling and Maya, is now represented by the dimensions of an *Edgeworth box*, (b, c). In the box, the distance from the left-hand edge to point E represents Liling's share of the endowment of broad beans, while the distance from the right-hand edge to point E represents Maya's share. The indifference curves through the endowment point, E, cross; and the area representing divisions of the endowment for which neither Liling nor Maya would be worse off than at E is shown by the lens bounded by the curves. Exchange of goods is certainly feasible: both Liling and Maya prefer any division of the endowment that lies in the shaded region to the initial division, E. Exchange naturally involves Liling giving up some of her broad bean crop for a portion of Maya's carrot crop.

> **By yourself**
>
> **X20.2** Define the marginal rate of substitution for Liling and Maya at the endowment, E. Explain how the difference in values means that trade is possible.
>
> **X20.3** In Figure 20.2, the endowment is at the lower-right corner of the lens. Under what conditions would the endowment be at the upper-left corner of the lens? What would be the outcome of trade in this case?
>
> **X20.4** Use Expression 20.2 to obtain an expression for the relative price of broad beans (the rate at which Maya gives up consumption of carrots in order to increase consumption of broad beans).
>
> **X20.5** Suppose that at the division, E, Liling and Maya were to have the same marginal rate of substitution. Sketch an Edgeworth box showing this outcome. What do you conclude about the possibility of exchange?

For there to be any trade, it is necessary that there are different marginal rates of substitution at the initial division of goods. Interpreting the marginal rate of substitution as the slope of the two participants' indifference curves through the initial division of goods, then if preferences are well behaved there will be a lens-shaped region, within which the division of goods at any point will be preferred by both partners. If Liling and Maya have the same MRS, then indifference curves through that division of goods touch but do not intersect, so there is no lens-shaped area. Any alternative division that lies in Liling's preferred set lies outside Maya's preferred set; and the reverse is also true. It is then impossible to find a new division that makes Liling and Maya better off, so they will not agree to exchange goods.

20.1.2   Pareto efficiency

Pareto improvement A division of endowment such that no one is worse off and at least one person is better off.

Pareto efficiency A division such that no further Pareto improvements exist.

In Figure 20.3, the division F lies on Liling's indifference curve through the initial division, E. However, it lies below Maya's indifference curve through E. Liling is no better off at F than at E, while Maya is definitely better off. We refer to such a change, in which at least one person is strictly better off and no one is worse off, as a **Pareto improvement**. We also note that since the indifference curves through F just touch, it would be impossible to make Liling better off without making Maya worse off. We refer to all such divisions – where indifference curves just touch, so that the intersection of preferred sets is a single division – as being **Pareto-efficient**, on the basis that

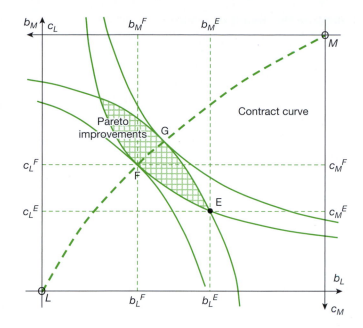

Figure 20.3 A Pareto-efficient outcome

having reached such a division it is impossible to make further Pareto improvements. Lastly, we define the **Pareto set**, which consists of all divisions of the endowment that are Pareto-efficient. In diagrams, we represent the Pareto set by the **contract curve**, which, as shown in Figure 20.3, will typically run from the bottom left to the top right corner of the diagram.

> **Pareto set (contract curve)** All divisions that are Pareto-efficient.

By yourself

X20.6   How likely do you consider it to be that Liling would accept the division of goods at F?

X20.7   Explain why division G is Pareto efficient, and discuss whether or not you consider it likely that it will be the outcome of exchange.

X20.8   The contract curve is sometimes defined as the portion of the Pareto set between F and G. Why might this be a useful definition? [*Hint*: Consider peoples' willingness to agree to any division of the endowment.]

There are at least three ways in which Liling and Maya might reach a new division of goods:

(a) One of them could impose a solution (as implied in the preceding discussion).

(b) They could negotiate an agreement. We might expect negotiations to reach a Pareto-efficient outcome on the contract curve, but without developing the theory of bargaining, we cannot easily specify the outcome.

(c) They could trade. Trade differs from negotiation, because we require the partners to fix terms of trade, agreeing the relative prices of the goods and then exchanging quantities of them. We demonstrate below that in this case both partners' marginal rate of substitution will be equal to the relative price. It then follows that the divisions, F and G, in Figure 20.3, cannot be reached by trade.

20.1.3 Exchange as the result of trade

We have claimed that point F in Figure 20.3 is one possible equilibrium division following negotiation between Liling and Maya, but that it cannot be reached by trade from the initial endowment, E. We now demonstrate this. Applying the requirement that in trade there are fixed prices, we represent the relative price of broad beans by the slope of the line EF:

$$\rho = \frac{c_L^F - c_L^E}{b_L^F - b_L^E} = \frac{c_M^F - c_M^E}{b_M^F - b_M^E} \tag{20.3}$$

In Figure 20.4, we draw a line from division E that passes through division F. Between E and F, Liling prefers all the divisions on the line to both E and F, while Maya prefers the divisions beyond F. We conclude from the diagram that, given the relative price of broad beans, ρ, Liling wishes trade to division G, while Maya would prefer trading to division, H.

Considering the preferred consumption bundles in Figure 20.4, we see that:

$$b_L^G + b_M^H > b; \text{ and } c_L^G + c_M^H < c \tag{20.4}$$

Having agreed to trade at the fixed relative price, ρ, Liling and Maya demand a greater quantity of broad beans than is in the endowment, but a smaller quantity of carrots. There is an excess demand for broad beans, but an excess supply of carrots. This cannot be an equilibrium state.

We have argued that, in any market, excess demand will be eliminated by prices increasing to the equilibrium level, $\rho^\star$, while excess supply (negative excess demand) will require a price fall to eliminate it. In this case, the relative price of broad beans, ρ, is the inverse of the relative price of carrots. By increasing ρ, broad beans become relatively more expensive for Liling and Maya, while carrots become relatively cheaper. Increasing ρ allows us to bring both markets into equilibrium. We show this in Figure 20.5, rotating the trading outcome

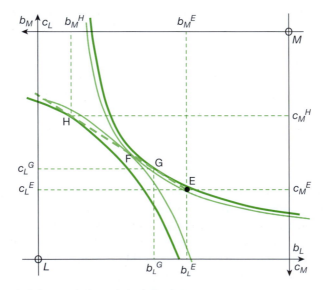

Figure 20.4 The market does not clear at market price ρ

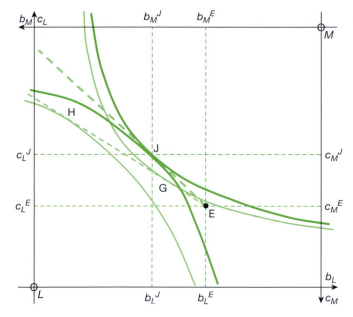

Figure 20.5 Trading to an equilibrium

line clockwise around the endowment point E. Drawing the line EJ, we see that at division J the requirement that both markets clear at the same time is satisfied. This division is Pareto-efficient and lies on the contract curve, with the relative price line EJ forming a common tangent to both curves. At division J, the relative price of broad beans, ρ^*, is equal to both Liling's and Maya's marginal rate of substitution. Given initial endowment, E, and relative price, ρ^*, they would both propose this division, J, on the basis that it maximizes their payoffs.

By yourself

X20.9   Suppose that Maya and Liling consider broad beans and carrots to be perfect complements, with their preferences represented by the utility function, $U : U(b_l, c_l) = \min(b_l, c_l)$. The total quantities of broad beans and carrots in their total endowment are equal.

(a) Explain why, in any division in which $b_L = c_L$, their indifference curves just touch.

(b) Suppose instead that Liling grows carrots and Maya grows broad beans. Using a diagram, show that if Maya can determine the division of the endowment, she can take all of Liling's carrots and offer no broad beans in return.

(c) Again, using the diagram, show that it is possible for Maya and Liling to trade to any division for which $c_L = b_L$.

X20.10 Now suppose that Maya and Liling consider carrots and broad beans to be perfect substitutes. However, while Maya would substitute 1 kg of broad beans for 1 kg of carrots, Liling would swap 2 kg of broad bean for 1 kg of carrots.

(a) Draw an Edgeworth box showing indifference curves, given that they wish to divide 12 kg of carrots and 20 kg of broad beans, and that Maya starts with all of the carrots, and Liling with all of the broad beans. On your diagram, indicate the region within which they might trade.

(Continued)

(b) Assume instead that their initial endowments are $\left(b_L^E, c_L^E\right) = (12, 6)$ and $\left(b_M^E, c_M^E\right) =$ (8, 6). Draw another Edgeworth box, and mark on it this endowment, E. Sketch the indifference curves through the endowment, and indicate the region within which trade might occur.

(c) What is the range of terms of trade which Maya and Liling might agree?

(d) Under what conditions might Liling end up with all of the carrots?

X20.11 Suppose that Maya and Liling have preferences represented by the utility function, $U : U(b_i, c_i) = b_i^{\frac{1}{3}} c_i^{\frac{2}{3}}$. The initial endowment, E: $\left(b_L^E, c_L^E\right) = (90, 0)$ and $\left(b_M^E, c_M^E\right) = (30, 120)$. Assume that they agree to trade 1 kg of carrots for 2 kg of broad beans.

(a) What is the opportunity cost of 1 kg of broad beans?

(b) Write down expressions for their marginal utility functions and their (common) marginal rate of substitution, *MRS*.

(c) Show that $MRS = -0.5$ whenever $b = c$. What do you conclude about the composition of the most preferred, affordable consumption bundle?

(d) Confirm that the division H : $\left(b_L^H, c_L^H\right) = (30, 30)$ and $\left(b_M^H, c_M^H\right) = (90, 90)$ is feasible, given the terms of trade; and that Liling's and Maya's indifference curves through H both have gradient $\rho = -0.5$.

(e) Sketch an Edgeworth box showing the endowment point; the terms of trade line; the indifference curves passing through the endowment point, E; and the indifference curves passing through the final division, H.

20.2   Trading to an optimum

In the example where goods are either perfect complements or else perfect substitutes, there is a range of relative prices, ρ, for which trade increases both participants' payoffs. Indeed, in the case of perfect complements, any choice of relative price could support one

Essential Maths 20.1: Constrained optimization, restated

We have met problems of the form:

$$\max_{(x_1, x_2)} f(x_1, x_2): g_0 - g(x_1, x_2) \geq 0 \qquad [\text{M20.1}]$$

where $y : y = f(x_1, x_2)$ is an increasing, concave function, and $g : g = g(x_1, x_2)$ is an increasing, convex function. We have solved such problems by using the method of equal gradients. The internal solution, (x_1^*, x_2^*), satisfies the conditions:

$$\left.\frac{\partial f}{\partial x_1}\right|_{(x_1^*, x_2^*)} \Big/ \left.\frac{\partial f}{\partial x_2}\right|_{(x_1^*, x_2^*)} = \left.\frac{\partial g}{\partial x_1}\right|_{(x_1^*, x_2^*)} \Big/ \left.\frac{\partial g}{\partial x_2}\right|_{(x_1^*, x_2^*)} \qquad [\text{M20.2a}]$$

$$g(x_1^*, x_2^*) = g_0 \qquad [\text{M20.2b}]$$

Expression M20.2a holds for all values of g_0, and we represent it in diagrams as the expansion path. Expression M20.2b confirms that the constraint is binding. We have generally been able to solve utility maximization and cost minimization examples by obtaining and solving the system of two equations in two variables, defined by Expression M20.2.

of the equilibrium outcomes. With perfect substitutes, though, there is no equilibrium. Instead, trade continues until one of the partners runs out of resources. These outcomes are the result of the nature of the underlying preferences.

- With perfect complements, people want to consume the goods in fixed proportions. Unless they already have a consumption bundle in which the goods have these fixed proportions, one good will be in excess supply and they would accept any terms of trade to reduce that holding.
- With perfect substitutes, trade increases utility when partners place different relative values on the goods. At any relative price that lies between the individual relative values, exchange will continue. With the partners' marginal rates of substitution remaining the same as they trade, once started there is no reason for them to stop.

Exercise X20.11 suggests that with a diminishing marginal rate of substitution, we might expect trade to lead to exactly one outcome, in which the division of the endowment has the property that the partners' marginal rates of substitution are equal to the agreed relative price. Given this relative price, both partners would choose the equilibrium division. We now develop that claim rather more formally.

20.2.1 A simple example

We now call the two partners Lukas and Michael, and consider their preferences over consumption bundles containing quantities of broad beans and carrots, as before. They have identical preferences, represented by the utility functions U_L and U_M: $U_i(b_i, c_i) = (b_i c_i)^{\frac{1}{2}}$. Lukas has grown a quantity of broad beans, b, while Michael has grown carrots, c, so that as before they only decide how to divide the endowment, (b, c). We assume that they have agreed a relative price for broad beans, ρ, so that 1 kg of broad beans will be exchanged for ρ kg of carrots.

Essential Maths 20.2: The Lagrangean function

Given the constrained maximization problem in Expression M20.1, we form the Lagrangean, Λ:

$$\Lambda(x_1, x_2, \lambda) = f(x_1, x_2) + \lambda[g_0 - g(x_1, x_2)] \qquad \text{[M20.3]}$$

The Lagrangean is a function of three variables:

- x_1 and x_2, over which the objective, f, and the constraint, g, are defined; and
- λ, the Lagrangean multiplier, which we introduce as a new variable.

We assert, without substantive proof, that if we are able to define the triple $(x_1^*, x_2^*, \lambda^*)$: $\lambda^* > 0$ which solves the problem

$$\max_{(x_1, x_2, \lambda)} \Lambda(x_1, x_2, \lambda) \qquad \text{[M20.4]}$$

then the pair (x_1^*, x_2^*) is the solution of Expression M20.1.

We shall only consider the first-order conditions for a maximum here, demonstrating that when they are satisfied, Expression M20.2 is also satisfied. (The second-order conditions required for concavity can be omitted from this discussion.)

Michael's problem

We consider Michael's problem first, ignoring Lukas's for the time being. He begins with endowment $(0, c)$ and exchanges carrots in return for some of Lukas's beans, so that he consumes (b_M^*, c_M^*). We can write Michael's objective function:

$$U_M(b_M, c_M) = (b_M c_M)^{\frac{1}{2}} \tag{20.5}$$

which Michael maximizes subject to the affordability constraint:

$$\rho b_M = (c - c_M) \tag{20.6}$$

Expression 20.6 sets out the rate at which Michael can acquire broad beans in exchange for some of his carrots. It has the same role as the expenditure constraint, introduced in Chapter 3. Expressions 20.5 and 20.6 therefore form a standard constrained optimization problem of the sort we have solved repeatedly. Applying the method of equal gradients, for the constraint:

$$\left.\frac{dc_M}{db_M}\right|_c = -\rho \tag{20.7}$$

by definition of the relative price. Considering the ratio of marginal utilities, we obtain the marginal rate of substitution:

> Applying the power rule of differentiation

> Rules of indices:
> $$\frac{1}{x^{\frac{1}{2}}} = \left(\frac{1}{x}\right)^{\frac{1}{2}}$$

$$MRS = -\frac{\partial U_M}{\partial b_M} \bigg/ \frac{\partial U_M}{\partial c_M} = -\frac{\frac{1}{2}\left(\frac{c_M}{b_M}\right)^{\frac{1}{2}}}{\frac{1}{2}\left(\frac{b_M}{c_M}\right)^{\frac{1}{2}}} = -\left[\left(\frac{c_M}{b_M}\right)^{\frac{1}{2}}\right]^2 = -\frac{c_M}{b_M} \tag{20.8}$$

Essential Maths 20.3: First-order conditions

Differentiating Expression M20.3, and setting these derivatives equal to zero:

$$\frac{\partial \Lambda}{\partial x_1} = \frac{\partial f}{\partial x_1} - \lambda^* \frac{\partial g}{\partial x_1} = 0 \tag{M20.5a}$$

$$\frac{\partial \Lambda}{\partial x_2} = \frac{\partial f}{\partial x_2} - \lambda^* \frac{\partial g}{\partial x_2} = 0 \tag{M20.5b}$$

$$\frac{\partial \Lambda}{\partial \lambda} = g_0 - g(x_1^*, x_2^*) = 0 \tag{M20.5c}$$

In Expression 20.5 all partial derivatives are evaluated at the optimum. Rewriting Expressions M20.5a and M20.5b:

$$\lambda^* = \frac{\partial f}{\partial x_1} \bigg/ \frac{\partial g}{\partial x_1} = \frac{\partial f}{\partial x_2} \bigg/ \frac{\partial g}{\partial x_2} \tag{M20.6}$$

Multiplying through Expression 20.6 by $\frac{\partial g}{\partial x_1}$, and dividing by $\frac{\partial f}{\partial x_2}$, we obtain Expression M20.2a. Adding $g(x_1^*, x_2^*)$ to both sides of Expression M20.5c, we obtain Expression M20.2b. If the pair (x_1^*, x_2^*) solves Expression M20.2, then it will also be part of the solution of Expression M20.5.

For the first-order condition to be satisfied, the marginal rate of substitution must equal the price ratio, and so equating Expressions 20.7 and 20.8:

$$\rho b_M = c_M \qquad\qquad [20.9]$$

Expression 20.9 is the expansion path, showing how Michael's preferred bundle changes with his endowment. Substituting for ρb_M in the resource constraint, Expression 20.6:

$$(b_M{}^*, c_M{}^*) = \left(\frac{c}{2\rho}, \frac{c}{2} \right) \qquad\qquad [20.10]$$

Michael gives up half of his endowment of carrots in exchange for a quantity of broad beans that has the same value in exchange. We have assigned Michael a Cobb–Douglas utility function of a form that we found in previous examples would lead to him allocating half of his expenditure to purchases of each good. The solution in Expression 20.10 is therefore consistent with that outcome.

Lukas's problem

It will be useful to write Michael's indirect utility, $V = V(b, c, \rho)$, which is the maximum utility given the endowment and the relative price, ρ:

$$V(b,c,\rho) = \left(\frac{c}{2\rho} \right)^{\frac{1}{2}} \left(\frac{c}{2} \right)^{\frac{1}{2}} = \frac{c}{2\sqrt{\rho}} \qquad\qquad [20.11]$$

We assume that Michael will insist upon reaching this utility level, which therefore becomes a constraint on Lukas's choices. As we show in Figure 20.6 (on the next page), this means that Lukas now faces two constraints:

(a) Affordability: Given the relative price, ρ, he must choose a consumption bundle in the triangle below the constraint, in the lightly shaded area of Figure 20.6.
(b) Acceptability: Michael must be able to obtain the level of utility in Expression 20.11, given Lukas's consumption. Lukas must choose a consumption bundle in Michael's preferred set, which is the more darkly shaded area in Figure 20.6.

Essential Maths 20.4: The Lagrangean multiplier

Expression M20.6 suggests that the Lagrangean multiplier, λ, indicates the rate at which relaxing the constraint to allow increased use of either input increases the value of the objective.

We define the value function, v:

$$v(g_0) = f(x_1{}^*(g_0), x_2{}^*(g_0)) = \Lambda(x_1{}^*(g_0), x_2{}^*(g_0), \lambda^*(g_0)) \qquad\qquad [M20.7]$$

The value function is the value of the objective, f, for the solution pair $(x_1{}^*, x_2{}^*)$, which depends on the constraining value, g_0. Since the constraint is always binding, $g(x_1{}^*, x_2{}^*) = g_0$, we obtain the second equality in Expression M20.7.

Differentiating Expression M20.7 with respect to g_0:

$$\frac{\partial v}{\partial g_0} = \left. \frac{\partial \Lambda}{\partial g_0} \right|_{(x_1{}^*, x_2{}^*, \lambda^*)} = \lambda^*(g_0) \qquad\qquad [M20.8]$$

As the constraining value, g_0, increases, the rate of increase of the value function is the Lagrangean multiplier, λ.

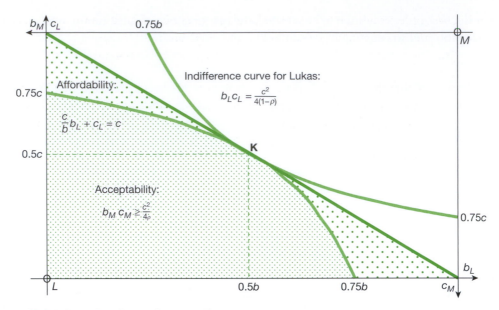

Figure 20.6 A Cobb–Douglas trading example

Essential Maths 20.5: **Multiple constraints**

We use the Lagrangean multiplier technique because it is possible to solve more general problems with it. Consider the alternative to the original problem, Expression 20.1:

$$\max_{(x_1, x_2)} f(x_1, x_2) : g_0 - g(x_1, x_2) \geq 0; h_0 - h(x_1, x_2) \geq 0 \qquad \text{[M20.9]}$$

which is the same type as Expression M20.1, but with two constraints. We form the Lagrangean, Λ:

$$\Lambda(x_1, x_2, \lambda, \mu) = f(x_1, x_2) + \lambda[g_0 - g(x_1, x_2)] + \mu[h_0 - h(x_1, x_2)] \qquad \text{[M20.10]}$$

and obtain the first order conditions for a maximum of Λ:

$$\frac{\partial \Lambda}{\partial x_1} = \frac{\partial f}{\partial x_1} - \lambda * \frac{\partial g}{\partial x_1} - \mu * \frac{\partial h}{\partial x_1} = 0 \qquad \text{[M20.11a]}$$

$$\frac{\partial \Lambda}{\partial x_2} = \frac{\partial f}{\partial x_2} - \lambda * \frac{\partial g}{\partial x_2} - \mu * \frac{\partial h}{\partial x_2} = 0 \qquad \text{[M20.11b]}$$

$$\lambda * \frac{\partial \Lambda}{\partial \lambda} = \lambda * [g_0 - g(x_1 *, x_2 *)] = 0 \qquad \text{[M20.11c]}$$

$$\mu * \frac{\partial \Lambda}{\partial \mu} = \mu * [h_0 - h(x_1 *, x_2 *)] = 0 \qquad \text{[M20.11d]}$$

Note that in Expressions M20.11c and M20.11d we multiply the partial derivative by the multiplier. With multiple constraints, not all are binding. With a slack constraint, the Lagrangean multiplier is zero.

For equilibrium, Lukas's most preferred consumption bundle satisfies both constraints. At division K, Lukas's and Michael's indifference curves just touch, with the common affordability constraint forming a tangent to both curves. We can write the equilibrium conditions as:

$$MRS_L(b_L^{\ K}, c_L^{\ K}) = MRS_M(b_M^{\ K}, c_M^{\ K}) = \rho \qquad [20.12]$$

By agreeing to trade to the division K, Lukas maximizes his own utility given his affordability constraint, while allowing Michael to trade to his own most preferred, affordable consumption bundle, given in Expression 20.10. In the diagram, we suggest that this will lead to Lukas and Michael dividing the goods equally.

By yourself

X20.12   In Figure 20.6, we suggest that Lukas and Michael will divide the endowment equally.

(a) Confirm (from Expression 20.10) that Michael's preferred bundle is half of the endowment if the relative price, $\rho = \frac{c}{b}$.

(b) Demonstrate that when the relative price, $\rho = \frac{c}{b}$, Lukas's most preferred affordable bundle $(b*, c*) = \left(\frac{b}{2}, \frac{c}{2}\right)$.

(c) Explain why we can write Lukas's problem as having two constraints: $\max_{b_L, c_L}(b_L c_L)^{½}$: $c_L = \frac{c}{b}(b - b_L)$ and $[(b - b_L)(c - c_L)]^{½} = \frac{1}{2}(bc)^{½}$. Form the Lagrangean, Θ, required to solve the problem.

(d) By obtaining the the first order conditions, confirm that $c_L* = \frac{c}{2}$.

The exchange process outlined here is very informal. Lukas and Michael meet and agree to an exchange of produce. We have shown that there is a unique relative price, ρ, at which they are able to trade to an outcome in which they maximize their payoffs subject to their affordability constraints. More generally, we treat the equilibrium of an exchange economy as a set of prices at which all markets clear simultaneously, irrespective of the number of people or the number of goods. For example, if Lukas and Michael had other goods that they wished to trade, such as onions, they would define a relative price, σ, so that 1 kg of onions would be traded for σ kg of beans. They would calculate the relative price of onions in terms of carrots as the ratio of relative prices, $\frac{\sigma}{\rho}$. It is therefore possible for us to determine relative prices or exchange ratios in an economy, using a unit of a single good as a reference.

Taking 1 kg of beans as the reference quantity, we suppose that Lukas and Michael use this as their **numeraire**, with the value of any quantity of other goods being expressed in terms of its exchange value in terms of kg of beans. The *numeraire* replaces money, emphasizing the fact that money is not by itself a good, and has no value in consumption. This arbitrarily fixes the price of one good, here $p_b = 1$. In an economy with m goods, only $m - 1$ of their prices can be determined independently.

Numeraire A good that serves as a unit of value in the economy.

20.3   Walrasian equilibrium

We have just defined the general equilibrium of an exchange economy in terms of a set of prices. We now develop this initial analysis, thinking about the way in which two people, Rachel and Sonja, reach their utility-maximizing choices. We use the fact that both Rachel and Sonja have preferred outcomes given any set of prices, and define the Walrasian equilibrium in terms of market clearing for all goods given a set of prices.

20.3.1 The offer curve

In Figure 20.7, Rachel faces the problem of finding her most preferred, affordable consumption bundle, given the feasibility constraint implied by the initial division, E, and the relative price, ρ, at which all exchanges must take place. We write Rachel's problem as:

$$\max_{b_R, c_R} U(b_R, c_R) : \rho b_R + c_R = \rho b_R^E + c_R^E \qquad [20.13]$$

We expect the usual first-order condition to be satisfied, and so at points J_1, J_2 and J_3 in Figure 20.7, Rachel proposes a division at which her indifference curve just touches the feasibility constraint associated with each price (shown in the diagram as a sequence of straight lines of increasing steepness). The curve $EJ_1J_2J_3$, which as in Chapter 7 we call the price offer curve, demonstrates how Rachel's optimal bundle changes as the relative price ρ changes. Remember that ρ is the opportunity cost of broad beans: the quantity of carrots Rachel must give up every time she increases consumption of broad beans by one unit (1 kg). As ρ increases, the slope of the constraint increases, and given the income offer curve in the diagram, she consumes more carrots and fewer broad beans.

Formalizing Rachel's problem, we form the Lagrangean, Λ:

$$\Lambda(b_R, c_R, \lambda) = U(b_R, c_R) + \lambda(\rho b_R^E + c_R^E - \rho b_R - c_R) \qquad [20.14]$$

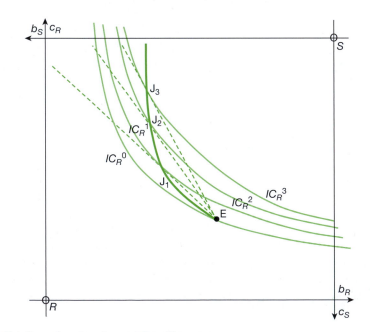

Figure 20.7 Relative price changes and the offer curve

We now write out the first-order conditions, noting that we have not specified the form of the utility function:

$$\frac{\partial \Lambda}{\partial b_R} = \frac{\partial U}{\partial b_R} - \lambda \rho = 0 \qquad [20.15a]$$

$$\frac{\partial \Lambda}{\partial c_R} = \frac{\partial U}{\partial c_R} - \lambda = 0 \qquad [20.15b]$$

$$\frac{\partial \Lambda}{\partial \lambda} = \rho b_R^{\ E} + c_R^{\ E} - \rho b_R + c_R = 0 \qquad [20.15c]$$

Equating the left-hand sides of Expressions 20.15a and 20.15b, we see that:

$$\frac{\partial U}{\partial b_R} = \rho \frac{\partial U}{\partial c_R} \text{ or that } MRS = -\frac{\partial U/\partial b_R}{\partial U/\partial c_R} = -\rho \qquad [20.16]$$

Expression 20.16 once again confirms that when Rachel maximizes her utility, her marginal rate of substitution is equal to the relative price, ρ; while Expression 20.15c demonstrates that her affordability constraint will be binding. This is simply a generalization of the argument in Section 20.2.

By yourself

X20.13   Assume that Rachel's maximization problem can be written as:

$$\max_{b_R, c_R} U(b_R, c_R) = b_R^{\ \alpha} c_R^{\ (1-\alpha)} : \rho(b_R^{\ E} - b_R) + (c_R^{\ E} - c_R) = 0$$

(a) By forming the Lagrangean or otherwise, confirm that Rachel's most preferred, affordable bundle (b_R^*, c_R^*) has the characteristic: $\frac{\alpha}{b_R^*} = \rho \frac{1-\alpha}{c_R^*}$.

(b) Hence or otherwise, demonstrate that Rachel's most preferred affordable bundle is (b_R^*, c_R^*):

$$(b_R^*, c_R^*) = \left(\alpha \left(b_R^{\ E} + \frac{c_R^{\ E}}{\rho} \right), (1-\alpha)\left(\rho b_R^{\ E} + c_R^{\ E} \right) \right)$$

(c) Show that as the relative price, ρ, increases, c_R increases, but b_R decreases.

(d) Write an expression for c_R^* in terms of b_R^*. (This is the equation of Rachel's price offer curve.)

Rachel allocates a fraction α of her endowment to financing consumption of broad beans, and a fraction $1 - \alpha$ to financing consumption of carrots. This is exactly what we would expect from previous discussion of the demand functions in Chapter 7. From Exercise X20.13c, note that the offer curve will always be downward-sloping. An increase in the relative price always leads to an increase in Rachel's demand, c_R, but a reduction in her demand, b_R.

By yourself

X20.14   Assume that Rachel continues to solve the problem in X20.13, but with the expenditure share parameter, $\alpha = \frac{1}{3}$, and initial endowments $(b_R^E, c_R^E) = (b_S^E, c_S^E) = (12, 12)$.

    (a) Obtain an expression for Rachel's optimal consumption bundle in terms of the relative price, ρ.

    (b) Show that if $\rho > 0.5$, Rachel will want to trade some of her broad beans for more carrots.

    (c) Evaluate the expression in (a) for Rachel's optimal consumption bundle for relative prices $\rho = 0.125, 0.25, 0.5, 1, 2,$ and 4. Are all of these choices feasible?

    (d) Sketch Rachel's price offer curve.

X20.15   Repeat X20.14 but for Sonja, whose utility function we write as $U(b_S, c_S) = b_S^{\frac{2}{3}} c_S^{\frac{1}{3}}$.

20.3.2   Market clearing

In Exercises X20.14 and X20.15, the price offer curves passing through the endowment are convex to the (respective) origins, as in Figure 20.8. The price offer curves indicate that as ρ increases, Rachel will substitute carrots for broad beans, and we represent this by a move upwards along the price offer curve. Sonja responds to an increase in ρ in a very similar way, although we would represent that by a move downwards along her price offer curve. Given the shape of the price offer curves in this case, they can have no more than two points of intersection. One will be the endowment, E. The other, if it exists, will be the division J_1, which they reach by trade.

At point J_1, both Rachel and Sonja maximize their utilities subject to the (common) affordability constraint. Rachel offers Sonja broad beans in return for more carrots; Sonja offers Rachel carrots, seeking broad beans in return. Both propose the same exchange rate,

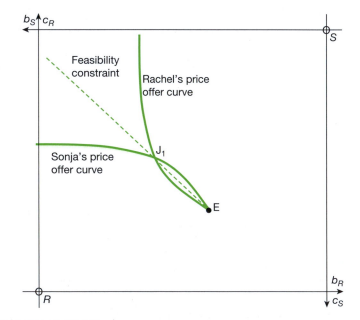

Figure 20.8 A Walrasian equilibrium

and so the markets clear. For both broad beans and carrots, the quantity supplied to the market equals the quantity demanded.

By yourself

X20.16   Given the endowments and utility function in X20.14 and X20.15, confirm that at the division $J : (b_R^J, c_R^J) = (8, 16); (b_S^J, c_S^J) = (16, 8)$ with relative price $\rho = 1$, Rachel and Sonja maximize their utilities and both markets clear.

X20.17   Suppose that the relative price increases, so that $\rho = 2$. Find Rachel's and Sonja's most preferred, feasible consumption bundles. Explain why these are not consistent with an equilibrium division.

X20.18   Repeat X20.17, but with the relative price decreasing so that $\rho = 0.5$. Without carrying out any further calculations, characterize the nature of the outcome for $\rho = 0.5$.

20.3.3   Eliminating excess demands

For both markets to clear simultaneously, the relative price has to be chosen in such a way that there are no **excess demands**. Starting from the endowment, E, in Figure 20.9, we see that for a relative price $\rho_0 : \rho_0 < \rho^*$, the shallow slope of the constraint means that it intersects Sonja's expansion path close to the left edge of the box, and Rachel's to the right of the endowment. Given the relative price, when they met Rachel would propose the division K_R, at which she would maximize her own utility, while Sonja would propose the division K_S. Both would seek to consume more than half of the

> **Excess demands** A demand for a good that is beyond the quantity in the endowment.

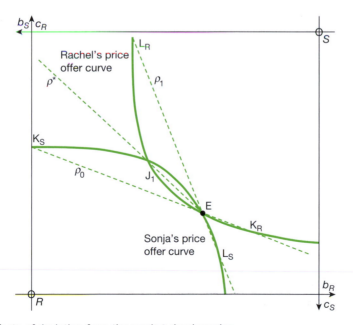

Figure 20.9 Effects of deviation from the market-clearing price

total endowment of broad beans, but even together, they would not seek to consume the whole division of carrots. At such a low relative price, there is an excess demand for broad beans, while there is excess supply (or negative excess demand) for carrots, and neither market is in equilibrium. In the same way, if we set the relative price to $\rho_1 : \rho_1 > \rho^*$ we obtain a very similar outcome, except that there is excess demand for carrots and excess supply of broad beans.

In Part II, we considered how a single person might most efficiently turn an endowment of money into a flow of utility. Here, we are considering how two people might most efficiently turn an endowment of goods into a flow of utility. In both situations, prices have an important role. As the partial equilibrium analysis of Part II indicated, if a consumer concludes that (at the margin) the cost of generating additional utility from increased consumption of one good is less than the cost of generating additional utility from consumption of a second good, then, by definition, the allocation of expenditure is not efficient. Such a consumer would increase utility by increasing consumption of the more efficient source of utility and reducing consumption of the less efficient source. To maximize utility, the consumer would necessarily increase spending on the good whose marginal consumption is considered to be the more efficient generator of utility. We see exactly the same process at work here.

- When the relative price is *less* than the market-clearing price, both Rachel and Sonja treat consumption of broad beans as a relatively cheap way of generating utility compared with consumption of carrots. Increasing the relative price reduces that effect. Reducing excess demand in the market for broad beans also reduces excess supply in the market for carrots.
- Similarly, when the relative price is *greater* than the market-clearing price, both Rachel and Sonja treat consumption of broad beans as a relatively expensive way of generating utility compared with consumption of carrots. Reducing the relative price reduces that effect. Reducing excess supply in the market for broad beans also reduces excess demand in the market for carrots.

In both cases, we see that the equilibrium is stable. The effect of price adjustment is to reduce both excess supply and excess demand.

20.3.4 Simultaneous market clearing

Walrasian equilibrium A set of prices that ensures that all markets clear at the same time.

When Rachel and Sonja meet, there is no requirement for them to rely upon market prices elsewhere: they can behave as a small exchange economy, and engage in trade at the relative price that will lead to their own, private market clearing. With the price offer curves through E both being convex to the origin for both participants, we would not expect to find more than one **Walrasian equilibrium** in which the markets clear and both Rachel and Sonja consume some positive quantity of both beans and carrots.

When Rachel and Sonja meet to trade their produce, we can imagine them going through a process in which one of them suggests a relative price, ρ, for the exchange, and both write down the amounts that they would seek to trade.

By yourself

X20.19   Continuing to use the endowments and utility functions in X20.14 and X20.15, suppose that Rachel initially proposes $\rho = 2$.
   (a) Confirm that Sonja will not wish to trade, but that Rachel would wish to acquire Sonja's endowment of carrots.
   (b) Calculate the excess demand for carrots and the excess supply of broad beans.
   (c) Repeat parts (a) and (b), assuming firstly that Sonja proposes a revised relative price, $\rho = 1.5$, and then that Rachel proposes a further revision, $\rho = 1.25$.

In the context of a 2×2 economy, this process of announcing a relative price and then seeking to enter into an exchange may seem unnecessarily complicated: we might instead expect Rachel and Sonja to make a series of offers and counter offers. In introducing the concept of an exchange economy, though, Léon Walras proposed that equilibrium prices would be obtained through a process of *tâtonnement*, or trial and error, and posited a role for an **auctioneer**, who would announce the set of relative prices for all goods, receive the amounts of each good that every person taking part in the exchange would either seek or offer, and, calculating in which markets there was either excess supply or excess demand, would either lower or raise the price for each good. In Exercise X20.19, Rachel and Sonja share the role of the auctioneer; their proposals should quickly take them to the equilibrium relative price, $\rho = 1$.

> **Auctioneer** A person who announces successive prices until declaring a set at which markets clear.

By yourself

X20.20   To prove some important results in general equilibrium theory, it is often convenient to rely upon Walras' Law: that the sum of values of excess demand across markets must be equal to zero.
   (a) Confirm that Walras' Law is satisfied in X20.19, so that at each relative price, the value of the excess demand for carrots is also the value of the excess supply of broad beans.
   (b) Given that Rachel and Sonja share a single feasibility constraint, use an Edgeworth box to demonstrate that if the market for carrots clears, the market for broad beans must also clear.
   (c) Show that if there is a Walrasian equilibrium, the division must also be Pareto-efficient.

20.4   Efficiency and equilibrium

In economics, we frequently refer to two *theorems of welfare economics*. We state these (loosely) in this way:

- Every Walrasian equilibrium is Pareto-efficient.
- There are divisions of the endowment in an exchange economy that support any possible Walrasian equilibrium.

We do not attempt to prove these theorems here. We can see that Figure 20.10 illustrates the Pareto efficiency of the Walrasian equilibrium in our examples, and we note that it follows directly from its definition. Beginning from the endowment, E, we have argued that at any given relative price, ρ, both Rachel and Sonja will propose divisions which maximize their

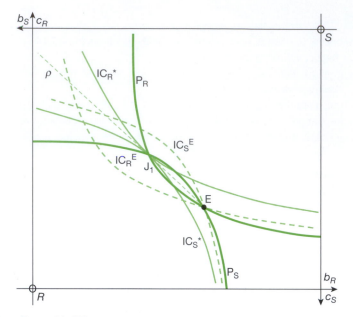

Figure 20.10 Price offer and indifference curves

own utility, and so each will choose a division on their price offer curves, P_R or P_S. We have argued that only where the price offer curves intersect (at division J_1 in Figure 20.10) can be an equilibrium division. In the diagram, we have shown that the indifference curves IC_R^* and IC_S^*, which pass through point J_1, have a common tangent whose slope is the relative price, ρ, and which passes through the endowment, E. We associate the common tangency property with Pareto efficiency: at every other division, either Rachel or Sonja (if not both of them) must have lower utility.

The second welfare theorem can be used to demonstrate how we might reach any division on the contract curve. While point J_1 in Figure 20.10 is the only efficient outcome that can be reached through trade, given the initial endowment, we show an alternative outcome in Figure 20.11. Given the initial division of the endowment, E, Rachel's share is noticeably smaller than Sonja's. She refuses to take part in trade unless she is able to obtain the payoff V_R^1, achieved on indifference curve IC_R^1 at the Pareto-efficient division, J_2. That forms a constraint for Sonja, who agrees to a two-stage process:

- Sonja transfers resources, so that trade does not begin from the initial division, E, but instead from the division, E_1.
- With the price offer curves, P_R and P_S, passing through E_1 and intersecting at J_2, Rachel and Sonja agree to trade at relative price ρ_1, so that (ρ_1, J_1) forms a Pareto-efficient Walrasian equilibrium.

In principle, then it is possible for Rachel and Sonja to achieve any equilibrium following a redivision of their endowments before trading, so that the new division will support the achievement of their desired equilibrium after trade. That is, we may associate a set of divisions, $A(J)$, and a set of prices, $\rho(J)$, with every Walrasian equilibrium, J. Trading from any division drawn from the set $A(J)$, the prices, $\rho(J)$, will clear the market. Exchange will conclude the division, J, being realized, and it will be both a Walrasian equilibrium and Pareto-efficient.

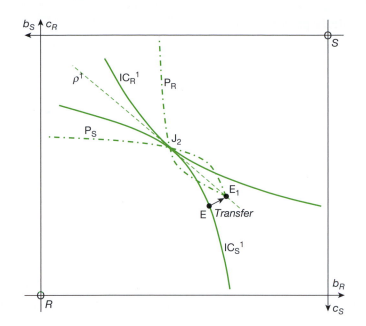

Figure 20.11 Trade after transfers

By yourself

X20.21 Using the results of X20.16, explain why we can be certain that the Walrasian equilibrium J_1 will be achieved through an exchange that begins from any division on the line $b_R + c_R = 24$.

X20.22 Assume that Rachel and Sonja have identical Cobb–Douglas preferences over consumption bundles containing broad beans and carrots:

$$U\left(b_R, c_R\right) = b_R^{\frac{1}{3}} c_R^{\frac{2}{3}}; \; U\left(b_S, c_S\right) = b_S^{\frac{1}{3}} c_S^{\frac{2}{3}}$$

with a total of 24 kg of both goods in every division.

(a) By partial differentiation, or otherwise, show that if Sonja has to meet a payoff target V_S: $V_S \geq (12)$, Rachel will propose a division in which $b_R = c_R$.

(b) Confirm that whatever division Rachel proposes, with $b_R = c_R$, her marginal rate of substitution, $-\frac{\partial U_R}{\partial b_R} \Big/ \frac{\partial U_R}{\partial c_R} = -0.5$.

(c) Hence confirm that if Sonja insists on receiving a payoff V_S, she will just meet that target if the initial endowment lies on the line $b_R + 2c_R = 36$.

X20.23 Rachel and Sonja seek to maximize their utilities, which have the same form as in X20.22. Suppose that Sonja has a utility target $V_S = 10$. Rachel's endowment $E_R = (18, 12)$; Sonja's endowment $E_S = (6, 12)$. Sketch a diagram showing (1) the initial endowment; (2) the Pareto set; (3) the relative price at which they will trade; and (4) the indifference curves (for Rachel only) at the initial endowment and after trade.

X20.24 Confirm that irrespective of her initial endowment, when Rachel's price offer curve intersects the Pareto set, $b_R = c_R$, her marginal rate of substitution, $MRS_R = -0.5$.

X20.25 What might be the policy implications of this capacity of an exchange economy to reach a competitive equilibrium from any initial division of endowments?

20.4.1 Monopoly power

We have claimed that every Walrasian equilibrium is Pareto-efficient. We have concluded that by leaving Rachel and Sonja to trade broad beans for carrots they will reach an efficient division of their endowments. They can even agree to transfer resources, so that they trade to a mutually acceptable, efficient outcome. And in doing all of this, they have been standing in for an economy in which n people exchange m goods. We should conclude that, possibly with the assistance of the auctioneer, it is in principle possible for a decentralized economy to reach a general equilibrium in which prices are set so that all markets clear. This outcome relies on the assumption that no one has large demands relative to the market, so that no one has market power.

We have already noted in our examples that were either Rachel or Sonja simply to choose the final division, each would maximize their own potential payoff by securing all of the gains from the exchange. We have argued that such a division cannot result from exchange because the common marginal rate of substitution at such a division would differ from the relative price required to reach it. It follows immediately that if Rachel or Sonja were to have monopoly power, and so could set the relative price arbitrarily, but lacked the capacity to impose the final division, the resulting equilibrium would be inefficient.

To confirm this, we turn once again to Rachel and Sonja's exchange of broad beans for carrots. In Figure 20.12, the exchange begins, as before, from the endowment E. Now, however, Rachel is able to determine the relative price, ρ^M, on her own, while Sonja proposes the final division, J_M, in order to maximize her utility, taking the relative price as given. We explain the diagram as follows:

- Rachel chooses the relative price, ρ^M, ensuring that the final division lies on the dashed line through the initial division, E, with slope, ρ^M.
- Sonja then proposes the division, J_M, at which the feasibility constraint set by Rachel meets her price offer curve, P_S.

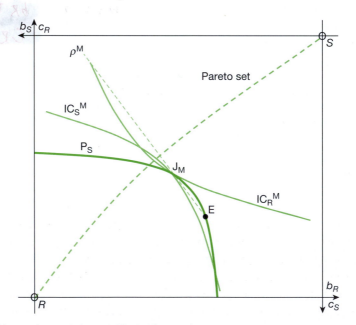

Figure 20.12 Monopoly power in quantity setting

- Rachel anticipates Sonja's decision, and so treats Sonja's price offer curve as her constraint. She therefore chooses the relative price, ρ^M, on the basis that Sonja's proposed division, J_M, is where her indifference curve, $IC_R{}^M$, touches, but does not intersect, Sonja's income offer curve, P_S.
- All of this happens away from the contract curve, and so at the division, J_M, Sonja's indifference curve, $IC_S{}^M$, intersects Rachel's indifference curve, $IC_R{}^M$. The lens that the indifference curves form above and to the left of J_M, confirms that J_M is not Pareto-efficient.

By yourself

X20.26 Using Figure 20.12, confirm that compared with the competitive equilibrium, J*, Rachel secures a larger share of the final division and so a higher utility when she is able to choose the relative price ρ^*.

X20.27 We can write Rachel's problem formally as:

$$\max_{\rho} U_R\left(b - b_S^*(b_S^E, c_S^E, \rho),\, c - c_S^*(b_S^E, c_S^E, \rho)\right),$$

$$\text{where } (b_S^*, c_S^*) : \max_{b_s, c_s} U_S(b_S, c_S) : \rho b_S + c_S = \rho b_S^E + c_S$$

(a) Set out Rachel's problem for the now familiar case in which the endowment of 24 kg of broad beans and 24 kg of carrots is divided equally between them, when Rachel's utility function $U_R(b_R, c_R) = b_R^{\frac{1}{3}} c_R^{\frac{2}{3}}$, and Sonja's utility function $U_S(b_S, c_S) = b_S^{\frac{2}{3}} c_S^{\frac{1}{3}}$.

(b) Solve Sonja's maximization problem, defining her demands b_S and c_S in terms of the relative price, ρ. Note: you can use the expressions for demands obtained in Chapter 9, to simplify calculations.

(c) Hence, solve Rachel's maximization problem, defining the relative price, ρ^M, so that Rachel maximizes her utility.

(d) Compare the outcome in parts (b) and (c) with the Walrasian equilibrium when prices are set competitively, confirming that with Rachel able to set the relative price, it is now higher, that Rachel's share of the endowment (and so her payoff) has increased, but that Sonja is worse off. Confirm that the monopoly outcome is not Pareto optimal.

X20.28 Repeat X20.27, but replacing the utility functions and endowments:
(a) Rachel: utility, $U_R(b_R, c_R) = b_R^{\frac{1}{3}} c_R^{\frac{2}{3}}$, endowment $E_R = (18, 12)$;
 Sonja: utility, $U_S(b_S, c_S) = b_S^{\frac{1}{3}} c_S^{\frac{2}{3}}$, endowment $E_S = (6, 12)$.
(b) Rachel: utility, $U_R(b_R, c_R) = b_R^{\frac{1}{2}} c_R^{\frac{1}{2}}$, endowment $E_R = (24, 0)$;
 Sonja: utility, $U_S(b_S, c_S) = b_S^{\frac{1}{2}} c_S^{\frac{1}{2}}$, endowment $E_S = (0, 24)$.

20.5 Conclusions

One of the most important claims of economic theory is that an economy does not need any form of central direction to set prices. In this chapter, we have illustrated this claim for the special case of an exchange economy: that is, one in which no production takes place and people simply trade goods and services at prices that are set so that all markets clear simultaneously. We have argued that where markets are not in such a Walrasian equilibrium, price adjustments are possible to resolve that. We have also demonstrated that it would be impossible to change the final division of an endowment without making at least one person worse off. Every Walrasian equilibrium is therefore Pareto-efficient.

Our last two examples are the start of important generalizations of this basic model. We argued that it is possible for people voluntarily to transfer resources to other people, and then to rely on trade to ensure that the final distribution of resources is efficient. We observe such transfers regularly. Within a family, parents make transfers to their children, who are then able to afford consumption patterns that they would not otherwise. In economics, we are interested to observe governments effecting such transfers, as when raising taxes that are then paid out in transfers to people who have low incomes. Using our understanding of the exchange economy, we might argue against transfers being made in kind, on the basis that it is most efficient for people simply to be given money with which they can finance consumption.

We also saw that our arguments about efficiency are dependent on there being no impediments to perfectly competitive outcomes. Where there is market power, we saw that the volume of goods that will be traded is less; and that while markets will clear, people with market power will be better off than when they face perfect competition, while people who lack it will be worse off. We cannot easily say that society is worse off, but the reduction in the volume of exchange ensures that the outcome is not Pareto-efficient, and it should therefore be possible to improve on these outcomes.

Summary

In an exchange economy, there is no production. People trade part of their endowment of goods and services at a set of prices, which ensures that markets clear.

The simplest exchange economy involves two people trading quantities of two goods. We can illustrate the process and the outcomes in an Edgeworth box, whose dimensions are the total endowment of the goods, and in which each point in the box represents a division of that endowment.

Divisions are Pareto-efficient if it is impossible to increase the payoff that one person in the economy achieves without reducing someone else's payoff. There is typically a continuum of Pareto-efficient divisions, which are represented in diagrams by the contract curve.

Markets clear when the excess demand is zero. When all markets clear simultaneously, there is a Walrasian equilibrium. When there is excess demand, prices rise (and when there is negative excess demand, or excess supply, prices rise). These effects bring the economy to a Walrasian equilibrium, which is Pareto-efficient.

There is a set of initial endowments and a set of prices that will support the emergence of every Walrasian equilibrium. We can therefore achieve every Walrasian equilibrium by appropriate transfers of resources before allowing exchange to occur.

Where some people have market power, they will use that to improve their own outcome from the exchange. In doing so, they distort prices, so that the final division is not Pareto-efficient and a Walrasian equilibrium is not reached.

Visit the companion website at **www.palgrave.com/mochrie** to access further teaching and learning materials, including lecturer slides and a testbank, as well as guideline answers and student MCQs.

21

Production and distribution

The standard model incorporates exchange, but also involves firms undertaking *production*, while people buy goods to generate utility. It is therefore sensible to extend our model of exchange to allow for production. In the context of a general equilibrium model, we drop the assumption that people have an endowment of money, assigning them instead an endowment of factors of production. People hire out their endowments to firms, who are then able to produce the output which they sell to people.

Throughout this chapter, we concentrate on the *efficiency* characteristics of outcomes. Our ultimate objective is the identification of conditions that give rise to the highest possible social welfare, which we define as a function of all individual utilities. Efficiency here implies trading off increases in one person's utility against reductions in another person's. The levels of utility that people can achieve will depend upon the consumption bundles that they can afford. Affordability depends upon the prices of goods, and the income that people can generate from hiring out factors of production.

In addition, though, the affordability of any consumption bundle depends upon total output of each consumption good, and this depends upon the allocation of factors inputs within production activities. We shall derive efficiency conditions for all of these situations, associating efficiency with the maximization of target variables.

We conclude by noting that there is nothing in the achievement of efficiency that implies equity in the *distribution* of final consumption. The mathematics of efficiency will hold equally well when one person consumes all output as when all people enjoy equal shares of output. We also note that it is in principle possible to increase social welfare by means of a *redistribution* of goods, but that if this redistribution is funded by the taxation of flows of money, it will lead to a loss of efficiency. This opens up the possibility that redistribution, while leading to a more equitable outcome, may end up reducing social welfare, so that people would prefer to retain the market-based distribution. Only lump-sum taxes, such as a poll tax, avoid this effect.

21.1 Production in general equilibrium

In Chapter 20, we considered behaviour within a model of exchange. While most of our examples involved a 2×2 model, they might easily be extended to analyse an economy in which n people, each seeking to maximize their own utility, trade quantities of m goods. To complete our general equilibrium analysis, we extend our model to include production, a process that requires the use of f factors of production. These factors are owned by people, but are then hired out to businesses, which use them to produce final goods for consumption.

In this chapter, we treat factors of production as one class of goods, used to produce the other class of final goods, which are the only sources of utility. In effect, this adds one step to our analysis of the generation of utility, so that we can, at least in principle, trace the whole circular flow of goods and services within an economy of given productive capacity. We concentrate on the efficiency conditions characterizing Walrasian equilibrium in the $2 \times 2 \times 2$ model in which two people rent out two factors of production, used to produce two final goods, while remembering that similar results would hold in an $n \times f \times m$ model with n people hiring out f factors of production, used to produce m final goods. The $2 \times 2 \times 2$ model is the simplest way of demonstrating the conditions that would hold in a more complete analysis, and, as before, allows us to illustrate our arguments using diagrams.

Rather than work with relative prices, as we did in Chapter 20, in this chapter we will use (nominal) prices. We note, from Walras' Law, that with two consumption goods and two factor inputs, there will be a total of four markets, but in only three of these will prices be set independently. Once we find a set of prices in which any three markets are in equilibrium, with supply equal to demand, it must be the case that the fourth market will be in equilibrium. This allows us to use one good as a *numeraire*, setting its price to one.

In Part III, we assumed that businesses are formed to produce goods and services. Here, we will see that businesses are in effect a convenient fiction, doing nothing more than coordinating a set of exchanges. In very small businesses, such as a café, or a florist, or a plumber, or a blacksmith, it is not unusual for a single person to provide all factor inputs. In the context of our approach here, such a business would be identical with the owner. We continue to assume that businesses seek to maximize profits: that is, the difference between the total revenue received from sales and the payments made to factors of production. In this chapter, we require all revenue to be passed on to factors of production, so that the maximum profit will be zero. To ensure this, in our $2 \times 2 \times 2$ models we assume that the firms' production functions exhibit constant returns to scale, since there will only be one firm in each market. In more general models, it would be possible simply to treat the zero-profit condition as being consistent with long-run equilibrium in perfectly competitive markets.

21.1.1   Robinson Crusoe

Before introducing the $2 \times 2 \times 2$ model, we consider the 'Robinson Crusoe' economy, a $1 \times 1 \times 1$ model in which one person hires out a single factor of production, used to produce a single good. In Daniel Defoe's novel of 1719, the hero, Robinson Crusoe, is shipwrecked and must survive by himself on an island. Here, we imagine Crusoe dividing his time between productive and leisure activities. It will be convenient to assume that there are two sides to his character: Robinson, who performs the work, and who also enjoys the leisure; and Mr Crusoe, who is effectively the owner of the island. Every day, Robinson and Mr Crusoe agree the terms of trade between them for the exchange of labour time for fish, the only good that Robinson consumes. We treat labour time as a factor of production; it therefore yields no utility to Robinson, but it does eat into his leisure time, which is costly. The final good in the model, fish, is a source of utility; and so Mr Crusoe, who owns the fishery, compensates Robinson for his labour time by giving him fish. Separating production from consumption in this way, we concentrate on the exchange rate between labour time and fish caught. We therefore predict that Robinson will maximize his utility by fishing until the costs, in terms of leisure forgone, and the benefits, in terms of fish consumed, are equal at the margin.

By yourself

X21.1 Suppose Robinson has a diminishing marginal product of labour, while he requires an increasing rate of compensation for his labour, on the basis that his preferences over combinations of leisure time and fish are well behaved.

(a) Sketch a diagram representing the total quantity of fish that Robinson can catch (as a function of labour time); and (at least) three separate indifference curves representing levels of preference over combinations of labour time and fish, one of which just touches the total quantity curve.

(b) Define the agreed wage w as the number of fish that Mr Crusoe gives Robinson per hour of labour time. Assume that Mr Crusoe will also pay Robinson a retainer – a quantity of fish, $F_0 = F(0)$, in addition to the wage paid for fishing. Sketch straight lines on your diagram showing the minimum wage that Robinson must be offered to reach each of the three indifference curves. Decide whether or not the implied production plans are feasible.

(c) On a separate diagram, show that the optimal outcome has the characteristics that:

   (i) the marginal rate of substitution of fish for labour time is equal to the marginal product of labour time, and also the agreed exchange rate for fish for additional effort (the wage);

   (ii) the total compensation which Mr Crusoe offers Robinson is the whole catch of fish;

   (iii) Mr Crusoe maximizes profit by just breaking even; and

   (iv) Robinson maximizes utility given the production constraint.

In some ways, there is nothing unexpected to see here. The main characteristics of the solution appear in Figure 21.1. We make the usual assumption of diminishing marginal product: the more time that Robinson Crusoe spends fishing, the more he will catch, but the rate at which he catches fish will fall. We also argue that his indifference curves should be upward-sloping, but convex. This captures the idea that he values both leisure time and

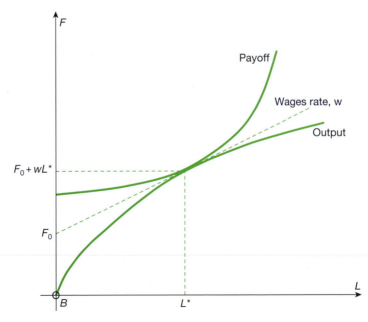

Figure 21.1 The Robinson Crusoe outcome

consumption of fish. We also see the retainer, which Mr Crusoe either keeps or passes on, as the intercept of the wage line with the vertical axis. It is the return on Mr Crusoe's capital. The 'wage income' is wL^*, and the wage rate, w, is the slope of the wage line.

The solution that emerges from trade, in terms of labour time and fish caught, would also emerge if Robinson were simply maximizing utility subject to the production constraint. Robinson works until the marginal product of effort equals the wage rate. At that wage rate, the marginal rate of substitution between leisure and fish is also equal to the wage rate. So, the marginal benefit and the marginal cost of fishing are equal. The advantage of the division that we set out here is that we assume Mr Crusoe brings the small amount of physical capital needed for the business – a boat, nets, lines, and hooks. Without Mr Crusoe's management, Robinson would have very limited fishing opportunities, so that it is quite reasonable that that Mr Crusoe should receive a share of the proceeds of the activity.

21.2   A two-person, two-factor, two-good model

Robinson Crusoe's problem provides us with a useful starting point for understanding how production and consumption activities will be related in a general equilibrium approach. We now introduce the $2 \times 2 \times 2$ model, which is the simplest model of an economy in which we can identify all conditions associated with a general equilibrium. We shall assume that production takes place within businesses, rather than allowing people to interact directly. We turn our attention to Richard and Seth, whose initial endowment, E, of capital, and labour (K, L), is divided so that:

$$K = K_R{}^E + K_S{}^E; \text{ and } L = L_R{}^E + L_S{}^E \qquad [21.1]$$

We assume that Richard and Seth set up businesses, a little like Robinson Crusoe in the previous example, with Richard's bakery producing bread and Seth's creamery producing cheese. We shall assume that their businesses are incorporated, so that they have legal identities separate from Richard and Seth. We therefore require the businesses to hire the factors of production that they need to operate. It would of course be possible for each business simply to hire its founder's endowment, but we would generally expect it to be more efficient for them to find a different allocation at which both firms would be able to increase production. Also, for efficiency, we shall assume that factor endowments are fully employed: this will certainly be the case if marginal products are always positive. As set out in the theory of production in Chapter 10, we assume that the firms have production functions, so that their outputs are (b, c), with $b = b(K_B, L_B)$, for the bakery, and $c : c = c(K - K_B, L - L_B)$ for the creamery. Production is of course technically efficient and there is no wastage of inputs.

In terms of its diagrammatic presentation, the problem of how firms should use their resources can be presented in much the same way as the problem of exchange, introduced in Section 20.1. With the whole endowment being used in production, we can represent any division of factors as a point within an Edgeworth box, as shown in Figure 21.2, whose dimensions are the total endowments of each factor. We might say that at the initial division, point E, the bakery hires Richard's endowment of capital and labour, while the creamery hires Seth's endowment. It might seem that all we are doing here is to complicate the

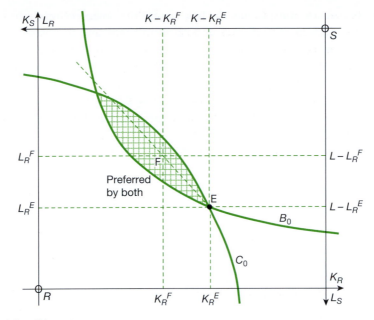

Figure 21.2 A feasible outcome

structure of the Robinson Crusoe economy, but we shall discuss a more general structure for the division of factor inputs shortly.

Since the businesses have their own identities, they *hire* the factors of production: Richard and Seth do not simply gift or lend them freely. At division E, both businesses pay the input owners the (market) prices, w_K and w_L, for the capital and labour that they hire. We next assume that Richard's and Seth's endowments of each factor are perfect substitutes. They can be used equally effectively in either business, ensuring that they will be hired at the same price when there is equilibrium.

By yourself

X21.2 If the bakery and the creamery operate in perfectly competitive markets, why might they decide not to use their founders' endowments of labour and capital?

X21.3 Suppose that Richard concludes that he could run the bakery more efficiently with less capital and more labour, while Seth would prefer to hire more capital and less labour. How might they be able to trade their endowments so that both firms can increase their output?

In a more complex model, with many firms, all facing perfectly competitive markets, we expect that in the long run, production will be economically efficient, with all firms operating at the most efficient scale. With perfectly competitive markets, profits are then eliminated and the average cost of production is minimized. In the long run, then, every firm has a finite demand for factors of production, and these demands are functions of their output.

In the case that we are considering, the bakery and the creamery might hire additional factor inputs if their founders' endowments were insufficient, and they would be able to do that in the market for these factors. In the same way, were their endowments not to be fully employed in their own businesses, Richard and Seth could hire out their unused factors. With only two firms, the only possibility is for Richard and Seth, in effect on behalf of their businesses, to exchange factors of production. In Figure 21.2, we show the creamery hiring some of Richard's capital, and the bakery hiring some of Seth's labour.

21.2.1 Efficiency conditions in production

In Figure 21.2, we draw isoquants, B_0 and C_0, through the division, E, which represents the initial division of factors. The isoquants show all combinations of factor inputs at which the firms might produce the same output as at E. Repeating an argument, which should be familiar from Chapter 20, since these isoquants cross, at any allocation represented by a point within the lens formed by the isoquants, both firms would be able to increase their output by trading some of their factors of production. Undertaking production at the endowment, E, firms achieve technical efficiency but not Pareto efficiency. An allocation such as F is therefore Pareto-improving. As in Chapter 20, we see immediately that Pareto efficiency requires an allocation for which the isoquants touch, rather than forming a lens.

Continuing to apply the argument from Chapter 20, suppose that the firms agree to trade factors of production, paying the same market prices, w_K and w_L, as they have already paid to rent the factors from Richard and Seth. For the allocation to be feasible, the rental values of the capital and the labour being traded are the same. The bakery can hire any combination of factors, (K_B, L_B) for which

$$w_K(K_B - K_B^E) + w_L(L_B - L_B^E) = 0 \qquad [21.2]$$

so that, at allocation F in Figure 21.2, Richard's income from renting capital, $K_B^E - K_B^J$, to the creamery exactly balances the cost of that the bakery must pay for hiring the additional labour, $L_B^J - L_B^E$. (We might also express this constraint in terms of Seth's income from renting out labour to the bakery being the same as the cost to the creamery of hiring additional capital.) Thus in Figure 21.2, we see the bakery and the creamery, and indeed Richard and Seth, agreeing to trade factor inputs. We might characterize this agreement in two ways:

- The bakery agrees to invest in the creamery, providing it with capital, while the creamery agrees to second its employee-owner, Seth, to work in the bakery. The creamery pays the bakery the interest on capital, which is then passed on to Richard; and the bakery pays the creamery the additional wages, which are then transferred on to Seth.
- Seth and Richard agree to exchange factor inputs directly, with Seth working with Richard in the bakery, and Richard providing Seth with capital which he uses in the creamery. The problem then seems very similar to the model of exchange introduced in Chapter 20.

We may wish to argue that businesses typically do not start from their owners' endowments, but will always hire all necessary input factors in markets. Within our simple $2 \times 2 \times 2$ model, this is not possible. We might expect that Richard and Seth would sit down together and agree how to use their resources most effectively.

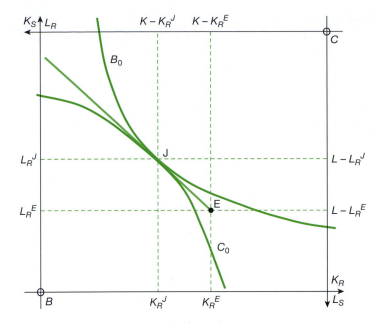

Figure 21.3 A Pareto-efficient allocation, reached by trade

Suppose that we define a Pareto-efficient allocation, J. We show such an outcome in Figure 21.3, in which, starting from an initial division of the endowment, which is hired by the bakery and the creamery from their owners, there is an exchange of factors. The exchange rate is represented by the slope of the line EJ, and is the ratio of input prices used by the both firms. In the Pareto-efficient allocation, J, the gradient of both firms' isoquants are equal to the relative input price. We use the notation of Chapter 10, defining the gradient of the isoquants, which is the marginal rate of technical substitution, as the ratio of marginal products. Then, for the bakery and the creamery:

$$MRTS^B = -\frac{MP_K^B}{MP_L^B} = -\frac{w_K}{w_L}; \text{ and } MRTS^C = -\frac{MP_K^C}{MP_L^C} = -\frac{w_K}{w_L} \qquad [21.3]$$

Whenever the allocation is Pareto-efficient, all firms hire inputs so that their marginal rate of technical substitution is the same. As in Figure 21.3, the isoquants just touch at division J, confirming that it is impossible to increase one firm's output without reducing the other's output. It is useful to rewrite Expression 21.3 in this alternative formulation:

$$\frac{MP_K^B}{w_K} = \frac{MP_L^B}{w_L} \text{ and } \frac{MP_K^C}{w_K} = \frac{MP_L^C}{w_L} \qquad [21.4]$$

Expression 21.4 is essentially the same condition as Expression 10.8, obtained in solving the resource allocation problem in a partial equilibrium approach. It confirms that at the margin, the return to expenditure is the same for both factors, and so neither firm can increase its output by varying its use of factor inputs, given the market-clearing constraint in Expression 21.2. At the Pareto-efficient allocation, production is economically efficient.

By yourself

X21.4 Suppose that the bakery has a production function $b(K_B, L_B) = K_B^{\frac{1}{3}}L_B^{\frac{2}{3}}$, while the creamery has production function $c(K_C, L_C) = K_C^{\frac{2}{3}}L_C^{\frac{1}{3}}$. Set out the firms' production problems where the total endowment, (K, L), is divided equally between them, and obtain the Pareto-efficient outcomes.

X21.5 Repeat X21.4, but replacing the production functions and endowments:
(a) Bakery: production, $b(K_B, L_B) = K_B^{\frac{1}{3}}L_B^{\frac{2}{3}}$; endowment, $E_B = (18, 12)$;
Creamery: production, $c(K_C, L_C) = K_C^{\frac{2}{3}}L_C^{\frac{1}{3}}$; endowment, $E_C = (6, 12)$.
(b) Bakery: production, $b(K_B, L_B) = K_B^{\frac{1}{2}}L_B^{\frac{1}{2}}$; endowment, $E_B = (24, 0)$;
Creamery: production, $c(K_C, L_C) = K_C^{\frac{1}{2}}L_C^{\frac{1}{2}}$; endowment, $E_C = (0, 24)$.

21.2.2 Profit maximization

To tie together production and consumption, we formalize the problem facing the bakery and the creamery. As firms, they wish to maximize profits, although we have already argued that in equilibrium there are no supernormal profits. The firms can sell any quantity of output at constant prices, p_b for the bakery, and p_c for the creamery:

$$\pi^B = p_b b(K^B, L^B) - w_K K^B - w_L L^B; \text{ and}$$

$$\pi^C = p_c c(K^C, L^C) - w_K K^C - w_L L^C = p_c c(K - K^B, L - L^B)$$
$$- w_K(K - K^B) - w_L(L - L^B) \tag{21.5}$$

These are not separate problems, given the assumption of full employment of resources. The whole of the endowment, except for the resources used in the bakery, is used in the creamery. Applying arguments developed in Chapter 20, this will be true so long as the production function is always increasing in both factors. We now partially differentiate the profit functions:

$$\frac{\partial \pi^B}{\partial K^B} = p_b \frac{\partial b}{\partial K^B} - w_K = 0; \text{ and } \frac{\partial \pi^B}{\partial L^B} = p_b \frac{\partial b}{\partial L^B} - w_L = 0$$

$$\frac{\partial \pi^C}{\partial K^B} = -p_c \frac{\partial c}{\partial K^B} + w_K = 0; \text{ and } \frac{\partial \pi^C}{\partial L^B} = -p_c \frac{\partial c}{\partial L^B} + w_L = 0 \tag{21.6}$$

This result depends on the full employment condition, since capital, K, is divided so that $K^C = K - K^B$, and the marginal product, $MP_K^C = \frac{\partial c}{\partial K^C} = -\frac{\partial c}{\partial K^B}$; and in the same way, $MP_L^C = \frac{\partial c}{\partial L^C} = -\frac{\partial c}{\partial L^B}$. This rather minor, technical result is very helpful because it means that we know how output in the creamery will change as factor usage in the bakery changes. Four useful results follow from Expression 21.6.

- The partial derivatives of output with respect to the factor inputs are the marginal products. Rearranging very slightly, we see that the conditions for Pareto efficiency in Expression 21.3 hold.
- Noting that the first term in each derivative is a product of the price of a good and the marginal product of a factor, which we define as the value of its marginal product, we rewrite the expression as:

$$\frac{\partial \pi^B}{\partial K^B} = VMP_K^B - w_K = 0; \text{ and } \frac{\partial \pi^B}{\partial L^B} = VMP_L^B - w_L = 0$$

$$\frac{\partial \pi^C}{\partial K^B} = -VMP_K^C + w_K = 0; \text{ and } \frac{\partial \pi^C}{\partial L^B} = -VMP_L^C + w_L = 0 \qquad [21.7]$$

At the margin, the rate at which revenue increases with the use of a factor input is also the rate at which costs increase. With constant returns of scale in production, marginal and average products are equal; and the firms both make zero (economic) profits, with the payments to the ultimate factor owners, Richard and Seth, equal to the firms' revenues.

• Next, we see that:

$$w_K = p_b \frac{\partial b}{\partial K^B} = p_c \frac{\partial c}{\partial K^C}; \text{ and } w_L = p_b \frac{\partial b}{\partial L^B} = p_c \frac{\partial c}{\partial L^C} \qquad [21.8]$$

We have again used the full employment condition, expressed in the form, $\frac{dK^C}{dK^B} = -1$. Expression 21.8 confirms that around a Pareto-efficient allocation, a change in the distribution of capital between the creamery, of size δK^B (or $-\delta K^C$) leads to a total change in revenues across the firms:

$$p_b \frac{\partial b}{\partial K^B} \delta K^B + p_c \frac{\partial c}{\partial K^C} \delta K^C = 0 \qquad [21.9]$$

The increase in the bakery's revenue from the increased use of capital, δK^B, matches the fall in the creamery's revenue. (In addition, starting from a Pareto-efficient allocation, the increase in the bakery's costs will be exactly equal to the reduction in the creamery's costs, confirming that at a Pareto-efficient allocation, both firms maximize their profits given resources.)

• Lastly, writing Expression 21.9 in terms of changes in output, we see that:

$$\frac{\frac{\partial b}{\partial K^B} \delta K^B}{\frac{\partial c}{\partial K^C} (\delta K^C)} = \frac{\frac{\partial b}{\partial L^B} \delta L^B}{\frac{\partial c}{\partial L^C} (\delta L^C)} = \frac{db}{dc} = -\frac{p_c}{p_b} \qquad [21.10]$$

In the first equality, we consider the effects of small changes in inputs on outputs. These give us a measure of the rate of change of outputs conditional on production remaining Pareto-efficient, which we can show in a diagram as a movement along the contract curve. Given the assumptions of perfect competition in product and factor markets, the expression indicates that at the profit-maximizing distribution, the rate at which production of bread would decrease as production of cheese increases is given by the ratio of the goods' prices. We infer from Expression 21.10 that around a Pareto-efficient allocation:

$$p_b db = -p_c dc \qquad [21.11]$$

As one firm expands its output, and hence its revenues, there will be an equal reduction in the other firm's revenues. It is this last result that enables us to link production and exchange.

As in Chapter 20, we might argue that there is a contradiction between the two ways in which we approach this problem. When we think of a single firm on its own, we treat it as going to the market and hiring factors of production at fixed prices: at this level, it does not matter that Richard is a baker, or Seth a cheesemaker. The firms simply hire factor inputs from Richard and Seth. Considering the economy as a whole, we have to be a little more careful. In Chapter 14, we argued that while one firm can take the price of both input factors and final goods as given, within the industry as a whole, prices are determined by the interaction of market supply and market demand. The same is true here. When we think of the bakery and the creamery as single firms, we treat them as price takers. But considering the economy as a whole, this can no longer be the case. There has to be a balance of supply and demand across the economy. Resources will flow, through the process of *tâtonnement*, to locations where they can be used most effectively. New businesses will enter the market, while others, already producing goods, can change the scale of their activities, or else shut down entirely. Given our treatment of profit maximization, firms will not wish to expand beyond the most efficient scale. But also, given the fact that resources are always productive, we would expect to see the entry of businesses until resources are fully employed.

21.2.3   The Pareto set and the production possibility frontier

In Figure 21.3, we constructed division J by allowing firms to trade production factors at their market prices. From the diagram, we see immediately that they were both able to increase their output and, given that they face constant prices, their revenues: division J lies in the lens formed by the isoquants through E. On the factor trade line, EJ, costs for both firms remain constant, so that the increase in revenues is also an increase in profits. We might also note that the firms' resource allocations between capital and labour at division J ensure that they produce the greatest possible output subject to the common affordability constraint. As when we consider the exchange of goods, we can be certain that when firms maximize profits simultaneously, the allocation of factor inputs will be Pareto-efficient.

> **Production possibility frontier** A curve formed from just feasible output combinations.

When firms maximize their profits, the allocation of factor inputs lies in the Pareto set, as shown in Figure 21.4a. For all allocations in the Pareto set, it is impossible to increase production of either good without also reducing production of the other one. We capture this fact in Figure 21.4b, where we show the **production possibility frontier**.

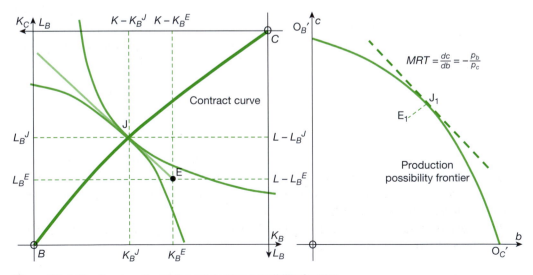

Figure 21.4 The Pareto set and the production possibility frontier

This curve shows the combinations of output that are achievable, given the total endowment. We show it as a downward-sloping, concave curve, which is consistent with the presence of diminishing returns to scale in production. Its intersection on the vertical axis represents point O_B in the Edgeworth box, with all resources being used to produce cheese; while its intersection on the horizontal axis represents point O_C, with bread being the only output. Point J_1 on the curve represents the product mix at allocation J. Point E_1, representing allocation E, lies inside the curve because it is not Pareto-efficient. The effect of the reallocation of resources from E to J in Figure 21.4a is shown in Figure 21.4b by the increased output, and therefore in more efficient factor input use. Lastly, we refer to the slope of the frontier, $\frac{dc}{db}$, as the **marginal rate of transformation**. This is a measure of the rate at which cheese production must fall as bread production increases, and we have already shown in Expression 21.11 that:

> **Marginal rate of transformation** A rate at which output of one good falls as output of another increases.

$$MRT = \frac{dc}{db} = -\frac{p_b}{p_c}$$

[21.12]

21.2.4 Production and exchange

The result is interesting because we can relate it our analysis in Chapter 20. Recall the examples in which Rachel and Sonja exchanged goods. They established an exchange rate, ρ, for the goods and then traded to a Pareto-efficient allocation, so that in any optimal allocation, $MRS_R = MRS_S = \rho$. Understanding the exchange rate as an opportunity cost, we now define it as the price ratio, $-\frac{p_b}{p_c}$. When firms maximize profits, they all undertake production efficiently. The marginal rate of transformation, the rate at which the creamery has to reduce production as the bakery increases its output, also equals the relative price. Having discussed the firms as profit maximizers, we can finish off our analysis by considering Richard and Seth as utility-maximizing consumers, and we approach this expecting to find that the price ratio has an important role in the discussion. Unlike Rachel and Sonja, who simply relied upon an endowment of goods, Richard and Seth depend upon the income derived from hiring out their endowment of factor inputs to firms to purchase goods. We continue to assume that firms make zero (economic) profits, so that Richard's and Seth's factor income is equal to the market value of the outputs available for purchase. Then:

$$p_b b + p_c c = w_k K + w_L L = M$$

[21.13]

where M is the market value of the total endowment of factor inputs, from which we can calculate the maximum quantity of each good, which Richard and Seth (together) might consume. Note that we do not know anything about the individual endowments, only about the total endowment and its market value.

We now repeat the analysis of exchange in Chapter 20, but incorporating production. We write Richard's utility function u^R as:

$$u^R = u^R(b^R, c^R)$$

[21.14]

Richard seeks to maximize his utility, subject to the constraint that Seth, who consumes everything that Richard leaves, is able to reach a utility constraint, u_0^S. For utility, u^S, expressed in terms of the total output achieved given the allocation of factor inputs between the bakery and the creamery:

$$u^S\left[b(K^B, L^B) - b^R, c(K - K^B, L - L^B) - c^R\right] \geq u_0^{\ S} \qquad [21.15]$$

Forming the Lagrangean Θ:

$$\Theta = u^R(b^R, c^R) + \theta\left\{u^S\left[b(K^B, L^B) - b^R, c(K - K^B, L - L^B) - c^R\right] - u_0^S\right\} \qquad [21.16]$$

Partially differentiating with respect to b^R and c^R, we obtain first-order conditions:

$$\frac{\partial\Theta}{\partial b^R} = \frac{\partial u^R}{\partial b^R} - \theta\frac{\partial u^S}{\partial b^R} = 0; \text{ and } \frac{\partial\Theta}{\partial c^R} = \frac{\partial u^R}{\partial c^R} - \theta\frac{\partial u^S}{\partial c^R} = 0 \qquad [21.17]$$

Rearranging the first-order conditions in Expression 21.17, we see that when they are satisfied:

$$MRS^R = -\frac{\partial u^R}{\partial b^R}\bigg/\frac{\partial u^R}{\partial c^R} = -\frac{\partial u^S}{\partial b^S}\bigg/\frac{\partial u^S}{\partial c^S} = MRS^S \qquad [21.18]$$

so Richard and Seth have the same marginal rate of substitution. Next, going back to the Lagrangean, and partially differentiating with respect to the factor inputs:

$$\frac{\partial\Theta}{\partial K^B} = \theta\left\{\frac{\partial u^S}{\partial b^S}\cdot\frac{\partial b}{\partial K^B} - \frac{\partial u^S}{\partial c^S}\cdot\frac{\partial c}{\partial K^B}\right\} = 0; \text{ and } \frac{\partial\Theta}{\partial L^B} = \theta\left\{\frac{\partial u^S}{\partial b^S}\cdot\frac{\partial b}{\partial L^B} - \frac{\partial u^S}{\partial c^S}\cdot\frac{\partial c}{\partial L^B}\right\} = 0 \ \ [21.19]$$

Interpreting the multiplier, θ, as the marginal value of slackening the constraint, then, given the assumption of well-behaved preferences, $\theta > 0$. Rewriting Expression 21.19, we obtain:

$$\frac{\partial u^S}{\partial b^S}\bigg/\frac{\partial u^S}{\partial c^S} = \left(\frac{\partial b}{\partial K^B}\bigg/\frac{\partial c}{\partial K^C}\right) = \left(\frac{\partial b}{\partial L^B}\bigg/\frac{\partial c}{\partial L^C}\right) = 0 \qquad [21.20]$$

The first term in Expression 21.20 is Seth's marginal rate of substitution, MRS^S. The other two terms have been defined in Expressions 21.10 and 21.12 as the marginal rate of transformation, MRT, the rate at which production of cheese falls. Since in deriving Expression 21.12 we have shown that MRT is equal to (-1 times) the price ratio, and in Expression 21.18 that $MRS^R = MRS^S$, we have confirmed that:

$$MRS^R = MRS^S = MRT = -\frac{p_b}{p_c} \qquad [21.21]$$

Expression 21.21 tells us that in general equilibrium, the (common) marginal rate of substitution is also the marginal rate of transformation. This condition seems very reasonable because it means that at the margin, the relative value of goods in production is also their relative value in consumption.

By yourself

- Richard and Seth, who have endowments (K_R, L_R) and (K_s, L_s) of capital and labour, form two companies, a bakery and a creamery, which produce bread and cheese.
- The companies hire factors (K_B, L_B) and (K_C, L_C) at prices w_K and w_L, producing outputs $b = \left[K_B^{\frac{1}{2}} + L_B^{\frac{1}{2}}\right]^2$ and $c = \left[K_C^{\frac{1}{2}} + L_C^{\frac{1}{2}}\right]^2$, which they sell at prices p_B (=1, so that bread is the *numeraire*) and p_c.

- Richard's and Seth's preferences over consumption bundles may be represented by the payoffs: $U_R(b_R, c_R) = \dfrac{b_R c_R}{b_R + c_R}$ and $U_S(b_s, c_s) = \dfrac{b_s c_s}{b_s + c_s}$.
- The companies seek to maximize their profits, given the production functions; and Richard and Seth seek to maximize their utilities, given affordability constraints.

X21.6   We first consider production.
   (a) Write down an expression for the bakery's profit, π_B.
   (b) By partially differentiating the expression for profit with respect to the factor inputs, K_B and L_B, show that the first-order conditions for profit maximization can be rewritten: $p_b\left(K_B^{\frac{1}{2}} + L_B^{\frac{1}{2}}\right) = K_B^{\frac{1}{2}} w_K = L_B^{\frac{1}{2}} w_L$.
   (c) Hence, obtain the equivalent conditions, which hold when the creamery maximizes its profits.
   (d) Show that the profit-maximizing conditions found in (b) and (c) imply that:
      (i) the firms employ capital and labour so that $\frac{L_B}{K_B} = \frac{L_C}{K_C}$;
      (ii) writing the total endowments, $L_B + L_C = L$ and $K_B + K_C = K$, $\frac{L_B}{K_B} = \frac{L}{K}$;
      (iii) $\frac{w_K w_L}{w_K + w_L} = p_b = p_c$, so that prices of the two goods have to be equal.
   (e) Hence, confirm that both firms maximize their profits at any allocation for which $(K_B, L_B) = \beta(K, L)$ and $(K_C, L_C) = (1 - \beta)(K, L)$. Sketch an Edgeworth box showing the allocations at which both firms maximize their profits.
   (f) Given the condition that when maximizing profits both firms hire factors so that the value of the marginal product equals the factor price, show that $w_K = 1 + \left(\frac{L}{K}\right)^{\frac{1}{2}}$ and $w_L = 1 + \left(\frac{K}{L}\right)^{\frac{1}{2}}$.

X21.7   Continuing with the production process:
   (a) Rewrite the problem facing the bakery so that it maximizes profit subject to the constraint of having a feasible production plan. Form the Lagrangean, Θ.
   (b) By solving the first-order conditions for a maximum of Θ, show that:
      (i) The multiplier, $\theta = p_b = 1$.
      (ii) For both factors, the (value of the) marginal product is the factor price; and the ratio of factor prices, $\frac{w_K}{w_L} = \left(\frac{L_B}{K_B}\right)^{\frac{1}{2}}$.
   (c) Similarly, obtain the first-order conditions associated with the profit-maximizing problem for the creamery, showing that the multiplier equals the price, p_c, and the ratio of factor prices, $\frac{w_K}{w_L} = \left(\frac{L_C}{K_C}\right)^{\frac{1}{2}}$. Hence confirm that $\frac{L_B}{K_B} = \frac{L_C}{K_C} = \frac{L}{K}$, so that the factor prices are $w_K = \dfrac{K^{\frac{1}{2}} + L^{\frac{1}{2}}}{K^{\frac{1}{2}}}$ and $w_L = \dfrac{K^{\frac{1}{2}} + L^{\frac{1}{2}}}{L^{\frac{1}{2}}}$ (and the final goods' prices are $p_b = p_c = 1$).

X21.8   If the firms reach the allocation $(K_B, L_B) = \beta(K, L)$; $(K_C, L_C) = (1 - \beta)(K, L)$:
   (a) Show that $MRTS_B = -\left(\frac{L}{K}\right)^{\frac{1}{2}} = MRTS_C$; and explain why this ensures that every allocation at which the firms maximize profits is also Pareto-efficient.
   (b) Confirm that for both businesses, $VMP_K = \dfrac{K^{\frac{1}{2}}}{K^{\frac{1}{2}} + L^{\frac{1}{2}}}$, and the marginal rate of transformation, $MRT = 1$. Interpret this result.

(Continued)

(c) In an Edgeworth box, sketch the Pareto set, and the isoquants passing through the allocation F: $(K_B, L_B) = \frac{1}{3}(K, L)$ and $(K_C, L_C) = \frac{2}{3}(K, L)$.

(d) Show that at the allocation H: $(K_B, L_B) = \beta(K, L)$ and $(K_C, L_C) = (1 - \beta)(K, L)$, the bakery produces $b = \beta(K^{\frac{1}{2}} + L^{\frac{1}{2}})^2$, while the creamery produces $c = (1 - \beta)(K^{\frac{1}{2}} + L^{\frac{1}{2}})^2$. Confirm that:

(i) total output, $b + c = (K^{\frac{1}{2}} + L^{\frac{1}{2}})^2 = y_0$;

(ii) the value of output, $p_b b + p_c c$, equals the cost of production, $w_K K + w_L L$;

(iii) both firms make zero profits.

(e) Sketch the production possibility frontier, illustrating on it point J', corresponding to input allocation J.

X21.9 Now consider the problem facing Richard and Seth.

(a) Write down an expression for Seth's utility, showing that he consumes the share of output (of both goods, and so of total output) that Richard does not. [*Note:* In other words, write down an expression for Seth's utility, given that $b_R + b_S = b$; $c_R + c_S = c$; and $b + c = (K^{\frac{1}{2}} + L^{\frac{1}{2}})^2$.]

(b) Assume that Seth meets a utility target $u^S(b_S, c_S) = u_s^0$. Write down an expression for Richard's utility maximization problem.

(c) Calculate Richard's marginal utilities, MU_B^R and MU_C^R, and his marginal rate of substitution, MRS^R. Repeat the calculations for Seth.

(d) Show that if the marginal rates of substitution are equal, then $\frac{c_R}{b_R} = \frac{c_S}{b_S} = \frac{c}{b}$. Using the argument developed previously, confirm that these conditions will be satisfied whenever Richard consumes a proportion α of the output of each good, and Seth a proportion $(1 - \alpha)$. [*Note:* This means that $(b_R, c_R) = \alpha(b, c)$, and $(b_S, c_S) = (1 + \alpha)(b, c)$.]

(e) On the diagram showing the production possibility frontier, add an Edgeworth box which has its upper right-hand vertex at J'. Within the Edgeworth box, show the Pareto-efficient allocations that satisfy the conditions obtaining in part (d).

(f) Calculate the common marginal rate of substitution for all allocations in the Pareto set. Add indifference curves for Richard and Seth to your sketch, assuming that $\alpha = \frac{1}{2}$, so that each consumes half of the output of both goods.

Explain why the allocation of goods in the Edgeworth box is not consistent with a general equilibrium.

(g) Show that the condition $MRS_R - MRS_S - MRT - \frac{p_b}{p_c}$ can only be satisfied when $b = c = \frac{1}{2}(K^{\frac{1}{2}} + L^{\frac{1}{2}})^2$. Sketch a new diagram showing the production possibility frontier; the allocation H' for which $b = c$ and the associated Edgeworth box; the Pareto set within the box; the Walrasian equilibria when (i) $\alpha = \frac{1}{4}$ and (ii) $\alpha = \frac{3}{4}$; the indifference curves passing through the equilibria; and the common tangents to the indifference curves at each equilibrium. Demonstrate that the equilibrium conditions are indeed satisfied.

We illustrate the links between production and exchange in Figure 21.5, while noting that the graph differs in some ways from the case analysed in detail in Exercises X21.6–X21.9. The production possibility frontier is derived from the Pareto set associated with firm profit maximization, and so shows the productive capacity of the economy. The allocation of factors inputs across firms determines the pattern of output in the economy. In a $2 \times 2 \times 2$ model, this is simply the quantity of bread and cheese, available to Richard and Seth for consumption. To study the division of goods, we draw an Edgeworth box whose dimensions are equal to the total outputs. Within the Edgeworth box, we show a Pareto-efficient division, J_1. As required in Expression 21.21, this has been chosen so that Richard's and

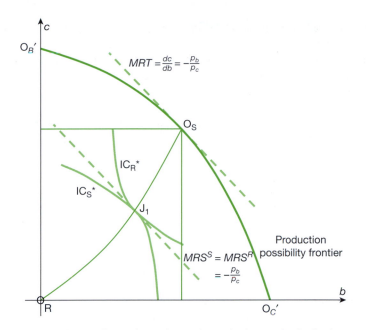

Figure 21.5 Equal marginal rate of transformation and marginal rate of substitution

Seth's marginal rates of substitution, the marginal rate of transformation, and the relative price of the final goods, are all equal. Our interpretation of the equilibrium division differs slightly from the one that we gave in Chapter 20. Richard and Seth no longer exchange final goods directly. Instead, they have realized the income from hiring out their endowment of factors of production. This gives them a common affordability constraint, the dashed line within the Edgeworth box. We know from our analysis in Chapter 20 that when they maximize their utility separately, subject to that common constraint, neither can do better than by consuming their share of division J_1. In the same way, we might here simply bypass the argument relating to the trading of resources between the two firms. In our introductory example, we created an artificial distinction between Robinson and Mr Crusoe. In this case, the firms might also be treated as a convenient fiction. It should be possible for Richard and Seth, recognizing that they share a common resource constraint, to agree to undertake production across the two activities, dividing the total endowment of input factors so as to achieve a Pareto-efficient outcome in both production and consumption.

In Exercises X21.6–X21.9, we make several simplifying assumptions. The production functions for both businesses have exactly the same form, with constant returns to scale. The average and marginal costs will be equal, irrespective of the scale of production, and for profit maximization, it follows that the prices of the goods have to be the same. In addition, since the bakery and the creamery face identical production constraints, they adopt the same labour:capital input ratio, shown by the Pareto set being the upward diagonal in the Edgeworth box; and with constant returns to scale, the production possibility frontier is also linear. This leads us directly to the result that the output of the two goods must be equal, for otherwise the marginal rate of substitution in exchange would not be equal to the marginal rate of transformation. By demanding a different product mix, the consumers increase their utility.

21.3   Distribution and equity

Our discussion has been couched in terms of (economic) efficiency. We briefly referred to distributional equity in Expression 21.12, where we noted that we only require the total expenditure on goods to be equal to the total income derived from the factors of production. This places no restriction on the initial division of the endowment of factor inputs, and thus the share of output that any individual will be able to afford. For example, in Exercise X21.9 we showed, in effect, that the market value of Richard's endowment of the factors of production can be any fraction of the total market value: he might have almost no resources, in which case he can generate almost no utility; or he might have almost all of the resources, and so be able to generate almost all of the utility.

Suppose that either Seth or Richard objects to an outcome on the basis that there is a large difference in the consumption levels. Simply requiring efficiency within the processes of production and exchange, we impose no condition stronger than that the outcomes should lie in the Pareto set. The attractive features of such a decentralized market system are that it is not possible:

- to increase the production of any good without reducing production of another one;
- to alter the mix of outputs without reducing their total value; and
- to increase the utility of any consumer without reducing the utility of someone else.

As in Section 20.4, we address concerns that if the outcome is agreed to be unfair, Richard and Seth might agree to change the way in which it is reached. Suppose that Seth has a much lower consumption level than Richard. Increasing Seth's share of consumption in Exercise X21.9, we should increase his share of the market value of factor incomes, $1 - \alpha$. We do not argue for changes in input prices, on the basis that this would create inefficiencies within the production process, including unemployment of input factors. Being consistent with our earlier argument, we should seek an increase in his share of the factor inputs. We will step outside the standard $2 \times 2 \times 2$ model here, and allow Richard either to transfer some of his capital to Seth, or else to transfer some of his factor income.

By yourself

X21.10   Consider the situation in X21.9 where $\alpha = \frac{3}{4}$. Suppose that Richard agrees with Simon to a reduction in the value of α to $\frac{1}{2}$. They then share the total factor incomes equally.

(a) Explain why we would not expect the product mix to change, so that the bakery and the creamery would continue to hire the same quantity of factor inputs, and the combination of outputs in the economy would remain unchanged.

(b) Sketch a diagram showing: the production possibility frontier; the Edgeworth box and the Pareto set; the allocations of final goods before and after the change in income shares; and also the indifference curves passing through the Pareto-efficient allocations before and after the income change.

Perhaps the most obvious point to emerge from Exercise X21.10 is that Richard appears to be acting against his own interests. He begins with a large share of factor endowments, but he gives some away. This suggests that he is concerned about Seth's welfare. Observing this, we might conclude that we have not described his preferences fully with his utility function. Instead of trying to explain resource sharing in this way, we shall discuss the design and operation of mandatory resource-sharing schemes.

21.3.1 The utility possibility frontier

The first step is to note that it is possible to construct a curve, analogous to the production possibility frontier from the Pareto set of final good allocations. This **utility possibility frontier** shows the payoffs that Richard and Seth receive. We note that since for every point on the production possibility frontier there is a distinct Edgeworth box showing feasible final good allocations, there is also a distinct utility possibility frontier for every point on the frontier. Think for a moment about the utility possibility frontier, UPF_1, in Figure 21.6. We would expect to find a single point on the curve representing an equilibrium allocation at which the marginal rates of substitution, MRS_R and MRS_S, are equal to each other and also to the marginal rate of transformation, MRT. At such an allocation, it would be impossible to reallocate factor inputs across firms in such a way that the resulting change in the combination of final goods being produced would lead to an increase Richard's and Seth's utilities.

> **Utility possibility frontier** A curve formed from utility combinations that are just feasible.

In Figure 21.6 we show three utility possibility frontiers, UPF_1, UPF_2 and UPF_3, as well as the curve UPF_0. Except at one point, where the separate curves touch UPF_0, each of the individual frontiers lies below that. We can define UPF_0 as an **envelope**. One way of thinking about points on this curve, UPF_0, would be say that they show the highest utility, $U_S = U_S(U_R)$, that Seth can achieve, given a specific target utility, U_R, for Richard. Starting from a point on the envelope, say J_1, and allowing Richard's target utility to increase while keeping the product mix constant, we expect the new allocation of goods to lie on curve UPF_1. If we allow the product mix to change appropriately, then in the

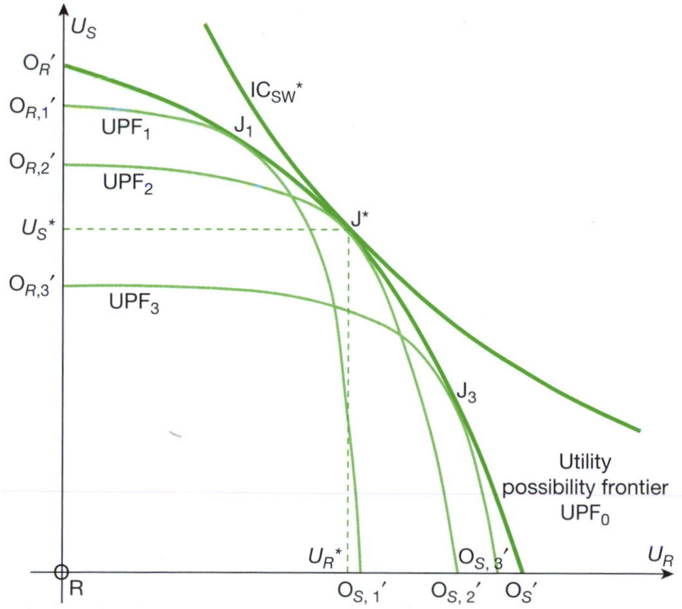

> **Envelope** A curve that forms a boundary of other curves.

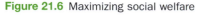

Figure 21.6 Maximizing social welfare

allocation of goods where Richard achieves his new target utility, Seth can obtain higher utility. At every point on UPF$_0$, though, to increase one person's utility, the other's utility has to fall. As argued above, the optimal product mix will change as Richard's utility target changes, with the marginal rate of transformation adjusting to the changing marginal rate of substitution. The utility possibility frontier, UPF$_0$, therefore shows the combinations of utility achievable at all Walrasian equilibria for which all markets clear and the efficiency conditions for production, distribution and exchange are all satisfied.

By yourself

X21.11   In X21.9, we obtained a linear production possibility frontier. Explain why we would obtain a linear utility possibility frontier. Confirm that if factor inputs are not allocated so that $b = c$, then even if production is efficient, the utility profile will lie in the interior of the utility possibility set.

Once again, in Exercise X21.11, we see that we have been analysing a rather special case. Given the constant returns to scale in production and the homogeneity of the utility functions, there is a single, efficient product mix. Every point on the utility possibility frontier represents a point on the Pareto set of final good allocations.

21.3.2 Social welfare

Assume that all of the efficiency conditions are satisfied, so that Richard and Seth's payoffs lie on the utility possibility frontier. This is a fixed constraint, and we are now used to thinking that, in the presence of such a constraint, it should be possible to maximize some objective. If we treat Richard's and Seth's payoffs, U_R and U_S, as goods, we might say that we can form a preference ordering over them. But whose preference orderings would these be? They cannot be Richard's or Seth's. Their preferences are represented by their payoffs. It also seems inappropriate to say that they are aggregate preferences, given that there is no absolute measure of utility, so we do not attempt to make inter-personal comparisons of utility. Instead, we shall rely on the concept of **social preferences**. Just as in discussing the incorporation of a *business*, which is a legal entity, and so capable of entering into contracts for its own benefit, so we can think of *society* as having an identity, which is distinct from the identities of its members. This social identity is not simply located in the government of a state, although representative, democratic governments will have preferences that relate in some way to the distribution of preferences of people generally.

Social preferences An aggregation of individual preferences over outcomes.

Social planner An individual with authority to allocate resources to maximize social welfare.

Social welfare function A function that weights individual preferences.

We shall assert that social preferences are the preferences of a **social planner**, and that they can be represented by a **social welfare** *function*, $w = w(u_R, u_S)$, and, as in Figure 21.6, by social indifference curves, such as IC$_{SW}$*. Along this curve, the social planner is of course indifferent between all utility bundles. We shall assume that preferences are well behaved, so that the socially preferred set is the whole area above and to the right of IC$_{SW}$*. Noting the point of tangency between the utility possibility curve and the social indifference curve, we see that the point J*:(u_R*, u_S*) is the most (socially) preferred, achievable utility profile.

By yourself

X21.12 Working with the utility possibility frontier in X21.11, calculate the most-preferred utility profile for the social welfare functions, w, where (a) $w(u_R, u_S) = \min(u_R, u_S)$; (b) $w(u_R, u_S) = \ln u_R + \ln u_S$; (c) $w(u_R, u_S) = u_R + 2u_S$; and (d) $w(u_R, u_S) = u_R^{\frac{3}{4}} u_S^{\frac{1}{4}}$.

X21.13 Using diagrams, explain why a social planner with a utility function such as (a) in X21.12 has a very strong commitment to egalitarianism.

X21.14 Suppose that the social planner's preferences are captured by form (b) of the social welfare function in X21.12. Sketch the social welfare indifference curves, $w = 1, 2$ and 3. What would you conclude about the slope of the utility possibility frontier on the line $u_R = u_S$ if the planner chooses the utility profile $(u_R{}^*, u_S{}^*)$: $u_R{}^* > u_S{}^*$?

The decision of the social planner reflects its preferences. We have restricted ourselves in Exercise X21.12 to CES functions. Where individual utilities are close complements, the planner will prefer there to be a largely equal distribution of resources; but where they are near-perfect substitutes, the planner will be concerned about the total value of the payoffs (ignoring the question of measuring utilities). To the extent that we are able to rely on the concept of social welfare, though, we have a basis for explaining how it might be that Richard is willing to give up some of his utility to Seth. The social plan has to have two elements. Firstly, the product mix must support the social optimum; and secondly, the incomes from hiring factors of production must also permit its achievement. To achieve the former goal, in our simple $2 \times 2 \times 2$ model, the social planner will instruct the bakery and the creamery to hire the optimal quantities of factor inputs. To achieve the latter, the planner will instruct Richard (or Seth) to transfer either part of his factor endowment or else part of the income he derives from it. We must also assume that all the actors in our model (businesses and people) agree in advance to follow the directions of the social planner.

If we identify the social planner with government, then we might expect transfers between people to be mediated through the tax and benefits system, and we shall discuss some possible distributional effects in Chapter 22 and 23. Explaining planned output is rather more difficult, though: since the collapse of the Soviet Union, there has been a substantial retreat from direct planning of the economy, although almost all governments have substantial programmes designed to direct business investment, and, through regulation and other measures, to control many elements of economic activities. For example, there are many countries in which a minimum wage is set for labour, irrespective of its productivity. In the context of our analysis, we can see this as another way of effecting resource transfers.

21.4 Conclusions

There have been two parts to our analysis. In Section 21.2, we have argued that in an entirely decentralized economy with production taking place in perfectly competitive markets, all efficiency gains from trade should be realized. Expressed in this way, economic theory suggests that there can only be a limited role for intervention (by government or other agencies) in markets. We have already seen, though, that some of the assumptions required for markets to be perfect can easily fail, with firms being able to exploit market power. This provides one role for public intervention in markets, and, in the remainder of the book, we shall see others.

The second part of our analysis is rather more normative, or value-based. We have claimed that in perfect markets, perfect efficiency is achievable. In such markets, there is no obvious role for intervention. More generally, we have seen that the distribution of incomes within a decentralized economy may be highly dispersed: the economy might operate very efficiently, but with some very rich, and some very poor, people. By introducing the social planner, we argued that members of society may enter into binding agreements to transfer income and resources to avoid any harmful concentration of resources. But while consistent with our technical arguments, the presence of a social planner has not been explained. We require a normative explanation of why utility-maximizing people would accept the imposition of such arrangements, unless they shared in the social planner's concerns about distribution; and were they to do so, it is unclear why they should require direction to undertake these transfers. As an explanation of the role of government, our theory is interesting. As an explanation of why governments choose to behave as they do, it has much less to say.

Summary

A full model of general equilibrium should take account of the production of final goods and services using factor inputs, which are owned by people, who consume the final goods.

It is possible to demonstrate all the results of a more general model, in which there are m goods, f factor inputs and n people using the $2 \times 2 \times 2$ model with two goods, two factor inputs and two people.

With four markets (two for factor inputs and two for final goods), the equilibrium is found by setting the prices of the inputs and final goods, recognizing that only three of them can be set independently, given that all markets clear in equilibrium.

For production to be efficient, then in the production of every good, $MRTS = -\frac{w_K}{w_L}$, so that the ratio of the value of the marginal product to the factor price is the same for every factor. It then follows that the marginal rate of transformation, or the rate at which production of one good falls as production of the other good increases, will satisfy the requirement, $MRT = -\frac{p_b}{p_c}$, and this is the gradient of the production possibility frontier.

Given factor incomes, for a general equilibrium, people will purchase goods, maximizing their utilities where individual $MRS = MRT$, and hence ensuring distributional efficiency.

Efficient outcomes may not be considered to be equitable. The utility possibility frontier demonstrates the capacity of the economy to generate combinations of utility for individuals. We argued that a social planner might then have preferences over these utility combinations, which could be represented by a social welfare function. The utility possibility frontier would then form a binding constraint on the planner's ability to achieve outcomes.

While invoking the planner, who might be associated with government or public authorities, we have not explained why individuals would be willing to accept direction from such a central authority.

Visit the companion website at **www.palgrave.com/mochrie** to access further teaching and learning materials, including lecturer slides and a testbank, as well as guideline answers and student MCQs.

22

Externalities

What we do in this chapter

In our models of general equilibrium, we have assumed that no actors' choices affect the outcomes of other agents. The utility of consumers depends only upon their consumption of traded goods. Firms' profits are the difference between the revenue that they receive from selling final goods for consumption and the costs of hiring factors of production. There are markets for all goods and services.

In this chapter, we ask what happens if we drop this assumption. We define an *externality* as an untraded good or service. We begin with a brief example, arguing that it is possible that so many agents may seek to use a publicly owned asset at the same time that they end up imposing costs on each other. In the absence of a market for access, its price is effectively set to zero; and, with the price fixed, the market fails to clear. We argue that this is essential for an externality: there has to be some untraded, or unpriced good, in whose market there is either excess supply or excess demand, preventing both market clearing and welfare maximization.

In the remainder of the chapter we use two examples of externalities in production, typical of the situation in which the production process for one good affects the production of another good. These are pollution, for which, as a waste product, there is no market; and the pollination services of bees, for which, in certain circumstances, markets will emerge. We argue that externalities in these circumstances change the costs of production for other firms, and that we should consider the full cost of production for the firm generating the externality as including the costs imposed on these other firms. For any level of output, where there is a negative externality, the marginal social cost exceeds its marginal cost, as usually measured, and some reduction in its output would increase social welfare. The reverse is true where there is a positive externality. Social welfare is increasing in output around its equilibrium level when no market exists.

Externalities provide a role for the social planner to become more actively involved in the operation of markets. We consider public solutions to managing output, including the imposition of quotas, the use of taxes and subsidies, regulation, and the creation of property rights. This last solution has increased in popularity in recent years, and is largely inspired by the analysis of Ronald Coase, who argued that the social costs of externalities and other market failures could largely be addressed by identifying the untraded property rights that give rise to the externalities, and creating a market for these artificially.

We have analysed general equilibrium models, in which people obtain utility from their own consumption, while firms' production decisions are determined by prices and the state of technology. Markets are perfect, and no single individual can affect overall market outcomes. In contrast, in the models of imperfect competition in Chapters 16–18 we showed how firms with market power can affect market outcomes, pushing up the market price to reduce the quantity traded. In Chapter 20, we showed that market power in an exchange economy will also affect prices and the extent of exchange, preventing the achievement of a Pareto optimum. Here, we introduce another type of market imperfection: the situation in which the decisions of one person directly affect the payoffs received by someone else. Unlike situations characterized by strategic interdependence, which we might explore by using game theory, we will try to understand what happens when there are spillovers in consumption and production.

Consider the situation facing people commuting to work, which we shall examine both here and in Chapter 23. A few cities around the world have started to introduce road-pricing mechanisms, but usually there is no market in a city for access to the road network. We can very quickly set out a contradiction between this fact and the efficiency results of our general equilibrium models. According to Walras' Law, the value of excess supply across all markets equals zero. A good that has a price of zero may therefore be trading in conditions of excess supply: the price cannot fall further. Treating access to the road system as a good, its supply is fixed, at least in the short run. For much of the day, that fixed supply will be sufficient to meet the demand and traffic will flow freely. For perhaps an hour or even two on every working day, though, there is a sudden increase in demand as people attempt to reach their work. Yet, in spite of there being substantial excess demand during this period, the access price remains zero.

We shall defer the question of why access charges are still relatively rare until Chapter 23. Here, we concentrate on the fact that there is an implicit price for road travel. Travel is not a final, consumption good, but instead an intermediate good, used in order to consume other goods – or, in the case of commuting, to engage in paid labour. As a baseline estimate of the direct costs of car usage, tax authorities in the UK typically allow payments covering the fully cost of travel, treating any higher payments as taxable income. To these costs, we should add the value of the time spent commuting. Suppose that as a result of congestion, journey times double, and that a typical journey, of 40 km, mostly on open roads, lasts one hour instead of taking 30 minutes. We say that during the peak period of excess demand, commuters impose an *externality* on one another: the value of the time that is lost, which can therefore never be used more productively. The externality associated with every car in excess of the full capacity of the system is very small, perhaps a fraction of a second. But this cost will be imposed on all of the drivers on that route, leading to the substantial costs noted above.

By yourself

X22.1   Assume that the value of an hour's leisure to a typical commuter is £15. If 20,000 cars enter a city during the period of excess demand, calculate the daily and annual costs of a 30-minute delay every day. What do you conclude about the size of the investment needed to eliminate congestion?

22.1 Externalities in production

One type of externality occurs when the production activities of one firm have an effect on those of another. We can classify these externalities as being either **positive**, in which case the effects are beneficial, typically lowering production costs; or else **negative**, in which case the externality has negative effects, increasing the total costs of production. An apple orchard presents a classic example of a positive externality. For an orchard to produce

Externality The effect of one individual's decisions on another's payoffs.

fruit, the blossoms have to be fertilized. A farmer might leave this to chance, but usually farmers agree with local beekeepers that they may place beehives among the trees at the appropriate time of year, usually in May. The bees fertilize the apple blossoms, and in doing so collect nectar, which they turn into honey. Since apple blossom appears relatively early in the year, there are also benefits to the beekeeper: the hive grows relatively rapidly, and so later in the year, when the hives have been moved to another location to benefit from the presence of later-blooming flowers, there will be more bees to feed on nectar and to collect pollen, and the output of honey will be higher. Both the farmer and the beekeeper benefit from the other's efforts in such an arrangement.

> **Positive externality**
> Externality with a beneficial effect.
> **Negative externality**
> Externality with a harmful effect.

In placing the hives in the orchard, the farmer recognizes his dependence on the beekeeper for the pollination of the apple blossom, and hence a good crop. Equally, the beekeeper benefits by being able to produce more honey throughout the year. To keep the analysis simple, let us begin with the case where the farmer does not make any payment to the beekeeper, so that, in consequence, the beekeeper does not recognize any obligation to the farmer. We shall also only consider short-run decision making, assuming that all markets are perfectly competitive.

22.1.1 The private solution

The private solution emerges when the beekeeper and the farmer make their decisions completely independently. We write the farmer's production function, A, as:

$$A = A(L_f, b_0, T_0) \tag{22.1}$$

where A is the harvest of apples, L_f is the labour usage throughout the year, b_0 is the size of the hive pollinating the blossom, and T_0 is the number of trees in the orchard. We use the subscript, 0, for those factors of production that the farmer cannot alter: trees cannot be planted and brought into production in the same year, while the beekeeper chooses the value of b. We shall also assume that the production function is well behaved, so that A is increasing and concave in all of the arguments of the production function, and with $\frac{\partial^2 A}{\partial L \partial b} > 0$. We interpret the cross partial derivative as meaning that as the beehive increases in size, the marginal product of labour will also increase, so that $\frac{\partial MP_L}{\partial b} > 0$. Writing the farmer's problem as:

$$\max_{L_f} \ p_A \cdot A(L_f, b_0, T_0) - w_f L_f - rT_0 \tag{22.2}$$

we can solve it in the usual way, obtaining the standard first-order condition for maximization, which we write as:

$$p_A \cdot MP_{L_f} - w_f = 0 \tag{22.3}$$

The value of the marginal product is equal to the wage paid to labour. Since a higher value of b_0 raises the value of MP_L for any given level of labour input, and the wage is fixed by conditions in the labour market, an orchard that allows more beehives to be placed in it will hire more labour. The additional labour usage increases output, as does the increase in the productivity of the labour that it has already hired.

By yourself

X22.2   In the short-run analysis of production, we argue that the marginal product of labour will be eventually diminishing, and this ensures that firms will not expand its use without limit. Explain why, given our present assumptions, we might expect the farmer to be happy always to have more beehives on the land. Criticize the argument. [*Hint*: Think of the problem of commuting.] *risk of congestion (密度过高: presumably densities)*

We can see that where a positive externality is unpriced, there will always be excess demand for it. This suggests that the farmer will pay the beekeeper to increase the number of beehives placed in the orchard. We therefore turn to the profits that the beekeeper makes. Suppose that it is possible to write the production function, h:

$$h = h[b(L_b, T_0)] \qquad [22.4]$$

where h is the quantity of honey, L_b is the labour effort that the beekeeper exerts, and, as before T_0 is the stock of fruit trees in the orchard. Again, we assume that the production function is well behaved, and so is increasing, but concave in both arguments. We also assume that the marginal product of labour increases with the size of the orchard, or that $\frac{\partial MP_L}{\partial T} > 0$. Effort is more productive where it is easier for the bees to find blossom. Not only is the stock T_0 determined by prior investment decisions, but even in the long run it would remain under the control of the farmer. This is the source of a second positive externality, from which the beekeeper, rather than the farmer, would benefit, but only in the long run. Continuing for just now with our short-run analysis, we use Expression 22.4 to write the beekeeper's profit-maximizing problem as:

$$\max_{L_b} p_h \cdot h[b(L_b, T_0)] - w_b L_b \qquad beekeeper's \qquad [22.5]$$

Then, differentiating to obtain the first-order condition:

$$p_h \cdot \frac{dh}{db} \cdot \frac{\partial b}{\partial L_b} = w_b \qquad \frac{\partial f}{\partial L_b} \qquad \frac{\partial b}{\partial L_b} \to beekeeper's \ MP_L \qquad [22.6]$$

$$\frac{\partial h}{\partial b} \cdot \frac{\partial b}{\partial L_b}$$

By yourself

X22.3   Show that there is a positive externality on production of honey from choice of orchard size, T. Explain how this affects the choice of labour input, L_b, and the quantity of honey produced. Confirm that so long as we assume $\frac{\partial MP_{L_b}}{\partial T} > 0$, the beekeeper would always prefer a larger to a smaller orchard. $\frac{\partial}{\partial T}\left(\frac{\partial b}{\partial L_b}\right) > 0 \quad T \uparrow MP \uparrow$

reach equilibrium with larger labor

22.1.2 The social optimum

We continue with the short-run analysis. We have already hinted that the private solution does not take account of the fact that the farmer benefits from larger beehives, by suggesting that she (or he) might pay the beekeeper to bring more hives into the orchard. But before exploring that possibility, we shall consider the problem that a social planner, as introduced in Chapter 21, might adopt. We shall assume that the planner is concerned with maximizing the joint profits of the two businesses, and so seeks to maximize:

$$\max_{L_b, L_f} \Pi = p_A \cdot A(L_f, b, T_0) + p_h \cdot h[b(L_b, T_0)] - w_f L_f - w_b L_b - r T_0 \qquad [22.7]$$

Expression 22.7 is simply the sum of the profit functions for the farmer and the beekeeper, except that the size of the beehives is no longer fixed for the farmer. We can write down the first-order conditions:

$$\frac{\partial \Pi}{\partial L_f} = p_A \cdot MP_{L_f} - w_f = 0 \qquad [22.8a]$$

$$\frac{\partial \Pi}{\partial L_b} = \left[p_A \cdot \frac{\partial A}{\partial b} + p_h \frac{dh}{db} \right] \frac{\partial b}{\partial L_b} - w_b = 0 \qquad [22.8b]$$

Expressions 22.8a and 22.3 are of course identical. The farmer's decisions do not affect the beekeeper's profits in the short run. But while we can see that the second term in the bracket in Expression 22.8b appears in Expression 22.6, the first term does not – this is the externality.

Figure 22.1 shows how the solutions to the private and social problems differ for the beekeeper. The value of the marginal product in the private problem is shown in the lower curve, VMP_b^P, which intersects the price schedule at output L_b^P. The higher curve, VMP_b^S, represents the value of the marginal product in the social problem. At the intersection with the price schedule, $L_b^S > L_b^P$. The horizontal distance between the two curves represents the additional labour which the social planner will direct the beekeeper to provide, recognizing the effect of the larger hives on the profits that the farmer can make.

Applying the argument used in the previous section about how the farmer will respond by increasing labour supply when there are more beehives, we identify two effects of the externality on behaviour. Firstly, for the planner, the marginal benefit to society of the beekeeper's labour is the sum of the value of the marginal product and the rate at which the farmer's revenues increase with the beekeeper's labour. This latter component does not enter into the beekeeper's calculations in obtaining the private solution. Secondly, we

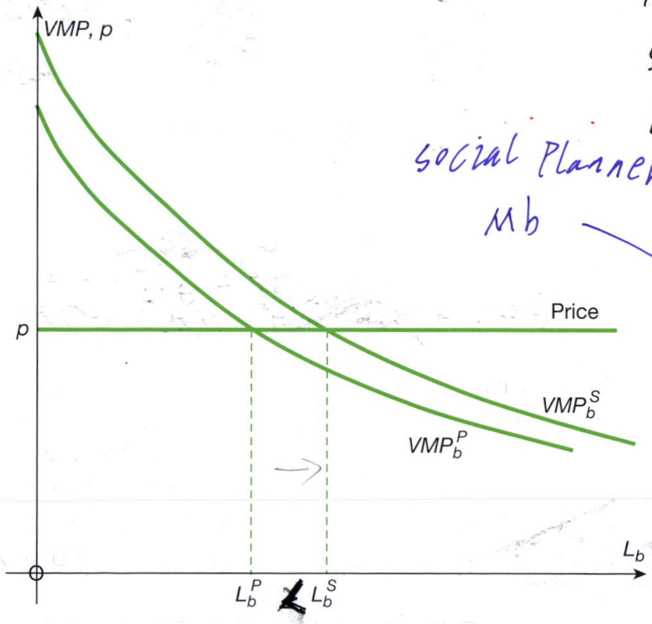

Figure 22.1 Private and social optima

know that there is an interaction between the size of the beehives and the farmer's labour productivity. So, while the planner directs the beekeeper to increase hours of work, no such direction is required for the farmer, who will choose to increase labour supply. This indirect effect is important.

We might question the role of the social planner here, who has somehow acquired the authority to direct the beekeeper to increase labour supply because that will benefit society. This runs rather counter to our assumption of individual agency, since it seems that the planner requires the beekeeper to work, but with the rewards accruing primarily to farmer. Another way of putting this is to note that in the private solution, the beekeeper and the farmer engage in the bare minimum of cooperation. The beehives are placed in the orchard, where they can be most productive. In the social optimum, though, they exploit all the benefits associated with their relationship. We shall have more to say on this matter in Chapter 23.

22.1.3 Positive externalities and the development of an industry

We have suggested that the social planner can have a role in coordinating the activities of firms, which is in some ways consistent with the assumption of the standard model that firms produce a single output. Effectively, in our example, we have continued with this convention. The farmer produces apples; and the beekeeper produces honey. For both, bees are an intermediate input, used in the production of both final goods. The farmer's and the beekeeper's decisions are certainly tied together. We might therefore argue that we should retire the social planner, replacing her with the owner of a single business which undertakes the production of both goods. The farmer and the beekeeper are then employees, working as directed by the owner. Increasing the hours that the beekeeper works, the owner increases firm profits from the increased revenues associated with the sale of more apples.

A slightly different way of thinking about this problem would be to consider how the farmer and the beekeeper come to collaborate. The farmer knows that it is risky to rely on the presence of natural pollinators – other insects that will provide the same service as bees. It is one step in the process of cooperation to invite the beekeeper to place hives inside the orchard, and subsequently only a short further step to offer payment to the beekeeper to elicit greater effort. We would expect the farmer to be willing to offer the wage at which the farmer's own profits are maximized.

> **By yourself**
>
> **X22.4** Consider the following situation. We write the short-term production function for the farmer, A: $A(L_f, b) = 50L_f^{0.5}b^{0.25}$; the short-term production function for the beekeeper, b: $b(L_b) = 4L_b^{0.5}$; and the associated output of honey, h: $h(b) = 125b$. The price of apples, $p_a = 2$, while the price of honey $p_h = 8$. The farmer's wage, $w_f = 10$, and the beekeeper's wage, $w_b = 20$.
>
> (a) Write down the farmer's profit function. Partially differentiate the derivative with respect to the labour input, L_f, and, by obtaining the first-order condition, show that the farmer maximizes profits by working $L_f^P = 25b^{1/2}$.
>
> (b) Write down the beekeeper's profit function. Partially differentiate the derivative with respect to the labour input, L_b, and, by obtaining the first-order condition, show that the beekeeper maximizes profits by working $L_b^P = 10,000$.
>
> (c) Calculate the size of the beehives, the total outputs of apples and honey, and the total revenues, costs, and profits of both the farmer and the beekeeper.

[handwritten margin notes, top right:]
$y = (x^a)^b$
$\dfrac{\partial y}{\partial x} = b \cdot (x^a)^{b-1} \cdot a x^{a-1}$

X22.5 Continue with the situation set out in X22.4.

(a) Write down the social planner's payoff function as the sum of the farmer's and the beekeeper's profit functions. Partially differentiate the function with respect to the labour inputs, L_f and L_b. Confirm that the optimal labour input for the farmer $L_f^S = 25b^{0.5}$, and that the socially optimal labour input for the beekeeper reflects both the optimal private use plus the positive externality on the farmer's production.

(b) Without attempting calculations, compare the socially optimal and the privately optimal sizes of beehives. Discuss the impact of beehive size on the total outputs of apples and honey, and the total revenues, costs and profits of both the farmer and the beekeeper. *optimal size ↑, because indirect effect, larger beehive, more apple and honey.*

X22.6 Discuss how the farmer might be able to encourage the beekeeper to increase the level of output from the privately optimal to the socially optimal level.

X22.7 Adapt Expressions 22.2 and 22.5, so that the farmer subsidizes the beekeeper's wage at a rate, s_b. Find the new first-order condition, and the value of the subsidy, s_b, that will lead to the socially optimal outcome.

if farmer able to pay subsidy = marginal benefit of the externality, beekeeper will choose socially optimal level of externality.

Coordinating activities in this way is effectively a form of innovation, with the farmer and the beekeeper working together to increase the value of their output. There is a tradition within economics, going back to Alfred Marshall (in *Principles of Economics*, 1920), that there are certain economies of scope associated with the physical concentration of an industry. For example, the ceramics industry in England gave a name, the 'Potteries', to the area in which production was concentrated (now largely the city of Stoke-on-Trent in Staffordshire). People who had the skills necessary to work in that industry tended to migrate there. People who had novel ideas, innovations that would improve the productive capacity of firms in the industry, tended to find it easiest to develop them there. Such conjectures led Marshall to suggest that within such an industrial district, the long-run supply curve would slope downwards, even where the market was perfectly competitive. Marshall's ideas have been developed in various ways, such as: the concept of *clusters*, examined particularly by Italian economists, seeking to explain the success of often dense networks of family owned, small- and medium-sized businesses in much of Central and Northern Italy; the theory of competitive advantage, developed in the work of Michael Porter; and the new economic geography, to which Paul Krugman is probably the most important contributor, which seeks to explain the rise of cities and the concentration of economic activity.

By yourself

X22.8 Sketch a diagram showing the situation facing a firm and the market in long-run equilibrium where there is perfect competition with the long-run supply curve: (a) perfectly flat; and (2) downward-sloping. Show how a change in demand conditions affects the equilibrium in each case.

X22.9 One important element of cooperation in an industrial district is the emergence of technical colleges, often funded with endowments by local businesses. Discuss their role in enabling businesses to increase productivity.

firm hiring ↑ positive externality

As a location for the development of a ceramics industry, the Potteries had natural advantages, with plentiful local deposits of clay and coal. The local industry first emerged in the 17th century; by 1760, early in the Industrial Revolution, Josiah Spode and Josiah Wedgwood, founders of businesses which continue to have a prominent role in the industry right up to the present day, had started business operations. Both Spode and Wedgwood were born into families that already owned potteries, and both made substantial improvements to manufacturing processes. So, it is easy to explain the emergence of a Marshallian industrial district in this area. But a concentration of industry also requires a concentration of specialist labour, which utilizes skills that are necessary to all of the businesses in the industry. We would expect economies of scale and scope in the provision of these facilities, and so industrialists would often endow specialist training colleges: in Stoke-on-Trent, this took place in the early 20th century.

22.2 Negative externalities (in production)

The beekeeper generates a positive externality, which benefits the farmer. Externalities can also be negative. In production, negative externalities typically arise when there is a by-product from the production of a good that has no market value, and which the producer simply dumps, effectively polluting the environment. Such pollution takes many forms. To an astronomer, both the heat and the light produced by a city makes observation more difficult. The cars that commuters drive into a city emit gases, which are potentially harmful to passers-by, as well as causing the congestion that we noted in the introductory example. A night club that plays music very loudly might affect neighbours. For our analysis, though, we shall assume that the by-product of production negatively affects the production of a second good. Thinking of production processes only, one of the most straightforward routes by which this could happen would be through the pollution of the water supply used by an industry.

Most large-scale electricity generating plants use a huge volume of water, which will often be drawn from a river, heated up, and then returned to the river. Water that is unusually warm may not seem to be a serious form of pollution when compared with the disposal of chemicals into a water supply, but we shall assume that there is a fish farm located close to a new power station. After the power station begins operations, the water that the fish farm draws from the river becomes warmer and supports a larger and more diverse population of bacteria, some of which cause infections in the fish stock. The fish farm responds by increasing its use of antibiotics to treat these diseases. The opening of the power station therefore increases the fish farm's production costs.

We present a simple analysis of the problem. Assume that the fish farm allocates its resources efficiently both before and after the opening of the power station. Denoting its total costs of output f after the power station opens as $C_1 = C_1(f)$, compared with total costs $C_0 = C_0(f)$, we assume that:

$$C_1(f) = h[C_0(f)]$$

[22.9]

where $C_1(0) = C_0(0)$ and $\dfrac{dC_1}{dC_0} > 1$.

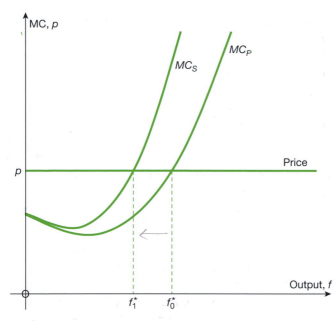

Figure 22.2 Externality in production on the fish farm

By yourself

X22.10 Confirm that for $f > 0$, average costs $AC_1(f) > AC_0(f)$, and marginal costs $MC_1(f) > MC_0(f)$.

These results follow directly from our definitions of average and marginal costs. Then, assuming that the fish farm faces a perfectly competitive market, and that it is the only business affected by the new power station, we expect it to be able to sell any output, f, at a given market price, p. Figure 22.2 illustrates the effects of the power station opening, and we see that the fish farm reduces its output from f_0^* to f_1^*.

By yourself

X22.11 To what extent is it reasonable to expect the owners of the power station to compensate the owners of the fish farm for the loss of profits that might occur as a result of the power station opening?

X22.12 Define the social costs of power production as the sum of the direct costs, measured by the power station's cost function, $C(w)$, where w is its output, and the costs experienced by other businesses, $S(w)$, which are directly attributable to pollution resulting from power generation. Assume that the power station has entered into long-term wholesale contracts, and so can sell any quantity of power at a constant price, p_w. Explain how the power station's optimal output would differ were the power station required to provide compensation for the loss suffered by other businesses.

22.2.1 The effect on the power station

We have argued that the fish farm either has to absorb an externality caused by the power station, or else should seek compensation for those costs. We might reasonably expect many other businesses to claim that the opening of the power station is having comparable effects

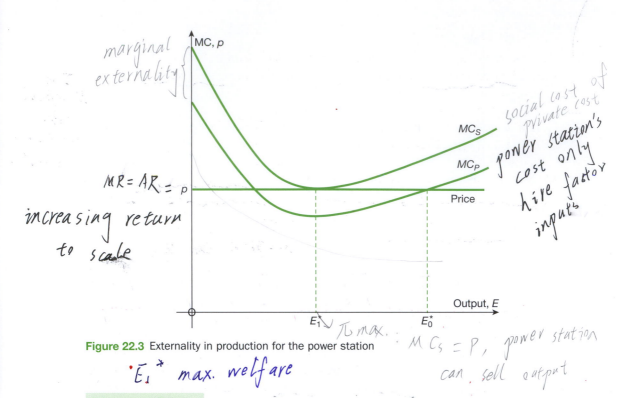

marginal externality

MR = AR = p

increasing return to scale

social cost of private cost

power station's cost only hire factor inputs

Figure 22.3 Externality in production for the power station

E_1^* max. welfare

$MC_S = P$, power station

can sell output

π max.

Private cost The cost borne by an individual in making a decision that gives rise to an externality.

Social cost The cost of activity, including negative externalities.

on their activities. From the point of view of the power station, then, the production externality is the sum of the costs that it imposes on these other firms. We illustrate this situation in Figure 22.3, where we assume that the power station faces a perfect market for its output. Again, for simplicity, we show the effect of the externality on the marginal costs. The lower curve, MC^P, represents the power station's costs when it has to pay only to hire factor inputs. These are the **private costs** of production. The higher curve, MC^S, represents the **social costs** of production. The gap between the two curves is the marginal externality. We have drawn the curves so that the profit-maximizing condition for production is just satisfied at output E_1^*, for which the social marginal cost, $MC^S(E_1^*) = p$, the price at which the power station can sell its output.

By yourself

X22.13 Confirm that where the private solution is allowed to emerge, the power station makes (economic) profits, but when the social optimum is imposed, it makes losses.

X22.14 We have argued that power networks are likely to experience increasing returns to scale in production. Adapting Figure 22.3, explain why this might increase the need to impose the socially optimal outcome *argue MC magg.*

$\uparrow$MC at every level of output

At the social optimum, the power station accepts liability for costs that other firms incur. It does so in a way that increases its marginal costs at every level of output, and so we can be certain that its profit-maximizing output will fall compared with the output at the private optimum.

π max. $\downarrow$, at output at the private optimum.

MC, P

P.

output, E

22.2.2 Socially optimal taxation

To ensure the social optimum, we assume that there is a social planner who is able to implement all necessary policies. We treat government as having this capacity.

The most obvious way for government to change prices is by imposing a tax. The ideal form of this tax – the so-called **Pigovian tax** – was first defined by Pigou in the 1920s: it should have a variable rate, the marginal social cost at every level of output. In Figure 22.3, such a tax would be the (vertical) distance between the two marginal cost curves at every level of output. The total revenue from the tax is then the total cost of the negative externality that the power company imposes on other producers. Were market conditions to change, the structure of such a tax would ensure that it would immediately adjust its output so that the new socially optimal outcome would be achieved.

> **Pigovian tax** A tax whose marginal rate is the marginal social cost less the marginal private cost.

The data required for the calculation of marginal tax rates under these circumstances is understandably difficult to collect. It may often be easier for a government to propose that there should be a simpler tax. We shall assume here that the tax is a simple lump-sum (flat-rate) tax or excise duty per unit of output produced, set so that a profit-maximizing firm, given the existing market conditions, will choose the socially optimal output. We illustrate this in Figure 22.4. The marginal cost curve increases at an increasing rate for all levels of output, as does the externality. The gap between the marginal social cost curve and the marginal cost curves becomes larger as output increases. To address the problem of the externality, the government sets the excise duty per unit sold, t. At the market price, p, which we assume remains unchanged, the power station will receive an amount, $p - t$. The profit-maximizing condition, $MC(E_1^*) = p - t$ is then satisfied, and the firm produces the output consistent with the social optimum.

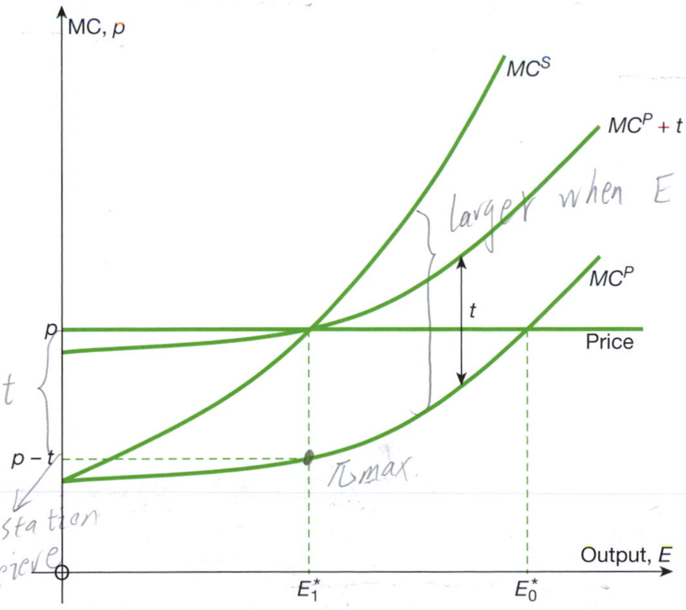

Figure 22.4 Correcting an externality using a flat-rate tax

Since it is unlikely that a government will introduce a tax that meets the Pigovian criteria, given the difficulties of identifying marginal effects of the externality, it will generally be necessary to adjust tax rates as market conditions change. The imposition of a tax will affect welfare in ways other than simply reducing or eliminating the externality. Firstly, a tax raises revenues, which the government must allocate in some way. If the government uses tax revenue to provide services directly, then this may increase concerns about there being welfare losses, which are caused by deviations from the efficient allocation of resources. We have also assumed that the collection of taxes, and the application of the revenue, can be undertaken costlessly, which is generally not the case. Facing a tax based on output, the power station might deliberately claim to have a lower output than is actually the case in order to reduce its liability. Were the tax to be imposed on the level of the externality rather than the level of traded output, then, since there is no market for the externality, it would be easy for firms to systematically under-report activity in order to evade the tax liability. Overall, even where such a tax might completely eliminate the negative externality resulting from the power station's activity, it would be likely to create new, efficiency-reducing distortions within the economy. For example, suppose that the effects of the pollution are particularly severe on farms raising livestock. If the compensation secured for these losses were sufficiently generous, then farmers might change their activities, increasing the size of their herds above the size they would have been had the power station not been built. A social planner may well consider such distortions to be so large as to make the cure worse than the initial problem.

By yourself

X22.15 We have assumed in this argument that there is no change in the market price, assuming that the power station faces perfect competition. Consider the situation facing the industry, and explain why this is unlikely. Indicate what you would expect to happen to the market price and the quantity produced, taking into account the likely effects on the market price and the quantity that each firm will produce.

X22.16 Compare the marginal tax rate imposed when applying the Pigovian and the flat-rate tax.

X22.17 Repeat the analysis of the imposition of a tax, assuming that the government applies an *ad valorem* tax (that is, a tax that is a constant proportion of the value of sales). Explain why the Pigovian tax will be an *ad valorem* tax when both the marginal private cost and the marginal social cost functions are linear.

X22.18 Treating the government as a social planner, what concerns might it have about the effect of a tax on a single good in general equilibrium? [*Hint:* Think of the condition that $MRT = MRS$ for all goods.]

22.2.3 Quantity restrictions and licensing

Given these problems with applying a tax, the social planner might seek other ways of managing the externality in production. We can summarize these as:

- Quantity restrictions, in effect administrative limits on output.
- Licensing arrangements, whereby businesses purchase the right to generate the negative externality. A recent extension of this approach has been to propose the creation of markets for negative externalities, so that businesses might trade such rights.

Simple quantity restrictions can be modelled in a very similar way to the taxes we have already imposed. In Figure 22.5, we assume that the government sets a maximum output of

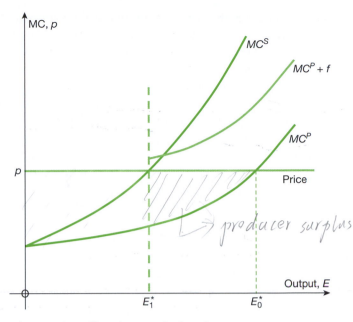

Figure 22.5 Correcting an externality using an output quota

Handwritten annotations (right margin):
$MC^P + f$
$> MC^P$
$f \geq t$
$MC^P(E) + f$
should it try to produce greater output

E_1^* for the power station. In effect, we have to assume that there is some sanction that could be imposed should the power station consciously exceed that goal. We also assume here that the government can verify output (costlessly) and that the business's operating licence permits the government to impose fines in the event of output being above the target. By the nature of the problem, the marginal (private) cost will definitely be greater than the marginal cost at output E_1^*. If the fine levied $f \geq t$, the excise duty from the preceding section, then the power station in Figure 22.4 will face a total marginal cost $MC^P(E) + f$, should it try to produce greater output.

Handwritten: $MC^P > MC$ at $\bar{E}_1^*$

By yourself

X22.19 Adapt Figure 22.5 to show the situation in which the combination of licence and fine fails to reduce the externality to the optimal level. *Handwritten:* E_1^* firm willing to pay fine, E above max. limit level

X22.20 Suppose that the government is able to require producers to pay a licence fee, without which all production is illegal. Indicate on your diagram the size of the largest fee that the government could persuade a power station to pay.

X22.21 Confirm that whether or not a licence fee is collected, the usual efficiency conditions for general equilibrium cannot be satisfied when production is restricted. [*Hint:* Concentrate on the values of the marginal products of input factors, assuming that businesses require both capital and labour inputs.]

X22.22 Suppose that the government issues licences allowing firms to produce any output up to the socially optimal output E_1^*, but with a fixed payment, irrespective of the scale of output. Assume that the government sets the fee so that it captures the entire surplus of a business operating at the maximum scale. Show that no business will wish to enter the market and operate at a smaller scale. Discuss why the businesses already in the market might be willing to accept such a restriction.

Handwritten (bottom): lump-sum tax → max. producer surplus

Handwritten (bottom left): firm will make loss, existing firm break even

We can see that a licence fee is rather like a tax in that it raises revenue for the government. We can also see that as a lump-sum levy it might act as a barrier to entry, and that in production the value of the marginal product for factors will be greater in the regulated industry than in other industries. The standard conditions for optimization will therefore not apply. Once again, we see that there is the possibility of the management of the externality leading to substantial divergences from the socially optimal use of resources. This is true here, where we assume that the government has complete information, and so can set tax or output levels perfectly for every power station, while also detecting all attempts to evade tax, and without there being any costs associated with these activities. We do not expect this to be the case, and so we look for other solutions to this problem.

In our analysis of general equilibrium, we found good reasons for supposing that an economy will achieve a Walrasian equilibrium, so that resource usage will reflect both technical and economic efficiency. Suppose that we begin from a situation in which a government recognizes that it might be desirable to undertake some form of licensing, capping the production of the externality for each business. It might seem that businesses have an incentive to seek a very large cap. In Exercise X22.20, we have argued that an effective licensing procedure should lead each business to pay the value of the surplus it would generate from production at the socially optimal level. In X22.22, we have argued that such a cap makes the structure of the industry very rigid, making entry difficult.

Assuming that regulation of the industry takes this form, suppose that some business develops an innovation that has the effect of reducing the extent to which it produces the externality. However, if firms are required to buy a licence that allows them to produce a set amount of the traded output, then the business that has developed the innovation will find it difficult to use it. The licence reflects the extent to which the existing technology generates the inequality, but on the basis that there is a fixed relationship between the production of the externality and the production of the traded good. To the innovator, planning on reducing emissions, acquiring a licence may well seem to be unnecessarily costly.

By yourself

X22.23 We continue to assume that the activities of a power station include pollution of the water supply for all firms operating downstream. Instead of licensing power generation, the government tolerates the production of the externality, here pollution. (It is still possible to detect all unlicensed emissions costlessly; and the fines imposed for failure to obtain licences in advance are large enough to ensure perfect compliance.) We also assume that the licensing environment involves two elements. Power stations can either:

- undertake to pay the costs of pollution recovery directly, $c = c_1 x + c_2 x^2$, where x is the level of pollution; or else
- purchase a licence permitting the production of a specific number of units of pollution, paying a fee f per unit.

    All power stations generate pollution $x = x_1 E$, where E is the plant's power output.

(a) Write down an expression for the costs of: (i) recovering the externality; and (ii) paying the licence fee in terms of the output of power.

(b) Calculate the level of output, x^*, above which a power station would prefer to pay the fixed licence fee rather than the recovery costs.

(c) Show that if process innovation leads to a reduction in the value of c_2, the value of x^* will also increase.

X22.24 We typically define the marginal abatement cost for a power station as being the rate of change in the cost of reducing production of an externality with the level of output. Assume that a power station is initially producing externality x_0, but recovers a quantity, x, and that its total abatement cost, $c = c_1x + c_2x^2$.

(a) Write down an expression for the marginal abatement cost.

(b) Sketch a diagram showing the marginal abatement cost (but show the unrecovered component of the externality on the horizontal axis, so that the curve is downward-sloping). Assume that the government charges a fee f for each unit of the externality that is not recovered. Show the power company's preferred level of recovery.

(c) Suppose that improvements in the recovery technology lead to a reduction in the value of c_2. Confirm that the power station will choose to increase the extent of recovery.

(d) Similarly, suppose that improvements in the production technology lead to a reduction in the value of x_1 at any level of output. Confirm that the power station will treat this as an improvement in technology that reduces its marginal cost, and will therefore tend to increase its output, while reducing production of the externality. $X_1 \downarrow MAC \downarrow$

(e) For marginal social cost $MC_s = s_1 + 2s_2x$, calculate the output at which the marginal recovery cost and the marginal social cost are equal. Explain why this is likely to be an economically efficient outcome. $MC = \dfrac{\partial c}{\partial x}$ $\quad c = c_1 x + c_2 (x - x_0)^2$

We have changed the focus of our analysis. In Exercise X22.23, the firm can avoid paying the licence fee for production of the externality by recovering it, thereby reducing its emission into the environment. For example, a power station, instead of simply returning waste water to the river might supply heating to nearby glasshouses, reducing their running costs. Exercise X22.24 illustrates that the effect of a proposal, which is often made in public debate, that there should be the complete elimination of an externality, may simply not be sensible in economic terms. The higher the level of the externality, the greater the marginal cost will be; but the higher the level of recovery, or **abatement**, the greater the marginal cost will be. If the extent of recovery is chosen so that the two marginal costs are equal, it will be as costly for the firm to reduce the externality further as it would be for society to accept a small increase in its level. We identify an optimal level of the externality, which is determined by the state of technology both for the production of the traded good and for recovery of the externality, and also by the impact of the externality on other producers.

> **Abatement cost** The cost borne by the producer in reducing an externality.

Note that this structure provides businesses with an incentive to reduce production of the externality, which a system of fixed-price licences would not. Figure 22.6 shows the effect of a business improving its recovery technology so that its marginal abatement cost falls from MAC_1 to MAC_2 for all levels of externality. Maintaining its output, and purchasing a licence to emit the externality at unit price, p, the firm increases recovery from $(x_1{}^* - x_0)$ to $(x_2{}^* - x_0)$. It therefore requires a licence only for the emission of a smaller amount of the externality.

22.2.4 Tradable permits

The last step in our analysis probably seems quite straightforward now. By licensing the production of the externality in such a way that businesses have an incentive to reduce its production, the government has transferred much of the responsibility for the management

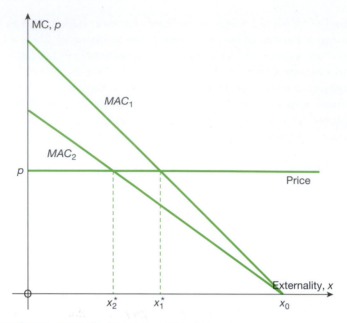

Figure 22.6 Correcting an externality by using variable licences

of the externality to its producers. Given concerns that managing an externality centrally is likely to be complex, and that by seeking to limit the effects of an externality through administrative means the government will introduce other inefficiencies into the economic system, this seems desirable in itself. It also suggests a rather different way of thinking about the problem, based on the identification of a missing market. We began by arguing that the externality would be in excess supply because no one demands it, even when the price is zero. In that analysis, we assumed that businesses had an unrestricted right to generate the externality. In developing the licensing solution, we have in effect placed restrictions on the right to produce, arguing that businesses may produce whatever amount of the externality they choose, so long as they are willing to pay for it. Allowing the government to represent the interests of society, we have in effect demonstrated that a firm in perfect competition will produce the externality to the extent that its willingness to pay $WTP_F = WTA_S$ – the government's, or the social planner's, willingness to accept. This is of course the fundamental condition for market clearing and efficiency, as introduced in Chapter 1.

There is an important difference between the arrangements we have been discussing and what we might consider to be a complete market: permits are not negotiable instruments. To vary its capacity to produce the externality, a business has to purchase or retire rights from the government. An alternative would be for the government to create negotiable, or tradable, instruments, typically in the form of permits, which would be divisible and which would also enable businesses to buy from one another and sell to one another the rights to generate the externality to. The government would retain a monopoly of permit issue, and so would be able to issue additional permits, or to purchase permits, or to cancel permits. For example, the governments of European Union states have developed markets for permits to produce emissions from industrial processes of gases that have been linked to climate change. This Emissions Trading Scheme (ETS) initially allocated rights to countries for a period of four years; in 2013, the lifespan for rights was changed to eight years, with much greater reliance on market-based allocations, typically in the form of the sale of rights through auctions, rather than on allocation based on historic usage. An active market for rights exists on the International Commodity Exchange, based in London.

With such tradable permits, the right to generate the externality becomes an asset of the business. For production to be technically efficient, we would expect businesses to hold the optimal quantity of assets. We would also expect the market price of permits to reflect demand, given the fixed supply (in any trading period). Governments have to anticipate the likely state of abatement technology during the lifespan of permits: excessive issue would fail to encourage abatement; but an overly restrictive issue would have a negative effect on total output. While attractive in principle, such a decentralized solution faces very considerable difficulties in implementation; as with the ETS, it often takes years for the system to operate as was originally intended.

22.3 Conclusions

We have concentrated in our analysis on externalities in production. Mention of the ETS should remind us that negative externalities may affect not only a specific community, but potentially the whole world, and for many years. The ETS is part of international efforts to address the widely recognized problem of climate change as an externality of production (and therefore, since production is not an end in itself, of consumption).

We have seen that there are many ways in which externalities can arise, but all take the form that there is a good for which the market is missing. In the case of the positive externality associated with the pollination activities of bees, we argued that resolution is very simple. Once the mutual benefit is identified, a market can be created. But in that case, the beneficiaries are easy to identify. We have also suggested that one element in the development of an industrial district is likely to be the emergence of specialist training institutions. This is a rather more complex example, because the beneficiaries of the development are not so easily defined. The social planner might impose the solution, but this again raises a question we shall address in the next chapter: how does the social planner obtain its authority? Thus far, we have assumed that the social planner is the government, or that the social planner behaves rather like a business that has identified an opportunity to exploit profit. In the case of skills training for industry, institutions might be formed (on a 'for profit' basis) by private individuals, effectively completing the missing markets. Other solutions are that (local) government, or some association of existing businesses, might sponsor them, using taxes or membership subscriptions to meet costs.

In the case of a negative externality, it is often sensible to look to government intervention for a solution, since very often the impact of the externality will be diffused across many people or businesses, making bilateral solutions more difficult. In addition, though, with a positive externality, there is excess demand for the good or service prior to the formation of a market. Without ignoring the possible difficulties, this often facilitates the emergence of a private solution. With a negative externality, the good associated with the externality is in excess supply at zero price. For this reason, the traditional economic analysis has been associated with the use of taxes or regulation to increase social welfare. The alternative solution, embodied in the ETS, is to rely on a definition of property rights that creates new goods, and hence new markets. We assume that the people suffering from the externality have a right to be free from it. Generation of the externality is then associated with loss of that good, and people and businesses are likely to be willing to accept sufficiently generous compensation their loss, whether mediated through market-based mechanisms, as with the ETS, or through the decisions of a social planner. With this in mind, we developed the concept of the optimal level of the externality, in which markets cleared. Frustrating as it might be when sitting in traffic that is not moving, so that our time is going to waste, we might hope that the capacity of the road network reflects such optimizing behaviour for society as a whole, and that the cost of additional road building would be less than the value placed on it. To understand better how we might perform those calculations is the object of the next chapter.

Summary

An externality is the effect of an action taken by a payoff-maximizing individual, which affects the payoffs of others, either positively or negatively. In our analysis, externalities are the result of the production decisions of firms and the consumption decisions of people.

Since an externality is a by-product of an activity, there is no market for it and it is unpriced. The value of the externality is therefore not included in decision making, with the result that with private decision making, the benefits of positive externalities will not be fully realized, while the costs of negative externality will not be fully met.

Where it is easy to identify both who produces and who is affected by the externality, it is relatively straightforward to resolve the problem. The producer can take account of the effect of the externality, and payments can be agreed reflecting marginal effects.

In other situations, it falls to the social planner to develop a solution. Treating the social planner as the government, the traditional response to a negative externality is the imposition of a tax. The ideal, Pigovian, tax is the marginal social cost at any level of activity. However, it is generally difficult to set such a tax, and approximations to it can distort economic behaviour. Such a policy can have unanticipated, damaging effects on welfare.

Alternatives to a tax are the imposition of price regulation, quantity regulation, or licensing arrangements. The use of tradable permits is an important development in licensing, in which there is a secondary market for permits. The social planner fixes the quantity of permits issued in any period, and allocates them according to some rules or else sells them through an auction process. Producers of the externality can then treat the permits as an asset, with holdings changing as need requires. A well-designed tradable permit scheme leads to an active market, and innovations that reduce production of the externality.

Visit the companion website at **www.palgrave.com/mochrie** to access further teaching and learning materials, including lecturer slides and a testbank, as well as guideline answers and student MCQs.

Public goods

What we do in this chapter

We have implicitly assumed that property rights over goods are well defined, so that it is possible to transfer ownership and rights of use. We classify such goods as *private* and introduce the concept of a *public good*, over which property rights are much more difficult to assert, and of which individual use does not imply consumption. Standard examples of public goods are broadcast signals, whether from a lighthouse, a radio or television mast, or a satellite orbiting the earth. No one can be prevented from receiving these signals, and their receipt does not diminish the quantity available for other people. The behaviour of the market for a public good is affected by these characteristics.

The need for public management and regulation of markets for public goods is rather more obvious than in markets for purely private goods. Rather than a law of one price in equilibrium, there is effectively a law of one quantity, with the whole quantity supplied of the public good being available to all potential consumers. We demonstrate that the efficiency condition for the supply of the public good can be expressed in terms of the equality of the marginal cost of expanding provision and the sum of all consumers' marginal *WTP*. We also show that

since individual use of the public good cannot be stopped, especially where there is redundancy in provision, there is a possibility of individual consumers withholding contributions to provision in the expectation that other consumers will fund provision. Such behaviour, which we call *free-riding*, has the capacity to reduce substantially the provision of the public good, or even to cause it to be abandoned.

With some degree of management of public good provision seeming necessary, we consider further the role of a social planner. We shall see that, as when considering externalities, the social planner has the capacity to impose the optimal outcome. This capacity seems most likely to emerge from consensus among economic agents, especially since, with even minimal restrictions on the form of social preferences, it is impossible for the social planner's actions to be fully democratic. Lastly, taking account of the analysis of public goods in terms of the nature of property rights, we demonstrate that it is possible to design a mechanism that supports truthful revelation of individual preferences. Using such a mechanism, for a project to go ahead it would need to generate a net benefit after deduction of costs.

23.1   Public goods

Congestion of a transport system every weekday morning reflects a negative externality which users impose upon each other. Applying our market-based approach, we should argue that a solution to this problem would be to charge for access to the system; but if we consider the public transport systems in most large cities, where most users have to pay to make a journey, the prices charged (at these peak periods) do not successfully ration usage to the point at which the externality is eliminated. Even though people stand in very crowded conditions, we argue that such an outcome reflects their optimal resource allocation, given the constraints they face. In this chapter, we shall argue that as well as the presence of externalities, there are other difficulties in allocating property rights which might lead to the failure of the spontaneous emergence of markets for certain goods and services.

Think of a very simple good, such as an apple. We know that there is a market for apples. Ownership rights in an apple seem quite easy to define in terms of physical possession. The owner can decide to allocate those property rights or to consume the apple, perhaps selling it to someone else or giving it to a child, or else eating it raw or using it in a recipe. We therefore say that the apple is **excludable**. The owner of the apple decides exactly who should be able to consume it. We also define it as being **rivalrous** *(in consumption)*. Once the right of use has been conferred by the owner, the apple is no longer available to be consumed by anyone else. Consumption involves the destruction of the apple, or at the very least its transformation and incorporation into another good. For more complex goods, we might say that for rivalrous goods, consumption of some quantity by one person reduces the quantity available to all other people. We define goods as being **private goods** when they are both excludable and rivalrous. Private goods therefore have well-defined property rights, and markets for them emerge quite naturally. In this chapter, we are interested in goods that do not have these properties. We begin with **public goods**, defined as having neither of these properties, so that they are both *non-excludable* and *non-rivalrous*.

Excludability
A property of a good that allows its owner to prevent others from using it.

Rivalrousness
A property of a good such that use by one person reduces the quantity available to others.

Private good A good that is excludable and rivalrous.

Public good A good that is both non-excludable and non-rivalrous.

By yourself

X23.1   Discuss the extent to which the following are likely to be either non-excludable or non-rivalrous in consumption:
(a) Air (that is, the gases constituting the atmosphere of the earth).
(b) Water held in a reservoir for domestic and industrial usage.
(c) The road system surrounding a city; and the pavements of the city streets.
(d) The public transport system (rail, buses, trams, etc.).
(e) The benefits of an inoculation campaign for an infectious disease such as polio.
(f) The national defence and security services provided by the government.
(g) Global positioning by satellite technology.

Of the items listed above, air appears both non-rivalrous and non-excludable. At birth, we all start to breathe the air around us. We continue to do that virtually continuously so long as we are alive, and so access to the atmosphere is non-excludable. The decision of one person to use more air (as a result of exercising vigorously) does not reduce the amount that is available to other people, or indeed to other animals. It therefore appears to be non-rivalrous. We might note, though, that for many centuries people have used the atmosphere as a dumping ground. They have released gases into it on the assumption that it was an inexhaustible reservoir and that their actions would not affect its properties. In many cities, however, that assumption has been demonstrated to be false, with the atmospheric pollution associated with industrial activity causing a substantial deterioration in air quality.

In the 1950s, alarmed by the increasing frequency of dense fog (smog) and the associated incidence of sometimes fatal respiratory diseases, the UK government passed the Clean Air

Act (1956), which placed substantial restrictions on the use of fossil fuels and industrial activities in many urban areas. Many other countries have since adopted similar legislative controls. More recently, as discussed in Chapter 22, concern that the changing composition of the atmosphere is leading to global climate change has led to concerted international action to restrict the release of potentially harmful gases into the atmosphere. Note that these steps involve the redefinition of property rights: if everyone has a right of access to the atmosphere, then emissions that threaten that right deserve to be restricted, either through regulation or through the creation of markets. In this case, note that we do not create a market for access to the public good, the atmosphere, but rather for the right to alter it, and so, potentially, to cause damage to it.

23.1.1 Broadcast signals as a public good

A lighthouse is a classic example of a public good; a much more current, and more widely used, version of the same service is provided by the global positioning system (GPS). A coastal navigation system, consisting mainly of buoys but also lighthouses, enables mariners to manoeuvre their vessels safely through hazardous waters. A ship's navigator can use marine charts to identify each light, and instruments to work out the ship's position. With the GPS, buoys and lighthouses are replaced by a chain of artificial satellites that orbit the earth, with never less than four visible at any time from any point on the earth's surface. Instead of a navigator having to calculate position, a GPS receiver can use the data transmitted by satellites to do this automatically. The lighthouse, the buoys and the satellites are all transmitters of broadcast signals: the users of these navigational systems simply receive them. As with terrestrial television or radio stations, there is no way of preventing these broadcasts from being received; and since satellites transmit their signals from high in the sky, the fact that one person receives them does not affect other users of the system in any way.

By yourself

X23.2   What evidence is there that people's *WTP* for the location identification services provided by GPS is greater than zero?

X23.3   GPS was developed by the Department of Defense in the USA for its own purposes. Why might we expect a government agency to have taken the lead in this project, rather than relying on market-based institutions to provide the investment?

X23.4   Consider a proposal to install streetlights in a small village. The proposal will go ahead if the amount that each villager is willing to contribute to the fund meets the cost of providing the lights. What difficulties might there be in relying only on voluntary contributions to fund the scheme?

The radio signals that GPS receivers use are transmitted continuously and reach across the whole surface of the earth. In principle, it is available to every driver, of any vehicle, who buys a satellite navigation receiver. Once the receiver has been purchased, though, the (marginal) usage cost is very close to zero. The *WTP* of users is therefore almost an irrelevance: the technology of production guarantees excess supply, with zero marginal cost to both supplier and the user. With perfect competition, we expect price to be set equal to marginal cost: a zero price suggests that private providers would not be able to provide the good. Instead, we would expect to see publicly supported provision.

Using the example of a lighthouse, economists have long noted that it is perfectly possible for a ship to pass by a lighthouse, using the signal to avoid hazards, and then to sail on. Were the lighthouse to be privately owned, then the owner would be unable to collect a fee directly from users. Nonetheless, every ship berths at some point, and the owners of ports may well find it to their advantage to make payments to the operators of nearby lighthouses (and other navigational aids) on the basis that shipowners are more likely to direct their traffic to a port at which the risk of loss is carefully managed. Following the work of Ronald Coase, some economists have argued in recent years that, as in the discussion of positive externalities in Chapter 22, the problem of provision of such goods lies in ensuring that property rights are well defined, so that some form of decentralized solution is viable. The important questions then revolve around the organizational structure of the industry. It seems unlikely, for example, that it would be more efficient for separate businesses to be formed to manage individual navigation buoys; indeed, we might argue that it would be most efficient to form a single business, granting it a monopoly over the management of a port and the neighbouring coastal waters. Rather than simply rely on the disciplines imposed by a market in the long run, private provision would take place in the context of a managed market with active regulation. As long ago as 1604, James I granted the Corporation of Trinity House a monopoly over pilotage in the Thames Estuary. Over the next 200 years, its authority and powers extended steadily further, until, in 1836, Parliament granted it the power to acquire and maintain all private lighthouses. As Britain became increasingly dependent on trade, regulation of coastal navigation steadily increased in order to realize the positive externalities associated with centralized management.

23.1.2 The free-riding problem

With the example of streetlighting in Exercise X23.4, it may seem that every household, h, in a village would benefit from its provision, valuing it at v_h. Supposing that someone living in the village simply proposes that there should be streetlights, sending every household an invitation to make a pledge of a contribution, c_h, to a joint fund, with the streetlights being installed should the pledged total across the n households in the village exceed the installation price, P:

$$C = \sum_{h=1}^{n} c_h \geq P \qquad [23.1]$$

- Using the concept of a best reply from game theory, suppose that a utility-maximizing householder believes that the value of other households' contributions $C_h^E > P$. The best reply, $c_h^*(C_h^E)$, of household h is then zero, since pledging money would not affect the provision of the service, but would reduce the household's ability to derive utility from other goods and services.
- Similarly, if a household believes that even pledging its full value, v_h, the total pledged $C < P$, or that the expected pledges of other households $C_h^E + v_h < P$, then all pledges in the range $0 \leq c_h \leq v_h$ are best replies, since they will not be called upon.
- Lastly, if the household believes that the total value of other households' pledges lies in the region $C_h^E \leq P - v_h \leq C$, then the household's best reply $c_h^*(C_h^E) = P - C_h^E$, so that the streetlighting is provided, but with the household making the minimum contribution required for provision to take place, since $C = P$.

By yourself

X23.5 Confirm that if the sum of household valuations, $V : V = \sum_{h=1}^{n} c_h < P$, then the proposal to install streetlights must fail.

X23.6 Assume that $v_h = v$, so that every household places the same value on the service, and that the feasibility condition in X23.5 is satisfied. Confirm that there are two symmetric Nash equilibria: (a) where $c_h = 0$ for every household; and (b) where $c_h = c$, and $C = nc = P$. Discuss whether equilibrium (a) or equilibrium (b) seems more likely to occur.

X23.7 Confirm that there is an equilibrium in which for household n, $c_n = 0$, but for all other households, $c_h = \frac{P}{n-1} < v$. Discuss the likelihood of being able to sustain such an equilibrium.

The game is similar to the *Stag Hunt* example in Section 18.4. People in the village would benefit from acting in concert; however, if they do not trust each other enough, then they will not make a pledge of support towards the provision of the streetlights; or else, if they do make one, they do so in the expectation that others will not pledge sufficient support for the project to go ahead.

Exercise X23.7 demonstrates a possibility that might arise when relying on voluntary contributions for the provision of a public good. Household n is known to be owned by a miser. Everyone else in the village expects that the miser will pledge nothing towards the provision of the streetlights, and so they realize that they must each make a slightly larger pledge than they would otherwise in order for provision to go ahead. We see that the payoff to the $n - 1$ households contributing c_h is:

$$0 < v - \frac{P}{n-1} < v \qquad [23.2]$$

The miser, by not contributing, obtains the payoff v from the streetlights, and is better off than all of the households that do contribute. Again, this reflects the structure of more complex *Stag Hunt* games than the two-player games that we have investigated: if there is redundancy in the hunting process, in the sense that the hunting party is larger than is required to catch the stag, every player has an incentive to be the first to defect, to go off and catch a hare, and then return to the party to obtain a share of the stag. We refer to such behaviour as **free-riding**: a player who is confident that others will make sufficiently large voluntary contributions so that the public good will be provided has no incentive to make any contribution towards its provision. The interesting question is not about the miser's failure to contribute, but rather about the others' willingness to do so.

Free-riding Obtaining access to a public good without contributing to the cost of its provision.

23.1.3 Optimal provision of a public good

In introducing the concept of market clearing in Chapter 2 for what we have here defined as a *private* good, we treated individual demands as the inverse of a person's *WTP*, with market demand simply being the sum of individual demands. Considering again a simple model of the market for apples, we can define each household's demand for apples, $q_h(p)$, and write the market demand, $Q^D(p)$, as:

$$Q^D(p) = \sum_{h=1}^{n} q_h(p) \qquad [23.3]$$

With a *public* good, the market demand has a different formulation. In our example of the streetlights in a village, in effect we added up individual households' *WTP* for a fixed supply of the good. Rather than define the market demand in the conventional way as a function of price, we should define the total willingness to pay across the *n* households in the village, so that for a level of provision, *S*:

$$WTP^n(S) = \sum_{h=1}^{n} WTP_h(S) \qquad\qquad [23.4]$$

The different forms of Expressions 23.3 and 23.4 reflect the distinction that with a private good, the market demand is the total sum of individual demands at a given price, while with a public good, the total willingness to pay for provision of the public good is the sum of each household's *WTP*, given the level of provision.

This analysis takes as given the extent of provision of the public good. Like any private good, there are costs of supplying the public good. We therefore expect to find some form of optimality condition that will be satisfied in equilibrium. Given the nature of the market demand, this turns out to be slightly different from the conditions we have obtained for private goods. We illustrate this in Figure 23.1. The downward-sloping, solid lines represent individual marginal *WTP* measures, which is to say that they measure the rate of change of *WTP* as provision of the good changes. Total *WTP* for each individual can then be measured as the area under the *MWTP* to the left of the output level, *q*. (Note that we refer to *marginal WTP* here because we are interested in finding out how total payments change with the level of provision of the public good.)

We construct the market *MWTP* curve, which is the dashed line, $MWTP^n(q)$, by taking the individual *WTP* curves and aggregating them vertically. We could call this curve the market demand for the public good, in effect inverting the relationship, but we avoid this terminology to emphasize the nature of the aggregation of individual *WTP* measures.

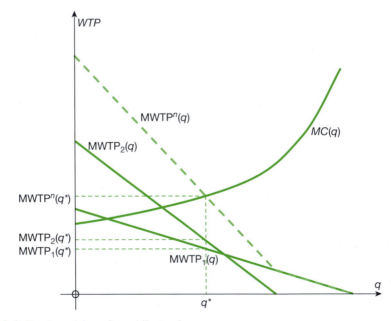

Figure 23.1 Optimal provision of a public good

The market *MWTP* curve is therefore a measure of the public good provider's marginal revenue, assuming that there is no free-riding. In this instance, we can treat the provider as a social planner, expecting the planner to expand provision until the marginal cost of provision equals the market *MWTP*. In the diagram, we show this outcome occurring where provision is q^*.

By yourself

X23.8 Suppose that Vishal and William live in houses at the end of a narrow track, 100 m in length. They have received an offer from a local contractor who is willing to pave and widen the track as part of a development project, but Vishal and William have to meet the cost of provision, which is £250 per metre. Assume that Vishal's marginal willingness to pay, $MWTP_V$ = £125/m; while for William, $MWTP_W$ = 250 − 1.25x, where x is the length of paved road.

   (a) Sketch a diagram to show the marginal cost, the individual *MWTP* curves, and the market *MWTP* curve. Indicate the economically efficient outcome, and confirm that this involves paving the full length of the track.

   (b) Suppose that the marginal cost of provision were to increase to £300/m. How would you expect the efficient outcome to change?

   (c) Suppose instead that Vishal's circumstances change and he has to use the track more often. Now $MWTP_V$ = 250. If William knows this, how might his behaviour change?

23.1.4 A utility-maximizing approach

Discussing optimal behaviour in terms of willingness to pay misses out much of the analysis, which we have developed already. With private goods, in Chapters 21 and 22, we obtained conditions necessary for general equilibrium in terms of efficient resource allocations. We now apply that approach to our preliminary analysis of the efficient provision of public goods. The general conditions for equilibrium will be very similar to the ones we have just identified.

Continuing with the example we have started to develop, we assume that as well as the road to their houses, Vishal and William obtain utility from consumption of a single private good, the floor area of their houses, and so we denote their consumption bundles, C_V: (R, S_V), for Vishal and C_W: (R, S_W), for William. Note that they both have access to the same quantity of the public good, but can choose to alter the size of their house without affecting the size of the other one. We shall define efficient resource allocation in terms of Vishal achieving utility maximization in the context of affordability and feasibility constraints, with the feasibility constraint taking the form of a utility target for William.

We write:

- Vishal's utility function, $U_V = U_V(R, S_V)$; William's utility function, $U_W = U_W(R, S_W) \geq U_0$.
- Unit price of road (per metre), $p_R = p$; marginal cost of floor space (per square metre), $p_S = 1$.
- Affordability constraint: $pR + S_V + S_W = m = m_V + m_W$, where m_I is the value of Vishal's and William's endowment; and m is the value of the total endowment.
- The problem:

$$\max_{R, S_V, S_W} U_V(R, S_V) : U_W(R, S_W) \geq U_0; \text{ and } pR + S_V + S_W = m \qquad [23.5]$$

By yourself

X23.9   Given the problem in Expression 23.5:

(a) Form the Lagrangean, and by partial differentiation with respect to R, S_v and S_w, obtain the first-order conditions (FOCs), which must be satisfied in a Pareto-efficient outcome. [*Hint*: Note that there will be two Lagrangean multipliers.]

(b) By expressing the multipliers in terms of the partial derivatives, confirm that for any Pareto-efficient allocation, (R^*, S_v^*, S_w^*):

$$\frac{\partial U_v}{\partial R} \bigg/ \frac{\partial U_v}{\partial S_v} + \frac{\partial U_w}{\partial R} \bigg/ \frac{\partial U_w}{\partial S_w} = p \qquad\qquad [23.6]$$

Expression 23.6 is a generalization of the result that we obtained relating to willingness to pay for a public good. The terms on the left-hand side are ratios of marginal utilities, or marginal rates of substitution. With pairs of private goods, we required everyone's *MRS* to be equal, but with a public and a private good, we instead require that the sum of *MRS* should be equal to the relative price of the public good.

This result is intuitively sensible. On the left-hand side, we have the rates at which Vishal and William would be willing to give up consumption of the private good as the quantity of the public good increases: holding their payoff constant, the better road that the builder lays, the smaller their houses need be. The difference from the analysis of private goods is that rather than the individual marginal rates of substitution being equal to the relative price, it is now the sum of their marginal rates of substitution, which equals the relative price. If Expression 23.6 did not hold, then Vishal and William could be made better off by altering the provision of the public good.

Example: quasi-linear utility

To adapt our graphical analysis to this more general approach, it will be convenient to consider the case of quasi-linear preferences, so that the marginal utility of private good consumption is constant.

We write Vishal's utility function:

$$U_V = u_V(R) + S_V \qquad\qquad [23.7a]$$

and William's utility function:

$$U_W = u_W(R) + S_W \geq U_0 \qquad\qquad [23.7b]$$

with the sub-utility functions u_V and u_W both increasing but concave.

By yourself

X23.10   Given quasi-linear preferences, as in Expression 23.7:

(a) Write down expressions for the marginal utilities and the marginal rate of substitution for both Vishal and William.

(b) Confirm that the marginal rate of substitution depends only on the level of provision of the public good.

X23.11   Suppose that there is only Vishal's house at the end of the track, and that his utility function, $U_v = R^\alpha$. We now write his problem, $\displaystyle \max_{R,\, S_v} R^\alpha + S_v : pR + S_v = m_v$.

(a) Confirm that the marginal rate of substitution, $MRS_v = -\frac{\alpha}{R^{1-\alpha}}$. Hence sketch the indifference curves $U_v = 1, 2$ and 3. Confirm that when $R = 1$, $MRS = -1$ on all three indifference curves.

(b) Show that if $p = \alpha = 0.5$, and if $m_v > 0.5$, Vishal's most-preferred, affordable consumption bundle, $(R^*, S^*) = (1, m_v - 0.5)$. On your diagram, sketch Vishal's income expansion path.

X23.12 We return to the situation where Vishal and William share the access road, writing William's utility function, $U_w = R^\alpha + S_w$.

(a) On a diagram, sketch both Vishal's and William's marginal rate of substitution as the value of R increases.

(b) Confirm that both for Vishal and for William, the marginal rate of substitution does not vary with the house sizes, S_v and S_w.

(c) Apply and interpret the condition in Expression 23.6 in this case.

In Figure 23.1, we derived the equilibrium outcome for the situation where consumption of private goods was (implicitly) held constant. In Exercise 23.12, we allow consumption of the private good, S, to vary, but we impose a particular form on preferences, so that Vishal's and William's MRS does not depend on their consumption of the private good. The condition in Expression 23.6 must always apply for an allocation to be Pareto-optimal, but usually the marginal rate of substitution between a private and a public good will depend upon consumption of both. In general, we do not expect it to be possible simply to sum individual marginal rates of substitution to find the optimal level of provision of the public good.

It is to construct Figure 23.2 that we assume that preferences are quasi-linear. Since the MRS measures can then be defined solely in terms of the level of provision of the public good, R, it is possible to add them together. The optimal level of provision is then defined

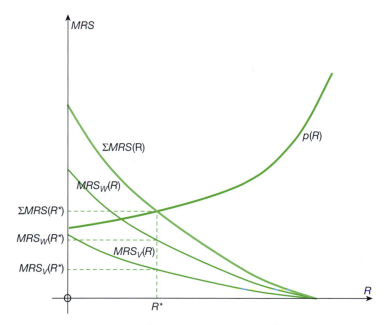

Figure 23.2 Pareto optimality conditions for supply of a public good, with quasi-linear preferences

so that the sum of the marginal rates of substitution, which is also the sum of the marginal utilities, equals the relative price of the public good. If we assume that all other markets, including those for factor inputs, are perfectly competitive, it follows that we can replace the supply curve with a marginal cost curve; and that at the Pareto optimum, the marginal rate of transformation, $MRT = MRS_V + MRS_W$. All the efficiency conditions of general equilibrium are then satisfied.

23.2   Managing public good provision

We have repeatedly demonstrated the capacity of decentralized structures to support efficient outcomes, most obviously in our derivation of a general equilibrium in Chapters 20 and 21. We have also noted: (1) that efficiency on its own does not allow us any way of choosing within the set of Pareto optimal outcomes; (2) that without property rights being cast in an appropriate form, externalities may lead to substantial inefficiencies; and (3) that reliance on voluntary contributions for the provision of public goods might lead to their under-provision. Our response to each of these situations has been to delegate the problem to a social planner, a single agent who has the capacity to direct otherwise independent agents' behaviour. We have associated the social planner with government, but we have said nothing about the nature of this government. It could have any form on a spectrum running from totalitarian dictatorship through to participative democracy.

23.2.1   Social welfare and preference aggregation

Given concerns we have expressed about intervention in markets, it may seem consistent for us to argue that the social planner's preferences should express and embody individual preferences over outcomes. Suppose, though, that we consider a small society, with three members, Anya, Brinda, and Claudia. They face three outcomes, which we shall label **x**, **y** and **z**: we can think of these as being allocations of their total endowment, expressed in the form of consumption bundles, consisting of a mixture of private and public goods. Now, suppose that we can write their preferences:

$$
\begin{array}{ll}
\text{Anya:} & \mathbf{x} > \mathbf{y} > \mathbf{z} \\
\text{Brinda:} & \mathbf{y} > \mathbf{z} > \mathbf{x} \\
\text{Claudia:} & \mathbf{z} > \mathbf{x} > \mathbf{y}
\end{array}
\qquad [23.8]
$$

By yourself

X23.13 Anya, Brinda, and Claudia want to find the socially preferred outcome.
- (a) Suppose that they each have one vote, which they may cast for their own most-preferred outcome. What will happen?
- (b) Suppose that they agree to engage in successive comparisons of pairs of outcomes. Show (i) that if **x** is compared with **y**, and then the more-preferred outcome is compared with **z**, they will choose **z**; but (ii) that if **y** is compared with **z**, and then the more-preferred outcome is compared with **x**, then **x** will be preferred.
- (c) Show that it is possible using successive pairwise comparisons for **y** to be most preferred.

> **X23.14** Claudia decides that this situation is too complicated and leaves. Anya and Brinda now try again, with each assigning three points to their most-preferred, two to their second-ranked, and one to their least-preferred, outcomes.
> (a) Confirm that on this basis they will choose outcome **y**.
> (b) Suppose instead that, before evaluating their preferences, they agree that since neither of them ranks outcome **z** highest, they should exclude it. How would this affect their choice?

Neither majority voting in Exercise X23.13, nor rank-order voting in Exercise X23.14, turns out to be entirely satisfactory. Even in these very simple cases, we see that it is possible to manipulate outcomes: with rank-order voting, simply by including seemingly irrelevant outcomes in the set of alternatives; and with majority voting, effectively by control of the order and the nature of the choices to be made. Of course, these are very simple examples, and so we might reasonably object that these examples cannot simply be carried over to more realistic situations.

Here, though, we can rely on an important result, first demon-strated by Kenneth Arrow: **Arrow's impossibility theorem**. We begin by assuming that the social welfare function takes the form of a ranked voting system reflecting individual preferences, and that the welfare function has similar properties to individual preferences. Specifically, we assume that both individual and social preferences are complete, reflexive and transitive. With n people involved in making decisions, each of whom forms a preference ordering, $\pi_i(A)$, over the set of possible outcomes, we can treat the social preference ordering, $\Pi(A)$, as a function of the individual preference orderings. The theorem states that it is then impossible for any social preference, $\Pi(A)$, to satisfy these three properties simultaneously:

> **Arrow's impossibility theorem** No rank-order voting system can convert individual preferences into a satisfactory social preference ordering.

- *Unanimity*: If in every individual preference ordering, π_i, for outcomes a and b, $a > b$, then in the social preference ordering, Π, $a > b$.
- *Independence of irrelevant alternatives*: Suppose that people are confronted with either one of two possible sets of outcomes, A_1 and A_2. Outcomes a and b are members of both outcome sets, so will be considered along with other possible outcomes. We define individual preference orderings $\pi_{1,I}$ over outcome set A_1, and $\pi_{2,I}$ over outcome set A_2. We also define social preference orderings, Π_1 and Π_2, over each outcome set. With outcomes a and b in both A_1 and A_2, everyone's pairwise comparison of a and b will be independent of the set of available alternatives. We then require that the ranking of a and b derived from the social preferences Π_1 and Π_2 will be independent of the other elements of the outcome set.
- *Non-dictatorship*: There is no individual, D, whose preference ordering, π_D, forms the social preference ordering, Π.

All three properties seem desirable for any social preference ordering. It would seem rather strange, were everyone to agree that outcome a is preferable to outcome b, that the social preference should then ignore such unanimity. Should the range of available outcomes change, it would also seem rather strange that either individual or social preferences between outcomes a and b should change. This leaves us with the matter of dictatorship. We would like the social preferences to reflect everyone's preferences. However, Arrow proved that for a social preference ordering to meet the requirements of consistency imposed by the unanimity and independence properties, it must be the ordering of a single person. This is not a recommendation for dictatorship, since it does not exclude representative democracy. We should understand the theorem as meaning that there will be circumstances in which people should be willing to accept the direction of a single social planner.

23.2.2 Managing free-riding

Vickrey–Clarke–Groves mechanism (VCG) A mechanism that charges people for the costs that their choices impose on others.

Mechanism An incentive structure designed to elicit the truthful revelation of type or preferences.

Until now, we have typically assumed that people will state their preferences truthfully, even though we know that it is possible that people will choose to free-ride. We therefore discuss a simple example of the Vickrey–Clarke–Groves mechanism (VCG), which can be applied in a wide variety of situations, and which is designed to ensure that people truthfully reveal their preferences. We need to define the term mechanism: a type of incentive structure, used extensively within economic theory, that is likely to ensure that people participating in some optimization process will reveal their type accurately. In this case, the VCG mechanism ensures that people who have access to a public good will declare their private valuations accurately. The social planner can then collect payments from them: the mechanism is the rule for the payment made to the social planner given declared valuations, and provides a strong incentive for truthful declarations in that any who lie about their valuation would reduce their net payoff. To free-ride in these circumstances, a person would have to state a value other than their true *WTP*. Compensating other people for the loss that they suffer as a result of the failure to make a truthful declaration is more costly than stating their true valuation, so everyone declares their true valuation. The social planner can therefore rely on the mechanism to generate a Pareto-efficient outcome in situations where there is incomplete information.

Central to the operation of the mechanism is the concept of the *pivotal participant*. The planner does not seek to collect payments from everybody, but only from those participants whose declarations affect the payoffs to other participants. We shall keep our analysis simple by assuming that the supply of the public good has already been determined, so that all that the social planner has left to do is to invite contributions. (For an efficient outcome, we therefore require the feasibility constraint, Expression 23.1, to be satisfied, so that the public good will be provided so long as the total declared values, $V \geq P$, the cost of providing it.) The social planner operates the mechanism by requiring each of the N possible beneficiaries of the provision of the good to pay an equal share, $p_i = \frac{P}{N}$, towards the cost of provision; and also, at the same time, to declare their valuation, v_i, of the good. So far, this is more or less what we might expect with voluntary provision, except that now people declare their *value*, rather than their voluntary contribution. This reflects the fact that the social planner now requires an additional set of transfers, but only from those people whose participation is pivotal, in the sense that their decision determines whether (or not) the public good will be supplied.

- If $V \geq P$, the planner concludes that provision is efficient, but requires additional payments to be made from among those participants benefiting from the decision to provide the good, for whom $v_i > p$, and who effectively impose costs on the participants, for whom $v_i < p$.
- If $V < P$, then the project will be cancelled, and the initial payments returned, but now payments will be collected from among those for whom $v_i < p$, who benefit from that decision, but who now effectively impose costs on participants for whom $v_i > p$.

Whatever the outcome, the transfers should just meet the externality associated with the social planner's decision about whether or not to proceed.

It may be easiest to work through an example of how the mechanism operates. Suppose that Vishal and William are now joined by William's brother Xavier. Together, they agree to buy a plasma TV so that they can watch the football World Cup finals. Treating this as a public good, they agree to use the VCG mechanism to calculate fair payments.

- They each agree to make an initial contribution, $p_i = 600$, meeting the total rental, $P = 1,800$.
- Vishal and William state that their values $v_V = v_W = 500$; Xavier states that his value $v_X = 800$.

We see that the sum of declared values, $V = P$, so that the total surplus, $S = V - P = 0$, and provision is (just) efficient. We conclude that in this situation, Xavier is pivotal, while Vishal and William are not.

- For both Vishal and William, the surplus from participation, $s_V = s_W = -100$; while for Xavier, $s_X = 200$.
- Considering the surplus, and ignoring either Vishal's or William's individual surplus, the total surplus, $S_{\sim V} = S_{\sim W} = 100 > 0$. (The notation '$\sim V$' means 'excluding Vishal', and '$\sim W$' means 'excluding William'.) Provision remains efficient.
- Excluding Xavier, the total surplus, $S_{\sim X} = -200$. Provision would become inefficient.
- Unsurprisingly, we see that the project goes ahead only because of Xavier's relatively high declared value, v_X. This confirms that Xavier is pivotal.
- The social planner therefore requires Xavier to make a transfer, $k_X = 200$. To avoid the possibility of Vishal and William understating their valuations, the planner does not distribute Xavier's payment to them.

By yourself

X23.15 Suppose that $v_X = 1,000$. Confirm that Xavier is still pivotal, and that the social planner will still require him to make a transfer, $k_X = 200$.

X23.16 Consider a case in which we have a public good for which total cost, $C = 5,000$, and with five possible participants, $i = 1, \ldots, 5$, benefiting from provision, with values $v_1 = 1,500$, $v_2 = 1,200$, $v_3 = 1,000$, $v_4 = 700$, and v_5 still to be declared. The social planner announces that the project requires initial contributions, $c_i = 1,000$. Show that:
(a) For $300 \leq v_5 < 600$, completion is inefficient; and participants 4 and 5 are pivotal, and so should transfer $k_4 + k_5 = 700$.
(b) For $600 \leq v_5 < 800$, completion is efficient: and participant 1 is pivotal, and so should transfer $k_1 = 1,300 - v_5$.
(c) For $800 \leq v_5 < 1,000$, completion is efficient; and participants 1 and 2 are pivotal, and so should transfer $k_1 + k_2 = 1,300 - v_5$.
(d) For $v_5 < 300$, the social planner will decide that completion of the project is inefficient; participant 5 is pivotal, and so should make a transfer $k_5 = 700$; and no participant is then worse off than if the project had gone ahead.

As the valuation, v_5, increases in Exercise X23.16, we see that the social planner's concern is Pareto efficiency. Whether or not the project is implemented, the application of the VCG mechanism ensures that no one is worse off than if the other decision had been made: this is plainly a simplification, since we here consider projects whose scope has been set in advance. We also note, though, how the nature of the transfers changes with the valuation, v_5.

In this example, the social planner will conclude that provision is (just) efficient for $v_5 = 600$. Suppose that we change the problem slightly, fixing v_5, but allowing this participant to declare any number c_5 as the valuation to the social planner:

- If $c_5 > 600$, then the project is certainly viable, but participant 5 is not pivotal.
- For $1{,}000 > c_5 > 600$, the surplus from participation $s_5(c_5) = v_5 - c_5 = 600 - c_5 < 0$.
- For $c_5 < 600$, then the project is not viable, and participant 5 is pivotal. The surplus from participation, $s_5(c_5) = -k_5 < 0$.
- For $c_5 = 600$, the project proceeds, so participant 5 is not pivotal; and $s_5(c_5) = 0$: a truthful statement of the valuation maximizes this participant's surplus.

The structure of this argument should seem familiar. Given the declared values of all other participants, this particular participant can do no better than to declare her or his valuation. Without referring to game theory at all, we have constructed the best reply for this participant.

Noting that we have made no assumptions about the form of declarations made by other participants, if we were to allow all participants' declared valuations to be an increasing function of their own private values and their beliefs about the values that other participants will declare, it is reasonable that there should be an equilibrium with truthful revelation of values. We do not seek to prove this claim here, but it turns out that in certain circumstances, where there are no opportunities for collusion among participants, truth-telling within the VCG mechanism is a dominant strategy.

23.2.3   Open access and common property

Open access resource A non-excludable but rivalrous resource.

Common property resource An excludable resource to which members of a group have access.

We began the discussion in Chapter 22 by considering congestion on a road system. Congestion is consistent with individual drivers making private optimizing decisions, but not taking account of the externality that they impose on each other. It also results, in part, from the decision that the road system should be an **open access resource**. It is not a public good, since there is plainly rivalry in consumption; at the same time, as an open access resource, it is not excludable. We can also define **common property resources**, to which members of a specific group have open access, but which are formally excludable to others. Since our interest here is in the management of such resources when private demands become so great that users begin to exert substantial negative externalities on each other, the distinction is not particularly important.

The classic statement of the need for management of such resources is Hardin's *Tragedy of the Commons*, a seemingly simple paper published in 1968. Hardin essentially notes that in the absence of property rights, the farmers of a village will continue to add to the herd of cattle which they keep grazing on the village's common land until there is no net private benefit at the margin. The farmer's marginal benefit, the revenue from being able to sell the cattle, is then equal to the marginal private cost. Considering the development of the village over time, we might expect to find that at very low stocking densities, there is no congestion of the common. Farmers can bring more cattle to graze without generating any externality. Gradually, though, as the stocking density increases, the cattle begin to exhaust their pasture. They put on weight more slowly, taking longer to be ready for market. At a high enough stocking density, even though there are more cattle grazing the common at any time, the rate at which they are brought to market declines as herd size increases further. It is only a social planner, and not the individual farmers, who takes account of the externality at the margin, and the gradually increasing gap between private and social outcomes.

By yourself

X23.17 Suppose that a village is surrounded by common land of 1,500 hectares. The farmers in the village use the common to graze cattle, achieving an output per hectare, C:

$$C = \begin{cases} y, y < 0.5 \\ -0.5 + 3y - 2y^2, 0.5 \le y < 1 \\ 0, otherwise \end{cases}$$

where y is the stocking density (cattle per hectare). All cattle may be sold for price $p = 1{,}200$, and we assume that the marginal cost of production, $c = 600y$.

(a) Show that the output per hectare, C is maximized at $y^* = 0.75$. Sketch a graph of the output per hectare. (Note that $C = 0$ if $y = 0$, or if $y > 1$.)

(b) If there is no management of the commons, farmers will continue to increase the number of cattle so long as the revenue that they obtain from selling the cattle exceeds the marginal cost. On your diagram, indicate what happens.

(c) If the commons are enclosed, so that a monopolist (a local landlord) is able to manage the land to maximize profits, the stocking density will be chosen to maximize profit. Show that this requires the landlord to maximize the stocking density.

The monopolist landlord is able to internalize the externality caused by congestion of the resource, while the individual farmers have no incentive to do so.

Note that the model we have just introduced is slightly unsatisfactory, in that it suggests that the marginal cost of production will remain constant as output increases. There are good reasons to expect there to be an increasing marginal cost of production: as the commons begins to be overgrazed, marginal costs might increase, perhaps because farmers have to buy additional feed for their animals and because other expenses, such as veterinary bills, increase. We have paid no attention to the effect of overgrazing on the future productivity of the land. In fact, we should expect overgrazing to reduce this considerably, so that the effects of the externality will continue to be felt not just this year, but also in future.

23.2.4 Fisheries management

Since Hardin wrote his paper, the global fishing industry has developed a substantial self-destructive capacity. Most developed countries limit access to their territorial waters, but until the mid-1970s, when countries started to assert management rights up to 200 miles from their coast, these were limited in extent. Until 1970, perhaps the most famous fishery in the world was the Grand Banks, off the coast of Newfoundland, Canada. Between 1900 and 1960, it produced between 200,000 and 300,000 tonnes of cod per year. Production then increased very rapidly, peaking at just over 800,000 tonnes in 1968 and 1969. In spite of an increasingly strict regulatory regime, the fishery was by 1991 largely exhausted. By 1994, Canada asserted its right to close the fishery entirely, with the moratorium on cod fishing remaining in place for over 20 years, during which the population has gradually recovered.

An open access fishery until 1978, for many years the Grand Banks attracted fishing boats from around the world: from the USSR, South Korea, and, towards the end of the period, boats registered in Central America but often owned by businesses based in the European Union, whose owners sought to avoid being required to adhere to regulation set by the North Atlantic Fisheries Organization. There is a certain irony that the actual destruction of the fishery occurred after Canada asserted its territorial rights in 1978, turning the fishery into a common property resource, which was open only to its own fishermen. The Canadian authorities set a quota of 250,000 tonnes per year in 1978. Fishermen and scientists realized that these quotas were higher than the sustainable level. By the early 1980s, the proportion of immature fish being caught started to increase rapidly, a sign that the population was reducing quickly. Nonetheless, provincial governments, such as Newfoundland's, continued to support increasing fleet capacity. Individual fishermen, who often incurred substantial debts in buying their boats, had no incentive to reduce their own efforts. This massive fishing effort appears to have almost eliminated the cod population, reducing the total biomass to an estimated 20,000 tonnes when the fishery was finally closed.

In fishery management, there are two principal methods: the management of effort; and the management of production. Management of effort will include such matters as fixing the number of days that a vessel can spend at sea, restricting the locations in which they might fish, placing limitations on vessels' size and power, and regulating the design of fishing nets (for example, using larger mesh so as to catch fewer small fish).

Management of production has traditionally been undertaken by setting quotas, usually for the entire fishery, in the form of a total allowable catch (TAC). The fishery authority divides the TAC among the registered vessels, perhaps using past catches as a guide to ongoing allocations. More recently, some countries, such as Canada and Norway, have developed systems of individual transferable quotas (ITQs). As the name suggests, rights are allocated to individual vessels, and because they are transferable it is possible to create a secondary market for them. However, in the face of a sudden collapse in a fish stock, even ITQs are not a sufficiently responsive policy instrument, and it will be necessary to manage the production capacity of the industry through such means as decommissioning grants that allow ships to be removed from the fleet.

23.3   Conclusions

With the examples of externalities and public goods used in the last two chapters, we have seen that it is often difficult to assign property rights in a way that leads to efficient resource allocation decisions. In the case of public goods, this results from the difficulties in excluding people from consumption, even where consumption is not rivalrous, since there is then a tendency towards free-riding. We assumed the existence of a social planner with the authority to make resource allocation decisions directly. We have been concerned, though, that such a process is not consistent with the decentralized approach to general equilibrium set out in Chapters 18 and 19, and so we have spent some time demonstrating how a social planner, or a government, might sidestep this problem by relying on mechanisms that encourage participants in a market to reveal their underlying preferences. Using the example of the Vickrey–Clarke–Groves mechanism we have shown that, so long as certain conditions hold, truth-telling is a dominant strategy. We have also seen that market-based rules increasingly have a role to play in the management of common property resources, such as fisheries, which are rivalrous in consumption, but non-excludable.

In developing our analysis of general equilibrium, we made a strong claim that it is possible to reach efficient outcomes without any management of the market. We then argued that it should be possible to construct a ranking of such outcomes. We have shown in this chapter that it is difficult to construct a social preference function that has certain desirable characteristics. Well-behaved social preferences cannot simultaneously demonstrate unanimity, independence (to irrelevant alternatives), and non-dictatorship. We are reluctant to abandon non-dictatorship, and it is easy to show that while independence might seem to be reasonable, it is violated in many choice processes that work effectively. If we observe the operation of any legislature, it should become clear that no government can pretend to be an omniscient social planner, and so tolerating imperfections in the choice process is probably generally desirable.

Summary

A good is non-rivalrous in consumption if use by one person does not restrict use by others. A good is non-excludable if it is impossible to restrict its use. A public good is non-rivalrous and non-excludable. A private good is both rivalrous and excludable. A common property resource is non-excludable (for members of a group), but is rivalrous.

The development of a market for a public good can be difficult. In many cases, public authorities have either granted a monopoly of supply or have undertaken supply directly.

This reflects the risk of under-provision of a public good because of lack of effective demand. If someone believes that other people will contribute enough to ensure the provision of the good, then that person has no incentive to contribute. We call this outcome free-riding. If one person decides to free-ride then free-riding can become endemic across the population, and the public good cannot be provided purely by voluntary contributions.

If the quantity of a public good that is provided is determined by the total volume of contributions, then individual contributions will be set so that the sum of marginal *WTP*s across the population is equal to the marginal cost of provision.

Agreement on the level of provision of a public good by voting may not be efficient. Arrow's impossibility theorem demonstrates that it is impossible for any rank-order voting system to convert individual preferences into a social preference ordering that possesses certain properties considered desirable for democratic decision making.

It may therefore be preferable to manage free-riding by use of a mechanism designed to elicit true preferences. The Vickrey–Clarke–Groves mechanism identifies the pivotal participants in a project, whose valuation affects whether or not the project will go ahead. By charging the pivotal participants, and only the pivotal participants, an amount equal to their surplus, which is not redistributed, the mechanism encourages truthful revelation of valuations.

With a common property resource, there are likely to be problems of excessive use, leading to rapid depletion. These are associated with the tragedy of the commons, in which users do not recognize the externality associated with their activity, although these can only be avoided through agreement about management of activity.

Visit the companion website at **www.palgrave.com/mochrie** to access further teaching and learning materials, including lecturer slides and a testbank, as well as guideline answers and student MCQs.

part **VI**

Behaviour

We have defined principles of resource allocation for individual decision makers, both people (as consumers) and firms (as producers), and we have explored outcomes of market exchange, showing how these depend on the structure of individual markets. We have also modelled the general equilibrium of a system of markets.

In Part IV, we moved away from the assumptions of perfect competition by allowing producers to have market power. We have assumed throughout our discussions that all activity, production, buying and selling, and consumption, takes place at a single point in time. Everyone has perfect information, so that all firms produce goods of the same quality, all potential customers know the prices that every firm will charge, and firms know how much of their output might be sold at any price.

The remainder of the book examines the implications for our models of relaxing these assumptions. Until now, we have said very little about people's preferences, beyond requiring these to be well behaved. Thinking about patterns of behaviour that we actually observe, we consider what we might infer about the form of utility functions. We shall analyse behaviour when people engage in a sequence of actions over time. We shall ask what happens when people do not have complete information, and

when obtaining information is an uncertain, costly activity. Information then becomes a good, which people can only acquire by allocating resources to that purpose.

This approach to information has led to many important developments in economic theory. For perfectly informed consumers, rational behaviour simply means calculating how to achieve the best possible outcome, given the available resources. This model will be a good predictor of behaviour where people are largely fully informed. There are many occasions when people make choices after only a brief review of the alternatives open to them, and so we develop models on the basis that the costs of becoming fully informed may exceed the benefits. Such decision-making processes can easily suffer from biases, leading to failure of the predictions of the standard (economic) model. In the last 30 years, behavioural economics has emerged as a substantial field in economics, providing, at least to some extent, an alternative to the standard theory. We explore some of these developments in Chapter 27.

The emphasis on behaviour, rather than on choice in consumption, changes the way that we undertake analysis. Sociologists have a well-developed critique of decision making in economics, and of the assumption of utility maximization. They tend to emphasize the extent to which choice is determined by social factors, with, for example, people behaving in ways that are recognized as being acceptable within the society in which they live. Even deviant behaviour can be explained by its relation to social norms. If young people choose to defy their parents' expectations, they may do so in order to conform to the expectations of other young people. Sociologists emphasize that such conformity – whether expressed through choices relating to clothing, physical appearance, music, use of alcohol, tobacco or drugs, religious behaviour, sexual activity, or in some other way – reflects the extent to which social context can shape behaviour, so we do not need to assume that there is any form of maximization of payoffs. Here, we can simply note that the standard economic theory presumes free will, but does not concern itself with the nature of individual utility functions. We can therefore reconcile the economic and the sociological approaches by suggesting that sociology can help economists to place restrictions on the form of the utility function in a particular situation.

Of course, no economist should be surprised by the thought that gaining the admiration of our peers might be a source of utility, for this is an important component of the understanding of the social context of behaviour in *Theory of Moral Sentiments*, the volume of social philosophy that Adam Smith published in 1759, seventeen years before the publication of *The Wealth of Nations*. We continue to use the tools of analysis that we have already developed, showing that they are versatile enough to be applied in this very different context.

24

Personal choice

What we do in this chapter

Until now, we have worked with the standard model of choice, considering in detail some very simple forms of resource allocation. In Part II, we developed an account of how someone might allocate money to buy the most-preferred, affordable consumption bundle. We now treat the principles developed in Part II as the starting point for wider analysis. We continue to assume that behaviour is rational, and intended to maximize utility.

We explore the claim that people who are close to a subsistence boundary will respond to an increase in the price of a staple good, such as rice or potatoes, by demanding more, rather than less of it. A necessary part of the argument is that there are combinations of goods that would not permit the achievement of the essential objective: survival. We also explore the claim that people can use goods to signal their wealth, and we set out conditions under which conspicuous consumption might lead to demand for a good increasing with the good's price. In this case, being able to afford such goods has a direct payoff, separate from their value in consumption.

Time and money are both basic resources. To generate well-being, or utility, people allocate time and money to activities. It is possible to exchange these resources: people can increase the amount of money available for consumption by working. We use the standard theory to obtain the labour supply function, the optimal amount of working time given the wage rate and prices of consumption goods. This leads naturally to discussion of time allocation decisions within households, where several people work together to generate utility.

We conclude with a broader discussion of the nature of goods. Here, we concentrate upon consumers' perceptions of quality, and the implications for product markets. We decompose goods into underlying characteristics, which are treating these as the sources of utility. This enables us to consider how we make choices between discrete goods where our needs are met fully by the purchase of a single unit of that good. It allows us to analyse the emergence of goods that vary in quality.

24.1   The Giffen effect

People living in advanced societies rarely confront subsistence, defined in terms of achieving a minimum caloric intake. Food is usually in plentiful supply: indeed, obesity is increasingly associated with relative poverty; and many people begin weight-loss programmes, even if the ubiquity, and cheapness, of food frequently leads to their failing to complete them. Achieving subsistence is still a consideration for a large fraction of the world's population. Failure to achieve this objective reduces life expectancy and increases death rates.

> **Subsistence** The minimum consumption required for survival.

   We consider the problem of a consumer who is close to the subsistence boundary, and who can buy consumption bundles containing quantities of two goods, beef and cassava. Cassava is grown widely, especially in South America and Africa: its tuberous root is a very simple source of calories. We shall treat it as the staple good, which forms the bulk of a subsistence diet. Beef is both rich in protein and calorie-intensive. As a source of calories it is much more expensive, and so in a subsistence diet, we expect it to be reserved for special occasions and celebrations. We begin with the simple assumption that, given prices p_b and p_c, someone able to spend an amount, m, can just reach the subsistence level by consuming only cassava, and no beef.

In Figure 24.1, the dotted line passing through consumption bundle A represents the subsistence constraint, and we treat this constraint as being rigid, so that this person will never choose a consumption bundle that lies below it. The solid line passing through A is the initial budget constraint. Again, this is rigid, so all consumption bundles above it are unaffordable. Then A is the only bundle that is affordable and that also permits subsistence.

Without showing indifference curves, we illustrate the effects of two equivalent changes – equivalent in the sense that they have the same effect on this person's utility. Firstly, we consider a fall in the price of cassava from p_c to p_{c1}, while the money available to finance consumption, m, remains the same. In the other, the price, p_c, does not change, but the money available to finance consumption increases from m to m_1. We might imagine both changes occurring as a result of government intervention. The price change could be a result of direct subsidy, reducing the price charged to the consumer, while the income change might be a result of social benefits being paid directly to the consumer.

By yourself

X24.1   We have mentioned very direct interventions in the market here. How might a government in a poor country intervene indirectly in the market, using *supply-side* policies to improve market efficiency so that food prices will fall?

In Figure 24.1, following the reduction in the price of cassava, p_c, we show the consumer choosing consumption bundle B: (b_1, c_1), while following the increase in m, the money

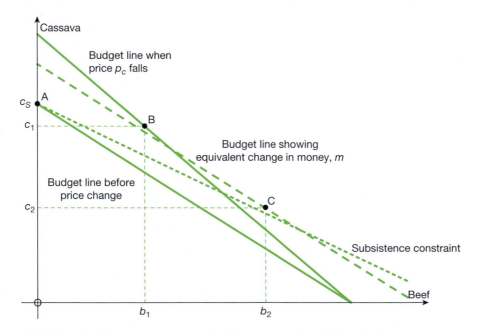

Figure 24.1 The subsistence constraint and indifference map for a Giffen good

available for consumption, we show the consumer choosing consumption bundle C: (b_2, c_2). As a result of the price change, the consumer who was previously at the subsistence level starts to consume beef, and reduces consumption of cassava. The change in the money available for consumption leads to a very substantial reduction in cassava consumption, as the consumer switches towards beef.

By yourself

X24.2 We define consistency of choices as follows: if a consumer chooses consumption bundle *X* before a reduction in the price of a good or before an increase in the money available for consumption, and consumption bundle *Y* afterwards, then the choice is consistent if *Y* was not in the original affordable set.
(a) Confirm that the choices in Figure 24.1 exhibit consistency.
(b) Indicate the income and substitution effects into which the total price effect might be decomposed. Classify beef and cassava as being normal or inferior goods, and state whether you consider them to be gross complements or gross substitutes.
(c) In Figure 24.1, a reduction in price p_c leads to a reduction in demand, *c*. Explain this outcome in terms of the income and substitution effects.

By emphasizing consistent choice we limit discussion of the utility function that might support **Giffen behaviour**, which is generally understood to relate to the increase in the price of a staple commodity causing an increase in its consumption. In Figure 24.1, as well as the consumption bundle, A, associated with subsistence, we define the bundle, B, chosen after the price change, and the bundle, C, chosen after the consumer has been given additional money. Requiring choices to be consistent, since bundle A lies in the affordable sets when bundles B and C are chosen, both B and C are preferred to A. If we now assume that this person is indifferent between B and C, so that the changes in the price, p_b, and money available, m, have the same effects on overall payoffs, then applying the decomposition from Chapter 8, the total (price) effect (from A to B) can be split into an *income effect* (from A to C), and a *substitution effect* (from C to B). Even though the substitution effect associated with a decrease in the relative price of cassava leads to an increase in demand, the income effect is negative and very strong, and so causes the total effect of the price change to be negative. Giffen behaviour therefore occurs when the money available for consumption increases, and demand for the staple, cassava, decreases rapidly. Cassava is shown here as an inferior good, for which the income effect associated with a price change is so strongly negative that it overwhelms the substitution effect.

> **Giffen behaviour** An increase in the price of a good leads to an increase in demand.

By yourself

X24.3 We have drawn the subsistence constraint as a straight line, but identified most-preferred, affordable consumption bundles at B and C.
(a) On what basis might we argue that beef and cassava are perfect substitutes on the subsistence constraint?
(b) Why is the preceding argument consistent with beef and cassava being imperfect substitutes when the subsistence constraint is not binding?
(c) Suppose that it is possible to become sated with cassava at relatively low levels of consumption. Sketch a preference map showing this property and the subsistence constraint.

We shall not try to characterize any further the nature of a utility function that supports Giffen behaviour. Exercise X24.3 suggests some of possible characteristics: that while the goods are close substitutes for low levels of expenditure, as the money available for consumption increases they cease to be so. Giffen behaviour therefore seems most likely to occur where there is substantial poverty.

24.2   Conspicuous consumption and positional goods

As the 19th century gave way to the 20th century, and the United States of America rose to economic pre-eminence, Thorstein Veblen developed his *Theory of the Leisure Class*. He argued that with increasing wealth, people would not work to achieve subsistence, and so could devote more time to leisure. (We shall explore the allocation of time to work and leisure in a more conventional economic model in Section 24.4.) He also argued that with changes in the distribution of income, people might wish to demonstrate their ability to enjoy leisure through displays of conspicuous consumption. In effect, Veblen argued that the value derived from acts of consumption depends on both the content of the consump-

> **Conspicuous consumption** A public display of consumption to demonstrate wealth.

tion bundle and the process of consumption. By being observed to consume a bundle of goods that would be affordable only by someone with great wealth, people assume that they secure the approval of their peers: consumption is therefore observable behaviour from which people might derive utility.

By yourself

X24.4   In our modelling, we have assumed that all economic agents have perfect information. Were that to include knowledge of everyone else's wealth, would there be any reason to engage in conspicuous consumption?

X24.5   Might any good be used in displays of conspicuous consumption? If not, what characteristics do you think are likely to make particular goods well suited to that purpose?

We assume that people are members of one of two classes, *L* and *W*. People of class *L* are conspicuous consumers. People of class *W* are not. In effect, people of class *L* form Veblen's leisure class, while people of class *W* form his working class. Conspicuous consumers believe that other people observe their consumption bundle and infer something positive about their wealth. Specifically, we assume that people of class *L* do not wish to be mistaken as being of class *W*. To demonstrate their type, they ostentatiously consume certain goods, deriving value from being seen to consume them.

In this analysis, consumption shifts from being a private activity to being a very public one. For example, someone who regularly works out in a gym might derive value from being known to exercise, with utility flowing from the reputation associated with the activity. In such circumstances, we might argue that exercise is a form of conspicuous consumption. Physical activity as leisure is interesting because historically much work involved physical effort: the leisure class now allows itself to be seeing engaging in activities that once would have been part of poorly paid, manual labour.

Until now, we have been interested in people only as consumers. We here switch attention to behaviour more generally, with consumption redefined as one particular kind of behaviour. In addition, though, note from Exercise X24.4 that conspicuous consumption is inconsistent with a model in which there is perfect information, or in which membership of class L is directly observable. If people of class L feel a need to demonstrate that they are wealthy by spending both time and money very publicly, and possibly wastefully, so that other people will infer that they are indeed wealthy, then this must be because other people cannot otherwise know how wealthy they are. The use of behaviour to disseminate information is very important, and a topic that we explore much more fully in Part VII.

By yourself

X24.6   We have suggested that conspicuous consumption might be wasteful. Suppose that people of type L demonstrate their wealth by burning money in public.
(a) Explain why this is wasteful.
(b) Why do you think that people of type W would not engage in it?
(c) What activities seem to you to be the closest approximation to the wilful destruction of property in order to demonstrate wealth?

X24.7   In a well-known account that sought to bring many of Veblen's insights into much more standard economic modelling, Harvey Leibenstein identified *snob* and *bandwagon* effects. How do these additional effects relate to Veblen's initial treatment of conspicuous consumption?

24.2.1   A model of positional consumption

We assume that consumers allocate their expenditure on the purchase of quantities of two goods, 1 and 2. Consumers of both classes have a fixed sum of money to spend, m_A and m_B, and both can buy any quantities of the goods at prices p_1 and p_2. We write the utility-maximizing, affordable consumption bundles as (l_1^*, l_2^*) and (w_1^*, w_2^*). We assume that class L consumers obtain utility not just from their own consumption bundle but also from w_2, the quantity of good 2 chosen by people of class W.

The two classes have different forms of utility function. While W's utility function is entirely standard, so that $v_W = v_W(w_1, w_2)$, we define L's utility function, $v_L = v_L(l_1, \frac{l_2}{w_2})$. Consumer L's utility here depends upon the amount of good 2 chosen relative to the amount that the other consumer, W, chooses. Note that as w_2 increases, the consumption relative $\frac{l_2}{w_2}$ decreases. If the utility function, v_L, is well behaved, v_L will then be decreasing in w_2. This goes beyond Veblen's arguments, in some ways, for Veblen simply argued that people wish to be seen to consume goods that are very costly in order to demonstrate their wealth. Here, people wish to be seen to consume a large quantity of certain goods compared to other people. We have laid aside the informational content of consumption patterns and the presumption that people are concerned about the inferences that other consumers make. It is enough to assume that some people benefit from being able to differentiate themselves from people of another class through their consumption choices. Type L consumers can obtain utility from believing that other people will infer their wealth from their consumption pattern. We call this **positional consumption**. This is a simpler and more general explanation than Veblen's. There is nothing in it, though, that is inconsistent with Veblen's model.

Positional consumption Utility depends upon the level of consumption relative to other consumers' consumption.

24.2.2 Analysis of the model

In Figure 24.2, we show the situation that consumer L might face. We do not need to analyse consumer W's decision in any detail. Assuming that W's preferences are well behaved, we might obtain demand functions, $w_1(p_1, p_2, m_w)$ and $w_2(p_1, p_2, m_w)$, which solve the standard utility-maximizing problem. We shall assume that for W, both goods are normal, so that $\frac{\partial w_2}{\partial m_w} > 0$. Then, from the law of demand, following a price rise $\frac{\partial w_2}{\partial p_2} < 0$.

> **By yourself**
>
> **X24.8** Using the Slutsky decomposition, confirm that $w_2(p_1, p_2, m_w)$ is decreasing in p_2.
>
> **X24.9** Suppose that for consumer W, demand for good 2 is price-elastic. What can you say about expenditure on this good following a price rise? How does this affect the budget constraint of consumer L?

Figure 24.2 captures the conclusion of Exercise X24.9. Note that instead of consumption of good 2, l_2, on the vertical axis, we show the *consumption relative*, $\frac{l_2}{w_2}$, the ratio of L's consumption of good 2 to W's consumption. Given that W's demand for good 2 is elastic, as price, p_2, rises, demand, w_2, falls so quickly that W reduces expenditure on the good. An increase in price p_2 therefore leads to a reduction in the implied price of the consumption relative, $\frac{l_2}{w_2}$, so that the budget constraint swivels clockwise, rather than anticlockwise. In Figure 24.2, we note that before the change in prices, L maximized utility by choosing bundle $X\left(l_1^0, \frac{l_2^0}{w_2^0}\right)$, and afterwards by choosing bundle $Y\left(l_1^1, \frac{l_2^1}{w_2^1}\right)$. The shift from X to Y is the total price effect.

In this case, the price increase leads to an increase in real income, rather than to a decrease in real income, and so in Figure 24.2, we show the income effect as the shift from

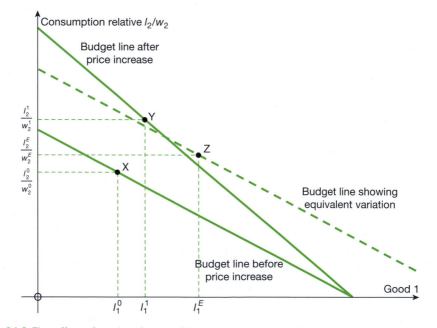

Figure 24.2 The effect of a price change with positional consumption

bundle X to bundle $Z\left(l_1^E, \frac{l_2^E}{w_2^E}\right)$. The substitution effect is then the shift from bundle Z to bundle Y. With price, p_2, increasing, the effective price, π_2, of the consumption relative has fallen, and as well as the income effect, there is substitution towards good 2.

By yourself

X24.10　Adapt Figure 24.2 so that the effect on the consumption relative of an increase in the price of good 2 is zero. Confirm that the income effect is then negative. Explain why this might happen and interpret the results.

X24.11　Suppose that consumer L has a Cobb–Douglas utility function. Adapt Figure 24.2 for this case, confirming that point Y would then lie directly above point X, and that consumption of good 2 would definitely increase following a price increase.

Even if the consumption relative is a normal good, it does not immediately follow that L will demand more of the positional good after a price increase. The consumption relative increases for any level of consumption because of the fall in the value of w_2. So, L might reduce consumption of good 2, while the relative $\frac{l_2}{w_2}$ increases. We show how this might happen in Figure 24.3, in which we go back to showing levels of consumption on the axes. In the diagram, the indifference curve through W cuts through the other indifference curves. This does not violate the assumption of transitivity of preferences. As prices change in this model, changes in w_2 lead to changes in L's preferences. The indifference curve through W reflects preferences before the prices change, while those through X, Y and Z reflect preferences after the prices change, and they do not intersect one another.

By yourself

X24.12　Initially, consumer L chooses consumption bundle V(l_1^0, l_2^0). When price p_2 increases, Ws demand for good 2, b_2, falls. What are the likely effects on:
(a) the total utility of bundle W;
(b) the marginal utilities, $MU_1(l_1^0, l_2^0)$ and $MU_2(l_1^0, l_2^0)$;
(c) the marginal rate of substitution $MRS = -\frac{MU_1}{MU_2}$?

X24.13　How does the change in the marginal rate of substitution affect the indifference curve through V? Suppose that bundle V was affordable after the price change. How would you expect A's demands to change?

In Figure 24.3, following a fall in w_2, we show the indifference curves through any bundle that L might choose becoming flatter. For consumer L, the effect of a change in w_2 will be apparent through an increase in the marginal utility of good 2, $MU_2(l_1, l_2)$. The marginal rate of substitution $MRS = -\frac{MU_1}{MU_2}$ will fall, and the indifference curves will become flatter.

Had consumer L faced the changed indifference map at the original prices, then instead of choosing bundle W, she would have chosen bundle X. This is an additional substitution effect, resulting not from the change in prices, but from the changes in the marginal utilities of the two goods because of the change in w_2. Perhaps the easiest way to explain this is to remember that the arguments of the utility function in this case are the contents of the consumer's own consumption bundle and the quantity of good 2 that other consumers

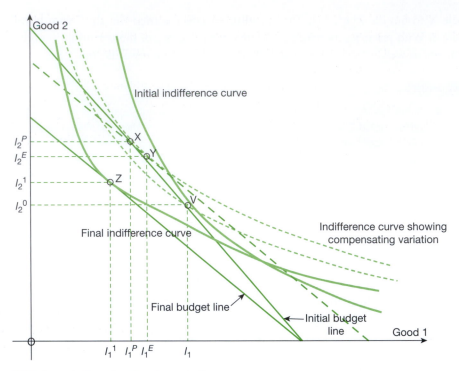

Figure 24.3 Impact of a price change on preferences

have chosen. The additional effect in the graph results from an exogenous change in this last variable. The crossing indifference curves in Figure 24.3 represent different sections of the utility function. Good 2 is normal, with the substitution effect and the income effect of the price increase reinforcing each other.

24.3   Negative prices

We have argued that goods have to have positive prices because of their scarcity. In our general equilibrium analysis, we found that the value of excess supply in a market is always zero, with a good that is abundant having zero price. What would it mean if a good had a negative price?

There are two ways in which we might think of this. Firstly, we may refer to the equimarginal principle: that for all goods whose consumption is not zero, the ratio of marginal utility to price has to be equal. So if we have a situation where there are two goods, A and B, and for some consumption bundle, $(a^{\star}, b^{\star})$

$$\frac{MU_A}{p_A} = \frac{MU_B}{p_B} \qquad [24.1]$$

then, if price $p_B < 0$, it must be that $MU_B < 0$. The price received is set so that at the margin it just compensates the consumer for the loss incurred from consumption. Such markets seem likely to be difficult to maintain. It is not unusual, for example, for someone who is likely to suffer a loss as the result of a major public work – perhaps a landowner across whose land a new road is to be built – to receive compensation. Where people consume goods that have negative value, it is generally because these goods are a by-product of some other process. We have treated air and water pollution as examples of such negative externalities, as analysed in Chapter 22.

We have assumed that there is a flow of goods and services from producers to consumers, with a flow of payments in the opposite direction. Suppose that we reverse the flow. Then people supply, while businesses and other organizations demand, these goods and services. The negative price in such a case reflects the fact that the quantity supplied (by business entities) is negative, because they are consuming them. Receiving payment, people supply or consume a negative quantity of the good. The obvious example is the labour that an individual supplies. Rather than assigning someone a sum of money to finance consumption, we assume that the person has skills that have a value in the labour market. We do not trade skills directly in the labour market, but instead provide them for a period of time to an employer. Assuming that this time is unpleasant, its marginal utility will be negative, and this justifies the negative price.

24.3.1 Labour supply

Formalizing this discussion, suppose that Dr M is able to work up to T hours in a month, receiving a wage w per hour. His consumption bundles, (b, c), consist entirely of bread and cheese, for which he pays unit prices (p_b, p_c). We may write the utility maximization problem:

$$\underset{b,c,T}{\max}\, U(b,c,l):wl \geq p_b b + p_c c \qquad [24.2]$$

We can form the Lagrangean:

$$\Lambda = U(b,c,l) + \lambda(wl - p_b b - p_c c) \qquad [24.3]$$

obtaining the usual first-order conditions:

$$\lambda = \frac{MU_b}{p_b} = \frac{MU_c}{p_c} = -\frac{MU_l}{w} \qquad [24.4]$$

The first two conditions are already familiar, and we have repeatedly interpreted them as indicating that in an optimal resource allocation, at the margin, consumers obtain the same return (in terms of utility) from expenditure across the available alternatives. The final term is new, and represents the rate at which loss of utility from working is compensated. (Since $MU_l < 0$, we require the negative sign here.)

By yourself

X24.14   In Chapters 3 and 4, we argued that for well-behaved preferences the assumptions of convexity and monotonicity have to be satisfied. Discuss the implications of these assumptions for the utility function $U = U(b, c, l)$ in Expression 24.4.

If preferences are still convex and monotonic, then we would expect to be able to find a unique, most-preferred, affordable consumption bundle. In Figure 24.4, we illustrate a simple situation in which there is a single, composite good, sold at price p, with the consumer choosing a quantity, G. Having no money initially, the consumer is able to finance consumption only by working, offering an employer labour time, L, at wage rate, w. Any consumption bundle for which $wL \geq pG$ is then affordable. With the equation of the

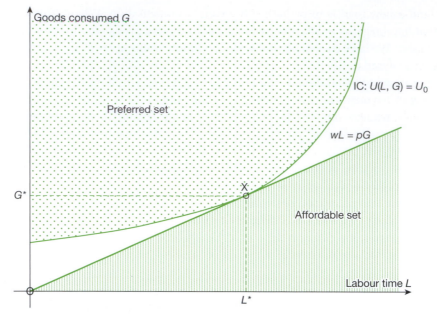

Figure 24.4 Optimal labour time

boundary, $wL = pG$, this affordable set is (weakly) convex. In the diagram, we can then draw a second (strictly) convex set, to which the affordability constraint forms a tangent. Consumption bundles in the interior of this latter set contain more goods but less labour time than the point of tangency, X. Given the assumption of monotonicity, all of these consumption bundles are preferred to X. If, in addition, we define the boundary of this set as the indifference curve passing through X so that IC: $U(L, G) = U_0$, then the upper-left set is the (weakly) preferred set for bundle X.

For the preferred set to be convex, on any indifference curve, the marginal rate of substitution must increase with the labour time and the quantity of goods in the consumption bundle. Since $MRS = -\frac{MU_L}{MU_G}$, sufficient conditions for this are that $\frac{\partial^2 U}{\partial L^2} > 0$, and $\frac{\partial^2 U}{\partial G^2} < 0$. The marginal disutility of labour time increases with labour time. This seems to be a perfectly reasonable assumption. Labour time is not pleasant, so we have to be compensated for our exertions. But the unpleasantness of additional labour time is greater if we are already working long hours. With a fixed wage w, and with labour time $L: 0 \leq L \leq T$, there will be an interior solution if the tangency condition

$$\frac{MU_L}{MU_G} = \frac{w}{p} \qquad [24.5]$$

is satisfied.

24.4   The choice between income and leisure

There is one small problem with our analysis in the previous section. It is plainly the case that we can define convex affordable and weakly preferred sets so that their intersection consists of a single point: the most-preferred, feasible resource allocation. Formally, to apply the Lagrangean multiplier method, we should maximize an objective function, f: $y = f(x_1, x_2)$, which is increasing and concave, subject to the constraint $g(x_1, x_2) \leq g_0$. The utility function defined in Expression 24.2 over quantities of consumption goods and labour time is increasing, but concave, in each of the goods, as we require. It is, however, decreasing, and convex, in labour time, and so does not have a form to which we can apply our mathematical solution processes safely without some adaptation.

To resolve these problems requires minimal change. While people use time in many different ways, we define as leisure all time other than that used for labour. Everyone has the same endowment of time, T, presumably 168 hours per week. We can then define leisure time, l: $l = T - L$. Switching our attention from labour to leisure is enough for us to be able to implement the standard constrained optimization approach. The consumer now has the problem of generating utility through the consumption of goods and services, financed by labour income, but requiring leisure time for it to be enjoyed. In this approach, leisure is a source of utility, while labour is entirely neutral: it is neither a source of utility, nor of disutility. (The disutility of labour in our previous discussion can be redefined as the value of forgone leisure.) In Figure 24.4, we show the optimal allocation of time to labour (and so the purchase of goods) and leisure. In this case, the consumer only has an endowment of time, which is partly converted into money earned as wages, subject to the constraint:

$$w(T - l) \geq pg \qquad [24.6]$$

Expression 24.6 defines the feasible set of attainable leisure time and expenditure combinations. We also assume that the utility function $U = U(l, g)$ represents (well-behaved) preferences over these combinations, so that the preferred sets are convex, with their boundary downward-sloping. This ensures that the conditions required to apply the usual approach to maximization can operate.

Writing the Lagrangean:

$$M = U(l,g) + \mu(wT - wl - pg) \qquad [24.7]$$

we can obtain the standard first-order conditions:

$$\frac{\partial M}{\partial l} = \frac{\partial U}{\partial l} - \mu w = 0$$

$$\frac{\partial M}{\partial g} = \frac{\partial U}{\partial g} - \mu p = 0 \qquad [24.8]$$

$$\frac{\partial M}{\partial \mu} = wT - wl - pg = 0$$

When these conditions are satisfied, it follows that:

$$\frac{\partial U}{\partial l} = \frac{w}{p} \frac{\partial U}{\partial g} \qquad [24.9]$$

so that for the most-preferred, feasible combination, the marginal utility of leisure equals the real wage multiplied by the marginal utility of expenditure. In terms of Figure 24.5, we find the standard tangency solution where the feasible and preferred sets just touch.

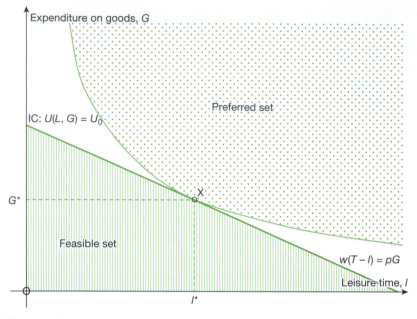

Figure 24.5 Optimal leisure time

By yourself

X24.15   Consider again the assumption that there should be neither utility nor disutility associated with labour time. How reasonable does this seem to be?

X24.16   Define $U = U(g, l)$ the utility generated from consumption of goods, g, and leisure time, l. For $U(g, l) = \frac{gl}{g+l}$, maximized subject to the feasibility constraint $w(T - l) \geq pg$, calculate the utility-maximizing combination (g^*, l^*). Suppose that the wage rate increases. Calculate the effects on leisure and purchase of goods.

X24.17   Suppose instead the utility function $U(g, l) = g + u(l)$, where u is increasing, but concave. Describe optimal choice (g^*, l^*), and explain how this changes with the wage rate.

24.4.1   The effect of changing wages

Any time taken as leisure reduces the hours of labour completed, and hence the quantity of goods that can be purchased. We therefore define the opportunity cost of labour as the ratio of the wage to the price of the composite good, $-\frac{w}{p}$, so that in effect an increase in the wage rate reduces the real price of goods, with purchase–leisure combinations becoming affordable that previously were not. In Figure 24.6, we show how the most-preferred purchase–leisure combination will change as the wage rate, w, increases. When the wage is zero, it is impossible to finance purchases from work, and so the consumer takes as much leisure as possible. As the wage increases, the consumer reduces leisure in order to finance consumption. In the diagram, we assume that both goods are normal. Were the initial endowment to increase, presumably by increasing the maximum time T available for leisure, or by providing an initial endowment of money to fund consumption (perhaps as interest from savings, or as transfer payments such as unemployment benefits), both leisure and consumption expenditure would increase.

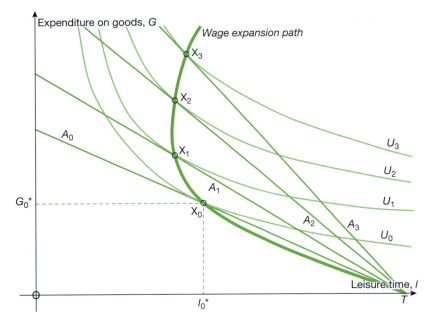

Figure 24.6 Wage expansion path

In Figure 24.6, at relatively low values of the wage, any increase leads to an increase in the quantity of goods purchased, g^*, but a reduction in the quantity of leisure, l^*. The substitution effect for leisure resulting from the change in the wage is large enough to outweigh the income effect. In the diagram, as the wage increases, the boundary of the feasible set rotates clockwise, the total effect of the price change on leisure becomes smaller, and eventually, at relatively high wages, the substitution effect is smaller than the income effect. When this happens, the consumer responds to further wage increases by reducing labour time. Both leisure time and the quantity of goods purchased increase. If goods are normal, then when the wage increases their price effectively falls, so that the substitution effect associated with a wage increase operates in the same direction as the income effect, and the quantity of goods purchased increases.

We show the effect of the increasing wage on labour time in Figure 24.7. Starting from a very low wage, the effect of an increase in the wage will be an increase in labour time. The supply curve is upward-sloping. But as the wage increases, even though the capacity to purchase goods from wages received continues to increase, further increases in labour supply eat into the available leisure. Even though this person's purchasing capacity continues to increase with increasing wages, the value attributed to leisure at the margin also increases, and so we have a situation in which the labour supply begins to decrease with further wage increases. We then have a backward-bending labour supply curve.[1]

---

1 Perhaps the most substantial piece of research in the online student essay bank is Connor Godsell's exploration of a natural experiment. He works for a company whose staff are employed with different contracts, and these provide different benefits for working on a public holiday. He explores how their time allocations decisions can be explained by the contract forms. You can read Connor's essay on the companion website for this book, at **www.palgrave.com/mochrie.**

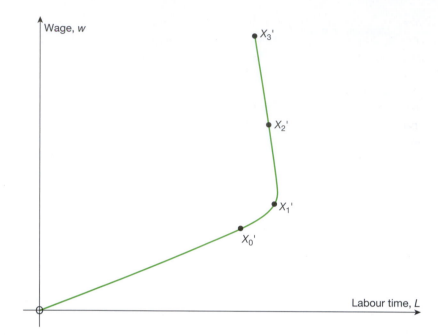

Figure 24.7 Labour supply curve

By yourself

X24.18   Exemptions from the European Union's Working Time Directive are generally available to senior managers, many of whom voluntarily work much longer hours than they can require their colleagues to work. How might we explain this observation?

X24.19   While senior managers have considerable freedom to choose their hours of work, other workers will often have to work fixed hours. Sketch diagrams showing the situation in which a fixed contract might lead to workers (i) working longer hours than they would ideally prefer, given the wage rate; and (ii) working shorter hours. If workers are required to be present at work for longer hours than they themselves require, how do you think they might respond?

X24.20   In order to elicit greater labour supply, firms may choose to offer their workers overtime payments. Sketch a diagram showing the effect of an increase in the wage from w_0 to w_1 after labour supply reaches L_0. Discuss how workers' labour supply decisions are likely to be affected by the marginal, rather than the average, wage. In terms of managing firms' costs, what do you conclude about offering overtime payments?

X24.21   We have assumed that the endowment consists solely of time. Suppose that we relax this to allow for the payment of social benefits, many of which are means-tested and are therefore gradually withdrawn as income rises. Many commentators have noted the presence of 'benefits traps' in which the tapering of benefits occurs alongside the imposition of income taxes, with reports (in extreme cases) of marginal tax and benefit reduction rates in excess of 100%. Explain how such benefits structures might lead people to decide not to enter employment.

We have assumed that people are able to choose their hours of work without any restrictions. This will often not be the case, with employers offering labour contracts that specify both the wage and the required labour time. The choice facing any employee is then not a standard resource allocation problem, but a rather more discrete one between accepting the fixed contract and remaining out of work. We analyse choices between combinations of characteristics that have been bundled together, as in this contract, in Section 24.6.

It is also very unlikely that the feasible set for any individual will be triangular. With incomes generally subject to a complex combination of taxes and benefits, even where an employer offers a fixed wage, the effective wage after receipt of benefits and payment of taxes will not simply be a linear function of labour time. It is possible for the boundary of the affordable set of leisure and consumption combinations to be neither smooth, nor convex. The standard solution methods have to be applied with some care, since it is possible that the equi-marginal conditions will not hold, and that we can have multiple local optima.

Exercise X24.21 suggests that both the provision of social benefits and their funding through taxes will have negative effects on labour supply. Social benefits enhance the individual's endowment. Resource combinations that were previously unaffordable now become affordable, but the opportunity cost of leisure remains unchanged. Assuming that leisure and consumption goods are normal, the introduction of social benefits will cause individuals to choose combinations with more of both goods, so that labour time will reduce. Similarly, except for people on high incomes, for whom the labour supply curve has attained a negative slope, the reduction in wage rates caused by income or sales taxes will lead to labour time falling. Aggregating across the economy, we might expect the effects of benefits and income taxes to include a reduction in total labour time, and therefore a reduction in the size of the economy. For government, though, it may nonetheless be desirable to impose such costs on society because of the benefits accruing from the provision of such a social safety net: people with zero income might have substantial leisure but be unable to survive, which we treat as the worst possible outcome.

24.5   The family: economics without markets

Suppose that someone's endowment includes a substantial quantity of money. Even without working, so that labour time $L = 0$, this person can buy consumption goods. In Figure 24.8, at the endowment $E(l_0, g_0)$, this person does not work, but can still buy goods. Note that we have shown the feasibility constraint extending beyond E. Until now, we have assumed that someone who is not in paid employment simply enjoys leisure time. There are, however, elements of behaviour, involving the production of personal services, which we might treat as leisure. Everyone has to eat. Generally, people have to set aside time to prepare food, even if only by heating a prepared meal in a microwave oven. Buying a prepared meal, rather than starting with fresh ingredients, we increase consumption of goods, but also leisure time.

We might contract out the provision of personal services. Instead of buying prepared food, we might hire a cook, whose job is to prepare meals. In effect, as well as supplying labour services, people might demand them. In Figure 24.8 (on the next page), with the marginal rate of substitution of leisure for consumption goods exceeding its opportunity cost at the endowment, E, this person chooses to increase leisure time by trading away part of the initial endowment of money.

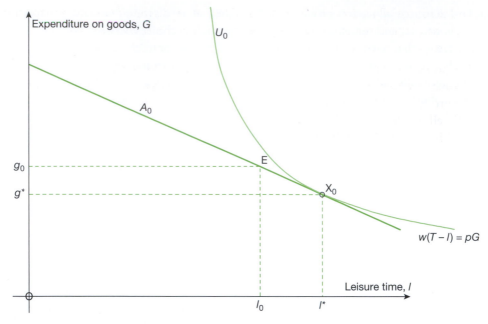

Figure 24.8 Financing personal services

By yourself

X24.22 In the preceding paragraph we assume that people buy personal services only after they have withdrawn entirely from the labour market. How would you explain the purchase of such services by people who are engaged in paid work?

24.5.1   Service production within a household

Treating people, as we have done up to this point, as if they only engage with each other through market exchange excludes some of the most important elements of human behaviour. Most people live in households, and interactions between household members do not usually involve exchange relationships. Parents tend not to charge children for board and lodging, while among adult members of a household there will often be a division of labour activities, with some more active in the production of what we have just defined as personal services than in the formal labour market.

We define a class of goods, **Z**, which are the personal services produced and consumed within a household. We also define a household as a group of people who, as well as sharing accommodation, have reached an informal arrangement relating to individual contributions to the production and distribution of personal services. Such arrangements are more complex than those which students typically make for sharing accommodation, but need not be as formal as those which are implicit in traditional marriages, in which the participants effectively agree to care for and support one another for the remainder of their lives. Conscious agreement to such an agreement is not necessary: young babies, crying in the middle of the night, are probably not even conscious of making demands on their parents. For simplicity, though, we shall assume that we are studying a household, H, with two adult members, $m = I, J$.

Since the model of household behaviour involves both the production and consumption of the Z goods, it has a rather more complicated structure than most of those that we have used before.

- For production of Z goods, we assign both members of the household an endowment of time T, which can be used either as labour time, L_m, paid at wage rate w_m, or else in the production of Z goods, $T - L_m$.
- As well as the time input, production also requires consumer goods, g, which are bought in the market, with their purchase at price, p, funded from wage income, $Y_H = w_I L_I + w_J L_J = pg$.
- In equilibrium, production is efficient. The household cannot reallocate its resources and increase the production of the Z goods. We can therefore define the production function, $\mathbf{Z} = [z_I(L_I^*, L_J^*), z_J(L_I^*, L_J^*)]$, where z_m is the quantity of Z goods consumed by household member, m, given that production is efficient.
- Each household member obtains utility from consumption, $u_m(z_I, z_J)$.
- One member of the household makes all decisions about time allocations and Z good production. This person seeks to maximize the payoff function, $U = U[u_I(z_I, z_J), u_J(z_I, z_J)]$. Given that the production and distribution of Z goods are fully determined once the labour requirement is set, we can treat the decision maker as maximizing the payoff $U = U[L_I, L_J]$.

Example

- We assume that the decision maker's payoff $U = \min[u_I(z_I, z_J), u_J(z_I, z_J)]$.
- We also assume that individual utilities have the form $u_m = z_m^a z_n^{(1-a)}$, where $a > 0.5$.
- The quantity of Z goods available to each member of the household, when offering L_m labour hours, $z_m = (T - L_m)(w_I L_I + w_J L_J)$.

These assumptions are sufficient for us to be able to demonstrate that both members of the household will divide their time equally between paid work and the production (and consumption) of Z goods.

Firstly, we note that for the decision maker in the household, it is essential that payoffs should be the same for both members of the household. Were there to be any difference in their payoffs, the decision maker would willingly reduce the higher one in order to increase the lower one. Secondly, individual payoffs are a weighted average of individual consumption of the Z goods. It is quite easy to confirm that the individual payoffs will only be equal if both household members consume the same quantity of Z goods. For this to happen, they must both offer the same labour time, $L = L_I = L_J$.

This means that we can simplify this problem to finding the labour time, L^*:

$$L^* = \overset{\max}{\underset{L}{}} (w_I + w_J)(T - L)L \qquad [24.10]$$

Differentiating, the first- and second-order conditions for a maximum are satisfied for $L^* = 0.5T$. This results directly from the form of the payoff function. The unit powers in the Cobb–Douglas production function for Z goods in Expression 24.10 mean that leisure and labour time are equally weighted.

We can see that this result emerges from the assumptions we have made about the generation of individual utility. We have included both members' consumption of Z goods in the individual utility functions, in effect assuming that they both care about the other's well-being, but not so much as they value their own. Yet in identifying one member as the decision maker in respect of production and distribution plans, we have had to allow that person to view the problem from two perspectives, firstly as a planner, and then as a consumer. Note that income from employment outside the household is shared equally between the two members of the household, even though they may have different wage rates.

Note that each member of the household has to spend time at home to generate Z goods, and we assume that they are both equally productive in this situation. In the example, even though income is pooled, Z goods are produced separately. If we allowed Z goods to be pooled, then we would expect to see a degree of specialization of activities, with the relatively high-wage household member spending more time working in paid employment, and the other spending more time in producing Z goods in the household.

By yourself

X24.23   Rework the example of household allocation, but with these alternative assumptions:
(a) The decision maker's payoff $U = \min[u_i(z_i, z_j), u_j(z_i, z_j)]$.
(b) Individual utilities $u_m = z_m^a$, where $1 > a > 0$.
(c) The quantity of Z goods available to each member of the household, when offering L_m labour hours, $z_i = (T - L_i)^{0.5b}(T - L_j)^{0.5(1 - b)}(w_i L_i + w_j L_j)^{0.5}$; $z_j = (T - L_i)^{0.5(1 - b)}(T - L_j)^{0.5b}(w_i L_i + w_j L_j)^{0.5}$.

X24.24   Rework the example of household allocation, but with these alternative assumptions:
(a) The decision maker's payoff $U = U_i U_j$.
(b) Individual utilities $u_m = z_m^a$, where $1 > a > 0$.
(c) The quantity of Z goods available to each member of the household, when offering L_m labour hours, $z_i = (T - L_i)^{0.5b}(T - L_j)^{0.5(1 - b)}(w_i L_i + w_j L_j)^{0.5}$; $z_j = (T - L_i)^{0.5(1 - b)}(T - L_j)^{0.5b}(w_i L_i + w_j L_j)^{0.5}$.

The examples in the preceding section are kept deliberately simple. They illustrate the fact that we can think of a household as being rather like a firm, a term that in law refers specifically to businesses organized as partnerships. Whereas a firm exists to make profits, the partnership in a household has the objective of generating utility for its members, achieved through the production and consumption of Z goods. The problem for the partners consists in balancing work outside the household and the generation of money income against work inside the household using wage income and labour time to generate the Z goods.

24.6   The characteristics approach to choice

Another way in which households are like firms is in their need for capital goods, the most obvious being the home in which the household members generate most of its Z goods. We have argued in Section 24.5 that the reach of markets as a resource allocation mechanism typically ends at the front door of the family home. Nonetheless, in the context of the family as an economic unit, we can think of a house as a large machine, used by members of the household to produce Z goods and hence to generate utility. We should also note that few people buy a single (physical) good that is more valuable than their family home. As a good, therefore, a house is very complex and strongly differentiated, particularly since, over time, most people adapt their home so that it might meet their needs and tastes more precisely. Taking all these factors into account, sale and purchase of a house generally involves quite a complex process of inspection, offers and negotiation.

Whether we think of a house as an asset or as a machine, we should recognize that it provides its occupants with a stream of services over a period of years. We might then classify a house as an experience good, on the basis that it is possible to appreciate fully its capacity to provide utility only after a period of living in it. The sort of inspection most people make before choosing to live in a house is quite cursory: assessment of the house's own qualities, and indeed those of the area in which it is located, will generally be quite

> **Experience good** A good whose nature can be confirmed only through use.
>
> **Characteristics (1)** Sources of utility embodied within a good.

approximate. While people may be aware of this at the time that they choose the house in which they will live, this limited knowledge suggests that they will make their choice among the various houses available by comparison of their (visible) characteristics, the set of properties associated with each one. Some are immediately apparent, and so the simple listings in sales' agents adverts will typically emphasize location, accessibility, standard of maintenance (the phrase 'development opportunity' warns of the need for costly repairs and renovations), size, number and type of rooms, and the nature of the heating system and insulation. In the UK, the vendor is required to provide potential purchasers with a report, which begins with a statement of the house's energy consumption, an analysis of any maintenance work that might be required, a valuation for both insurance and sale, and a statement of how the current occupant has adapted it. With this information, a potential buyer can make more informed comparisons between houses. Across all the range of possible measures that we identify, every house entering the comparison process will be different.

Each house can therefore be described as a bundle of characteristics. People typically choose to live in one and only one at any time, so it is impossible to buy and 'consume' a fraction of a house, while multiple purchases are relatively rare. It is also impossible to buy several fractions of houses, and then to combine them into the preferred home. Choice therefore involves preferences among houses, each of which we now treat as a bundle of characteristics. One person might value an ensuite bathroom beside a bedroom very highly, while another might be more interested in the layout of the kitchen, and a third in the extent of storage facilities. Individual valuations, and preference orderings, over a set of houses might differ substantially.[2]

24.6.1 Applying the characteristics approach

The characteristics approach can be applied not just to complex goods, such as a house, but also to relatively simple ones. Consider an apple. Going into any fruit shop, we expect to encounter perhaps half a dozen varieties. There are, in fact, at least 8,000 varieties of apple worldwide, differing in size, in colour, in firmness, and in flavour, all of which

---

2 For a discussion of the difficulty of deciding upon how to identify the characteristics of a house, while also treating it as a source of services, please read the essay 'Rental Prices' by Malin Bjaroy on the online student essay bank. While largely an interesting exploration of personal experience, covering budgeting as well as the rental decision, this essay emphasizes that utility depends on much more than the simple volume of goods in a consumption bundle. The essay bank is accessible through the companion website for the book, at **www.palgrave.com/mochrie.**

are characteristics. Until now, we have treated all apples as being identical, but here we assume that it is possible for us to make a comparison between different types of apple. Applying the characteristics approach, we concentrate instead on the comparison between apple varieties. Suppose for the moment that it is possible for us to create an index of sweetness (flavour) and crispness (texture). Measuring each variety against these criteria, people can express preferences over the available combinations of characteristics. It is then possible for us to identify someone's most-preferred variety in terms of its combination of characteristics.

Now, think of apples from the perspective of a farmer. It takes approximately eight years for an apple tree to reach maturity and to start producing fruit. For any orchard, then, the short run is quite a long period. In selecting the variety of trees to plant, a farmer has to predict the distribution of tastes over the possible characteristics of apples among consumers some years in the future. With so many varieties available, we expect the farmer only to choose varieties that are in some way efficient: we are interested in varieties whose characteristics mean that they cannot be dominated by other varieties.

By yourself

X24.25   Explain why it is not possible to include price as a characteristic of a good.

X24.26   List the possible characteristics of an apple that you consider relevant to this analysis. Choosing any two, sketch a diagram showing a variety of possible combinations of characteristics. Explain which ones might be chosen by growers. Indicate the preferences of a consumer over these characteristics, and identify the utility-maximizing combination.

X24.27   Through experimentation and selective breeding, it is possible for farmers to create new breeds of apple. Discuss how such processes might change the analysis.

In the preceding exercises, we did not consider the price of the apples that are being sold. Assuming that markets are perfectly competitive, then we expect to obtain the standard equilibrium conditions:

- For consumers, we expect to find that for the optimal apple, $MU_A = \lambda p_A$, where MU_A is the marginal utility of the apples, p_A is the price and λ is the Lagrangean multiplier, which we have interpreted as the marginal value of additional money. We can think of the utility of an apple as being derived from its characteristics.

- Growers will want to produce the variety of apples for which its customers will pay the highest amount. Assuming perfect competition, then in the long run growers will make zero profits, producing output at minimum average cost, which for long-run equilibrium will also be the price at which apples are sold. We can therefore think of the efficient boundary in Exercise X24.26 as showing the combinations that a grower might produce for any given price.

- The gradient of this efficient boundary indicates the rate at which farmers have to reduce the strength of one characteristic of an apple in order to increase the strength of another. It is therefore a *marginal rate of transformation*, as defined in Chapter 21.

- For the optimal characteristic set, the consumer's marginal rate of substitution between characteristics will be equal to the marginal rate of substitution. The utility-maximizing consumer therefore treats the efficient boundary as defining (the edge of) the feasible set, selecting the apple embodying the characteristics for which $MRS = MRT$, as illustrated in Figure 24.9.

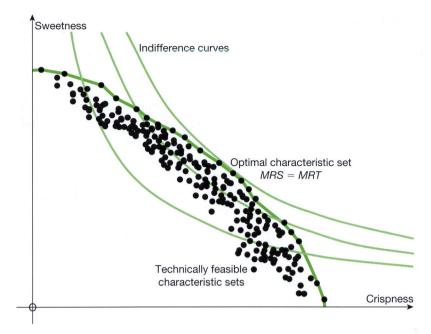

Figure 24.9 The optimal apple

Despite there being over 8,000 varieties of apple, few supermarkets stock more than one dozen. We can explain this difference by noting that many 'antique' varieties of apple may well be very good fruit, but the trees on which they grow take longer to reach maturity, or else have relatively low fruit yields. A farmer growing them would not reach the technically efficient frontier. Of course, this does not mean that these apples have been abandoned entirely. Some consumers can afford to pay much more than the market price. The (re-) emergence of farmers' markets in many countries can sustain a market for highly valued input combinations which would fail the efficiency criterion stated above.

> **By yourself**
>
> **X24.28** We have concentrated our discussion on characteristics of apples in consumption. In considering production and distribution, we might also expect there to be characteristics that affect the varieties chosen, such as the length of time for which each might be stored, or the robustness of the fruit in the mechanized harvesting process. What effects might such characteristics have on the choice available to the consumer?
>
> **X24.29** How would you explain the fact that supermarkets continue to stock several apple varieties? On what criteria would you expect the decision to stock any particular variety to be based?

From the point of view of production, we expect farmers to grow varieties that they expect to be able to sell profitably. With supermarkets playing a very large role in distribution, farmers will enter into long-term supply contracts. Market coverage involves providing a sufficiently wide choice to consumers so that no characteristic combination that is profitable at the scale required for this distribution system is omitted. However, alternative, locally based distribution systems may provide consumers with greater variety. The Italian 'Slow Food' movement is perhaps the best known of these, and encourages people to value consumption more carefully.

24.7   Conclusions

We have surveyed a broad range of applications of our standard model of resource allocation. The argument about Giffen behaviour requires the goods purchased for bare subsistence to be so strongly inferior that as their price falls, and real income increases, they
quickly drop out of the consumption bundle. We now have some quite robust evidence
from development economics that this is indeed the case. The situation of people using
consumption to demonstrate their wealth is almost the opposite. There is a popular misper-
ception that economists believe that Veblen effects, like the Giffen effect, are associated
with an upward-sloping demand curve. We have shown that all that is required is for some
people to increase their consumption relative to others following a price increase. It is not
that such consumers' demand increases, but that it falls relatively slowly.

We also modelled resource allocation in terms of managing an endowment of both
money, which has to be allocated for purchase of goods, and time, which has to be allocated to labour and leisure. Through paid work, it is possible to turn time into money.
The more hours that we work, the more money we will have to pay for consumption,
but the less time will be available in which to enjoy it. From this we obtain the theory of
labour supply; the subsequent discussion of hiring servants to undertake relatively menial
tasks, permitting wealthier people to extend their leisure time, is entirely consistent with
Veblen's arguments.

Not only does consumption require time, but it is also a social process which can be
undertaken with other people. Attending a concert with several thousand other people is
a different experience from listening to the concert being streamed across the internet. We
have considered how consumption might take place within a household, in which resources
are pooled among its members, so that the household's members share in consumption, for
example sharing meals.

Rather than simply thinking about consumption decisions, we have started to explore
behaviour by using the tools of standard economic theory. We have not abandoned these
tools, but turned them to a wide range of new tasks. Our strategy has been to make a series
of small changes to the standard model, each of them appropriate for the situation we are
trying to understand. This will be our strategy throughout this part of the book, as we seek
to widen further the range of behaviours that we try to understand as economic phenomena.

Summary

The Giffen effect is often associated with
demand for a staple good that forms
a substantial part of the consumption
bundle chosen by people who are close
to a subsistence boundary. We assume
that the Giffen and alternative goods are
perfect substitutes along the subsistence
constraint only.

A Giffen good is strongly inferior. If real incomes
increase because of a fall in the price of the
Giffen good, then the relatively small substitution
effect will be swamped by the negative income
effect, leading to a reduction in demand.

Conspicuous consumption consists of activities
involving publicly observable consumption of
particular goods, intended to demonstrate

a person's wealth. We define positional consumption similarly, but involving the demonstration of a person's position in a distribution of wealth.

For positional consumption, it is enough that individual utility depends not only on the bundle of goods consumed by the individual, but also upon the consumption of some good by a reference consumer. The higher the level of reference consumption, the lower the utility obtained from a given consumption bundle by someone engaging in positional consumption.

Treating the good over which positional consumption occurs as price-elastic, we note that an increase in its price leads to a reduction in the demand among the reference group. This leads to an additional substitution effect for the positional consumers. Lower reference consumption alters the positional consumers' utility functions. If this substitution effect is strong enough, conspicuous consumers' demand can increase following a price increase.

We may define a good with a negative price either as a good that the consumer supplies, or else as a good whose marginal utility is always negative.

Defining labour in this way, people will work until the wage compensates them for the (marginal) loss of utility from working. We can also associate a positive utility with leisure, rather than a negative utility with labour. Treating labour and leisure as alternative ways of spending time, we assume that the purpose of labour time is to convert time into money to finance expenditure.

Defining the resources available to the consumer as time and money, the most-preferred, feasible resource allocation occurs where the marginal value of additional leisure is the product of the real wage and the marginal value of additional goods.

We argue that with many forms of well-behaved preferences the wealth effect of an increase in the wage rate will eventually lead to people increasing both leisure time and the purchase of goods. In such circumstances, the labour supply curve bends backwards.

We assume that households exist to produce Z goods, which are not subject to market exchange, but allocated within the household. Z goods require time inputs (within the household) and money (earned through external labour).

To simplify our models, we assume that one member of the household is able allocate all members' time, solving a single time allocation problem for the efficient production and distribution of Z goods. Allowing for differing relative returns among household members, we predict a degree of specialization in the roles taken on by household members.

It is sometimes useful to treat goods as a bundle of characteristics, and then to model utility as a function of the characteristics of a particular example of a good. Firms will often produce varieties of the good that are efficient in the sense that their characteristics are not dominated by any other variety.

We also expect producers only to produce such a range of varieties as will allow them to avoid losses; given the price of the good, determined in a competitive market, we therefore expect them to choose a scale of production at which efficient bundles of characteristics can be sold at a price equal to (minimum) average cost.

We then expect people to choose the variety of the good for which the marginal rate of transformation across characteristics in production is equal to the consumer's marginal rate of substitution in consumption.

Visit the companion website at **www.palgrave.com/mochrie** to access further teaching and learning materials, including lecturer slides and a testbank, as well as guideline answers and student MCQs.

25

Inter-temporal choice

People need time both to work and to enjoy consumption. In addition, time passes, so that we cannot undo prior actions, and we can only prepare to act in the future. We model fully informed, rational decision makers, who plan resource allocations to maximize utility not just at the present moment, but over time.

In this chapter, we concentrate on personal choice, adapting the standard model to examine the characteristics of the equilibrium where consumption takes place in two time periods. We introduce the concepts of *income* and *consumption profiles*, which show the flow of money to finance consumption across the current and the future period, and the pattern of expenditure across the two periods. The problem is then to allocate expenditure across periods so as to maximize the value of the flow of consumption over time.

We adopt the convention that future consumption is valued less than future present consumption, saying that people discount future utility. We also assume the existence of *asset markets*, allowing both borrowing and saving, so

that people are able to choose how to allocate their expenditure across time, rather than having to spend money when they receive it. This allows us to define a single expenditure constraint across the two time periods, and so to obtain the utility-maximizing level of consumption in each period. We also discuss the pricing of *perpetual bonds*, a simple class of traded financial assets, which allow people to save and borrow, and so to manage their pattern of expenditure across time.

Our concluding discussion turns to the value of education, or, more generally, *human capital.* Capital markets allow young people to anticipate future income. It is possible that they might decide to forgo current income, spending a period in training, but knowing that they will thereby increase their future income. In the context of our model, we are able to show that the optimal choice for an individual should involve maximizing the present value of their income profile, so that at the margin, the return to this personal investment is equal to its cost.

25.1   Inter-temporal choice

In this chapter, we discuss resource allocation over time. This requires a two-period model, in which saving and borrowing allow the linking of expenditure decisions across the two periods. For example, people engaging in training have no income, and indeed must pay often tuition fees in order to complete their studies. Such students have to borrow money, and lenders will only be willing to lend to them if it is reasonable to expect repayment in full. The resource allocation problem now extends over those two distinct time periods, and so we have a problem of *inter-temporal choice*.[1]

---

1   Central to such an approach is the treatment of money as an asset. In the online student essay bank, Witu Willman reminds us that durable goods are also assets from which utility will be derived, and suggests how we should accommodate such purchasing decisions within this type of modelling framework. You can read Witu's essay on the companion website for this book, at **www.palgrave.com/mochrie.**

A similar and closely related problem concerns people in work who are planning for retirement, a period that will nowadays often last twenty years or more. Such people need to save enough money during their working lives to be able to finance consumption in this later period. So, while we expect students to borrow money in the expectation of future income, we expect pensioners to draw down savings made while they were in work. Again, to understand these decisions, we have to develop a model of inter-temporal choice. Both the funding of student tuition and the encouragement of saving for retirement are substantial problems in public policy.

25.1.1 A simple model of inter-temporal choice

Once again, we adapt the standard model of resource allocation, using the simplest possible specification that allows illustration of the most important assumptions required for, and implications of, our analysis. We begin by defining notation, and setting out assumptions.

Consumption profiles

- We assume that there are two periods: $t = 0, 1$, where $t = 0$ is the *current* time period and $t = 1$ is the *future* time period.
- Everyone has to consume goods and services in both time periods.
- We therefore define an *inter-temporal* consumption profile $C = (c_0, c_1)$, where c_t represents the amount of money used to finance consumption in each period. We do not analyse the choice of goods within each period.

> **Consumption profile** A list of total expenditure in a sequence of time periods.

Preferences

- We assume that our consumer has preferences over the profile C, which we can represent by the utility function $u = u(c_0, c_1)$.
- Preferences over consumption profiles are well behaved, so that, as in Figure 25.1, indifference curves showing consumption profiles associated with a given value of the utility function have the standard properties: smooth, downward-sloping, convex to the origin, and never intersecting.

Financing consumption

- We assume that people receive a fixed amount of money, m_t, to spend in each period. We define the income profile $M = (m_0, m_1)$.
- Money has a role as a store of value. Money that is received in the current period, $t = 0$, can be saved to finance consumption in the future period, $t = 1$.
- We assume that it is possible to save money with banks or other financial institutions, which offer a fixed return, r, on savings deposited in the current period, and withdrawn in the future period.
- This means that a person receiving m_0 and spending c_0 in the current period, where $m_0 > c_0$, saves $s_0 = m_0 - c_0$. In the future period, the bank repays $(1 + r)s_0$.
- We assume that financial institutions channel savings to people who wish to borrow. We assume that these financial markets are perfect, in the sense that the cost of borrowing, r, is exactly the same as the return obtained by savers.

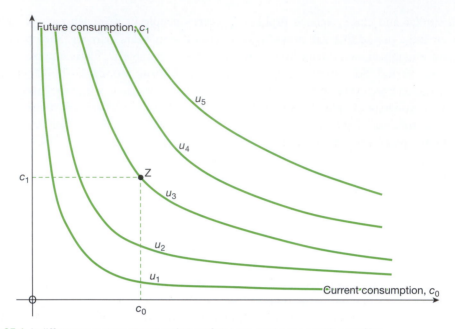

Figure 25.1 Indifference curves representing preferences over consumption profiles

- A person receiving m_0 and spending c_0 in the current period, where $m_0 < c_0$, borrows $b_0 = m_0 - c_0$. In the future period, the borrower repays $(1 + r)b_0$.
- We assume that people begin the current period with no money, and (by the assumption of non-satiation) maximize utility by spending all of the money received over the two periods. Any savings from the current period will be spent in the future; and borrowing in the current period has to be repaid. In both cases, it has to be the case that:

$$m_1 - c_1 = -(1 + r)(m_0 - c_0) \qquad [25.1]$$

It will often be useful to write Expression 25.1 as:

$$(1 + r)m_0 + m_1 = (1 + r)c_0 + c_1 \qquad [25.2]$$

or else as:

$$m_0 + \frac{m_1}{1 + r} = c_0 + \frac{c_1}{1 + r} \qquad [25.3]$$

The first version, Expression 25.1, confirms that net saving in one period finances net borrowing in the other one. More generally, the differences between income and expenditure in each of the two periods have to be equal and opposite, although both have to be evaluated at the start of the future period to allow for the return on saving and the cost of borrowing. The alternatives, Expressions 25.2 and 25.3, state that the value in period $t = 1$ of all income is exactly the cost of financing the consumption profile, were all funds actually received in period $t = 1$. Any consumption profile that satisfies the linear expression in Expression 25.2 is then affordable.

By yourself

X25.1   Given the expenditure constraint, Expression 25.1, calculate:
(a) The opportunity cost of current consumption.
(b) The opportunity cost of future consumption.
(c) The level of consumption in the current period ($t = 0$) if consumption in the future ($t = 1$) is set to zero.
(d) The level of consumption in the future if consumption in the current period is set to zero.

Expression 25.2 defines the consumption profile, using the value of income flows and payments for consumption as if they were all realized in the future, when $t = 1$. We therefore say that it represents the inter-temporal consumption constraint in terms of **future values**. Similarly, we say that Expression 25.3 expresses the constraint in **present value** terms, as if all income were to be received, and payments made, in the current period, $t = 0$. Given that people who save in the current period receive a return, r, in future, while people who borrow have to repay their loans with interest, spending a given amount in the current period means giving up more spending in future. We see this in Figure 25.2, where we indicate the affordability constraint for a consumer with income profile $M = (m_0, m_1)$.

Future value The value of a sum of money available at the present time, evaluated at a certain time in the future.

Present value The value of a sum of money available at some future date, as if available now.

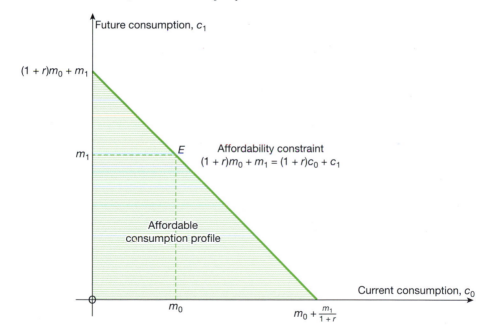

Figure 25.2 The affordable set of consumption profiles

By yourself

X25.2   Suppose that the interest rate increases. Adapt Figure 25.2 to show how this will affect the affordable set.

X25.3   We have assumed that financial markets are perfect, so that consumers can borrow and lend at the same interest rate. In reality, the interest rate paid by borrowing consumer is usually higher than the interest rate received by savers. Adapt Figure 25.2 to show this effect.

25.1.2 The optimal consumption profile

The form of the constrained maximization problem is familiar. Bringing together the preference map of Figure 25.1 and the affordable set of Figure 25.2, we find that we have the usual solution to the optimization problem, where the consumer achieves the highest possible payoff by selecting the consumption profile on the affordability constraint whose marginal rate of substitution equals the opportunity cost. We illustrate this outcome in Figure 25.3.

From Exercise 25.1, we know that the opportunity cost of current consumption, the gradient of the affordability constraint, may be written:

$$\left.\frac{dc_1}{dc_0}\right|_{m_1 - c_1 = -(1+r)(m_0 - c_0)} = -(1+r) \tag{25.4}$$

We do not know anything more about the marginal rate of substitution than its definition as the ratio of the marginal utilities of consumption:

$$MRS = \left.\frac{dc_1}{dc_0}\right|_{u=u_0} = -\frac{\partial u}{\partial c_0}\bigg/\frac{\partial u}{\partial c_1} \tag{25.5}$$

For the optimal consumption bundle, Expressions 25.4 and 25.5 are both satisfied, and so:

$$\frac{\partial u}{\partial c_0}\bigg/\frac{\partial u}{\partial c_1} = 1+r \tag{25.6}$$

The right-hand side of Expression 25.6 is the opportunity cost of current consumption, or, in Figure 25.3, the slope of the affordability constraint. The left-hand side is the marginal

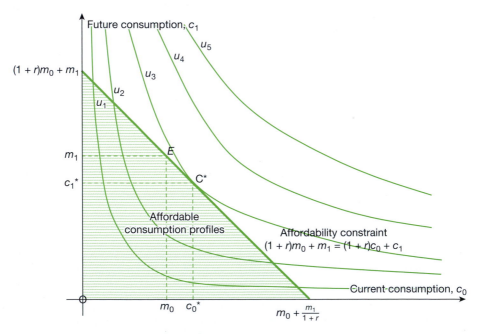

Figure 25.3 The optimal consumption profile

rate of substitution, or, in the diagram, the slope of the indifference curve. Given the assumptions set out above, we can be certain that Expression 25.6 holds true for a single consumption profile on the affordability constraint, $C^* = (c_0^*, c_1^*)$, at which the affordability constraint forms the tangent to the indifference curve, $u = u_0$. The form of the diagram should be entirely familiar from previous examples. All that we have done is to introduce the return on funds across the two time periods, and to consider how that affects the equilibrium in the model.

By yourself

X25.4 Suppose that there are two individuals, whose utility functions may be written $u_A = c_0^a c_1^{1-a}$, and $u_B = c_0^a + c_1^a$. Their income profiles are $M_A = (m_A, 0)$ and $M_B = (0, m_B)$. For each individual, write down the relationship that must exist between the level of consumption in the current period and that in the future period, and obtain the consumption profile. Indicate clearly the amount that individual A saves, and the amount that individual B borrows in the current period ($t = 0$).

X25.5 Assuming perfect capital markets, explain how the consumption profiles would change if the income profiles became $M_A' = (0, (1 + r)m_A)$ and $M_B = (\frac{m_B}{1+r}, 0)$. Explain why the consumption profile will always stay the same if the future (or present) value of the income profile remains constant.

X25.6 Suppose that there is a minimum level of consumption that must be reached in both periods, c_{min}. By sketching an indifference map of the utility function $u = (c_0 - c_{min})^a (c_1 - c_{min})^{1-a}$, explain how this characteristic is captured.

25.1.3 Changing price levels

We do not consider the price of goods in each period, but only the price level, p_t. We shall assume that $p_0 = 1$, so that the current period is the base year, and that $p_1 = (1 + \pi)p_0$, with π the rate of inflation between the two periods. The amount of money received in each period, m_t, is expressed in nominal, rather than real terms; it follows that with inflation, a given amount of money can purchase fewer goods and services in the future period ($t = 1$) than in the current period ($t = 0$).

We can quite easily incorporate a change in prices into the affordability constraint, Expression 25.1, writing it as:

$$m_1 - (1 + \pi)c_1 = -(1 + r)(m_0 - c_0) \qquad [25.7]$$

Once again, we can interpret this as saying that saving (borrowing) in the current period ($t = 0$) must be spent (repaid) in the future period ($t = 1$). We can imagine the income profile, $M = (m_0, m_1)$, remaining exactly the same as it was in the earlier discussion.

By yourself

X25.7 In Expression 25.7, explain in words the term $(1 + \pi)c_1$. Confirm that the consumer forgoing consumption in the future period is not affected by the increase in inflation, while a consumer who abstains from current consumption cannot purchase as large a bundle after an increase in inflation. Hence, show in a diagram the effect of an increase in the value of the inflation rate, π, on the affordability constraint.

(Continued)

X25.8   Show that the opportunity cost of current consumption, $\frac{dc_1}{dc_0} = -\frac{(1 + r)}{(1 + \pi)}$. Confirm that this opportunity cost falls as inflation, π, increases.

X25.9   When the interest rate, r, and the inflation rate, π, are small, we approximate the *real interest rate* by the term $r - \pi$. Show that if the real interest rate is negative, then the consumer can purchase more goods with a fixed sum of money in the current period ($t = 0$) than in the future period ($t = 1$).

X25.10   Assume that consumption at time t is a normal good. Sketch a diagram indicating clearly the decomposition of the total effect on the consumption profile of an increase in inflation through (a) the real wealth effect, associated with a shift in the consumer's affordability constraint; and (b) the substitution effect, associated with the change in the opportunity cost of current consumption.

Exercises X25.7–X25.10 illustrate further how we can use the approach of the standard model to analyse inter-temporal choice. An increase in inflation has the effect of increasing the cost of future consumption. For a consumer with a fixed income profile, M, higher inflation reduces both wealth and the opportunity cost of current consumption. In X25.10, the wealth effect reduces consumption in both periods, while the substitution effect causes consumption to be brought back from the future to the current period.

25.1.4   Discounting the future

Consider the utility function:

$$u = u(c_0, c_1) = c_0^{0.5} + \delta c_1^{0.5}, \text{ with } 0 < \delta < 1 \qquad [25.8]$$

Many properties of this utility function should already be familiar: it is homogeneous of degree 0.5, and it is a member of the family of CES utility functions, but it is *separable*: the payoff to the consumption profile is a weighted sum of a function of the level of consumption in each period, $u_t(c_t) = c_t^{0.5}$.

Instantaneous utility
The utility generated in a specific time period.

A consumer with utility function of the form of Expression 25.8 obtains **instantaneous utilities** $u_t(c_t) = c_t^{0.5}$ from consumption in the current period ($t = 0$), and also in the future period. Given that the form of the function does not change, a consumer enjoying the same level of consumption in both periods would derive equal instantaneous value from consumption in each period. Then, moving from the instantaneous utilities back to the utility function in Expression 25.8, we note that we do not simply add up the two

Discount factor The ratio of the present value of money to its future value.

instantaneous utilities, but instead first multiply the future utility by some positive fraction. Treating the function in Expression 25.8 as the consumer's valuation of the consumption profile at the start of the current period, if parameter $\delta < 1$, the consumer does not value consumption in the future period as highly as consumption in the current period. We say that the consumer *discounts* the future, calling the parameter δ the **discount factor**.

By yourself

X25.11   Calculate the total utility of the consumption profiles:
(a) (100, 100), with discount factor 0.95;
(b) (121, 144), with discount factor 0.9;
(c) (64, 256), with discount factor 0.5.

X25.12   Calculate the marginal rate of substitution, $\frac{dc_1}{dc_0}\Big|_{u(c_0, c_1) = u_0} = -\frac{\partial u}{\partial c_0} \Big/ \frac{\partial u}{\partial c_1}$, for a consumer with utility function of the form in Expression 25.8. Confirm that as the discount factor, δ, increases, the marginal rate of substitution also increases.

X25.13   Using the results of X25.12, sketch an indifference map for the utility function $u = c_0^{0.5} + \delta c_1^{0.5}$, where the discount factor $\delta \approx 0$. Interpret the diagram in terms of the consumer's present valuation of current and future consumption.

X25.14   Assume that the consumer has an income profile, $M = (m_0, m_1)$, with price level $(p_0, p_1) = (1, 1 + \pi)$, and can borrow or save any amount of money on a perfect capital market, so that the interest rate on loans and savings is r.
  (a) Write down an expression for the consumer's affordability constraint over consumption profiles, $C = (c_0, c_1)$.
  (b) Write down an expression for the opportunity cost of current consumption, $\frac{dc_1}{dc_0}\Big|_M$.
  (c) Find the relation between current and future consumption on the consumer's wealth expansion path, associated with changes in the income profile.
  (d) Find the consumer's optimal consumption profile.

In Exercises X25.12–X25.14, we obtain the optimal consumption profile for a consumer with a given instantaneous utility function, but we allow for any value of the discount factor, δ, and also any level of the interest rate, r, and any level of price inflation, π. Here we consider a specific case, where $\delta = 0.9$, $r = 0.05$, and $\pi = 0$. The price level is constant, it is possible for the consumer to borrow or lend at an interest rate of 5%, and any level of future consumption has only 90% of the value of the same level of consumption in the current period.

This consumer has income profile $M = (m_0, m_1)$. We can apply the affordability constraint, Expression 25.1, for the given values of the interest rate, r, and inflation, π.

$$m_1 - c_1 = -1.05(m_0 - c_0) \qquad [25.9]$$

From this we can calculate the slope of the affordability constraint:

$$\frac{dc_1}{dc_0}\Big|_{(m_0, m_1)} = -1.05 \qquad [25.10]$$

Turning to the utility function, Expression 25.8, with $\delta = 0.9$, $u(c_0, c_1) = c_0^{0.5} + 0.9c_1^{0.5}$. Taking the total differential on the indifference curve, $u = u_0$:

$$0.5 c_0^{-0.5} dc_0 + 0.45 c_1^{-0.5} dc_1 = 0 \qquad [25.11]$$

And so, rearranging this expression, we obtain the total derivative:

$$\frac{dc_1}{dc_0}\Big|_{U_0} = -\frac{10}{9}\left(\frac{c_1}{c_0}\right)^{0.5} \qquad [25.12]$$

We know that for the consumer to achieve the maximum possible utility, the values of Expressions 25.10 and 25.12 have to be identical, so that $\frac{10}{9}\left(\frac{c_1}{c_0}\right)^{0.5} = \frac{21}{20}$. Rearranging, we find that:

$$c_1 = \left(\frac{189}{200}\right)^2 c_0; \text{ or } c_1 \approx 0.893 c_0 \qquad [25.13]$$

Substituting Expression 25.13 back into the affordability constraint, Expression 25.9:

$$m_1 - \left(\frac{189}{200}\right)^2 c_0 = -1.05(m_0 - c_0) \qquad [25.14]$$

Then, for any income profile with future value $M = m_1 + 1.05m_0$, this consumer's consumption profile:

$$C \approx (0.515\,M,\, 0.460\,M) \qquad [25.15]$$

The values of the discount factor, δ, and the market interest rate, r, chosen in this example lead to the consumer spending slightly more in the current period ($t = 0$) than in the future period ($t = 1$).

We can think of the discount factor as a measure of foresight, or patience. The income profile $M = (m_0, m_1)$ is an endowment of income, which the consumer is certain to receive. Partly for that reason, it is sensible that a consumer who receives the bulk of his or her income in future should be able borrow in the current period ($t = 0$), relying on the receipt of the funds for repayment in the future period ($t = 1$). Such a consumer will decide how much to borrow in the current period. The higher the value of the discount factor, δ, the more patient the consumer is, and the higher the level of consumption in future will be compared with the level of consumption at present. Indeed, in Exercise 25.14c, we have found the equation of the wealth expansion path:

$$c_1 = \frac{\delta^2(1 + r)^2}{(1 + \pi)^2} c_0 \qquad [25.16]$$

We can see from Expression 25.16 that when the discount rate, $\delta > \frac{1 + \pi}{1 + r}$ (that is, the inverse of the real interest rate) patient consumers will defer consumption until the next period. Where an economy is characterized by low price inflation and high nominal interest rates, we expect that net saving will be high. From a macroeconomic perspective, this is a channel for higher investment across the economy and sustained growth of national income.

By yourself

X25.15   Use the optimal consumption profile stated in Expression 25.16:

$$C = (c_0,\, c_1) = \left[M\left(\frac{1 + \pi}{1 + r}\right)\left(\frac{1}{1 + \pi + \delta^2(1 + r)}\right),\, \delta^2 M\left(\frac{1 + r}{1 + \pi}\right)\left(\frac{1}{1 + \pi + \delta^2(1 + r)}\right) \right]$$

(a) to confirm the optimal consumption profile in Exercise 25.14;

(b) to find the optimal consumption profile for the parameter values $\delta = 0.95$, $r = 0.1$, $\pi = 0$;

(c) to find the optimal consumption profile for the parameter values $\delta = 0.6$, $r = 0.5$, $\pi = 0.4$.

In Figure 25.4, we can see the effect on consumer preferences of different values of the discount factor, δ. There are three indifference curves, the lowest representing the situation where $\delta = 1$, so that the consumer values current and future consumption equally. For the middle curve, the discount factor $\delta = 0.95$, so that we might consider this consumer to be patient. The uppermost curve is the indifference curve for a third consumer, a relatively impatient one, for whom the discount factor is 0.7. We see the three curves as having the

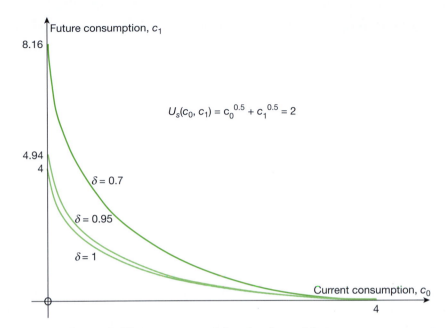

Figure 25.4 The effect on indifference curves of changing discount factors

same intersection on the horizontal axis, indicating that they all represent the same level of utility. The lower the value of the discount factor, the higher the intersection of the indifference curve with the vertical (future consumption) axis. As the discount factor reduces, indifference curves stretch vertically. As the value of δ approaches zero, indifference curves gradually tend towards vertical lines.

By yourself

X25.16 In X25.12, we found that for the utility function, $u(c_0, c_1) = c_0^{0.5} + \delta c_1^{0.5}$, the marginal rate of substitution, $\frac{\partial c_1}{\partial c_0}\big|_{U=U_0} = -\frac{c_1^{0.5}}{\delta c_0^{0.5}}$.

  (a) Setting utility $u = u_0$, write an expression for the level of future consumption, c_1, in terms of the utility obtained and the level of current consumption, c_0.

  (b) Using the expression found in part (a), rewrite the marginal rate of substitution in terms of the utility, $u = u_0$ and the current consumption, c_1.

  (c) Confirm that for a given value of current consumption, c_0, and utility, u_0, as the value of the discount factor, δ, decreases, both future consumption, c_1, and the marginal rate of substitution decrease.

X25.17 Sketch a diagram showing the optimal consumption profile for a consumer with this utility function. Indicate the effect of a reduction in the discount factor on the marginal rate of substitution, and explain how the consumption profile will change, assuming that the affordability constraint remains the same.

X25.18 Throughout our discussion we have adopted an additive CES utility function, choosing parameter values that have the effect of turning current and future consumption into substitute goods. How reasonable do the assumptions of additivity and inter-temporal substitutability seem?

(Continued)

X25.19   Replace the utility function in Expression 25.8 with the Cobb–Douglas utility function:

$$u(c_0, c_1) = c_0^{0.5} c_1^{0.5\delta}$$

Repeat X25.14 using this utility function, obtaining the optimal consumption profile. Explain how the optimal consumption profile will change as the value of δ increases.

25.2   Discounting over multiple periods and time intervals

The discount factor and the real interest rate together tell us how much an individual values current consumption over future consumption. The analysis of Section 25.1 allows us to represent these effects in a model with only two periods. The basic result is quite straightforward: the smaller the discount factor, the more that current consumption is valued relative to future consumption, and so the greater the bias in favour of the former.

As with our discussion of the standard model, having two periods is enough for us to be able to demonstrate the main principles. But there are often situations where a project lasts for several years, with revenues received and costs incurred from time to time during the project's life, or where someone might have to decide on an expenditure profile given a flow of income across some longer time span. Finding optimal outcomes in such cases requires rather more complex calculations than for a two-period model; here, we simply introduce some additional rules required to solve them.

25.2.1   Multi-period discounting of income

In examples with only two periods, we have taken advantage of there being only a single future period; thus, we wrote the affordability constraint in terms of future values. With multiple future periods, it makes our calculations a little easier if we instead use the present value of income and expenditure.

Suppose that as well as the current period ($t = 0$), there are T future periods ($t = 1$, $2, \ldots, T$). We shall assume that the consumer's income profile, $M = (m_0, m_1, \ldots, m_T)$, that the interest rate between any two periods, r, is constant, and that the price level, $p_t = 1$, so that there is no inflation. Alternatively, we might say that we carry out our analysis using a

Essential Maths 25.1:   Future value, present value, and discounting

Future value: For a sum of money, S_0, placed on deposit in the current period ($t = 0$) at interest rate r, for one period, the *future value*, $v_F(S_0) = S_1 = (1 + r)S_0$. More generally, for a sum S_0 placed on deposit at interest rate r for T periods, the future value $v_F(S_0) = S_T = (1 + r)^T S_0$.

Present value: For a sum of money, S_1, which will be received in the next period, when the interest rate r is charged on loans, the *present value*, $v_C(S_1) = S_0 = \frac{S_0}{1+r}$. More generally, for sum S_T due to be received in T periods, the present value $v_C(S_T) = S_0 = \frac{S_0}{(1+r)^T}$. The present value is therefore the amount of money that can be borrowed in the current period, with repayment being made from the income received in future. In considering a stream of receipts and expenditure received at different times, it is generally easiest to calculate their present values. In doing so, we *discount* these financial flows, applying the *discount factor* $\rho = \frac{1}{1+r}$ in every period.

real income profile, so that the elements of M, the return to saving, and the cost of borrowing have already been adjusted for price inflation.

We also define a consumption profile, $C = (c_0, c_1, \ldots, c_T)$. We want to know which profiles are (just) affordable. After allowing for the return to saving and the costs of borrowing, the profile will be affordable if the consumer is not in debt at the end of period T.

We first add a third period ($t = 2$) to the model of Section 25.1, so that there are two future periods. We assume for the moment that all income is received in the initial period, so that the income profile, $M = (m_0, 0, 0)$. The (one period) interest rate is fixed, so that $r_0 = r_1 = r$. Spending c_0 in the current period, the consumer saves $s_0 = m_0 - c_0$, which, carried forward to the next period, gives the consumer $(1 + r)s_0$. Of this amount, c_1 will be allocated to finance consumption, and s_1 will be saved, so that in the last period ($t = 2$), the consumer can spend $(1 + r)s_1$. Any income profile for which $c_2 \leq (1 + r)s_1$ is then affordable.

By yourself

X25.20 By defining s_1 firstly in terms of s_0 and c_1, and then by defining s_0 in terms of m_0 and c_0, show that the affordability constraint can be written in terms of future values (at $t = 2$) as $(1 + r)^2 m_0 = c_2 + (1 + r)c_1 + (1 + r)^2 c_0$. Write the constraint in terms of present values as well.

X25.21 Repeat the argument of X25.20, but for the case where there are three future periods, so that $t = 0, 1, 2, 3$.

X25.22 Using the results of X25.20 and X25.21, show that the affordability constraint when there are T future periods may be written: $(1 + r)^T m_0 \geq \sum\limits_{t=0}^{T} (1 + r)^{T-t} c_t$, or equivalently as:

$$m_0 \geq \sum_{t=0}^{T} (1 + r)^{-t} c_t. \qquad [25.17]$$

X25.23 How do the expressions found in X25.22 change if instead of an endowment received in the current period, m_0, the consumer receives an endowment m_T in the final period ($t = T$).

X25.24 Now suppose that the consumer receives income in every period, so that the income profile $M = (m_0, m_1, \ldots, m_T)$. Show that the affordability constraint can be written:

$$\sum_{t=0}^{T} (1 + r)^{-t} (m_t - c_t) \geq 0 \qquad [25.18]$$

Expression 25.18 has a very simple interpretation. The present value of the expenditure stream cannot be greater than the present value of the income stream. When this constraint is satisfied, a consumer who is facing perfect capital markets, and so is able to borrow and save any amount at an interest rate r between periods, and who is considering expenditure plans from the current period ($t = 0$) until the last period ($t = T$), will be able to finance the planned expenditure in each period, t, from current income, prior savings, or borrowing on the strength of certain future income.

25.2.2 Multi-period discounting of utilities

Having defined the inter-temporal affordability constraint, we define the inter-temporal utility function. In Section 25.1, we introduced a separable utility function, which took the form of a weighted sum of the value of the total expenditure in the current period and the future period, c_t ($t = 0, 1$), with the within-period valuation, $u(c_t)$, being the same across both periods. We use this form of utility function here, but with multiple future periods, rather than just one. We assume that we can apply a constant one-period ahead discount factor, δ.

We calculate the present value of the consumption profile, $C_T = (c_0, c_1, c_2, \ldots, c_T)$, defined across the current period and T future periods. We have already defined the present (or discounted) value of the consumption profile, $C_1 = (c_0, c_1)$:

$$U(C_1) = u(c_0) + \delta u(c_1) \tag{25.19}$$

for the case where $T = 1$, and for discount factor $\delta : 0 < \delta < 1$.

With two future periods, we can define the function $U_1(C_2)$ as the present (or discounted) value of the portion of the consumption profile, C_2, which begins in period $t = 1$. Adapting Expression 25.19:

$$U_1(C_2) = u(c_1) + \delta u(c_2) \tag{25.20}$$

We now obtain the present value of the consumption profile:

$$U_0(C_2) = u(c_0) + \delta U_1(C_2) = u(c_0) + \delta u(c_1) + \delta^2 u(c_2) \tag{25.21}$$

By yourself

X25.25 Confirm that we can write the present value of consumption profile C_T as:

$$U(C_T) = \sum_{t=0}^{T} \delta^t u(c_t) \tag{25.22}$$

X25.26 Using Expressions 25.18 and 25.22, write down the constrained maximization problem facing the consumer in terms of present values.

In Section 25.1, with only one future time period ($T = 1$), we were able to use the method of equal gradients to find the present-value-maximizing consumption profile. Here, with $T > 1$, we have to rely on the Lagrangean multiplier technique. Using the result of Exercise X25.26, we can write the Lagrangean:

$$\Lambda = \sum_{t=0}^{T} \delta^t u(c_t) + \lambda \sum_{t=0}^{T} (1 + r)^{-t} (m_t - c_t) \tag{25.23}$$

Expression 25.23 might seem complex at first sight because of the appearance of the summation signs. So, we shall consider an example where $T = 2$. With only two future periods, this is the simplest possible case with more than one future period.

By yourself

X25.27 Consider the maximization problem:

$$\max_{c_0, c_1, c_2} [u(c_0) + \delta u(c_1) + \delta^2 u(c_2)] : c_0 + \frac{c_1}{1 + r} + \frac{c_2}{(1 + r)^2} \leq m_0 + \frac{m_1}{1 + r} + \frac{m_2}{(1 + r)^2} \tag{25.24}$$

Form the Lagrangean, as in Expression 25.23. By partially differentiating with respect to the levels of consumption, c_0, c_1, and c_2, and setting the derivatives to zero, confirm that the optimal consumption profile C_2* will satisfy the condition:

$$\lambda = \frac{\partial u}{\partial c_0} = \delta(1 + r) \frac{\partial u}{\partial c_1} = \delta^2 (1 + r)^2 \frac{\partial u}{\partial c_2} \tag{25.25}$$

Expression 25.23 and the subsequent exercises indicate that for the optimal consumption profile, C_T^*, defined with consumption in the current and T future periods, there is a simple relationship between the marginal utilities of within period consumption:

$$\frac{\partial u}{\partial c_{t+1}} \bigg/ \frac{\partial u}{\partial c_t} = \frac{1}{\delta(1+r)} \qquad [25.26]$$

Expression 25.26 defines the common ratio of a geometric sequence, as defined in Essential Maths 25.4. Making the usual assumption that the marginal utility of consumption is a decreasing function,

By yourself

X25.28 Suppose that $\delta = (1 + r)^{-1}$. Explain what this means in terms of personal and market discount rates. What do you infer about the optimal level of consumption in the three time periods in X25.27?

X25.29 Suppose that $\delta(1 + r) < 1$. What do you infer about the optimal consumption profile?

then if a consumer is impatient, so that δ is small and $\delta(1 + r) < 1$, the marginal utility of consumption increases across periods. Without calculating the exact time path of consumption, we conclude that it must steadily decrease as time passes.

25.3 Further modelling of inter-temporal choice

Our primary interest throughout this book has been to understand problems of resource allocation. In this context we have characterized optimal consumption profiles in an idealized situation, with perfect capital markets and constant discount rates. To analyse behaviour in even the simplest capital markets in a multi-period setting, it is very useful to be able to do some standard calculations that allow us to extend and apply our understanding of discounted (or present) values.

Essential Maths 25.2: Applying simple and compound interest

Simple interest: Given initial savings, S_0, lodged in the current period ($t = 0$), interest rS accrues each period, but is not credited to the account until the last period ($t = T$), when the savings are repaid, with interest. There will be T accruals (at the end periods, $t = 0, 1, \ldots t - 1$), so the total repayment

$$S_T = (1 + rT)S_0 \qquad [M25.1]$$

Compound interest: Interest is added to savings each period, with the interest for the following period calculated on the sum of the original amount saved and interest that has already been paid. We define compounding factor $\rho = 1 + r$. We now multiply together successive compounding factors. For savings S_0 in the current period ($t = 0$), held until period T, the total sum due

$$S_T = (1 + r)^T S_0 = \rho^T S_0 \qquad [M25.2]$$

Unless specified otherwise, we shall assume that interest accrues on a compound basis.

25.3.1   Published and cumulative interest rates

Most people in regular employment are paid a salary every month, and so also make monthly payments on outstanding loans and to regular saving schemes. Partly as a result, instead of interest being applied annually on these financial products, it is more typically applied every month. The advertised headline rate of interest for a loan is r, while there are $n = 12$ charging periods in the year. Then, applying Expression M25.3, the cumulative applied rate of interest, r_C, may be written:

$$r_C = \left(1 + \frac{r}{12}\right)^{12} - 1 \tag{25.27}$$

Consider the case in which at the start of the year the amount outstanding on the loan is L_0. Then, were the borrower to make no repayments on this loan account, at the end of the year the amount outstanding would increase to:

$$L_1 = (1 + r_C)L_0 \tag{25.28}$$

> **By yourself**
>
> **X25.30** Suppose that the advertised rate of interest on a loan is 12%, so that $r = 0.12$. Calculate the cumulative applied rate when compounding takes place (a) quarterly (every 3 months), (b) monthly, (c) weekly, and (d) daily. Using Expression M25.4, calculate the cumulative applied rate of interest when there is continuous compounding.
>
> **X25.31** For many centuries, it was standard for the monthly charging rate of interest on loans to be set at 1%. Much more recently, payday lending has emerged, and in this market interest accrues at a rate of up to 1% per day, with the loan and interest being repaid in full when it falls due. Compare the cumulative applied rates of interest in these cases:
> (a) a loan of £1,500, taken from a conventional lender, with a monthly charging rate of 1%, repaid in a year;
> (b) a loan of £400 taken from a payday lender, which sets a charging rate of 1% per day, and repaid after 15 days (you may assume that compounding would occur every 15 days);
> (c) a loan of £300 on which there is daily compounding of the interest of 0.5% per day, with repayment in full after 15 days.

Across Europe, lenders are required to state the cumulative applied rate of interest on loans, allowing for other fees that might be charged, such as facility arrangement and repayment fees. This requirement is designed to ensure that potential borrowers are able to see clearly what the cost of credit will be across a range of loans. Specialist, short-term lenders, often called payday lenders, complain that a measure of annualized interest is inappropriate for their products because their loans are typically repaid in a matter of weeks or even days. Their business model involves the charging of a very high rate of interest, often 1% per day, but relatively low fixed fees. Exercise X25.31 indicates the extent to which increasing the frequency of compounding increases the cumulative applied rate of interest. The annualized interest rate on a payday loan will typically be at least 200 times as great as the interest rate on a more conventional loan; and for anyone who is unable to repay such a loan in full, on time, the interest rate multiple will be even higher.

25.3.2 Repayment instalments on a loan

In the preceding section, we implicitly assumed that although interest is compounded over time, the whole repayment of the loan, both principal and interest, would take place at the loan's maturity, or at least at the end of a year. In reality, repayments of the loan principal are often made throughout its term. We write the loan principal (the amount borrowed) as L_0, the published annual interest rate as r, the number of subdivisions of the year as n, and the term of the loan (in years) as T. We wish to find the repayment instalment, R, defined so that at the end of the T periods, the sum outstanding, $L_T = 0$. In these calculations, we take account of the fact that the principal, L_0, is repaid steadily out of the repayment instalments, rather than in one amount in period T, when the loan matures.

Essential Maths 25.3: **Subdivision of time periods**

Given time periods $t = 0, 1, \ldots , T$, suppose that we can divide each period into n smaller intervals, of equal length, with the compounding of interest occurring within each of these. If the published annual rate of interest paid on savings (charged on loans) is r, then the rate applied in each of the n sub-intervals is $\frac{r}{n}$. The cumulative applied rate, allowing for compounding across these intervals,

$$r_c = \left(1 + \frac{r}{n}\right)^n - 1 \qquad \text{[M25.3]}$$

Increasing the number of sub-intervals, the interest rate applied decreases. In the limit, as $n \to \infty$,

$$r_c = \lim_{n \to \infty} \left(1 + \frac{r}{n}\right)^n - 1 = e^r - 1 \qquad \text{[M25.4]}$$

where the constant $e \approx 2.7813$, the Euler number, is a fundamental mathematical constant. We say that as $n \to \infty$, compounding becomes continuous, and the cumulative applied rate is the (constant) continuous growth rate of the sum to which it is applied.

Essential Maths 25.4: **The sum of a geometric sequence**

We define a geometric sequence s_t: $s_t = ar^t, t = 0, 1, 2, \ldots$, so that $S = a, ar, ar^2, \ldots$ Since $s_0 = a$, the parameter a is the initial term of the sequence; and since $s_t = rs_{t-1}$, the parameter r is the common ratio of all pairs of successive terms.

We may define the sum of the first T terms of the sequence

$$S_T = s_0 + s_1 + \ldots + s_{T-1} = a + ar + ar^2 + \ldots + ar^{T-1} \qquad \text{[M25.5a]}$$

$$\text{and} \qquad rS_T = rs_0 + rs_1 + \ldots + rs_{T-1} = ar + ar^2 + ar^3 + \ldots + ar^T \qquad \text{[M25.5b]}$$

Subtracting Expression M25.4a from Expression M25.4b, and cancelling terms, $(r - 1)S_T = ar^T - a$, so that

$$S_T = \frac{r^T - 1}{r - 1} a \qquad \text{[M25.6]}$$

then as $T \to \infty$, if $|r| < 1$, $r^T \to 0$, and we can simplify Expression M25.5:

$$S_T \to \frac{a}{1 - r} \qquad \text{[M25.7]}$$

By yourself

X25.32   Given the principal, L_0, the charging rate of interest, $\frac{r}{n}$, and the loan term, T, obtain expressions for:

(a) the number of repayment instalments;

(b) the amount outstanding on the loan after one, two, and three repayments.

X25.33   Confirm that we can write the amount outstanding after t repayments as:

$$L_t = \left(1 + \frac{r}{n}\right)^t L_0 - R \sum_{s=0}^{t-1} \left(1 + \frac{r}{n}\right)^s \qquad [25.29]$$

X25.34   Applying the formula for the sum of a geometric sequence, Expression M25.6, show that the loan repayment, R, may be written:

$$R = \frac{\dfrac{r}{n} L_0}{1 - \left(1 + \dfrac{r}{n}\right)^{-nT}} \qquad [25.30]$$

Expression 25.30 defines the repayments associated with a loan. Especially with long-term loans – such as those typically required for house purchase, where the charging rate of interest is not fixed – it is sensible to be aware of the effects of changes in the interest rate on the regular repayment amount. Following the onset of the financial crisis in 2008, interest rates in many countries fell to historically low levels, and were kept at these levels for many years. These rates were so close to zero that the only possible change was for them to increase; and as they were so low, it was clear that even a modest rise (of say 2–3%, so that they returned close to historically normal levels) would nearly double the charging rate on many long-term loans. We have already considered the effects of very large differences in the published interest rate and more frequent compounding on the interest rate, but here we are interested in finding the effects of relatively small changes in the interest rate.

By yourself

X25.35   Using Expression 25.29, calculate the monthly repayment on:

(a) A loan of £160,000, repayable over 10 years in 120 monthly instalments, when the advertised simple interest rate is 3.5% p.a.

(b) A loan of £280,000, repayable over 25 years in 100 quarterly instalments, when the advertised simple rate of interest is 6.5% *per annum*.

X25.36   For each of the loans in X25.35, calculate the effect on the monthly repayment of an increase in the interest rate of (a) 1% p.a. and (b) 3% p.a.

25.3.3 Investing for income

The only financial transactions we have considered so far are term deposits and loans, operated by a bank. Such deposits are typically not negotiable assets. A depositor cannot sell a claim on the bank to someone else. The only way to realize the capital at the bank is to withdraw funds from the account. For other types of financial investment, though, there will typically be secondary markets for the underlying financial assets. In this chapter we shall only consider the very simplest of these, bonds.

We define a *bond* as a negotiable debt, characterized by a nominal value, V, and a maturity, or redemption date, T. The issuer of the bond promises to pay the nominal value of their holdings to all investors at maturity, thereby redeeming the outstanding stock, and extinguishing the debt. Given that bonds are typically issued to provide long-term debt finance, bond holders require interim payments during the life of the bond, as well as the payment, V, at redemption. This stream of ongoing payments usually takes the form of a fixed sum, the *coupon*, C, paid to all bond holders at regular intervals, most often annually or semi-annually. It is usual to express the coupon as a percentage of the nominal value, V. This is all the information that we require to describe a bond; for example, '6% Treasury Stock, 2020' would define a bond issued by the UK government, maturing in 2020, and through its lifetime paying a coupon of £6 per year, per £100 of nominal stock.

As they have these characteristics, bonds, or fixed income securities, are very attractive to institutional investors, such as pension funds and insurance companies, which typically have well defined liabilities and which therefore need to hold assets that will generate a certain flow of income over time. Such investors will often think about any financial asset as being a sequence of claims for payment on the issuer of the asset. In the case of bonds, the (nominal) value of these claims is certain, but for other financial assets, such as the shares issued by a company, there are no guaranteed future payments. As we shall see below, given the presence of a secondary market for bonds, it is possible that their present value, and thus their market price, will change during a bond's lifetime. These characteristics should be taken into account when deciding whether or not to hold bonds as an alternative to bank deposits.

The certainty of the stream of payments associated with a bond means that it is very easy to calculate its value, given the coupon, C, the redemption value, V, and the maturity date, T. If we continue to assume that the market rate of interest, r, is constant, then it is very easy to obtain the present value of a bond:

$$PV = \sum_{t=1}^{T-1} \frac{C}{(1+r)^t} + \frac{V}{(1+r)^T} \qquad [25.31]$$

For simplicity, we have assumed in the formula in Expression 25.30 that there is an annual coupon payment, C, with the first payment made one year from now, continuing for each of the T years until redemption. We have therefore assumed that the final coupon payment is made at the same time as the bond's redemption. It can sometimes be useful to think of the redemption payment as an alternative to the right to a stream of payments continuing into the future. There is nothing to prevent the bond issuer from funding the redemption of a bond through the issue of more bonds: governments, the largest issuers of bonds, frequently manage their financing needs in this way.

The discounted values, or present values, of the T coupon payments in Expression 25.31 form a geometric sequence with T terms, and so we can obtain a simpler expression for the present value.

By yourself

X25.37 Confirm that the present value of the bond, as given in Expression 25.31, may be written:

$$PV(V,T,C) = \frac{C}{r}(1 - (1+r)^{-T}) + V(1+r)^{-T} \qquad [25.32]$$

X25.38 Perpetual, or undated, bonds offer their holders an indefinite income stream from the coupon, so that there is no redemption date: the issuer in effect promises to continue to make payments forever.

(Continued)

(a) Show that we can write the present value of a perpetual bond $PV(C)$:

$$PV(C) = \lim_{T \to \infty} PV(V, T, C) = \frac{C}{r}$$ [25.33]

(b) Confirm that if $C = rV$, then the present value of the perpetual bond in Expression 25.33 is equal to the present value of the redeemable bond in Expression 25.32.

X25.39   We have defined a bond in terms of the stream of payments associated with it, all of which are certain. Why might the present value of a bond change over time? [*Hint:* Think about both the nominal value and the real value of the bond.]

X25.40   The UK government last issued perpetual bonds in 1946. Why do you think that few governments are willing to issue such securities to fund expenditure? [*Hint:* Think about why investors might prefer to hold a sequence of redeemable bonds, rather than a perpetual bond.]

X25.41   Most large companies will finance their activities through a mixture of debt finance (bond issue) and equity finance (share issue). We have defined bonds in terms of the flow of income associated with them. Shares in a company can similarly be defined as a claim on a share of the profits that the company will make in future, distributed through a sequence of dividends, agreed by shareholders, usually at the company's annual meeting. Explain why it is more difficult to calculate the present value of the equity of a company compared with the present value of its debt.

In these exercises, we push against the limits of the simple examples which we can explore here. Thinking in terms of the opportunity cost of holding a bond rather than money, we should treat the present values in Expressions 25.32 and 25.33 as the market price of these bonds. We may argue that people decide to hold bonds, in preference to money, because it is easier to liquidate a bond holding than a term deposit in a bank. We should also note the prediction of Exercise X25.39, that if the interest rate goes up (down), then the bond price should go down (up).

Imagine a situation in which a potential buyer expects interest rates to fall, while a potential seller expects interest rates to rise. The buyer expects the market prices of bonds to rise, while the seller expects them to fall. We might say that the buyer expects to make a *capital gain* from buying the bond now and then selling it, while the seller fears making a capital loss from continuing to hold it. Such capital gains and losses are of course additional to the stream of income associated with holding the bond. We can use such divergences in beliefs to explain the existence of an active secondary market with willing buyers and willing sellers. However, we can only have such divergent beliefs if people are not fully informed about the market, so that they do not all know what the interest will be in future. This lack of complete information about the future is necessary for the price of a bond to change over time: not only is it possible that there will be changes in the market interest rate, but such changes might be unforeseen, and therefore cannot be (fully) anticipated.

By yourself

X25.42   We sometimes refer to a *speculative motive* for holding money.
(a) Under what circumstances might an investor might prefer to hold cash assets in a bank account rather than in (perpetual) bonds?
(b) What might cause such an investor to withdraw savings from a bank, using the funds to purchase bonds?

Investment for capital gain requires a judgement that it will be possible to find two other investors at different points in time, whether the investment is held for years, for days, or even, with automated trading platforms, for fractions of a second. There must currently be a willing seller at the existing market price, while in the future there must be a willing buyer, even though the market price of the bond has risen in the intervening period. Finding a willing seller just now may be reasonably straightforward. In the absence of perfect information, though, the future is uncertain. There can be no guarantee of finding a buyer willing to pay a higher price at any time in the future. Such investment is therefore inherently risky, since there is no guaranteed return. We consider the economic analysis of risk in Chapter 26.

25.4 Education as an investment

From the perspective of the company, bond issue involves the ingathering of financial capital, and the purchase of (physical) assets to be used within the company's activities to generate profits (even after allowing for the coupon payments), and the eventual return of the loan capital to investors. As noted in Section 25.3, from the perspective of a long-term investor, bond issue involves the right to a stream of future payments; it is therefore rational to invest in the bond issue if the present value of the stream of payments is greater than the issue price.

We now turn to a rather different kind of investment project: participation in education. Everyone reading this book has had some experience of it, since learning to read is one of the most important investments of this type.[2]

In many countries, parents are required to demonstrate that they have made arrangements for their children's education, with universal primary education being provided without any tuition fees. Of course, there is a substantial difference between requiring children's attendance in education and ensuring their active participation, or even their achievement of particular outcomes. Improving the effectiveness of education systems is treated as an important goal of government policy, not least because it is considered that this will have economic benefits over time. In contrast, even where public policy is designed to encourage people to continue their studies to degree level, there is no compulsion to do so. We now explain participation in higher education as an investment whose returns are derived from higher wages in future.

In modelling labour supply in Chapter 24, we assumed that people work to generate the money required to purchase consumption goods, but that in working they also reduce the leisure time available to enjoy that consumption. Generally, students pay fees to take part in higher education. In the context of our earlier model, education would be classed as consumption, so that we have to consider time spent studying, or in a classroom, as a source of utility, undertaken because it is pleasurable. We can probably agree, relying on our own experience, that this seems improbable. Treating education as work is also

---

2 Diarmuid Cowan, in an essay on how people use their time, discusses how what we choose to learn depends in part on the opportunities that are open to us. He treats education as an investment, but also discusses its role in society, emphasizing that human capital is not simply the acquisition of knowledge, but also an accumulation of experiences. Diarmuid's essay is available through the companion website for this book, at **www.palgrave.com/mochrie.**

problematic. Study is unpaid, and generates no marketable output. Treating study as a form of investment, involving the purchase of a payment stream, resolves this difficulty.

We shall treat people as being like companies, assuming that they have to enter into debt contracts to finance their academic studies, and that they use resources, expending mental effort during the current period, to increase future productive capacity, rather than producing marketable labour immediately by entering employment. Just as investment by a company increases the capital stock used in its production activities, we treat the acquisition through education of skills, knowledge, and attributes, which are of value to an employer, as investments in *human capital*. In this approach, someone completing a university degree will be able to offer employers higher-quality labour services in future. Education increases labour productivity, and therefore wages.

25.4.1 Modelling the participation decision

We use a two-period model, considering education and labour supply decisions which individual people will make across the two periods. We assume that in the current period ($t = 0$), people choose between going into employment and completing a course of study at a university. The wage that they will receive in the future period ($t = 1$) depends upon whether or not they have graduated from university: we shall assume that graduation requires satisfactory completion of the course of study, and not simply willingness to spend the whole of the current period at university. Given that university education is voluntary, we want to develop a model in which some fraction of the total population will go to university, while the remainder will not.

Assumptions

- There are two types of people: type A who have high productivity; and type B, who have low productivity.
- In the current period, $t = 0$, anyone (of either type) going into employment is paid wage w_0.
- In the future period, $t = 1$, someone of type A with work experience from the current period earns wage w_1^N, while someone of type B obtains wage w_1^S, with $w_1^N = nw_1^S$, where $n > 1$.
- In the current period, anyone (of either type) going to university must pay fees F.
- In the future, a graduate of type T obtains wage $(1 + g)w_1^T$, where g is the graduate premium.
- Capital markets are perfect, so that both the charging rate on loans and the interest paid on savings is r, and people can borrow or save any amount in the current period.
- There is perfect information, so that employers can identify a person's type costlessly.

Classifying people in this way makes the analysis very simple. Type A people are certain to obtain a higher salary (in the future period) than those of type B. While the proportionate graduate premium is the same for people of both types in the future period, the total premium for type A people will be larger than that for type B people.

By yourself

X25.43 Explain why we might expect there to be a wage differential between people of types A and B in future, if neither complete a university degree.

X25.44   Write down an expression for the present value of income received over the current and future periods, less any education costs, for:

(a) someone of type A who does not attend university;

(b) someone of type A who attends university;

(c) someone of type B who does not attend university;

(d) someone of type B who attends university.

X25.45   Confirm that if $gw_1^S < (1 + r)(w_0 + F)$, people of type B would choose to go straight into employment, rather than going to university; while if $gw_1^N > (1 + r)(w_0 + F)$, people of type A would choose to go to university, rather than going straight into employment.

X25.46   Using the results of X25.45, explain the circumstances under which low-productivity people go straight into employment, and high-productivity people go to university. Compare the present value of lifetime earnings of high- and low-productivity people.

The investment of time and effort in a university education is worthwhile so long as the financial returns are great enough. With perfect capital markets, the affordable set for an individual is determined purely by the present value of income. People choose between going to university and going into employment in the current period in order to maximize this present value. We have illustrated the situation where wage $w_1^N > w_1^S$, so that type A people earn more than type B people in the future, even if neither go to university. We have also considered the possibility that university fees might be set so that the present value of acquiring a degree is positive for people of type A, but negative for people of type B. During the current period, $t = 0$, everyone of type A goes to university, while everyone of type B goes into employment.

We do not consider the optimal consumption profile because the driver of education choices is the effect on earning potential. Notice that we have assumed that students have no income in the current period, and that they must borrow in order to finance their studies. We can easily imagine some students who draw on existing family savings in order to fund their studies, and who therefore borrow nothing. Whether self-funding or borrowing the funds required for study, the opportunity cost of study is still the sum of the tuition fee, F, and the wages forgone, w_0. The source of funding should not affect the returns from studying, and therefore should not affect the participation decision.

By yourself

X25.47   Suppose that the public authorities in a country pay tuition fees directly to a university, and offer a study stipend to students. How do you think that this would affect participation in education? Think carefully about how the government would raise the money necessary to pay these fees.

In our example, we have assumed that the future wage will be greater than the current wage for people who do not go to university. It is easy for us to explain this in terms of our definition of human capital. We should expect formal education to be only one way of generating such capital, with experience gained from working, and either formal or informal 'on the job' training, providing alternatives to university education.

We have also in effect distinguished between people of types A and B on the basis of their ability to generate returns from the same investment in human capital. Through both on-the-job training and university education, people of type A are able to secure higher wages in the future than those of type *B*. We might relate this to some underlying characteristics of members of the two groups, perhaps as simple as differences in their attitude both to study and work. We might also note that all we have discussed in this example is the capacity of these two types to generate income. This could also reflect differences in preferences between the two types, with people of type *B* valuing leisure time rather more than people of type *A*. Thinking about broader issues of quality of life, it is by no means clear that the higher income-generating capacity of people of type *A* means that they are better off than people of type *B*.

25.5   Conclusions

We have extended the standard model to consider the allocation of expenditure over time within a fixed affordability constraint. In making decisions in the current period, people are aware that they will also take actions in future, with their current actions constraining possible future actions. In making such choices, we have argued that people will place a value on future outcomes as well as current outcomes, although they will put greater weight on the present than the future. Jam today is better than (the same quantity of) jam tomorrow.

Our models are very simple. We assume that there is perfect information about the present and about the future. We have assumed that interest rates are constant over time, and we have assumed that capital markets are perfect. None of these assumptions seem to be at all realistic. In particular, it seems very unlikely that there can be any certainty about the state of the world tomorrow. For most people, in any day, entirely unforeseen events, such as a road accident, a house fire, or sudden heart failure, might prevent them from putting their plans for the future into effect. The pervasiveness of such uncertainty is one reason for not valuing future consumption as highly as current consumption, and this will be the next area we consider.

Summary

We have extended the standard model of resource allocation to problems where decisions have to be made at different times. In doing so, we have assumed that time is divisible into finite periods, rather than being a continuous variable, with resource allocation decisions being made during each period.

We have concentrated on the behaviour of individuals as consumers. An individual's within-period utility function remains the same across time periods. Implicitly assuming that people are able to solve the within-period resource allocation efficiently, we concentrate on the allocation of money for consumption purposes across time.

The objective of maximizing inter-temporal utility requires an inter-temporal affordability constraint. We assume that people have access to perfect capital markets, and so can save and borrow any amount for any length of time, at a fixed interest rate r between periods. A consumption profile is affordable if it can be financed entirely from the initial endowment and money borrowed in the initial period, to be repaid from future income.

The rate of time preference is the counterpart to an interest rate on borrowing and saving. The effect of time preference is that future utility is discounted relative to present utility, and so the inter-temporal utility function is a weighted sum of within-period utilities. The smaller the discount factor, the greater the relative weight put on current consumption. With future discounting, current utility weighs more heavily in the inter-temporal utility function than future consumption. Where the discount factor takes a low value, this will lead to consumption decreasing over time periods.

As well as being able to finance future consumption by saving money, people can invest savings in (secondary) capital markets. The simplest financial assets available for saving are bonds, tradable securities issued by governments and companies, which are a form of debt. The market value of a bond is negatively related to the market interest rate: should the interest rate go up, then the bond value will go down.

In the case of perpetual bonds, investors buy the right to an indefinite stream of interest payments and nothing else. Given a constant market interest rate, the bond price is inversely related to the interest rate.

We have applied the model to personal investments made by individuals. Using the example of the decision to continue in education beyond compulsory schooling, we treated the skills acquired through education as a capital stock. For any individual, the participation decision will then be based on financial returns, accrued through increased earnings in work during future periods. By allowing these financial returns to differ across people, we show that only some people will choose to continue in education.

Visit the companion website at **www.palgrave.com/mochrie** to access further teaching and learning materials, including lecturer slides and a testbank, as well as guideline answers and student MCQs.

26

Choice and risk

After extending the standard model so that it can incorporate inter-temporal choice, it is natural to consider choice under *risk*, when both outcomes and payoffs are uncertain. Assuming that we can define a probability distribution over all possible outcomes, we set out the assumptions required for preferences across outcomes to be represented by the members of the family of the so-called *von Neumann–Morgenstern utility functions*. We demonstrate that it is necessary to treat these functions as cardinal measures, abandoning the ordinal interpretation used up to this point.

We define *utility* in any state of the world as a function of wealth in that state, so that expected utility is a probability-weighted sum of payoff values in each state. Defining a *lottery* as the set of outcomes together with the associated probability distribution, we apply arguments about expected utility to understand preferences over lotteries. In particular, we are able to compare the expected utility of a lottery with the utility of its expected wealth, received with certainty. From this, it is possible to develop measures of risk aversion, such as the *risk premium*, a measure of the wealth that someone would give up in order to avoid participating in a specific lottery.

Since someone who is risk-averse would prefer a smaller, certain income to the expected income associated with risky outcomes, it should be possible to persuade such a person to buy insurance against the risk of loss. We note, though, that there are many cases where people choose to gamble, indicating that they are willing to embrace some risks, while still buying insurance, which suggests a desire to avoid risk. We provide an explanation for this in terms of *reference-dependent utility*, which we explore in much more detail in Chapter 27.

Insurance markets are means of trading risk. We explore their emergence, noting that by pooling risks, a group of risk-averse people can increase their utility. In the same way, it is possible for a risk-neutral business to offer fair, full insurance to risk-averse customers, so that there is a full transfer of risk from the customer to the insurer. The customer pays an insurance premium, which pays out the full value of any loss suffered, with the premium calculated so that it equals the expected payout exactly. Should the insurer offer policies under which it expects to make a profit, then customers will prefer to bear some of the risk.

26.1   The nature of risk

'In this world nothing can be said to be certain, except death and taxes' (Benjamin Franklin, Letter to Jean-Baptiste Leroy, 1789). We frequently encounter situations in which people face risks. Gamblers in a casino embrace it. The builder of a house in a flood-plain seems oblivious to it. A firm producing some new good, even after extensive research into demand, faces the risk that there will be no market for it. Governments introducing taxes intended to change behaviour risk many unforeseen consequences.

We have assumed that people making decisions have perfect information. Risk occurs where people have to make choices without knowing what the state of the world will be. As a result, they cannot be certain about the effect – in terms of generation of utility – of their actions. In some situations, people actively assume risk. For example, when buying lottery tickets, people select a set of numbers, doing so before the winning numbers have been selected. People also engage in a wide range of risky behaviours. For example, it is well known that regular use of tobacco products may lead to crippling illness and even premature death, yet in advanced economies somewhere between 20% and 30% of the population continue to smoke. In other situations, though, people avoid risk: following instructions on road signs, exercising regularly, and following nutritional advice, for example. In these cases, we might say that people seek to manage or mitigate risk, where *management* involves actions that mean that an adverse outcome is less likely, and *mitigation* involves actions designed to reduce the impact of adverse outcomes.

Much of our attention in this chapter will be on the operation of those markets in which risks can be traded. If there are some people who are willing to bear risks, while at the same time there are others who would like to shed them, then it may seem obvious to try and find a price at which there will be willing buyers, and willing sellers, of exposure to risk. Insurance policies are financial contracts that make this possible. We might wonder who is most likely to want to purchase insurance, noting that enjoyment of taking risks does not necessarily mean willingness to pay the costs after the event. Consider an enthusiastic, but accident-prone, skier: with full insurance, the skier knows that someone else will pay all of the (financial) costs associated with an accident. We might predict that this skier will take greater risks when insured than when uninsured.

By yourself

X26.1 In commercial law, the principle of *caveat emptor* (let the buyer beware) is generally honoured. Why might it not be appropriate to apply this in the case of bank deposits? What undesirable effects might a universal guarantee, supported by public authorities, have on: (a) banks' behaviour; and (b) depositors' behaviour?

X26.2 Some surgeons, prior to operating on a patient, will require the patient to alter a risky behaviour, perhaps changing diet to reduce weight and blood pressure, stopping smoking, or reducing alcohol consumption. Explain how the surgeon might consider this to be part of a risk-management or risk-mitigation strategy.

X26.3 Governments in all developed countries have had to recognize that demographic change – people living longer (about 2.5 extra years per decade), with populations stabilizing as fertility rates fall below 2 live births per woman – will require careful management. How might governments encourage people to engage in financial planning for a lengthy period of retirement?

26.1.1 A motivational example

We begin with a very simple example: *A* tosses a coin, with both *A* and *B* observing how it lands (head side up or tail side up). They agree that if the coin lands head side up, *A* will pay *B* £10, while if it lands tail side up, *B* will pay *A* the same amount. In this situation:

- We have an experiment or trial that yields one, and only one, of two outcomes, *H* and *T*.
- There are values of the outcomes for *A* and *B*, $(v_A(H), v_B(H)) = (-10, 10)$ and $(v_A(T), v_B(T)) = (10, -10)$.

- In the experiment, we treat both outcomes as being equally likely to occur, represented by the probability distribution, $\Pr(H) = \Pr(T) = 0.5$.
- Assuming that player i is concerned only about the financial value of participation, the expected value, $E[v_i] = \Pr(H)v_i(H) + \Pr(T)v_i(T) = 0$.

This situation involves A and B engaging in a very simple gamble. We could describe it in a slightly different way,: both players contribute £10 to a shared pot, with B taking the pot when outcome H occurs, and A taking it under outcome T.

By yourself

X26.4   Confirm that when the pot is shared, each player receives an expected payment of £10, so that the value of participation in the game, net of the initial contribution, is zero.

26.1.2   The nature of probability

Randomness A quality of a trial such that all outcomes are equally likely to occur.

Probability distribution A function that measures the likelihood of particular events occurring.

In the example, we might reasonably assume that when the coin is tossed in the air and caught, it can only land with one face up, and so will not land balanced on its rim, which would be a third result of the trial. The structure of the proposed payoff is consistent with a belief that the coin toss is **random**, with each outcome equally likely to occur. We can capture these beliefs slightly more formally in the form of the probability distribution over the possible outcomes.

A **probability distribution** is simply a rule, or function, which allows us to measure how likely it is that each of the results of an experiment – or some event, or combination of results – will occur.

- We assign an event that is certain to occur a probability of one; and its complement, an event that is certain not to occur, a probability of zero. (We could restate Franklin's belief that death and taxes are certain by saying that these are events with a probability of one.)
- Since the experiment will definitely take place, with A tossing the coin in the air, and there will certainly be a result, the sum of probabilities over the results:

$$1 > \Pr(H), \Pr(T) > 0, \text{ and } \Pr(H) + \Pr(T) = 1 \qquad [26.1]$$

Expression 26.1 simply formalizes our intuitive understanding that there are two possible results, of which one or other must occur, so that neither is certain.

- In defining the coin toss as an experiment, we mean that the result is entirely random and unpredictable; in the absence of any reason not to do so, we assign equal probability to each result. With only two possible results, $\Pr(H) = \Pr(T) = 0.5$. More generally, the probability of any event which might occur, but which is not certain, lies between 0 and 1.

The assumption that both results are equally probable in the experiment is grounded in experience. Most people will have seen coins being tossed in the air many times, but will never have developed any accurate way of predicting how they will land. One way of treating the probability distribution across the results of this single trial is the use of the relative frequency of outcomes in repeated trials, where each trial is independent of the others. (Famously, during World War II, a South African mathematician interned in Denmark, John Kerrich, carried out a trial of 10,000 repeated tosses of a single coin, obtaining 5,067 heads and 4,933 tails, and so concluded that both results were equally likely to occur in any single trial.)

Had Kerrich's coin been used in the situation described above, then there would have been little doubt of the fairness of the coin being used, and the probability of each outcome. But, we do not expect A and B to have checked the fairness of the coin through similar repeated experiments. To maintain an objective model when there is only a single trial, we might interpret the probability distribution over the possible states as incorporating the unmeasurable characteristics of the system that leads to the coin toss: the force exerted on the coin, the angle at which it is launched into the air, and the face that is upward when it is tossed, for example. It seems much easier with a trial based on such a coin toss simply to assume that both results are equally probable.

We treat a single coin toss as an experiment with two possible results. We may face situations where we have to predict the probability distribution of a series of experiments, or of multiple simultaneous experiments, each of which we treat as being **independent** of each other. In this situation, knowing the result of one experiment does not help us predict the outcome of any other experiment.

> **Independence** A quality of successive trials, such that the outcome of one cannot be (causally) related to the outcome of the others.

By yourself

X26.5 The *gambler's fallacy* is a belief that if successive trials are truly random, then if one result occurs more frequently than expected in a sequence of trials, in subsequent trials it is likely to occur less frequently. (The most famous example of this occurred at a casino in Monte Carlo in 1913: the ball landed on 'black' in a roulette wheel in 26 successive trials, and gamblers, convinced that the sequence was highly improbable, behaved as if they believed that with each successive spin of the wheel, the probability of the ball landing on 'red' was increasing.) Explain why the fallacy is inconsistent with the belief that successive trials are independent.

26.1.3 Probability distributions

A sequence of coin tosses is a simple example of a compound experiment in which the probability distribution in individual trials remains constant throughout. There will be a probability distribution over the outcomes of the entire sequence of experiments.

By yourself

X26.6 Consider an experiment in which we throw four coins in the air simultaneously.
(a) By listing possible results, confirm that there are 16 in total.
(b) If we assume that for all four coins, $Pr(H) = Pr(T) = 0.5$, explain why the results *HTHH*, *HHHT* and *HHHH* are equally probable. What do you conclude about the probability of every result?
(c) Define the events $n_H = 0, 1, 2, 3$ and 4, where n_H is the number of coins facing head up. Using the listing in part (a), calculate the probabilities $Pr(n_H = 0)$, $Pr(n_H = 1)$, $Pr(n_H = 2)$, $Pr(n_H = 3)$, and $Pr(n_H = 4)$.

X26.7 For an experiment in which we toss two dice at the same time, summing together the numbers showing on the upward faces:
(a) Confirm that there 36 possible results, which can be classified into 11 events, according to the value of the sum, s. Calculate the probability of each event.

(Continued)

(b) Hence calculate the probabilities of the value of s being:

    (i) 11 or 12;

    (ii) 7 or more; and

    (iii) a multiple of 4.

X26.8 We carry out a very similar experiment, throwing two dice. On this occasion, we define the associated events as the product, π, rather than the sum, of the numbers showing on the upward faces of the dice.

(a) In this case, $1 \leq \pi \leq 36$. Calculate the probability of each value. [*Note*: There are several events for which the probability is zero.]

(b) Calculate the probability of the following events:

    (i) obtaining a multiple of three;

    (ii) obtaining a multiple of four;

    (iii) obtaining a number greater than or equal to 24; and

    (iv) obtaining a number less than or equal to 8.

Random variable
A function whose value is determined by random events.

In these experiments, the measures n_H, s and π summarize characteristics of their results. More generally, we can think of such measures as examples of **random variables**, numbers whose value is determined by the result of an experiment. Going back to our original example of the coin toss, we can think of the payment that A makes to B as a random variable, p_A: $p_A \in \{-10, 10\}$. We then define the probability distribution as a function of the random variable, here $\Pr(p_A) = 0.5$.

We shall typically carry out analysis in this chapter in terms of random variables, V, which can take exactly two values, so that $V \in \{v_1, v_2\}$, with the associated probability distribution across the realized values:

$$\Pr(V = v) = \begin{cases} \Pr(v_1), & \text{if } V = v_1 \\ 1 - \Pr(v_1), & \text{if } V = v_2 \end{cases} \quad [26.2]$$

As usual, to simplify our presentation we allow there to be only two outcomes, confident that most of the results we obtain can be easily applied to more complex situations.

26.1.4 Valuing risky outcomes

We define events, or states of the world, in terms of total (personal) wealth. We shall define the utility achievable in each state with the realized wealth. In addition, although we use the term 'experiment' and indeed examples in which people choose whether or not to bear particular risks, we shall often recognize that people have no control over the risks that they face. Even in such cases, though, we shall talk about 'trials' to emphasize that in such situation, people might respond to inherent risks, either embracing them, or seeking to mitigate their effects.

Treating wealth after bearing risk as a random variable, we can define its expected value. For a random variable $X \in \{x_1, x_2, \dots, x_n\}$, with associated probability distribution $\Pr(X = x_i) = \{p_1, p_2, \dots, p_n\}$, the expected value

$$E[X] = \sum_{i=1}^{n} p_i x_i \quad [26.3]$$

This **expected value** is a probability-weighted sum of the outcome values for the experiment. More probable events have greater weight in the sum than less probable events. In our initial coin toss example, with only two possible results to the experiment, and with outcome values equal and opposite, the expected value was zero.

> **Expected value** A probability weighted sum of all possible values of a random variable; the mean value of the variable.

By yourself

X26.9 Calculate the expected value of the experiments in X26.6–X26.8.

Suppose that before taking part in the coin-toss experiment, the participants, A and B, have wealth, w_{A0} and w_{B0}. After participating in the experiment, their wealth changes to:

$$w_{i1} = w_{i0} + v_i \qquad [26.4]$$

where v_i is the payment which player i makes (or receives). In the example, $v_A \in \{10, -10\}$, with probability distribution, $\pi(10) = \pi(-10) = 0.5$; and $v_B = -v_A$. Note that since v_A is a random variable, v_B, defined as a function of v_A, is also random. Since w_{i0} is certain, the probability distribution of wealth after the experiment, w_{i1} is the distribution of the payment, v_i, and so the expected value of wealth after the experiment, $E[w_{i1}] = w_{i0}$. The participants in this experiment finish with expected wealth equal to their original wealth, although neither of them have their original wealth.

By yourself

X26.10 Working with the experiments in X26.6–X26.8, calculate the expected change in wealth, $E[w_1] - w_0$:
(a) The experiment consists of four coin tosses. A participant in the experiment is required to pay an initial stake of £4. In return, the participant receives a payout $v(r) = 2^r$, where r, the result of the experiment, is the number of heads in the sequence of four coin tosses.
(b) When summing the values on two dice, say that the participant receives the value if the total is an even number, but has to pay the value if the total is an odd number.
(c) When multiplying the values on two dice, the participant has to pay a stake of £10 at the start of the experiment, but receives a payout of £25 if the product is greater than 12.

26.2 Expected utility

Calculating the change in expected wealth is one way in which people might decide how to respond to situations involving risk. Remember though, that money is only useful because it permits the purchase of goods, and thus the generation of utility. If the sum of money available to finance consumption is a random variable, then so is the realized utility after bearing the risk. If we define utility as a function of wealth, which is not a linear, the value of a given loss will generally be different from the value of a gain of the same amount. Instead of simply calculating the amount of money expected at the end of one our experiments, we would expect responses to risk to be made on the basis of the expected value of the utility achievable after bearing it.

The idea of basing decisions on expected utility, rather than on expected monetary value, has a very long history. Consider the following example, first presented by Daniel Bernouilli in 1738. A casino offers the following wager, based on a succession of coin tosses. The game continues for t coin tosses, ending after T coin tosses, or else on the first occasion on which the coin lands head up, if this occurs first. Such a sequence must consist of $t - 1$ *Tails*, following by 1 *Head*; or else T *Tails*.

By yourself

X26.11   For the sequence of coin tosses described above:
(a) Calculate the probability of the first *Head* occurring on the tth toss, assuming that the coin is fair, and that each toss forms a distinct experiment (so that successive coin tosses are independent of each other).
(b) Suppose that the casino offers a payment of 2^{t-1} at the end of each sequence, up to a maximum length $T = 20$. (This means that after a sequence of 20 *Tails*, the casino ends the game, and the gambler loses the initial stake.) Calculate the expected value of the payment the casino would make.
(c) Suppose that the casino offers a payment of 2^{t-1}, irrespective of the length of the sequence. Confirm that the expected value of the casino's payout is infinite.

The *St Petersburg Paradox* refers to the contradiction between the observation that as the maximum length of the sequence of coin tosses increases without limit, so that as $T \rightarrow \infty$, the expected value of the payout is infinite, and yet if people are offered this gamble, they rarely indicate a willingness to pay a stake of more than £25.

The traditional resolution of the paradox, first set out by Bernouilli, rests on two assumptions: firstly, that there is an increasing, concave utility of wealth function; and secondly, that it is the expected utility from participation in the gamble, rather than the expected wealth, that determines behaviour. In this case, suppose that we define the utility of wealth as:

$$U(W) = \sqrt{W} \qquad\qquad [26.5]$$

where W is the wealth after taking part in the gamble, consisting of initial wealth, W_0, and the payment received (net of any participation fee, or stake money), $W - W_0$.

By yourself

X26.12   Assume that $U(W_0) = 0$ and that there is no stake money paid to take part in the gamble.

Calculate the utility $U(W(t))$ obtained when the casino pays out at the end of a sequence of length, t. Defining the expected utility as a probability-weighted sum of the utilities obtained from sequences of coin tosses of all possible lengths, write out the first terms as the product of the probability of a sequence occurring and its payoff. Hence confirm that the expected utility may be written:

$$E[U(W)] = \tfrac{1}{2}\sum_{t=1}^{\infty} 2^{-\frac{t-1}{2}} = 1 + 2^{-\frac{1}{2}} \qquad\qquad [26.6]$$

The calculations in Exercises X26.11 and X26.12 demonstrate that whereas the expected payment is infinite, the value of the expected payment in Expression 26.6 is finite. All that is required to resolve the paradox is to assume that the expected utility function is strictly concave, but increasing, so that:

$$U'(W) > 0; \text{ and } U''(W) < 0 \tag{26.7}$$

The greater an individual's wealth, the greater will be the achievable utility from consumption; but the rate of increase of utility – the marginal utility of wealth in effect – will decrease with wealth.

26.2.1 Properties of an expected utility function

Until now, we have referred to people taking part in experiments, with the results being grouped together into a set of events, or outcomes, of the experiment, and with a probability distribution being defined across the events. We now change our language very slightly, supposing that people in effect participate in lotteries, whether voluntarily or as a result of events beyond their control. As with experiments, we define each lottery, L, in terms of the

> **Lottery** A description of an experiment in terms of the values taken by a random variable, representing outcomes and their associated probability distribution.

outcome set, $W = \{w_1, w_2, \dots, w_n\}$, which consists of all possible values of total wealth after participation in the lottery, as well as the probability distribution over these values, $\Pi = \{\pi_1, \pi_2, \dots, \pi_n\}$,. We then define the expected utility of the lottery prior to participation:

$$E[U(L)] = \sum_{i=1}^{n} \pi_i u(w_i) \tag{26.8}$$

The expected utility function measures how much value a person might reasonably expect to obtain through participation in the lottery; in effect, it is simply the probability-weighted sum of the possible realizations of wealth after participation. After the lottery is drawn, the actual utility of wealth will be certain, and determined by the person's wealth in the usual way. Using an expected utility function, it is possible for someone to choose between different lotteries (or indeed to choose between participation in a lottery and an alternative, certain outcome). With such a function, utility is derived only from the realized wealth. Relying on a measure for making participation decisions that is additive means that we exclude the possibility of interactions across the various outcomes. For example, we do not consider a large gain to be especially valuable just because it is relatively unlikely to occur: its achievement is not, by itself, a source of utility. Equally, we do not consider there to be any regret when the outcome involves a loss (relative to wealth under certainty), or a loss occurring when a small gain was more likely.

> **Expected utility** A probability weighted sum of all the possible values of utility scores from a lottery; the mean of utility.

By yourself

X26.13 In our analysis, we will assume (1) that participation in a lottery is not a source of utility; (2) that the probability distribution across outcomes is objective, and known; and (3) that all people choosing whether or not to participate in the lottery have the same information available to them. To what extent might we appeal to deviations from such assumptions in seeking to explain why people actively assume risks? [*Note:* You may wish to distinguish between three types of activity: (a) buying lottery tickets; (b) playing a card game, such as poker or bridge; and (c) betting on the outcome of sporting contests, such as horse races.]

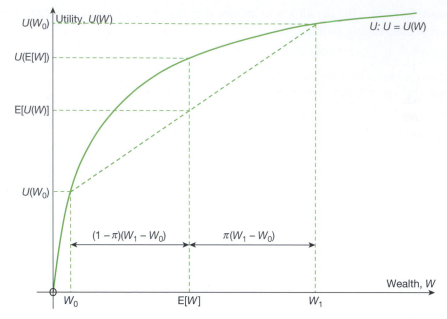

Figure 26.1 The expected utility of wealth

The calculation of expected utility in a simple lottery is shown in Figure 26.1. There are two possible outcomes, one with wealth W_0 and one with wealth W_1, with associated probabilities, π and $1 - \pi$. Applying the formula for the expected value in Expression 26.3 and rearranging it, we see that:

$$E[W] - W_0 = (1 - \pi)(W_1 - W_0) \qquad [26.9]$$

The higher the probability of obtaining wealth W_0, the closer $E[W]$ will be to W_0 in the diagram.

Similarly, applying the formula for the expected utility, Expression 26.8, and rearranging:

$$E[U(W)] - U(W_0) = (1 - \pi)[U(W_1) - U(W_0)] \qquad [26.10]$$

Expressions 26.9 and 26.10 hold because the expected value and the expected utility are identically weighted sums of these two different outcome measures. Taking part in the lottery, $L = (W_0, W_1, \pi)$, a person with utility of wealth $U = U(W)$, as illustrated in Figure 26.1, has expected wealth (after participation), $E[W]$, but expected utility, $E[U(W)]$. Were we able to offer the certain alternative, $E[W]$, it would yield certain utility, $U(E[W])$. Note that in Figure 26.1, the utility of certain wealth is greater than the expected utility of wealth after participating in the lottery. This is an immediate result of the concavity of the utility of wealth curve in the diagram. The assumption of a concave utility of wealth function is intuitively appealing, since the marginal utility of wealth is then decreasing; and as we saw in the discussion of the St Petersburg Paradox, this characteristic has traditionally been used to explain some features of observed decision making.

26.2.2 Attitudes to risk

We define concavity in terms of the sign of the second derivative, with $\frac{d^2U}{dW^2} < 0$. For the chord joining any two points on the graph of an increasing, concave utility of wealth function, the chord lies below the graph. That is, for any utility function for which $U = U(W)$, with $U''(W) < 0$, the chord joining any pair of points, A(W_A, U_A) and B(W_B, U_B), on the graph of the utility of wealth passes through the point, C($tW_A + (1 - t)W_B, tU(W_A) + (1 - t)U(W_B)$), with $U(tW_A + (1 - t)W_B) > tU(W_A) + (1 - t)U(W_B)$. It follows that certain wealth, W_0, is always preferred to participation in a lottery, L, where the expected wealth from participation, $E[W] = W_0$. We therefore associate a concave utility of wealth function with *risk-averse* behaviour, such as avoiding active participation in lotteries, and reducing exposure to risk wherever possible.

By yourself

X26.14 Sketch a diagram showing a utility of wealth function, which is convex. Demonstrate that the expected utility, $E[U(W)]$, from participation in the lottery, $L = (W_1, W_2, \pi)$ is greater than the utility of certain wealth, $U(E[W])$. Compare the differences in attitude to risk between two people, one with concave, and the other with convex, utility of wealth functions.

We have seen that if someone is **risk-averse**, and faces the lottery, L, with expected wealth, $E[W]$, then given the choice between certain wealth equal to the expected wealth after participation in the lottery and participation in the lottery, this person will choose the certain outcome rather than the risk of participation. Alternatively, if

> **Risk aversion** Behaviour that reflects a preference for a certain outcome rather than participation in lotteries.

$$U(E[W]) > E[U(W)]$$
$$[26.11]$$

then this person is risk-averse. We noted above that the condition in Expression 26.11 is satisfied whenever the utility of wealth is concave. From Exercise X26.14, we may conclude that this is also a sufficient condition. When the utility of wealth is convex, Expression 26.11 fails. A person choosing between participation in lottery, L, with expected wealth, $E[W]$, and receiving wealth, $E[W]$, with certainty, will choose the lottery. We say that such a person is **risk-loving**.

> **Risk-loving** Behaviour that reflects a preference for participation in lotteries rather than a certain outcome.

Formally, for risk aversion we require strict concavity. Likewise, love of risk requires strict convexity. If utility is linear in wealth, we can demonstrate that in any lottery, L, the expected utility from participation equals the utility of the expected wealth, when offered as a certain alternative. We say that if

$$U(E[W]) = E[U(W)]$$
$$[26.12]$$

the person is **risk-neutral**. A risk-neutral individual is only concerned about the expected outcome of the lottery. We can imagine this as being a natural position for a business, which has to take many risks, all of which are statistically independent. As we shall argue in more detail below, we expect the frequency distribution of outcomes across many risks to approximate the underlying probability distribution of the population very well. For a business that knows the probability distribution, the sum of the expected values of each risky outcome is likely to be a very good approximation to its realized income after bearing the risks. With gains and losses from lotteries tending to cancel each other out, the risk from simultaneous participation in many identical, independent lotteries is often close to zero.

> **Risk neutrality.** Indifference between certain outcomes and participation in lotteries.

By yourself

X26.15 Demonstrate that for the utility function, U: $U(W) = a + bW$, then the expected utility, $E[U(W)]$, from participation in the lottery, $L = (W_0, W_1, \pi)$, equals the utility of the expected wealth, $U(E[W])$.

26.2.3 The risk premium

In Figure 26.2, we have again drawn the graph of a concave utility of wealth function, so that the utility of the worse outcome, $U(W_0)$, is less than the expected utility of wealth, which is itself less than the utility of expected wealth:

$$U(W_0) < E[U(W)] < U(E[W]) \qquad [26.13]$$

Assuming that the utility of wealth is a continuous function, there must be some level of wealth, W_δ:

$$E[W] > W_\delta > W_0; \text{ and } U(W_\delta) = E[U(W)] \qquad [26.14]$$

There is some level of wealth, W_δ, strictly less than the expected wealth after participation in the lottery, L, whose utility is the expected utility, $E[U(W)]$, from participation. Offering someone whose utility of wealth is as shown in Figure 26.2 a choice between participation in the lottery $L(W_0, W_1, \pi)$ and certain wealth, $W_\delta = E[W] - \delta$, this person would be indifferent between the alternatives. Another way of thinking about this is to say that δ is the maximum sum of money that this person would be willing to give up in order to avoid participating in the lottery. We therefore refer to δ as the **risk premium**.

Risk premium The payment that a risk averse person will make to transfer the risk to someone else.

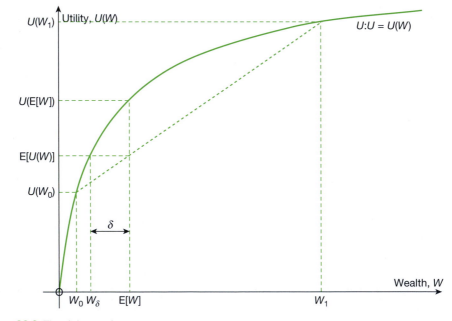

Figure 26.2 The risk premium

Think about what it would mean for a risk-averse person, A, to pay to give up the risk. Another person, B, must agree to bear the risk instead if risk mitigation is not possible. We define a contract in which A and B agree to payments, c, which depend on A's wealth after bearing the risk and which are designed to ensure that whatever the realized outcome of the lottery, L, might be, A's wealth, W, will be certain.

By yourself

X26.16   Write down the terms of the contract between A and B that would ensure that: (a) A obtains expected wealth $E[W] - c$ with certainty; (b) A is indifferent between entering into the contract and bearing the risk; and (c) B, who loves risk, would be willing to enter into the contract.

Should B offer to take on the risk that A would otherwise face, while leaving A with certain wealth, $W > E[W] - c$, then A will strictly prefer the certain outcome to bearing the risk. We have here the basis for an insurance contract, even though we usually define insurance in a slightly different way.

26.2.4 Insurance contracts

Suppose that participation in the lottery is not voluntary. There are some risks that people have to bear unless they take steps to avoid them. A car might break down, or slip on ice and crash, or be stolen. Let us suppose that there is a small probability, π, of such an event occurring, reducing wealth from W_0 to $W_0 - D$ in Figure 26.3. This is the involuntary lottery, $L^A = (W_0, W_0 - D, \pi)$.

We allow a person facing this risk to purchase insurance. The insurance contract has a slightly different structure from the simple transfers after realization of wealth considered

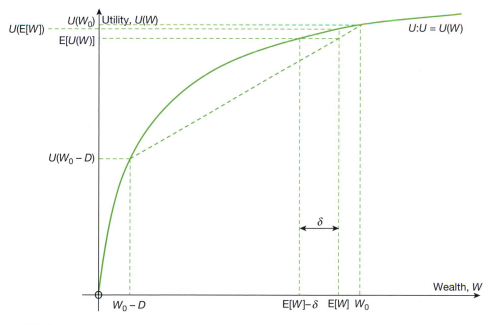

Figure 26.3 The maximum insurance premium

in Exercise X26.16. Typically, the person seeking insurance provides information to the insurer, which the insurer uses to determine the terms under which the policy will be granted. We would normally expect the proposal and the subsequent policy to be defined in terms of:

(a) the insured event, N, which we can define in this case as theft or accidental damage to the car, but which is not the result of negligence on the part of the proposer;

(b) the sum assured, B: the amount of money that the insurer will pay in the event of the insured event occurring;

(c) the premium, R: a fee set for the purchase of the insurance policy.

We assume that there is only one event, N, that can lead to a loss, whose value, $D(N)$, the associated damage, is certain. We also assume that the probability, $\Pr(N)$, is known to the insurer and to the policyholder.

If N does not occur, then the insured policyholder will have wealth:

$$W(0) = W_0 - R \qquad\qquad [26.15]$$

While if the insured event does occur, the policyholder's wealth will be:

$$W(N) = W_0 - D - R + B \qquad\qquad [26.16]$$

For simplicity, we shall assume that the policy offers *full insurance*, so that the payout when N occurs, $B = D$. Then $W(0) = W(N) = W_0 - R$. With full insurance, wealth is certain, $W = W_0 - R$. For anyone who is risk-averse, so long as

$$U(W_0 - R) > E[U(W)] \qquad\qquad [26.17]$$

the insurance policy increases utility. By definition of the risk premium, δ, the condition in Expression 26.17 will be satisfied if $R < \delta$. Quite reasonably, so long as the insurance premium is not too high, someone who is risk-averse will buy a policy, enjoying certain utility greater than the expected utility from participation in the lottery.

By yourself

X26.17 For the following situations, calculate the risk premium (the maximum insurance premium that an individual would pay).

(a) Wealth $W_0 = 1,000$, loss $D = 1,000$; probability of loss, $\pi = 0.1$; utility $U : U(W) = W^{\frac{1}{3}}$.

(b) $W_0 = 200$; $D = 100$; $\pi = 0.05$; $U(W) = W^{\frac{1}{2}}$.

(c) $W_0 = 500$; $D = 200$; $\pi = 0.2$; $U(W) = \ln(1 + W)$.

X26.18 Using diagrams, demonstrate that no one who loves risk will want to buy insurance.

26.2.5 Mutual insurance

From Exercises X26.17 and X26.18 we can see that it will always be possible for someone who loves risk to sell an insurance policy to someone who wants to avoid it. But this does not really help us to explain the foundation of societies designed for the purpose of providing mutual insurance. For example, until the Battle of the Little Big Horn (in what is now Montana) in 1876, army officers serving on the (Western) frontier of the USA 'passed the hat' following the death of a comrade. This raised enough money to transport dependents back to the settled areas of the United States, usually near the East coast, where they might more easily be supported by their friends and relatives. At Little Big Horn, the 7th Cavalry were slaughtered. With few survivors, the system of 'passing the hat' failed. A direct consequence of the battle was therefore the foundation of the Army Mutual Aid Association in January 1879, formed to 'aid the families of the deceased members in a prompt, simple and substantial manner'. It continues today as the American Armed Forces Mutual Aid Association.

Suppose that we have a group of S soldiers, all serving officers in an army, all awaiting their assignment to duties. They all face the involuntary lottery, $L = (W_0, W_0 - D, \pi)$. Each faces the same probability, π, of loss, D, associated with event N, death in battle. We assume that every officer has a given concave utility function, U: $U = U(W)$, so that all are equally risk-averse. In addition, we shall assume that only serving officers face such risks; and that the risk of any single member of the group experiencing the loss is independent of any other member suffering it.

To analyse the reduction of risk, recall our initial definition of probability in Section 26.1.1. Thinking in terms of relative frequency, we simply believe that a proportion, π, of the population, N, will suffer loss, D. In a strict relative frequency interpretation, the casualty rate would be the proportion of serving officers who die in service. Assuming that there are no costs to writing or administering the insurance policies, and that the proportion of fatalities is certain, then the officers' corps might treat the total loss that they will suffer jointly as a certain event. The insurance premium payable to the mutual society is then a contribution to a common fund that will meet those losses. Individually risk-averse, by joining together in this way members of the group are able collectively to eliminate the risk (of financial loss).

Abstracting from this example, we see that in defining policy the insurance society must make a judgement about the probability of loss in the future. Even with an objective model to determine the probability distribution of losses, and which is a good approximation to the true one, the relative frequency of losses, ρ, cannot be predicted completely with any accuracy. We expect though, that as the population size $N \to \infty$, $\rho \to \pi$. In other words, in a very large population, we expect the proportion of people suffering losses to be very close to the probability of any individual suffering a loss, assuming that the objective model generating that probability is correct. While we cannot be certain about the relative frequency in the population, just as Kerrich found with his coin (Section 26.1), with a large enough population, or even a large enough sample drawn randomly from the whole population, the observed deviation across the sample from the predicted relative frequency of losses, will typically be very small. Allowing for the costs of writing and administering the insurance policies, it is possible for members of the group facing the common risk to insure against it, and thereby to increase their utility.

There are two particular problems associated with the future value of individual probabilities of loss. The first is *adverse selection*. Those officers who expected to face a high risk of death would have been much more likely to seek insurance than others who did not. With the characteristics of the group buying insurance being different from those of the whole population, then if the insurance society wrote only a single, standardized policy, which took no account of these differences in (potential) members' risk profiles, it would systematically underestimate the risk of death among those purchasing its policy. With substantial differences between the risk profile of the population and the group taking out insurance, the insurer faces a substantial risk of losses. The second problem is *moral hazard*. It might be argued that in purchasing insurance, soldiers would free themselves from restraints on their conduct; indeed there has been much debate about 7th Cavalry's tactics at Little Big Horn. Once insured, they might be more willing to risk their lives in the course of their duties. Simply by being insured, the risk profile of the insured is different from the risk profile of the whole population. To avoid this effect, many insurance policies will become invalid if the policyholder acts negligently or is responsible for the occurrence of the insured event. With life assurance, for example, there is a general assumption that death is not sought, and so suicide is very often excluded from the insurance.

By yourself

X26.19 Explain why most health insurance schemes give the general population limited control over whether or not they participate.

X26.20 Why might it be more difficult for a market to exist for flood insurance than for fire insurance?

X26.21 The European Court of Justice has held that there should be no differences in the motor insurance premiums offered to men and women. On what basis might there be differences? How reasonable is it to make the practice unlawful? Given that equalities legislation recognizes other protected characteristics, such as age, how might insurers determine risk classes without relying on this characteristic?

X26.22 Within analysis of bank deposit insurance, we sometimes refer to *double moral hazard*. Explain why the existence of insurance might cause (a) the depositors and (b) the managers of an insolvent bank to take more extreme risks.

X26.23 Why might a casino offering a game with the structure of the one in the St Petersburg Paradox find it difficult to buy insurance against that risk?

X26.24 Many people who insure their home contents, their car and even their lives will happily gamble. How would you explain the seeming contradictions in this behaviour?

X26.25 Economists sometimes argue that in many poor countries, by enabling people to pay for high-value goods at the time they need them, informal, often community-based, lending channels are effectively a form of insurance. Explain why people might need to rely on such methods of insurance.

26.3 The von Neumann–Morgenstern axiomization

We have simply defined the expected utility function, without providing any justification for its adoption apart from its value in assisting with the resolution of the St Petersburg Paradox. In Exercise X26.13, we have considered some reasons for believing that an expected utility approach is necessarily incomplete, particularly the way in which it assumes that we only need to consider outcomes and not behaviour.

In 1947, von Neumann and Morgenstern set out a justification for the use of the expected utility approach in terms of a set of axioms, all of which appear to impose entirely reasonable constraints on preferences over lotteries. We shall state these axioms in terms of three lotteries, L^A, L^B and L^C. As in Chapter 4, preferences are a binary relation, and we denote weak preference for one lottery over another by the operator '$\succcurlyeq$'.

- *Completeness:* For any pair of lotteries, L^A and L^B, either $L^A \succcurlyeq L^B$, or $L^B \succcurlyeq L^A$, or both (in which case the person is indifferent between the lotteries). *Therefore:* It is possible to rank every pair of lotteries.

- *Transitivity:* For any triple of lotteries, L^A, L^B and L^C, assume that $L^A \succcurlyeq L^B$, and $L^B \succcurlyeq L^C$. Then $L^A \succcurlyeq L^C$. *Therefore:* We rule out cyclic preferences over lotteries.

- *Continuity:* For any triple of lotteries, L^A, L^B and L^C, again with $L^A \succcurlyeq L^B$, and $L^B \succcurlyeq L^C$. Then there is some value $v : 0 \leq v \leq 1$, for which $vL^A + (1 - v)L^C = L^B$: *Therefore:* It is always possible to construct a new lottery that is a combination of the most and least preferred of the triple, and which is ranked equally with the middle-ranked lottery.
- *Independence of irrelevant alternatives:* For any triple of lotteries, L^A, L^B and L^C, again with $L^A \succcurlyeq L^B$, and some value $v : 0 \leq v \leq 1$, then $vL^A + (1 - v)L^c \succcurlyeq vL^B + (1 - v)L^c$. *Therefore:* Constructing a pair new lotteries that are identical except for a component, which we can already rank, the ranking of the new pair will be the same as the ranking of the original pair.

Whenever a person's preferences over lotteries satisfy these axioms, then it is possible to represent them by an expected utility function. We define two lotteries, $L^A = (w_1^A, w_2^A, ..., w_n^A; \pi_1^A, \pi_2^A, ..., \pi_n^A)$ and $L^B = (w_1^B, w_2^B, ..., w_m^B; \pi_1^B, \pi_2^B, ..., \pi_m^B)$. Then $E[U(L^A)] \geq E[U(L^B)]$ if, and only if, $L^A \succcurlyeq L^B$.

Note that the first three assumptions were first introduced in Chapter 4 as being necessary for the existence of a utility function. The fourth assumption, *independence of irrelevant alternatives*, ensures that the expected utility function will be additive, with no interaction between alternatives.

There are two important properties of preferences which can be represented by an expected utility function, which we shall simply state without any derivation. Firstly, with the expected utility function, we can rank complex lotteries, with multiple outcomes, by calculating the expected utilities of the constituent simple lotteries, each of which has only two outcomes. Secondly, in Chapter 5, we argued that a utility function should be unique up to a monotonically increasing transformation. The nature of the expected utility function as a weighted sum of the possible outcome utilities means that the expected utility function is unique up to a linear transformation. This means that while it is possible for us to add a constant to a utility function, and also to multiply through it by a constant, and for the transformed function to represent the same preferences over lotteries, after a non-linear transformation of the expected utility function, the transformed function will no longer represent the original preferences.

By yourself

X26.26 Consider the utility of wealth function, $U(W) = W^{0.75}$.
  (a) Confirm that the function is concave.
  (b) Confirm that any linear transformation, $V_1 = a + bU$, is also concave.
  (c) Confirm that the transformation $V_2 = U^2$ is (i) monotonically increasing; and (ii) convex.

X26.27 Alex believes that at the end of this time period his wealth, W, will either be 16 or 64. He believes that $Pr(W = 16) = Pr(W = 64) = \frac{1}{2}$. He considers his utility to take the value $U(W) = W^{0.75}$.
  (a) Calculate his expected wealth, $E[W]$, at the end of this time period.
  (b) Calculate his expected utility of wealth, $E[U(W)]$ at the end of the period, confirming that $U(E[W]) > E[U(W)]$.
  (c) Suppose that there is a change of circumstances. Alex now believes that his wealth at the end of the period will be $W = 24$, or else $W = 56$, with probabilities as before, $Pr(W = 24) = Pr(W = 56) = \frac{1}{2}$. Confirm that Alex's utility of expected wealth, $U(E[W])$, does not change, but that his expected utility of wealth, $E[U(W)]$ increases (from approximately 15.3 to 15.7).

(Continued)

X26.28   Alex's friend Bianca faces almost exactly the same situation as Alex, except that her utility of wealth, $V : V(W) = 0.05[U(V)]^2$. Calculate Bianca's expected utility from participation in the lotteries in X26.27b and X26.27c. Confirm that Bianca's expected utility, $E[U(W)]$, decreases (from 14.4 to approximately 13.4), and that the utility of her expected wealth, $U[E(W)] \approx 12.6$.

X26.29   Consider the two utility of wealth functions, $U = U(W) = W^{3/4}$, and $V = V(W) = 0.05[U(V)]^2$.
(a) Confirm that V is a monotonically increasing transformation of U.
(b) Show that the marginal utility, $\frac{dU}{dW}$, is decreasing in W, but that $\frac{dV}{dW}$ is increasing in W.
(c) For the lottery, $L = (W - \delta, W + \delta, \frac{1}{2})$, confirm that expected wealth $E[W] = W$. Show that the expected utility $E[U(W)]$ is decreasing in δ, while the expected utility $E[V(W)]$ is increasing in δ. Relate these results to the underlying attitude to risk implied by the utility function.

26.3.1   Representing preferences over lotteries

Until now, we have worked in terms of the utility of wealth, comparing the expected utility after participation in a lottery, L, with the certain utility of an alternative. Having now defined the expected utility function in a way that allows us to compare lotteries, we extend our analysis. In Figure 26.4, we show a situation in which there are two alternative states of the world, the outcomes of the (involuntary) lottery $L = (W_1, W_2, \pi)$. In the good state of the world, Christopher drives his much-loved but very run-down car without any accident. His wealth at the end of the year is then W_1. In the bad state, he writes the car off, and has to buy a replacement, at cost D, so that his wealth at the year end is $W_2 = W_1 - D$.

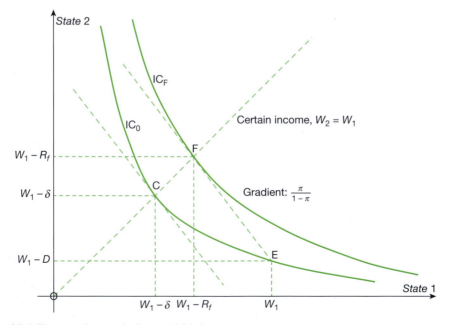

Figure 26.4 The certainty equivalent and fair insurance

The probability of such an accident occurring is π. The probability distribution over the two states is fixed, but Christopher can take actions, such as purchasing insurance, so that the wealth achieved in each state varies. In Figure 26.4, we indicate Christopher's preferences over possible lotteries by indifference curves. The indifference curves suggest that preferences are well behaved, so that it should be possible to identify a unique, expected utility-maximizing, state-contingent income profile. Without insurance, his state-contingent wealth profile, $E : (W_1, W_2) = (W_0, W_1 - D)$.

We also show the line $W_1 = W_2$, in which the wealth in the two states is equal. This is effectively the full insurance line, in which wealth and utility are both certain, so that there is no risk associated with participation in the lottery. Note that the indifference curve through E cuts through the certainty line at $C : (W_0 - \delta, W_1 - \delta)$. The term δ, as in Section 26.2.3, represents the risk premium for the lottery, L, and so is the maximum payment that a person might be persuaded to give up to eliminate exposure to risk.

> **By yourself**
>
> **X26.30** Show that where indifference curves are convex, the person is risk-averse.

A risk-averse person, such as Christopher, who has access to insurance, can manage exposure to risk. Assume that it is possible to buy full insurance, so that paying a premium, R, the policyholder obtains payment, $B = D$, should state 2 occur. The expected profit from the transaction for the insurer is the difference between the premium, R and the expected payment, $(1 - \pi)B$. If the firm expects simply to break even, it charges premium R_f:

$$R_f - (1 - \pi)D = 0 \qquad [26.18]$$

If we assume that at point F it has been possible to buy full, fair insurance, the slope of the line EF can be written:

$$\frac{dW_2}{dW_1} = \frac{R_f - D}{R_f} = \frac{(1 - \pi)D - D}{(1 - \pi)D} = -\frac{\pi}{1 - \pi} \qquad [26.19]$$

The slope of this line is therefore the ratio of the probability of states, also known as the *odds ratio*. We can also think of the probability of loss, $1 - \pi$, as being the fair premium rate: the price of purchasing a unit value of insurance cover.

Now let us think of the slope of the indifference curve. For the utility function, $u = u(W_1, W_2)$, we write the differential:

$$du = \pi MU_1 dW_1 + (1 - \pi)MU_2 dW_2 = 0 \qquad [26.20]$$

The marginal rate of substitution, $MRS = \frac{dW_2}{dW_1}$:

$$MRS = -\frac{\pi MU_1}{(1 - \pi)MU_2} \qquad [26.21]$$

Note that we can immediately evaluate the marginal rate of substitution when wealth is certain. Since $W_1 = W_2$, it follows that $MU_1 = MU_2$, so $MRS = -\frac{\pi}{(1 - \pi)}$. This means that for all certain wealth levels, the marginal rate of substitution equals the odds ratio (or ratio of probabilities), as illustrated in Figure 26.4, where the indifference curves at C and F have the same slope, and the fair-odds line EF is the tangent to the indifference curve at F.

We conclude that a risk-averse individual, offered insurance on these terms, will purchase full insurance and so avoid bearing any part of the risk.

By yourself

X26.31   Suppose that the risk of loss increases, so that the probability of the better outcome, π, falls from π_0 to π_1. On a diagram, illustrate the impact of this change on: (a) the slope of the fair-odds line; and (b) the gradient of the indifference curves where they intersect the certainty line.

X26.32   Explain why no insurer would offer an insurance policy with premium rate $\rho : \rho < 1 - \pi$, the risk of loss. Discuss whether or not it is reasonable to expect an insurer to offer a policy for which the premium rate, $\rho : \rho > 1 - \pi$.

X26.33   Suppose that the involuntary lottery, $L = (400, 100, 0.9)$, and that the utility of wealth, $U(W) = W^{\frac{1}{2}}$.
   (a) Calculate the expected utility after participation.
   (b) Calculate the risk premium, δ, the certainty equivalent, $W_0 - \delta$, and the wealth when it is possible to buy full, fair insurance.
   (c) Obtain the equation of the fair-odds line.
   (d) Confirm that the gradient of the indifference curve passing through the intersection of the certainty line and the fair-odds line is the slope of the fair-odds line.
   (e) Assume that it is possible to purchase an insurance policy for any sum, B, at the fair premium rate, $\rho = 1 - \pi$. Write down an expression for the expected utility on purchasing insurance, B. Confirm that the purchase of full insurance maximizes utility.
   (f) Suppose that the premium rate, $r > 1 - \rho$. Rework the calculations in part (e) and explain when it will be optimal to purchase partial insurance. Illustrate your conclusions.

Where insurance is fair, someone who is risk-averse chooses full insurance. When insurance is not fair, a risk-averse individual, as we see in Figure 26.5, prefers partial insurance. The lowest premium rate is higher than the fair rate, so that $\rho > \rho_f = (1 - \pi)$, the risk of loss. The best (available) odds line, starting from the endowment, point E, is flatter than the fair-odds line, whose slope is the marginal rate of substitution over wealth profiles at every point on the certainty line. The marginal rate of substitution is shown as being equal to the slope of the best-odds line at wealth profile G : $W_1 > W_2$.

While it is possible that people will be unable to purchase full, fair insurance because insurers need to cover administrative costs, we might note a different reason. There are often differences in the risks that people face. Suppose that Christopher, driving his old Skoda, lives in a rural area. His risk of loss is relatively low, compared with Diana, who lives in a large city. Otherwise, the situations in which Christopher and Diana make insurance decisions are identical. They have the same wealth profile and the same underlying preferences. In Figure 26.5, we only show Christopher's indifference curves. Facing a higher risk of loss, Diana's *MRS* is less than Christopher's for every consumption bundle. If the insurance society does not recognize these differences, it might offer Christopher and Diana a single contract, designed so that it should break even across both of them. In effect, people like Christopher then subsidize people like Diana; but facing a lower risk of loss, they buy less than full insurance, and bear some share of the risk themselves. With differences in the underlying risks facing people, full insurance cover tends to be bought by the people with the greatest risk of loss.

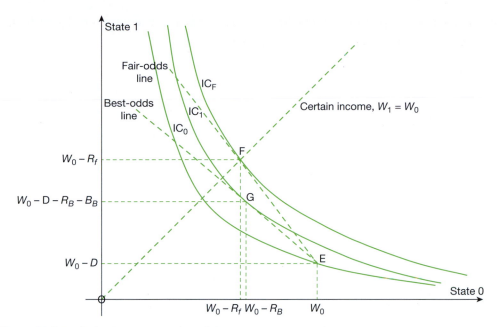

Figure 26.5 Profitable insurance and partial cover

By yourself

X24.34 Suppose that competition in the insurance industry means that every insurance company expects to make zero profits. Sketch a diagram illustrating the fair-odds lines where the probability of loss: (1) for the lowest-risk person is 0.05; (2) for the average person is 0.2; and (3) for the highest-risk person is 0.5. Given that they all can buy insurance at the same premium rate, explain how the coverage they purchase will differ.

26.4 Conclusions

People face risks every day, sometimes choosing to embrace them, and sometimes seeking to manage their effects, where they cannot avoid participation. In modelling risks in terms of a probability distribution over the state of the world, we assume that it is possible to identify the probabilities of events occurring, and this requires us to be able to analyse the relative frequency with which outcomes arise, or else to be able to define a model so that we can calculate the probabilities. We have also proposed that in making decisions, people are motivated to maximize their expected utility. The axiomization of preference under conditions of uncertainty developed by von Neumann and Morgenstern adds the independence of irrelevant alternatives to the usual axioms, but then specifies that the expected utility function must be a probability-weighted sum of the possible realizations of utility. Representing a well-behaved preference ordering defined over all possible lotteries, we have used the expected utility function to consider the extent to which risk-averse people purchase insurance as a means of reducing their exposure to risk. We have argued that the people with a low probability of an accident may be offered poor terms by insurers, and so only purchase partial insurance. We have also demonstrated that it is possible for a group of risk-averse individuals to work together to provide mutual insurance, on the basis that through the sharing of losses, they buy a degree of certainty.

Summary

We define a probability distribution over a set of events as a measure of the relative frequency with which each event occurs. Where people have to make a decision, knowing only the probability distribution of outcomes that might occur, we say that they face risk.

We define the expected value of an experiment as the probability-weighted sum of outcomes. We usually distinguish between the expected financial value of an experiment and its expected value in terms of utility.

In many situations we assume that the utility of (realized) wealth is an increasing, concave function. This supports the assumption of risk aversion, with the utility of expected wealth being greater than the expected utility of wealth in an experiment.

There is no requirement that people be risk-averse. People sometimes choose to assume risk, as when they willingly gamble. The utility of wealth of someone who is risk-loving is convex. In the same way, if someone is risk-neutral then they are only concerned with the financial values of outcomes, and this requires the utility of wealth to be linear.

Insurance is a contract allowing the transfer of (financial) risk. The insurer receives a premium from the policyholder, while agreeing to make payments that are contingent on the policyholder experiencing losses. We define as full insurance the situation in which the insurer accepts the whole risk of loss. We define as fair insurance the situation in which the insurance premium rate is the probability of loss.

Where a group of people face a similar distribution of outcomes, they can agree to pool the risks, forming a mutual insurance society. In pooling the risks, the expected loss that each faces is substantially reduced, so that in effect they purchase certainty.

Visit the companion website at **www.palgrave.com/mochrie** to access further teaching and learning materials, including lecturer slides and a testbank, as well as guideline answers and student MCQs.

chapter 27

Rationality and behaviour

What we do in this chapter

We conclude our exploration of the standard model with some trenchant criticism. The great advantage of the standard model is that it provides us with a coherent framework in which to analyse the choices made by people or firms, while recognizing how these depend on the nature of the choice environment facing them. We now ask whether or not it is inevitable that people will appear to behave rationally. Effectively redefining *rationality* as a scarce resource, we argue that in certain situations it is sensible for us to treat choice as a *learned response*. While learned responses have a cost advantage over conscious consideration, we show that it is possible for them to be used excessively, in situations where conscious consideration would lead to a better outcome. We argue that learning involves exploration of the choice environment over time; as people do the best they can, their behaviour adapts to the situation. Often, they will make (small) adjustments in their resource allocation until such adjustments do not seem to offer any further benefits. Nevertheless, such processes of gradual adjustment can lead to deviation from the best outcome of conscious consideration, even allowing for the additional decision making costs.

As well as the failure of adaptive processes, learned behaviour might fail to guide resource allocation perfectly because of biases, which seem almost inevitably to affect the process. Using learned behaviour, people seem to treat some alternatives within choice sets as more prominent than others, increasing the probability of these alternatives being chosen. For example, within a sequence of choices, the belief that an outcome that has been acceptable in the past is likely to be acceptable now leads to *status-quo bias*. Allowing for willingness to adjust and to adapt behaviour, previous choices can act as an anchor for future choices.

In addition, we shall also set aside the assumption that conscious consideration leads to fully rational outcomes, on the basis that having evolved over time, such consideration is most effectively applied in situations whose characteristics are similar to those of choices that have been faced throughout human development. We concentrate on a single type of deviation from perfect rationality: the tendency of people to behave as though they are averse to losses, which allows us to understand behaviour in situations of risk more fully.

27.1 Rationality as a scarce resource

We go back to the assumptions of the standard model, first introduced in Chapter 2. Assumption A2.6, *Free access to information*, has been an essential underpinning of all of our analysis up to this point. From this point onwards, we consider how it might be set aside. In this chapter, we assume that processing data about the choice environment takes time and effort. Identifying optimal behaviour using conscious consideration behaviour becomes a costly activity, used only where people believe that it is valuable.

By yourself

X27.1   Suppose that Anthony is choosing a new car. (We shall assume that he has made the decision to buy a car, but has still to choose between the variety of models available.) To what extent might we expect the choice to be a result of conscious consideration? To the extent that information is costly to acquire and to process, how might this affect his decision?

We argue that in the absence of conscious consideration, people will make choices unconsciously, and so might fail to achieve their (consciously) desired outcomes in two ways. Firstly, in responding to the choice environment, people's cognitions might direct them. With people managing the acquisition and processing of information in a variety of ways, it is possible that there will be systematic differences across people in the ways in which they use the same information. For example, approximately 8% of men are colour-blind, which often means that they are unable to distinguish red from green. Presented with the same information as someone who can distinguish these colours, they reach different conclusions. In much the same way, we might argue that product branding is designed to affect cognitions. Buying a well-known brand reduces the costs of decision making, particularly when the branded good has been placed prominently

Cognitions Mental processes involved in knowledge acquisition.

within the choice environment. Knowing this, businesses often make considerable investments that are intended to enable them to manage and to alter perceptions of the characteristics of goods, and so guide potential customers towards purchase of their goods and services.

A related, but distinct, problem might arise where the potential costs and benefits of different patterns of behaviour are not fully understood at the time of making a choice. The classic example is cigarette smoking. In advanced economies, there can be few people who are unaware of the fact that this activity is associated with chronic illness and premature death. Partly as a result, prevalence of smoking in many countries has fallen substantially, with the proportion of smokers often between 20% and 30% of the adult population. For young people, the accumulated costs of tobacco use will typically be evident many years from now. There is very considerable uncertainty about both the timing and the extent of such effects. In contrast, the benefits of consumption, due to the absorption of nicotine into the bloodstream, can be felt in seconds.

By yourself

X27.2   Suppose that Britney smokes regularly. What differences might there be between making the decision: (a) to have the first cigarette of a particular morning; and (b) to stop smoking?

If we define choice in terms of smoking a single cigarette, at a single point in time, it seems entirely reasonable to concentrate on the short-term impact. Instead, treating smoking as a sequence of choices, the potential long-term effects will be much more prominent in decision making.

For a regular smoker, gradually becoming concerned about the long-term effects, it might seem reasonable to reduce the rate of consumption. The tension between choosing a single action and considering the possible effects of the sequence of actions is important here.

As well as causing an immediate pleasurable sensation, absorption of nicotine leads to a complex series of effects on brain activity, which increase desire for consumption of the drug. Smoking regularly then becomes a habit, which is difficult to give up. Regulating the habit, so that it is just an occasional activity, may be optimal when using conscious consideration, but may be difficult to achieve in practice, when choosing whether or not to smoke at particular times. We often find that people either do not smoke at all or else smoke habitually. According to the standard theory, regular smokers act as if they have consciously chosen to adopt the habit, and their chosen frequency of smoking optimizes the payoff to the activity. Admitting different cognitions, and allowing for the impact of habituation on the choice environment, we might argue that, having acquired the habit, people can maintain it without conscious thought, irrespective of its underlying usefulness.

27.1.1 A behaviourist approach to choice

For a few moments, we shall stop thinking solely about human behaviour. We can easily find evidence of a wide range of animals having the ability to learn how to behave in the choice environment that they face. There are good, essentially economic, reasons for this. Consider, for example, the foraging behaviour of two animals. One animal simply wanders around its territory randomly, consuming opportunistically. This is typical of primitive mammals, such as the American opossum. The other remembers the location of an abundant resource found the day before and starts foraging there – behaviour we might associate with many rodents, for example mice and rats. We expect the animal that has the ability to learn where food supplies are likely to be found to be more efficient, in the sense that its cost of effort to achieve a sustainable caloric intake will be lower. In a situation in which resources are very scarce, this ability could substantially affect the probability of survival. More generally, we might argue that having the capacity to learn increases an animal's evolutionary fitness.

We might write down the model of learning implied in this description as follows:

- Animals feel a need (hunger), which they can satisfy only by obtaining an external resource (food):
  - animals can obtain that resource by undertaking certain actions (foraging); and
  - since it satisfies a need, obtaining and consuming the resource is rewarding.
- The environment in which foraging takes place is stable:
  - actions that have secured the resource in the past are therefore more likely to yield the resource in future; and so
  - learning consists of identifying actions that are associated with the satisfaction of a need.

The psychologist B. F. Skinner explained these processes in terms of operant conditioning. To carry out experiments on learning through conditioning, he devised an experimental apparatus, the Skinner box, into which an experimental subject, often a rat or a pigeon, is placed. Within the box, there will typically be a mechanism such as a lever which, when pressed (often enough), will deliver food. There will also be other sources of external stimulation, such as coloured lights, a loudspeaker, and a metal grid in the floor, through which an electric current might be passed. The box is designed so that experimenters can in effect alter the operation of the choice environment.

> **Operant conditioning**
> Learning based on the acquisition of rewards (or the experience of punishment) for behaviour.

Assume that when a subject is first placed in a box, it has never been in an environment in which pressing on a lever will deliver food. Feeling hungry, it will go through its usual repertoire of foraging activities (unsuccessfully) until sooner or later it presses the lever. To ensure that the subjects learns to associate pressing the lever with food, during this initial conditioning period, a large pellet of fodder will be delivered every time that the subject presses the lever. Once the subject has come to associate pressing the lever with the delivery of food, the experimenter can make the choice environment more complicated. For example, food might be delivered only when a green signal light is switched on; or pressing the lever might stop food being delivered for a short period of time; or food might only be delivered on every fifth press of the lever, or else with some probability on each press of the lever, with the probability of delivery decreasing in the frequency of the lever presses.

By yourself

X27.3   We introduced Clive, a large white rat, to the Skinner box yesterday. He now happily presses the lever, gobbling up his rewards. Explain how you think his behaviour will change – that is, what he will learn to do – as the reinforcement (reward) changes in the ways suggested above.

X27.4   We have only discussed positive reinforcers in the example above (the delivery of food). Within the analysis of operant conditioning, there are also roles for negative reinforcers, effectively punishments for behaviour. Giving possible examples of these, explain their role.

Defined in this way, animal subjects seem to possess quite a high degree of rationality. Experimental psychologists do not typically model their subjects' behaviour by assigning them a utility function, and calculating an optimal response rate, given the reinforcement schedule of the experiment: their interest tends to be much more in the process of adjustment to changing external circumstances, rather than in simply predicting the eventual steady state. Even with as simple a tool as a Skinner box, we might consider the choice environment of experiments to be quite complex, yet the pattern of responses that subjects exhibit typically conforms quite well to predictions.

By yourself

X27.5   In a *variable ratio* reinforcement schedule, reinforcement occurs after a randomly determined number of actions, with the expected frequency of reinforcements set in advance. How might conditioned subjects behave in this case?

X27.6   How might we expect experimental subjects to respond during the *extinction* phase of an experiment, when they are still in the box, but reinforcements are no longer available?

Operant learning presents a substantial challenge to our understanding of rationality. If rats' behaviour can have the appearance of rationality, to the extent that human behaviour is largely unconscious and driven by a desire to satisfy basic needs, we cannot be certain that human behaviour is truly rational. The coolly rational decision maker of the standard theory might be replaced by a rather more interesting person, whose decision making includes a repertoire of learned responses. Feeling tired, this person simply falls asleep; feeling hungry, much like an experimental animal, she finds food; or feeling cold, she switches on the central heating. Almost everyone, even babies and the chronically ill, can fall asleep when it is necessary. Yet even the basic skills of foraging for food have to be acquired, and, as we shall argue below, much more complex decisions than switching on a central heating system might simply be learned responses.

Treating choice as coolly rational is no more an abstraction from reality than treating behaviour as learned responses. We should expect a complete model of economic decision making to recognize that there will be times when conscious consideration predominates: for example when the choice is well defined, the payoffs are large, and all the required information is to hand. There will also be times when learned responses predominate, for example when the choice is one that has to be made frequently, possibly as part of a sequence, when the payoffs are small, and where the cost of becoming fully informed is very large. Thinking back to our example of smoking, we might well consider day-to-day choices simply to be an example of learned responses. However, in seeking to manage behaviour, it seems desirable to invoke conscious consideration.

27.1.2   The kinked demand curve

One way of modelling choice as learned behaviour is to treat people as typically making small experiments, adapting their choice pattern slowly. If we believe that the choice environment that we face today is very similar to the choice environment that we faced yesterday, those choices which seemed previously to meet our needs are likely to continue to do so.

By yourself

X27.7   Consider 'Example: petrol stations in a city' (Section 1.2.4). There is substantial competition in supply, and across petrol stations fuel is a perfect substitute. The standard model predicts a single market price.

(a) Use a price comparison website (e.g. www.fleetnews.co.uk/static/tools/compare-fuel-prices) to find out the extent of variation that occurs in the city in which you live, or one nearby.

(b) Discuss how our analysis might change if we treat buying fuel as a learned behaviour.

(c) We have suggested that people are likely to treat the choice environment as relatively stable. Suppose in this case that they will only carry out local experiments (buying from another petrol station) if there is some relevant change to the environment. Consider the possible effects on behaviour of: (i) an increase in the price charged by the most frequently used petrol station; (ii) a decrease in that petrol station's price; (iii) an increase in the price charged by a competing petrol station; and (iv) a decrease in the competing petrol station's price.

(d) What might we conclude about the price elasticity of demand when there are: (i) price increases; and (ii) price decreases? What does this suggest about the marginal revenue function around the current level of sales?

Exercise X27.7 suggests that behaviour will involve an asymmetric response to price changes. We suppose that a price increase at the favoured petrol station is more likely to trigger search activity than a price decrease; and that a price decrease at another petrol station is less likely to trigger search activity than a price increase at the favoured one. Such behaviour seems intuitively reasonable, if only because it is very similar to the discussion of foraging behaviour with which this section began.

In Figure 27.1, we illustrate how this behaviour might affect the demand for petrol facing any petrol station. Initially, the market is in equilibrium, with a price, p_0, charged at all

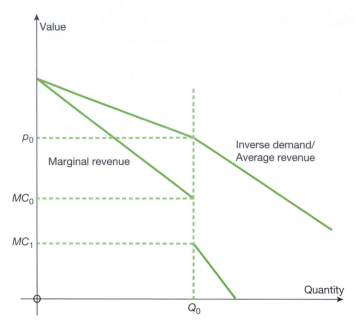

Figure 27.1 Asymmetric responses to price changes

petrol stations. Demand at this petrol station is then $Q_0 = Q(p_0)$. With the petrol station maximizing profits, the marginal cost and the marginal revenue will be equal, so that $MC(Q_0) = MC_0$. The kink in the demand curve reflects differences in consumers' responses to price rises and price cuts. These differences also mean that the marginal revenue curve is discontinuous when $Q = Q_0$.

By yourself

X27.8 Suppose that the petrol station faces (a) an increase in its costs and (b) a small decrease in its costs, so that $MC_1 < MC(Q_0) < MC_0$. Describe its profit-maximizing behaviour in each case.

In this kinked demand curve model, if a petrol station faces an increase in costs, then it maximizes profits by increasing price, and selling a smaller quantity of petrol. Facing a small reduction in costs, it maintains price, and its profit margins increase. In the short run, at least, we expect prices to be 'sticky'. The behavioural response of customers to price changes lead to petrol stations being reluctant to reduce prices, at least as an immediate response to cost reductions.

This example suggests that it is quite easy to develop models within which learned responses affect economic behaviour. Our explanation presumes that people make a sequence of choices facing what they believe to be a relatively stable choice environment – without that, behavioural learning would not occur. Simply repeating previous behaviour minimizes the costs of making choices. Even when considering alternatives, it will often be more effective to begin from previous behaviour, and to think about how this might be adapted. In Section 27.2, we shall specify some ways in which decision making can be biased because of limitations in the cognitive processes that seem to be used in decision making.

27.1.3 Bounded rationality

First, though, we introduce Herbert Simon's concept of *bounded rationality* or **procedural rationality**. Seth assumed that in many situations it would be very costly for people or firms to identify optimal (maximizing) actions. Instead, he proposed treating choice as the outcome of exploration of the environment, with exploration stopping at the first acceptable (satisfactory) outcome. To distinguish this resource allocation process from the maximization of standard theory, we call it **satisficing**: doing well enough. For someone who is satisficing, we can treat the payoff function as a constraint, rather than as an objective. In Figure 27.2, we show the set of acceptable combinations for someone choosing a consumption bundle containing quantities of goods B and C, (B, C). As usual, we impose an affordability constraint, showing the maximum possible expenditure. Now, though, we complement this with a payoff constraint, which we show as an indifference curve. We assume that this is associated with the minimum acceptable utility. The intersection of the two constraints is shown as a shaded area. The consumer's objective is now to find any consumption bundle within that area. To abandon maximization for satisficing, we must believe that the consumer cannot behave as though fully informed. In particular, we might wish to argue that there is:

> **Procedural (bounded) rationality** Making choices using some prescribed decision making process.
>
> **Satisficing** Setting an acceptability target for a choice, and stopping a procedurally rational process as soon as the target is reached.

- uncertainty about the preference relation over consumption bundles;
- the lack of a fully formed preference relation;
- uncertainty about the affordability constraint, for example because of uncertainty over the real value of income (over time).

We imagine such a consumer constructing a consumption bundle by adding small amounts to it, stopping when the payoff and acquisition cost both seem reasonable.

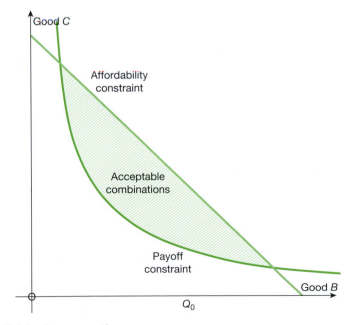

Figure 27.2 Satisficing in consumption

By yourself

X27.9 For a person with utility, $U : U(B, C) = B_{0.5} C_{0.5}$ where utility is derived from consumption bundle, (B, C), and where choice is defined by the affordability constraint $B + C < 20$ and the payoff constraint $U(B, C) \geq 8$, sketch a diagram indicating the set of acceptable combinations.

X27.10 Using the example in X27.9, suppose that this person initially chooses the consumption bundle (B, C), for which the affordability and payoff constraints are met, but do not bind. Making a sequence of choices, this person gradually adjusts the consumption bundle.

(a) Given an adjustment cost of 0.05, in terms of payoff, with consumption of good B increasing by 0.1 units on every occasion, explain why this consumer might not reach the affordability constraint.

(b) Repeat the argument of part (a) for consumption of good C.

(c) Given an adjustment cost of 0.1, the consumer experiments by increasing consumption of both goods by one unit. Discuss whether or not this consumer will continue experimenting until income is exhausted.

Someone tentatively exploring the choice environment following very simple rules such as the ones in Exercise X27.10 may end up making a final choice that is some distance away from the optimum. We might also note that there is no obvious reason for there being an adjustment cost in these exercises, other than people being in a situation where there is considerable uncertainty, so that the evaluation of alternatives has substantial costs.

In Figure 27.2, we have in effect assumed that preferences, even if not well understood, are at least well behaved. In principle, this means that it is possible to reach the unique, utility-maximizing consumption bundle through a process of experimentation. Suppose, however, that preferences are not well behaved. In Figure 27.3, we show how this might lead to someone choosing a sub-optimal outcome. We assume that preferences are not convex, but that the affordable set is well defined, and so assume that the acquisition cost of the chosen bundle will be the maximum possible. Given the constraint on expenditure, we can show the realizable utility in terms of the quantity of good B in the consumption bundle. In the diagram, as consumption of good B increases, utility first increases, reaching a maximum at $B = B^*$, then decreases until $B = B_0$, and then increases again, reaching a local maximum at $B = B_1$. We now set out assumptions about the way in which the consumer approaches this situation:

- The first choice is made randomly.
- After making the first choice, the consumer will carry out an experiment, increasing consumption of good B by a small amount, δB.
- If the increase in payoff is large enough, then the consumer will repeat the experiment, stopping when the increase in payoff falls below δV.
- If there is a decrease in payoff, the consumer will reduce consumption of good B.

If the payoff (utility) function is single-peaked, as in the standard theory, then the choice of starting point for the adjustment process is unimportant. There is a single constrained optimum, and while we have noted in Exercise X27.10 that someone might not reach it simply because adjustment costs seem likely to outweigh the potential gains, the starting point for these experiments should not substantially affect the eventual outcome.

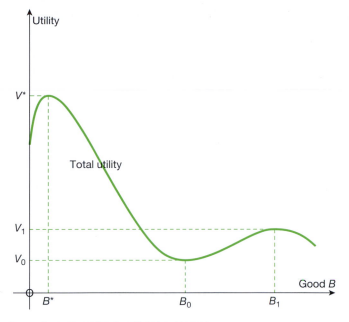

Figure 27.3 Local experiments and sub-optimal outcomes

However, as shown in Figure 27.3, we can easily imagine situations in which the payoff function has two maxima. The rules that we have set out, by which an experiment will continue if it leads to an increase in payoffs, imply that if someone starts from a relatively high level of consumption of good B, $B > B_0$, then experiments will continue until $B \approx B_1$, and the chosen bundle represents the achievement of a local maximum, rather than a global one.

By yourself

X27.11 Discuss the range of outcomes that might emerge in this example. Define the range of initial choices that will lead to the consumer reaching (at least approximately) the optimum, B^*, and those that might lead (approximately) to the local maximum, B_1.

X27.12 What elements of habituation does this model possess, which would not emerge in the standard model?

27.2 Biases and heuristics in choice processes

If choice is a learned behaviour rather than the result of conscious consideration, decision making might exhibit largely predictable deviations from the predictions of the standard model, which can be classified under a few headings. By identifying frequently occurring biases within decision making, it has been possible to explain their origin by proposing **heuristics**, or decision rules. Decision processes defined by these heuristics allow us to explain the observed data, and in particular deviations from what might be predicted, assuming choice to be the result of conscious consideration. Knowing how decisions typically deviate from the

Heuristic A decision-making rule.

rational choice in a given situation, then we form inferences on the nature of the choice process. This research has been very fruitful, and has deepened our understanding of choice in economics very substantially, but we shall also argue that it offers little more than a critical perspective on the standard model. As yet, there is no consistent behavioural model that might sit alongside the standard one.

27.2.1   Status-quo bias

Status-quo bias has already emerged within our discussions. It can emerge within any sequence of choices. After the initial choice, there is implicitly an asymmetry among the alternatives, since one (and only one) is the most recently chosen. Simply repeating the previous choice is then likely to minimize the costs of decision making. We have observed that where the choice environment is stable, then if the original choice proved satisfactory, repetition should also be satisfactory. Repetition of an action is not necessarily evidence of status-quo bias: we would need to find evidence of people preferring an action solely because they have chosen it already.

Indeed, there is a further explanation, which is largely consistent with the standard theory, in which status-quo bias results from asymmetries in transaction costs.

> **By yourself**
>
> X27.13   Standard leases over a residential property run for one year, but can then be extended on a monthly basis without a further agreement being signed.
> (a) Discuss the extent to which conscious consideration might guide choice: (i) when first entering into a lease; and (ii) when deciding whether or not to terminate a lease on its anniversary.
> (b) What do you consider to be the transaction costs associated with moving house? Estimate their size, relative to the monthly rental that you would have to pay.

As discussed in Chapter 24, a house is a complex capital good, a bundle of characteristics, so that each one is differentiated from all others. We might expect decisions made on conscious consideration to involve a survey of all available properties when first choosing to rent one. At the end of the lease, the tenant might be content that the outcome of the initial search – that at the time the chosen property was the best available – is still broadly valid. The tenant now knows more about the house than any alternative, and so the risk of disappointment can be reduced by renewing the lease. Then there are the direct costs associated with moving house, such as packing and transporting possessions, and setting up new utility accounts. We could make similar arguments about other types of contracts, such as those for mobile phones or bank accounts. Preference for the status quo based on *transition costs* or *switching costs* need not be the result of bias.

True status-quo bias requires the relative valuation of alternatives to change purely because one of them has been chosen previously, possibly in an entirely random allocation. A well-known example is the *endowment effect*, reported in laboratory experiments. Imagine a situation in which some participants in an experiment are given an object which they can exchange for money, while others are given money with which they might bid for the object. (All of the potential sale and purchase transactions take place only with the experimenters: there is no attempt to create a market among participants.) The endowment effect arises where the mean *WTA* among those given the object is significantly greater than the mean *WTP* among bidders. Indeed, in some cases, experimenters report a mean *WTA* above the market price of the object. This is not consistent with the standard model, for if the participants did value the good so highly, they should already have bought it in the open market.

In the experiment, the status-quo is manipulated by the experimenter: participants are allocated either the object or else some money. This manipulation does not require any action on the part of the participants. Even though participants cannot use the object during the experiment, they still revalue it. The result does seem difficult to explain, unless we accept that simple possession of an object leads people to revise their estimates of its value. Status-quo bias here means that people who have been given the object have a stronger preference for states of the world in which they keep it.

There is evidence of status-quo bias in both field, and natural, experiments. One well-known example relates to the legal framework for car insurance introduced in the early 1990s in the neighbouring US states of New Jersey and Pennsylvania. Each of the two states defined an insurance contract that had to be offered as the default option, but each permitted policyholders to choose instead the contract of the other state. The standard contract in New Jersey had lower premiums than the contract in Pennsylvania; however, it placed greater restrictions on drivers' right to sue for damages after an accident. If they wished to choose the alternative contract, only minimal action was required of drivers. In each state, although the default option in the other state was available to all drivers, the majority chose the default option in their own state. The default rule defined the status quo. The difference in behaviour among drivers in adjacent states can be explained most easily by appealing to some form of status-quo bias.

By yourself

X27.14 Pensions are long-term saving contracts. Governments in many countries wish to encourage greater private provision. Discuss measures that might be taken to make increased participation become the default option. Explain the importance to these of status-quo bias.

We have concluded that people have a preference for the existing state of the world. To explain the existence of such a preference, we draw on the concept of cognitive dissonance, which has been widely used in psychology for many years. A state of *cognitive consistency* occurs when all of our perceptions of the world are consistent with there being a single reality. We suppose that people desire consistency, finding dissonances within their cognitions unpleasant. We might expect people to take action intended to restore consistency. A standard example uses behaviour in experiments. Suppose that a participant in the experiment has just chosen alternative *A* when alternative *B* was also available. After the participant has made that first choice and before he makes a subsequent one, the experimenter provides information, perhaps in the form of advertising, about each of the alternatives. The information in advertising is intended to encourage the choice of only one alternative. To maintain cognitive consistency, the person might choose to read the advertising for alternative *A*, rather than alternative *B*, in effect selecting the evidence that will reinforce their previous choice.

Cognitive dissonance
Mental tension caused by mutually incompatible cognitions.

By yourself

X27.15 In the following examples, discuss whether you think that there is evidence of dissonant cognitions, and how you think people might resolve them.

(a) (i) 'Smoking kills.' (ii) 'I enjoy smoking.'

(b) (i) 'Theft is wrong.' (ii) 'I could use these office supplies at home.'

(c) (i) 'We need to reduce our carbon footprint.' (ii) 'I could never be a vegetarian.'

(d) (i) 'You can never be too cautious.' (ii) 'Wait until I win the lottery.'

Another explanation of status-quo bias in psychology is **self-perception theory**. In the context of a sequence of choices, this claims that people form their attitudes to alternatives after making their initial choice. It may be that it is only *after* choosing alternative *A* that someone concludes that they have a preference for that alternative. In effect, we suppose that even if initial choices are entirely random, people tend to assert that they have chosen their preferred alternative. To explain how this might arise, suppose that most people believe that they are rational decision makers, as defined in standard economic theory. To decide, having chosen alternative *A*, that alternative *B* would have been better challenges that self-concept. Therefore we are more likely to repeat choices. Status-quo bias emerges to maintain cognitive consistency. Note that this goes beyond the argument about cognitive dissonance: we assume that people may anticipate the experience of dissonance, and so may alter their choices to avoid its occurrence.

Self-perception theory Justification of a choice by assertion of the existence of preferences.

27.2.2 Anchoring and adjustment

In Section 27.1.3, we examined how people, lacking the ability to identify the optimal outcome, might adapt their behaviour as they searched for higher payoffs within an acceptable set. We supposed that each experiment would begin from a previous choice and involve a small adjustment, with people carrying on either until they reached a constraint, or else until the experiment failed. In this situation, we can describe the original choice as an **anchor**.

Anchor Information used as the starting point for making a decision.

Experiments carried out by psychologists typically seek to demonstrate the process of anchoring and adjustment in terms of failure to improve fully over an initial estimate that people know cannot possibly be correct. For example, suppose that you are told that the USSR launched *Sputnik 1*, the first artificial satellite to orbit the earth, in October 1957. You now have to estimate when the US *Apollo 11* mission reached the moon. Plainly, since *Sputnik 1* was the first satellite to be launched, the *Apollo 11* mission must have occurred later. In experiments, one way of asking participants to state their beliefs is to ask both for a point estimate, in this case the single date on which the moon landing is most likely to have occurred, and for a range, in this case a range of dates that may be plausible estimates.

By yourself

X27.16 For each question, estimate the smallest and largest reasonable values for the answers, and also a single point estimate.

(a) In 1603, Queen Elizabeth of England was succeeded by James VI, King of Scotland. During Elizabeth's reign, Spain assembled a large fleet, the Armada, with which it intended to invade England. In what year did the Armada sail?

(b) Between February 1931 and September 1937, Malcolm Campbell broke the world land speed record five times. He reached a speed of 246 mph in February 1931. What speed did he achieve in September 1937?

(c) The Star of Africa, which weighs 530 carats, was for many years the largest cut diamond in the world. It is only one of 104 diamonds cut from the Cullinan diamond. What is the weight (in carats) of the second largest diamond?

(d) The orbital period of Mercury (the planet closest to the sun) is 88 days. What is the orbital period of Venus (the planet second closest to the sun)?

(e) In 1066, William I won the Battle of Hastings and secured the English throne. William undertook a comprehensive survey of landholdings, recorded in what is known as the Domesday Book. In what year was the survey completed?

(f) At its completion in 1311, Lincoln Cathedral had the highest spire in the world. After its collapse in 1549 and partial rebuilding, the spire is now 83 m high. What was its original height?

(g) The Greek philosopher, Socrates, was executed in 399 BC. When was his pupil, Plato, born?

Choices made using techniques of anchoring often seem to involve a smaller adjustment than might be optimal. In questions of the type set out in Exercise X27.16, the anchor is the information given in the question, which cannot be the best point estimate, and which also indicates the direction, but not necessarily the size of the necessary adjustment. You should find that at least some of your point estimates in these questions will be between the anchor and the true value. In addition, though, when using anchoring, point estimates will often not be at the mid-point of the range of possible values, but instead quite close to the boundary of the interval nearer to the anchor. This implies that people generate a probability distribution across plausible estimates, which is skewed towards the anchor.

It is relatively easy to find evidence that anchoring affects choice, but to explain its emergence, and persistence, is rather more difficult. The most obvious explanation relies upon satisficing behaviour. We can think of the anchor as lying outside the acceptable set. This would certainly be the case if we think of adjustment as being both a continuous and a costly process. People tend to stop when further adjustments seem unlikely to yield substantial benefits. Yet this does not seem to explain what happens in situations where people are adjusting choices from anchors, such as the ones in the exercise, that utilize external information. In such cases it is not clear that adjustment costs increase in the size of adjustment.

It may be useful to consider other types of behaviour. If people use anchoring and adjustment in decision making in the real world, they will often have to generate their own anchors. For example, in most sports, professional players will have years of experience of solving particular problems that depend upon being able to automatically adjust motor skills very finely, avoiding conscious consideration. In order to play a good shot, a golfer has to manage such attributes as stance, grip address and follow through. If they play regularly, golfers are likely to be able to make adjustments to the conditions on a specific course very easily. The loss of this ability, a condition sometimes called 'the yips', can end a successful career.

Returning to the examples in Exercise X27.16, it would be possible to invite people to generate their own anchors before asking them to answer the questions. For example, while relatively few people know the orbital period of Mercury, the Earth's orbital period is a year, or 365 days. So, to estimate the orbital period of Venus, we use the value of 365 days as a self-generated anchor. If we think of the cognitive process with an externally provided anchor, it may simply be the salience of the anchor that causes bias. When we are asked to give a single point estimate, the anchor enters into our consideration. Even when we are convinced that it has limited value as a guide to the true value, we cannot easily ignore it.

Having generated our own anchor, it seems likely that in some sense we have to go through an adjustment process. Experimental work in psychology and economics since 2000 does indeed suggest that this is the case: if people are distracted, perhaps by asking them to complete multiple tasks simultaneously, they find it more difficult to make these adjustments. When there is a self-generated anchor, this affects their estimates, but not when there is an external anchor.

27.2.3 Salience, availability, and representativeness

We have already introduced the concept of *salience* in terms of the ease of accessibility of particular pieces of information when making decisions. Building on Simon's arguments that decision making might be procedurally, rather than substantively, rational, behavioural economics has sought to identify heuristics, or decision protocols and rules, which reduce the costs of decision making and which frequently, but not always, prove satisfactory. We argue that the salience of information is likely to affect the outcome of choice processes, concentrating on two of the first heuristics developed in this area: *availability* and *representativeness*.

> **Availability** The ease of recall of an item, taken as a measure of its relative frequency.

The availability *heuristic* is based on the fact that the more frequently events occur, the easier they are to remember. Asked to estimate the probability of an event occurring, someone using the heuristic will rely on how easy it is to recall. The failures of the heuristic may therefore be observed in experimental processes in which experimenters are able to manipulate the ease with which participants might recall particular events. The classic experiment, reported by Tversky and Kahneman in 1973, involved participants being presented with a recording of one of four lists of names being read out. Two lists consisted of the names of 19 famous men and 20 less famous women; the other two consisted of the names of 20 famous men and 19 less famous women. Two lists were of entertainers, and two were of other public figures. After listening to each recording, participants were asked either to recall names on the list or else simply to state whether there were more men's or women's names on the lists. Unsurprisingly, participants asked to recall names tended very strongly to list the famous ones more frequently than the less famous ones. Almost 80% of the participants required simply to state which gender appeared more frequently on the list said that the gender of the more easily recalled names were in the majority.

The experiment succeeds because of the manipulation of cognitions. In this situation, fame means that it is more likely that particular names will already be familiar to participants. These names have greater salience, and so are easier to remember. The availability heuristic seems likely to be important in situations where there is uncertainty, and where we wish to generate a subjective probability distribution over states of the world. For example, during an election campaign, we might form our own estimates of the probability of the incumbent being re-elected by thinking of the opinions expressed by our acquaintances. Our sampling technique means that the result is likely to be seriously biased.

X27.17 Consider these two structures, *A* and *B*. A path in a structure consists of one element in each row, from the top to the bottom.

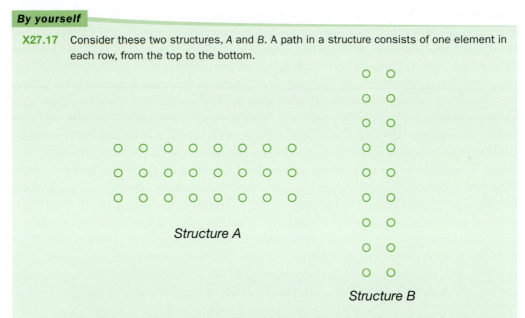

Structure A

Structure B

Without attempting calculations, state whether you believe the number of paths to be greater in structure *A* or in structure *B*; and then estimate the number of paths in each structure.

X27.18 There are 10 intermediate stops on a bus route between two cities. Services can stop at any combination of *r* out of the 10 stops.

START	1	2	3	4	5	6	7	8	9	10	TERMINUS

For *r* = 2, 3, 4, 5, 6, 7, and 8, without carrying out any calculations, estimate the number of service patterns that are possible.

X27.19 Consider structure *C*, below. We again define a path as consisting of one element from each row.

```
X O X X X X
X X X X O X
X X O X X X
X X X O X X
X X X X X O
O X X X X X
```

Structure C

Estimate, without any calculations, for *r* = 0, 1, 2, 3, 4, 5, and 6, the percentage of paths that pass through *r* 'O' nodes and 6 − *r* 'X' nodes. [*Note:* The sum of your estimates should be 100.]

X27.20 Now consider a situation in which 6 players are each dealt a single card from a deck in which $\frac{1}{6}$ of the cards are marked 'O' and $\frac{5}{6}$ are marked 'X'. In a long sequence of deals, estimate, without any calculations, for *r* = 0, 1, 2, 3, 4, 5, and 6, the percentage in which *r* players receive 'O' cards and 6 − *r* receive 'X' cards. [*Note:* Once again, the sum of your estimates should be 100.]

Exercises X27.17–X27.20 are adapted from Tversky and Kahneman (1973), who reported that participants in their experiments tended to behave as though using the availability heuristic in the first three. It is easier to see many paths in Structure A than in Structure B: there are eight columns in Structure A, but only two in Structure B. The probability of two paths sharing a node is only $\frac{1}{8}$ in Structure A, but ½ in Structure B. Similarly, in X27.18, participants in experiments tended to underestimate the number of possible combinations of service patterns, except in the case $r = 2$. Again, it is easier to construct examples of such service patterns quickly. Lastly, in X27.19, the experimental subjects tended to overestimate the frequency of paths for which $r = 0$, and to underestimate the frequency with which $r = 1$. Again, this is consistent with people using availability to make decisions. In each row of Structure C, there are five 'X' nodes and only one 'O' node. It therefore seems much easier to construct 'X'-only paths. In all of these cases, availability is misleading.

If you completed Exercises X27.19 and X27.20 with minimal calculation, then it may not have been obvious that the answers are exactly the same. Certainly in Tversky and Kahneman's original experiments participants responded in very different ways to problems of this type. We can understand their responses quite easily by noting that the two exercises are set out so as to direct people's attention to different characteristics of the distribution. In Exercise X27.19, the graphical representation makes it easy for people to see paths which pass through 'X' nodes only, so that the availability heuristic guides the response. In Exercise X27.20, the instructions emphasize the probability of any card being an 'O', effectively drawing attention to the mean number of 'O' cards in any deal. We therefore expect experimental participants to be guided by what Tversky and Kahneman (1974) called the **law of small numbers** associated with decisions made using the **representativeness** *heuristic*. This 'law' is a belief that a sample drawn from a population should be representative of the underlying population. It predicts that when told, in Exercise X27.20, that 'O' cards comprise $\frac{1}{6}$ of the population, people correctly expect the outcome with one 'O' card in a sample of six to have the highest probability.

> **Law of small numbers** The belief that a sample should have the distributional properties of the whole population.
>
> **Representativeness** The probability of an outcome greater where the sample's distributional properties are the same as those of the population.

By yourself

X27.21   Suppose that we consider a sequence of nine tosses of a fair coin. Rank the following outcomes by probability of occurrence:

(a) H   H   H   H   H   H   H   H   H
(b) H   H   H   H   H   T   T   T   T
(c) T   H   T   H   T   H   T   H   T
(d) T   H   T   T   T   H   T   H   H

Answering Exercise X27.21 by using the representativeness heuristic, we might believe that the outcome of a sequence of coin tosses should have the characteristics of the underlying distribution of an infinite sequence of coin tosses. There would then be an (approximately) equal number of 'H' and 'T' outcomes, but without any ordering within the sequence. Using these rules, we correctly consider case (a) to be improbable. We might also consider the sequence of 'H' outcomes followed by a sequence of 'T' outcomes in case (b) to be improbable. We might even consider that the alternating 'H' and 'T' outcomes in case (c) have an improbable structure compared with the seeming randomness of case (d). But in making such an argument, we overlook the fact that all of the 512 possible sequences are equally probable: by inviting you to rank the probability of the outcomes, the exercise is framed to direct you towards use of the heuristic in a situation where it is will be misleading.

27.3 Loss aversion

Reliance on choice heuristics and learned behaviour may lead to predictable deviations from what might reasonably be considered rational choices in very particularly prescribed situations. The availability heuristic can lead us to conclude that a memorable event occurs more frequently than it actually does. The representativeness heuristic might cause us to believe that an outcome that corresponds to our mental image of a class of events is more probable than it actually is. The framing of a problem might direct us to solve it in a particular way. The previous occurrence of a particular state of state of the world might lead us to prefer that state over others. These results may be interesting, but they do not give us direct insights into economic behaviour. They do, though, give some of the context in which economic decisions might be made.

Consider decision making in the face of risk or uncertainty, such as might confront a group of foraging animals. Specifically, consider how our ancestors, perhaps 50,000 years ago, might have approached decision making. There is widespread agreement among scholars that by this time period, humans had developed reasonably sophisticated languages: sufficient, for example, to be able to share knowledge of how to make tools. For our purposes, we might reasonably suppose that these language skills enabled people to encode descriptions of choice environments, and so to engage in conscious consideration. When scientists report that people seem to rely on representativeness to calculate a probability, instead of systematically applying all of the information contained in a problem, we might infer that greater abilities would not have conferred benefits in any situation where early humans had to estimate the probability of a state of the world. The use of heuristics, such as availability and representativeness, were 'good enough' guides to choice. In the context of foraging, representativeness would mean nothing more than that people would consider an area with abundant pickings to conform to a set of observable characteristics. This does not seem unreasonable.

Nonetheless, by being able to abstract from reality, and to encode problems using language, people could find different ways of solving those problems. We might think of behavioural economics as a new way of encoding economic problems, intended to allow us to solve problems that are anomalous within the standard theory. We have already seen this in Exercises X27.19 and X27.20. Differences in the way in which we set out that problem affected the way in which people tended to solve them. Turning to analysis of decision making under risk, we begin with a well-known problem, the Allais' paradox.

By yourself

X27.22 Consider the following pairs of lotteries. [*Note:* Remember our definition of a lottery in terms of a set of outcomes, and a probability distribution over these.]

- A: L_{A1} = (2,500, 2,400, 0; 0.33, 0.66, 0.01) and L_{A2} = (2,400; 1).
- B: L_{B1} = (2,500, 0; 0.33, 0.67) and L_{B2} = (2,400, 0; 0.34, 0.66).

Decide whether you would prefer the opportunity to participate in lottery A1 or in lottery A2. Repeat this for pair B. Briefly explain your choice.

(Continued)

X27.23 Review the von Neumann–Morgenstern axiomization in Section 26.3.

(a) Calculate the expected value of participation in lotteries, L_{A1}, L_{A2}, L_{B1}, and L_{B2}.

(b) Assume that $u(0) = 0$.

    (i) Suppose that lottery L_{A2} is preferred to lottery L_{A1}. What condition must hold between $u(2,500)$ and $u(2,400)$?

    (ii) Repeat part (i), given that lottery L_{B1} is preferred to lottery L_{B2}.

(c) Discuss the differences between lotteries L_{A1} and L_{B1}; and between L_{A2} and L_{B2}.

(d) Many people prefer L_{A2} to L_{A1}, but L_{B1} to L_{B2}. Discuss whether or not this is likely to be consistent with the axiom of the independence of irrelevant alternatives.

In Exercise X27.22, we cannot say that any preferences are correct: these are of course personal. Most people claim that they prefer the certainty of lottery L_{A2} to the risk of L_{A1}, while also preferring the slightly lower probability of a noticeably larger gain from lottery L_{B1} to the slightly higher probability of a noticeably smaller gain from L_{B2}. This combination turns out to be problematic in terms of expected utility theory. Firstly, we note that in both situations A and B, the expected payoff from participation in lottery 1 is greater than that from participation in lottery 2. Someone who is risk-neutral should prefer participation in lottery 1 in both situations. We expect most people to be risk-averse, but we find the same problem arising. Anyone preferring participation in L_{A2} should also prefer participation in L_{B2}. This is unsurprising when we realize that moving from L_{A1} to L_{B1}, and from L_{A1} to L_{B1}, we simply reduce the probability of winning 2,400 by 0.66. In the von Neumann–Morgenstern axiomization of expected utility (Section 26.3), we include the axiom of independence. This asserts that the preference over lotteries should not be affected by the presence of a probability of winning a fixed amount that is common to every alternative, but only by the elements that differ. We should ask ourselves whether we prefer to win 2,500 with probability 0.33 and 0 with probability 0.01, or 2,400 with probability 0.34.

Loss aversion A desire to avoid losses.   In Chapter 26.2, we introduced the concept of risk aversion, according to which people may wish to avoid risk. For example, given a choice between certain wealth to participation in a lottery where the expected wealth after participation equals the certain wealth that would otherwise be available, someone who is risk-averse would choose the certain wealth over participation in the lottery. Within behavioural economics, **loss aversion** plays a similar role. We apply a very simple decision-making process to the comparison of lotteries in Exercise X27.22. The lotteries in situation A are different from those in situation B, since L_{A2} has a certain outcome. People might therefore tend to use this lottery, whose outcome is very easy to interpret as an anchor. Lottery L_{A1} then offers a very small expected gain, partly because of the small probability of doing much worse. For someone who is loss-averse, that last outcome might enter heavily into decision making, so that L_{A2} is preferred. In situation B, the zero outcome is most probable in both lotteries, so people might use this as the anchor. Then L_{B1} is preferable because it offers a slightly higher expected payoff. We do not have to take account of a loss. The preference reversal can then easily be explained as a combination of a framing effect and an approach to decision making that may well have had value in evolutionary terms. For early humans, living in an environment where uncertainty was rather more prevalent than in developed economies, guarding resources to avoid losses may have been very important for survival.

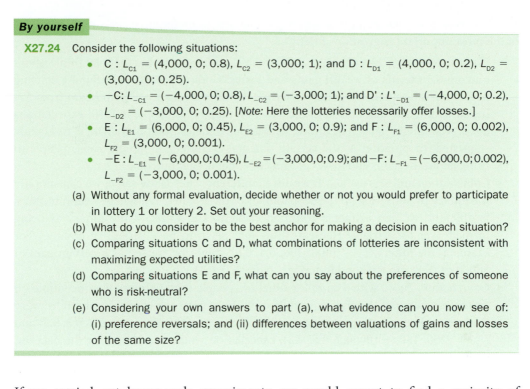

By yourself

X27.24 Consider the following situations:

- C : L_{C1} = (4,000, 0; 0.8), L_{C2} = (3,000; 1); and D : L_{D1} = (4,000, 0; 0.2), L_{D2} = (3,000, 0; 0.25).
- −C: L_{-C1} = (−4,000, 0; 0.8), L_{-C2} = (−3,000; 1); and D' : L'_{-D1} = (−4,000, 0; 0.2), L_{-D2} = (−3,000, 0; 0.25). [*Note:* Here the lotteries necessarily offer losses.]
- E : L_{E1} = (6,000, 0; 0.45), L_{E2} = (3,000, 0; 0.9); and F : L_{F1} = (6,000, 0; 0.002), L_{F2} = (3,000, 0; 0.001).
- −E : L_{-E1} = (−6,000,0; 0.45), L_{-E2} = (−3,000,0; 0.9); and −F: L_{-F1} = (−6,000,0; 0.002), L_{-F2} = (−3,000, 0; 0.001).

(a) Without any formal evaluation, decide whether or not you would prefer to participate in lottery 1 or lottery 2. Set out your reasoning.

(b) What do you consider to be the best anchor for making a decision in each situation?

(c) Comparing situations C and D, what combinations of lotteries are inconsistent with maximizing expected utilities?

(d) Comparing situations E and F, what can you say about the preferences of someone who is risk-neutral?

(e) Considering your own answers to part (a), what evidence can you now see of: (i) preference reversals; and (ii) differences between valuations of gains and losses of the same size?

If we carried out larger-scale experiments, we would expect to find a majority of participants expressing a preference for participation in lotteries L_{C2} and L_{D1}, but also in lotteries L_{-C1} and L_{-D2}. Similarly, we would expect to find preferences for participation in lotteries L_{E1} and L_{F2}, but also in L_{-E2} and L_{-F1}. This immediately suggests differences in the way in which we process decisions defined as involving gains and losses. We also seem, in situations E and F, to have evidence of the way in which we process decisions when the probability of gain is either reasonably large or very small. Once again, we have evidence of ways in which choices might be affected by the way in which we describe the situation.

27.3.1 Prospect theory

Firstly, a brief definitional note. Lotteries, defined as a set of outcomes and the probability distribution over them, may also be called **prospects**. What has become known as **prospect theory** is simply an alternative to expected utility theory: it takes account of the anomalies that we have just reviewed, especially through loss aversion. It illustrates very well both the flexibility of this approach grounded in empirical observation and its limitations in terms of being unable to rule out any particular form of behaviour.

Prospect An alternative name for a lottery.

Prospect theory A behavioural theory of decision making when faced with uncertainty.

Prospect theory presumes that there are two parts to making a choice among lotteries. Before evaluating the alternatives, these have to be edited. This can be done in several different ways, and differences in personal evaluations can be explained to some extent by people using different editing processes, or by using the same set of processes but applying them in a different order. Given the rather speculative nature of these processes, which tend to be inferred from observation of seeming anomalies in preferences, we simply list some of the most important suggestions briefly.

- *Coding.* We have already met this process, in arguing that people think about outcomes in terms of wealth gains and losses. Coding entails identifying a starting point (for subsequent evaluations). While it will often be sensible to begin from the initial wealth, the description of the situation may cause people to form expectations about what might happen in future, so that the reference point may change. As already suggested, in situation A, the certain outcome of lottery L_{A2} might cause people to think about the gains and losses of lottery L_{A1} net of that outcome.
- *Combination* and *segregation.* If wealth in different states is the same, we can simplify the lottery by summing up the probabilities of these states. But where wealth in states is different, we can extract a common element, and think of the lottery as being formed over the variable element. (This may seem to be a variant of coding.) For example, the lottery, $L_G = (400, 300; 0.4, 0.6)$, might be treated as a certain gain of 300, together with a second lottery, $L_{G'} = (100, 0; 0.4)$.
- *Cancellation.* Faced with a complex situation, people might choose to concentrate on certain elements of the choice, setting aside those parts which are common to every alternative. For example, defining situation H : $L_{H1} = (200, 100, -50; 0.2, 0.5, 0.3)$ and $L_{H2} = (200, 150, -100; 0.2, 0.5, 0.3)$, cancellation would mean making the decision by comparing the lotteries J : $L_{J1} = (100, -50; 0.625, 0.375)$ and $L_{J2} = (150, -100; 0.625, 0.375)$. Noting that in situation H, the probability of obtaining the payoff of 200 is the same in both lotteries, we concentrate on the differences. In effect, cancellation involves isolating the differences, shown in the compound lotteries in the decision trees in Figure 27.4. The lower arm of the tree is the same in both lotteries. The upper arms lead into the lotteries in situation J, which are rather easier to consider.

Given that there is no unique, or correct, method of editing the description of a situation, we can easily explain anomalies in preferences in terms of the ways in which editing is carried out. Indeed, we have typically inferred the nature of editing from observation of anomalies in preferences, rather than from introspection.

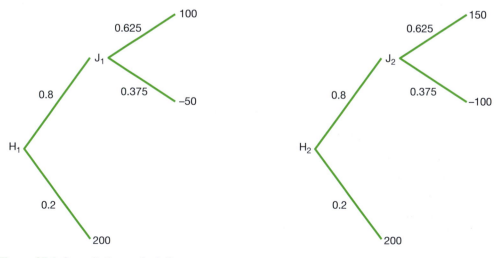

Figure 27.4 Cancellation as isolation

It is only after editing that people evaluate the lotteries. Firstly, let us suppose that there is an objective probability distribution, P. We shall assume that people do not use this probability distribution, but instead a subjective weighting, Π, which will not necessarily conform to some of the restrictions we would place on a probability distribution. In addition, we need a valuation scale, V, defined over the outcomes, x, expressed in terms of gains and losses relative to the anchor for these calculations.

Let us now consider a simple lottery, $L = (x_1, x_2, 0; p_1, p_2)$, so that there are at most two non-zero outcomes. We say that a lottery is regular if $x_1 x_2 \leq 0$ or $p_1 + p_2 < 1$. Either the lottery has a gain and a loss, or else there is a positive probability of receiving the anchor outcome.

> **By yourself**
>
> **X27.25** In situations A–F, H and J which lotteries are regular?

We may propose a value for this lottery:

$$V(L) = V[x_1, x_2, 0; p_1, p_2] = \pi(p_1)v(x_1) + \pi(p_2)v(x_2) \qquad [27.1]$$

Note that the function V determines the value of participation in the lottery, while function v is the value of a particular payoff. Given that evaluation is defined in terms of gains and losses relative to the anchor, we shall assume that $v(0) = 0$. We shall also assume that people evaluate certain events accurately, so that $\pi(0) = 0$ and $\pi(1) = 1$, and $V(x; 1) = v(x)$.

> **By yourself**
>
> **X27.26** We also define a positive lottery, $L : x_1 > x_2 > 0$, and $p_1 + p_2 = 1$. Assume that we edit a positive lottery by extracting the certain gain, x_2. Write down an expression for the value of the lottery, $V(L)$, in terms of the certain gain and the perceived value of the possible further gain.
>
> **X27.27** Define a negative lottery, using the definition in X27.26 as a guide, and then write down an expression for its value.

27.3.2 Constraints on valuation and weighting functions

These rules for valuation of a lottery allow us to explain the anomalies in choice that we have observed in situations A–J. But they do so by taking us away from the world in which people behave consistently, as though following principles of conscious consideration. Behaviour conforming to such a pattern is not irrational, but we might assume that the potential losses from this pattern of behaviour are not obvious to the person making these choices. Given the substantial volume of evidence relating to choice that we have now reviewed, we can nonetheless suggest some constraints on the form of the valuation and weighting functions that people might use.

Firstly, when we consider valuations of losses and gains around an anchor, we should treat losses and gains separately to emphasize the characteristic of loss aversion, with the value of a loss of fixed size larger than the value of an equivalent gain. Secondly, we expect valuations to be concave in gains, but convex in losses. Then, for change in wealth, x:

$$v(x)\begin{cases} > 0 \text{ if } x > 0 \\ < 0 \text{ if } x < 0 \end{cases}; \ v'(x) > 0; \text{ and } v''(x)\begin{cases} < 0 \text{ if } x > 0 \\ > 0 \text{ if } x < 0 \end{cases} \qquad [27.2]$$

$$-v(-x) > v(x) \qquad [27.3]$$

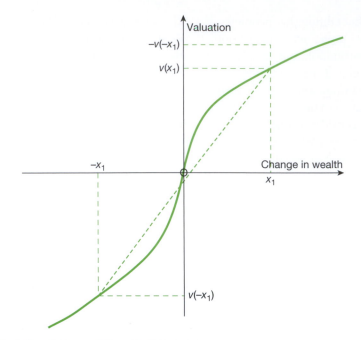

Figure 27.5 The inferred shape of the valuation curve

In Figure 27.5, we illustrate these constraints on the valuation of changes in wealth in a single curve, drawn so that it is always steeper and further below the axis for a loss of given size, $-x$, than it would be above the axis for a gain of the same size.

> **By yourself**
>
> **X27.28** Suppose that you are offered the choice of participation in the lotteries in situations K and M:
>
> $$L_{K1}: (900,0; 0.25, 0.75); \quad L_{K2}: (600,300,0; 0.25, 0.25, 0.5);$$
> $$L_{M1}: (-900, 0; 0.25, 0.75); \quad L_{M2}:(-600, -300, 0; 0.25, 0.25, 0.5).$$
>
> Making your choice, given the constraints in Expressions 27.2 and 27.3, in which lotteries would you prefer to participate?
>
> **X27.29** Suppose that you are offered the choice between participating in the lotteries in situation N:
>
> $$L_{N1}: (200, -200; 0.5, 0.5); \quad L_{N2}: (100, -100; 0.5, 0.5)$$
>
> Which would you choose, assuming that your valuations abide by these constraints?

The rules that we have imposed here seem intuitively reasonable and again have empirical support. People tend to be very averse to gambles of the sort described in Exercise X27.29, and so will try to reduce their exposure to them, choosing to participate in the lottery with the smallest change in assets. Similarly, with the valuation function convex when there are losses, but concave when there are gains, the value of a gain of 600 will be greater starting from zero than from 300, so that people often prefer lottery L_{K2}, but also lottery L_{M1}.

As well as restrictions on valuations of outcomes, we also impose restrictions on the weighting function, which replaces the probability distribution used in utility theory. Rather than demonstrate their origin, we simply state them here, illustrating the inferred relationship between the probability distribution and the decision weights in Figure 27.6.

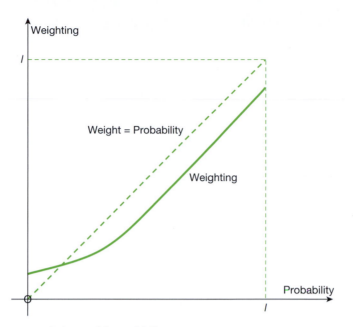

Figure 27.6 The proposed shape of the weighting curve

Firstly, we consider that people weight certain events, which occur with probability $p = 0$ or else $p = 1$, perfectly, so that $\pi(0) = 0$ and $\pi(1) = 1$. However, we shall also assume that in general:

$$\pi(p) + \pi(1 - p) < 1 \hspace{4cm} [27.4]$$

When the condition in Expression 27.4 is satisfied, people typically underweight the gains in positive lotteries, and this is sufficient to explain the results of Allais' paradox in situations A and B. However, the comparison between situations E and F (and also between situations −E and −F) suggest that this underweighting of probabilities will not occur for very small probabilities. Rather speculatively, we might conclude that once people realize that there is non-zero probability of an event, they assign it a decision weight that is rather greater than its true probability, but that decision weights thereafter increase more slowly than probabilities, until people realize that the events are certain. We show a possible relationship between weights and probabilities in Figure 27.6.

By yourself

X27.30 Explain how non-linearities in the weighting function might help to explain the differences in preferences over the lotteries in situations E and F in X27.24.

X27.31 Show that it is possible to explain the version of Allais' paradox used in X27.22 by using the weighting rule $\pi(0.34) + \pi(0.66) < 1$. [*Hint:* You should write down expressions showing what we might infer about the valuation of the lotteries when there is a seeming preference reversal.]

We now have a model of decision making in situations where there are risks that is in many ways an adaptation of expected utility theory. The valuation of a lottery is still a weighted sum of valuations of individual outcomes, but the weights on the valuations do not have the properties of a probability distribution. The restrictions on the valuations reflect the fact that we measure these in terms of gains and losses either from *initial* wealth or from *expected* wealth. This is obviously problematic. In experiments, for example, if we manipulate the framing of the decision, then we expect to observe different choices. For example, it is possible to explain status-quo bias in this way. When people are given an object to keep or to sell, it seems likely that they frame the valuation problem on the basis that they will keep the object. Simply giving it away would involve an element of loss. This framing effect introduces an asymmetry when we compare it with the situation in which participants are given money, which they can keep, or else trade for the object; in fact, the object will be a source of value by itself, while the value of money is derived from our ability to use it to acquire goods and services. Having introduced prospect theory to explain loss aversion, we can see that it provides a theoretical basis for investigating a much wider class of decisions.

27.4   Conclusions

The standard model of economics can be derived simply from introspection. In Parts II–IV, we set out a series of axioms that restrict both the nature of preferences for people and the state of technology available to firms, and then followed through their implications, assuming that decision makers have limited resources available to reach their goals. Throughout the book, we have followed the strategy of asking how we can adapt our theory to more complex situations. In some ways, when we reach this chapter that approach breaks down. For the first time, we have looked to disciplines other than economics to provide us with assumptions to motivate our economic analysis.

Nonetheless, the approach in this chapter is consistent with the argument of the book, if we understand it as a response to the question of how to model economic behaviour in circumstances in which conscious consideration is a scare resource. Our initial response was to reflect upon the nature of learning, developing the notion that learning, in the sense of adapting to a choice environment, would continue for as long as it appeared to be productive. This much is certainly consistent with the standard theory.

The grounding in observation means that the theories presented in this chapter are rather different in nature from the standard theory. Reviewing a substantial volume of research findings, we have set out a body of anomalies, which are interesting because they are difficult to accommodate within the context of the standard model. For example, within the standard model, our description of the world does not affect decisions. There is, in any case, a single, objective reality. Within what we defined as prospect theory, the description of the world that someone is given, or indeed their own perception of the world, might be expected to affect their interactions with it. We see this in evidence such as the finding of status-quo bias. There is at least a risk within behavioural economics of never being surprised by any pattern of outcomes because the explanations and definitions are so elastic. This should lead us to question just what we are able to explain using behavioural economics. If we are able to explain every pattern of events after they occur, but by reference to an *ad hoc* adjustment to our definition of weighting functions or editing processes, then we might consider that in effect we have explained nothing. More than in any other chapter, we are considering insights that are still being developed, and that are therefore contentious within the research community.

Summary

We treat behavioural economics as an exploration of the implications for economic theory of allowing decision making to be a costly process. We abandon the presumption that all decisions should be treated as if they were the outcome of some optimizing process.

A full account of behavioural economics requires an understanding of the development of decision-making capacities during the evolution of humans through processes of natural selection.

Behavioural economics draws on the insights of behavioural psychology, especially as these relate to learned behaviour, which is recognized to be appropriate as a result of experience.

An important precursor of behavioural models in economics was the concept of procedural or bounded rationality, according to which decision makers cannot optimize because of the impossibility of identifying optimal outcomes, and so set themselves the goal of satisficing: of finding an acceptable outcome. Satisficing behaviour might lead to people reaching a local, rather than a global, optimum as the result of only being willing to make small adjustments to behaviour.

There is evidence of systematic biases within decision making. These have been found to be consistent with the use of simple heuristics, or decision protocols, such as anchoring to guide actions, and availability and representativeness to identify the most likely state of the world.

Prospect theory offers a general structure that specifies the nature of decision making under conditions of uncertainty. It uses careful classification of behaviour, demonstrating that behaviour tends to be consistent with parsimonious decision-making processes which are used to explain otherwise anomalous behaviour.

Within prospect theory, we replace the assumption of risk aversion with the assumption of loss aversion, in which people wish to avoid probable losses in situations of uncertainty. We also assume that people do not necessarily apply a probability distribution when evaluating how likely it is that outcomes will occur, but instead apply a more general weighting function. Lastly, to simplify the evaluation of alternatives, we assume that people edit prospects, so that they can concentrate on the most important features of those prospects.

Visit the companion website at **www.palgrave.com/mochrie** to access further teaching and learning materials, including lecturer slides and a testbank, as well as guideline answers and student MCQs.

In Part IV, we concluded our analysis by using game theory to show that firms in an oligopolistic market may behave in very different ways. They may or may not have market power; they may cooperate with each other, or breach agreements; and they may compete as equals, or be willing to follow another firm's lead. In Part VI, we analysed people's behaviour, suggesting ways in which the standard model might have to be adapted when there is a cost to acquiring and processing information. We now bring these ideas together.

In any transaction, we might reasonably expect the seller to have a better knowledge of the quality of the good than the potential buyers. The seller possesses the good, and so has had an opportunity to inspect, and perhaps even to test, the good. Buyers do not typically have this opportunity. This introduces a situation in which there is asymmetric information. We shall argue that in such situations, the people who are most obviously inconvenienced are potential sellers bringing high-quality goods to the market. Sellers of low-quality goods have no problem: in effect they state that the goods are of low quality by confirming that they have a relatively low *WTA*. People willing to buy low-quality goods at the sellers' *WTA* also have no problem. They are able to complete transactions. For potential

sellers of high-quality goods, though, it is not possible simply to announce a high *WTA* to demonstrate that their goods are of high quality, because anyone could make such a claim. An unscrupulous seller of low-quality goods, noting assertions made by sellers of high-quality goods, might see mimicry as an easy way to make quick profits. Potential buyers, realizing this, and aware of their inability to test sellers' claims, might reasonably buy the goods that they know are of low quality because they are sold at a low price. In these circumstances, we shall argue that the presence of sellers of low-quality goods exerts a negative externality on sellers of high-quality goods. The latter may be unable to sell as much as they would otherwise, or else they may be unable to sell their output for as high a price as they would otherwise.

In discussing behaviour, we suggested that people may be misled by reliance on choice heuristics because the potential benefits of making choices by using conscious consideration are not apparent. We now want to understand behaviour in situations in which only some of the people considering taking part in a transaction possess relevant information. This is a more general problem than the one discussed above. The problem is to find a way of making credible claims. Solutions might emerge through the structure of the market, the form of contracts which the market supports, and observable actions that are understood to demonstrate credibility. Typically, these methods will add to the costs of conducting business. It is even possible that the costs of communicating information in a credible manner will be so high that people decide that it is not worthwhile trying to mitigate the costs imposed by information asymmetries. In such cases, the benefits that accumulate from making sure that other people are well informed are too small for people to want to do this.

Typically, we shall be thinking about situations in which there are two parties involved. We shall therefore use the methods of game theory to understand outcomes. This will involve analysis of more complex games, and therefore the introduction of solution concepts that allow us to consider only a subset of the Nash equilibria of these games, on the basis that only the members of the subset have characteristics that seem reasonable.

28

Games with incomplete information

What we do in this chapter

When we introduced game theory in Chapter 18, we considered strategic games with *complete information*. Before the game began, the players could identify the actions that they should choose, given beliefs about the actions of other players. We defined the Nash equilibria of the game as the set of action profiles in which every player's beliefs about the other players' actions were correct. Apart from the actions that the other players might choose, everything in these games was perfectly understood.

We now consider a wider class of games, allowing for differences in the information available to the players, or *asymmetric information*. We model such cases by supposing that there are two states of the world, with only one player knowing which state has actually occurred. For the fully informed player, analysis of best replies changes very little, but the imperfectly informed player uses a strategy with actions depending on beliefs about the state of the world. The uninformed player has to assume that actions will be chosen according to the probability distribution over states of the world. For consistent best replies, we obtain the *Bayes–Nash equilibrium*.

We use an example in which sellers come to market knowing the quality of the product

that they are selling, but buyers know only the proportions of high- and low-quality goods in the market. We set up the model as a game, in which potential buyers and sellers announce *WTP* and *WTA* at the same time, with the transaction being concluded if *WTP* > *WTA*. After noting that in this game only the low-quality goods will be traded, we consider a generalization to a continuum of different qualities, concluding that it is possible for asymmetric information to cause the complete collapse of the market.

Such a situation is plainly unsatisfactory. We conclude our discussion by considering how it might be possible for the informed player to communicate with the uninformed one. We see that *communication* is necessarily costly, not least because some informed players may actually benefit from the information asymmetry, and those players who do decide to communicate must bear costs to demonstrate their sincerity. As an example, we concentrate on a simple labour market, showing the ways in which employers might be able to use observable characteristics of potential employees to infer their unobservable productivity.

28.1 Problems of coordination

While drafting the novel, later published (in 1813) as *Pride and Prejudice*, Jane Austen used the title *First Impressions*. The plot is simple: two young people, Elizabeth Bennet and Fitzwilliam Darcy, meet, and although initially unable even to form a friendship, they gradually begin to admire and love one another. To this extent, it may seem no more than a romantic comedy; its place as a classic depends indeed very much on Miss Austen's insights into the nature of learning and decision making. Her heroine, Miss Bennet, places great store on her ability to judge other people's character: learning that she has allowed herself to be easily misled is central to her character's development. Mr Darcy follows a similar path, initially being dismissive of the woman whom he ends up asking (twice) to be his wife. It is only when he has recognized her merits that he can frame that request so that it is accepted.

The book explores the development of their relationship over time. We here consider a point relatively early in the account, when both Darcy and Elizabeth are interested in, but also puzzled by, the other. Social conventions prevent direct exploration of their attitudes and feelings: of necessity, they have to infer these from observation of each other's behaviour.

We set up a simple version of the two-player, two-action game commonly called *Battle of the Sexes*. The game's Nash equilibria result from the players not knowing what the other will do. Both players enjoy a higher payoff from an action when the other player chooses the same one. Their rankings of actions are, however, different. So, in the example shown in Table 28.1, Miss Bennet would prefer to be at a ball; and Mr Darcy would prefer to stay at home and have dinner.

Battle of the Sexes (1)		Miss Bennet	
		Ball	Dinner
Mr Darcy	Ball	(6, 12)	(2, –2)
	Dinner	(4, 2)	(8, 4)

Table 28.1 A preference for being together

By yourself

X28.1   Confirm the following:
(a) There are two Nash equilibria in pure strategies: both choose to go the ball; or both choose to go to the family dinner.
(b) Neither player has a dominant strategy.
(c) Miss Bennet's best reply, $\beta*$, is a function of her beliefs, δ^e, about Mr Darcy's probability distribution over the actions, and may be written:

$$\beta*(\delta^e) = \begin{cases} 0, \delta^e < \frac{1}{8} \\ [0,1], \delta^e = \frac{1}{8} \\ 1, \delta^e > \frac{1}{8} \end{cases}$$

(d) Mr Darcy's best reply, $\delta*$, is a function of his beliefs, β^e, about Miss Bennet's probability distribution over the actions, and may be written:

$$\delta*(\beta^e) = \begin{cases} 0, \beta^e < \frac{3}{4} \\ [0,1], \beta^e = \frac{3}{4} \\ 1, \beta^e > \frac{3}{4} \end{cases}$$

(e) There is a Nash equilibrium in mixed strategies in which Mr Darcy chooses to go the ball with probability, $\delta = \frac{1}{8}$, and Miss Bennet chooses to go to the ball with probability, $\beta = \frac{3}{4}$.
(f) In this Nash equilibrium, Mr Darcy has an expected payoff of 5, and Miss Bennet an expected payoff of 3.25.

Remember that in a game where players can adopt a mixed strategy, their strategies cannot be described simply in terms of actions. Instead, players' strategies are probability distribution over their actions. With a two-player, two-action game, once we have defined the probability, π, of one action being chosen, the probability of the other being chosen is simply $1 - \pi$. Both players can choose either action, and so every action occurs with a non-zero probability. The intuition for the mixed-strategy equilibrium emerging in this situation is not particularly obvious. We have to imagine that the two players are unable to communicate with each other, so that they cannot coordinate their actions. In addition, we imagine that the game is played once, and once only, with these players. Were Mr Darcy and Miss Bennet to fail to meet, the game would be over, and there would be no opportunity for them to learn from experience. In that case, only one outcome is observed. Given how we defined probability distributions in Chapter 26, it would be difficult to model the situation as some form of objective distribution reflecting the behaviour of populations of men and women, from whom Mr Darcy and Miss Bennet have been drawn at random.

This suggests that we have to rely on a *subjective* interpretation of all probabilities. Beliefs about the other player's probability distribution are perhaps best treated as a **Bayesian prior**, a subjective probability distribution, which might change as more information about the other player's intentions is revealed. This Bayesian prior informs the best reply of the players. In addition, to play a mixed strategy, it is essential that a player is indifferent between the expected outcomes

> **Bayesian prior** A random variable, defining beliefs, whose subjective probability distribution changes as information is received.

of actions chosen with non-zero probability: all must have the same expected payoff; and no other action can have a higher expected payoff. There is the same expected payoff to all actions, and also to any probability distribution over these actions.

We demonstrate the existence of the three Nash equilibria in Figure 28.1 by setting out the players' best replies:

- For Miss Bennet:
  - Should she believe that there is a probability, $\delta = \frac{1}{8}$, of Mr Darcy deciding to go the ball she would be indifferent between the two actions. Her expected payoff, $E[v_B]$, to either action, or indeed to any linear combination of the actions, is defined by the probability, β, of her going to the ball, $E[v_B] = 3.25$.

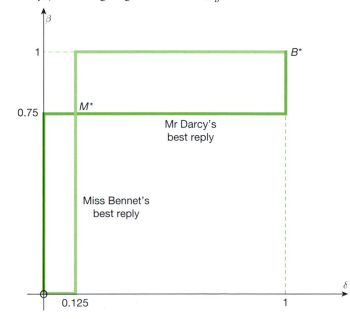

Figure 28.1 Best replies in the *Battle of the Sexes* example

- Should she believe that it is less probable that Mr Darcy will go to the ball, then she maximizes her expected payoff by going to dinner, and so she chooses that action with certainty.
- Lastly, should she believe that it is more probable that Mr Darcy will go to the ball, then she will maximize her expected payoff by choosing that action with certainty.
- For Mr Darcy:
  - Should he believe that with probability, $\beta = \frac{3}{4}$, Miss Bennet will go to the ball, then he will be indifferent between the actions.
  - He will prefer to go the ball if he considers it even more probable that Miss Bennet will be there.
  - He will prefer to stay at home if he believes it less probable that Miss Bennet will be at the ball.

In Figure 28.1, the probability, δ, of Mr Darcy attending the ball is represented on the horizontal axis, and the probability, β, of Miss Bennet attending the ball is on the vertical axis. Mr Darcy's best reply is drawn in the darker, and Miss Bennet's in the lighter, shade of green. The graphs of the best-reply functions indicate that for each player there is a critical value of their prior for which they are indifferent between actions, and that for any other values, there will be a unique best reply.

In Figure 28.1, we see the three Nash equilibria of the game where the best-reply curves intersect. Two of them are in pure strategies, where both Elizabeth and Darcy choose with certainty to go either to the ball or to dinner. We could identify these as soon as we set out the payoff matrix, Table 28.1. The third Nash equilibrium is in mixed strategies: $(\delta^\star, \beta^\star) = (0.125, 0.75)$ and occurs when both choose to go to the ball with a probability equal to the prior for which the other player is indifferent between actions. Explaining this outcome may seem difficult, because it suggests that people act randomly. In the games that we explore in this chapter, failures of coordination tend to result from difficulties in communicating information in a credible way. It might seem that this particular coordination problem could be solved through the use of social media, but we shall build on our argument from discussion of the Prisoners' Dilemma and the *Stag Hunt* in Chapters 18 and 19 that it is very easy for someone to announce an intention to choose some action, but then not to carry out that action. In this chapter, we argue that it is also very easy for players in a game to make false claims about the nature of their private information, in an attempt to deceive other players.

28.1.1   A Bayesian game

We have presented *Battle of the Sexes* as a strategic game with complete information. Our interest here is in its extension to a situation in which there is incomplete information, considering the point in *Pride and Prejudice* where the protagonists have met, but not understanding each other well, are uncertain how to behave. Mr Darcy wishes to meet Miss Bennet once again (but has been careful not to communicate that to anyone, possibly even suppressing any conscious acknowledgement of the fact). He does not know, though, whether or not Miss Bennet wishes to meet him (although frequently when they meet, she makes clear her distaste for his conduct). In effect, Mr Darcy knows that there are two states of the world, one in which they both wish to meet, and one in which Miss Bennet wishes to avoid him. Should she wish to meet him, then they will play the game set out above in Figure 28.1. If she wishes to avoid him, the situation might usefully be summarized in a different game, shown in Figure 28.2. In the alternative version of *Battle of the Sexes*, Mr Darcy has exactly the same preferences as before (represented by the same payoffs). Miss Bennet's preferences have changed, and the payoffs indicate that she prefers to avoid Mr Darcy.

Battle of the Sexes (2)		Miss Bennet	
		Ball	Dinner
Mr Darcy	Ball	(6, 2)	(2, 6)
	Dinner	(4, 8)	(8, −2)

Table 28.2 A preference for avoiding Mr Darcy

By yourself

X28.2 Confirm the following:
  (a) There is no Nash equilibrium in pure strategies.
  (b) Neither player has a dominant strategy.
  (c) There is a Nash equilibrium in mixed strategies in which Mr Darcy chooses to go the ball with probability, $\frac{5}{7}$, and Miss Bennet chooses to go to the ball with probability, $\frac{3}{4}$.

X28.3 Illustrate the best replies of this game in a diagram similar to Figure 28.1. Explain why the Nash equilibrium in mixed strategies is unique.

From the way that we have presented the problem, it might seem that Mr Darcy has first to decide which version of the game he is playing. This is not possible in a situation of **incomplete information**, for that would mean understanding Miss Bennet, and perhaps himself, better than he does. The best that he can do is to assign probabilities to each version of the game, and then to calculate the expected payoffs to each action, defining best replies to each possible strategy that he might encounter.

> **Incomplete information** The situation in which a player in a game lacks information relevant to a decision.

We therefore model his analysis by saying that he expects to play the version, G_1: *Prefers to meet*, with probability p, and version, G_2: *Prefers to avoid*, with probability $1 - p$. Another way of thinking about this is that Mr Darcy is participating in a lottery, $L = (G_1, G_2; p, 1 - p)$, in which the outcomes are the right to participate in one version of the game. This means that he is no longer a player in a strategic game with complete information, but rather in a game, G, of incomplete information, as illustrated in Table 28.3. We will not ask how Mr Darcy might come to assign these probability weights to the versions of the game. Indeed, given the discussion of prospect theory in Chapter 27, we might question whether reliance on expected payoffs is appropriate.

Battle of the Sexes		Miss Bennet (1); prob^y p		Miss Bennet (2); prob^y $1 - p$	
		Ball	Dinner	Ball	Dinner
Mr Darcy	Ball	(6, 12)	(2, −2)	(6, 2)	(2, 6)
	Dinner	(4, 2)	(8, 4)	(4, 8)	(8, −2)

Table 28.3 The game G in normal form

We have already applied the concept of Nash equilibrium in mixed strategies to both G_1 and G_2 separately, showing that if Miss Bennet follows the strategy $\beta = 0.75$, Mr Darcy

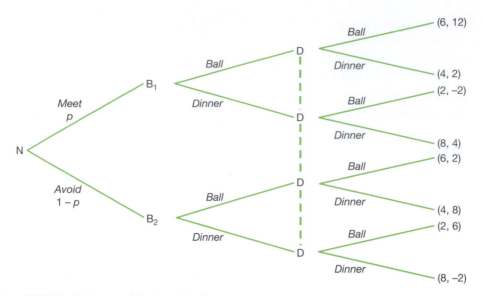

Figure 28.2 The full game of *Battle of the Sexes*

has the same expected payoff to both actions. We follow a similar process here, but rather than Miss Bennet choosing her action randomly, nature now chooses Miss Bennet's type randomly: the game does not begin with her deciding between playing version 1 or version 2 of the game. The game, G, can then be set out in extensive form in Figure 28.2, beginning with a move by player *N*, nature, which determines Miss Bennet's type.

The next stage of our solution needs a little thought. We define a strategy as the set of actions that a player chooses prior to the start of the game, assuming that the game will reach a particular decision node during the play of the game. For Miss Bennet, this means that before the move of nature takes place, she decides what actions she will choose both in the case that she wishes to meet and in the case that she wishes to avoid Mr Darcy. We can therefore define the strategy set for Miss Bennet, $\sigma_B = \{(Ball, Ball), (Ball, Dinner), (Dinner, Ball), (Dinner, Dinner)\}$, where the first element in each pair is the choice she makes at node B_1, in the '*would like to meet*' version, while the second is the choice made at node B_2, in the '*would like to avoid*' version.

Once the 'move of nature' has happened, and she is certain in her intentions, she implements her strategy. Notice that Mr Darcy acts at the same time as Miss Bennet. This means that he cannot observe her decision. We show this in Figure 28.2 by connecting the four 'D' nodes with a dashed line, representing the fact that Mr Darcy cannot distinguish between them.

The best that Mr Darcy can do is to determine the best reply to each of Miss Bennet's possible strategies. For this, he has to calculate the expected payoff from each of his actions, given the probabilities of each of the sub-games being played out.

Mr Darcy's expected payoffs		**Miss Bennet's strategy**			
		Ball, Ball	*Ball, Dinner*	*Dinner, Ball*	*Dinner, Dinner*
Mr Darcy's action	*Ball*	6	$6p + 2(1-p)$	$2p + 6(1-p)$	2
	Dinner	4	$4p + 8(1-p)$	$8p + 4(1-p)$	8

Table 28.4 Mr Darcy's expected payoffs

By yourself

X28.4 Confirm the following, when $p = 0.5$:

(a) In pure strategies, Mr Darcy's best reply, $\delta^*(\sigma_B)$, to Miss Bennet's possible (pure) strategies are: (i) for $\sigma_B = $ (Ball, Ball), $\delta^*(\sigma_B) = $ Ball; and (ii) $\delta^*(\sigma_B) = $ Dinner, otherwise.

(b) When playing his best reply, Mr Darcy's expected payoff to these strategies, $E[v(\delta^*)]$: (i) for $\sigma_B = $ (Dinner, Dinner), $E[v(\delta^*)] = 8$; and (ii) otherwise, $E[v(\delta^*)] = 6$.

(c) There is a Nash equilibrium in pure strategies, $(\sigma_B, \sigma_D) = $ ((Dinner, Ball); Dinner).

X28.5 Confirm that the Nash equilibrium in X28.4c is the only one in pure strategies, given that $0 < p < 0.75$.

X28.6 Confirm that when $p > 0.75$, there is a Nash equilibrium in pure strategies $(\sigma_B, \sigma_D) = $ ((Ball, Dinner); Ball).

From Table 28.4, we see immediately that Mr Darcy will choose the same action as Miss Bennet if he believes that she is certain to choose one or other of them. But if Miss Bennet's strategy involves different actions in each sub-game, then Mr Darcy will choose *Ball* if he believes that the probability of her choosing *Ball* is at least 0.75. Otherwise, he will choose *Dinner*. This is entirely consistent with our analysis of the pure strategy equilibria in the simpler game of complete information with which we started the discussion. We can also see that if Mr Darcy formed the belief that $p = 0.75$, he would be willing to adopt a mixed strategy. Analysis of equilibrium in mixed strategies in this case adds little to our understanding of the situation, and so we have omitted it.

We concentrate on the Nash equilibrium, $(\sigma_B^*, \sigma_D^*) = $ [(Ball, Dinner); Ball]. In the subgame, G_1, both make the decision to go to the ball, so that they meet. In the subgame, G_2, Mr Darcy goes to the ball and Miss Bennet goes to the dinner. This equilibrium is sustainable because of the changes in Miss Bennet's payoffs across the states, but also the probability of her wishing to meet Mr Darcy. It seems that were it not for his wish to meet Miss Bennet, he would go to the dinner. So, he has to be quite certain that she wishes to meet him in order for him to go to the ball. But if Miss Bennet actually does not wish to meet him, and she believes that Mr Darcy will go to the ball, she will prefer to go to dinner.

It is perhaps best for us to stop at this point, recognizing that there are at least two ways in which this model still falls short of the plot in the book. We have assumed that Mr Darcy's intentions are clearly understood, and that the uncertainty only relates to Miss Bennet's intentions. For a large part of the book, both seem to have poorly defined preferences, and so there is very considerable uncertainty. The title that Jane Austen laid aside, *First Impressions*, was intended to convey the importance of the protagonists gradually understanding each other's character and preferences over a period of time, which happens through repeated interactions and observation. To model the plot as a strategic game, in which all actions take place at the same time, is therefore a gross simplification. We should instead think in terms of models in which the observation of actions leads to *learning*, defined in terms of the updating of the protagonists' Bayesian priors. That is, as the novel progresses, repeated interactions will lead Mr Darcy and Miss Bennet to form more certain, and more accurate, beliefs about each other, so that they find it easier to coordinate their actions.

28.2   A market for secondhand cars

Anya buys a new car for £20,000. After a month, she is unexpectedly offered a job in another country. So she decides to sell the car, privately. It is still under warranty, and she has only travelled about 400 miles in it. She struggles to obtain more than £18,000 for it. How might we explain the sudden loss of value?

We begin with two observations. We should think of a car as an experience good. If the owner has had a car for a month, potential buyers might conclude that the owner has had sufficient time to assess its quality, and expect the owner to be satisfied with the purchase. In general, therefore, the offer of a car for sale very soon after the original purchase should then raise suspicions in the minds of potential buyers. Rather than inferring that the sale is motivated by a change in personal circumstances, potential buyers might well conclude that there is a high probability that the car being offered for sale is of poor quality – that the owner of the car is not satisfied with it, and so wishes to dispose of it. This is a simple example of **Bayesian learning**. Potential purchasers will treat the fact of a nearly new car being offered for sale as informative, and will update their priors about the car's underlying quality.

Bayesian learning
Revision (or updating) of a prior on receipt of information.

Let us now be more precise about the underlying model. Our analysis will proceed on the basis that there can be substantial differences in quality among cars that, on a simple visual inspection, appear to be identical. To simplify further, we shall suppose that there are exactly two types of car: those of standard quality ('peaches'), and those of low quality ('lemons'). The actual quality of any individual car can only be verified by driving it for some time. As a result, the car manufacturer cannot deliver a new car with a guarantee that it is of standard quality: instead, the manufacturer's warranty will typically include an offer to undertake remedial repairs free of charge if a car turns out to be of low quality.

Assume that all potential buyers would be willing to pay $WTP_S = 20,000$ for a new car guaranteed to be of standard quality, but only $WTP_L = 15,000$ for one of low quality. They also believe (correctly) that the proportion of low-quality cars in the population, $\pi = 0.01$, and they are all risk-neutral. Ignoring all the possible complications of behavioural models – including the possibility of regret on discovering a car to be of poor quality – we can rely on WTP as a measure of the expected value of payoffs from ownership and use of the car. When buying a new car, then, we calculate Anya's WTP as:

$$WTP = \pi_S \cdot WTP_S + \pi_L \cdot WTP_L = 0.99*20,000 + 0.01*15,000 = 19,950 \qquad [28.1]$$

After a month, though, when she makes the decision to sell it, Anya is certain that the car is of standard quality. This means that she would like to obtain a price of £20,000 for it. Remember that when she bought the car, she did so believing that the probability of it being low quality, $\Pr(Low) = \pi = 0.01$, which is simply the Bayesian prior of any car of this type, chosen at random, being of low quality. We have suggested that potential buyers will treat the fact that she is bringing it to market as an informative event, and so will revise their prior. Suppose that potential buyers now believe $\Pr(Low|\text{For sale}) = \lambda = 0.9$. Then for a buyer:

$$WTP = \lambda \cdot WTP_L + (1 - \lambda) \cdot WTP_S = 0.9*15,000 + 0.1*20,000 = 15,500 \qquad [28.2]$$

By yourself

X28.7 Suppose that Brinda buys a car of exactly the same type at the same time as Anya. She identifies it as a peach, but after a month she is bored with it, and would simply like to replace it. For Brinda, $WTA_B = 18,000$; that is, she is willing to accept a loss of nearly £2,000.
(a) Confirm that if the prior $\lambda = \pi = 0.01$, so that there is no learning, then Brinda will be able to find a willing buyer.
(b) Confirm that if the prior $\lambda = 0.9$, so that potential purchasers consider the fact that the car is offered for sale to be highly informative, then Brinda will not be able to find a willing buyer.
(c) Find the range of values of λ for which Brinda will find a willing buyer.

X28.8 Explain why for Anya, $WTA = 0$; and that irrespective of the value of λ, she will be able to find a willing buyer.

X28.9 Suppose that among the 10,000 people who buy their cars at the same time as Anya and Brinda, there are 25 forced sellers, like Anya; 25 willing sellers of standard-quality cars, like Brinda, with $WTA = 18,000$; and 100 willing sellers of low-quality cars, with $WTA = 15,000$.
(a) Calculate the average value to a potential buyer of a car that will be brought to market, given that: (i) potential buyers believe that only low-quality cars and forced sellers will bring cars to market; and (ii) potential buyers believe that all three groups of cars will be brought to market.
(b) Explain why the revision of the prior in (i) is consistent with the market reaching equilibrium, but the revision in (ii) is not.

X28.10 Suppose that there are no forced sales. Assuming that there are n potential sellers of standard-quality cars, what is the highest WTA that Brinda could set if she is to succeed in selling her car?

Potential buyers know that almost all owners of peaches have no intention of selling their cars. So, the question arises of just how many will actually want to sell them. From Exercises X28.9 and X28.10, it may seem that voluntary sellers of peaches have either to be implausibly frequent (relative to people trying to offload lemons) or else willing to accept a relatively large loss from the sale. This suggests that it should be possible to design a simple model in which all peaches are withdrawn from the market, all potential buyers are aware that only lemons are available, and so, in equilibrium, the prior $\lambda = 1$ and the market price $p = 15,000$ – the WTP for a lemon.

In such a market there is **asymmetric information**, because only the seller knows fully the characteristics of the good brought to market. We usually assume that potential buyers only know the underlying distribution of characteristics across the population of goods. Allowing for Bayesian learning, however, we often predict a problem of **adverse selection**, with buyers inferring that only poor-quality goods will be brought to market. Sellers of lemons therefore exert an externality on potential sellers of peaches, who will either decide not to offer their goods for sale, or else will have to accept a much lower price than they would were there to be perfect information.

Asymmetric information The situation in which players' information sets differ.

Adverse selection Asymmetric information exerts a negative externality on sellers of high quality goods.

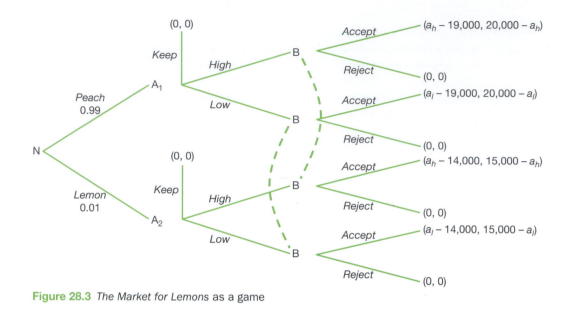

Figure 28.3 *The Market for Lemons* as a game

28.2.1 Adverse selection in a game

It seems straightforward to use the structure of a Bayesian game to analyse the problem facing Anya and Brinda. We show this in Figure 28.3, where we call the game *The Market for Lemons*. The title comes from an important paper by George Akerlof, which was one of the earliest attempts to explain how information asymmetries lead to adverse selection, and, in certain circumstances, to the total collapse of the market. The game begins with a move of nature. As before, with probability $p = 0.99$, any car chosen at random is a peach; the buyer, A, cannot distinguish a peach from a lemon at the time of purchase. As before, after a month has passed, the owner, A, who now knows the quality of the car with certainty, decides whether or not to try to sell it. We assume that A has three actions available to her.

- She can keep the car, in which case the game will end immediately.
- She can offer it for sale at a high price, a_h, claiming that it is a peach.
- She can offer it for sale at a low price, a_p, implicitly admitting that it is a lemon.

We assume that the potential buyer, B, believes that cars are brought to the market voluntarily. Observing the price set by A, B chooses between *Accept* or *Reject*. There is no haggling over the price. The payoffs from the game are then expressed in terms of net benefits after the game has ended. So that there is some consumer surplus to be divided, we have assumed that $WTA_A = WTP_B - 1{,}000$. Were we to assume that B had perfect information, then there would be a range of possible offers, a, for which $WTA_A > a > WTP_B$, and the transaction would proceed. Any failure to complete the sale is therefore a result of the information asymmetry and the subsequent problem of adverse selection.

As in *Battle of the Sexes*, we show in the diagram a potential buyer's uncertainty over the state of the world, arguing that when making decisions the buyer cannot determine which node the game has reached. The structure of the game is slightly more complicated, with A now making an offer to B, and B deciding whether to accept or to reject it. At first sight, it may seem that this structure will allow the buyer to decide whether the car is a peach or a lemon, so that the offer is informative.

By yourself

X28.11 Consider the situation facing the potential buyer, B. Confirm that with perfect information, B:
(a) facing a high price, would pay a_h only for a peach; and
(b) facing a low prices, would pay a_l for any car.

X28.12 Assume now that there is asymmetric information. The buyer assumes that the car is a lemon with probability λ_h, when the seller announces the high price, a_h; and with probability λ_l, when facing the low price, a_l.
(a) Confirm that: (i) the seller of a peach will set a price of at least £19,000; and (ii) the seller of a lemon will set a price of at least £14,000.
(b) Suppose that all sellers of peaches set a price of £19,000; and all other sellers of lemons set a price of £14,000. What might B infer about A's car if A sets a price of £19,000, even though the car is a lemon?
(c) Explain why you think that the situation outlined in part (b) is unlikely to arise. [*Hint*: If A believes that there is an advantage to setting a high price when selling a low-quality car, how will other sellers of lemons behave?] Discuss why it is unlikely that B will consider the price set by A to be informative about the quality of the car, so that $\lambda_h = \lambda_l = \lambda$.
(d) Show that if $\lambda < 0.2$, then the expected value of a car to a buyer, $E[v_B] > 19,000$, and peaches will be offered for sale.
(e) Show that if $\lambda > 0.2$, then the expected value of a car to a buyer, $E[v_B] < 19,000$, so that only lemons will be offered for sale.
(f) Confirm that there is a Bayes–Nash equilibrium in pure strategies, $(\sigma_A, \sigma_B, \lambda)$, with σ_A = (Keep, Low); σ_B = (Reject, Accept); and $\lambda = 1$. [*That is*: A keeps a peach, and offers a lemon for sale at a low price; B believes that all cars offered for sale are lemons, and so will only buy cars offered at a low price.]

The structure of the game in Exercise X28.12 is slightly more complex than *Battle of the Sexes*. There, we did not allow Darcy and Elizabeth to communicate at all, and so there was no opportunity for (Bayesian) learning in the form of updating of priors. In this example of adverse selection, we see that learning does take place. When people go to buy a new car, they have a prior, $\lambda = \pi$, so that the probability of the car they buy being a lemon is simply the probability of any car chosen at random being a lemon. Anyone who sells a nearly new car, though, faces the problem that potential buyers will have formed a very different prior, $\lambda > \pi$, on the basis that a larger proportion of lemons than peaches will be offered for sale. Indeed, if the potential buyer B believes that λ is large enough, owners of peaches will withdraw their cars from sale, preferring to keep them; potential buyers will revise their beliefs, so that $\lambda^* = 1$; and we will obtain the Bayes–Nash equilibrium in which only lemons are traded. Note that the Bayes–Nash equilibrium involves both a strategy for each player, and also a set of beliefs with which their actions are consistent.

By yourself

X28.13 Confirm that when half of the people who purchase lemons, and 2.5% of the people who buy peaches, seek to trade their cars in shortly after purchase, there is a second Bayes–Nash equilibrium in pure strategies in the game illustrated in Figure 28.3: $[\sigma_A*, \sigma_B*, \lambda*]$ = [(High, High), (Accept, Accept), 0.17], with 'High' price, $p*$: £19,000 < $p*$ < £19,150.

The Bayes–Nash equilibrium in Exercise X28.13 still involves all cars being sold at the same price. Note the difference in beliefs compared with the equilibrium identified in Exercise X28.12: there all cars brought to market were lemons. Here, approximately 3% of cars are traded, with a little over $\frac{1}{6}$ of these being lemons. The proportion of peaches remains large enough, given the difference in the valuations of types of car, that potential buyers' *WTP* will be greater than the *WTA* of sellers of peaches. In this case, then, the peaches are not withdrawn from the market, but their sellers still have to accept a lower price than if the cars were traded in a market with full information.

28.2.2   Unobservable product variety and market collapse

With only two qualities of car, we have argued that in the secondhand market (at least for nearly new cars), beliefs about the quality of the cars brought to market can lead to an outcome in which only the lower-quality cars are traded. A forced seller, such as Anya, has to accept a price that is lower than she would ideally like; but she concludes that such a sale is better than keeping the car. We now consider a more general case than our previous example, the basis of Akerlof's 1970 paper, *The Market for Lemons*, in which the quality of a car is a continuous random variable. The equilibrium is much the same as in the previous example. The market collapses completely, with only the very poorest-quality car being traded.

We assume that new car quality, q, is uniformly distributed: $q \sim U[0, 2]$. We write the probability of a new car's quality, q, being less than some value, q_0, as:

$$\Pr(q < q_0) = F(q_0) = 0.5q_0 \qquad [28.3]$$

and the marginal probability, f:

$$f(q_0) = \frac{dF}{dq} = 0.5 \qquad [28.4]$$

Average car quality, $\mu = E[q] = 1$. We also assume that there are N potential sellers, each of whom wishes to sell one car only. The number of potential buyers is at least N, with each potential buyer seeking to purchase one unit.

To ensure that under conditions of perfect information, all cars are traded, we define sellers' valuations, V^S:

$$V^S = WTA(q) = 10,000q \qquad [28.5]$$

while buyers value quality according to the function, V^B:

$$V^B = WTP(q) = 15,000q \qquad [28.6]$$

We also change the structure of the sale process. Instead of sellers announcing their *WTA*, buyers announce their *WTP*, with sellers deciding whether or not to accept the potential buyers' bids.

> **By yourself**
>
> **X28.14** Assume that there is perfect information, or that q is observable. Show that when a buyer and a seller meet, *WTP* > *WTA*, and the transaction will proceed.
>
> **X28.15** Now assume that there is asymmetric information. Sellers know the value of q, while buyers only know the distribution of q.
>   (a) Confirm that buyers are risk-neutral.
>   (b) Explain why we should not expect buyers to offer to pay more than 15,000 for any car.
>   (c) Suppose that a potential seller owns a unit of the good for which $q > 1.5$. Explain why this seller will not be able to complete a sale.
>   (d) Suppose that all goods for which $q \leq 1.5$ are brought to the market. Show that *WTP* = 1,125, so that goods for which $q > 1.125$ remain unsold.

(e) Suppose that all goods for which $q \le q_0$ are brought to market. Show that $WTP = 0.75q_0$, so that goods for which $0.75q_0 < q \le q_0$ remain unsold.

(f) Show that the equilibrium condition for this market can be written, $WTP = E[q | q < q_0] = q_0$; and that this is satisfied when $q_0 = 0$.

Given the distribution of quality, we might expect there to be a viable market, as in Exercise X28.14. With buyers placing a higher value on every unit of the good than the seller, irrespective of the realization of the quality measure, q, all goods would be traded. In Exercise X28.15, with asymmetric information, whatever the proportion of sellers, q_0, who bring their goods to market believing that they will be able to sell them, a quarter of them will be disappointed. In Figure 28.4, we show that buyers, knowing the proportion of the population of cars, q_0, brought to market, will set their WTP, and hence their bids, $b = \frac{3}{4}q_0$. For potential sellers for whom $\frac{3}{4}q_0 < WTA < q_0$, the sale fails. As a result, the proportion of cars brought to the market is again reduced by a quarter to $q_1 = \frac{3}{4}q_0$. As a result, buyers' WTP also falls by 25%, and so, once again, does the proportion brought to market. We can work through multiple iterations of this process until the market collapses with $b = q^* = 0$. In effect, we conclude that for any price, $p > 0$, and so any quantity supplied, $q \le N$, $WTP(q) < WTA(q)$, and the market does not clear.

The result that with asymmetric information a market might collapse is probably interesting rather than instructive. As we shall see in Section 28.3, market participants can often take actions that reduce the effects of asymmetric information. There are, in fact, three assumptions causing the collapse of the market in this case: the uniform distribution of quality; the zero value placed on the lowest-quality good; and the ratio of the buyers' and the sellers' quality valuations. Adapting any of them would allow some of the good to be traded.

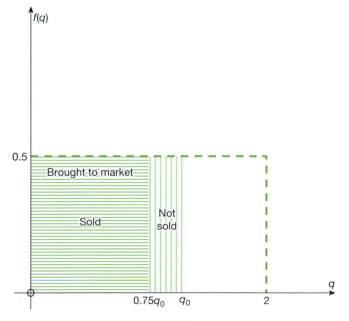

Figure 28.4 Goods brought to market and goods traded

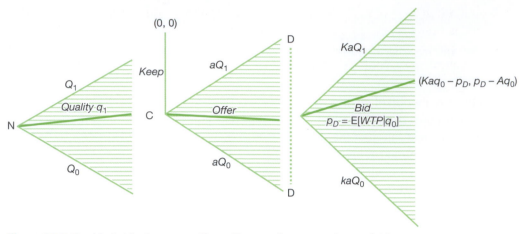

Figure 28.5 *The Market for Lemons*, with quality a continuous random variable

From Figure 28.5, we can see the operation of adverse selection in the case where the lowest possible value of quality, $Q_0 > 0$. Here, the value of the quality index, q, is a continuous random variable, and so is shown as a move of nature in which $Q_0 \leq q \leq Q_1$, taking the value $q = q_1$ in the diagram. Owning this unit of the good, Charles knows its quality with certainty. He now considers selling to a prospective purchaser, Denise. As before, Denise knows the distribution of quality across all cars, and she, in common with all other possible buyers, also knows that Charles always has the option of withdrawing the good from sale, if the price which she offers, p_D, is less than his *WTA*. For the exchange to be possible:

$$p_D \geq WTA(q_1) = aq_1 \qquad [28.7]$$

Believing that all goods of quality $q \leq q_0$ will be offered for sale, Denise will be willing to pay the expected value of her *WTP*, conditional on this fraction of cars being traded. For price, p_D:

$$p_D = E[WTP(q|q \leq q_0)] = KaE[q|q \leq q_0] \qquad [28.8]$$

Then, in equilibrium, for the marginal transaction, $WTA(q_0) = E[WTP(q|q \leq q_0)]$, so that the value of the best-quality traded good to the seller is just equal to its expected value to the buyer. Equating the values in Expressions 28.7 and 28.8:

$$KE[q|q \leq q_0] = q_0 \qquad [28.9]$$

By yourself

X28.16   Suppose that we defined the index of quality $q \sim [0, 1]$, with $WTA = 1{,}000(14 + 5q)$ and $WTP = 1{,}000(15 + 5q)$. By applying the equilibrium condition in Expression 28.9, explain the outcome in this market.

X28.17   Suppose that we define the index of quality $q \sim [0, 2]$, as in the Akerlof paper, but define $WTA = 1{,}000(a + q)$, and $WTP = 1{,}000(a + 1.5q)$. Confirm that the market will always collapse, irrespective of the value of a.

X28.18   Repeating X28.17, but with $WTP = 1{,}500(a + q)$.
(a) Show that if $a = 0$, then the market collapses.
(b) Show that if $0 \leq a \leq 1$, then $q* = 2a$.
(c) Show that if $a > 1$, then $q* = 2$, and the full market is served.

The equilibrium condition, Expression 28.9, is that the average value to a buyer of a car that is traded is the value to its seller of the car of highest quality, among those traded. Since the buyer cannot tell the quality of the car being purchased, for consistency with the principle of voluntary exchange, the buyer's expected value can never be less than the seller's valuation.

28.3 Signalling

In introducing the problems caused by asymmetric information, we suggested that people might try to indicate the quality of the goods that they are bringing to market by stating a high *WTP*. We concluded that this could not work because there is nothing to stop someone who is bringing low-quality goods to the market from simply imitating this behaviour. As a result, we have a situation in which the law of one price applies to sales of all observationally identical units of a good, whether or not these units are actually identical. We also saw that the market outcome is driven by beliefs about the proportion of low-quality goods (and therefore also of high-quality goods) being traded, which can turn out to be self-reinforcing. For the sellers of high-quality goods, it seems desirable to be able to affect the process whereby buyers update their beliefs, so that potential buyers of their goods will recognize these to be of high quality.

We now distinguish between the underlying characteristics of a unit of the good, and its attributes. In the examples used in Section 28.2, we have assumed that there is a single characteristic, quality. Neither buyer nor seller can alter the value of characteristics and we assume that only the seller can observe them. Attributes, though, are observable by both parties to the transaction, and can be manipulated by the seller. We shall assume that it is costly for the seller to undertake that manipulation, but also that the cost of manipulation is higher for sellers of low-quality goods than for sellers of high-quality goods.

> **Characteristics (2)** Underlying (unobservable) qualities of a good, which nevertheless determine its value.
>
> **Attributes** Observable signs, which can be manipulated by informed players and whose value is used by uninformed players to update priors.

Before presenting any formal examples, it should be possible to see that potential sellers, through manipulation of an attribute, might signal the value of the underlying characteristic. They do so on the basis that potential buyers believe that they might infer the true value of the characteristic from the observed value of the attribute; and that in equilibrium, these beliefs will be correct. The manipulation of an attribute differs from the simple announcement of *WTA* because of the variation in the cost of manipulation with the value of the characteristic. If effective, signalling will only be used by sellers of high-quality goods, who then obtain a higher price for the goods that they bring to market. Is it important that sellers of high-quality goods should obtain a (positive) net benefit from generating the signal, while sellers of low-quality goods would experience negative net benefits. Underlying this outcome is Bayesian learning, with potential buyers, upon observing the signal, revising their prior and seeing the good as being of high value.

> **Signal** Manipulation of an attribute to convey information about a characteristic.

By yourself

X28.19 Explain why the willingness of a seller to provide a warranty to the buyer of a car, such as undertaking to pay the costs of repair of any mechanical faults arising in the 12 months following the purchase, might be interpreted as a signal that the car being offered for sale is a peach.

28.3.1 The information structure of a game with signals

We illustrate the nature of a signalling game in Figure 28.6, which builds on the *Market for Lemons* example. Initially, a move of nature will determine the quality of the good, Q. We assume that there are only two possible values, $Q = 1$ and $Q = 0$, with the higher quality being achieved with probability, α. As before, quality is the underlying, unobservable characteristic. The producer of the good, A, must make a decision about whether to emit the signal, $S = 1$, consistent with the good being of high quality, or else the signal $S = 0$, consistent with low quality. The potential buyer, B, then observes the signal, and on the basis of the observation updates the prior, assigning probability β_i to the good being of high quality. If the signal conveys information, $\beta_1 > \alpha > \beta_0$, and the buyer revises the prior after observing the signal. The buyer then offers to pay a price p_1 or a price p_0. We will assume that the difference in prices should reflect beliefs about the quality of the good. In the cases that we have examined until now, there have been no effective signals, so that $p_1 = p_0$, and this has led either to the withdrawal of the high-quality goods, or to a price lower than the seller would achieve with full information. The payoffs to the seller depend upon the price achieved, the cost of producing the good, and the cost of emitting the signal, with both costs dependent on the value of the quality characteristic, Q. The payoff to the buyer is simply the difference between the value in consumption and the price paid.

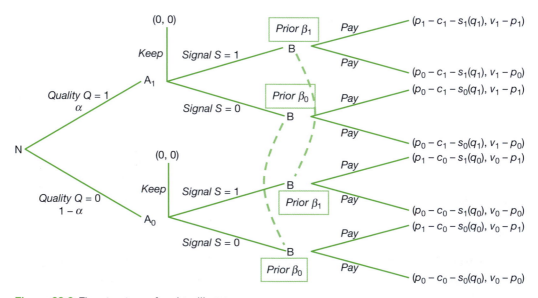

Figure 28.6 The structure of a signalling game

Without solving the game in Figure 28.6, we can explore the implications of this structure. We simplify the analysis by assuming that the signal, S, allows *perfect* separation. If $Q = 1$, then the signal will definitely be emitted (at node A_1) and if $Q = 0$, then the signal will definitely not be emitted. In addition, for equilibrium (strictly, for **perfect Bayesian equilibrium**), player B's beliefs should be consistent with this behaviour, so that the priors $\beta_1 = 1$ and $\beta_0 = 0$. Player B, observing the signal, forms a certain belief that the game has reached the higher node consistent with nature having chosen $Q = 1$, so that the value of the good in consumption is v_1. Failing to observe the signal, player B forms a certain belief that the game has reached the lower node, so that $Q = 0$, and the value in consumption is v_0. We therefore expect player B to offer the higher price, p_1, on observing the signal and the lower price, p_0, otherwise. The perfect Bayesian equilibrium of the game can therefore be written in terms of the players' strategies, and the updating of player B's beliefs after observing the value of the signal: $[\sigma_A, \sigma_B, \beta] = [(1, 0), (p_1, p_0), (1, 0)]$.

> **Separation** The outcome of a game in which a signal allows correct identification of types.
>
> **Perfect Bayesian equilibrium** Equilibrium of an extensive game with incomplete information, in which all players' revisions of priors and strategies are consistent.

By yourself

X28.20 For this outcome to be a perfect Bayesian equilibrium, it must satisfy certain conditions. Derive expressions for which each would be satisfied.

(a) Player A, given $Q = 1$, obtains a higher payoff from choosing signal $S = 1$, and receiving payment p_1, than from signal $S = 0$, and receiving payment p_0.

(b) Player A, given $Q = 0$, obtains a higher payoff from choosing signal $S = 0$, and receiving payment p_0, than from signal $S = 1$, and receiving payment p_1.

(c) Player B, observing $S = 1$, will offer p_1; and observing $S = 0$, will offer p_0. [*Note:* Remember that this action has to be consistent with player A choosing $S = 1$ in order to lead player B into believing $Q = 0$.]

(d) Both players must be better off from taking part in the game than from not taking part. In particular, player A should not decide to keep the goods.

When we introduced the concept of sub-game perfection in Chapter 19, we argued that it had the advantage that all players would make their decisions based on the previous history of the game, while anticipating that all future decisions would be made so that the players making them would maximize their payoffs. In the game illustrated in Figure 28.6, we cannot use the sub-game perfect concept because player B cannot be certain of the point that the game has reached when called on to make a decision. We therefore rely on the equilibrium beliefs being consistent with player A's strategy, as well as supporting (expected) payoff-maximizing behaviour for player B. We will not define the concept rigorously here, but the requirement of consistency between revision of beliefs through Bayesian learning and players' strategies is the basis of *perfect Bayesian equilibrium*.

28.3.2 Job market signalling

Our last example applies the signalling model in a very simple context. We assume that:

- There are two types of worker, for whom nature selects $Q = 1$ or $Q = 2$.
  - The proportion of type 2 workers in the population is f.

- In employment, the value of the marginal product of worker, w, $VMP_w = Q_w$.
  - There is perfect competition in both product and labour markets.
  - With perfect information, employers would pay workers wage $m_w = VMP_w$.
  - Workers obtain no utility (or disutility) from working.
- Potential employers cannot observe the type Q; but they can observe the level of education obtained by a worker, e.
  - For $Q = 1$, the marginal cost of education, $c_1 = 2$, irrespective of the total level of education.
  - For $Q = 2$, the marginal cost of education, $c_2 = 0.5$.
- It is common knowledge that employers believe, with certainty, that any worker with education, $e_w \geq e^*$, is of type $Q = 2$; and that any worker with education, $e_w < e^*$, is of type $Q = 1$.

If we are to accept the reasoning behind this model, there is a sense in which education is a sham. We put aside explanations based on the formation of human capital. Instead, people have innate ability, leading to variation in workplace productivity: in this model, education, e, is simply considered (by employers) to enable those with high ability to signal the high value of the unobservable characteristic, Q. It is not an investment on which returns are obtained, but simply the cost of an activity undertaken to reduce the effect of the externality caused by the presence of low-productivity workers.

We illustrate the structure of the model in Figure 28.7. As in the discussion of the general model, the game begins with a move of nature, which determines the worker's type, Q. The worker then has a decision to make, which is to invest in a level of education, e, or else to quit this labour market. Given employers' belief that a sufficiently high education level is a signal of higher productivity, if there is to be an equilibrium, then in equilibrium the level of education, e_2, chosen by workers of type $Q = 2$ should be sufficiently high that workers of type $Q = 1$ will prefer to obtain education, e_1, although this allows employers to identify their type. It follows that $e_2 \geq e^* > e_1$.

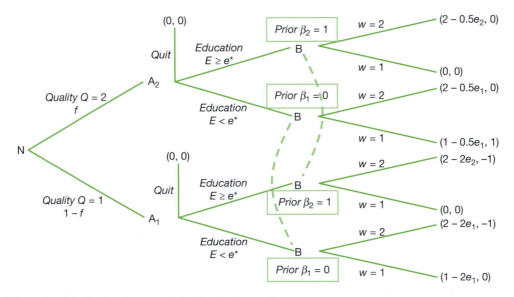

Figure 28.7 A simple labour market signalling example

By yourself

X28.21 Confirm that there is a perfect Bayesian equilibrium of this game, $[\sigma_A, \sigma_B, \beta] = [(0, 0.5),$ $(1, 2), (0, 1)]$. Confirm that here $e_2 = e^*$, so that workers of type Q_1 maximize their payoff (with education $e_1 = 0$); just preferring this to obtaining education, $e^* = 0.5$.

X28.22 Explain why we expect any firm that sets wage $w = 1$ for workers who emit $E = e_2 \geq e^*$ to be unable to hire any. What would we conclude about the labour force of such a firm?

X28.23 Explain why we would not expect any firm that offers a wage $w = 2$ to *all* workers to be able to trade.

X28.24 Find conditions that must be satisfied (i) for workers of type $Q = 2$ to choose education $E = e^*$; and (ii) for workers of type $Q = 1$ to choose education $E = 0$.

X28.25 Suppose that $f > 0.75$. Demonstrate that workers of type $Q = 2$ will then prefer to set $e = 0$, so that there is a pooling equilibrium, in which all workers obtain the same wage, $w_{ave} = 1 + f$, rather than investing in education to obtain the wage $w_2 = 2$.

X28.26 Confirm that whether there is a pooling or a separating equilibrium, workers of quality $Q = 1$ obtain the same payoff as they would under conditions of perfect information.

Observing any value for e, an employer updates the prior β: $\beta = \begin{cases} 1, \text{ if } E \geq e^* \\ 0, \text{ otherwise} \end{cases}$. The simple binary rule means that employers, observing the signal being given, are certain about the worker's productivity. Given that education is costly, both types of worker will want to minimize the quantity that they obtain. It then follows in this case that by setting $e^* = e_2 = 0.5$, employers do just enough to discourage low-productivity workers from attempting to signal that they are actually of high productivity. Rather than attempting to mislead employers, they are better off choosing education, $e_1 = 0$, and being treated as being of low productivity. Such signalling is costly for the higher-productivity workers of type $Q = 2$; Exercise X28.25 demonstrates that in this situation, if the proportion of low-productivity workers of type $Q = 1$ is low enough, higher-productivity workers will prefer to accept the reduced wage in a pooling equilibrium rather than to invest in the education needed to support the separating outcome. We note, though, in Exercise X25.26, that low-productivity workers are no worse off than they would be in a situation with perfect information. *Signalling*, in this case, is a response to the externality imposed on workers of high productivity by the presence of low-productivity workers. It does not overcome the problem of asymmetric information, but by allowing high-productivity workers to reveal their type, it can reduce the associated externality.

28.4 Conclusions

In simple strategic games, such as the Prisoners' Dilemma or *Stag Hunt*, we recognized that players would find it difficult to achieve the Pareto-optimal outcome, but that these difficulties might be resolved through commitment devices, or by the players trusting one another enough. In this chapter, we began by introducing strategic games in which one player did not know the other player's type. We argued that in such circumstances the uninformed player has to form a probability distribution over the games which might be played in different states of the world, and so to decide upon equilibrium behaviour given beliefs about the state of the world. The remainder of the chapter is largely concerned with the fact that we have set out a situation in which information is asymmetric. We are interested in situations in which all information is known, but in which only one of the two players is fully informed. It is evident that fully informed players will often have an interest in finding ways to communicate what they know: in the case of the *Market for Lemons*, almost every potential buyer and seller could be better off.

The problem facing the informed players is that to the uninformed players they are all perfectly indistinguishable. Simply announcing potentially valuable information is therefore not credible because claims can easily be mimicked. The *Market for Lemons* is an extreme example in which there is complete market collapse, but in general we may conclude that the presence of goods that are of low quality exerts a negative externality on suppliers of high-quality goods. This takes the form of reducing either the volume of high-quality goods that are traded, or else the price that their sellers can obtain.

As with discussion of externalities in Chapter 22, we have a problem in which there is effectively a good for which there is no market. In the earlier chapter, we concentrated on how it might be possible to create markets for these untraded goods. That solution, in many ways the most straightforward one, does not work here, because it is not possible to create a market for the unobservable characteristic, which is the source of the externality. Instead, we have suggested that people who are fully informed, and who want to communicate information, might engage in costly activities, or signals, that cannot easily be mimicked by other fully informed people. In the market for used cars, for example, this might take the form of a warranty, with the seller agreeing to accept liability for future repairs. In labour markets, we have suggested that education might be a signal of underlying productivity. In both cases, the signal gains credibility because a seller of a low-quality good would find it relatively costly to mimic the signal. In effect, in the absence of separate markets for goods of different qualities, signalling allows the creation of markets in which goods are traded according to whether or not they are certified as being of high quality. Unable to create a market for the underlying quality, effectively we separate out the markets for the certified and the uncertified goods.

Summary

In a strategic game of incomplete information, at least one player is not fully informed about the state of nature, and we apply our analysis of risk to that player's strategic interactions with the other players in the game.

The appropriate equilibrium concept is then the Bayes-Nash equilibrium, in which players seek to maximize their expected payoff, conditional on the information that they possess about the state of nature.

We have examined the Bayes–Nash equilibrium of games in which fully informed sellers are unable to communicate credibly the quality of the goods that they bring to market. With these goods appearing indistinguishable to potential

buyers, we have considered examples in which markets collapse completely. We have argued that, in general, we should expect the presence of low-quality goods to reduce the market price or the quantity traded.

In more complex games, we permit the communication of information. Potential buyers know that the cost of generating a signal is greater for a seller of low-quality goods than for a seller of high-quality goods. On observing both a positive and a zero value for a signal, potential buyers update their prior, which is their estimated probability of the good being of high quality, increasing it when the signal has a positive value, and reducing it when it has zero value.

Buyers' *WTP* therefore increases on observing a positive value of the signal, and falls on observing a zero value. If the difference in *WTP* is greater than the cost of signalling for a high-quality seller, but less than the cost for a low-quality seller, then separation occurs, with only high-quality sellers signalling, and buyers treating signals as certain indicators of high quality.

The appropriate equilibrium concept is now the perfect Bayesian equilibrium: in this, when players are called upon to make a decision, their actions maximize the expected payoff in the remaining part of the game, conditional on their beliefs, which incorporate all of the information available to them.

Visit the companion website at **www.palgrave.com/mochrie** to access further teaching and learning materials, including lecturer slides and a testbank, as well as guideline answers and student MCQs.

29

Product differentiation

Firms seek opportunities to make economic profits, and we tend to associate these with the ability to exert market power. In this chapter, we concentrate on two possible forms of *product differentiation*. We assume that product differentiation is real, in the sense that when competing firms bring their products to market, potential buyers are able to discern differences between them, and so will not consider products to be perfect substitutes. We will also generally assume that it is possible for potential buyers of the good to rank alternatives, considering both situations of *horizontal differentiation*, in which purchasers' rankings differ, and situations of *vertical differentiation*, in which purchasers' rankings are identical, so that it is reasonable to talk of there being quality differences across products.

In both cases, we think of product differentiation as being based upon a characteristic of a good, which we will often call its *location*. We shall typically assume that this characteristic is observable, so that our models are extensive games of perfect information, played between businesses: their potential customers are passive, non-strategic actors. In our models, businesses will have up to three decisions to make: (1) whether or not to enter the market; (2) their location (or the value of the characteristic); and (3) their price. Given this structure, we apply the process of backwards induction to obtain the sub-game perfect equilibrium. In analysing the equilibria of these games, we consider in particular the extent of product differentiation, and its implications for pricing and entry. We conclude that, typically, the ability of businesses to make profits depends upon the degree of non-price competition; but we also note that it is possible for economic profits to be eliminated in situations in which the number of businesses entering a market is more than would be socially optimal.

29.1   The linear city

Although game theory was first formally defined in the 1940s by mathematicians, even before then, some economists had anticipated these advances. Harold Hotelling's paper, *Stability in Competition*, of 1929, which seeks to build upon the insights of Cournot (competition in quantities) and Bertrand (competition in prices), is one of the best-known examples. Hotelling begins by noting that even where strategic interactions are important, it is implausible to suggest that there will be wholesale switching among groups. Going back to our examples from Chapter 1, we can often find limited variation in the prices set by petrol stations, of perhaps 1–2% around the average. We have explained the persistence of such differences on the basis that changing supplier is not a costless process, suggesting that the costs of travelling between petrol stations will often be enough to persuade people to return regularly to the same supplier. Customer loyalty is the result of different transport costs.

Hotelling's model simplifies the structure of a city to a single roadway, which is of unit length. As shown in Figure 29.1, we assume that there are two firms in the market, *A* and *B*, who choose their positions. The map is orientated in the conventional manner. The distance

Figure 29.1 Distribution of firms in the linear city

to the western edge of the town for firm A is a and the distance to the eastern edge for B is b. We assign every house on the road a location, x: $x \sim U[0, 1]$. That is, the density of housing in the city is entirely uniform, as might be found in a model town of the sort laid out in the 18th century at the start of the Industrial Revolution. We assume that the firms sell perfect substitutes, at the same price, so that they can only differentiate themselves on the basis of the transport costs to their premises, which we treat as quadratic. For location x:

$$C_A(x) = (x - a)^2; \text{ and } C_B(x) = (1 - b - x)^2 \qquad [29.1]$$

With costs increasing in the distance travelled, people will always choose the firm that lies closer to their house. We define the *marginal consumer*, located at x^*, as being indifferent between the two firms, so that $C_A(x^*) = C_B(x^*)$. Then:

$$(x^* - a)^2 = (1 - b - x^*)^2 \qquad [29.2]$$

Solving Expression 29.2, we obtain:

$$x^* = \tfrac{1}{2}(1 - b + a) \qquad [29.3]$$

Perhaps unsurprisingly, this location lies exactly halfway between a and b.

29.1.1 Minimum differentiation

We now treat the situation as a strategic game, with firms A and B selecting their locations at the same time. We assume that they are interested in maximizing market share and that there is no cost to choosing any location (or no differences in costs associated with choice of location). The firms obtain market shares:

$$f_A(a, b) = \begin{cases} \tfrac{1}{2}(1 - b + a), \text{ if } a \leq 1 - b \\ \tfrac{1}{2}(1 - a + b), \text{ if } b < 1 - a < a + b \leq 2 \end{cases}; \text{ and } f_B(a, b) = 1 - f_A(a, b) \quad [29.4]$$

From Expression 29.4, firm A obtains the market segment to the west of x^* when $a < 1 - b$, so that A is located to the west of B, the market segment to the east of x^* when A is east of B, and half of the market when both firms choose the same location.

> **By yourself**
>
> **X29.1**   Confirm that if $y = x(1 - x)$, then y is maximized when $x = 0.5$. Hence demonstrate that if $a(1 - a) > b(1 - b)$, firm A has greater market share.
>
> **X29.2**   Given that firm A believes that firm B will choose location b^e, where should firm A locate? How would you expect firm B to respond? Show that $(a^e, b^e) = (\tfrac{1}{2}, \tfrac{1}{2})$ is the only set of consistent conjectures, and the only possible Nash equilibrium in pure strategies.

The conclusion of Exercise X29.2 is very straightforward. Whatever location one firm chooses, its competitor cannot do better than choose a location as close to it as possible, but slightly nearer the centre of the town. The only way to ensure stability is for both firms to choose the same location, at the centre, so that both obtain equal market share. Any deviation would then involve loss of market share. We obtain an outcome in which there is minimum differentiation between products.

By yourself

X29.3   This model has frequently been related to competition between political parties in an election. Suppose that there are two political parties, K and L, and that it is possible to locate their electoral platforms, k and l, on a line between 0 (the most left-wing position) and 1 (the most right-wing position). We assume that voters' preferred positions, $x \sim U[0, 1]$, and that they will vote for the party closer to their position.

(a) Confirm that if $a = 0.5$, then the best reply $b*(0.5) = 0.5$; and that if $a \neq 0.5$, then $b*(a)$: $a < b* < 1 - a*$.

(b) Sketch a diagram showing these best replies.

(c) Confirm that $(a, b) = (0.5, 0.5)$ is the only Nash equilibrium in pure strategies.

Median voter theorem The claim that the manifestos of political parties are very similar on the basis that to win power each party requires the support of the median voter.

Median voter A person at the centre point of a one-dimensional distribution of political beliefs.

Again, we see the principle of minimum differentiation, often formulated here in terms of a **median voter theorem**. In order to win an election, a candidate needs to win a majority of votes. Typically, a majority of one is sufficient. This will happen whenever that candidate's position is closer to that of the **median voter** than the other candidate's. In order to avoid losing, both candidates choose the position at the median of the distribution of voters, and the election is tied (so that they share power).

The median voter interpretation naturally extends itself to a more general economic interpretation in terms of horizontal differentiation. We already know that firms can make supernormal profits when they have market power, and have argued that one form of market power is product differentiation. We now make two distinctions:

- In *non-address* models, products are different, but there is no scale on which differences can be measured: a preference for wearing black, rather than brown, blue or red shoes might fall into this category.
- In *address* models, there is some observable, measurable characteristic of a good.
  - Within address models, *vertical differentiation* occurs when all consumers agree on the ranking of the products. For example, were two mobile phones identical in every characteristic except their speed of connection to the internet, we would expect all consumers to prefer the faster one.
  - Horizontal differentiation emerges when consumers' rankings of products (by the value of the characteristic) differ. Building on the median voter example, we might rank newspapers according to their position on the political spectrum, from liberal to conservative. We might reasonably expect people to prefer to read newspapers whose stance is broadly consistent with their own political beliefs.

Horizontal differentiation Spatial differentiation such that consumers' preferences over characteristics differ.

Spatial differentiation The distribution of goods' characteristics that can be measured.

Given these distinctions, Hotelling's model allows us to explore horizontal differentiation within the framework of an address model. The prediction of our introductory analysis, that with two firms in the market there will be minimum differentiation, may seem counter-intuitive. We have to remember that we have allowed businesses to choose location freely, but without competing in price. Given that it is generally much easier for firms to alter prices than location, we should also analyse competition in prices, with firms having fixed locations. We might interpret this either as the short run, or else as the last stage in an extensive game.

29.1.2 Competition in prices

We begin by assuming that $a = b = \frac{1}{4}$, but that the firms compete by setting prices p_A and p_B. Apart from their location, products are identical, so that all consumers obtain value v from consumption. For a consumer at location x, the costs of the products are:

$$C_A(x) = p_A + (x - \tfrac{1}{4})^2; \text{ and } C_B(x) = p_B + (\tfrac{3}{4} - x)^2 \qquad [29.5]$$

We shall also assume that the firms set their prices, p_A and p_B, subject to the restriction:

$$p_A, p_B < v - \tfrac{1}{16} \qquad [29.6]$$

So long as Expression 29.6 is satisfied, all consumers obtain some surplus from buying the good, and so we say that the market is covered. Our last assumption is that firms have no costs of production. An alternative would be to define prices net of constant marginal costs, noting that in the short run fixed costs do not affect decisions about the production level, and that exit is not possible.

> **Market coverage**
> Firms' strategies ensure that all consumers are in the market, with no unmet demand.

Given any pair of prices, (p_A, p_B), we define the marginal consumer, who is indifferent between products A and B, by the location, x^*, for which:

$$p_A - p_B = (x^* - \tfrac{3}{4})^2 - (x^* - \tfrac{1}{4})^2 \qquad [29.7]$$

By yourself

X29.4 Confirm that on simplifying Expression 29.7, we obtain:

$$x^* = \tfrac{1}{2} - (p_A - p_B) \qquad [29.8]$$

Expression 29.8 seems intuitively reasonable. When $p_A = p_B$, $x^* = \frac{1}{2}$, the firms share the market equally; but were $p_A > p_B$, then firm A would have lower market share.

By yourself

X29.5 Given our assumptions, firm A's objective is to maximize revenues.
  (a) Show that its revenue, $R_A(p_A; p_B) = p_A[\tfrac{1}{2} - (p_A - p_B)]$.
  (b) Both firms set their price at the same time. Denote firm A's belief about the price that firm B will set as p_B^e. Confirm that firm A's best-reply function, $p_A^*(p_B^e) = \frac{1}{2}(p_B^e + \frac{1}{2})$.
  (c) Show that firm B's best reply may be written: $p_B^*(p_A^e) = \frac{1}{2}(p_A^e + \frac{1}{2})$.
  (d) Confirm that there is a Nash equilibrium, $(p_A^*, p_B^*) = (\frac{1}{2}, \frac{1}{2})$; so that the firms achieve revenues $R_A(p_A^*, p_B^*) = R_B(p_A^*, p_B^*) = \frac{1}{4}$, and that the market will be covered if $v > \frac{9}{16}$.

The (quadratic) travel cost function is convex, so that the marginal cost of travel is increasing. It is easy to justify the non-linear form by arguing that we are considering differences in tastes. Consumers do not consider small deviations from their ideal specification of the good to be particularly costly, but feel that the loss of having to compromise on specification increases more quickly than the scale of the compromise. We also note that in choosing the locations $(a, b) = (\frac{1}{4}, \frac{3}{4})$, or being directed there by a social planner, the firms in this case minimize the average distance that consumers will travel, and so the total travel costs. However, this is not enough for the outcome to be considered socially optimal.

By yourself

X29.6   Suppose that a social planner insists upon minimum differentiation, so that $a = b = 0.5$.

(a) Confirm that if $v - \frac{1}{4} > p_A > 0$, firm B can obtain the whole market by setting a price $p_B : p_A > p_B > 0$, but that if $p_A = p_B$, then the firms share the market entirely.

(b) Hence confirm that the only Nash equilibrium in prices is $(p_A^*, p_B^*) = 0$.

X29.7   Suppose that the firms have chosen to engage in maximum differentiation, so that they select the locations at the end points of the line segment: $a = b = 0$.

(a) Confirm that if the firms set prices p_A and p_B, then the location of the marginal consumer will be $x^* = \frac{1}{2}[1 + p_B - p_A]$.

(b) By obtaining the revenues of each firm, show that their best-reply functions may be written in implicit form as:

$$p_A^*(p_B^e) : 2p_A^* - p_B^e - 1 = 0; \text{ and}$$
$$p_B^*(p_A^e) : 2p_B^* - p_A^e - 1 = 0;$$

where p_B^e is firm A's conjecture of price, p_B, and p_A^e is firm B's conjecture of price p_A.

(c) Show in the Nash equilibrium (where there are consistent conjectures), $(p_A^*, p_B^*) = (1, 1)$.

(d) Confirm that for the market to be covered, $v > \frac{5}{4}$.

Unsurprisingly, with the two firms choosing the same location, so that there is minimum differentiation, they will share the market equally, setting price to marginal cost. We therefore eliminate supernormal profits, but increase the average travel cost, and this may be preferable for society. In contrast, when the firms are able to maximize product differentiation, they are able to set higher prices than with minimum differentiation. The average travel cost is just the same as with minimum differentiation, although individual consumers face different travel costs. With firms charging a higher price, and average travel costs unchanged, maximum differentiation appears to be a worse outcome for consumers than minimum differentiation. Intuitively, it seems reasonable that firms competing in prices should want to increase product differentiation and hence their market power. We confirm this by developing an extensive game in which firms choose first their location and then their prices.

29.1.3   Choice of location and prices

The nature of competition in our model does not change. There are only two firms in the market, A and B. The market remains a line segment of unit length. Travel costs also remain as before, and we assume that the value in consumption, $v = \frac{5}{4}$, which turns out to be sufficient to ensure that the market is covered, irrespective of the locations that the firms choose. In the two-stage game, shown in Figure 29.2, firms observe their competitors' choice (of location) before choosing their price. It is only in the choice of prices in the second state that there is any strategic interaction between the firms, as shown in the diagram by the best-reply lines, $p_B^*(p_A^e)$ and $p_A^*(p_B^e)$. In the first stage of the game, firms choose their own location, taking into account the effect that their choice will have on their profits in the second stage.

We shall see that varying location in the first stage of the game leads to parallel shifts in the best-reply lines in the second, and this affects both the equilibrium price and firms' profitability. Without further analysis, by examining Figure 29.2 you should be able to convince yourself that by altering their location, the firms can shift the best-reply curves

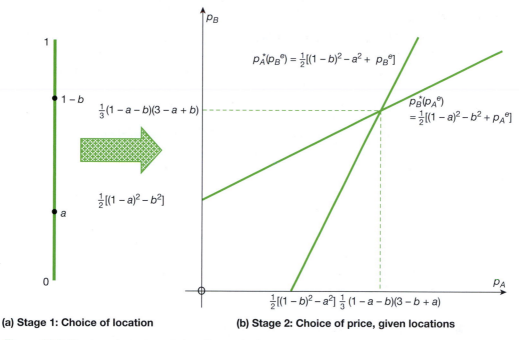

Figure 29.2 The two-stage game in location and prices

away from the origin, and so increase the equilibrium prices. We interpret such shifts as a reduction in competition, which will lead to increased profits. To confirm these intuitions, we formally introduce the two-stage game.

- *Stage 1*: Firms A and B choose locations a (from the bottom) and b (from the top) of the line segment. We assume that $a + b \leq 1$, or that $a \leq 1 - b$.
- *Stage 2*: A and B choose prices p_A and p_b, which are best replies to their conjectures about the other firm's price, given chosen locations, a and b. Equilibrium occurs when conjectures are consistent.

To obtain the sub-game perfect equilibrium, we first analyse *Stage 2*, obtaining the location of the marginal consumer, which is enough for us to find each firm's market share (assuming that the market is covered), and then the reaction functions and the Nash equilibrium prices, conditional on the firms' locations. We then demonstrate that these prices (and the firms' revenues) will be higher the greater the distance between locations a and b, which the firms choose in *Stage 1*.

Step 1: Market shares

We define the costs, C_A and C_B, facing the marginal consumer, located at x^* as:

Total cost equals price + travel cost

$$C_A(x^*) = p_A + (x^* - a)^2 = C_B(x^*) = p_B + (1 - b - x^*)^2 \qquad [29.9]$$

Equating the expressions for costs:

Multiply out expressions in brackets; treating $1 - b$ as single term

$$p_A + (x^*)^2 - 2ax^* + a^2 = p_B + (1 - b)^2 - 2(1 - b)x^* + (x^*)^2$$

On rearranging:

$$p_B - p_A = a^2 - (1 - b)^2 + 2(1 - a - b)x^* \qquad [29.10]$$

We can rewrite Expression 29.10 with x^* defined explicitly in terms of the prices and the locations:

$$x^* = \frac{1}{2(1 - a - b)}\left[p_B - p_A + (1 - b)^2 - a^2\right] \qquad [29.11]$$

We know that the market share of firm A will be x^*, while the market share of firm B will be $1 - x^*$. In *Stage 2*, with locations chosen, firms can only affect market shares (and so their revenues and profits) by choosing prices, p_A and p_B.

Step 2: Reaction functions

Concentrating on the decisions made by firm A, we write its conjecture of firm B's price, p_B^e, and its conjectured revenue $R_A^e = x[p_A^*(p_B^e)] \cdot p_A^*(p_B^e)$:

Expected revenue is the product of price and expected market share

Substitute in [29.11], with expected price, p_B^e

$$R_A^e(p_A, p_B^e, a, b) = \frac{p_A}{2(1 - a - b)}\left[p_B^e - p_A + (1 - b)^2 - a^2\right] \qquad [29.12]$$

R_A is quadratic in p_A

Taking the partial derivative with respect to p_A:

$$\frac{\partial R_A}{\partial p_A} = \frac{p_B^e - 2p_A + (1 - b)^2 - a^2}{2(1 - a - b)} \qquad [29.13]$$

Multiply through terms in square brackets by p_A **or** use the product rule

Setting this partial derivative to zero, we define the best reply, $p_A^*(p_B^e)$:

Set the numerator of [29.13] to zero

$$2p_A^*(p_B^e) - p_B^e = (1 - b)^2 - a^2 \qquad [29.14]$$

Add $2p_A^* - p_B^e$ to both sides

By yourself

X29.8   Given firm B's conjectured revenue, $R_B^e(p_B) = \{1 - x[p_B^*(p_A^e)]\} \cdot p_B^*(p_A^e)$, show that firm B's best reply, p_B^* satisfies the condition:

$$2p_B^*(p_A^e) - p_A^e = (1 - a)^2 - b^2 \qquad [29.15]$$

We have shown the best-reply curves defined in Expressions 29.14 and 29.15 in Figure 29.2. We note that these curves are upward-sloping lines, indicating that the products are *strategic complements*. Both firms' best replies increase in the price that they expect their competitor to set.

Step 3: Equilibrium prices

Having obtained the best-reply functions, we find the Nash equilibrium of the *Stage 2* subgame. Requiring consistent best replies, we can rewrite the best replies in Expressions 29.14 and 29.15 as:

Need: $(1 - b)^2 = 1 - 2b + b^2$

$$2p_A^* - p_B^* = (1 - b)^2 - a^2 \qquad [29.16a]$$

Multiply [29.15] by 2 $$4p_B^* - 2p_A^* = 2(1 - a)^2 - 2b^2 \qquad [29.16b]$$

... and $2(1 - a)^2 = 2 - 4a + 2a^2$

Adding these two expressions together:

Use $a^2 - b^2 = (a - b)(a + b)$

$$3p_B^* = 3 - 4a + a^2 - 2b - b^2 \qquad\qquad [29.17]$$

Write $3 - 4a - 2b =$
$3(1 - a - b) - (a - b)$

Then gather together
terms in $(a - b)$ to obtain

$$p_B^* = \tfrac{1}{3}(3 - a + b)(1 - a - b) \qquad\qquad [29.18]$$

By yourself

X29.9 Demonstrate that in equilibrium, firm A sets price, p_A^*:

$$p_A^* = \tfrac{1}{3}(3 - b + a)(1 - a - b) \qquad\qquad [29.19]$$

X29.10 Given the Nash equilibrium prices, (p_A^*, p_B^*) in *Stage 2* of the game, confirm that the marginal consumer is located at position $x^* = \tfrac{1}{6}(3 - b + a)$.

X29.11 Substituting from Expressions 29.11, 29.18 and 29.19:
   (a) Confirm that firm A's revenue in equilibrium, R_A^*, can be written as:

$$R_A^*(a, b) = \tfrac{1}{18}(1 - b - a)(3 - b + a)^2 \qquad\qquad [29.20]$$

   (b) By partially differentiating Expression 29.20 with respect to location, a, confirm that:

$$\tfrac{\partial R_A^*}{\partial a} = -\tfrac{1}{18}(3 - b + a)(1 - b + 3a) < 0 \qquad\qquad [29.21]$$

Step 4: Equilibrium locations

In Exercise X29.11, we consider the effect of the choice of location in *Stage 1* on firm A's revenues, anticipating expected revenues in *Stage 2*. This ensures that our solution is sub-game perfect. We assume that firm A's choice of location, a, is independent of firm B's choice, b. Firm A chooses location a^*, in order to maximize its revenue, without needing to form a conjecture, b^e.

To determine the optimal location, a^*, we partially differentiate revenue, R_A^* with respect to location, a. Note from Expression 29.21 that the usual first-order condition, $\tfrac{\partial R_A}{\partial a} = 0$, cannot be satisfied. The partial derivative is certainly less than zero, meaning that the firm's revenue is a decreasing function of its location, or, more strictly, its distance from the edge of the interval. It is easy to check both that firm A's revenue is decreasing in b, and that firm B's revenues, R_B^*, decrease in both a and b. Both firms' profits increase in the degree of product differentiation, and since the first-order condition for profit maximization is never satisfied, we predict maximum product differentiation, with the sub-game perfect equilibrium $(a^*, b^*, p_A^*, p_B^*) = (0, 0, 1, 1)$.

To understand the effect of the location choice in *Stage 1* on the outcome in *Stage 2*, shown in Figure 29.3, we begin from minimum differentiation, with $a = b = \tfrac{1}{2}$. In *Stage 2*, this gives rise to the lighter green reaction lines, both of which pass through the origin, so that the profit-maximizing prices $(p_A^*, p_B^*) = 0$. With minimum differentiation, the firm's make zero profits.

If we allow firms to change their location, moving towards the end points, the reaction curves in the right-hand panel move out from the origin. In the limit, with maximum product differentiation, the reaction curves are the dark green lines, with profit-maximizing prices $(p_A^*, p_B^*) = (1, 1)$. Increasing product differentiation reduces the intensity of competition between firms, increasing their market power, and so their profits. Both firms benefit when locations are further apart.

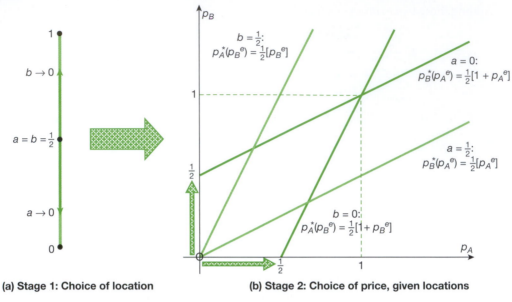

(a) Stage 1: Choice of location   **(b) Stage 2: Choice of price, given locations**

Figure 29.3 The effect of changes in location

We should not think of horizontal differentiation as relating simply to physical distance. Instead, with this model people differ in their ideal specification of a good, defined in this case by a single characteristic, such as the sweetness of an apple, the length of time for which a cheese has been matured, or the policy position of political parties. In our simple model of political processes, we assumed that political parties are only concerned with winning the election, and so have no strong policy position. If instead we were to assume that parties need to raise campaign finance to communicate their policy position, then some degree of product differentiation would become necessary. If, in addition, parties are seen as being further from the centre than their opponents, then they will lose. In these circumstances, maximum product differentiation cannot be the solution, and we might expect to see parties appealing to more extreme positions in non-election years to raise funding, and then to the median voter when campaigning in elections.

29.2   The circular city

In the previous examples, we have only considered duopolies, with two firms competing for market share. It is difficult to add additional firms to a model in which the market is represented by a line segment, because of the effects of end points. Suppose that we add a third firm, *C*, to the introductory model set out in Expressions 29.1 and 29.2. It is then impossible to find a set of consistent conjectures in which the each firm maximizes its market share given beliefs about the other firms' choices, which turn out to be correct. In fact, with more than two firms, it is impossible to find a Nash equilibrium in pure strategies. (If you doubt this, try experimenting with situations in which two firms have chosen their locations, then locate a third firm so that it maximizes its market share; and then review the decisions of the first two firms. Can you find locations at which none of the three players will seek to change position?)

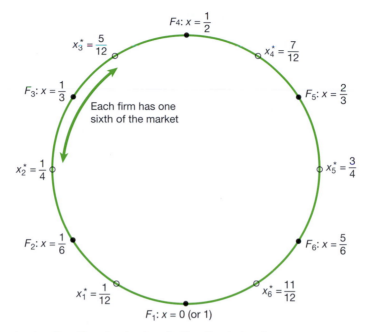

Figure 29.4 The circular city, with entrants choosing location to break even

A firm located at an end point of a line can only attract consumers from one direction, whereas other firms will face marginal consumers in both directions. With more than two firms in the market, it will often be useful to know what the optimal number of firms might be: in the following analysis, firms enter the market until all profits are eliminated. The market is still one-dimensional, with consumers able to move in either of two directions, so there is still horizontal differentiation, with consumers having some preferred location, x. This is only possible if we replace the line segment with a closed loop, usually taken to be a circle. As shown in Figure 29.4, firms choose locations around the circle such that each serves the market segment in which, because of transport costs, consumers prefer their firm's product to that of their competitors.

In studying the entry decision, we only consider symmetric outcomes, as in the diagram. We model the market as a circle of unit circumference. With six firms in the market, we index their locations, x, from 0 to 1, beginning with firm F_1, whose location $x_1 = 0$ (or 1). We then define all other locations by their distance clockwise around the circle. In a symmetric outcome, firms choose evenly spaced locations around the circle. They all set the same price, p^*, which is low enough that, allowing for transport costs, the market is covered. The marginal consumer between any pair of firms will then be located in the midpoint of the segment of the circle connecting them. Unsurprisingly, each firm obtains $\frac{1}{6}$ of the total market.

This development of Hotelling's model was first proposed by Salop in an article published in 1979. It simplifies the problem of spatial competition very nicely, but at the cost of giving up some realism in the assumptions. It is perhaps easiest to imagine a city as being bounded by a major road, so that travel around the city has much lower costs than travel across it. Businesses that rely on customers being able to reach them easily, such as supermarkets or petrol stations, might then choose locations on the edge of town (as has happened increasingly in recent years). We have seen in our previous discussion that distance from competitors reduces price competition, and with equal spacing no firm can be further away from both neighbouring competitors.

29.2.1   Free entry in the Salop model

Again, formalizing this intuitive explanation, we assume that:

- There are N firms which might enter the market.
  - Each firm faces constant marginal costs of production, which as before we set to zero so that prices are stated net of marginal costs.
  - Firms must pay a fixed cost, F, in order to enter the market.
- *Stage 1*: Each of the N firms decides whether or not it will enter the market.
  - Once the number of firms in the market, $n \leq N$, is known, they choose locations, $x_f = \frac{f-1}{n}$, around the circle, which are evenly spaced.
- *Stage 2*: The n firms compete in prices, p_f.
  - All consumers, given their location on the circle, $x: 0 \leq x \leq 1$, buy from the firm, f, that minimizes the cost of purchase, $C_f(x) = p_f + (x - x_f)^2$.

We deliberately avoid analysis of the location of firms. If we continue to assume that transport costs are quadratic, it is possible to demonstrate that there is a perfect equilibrium in which n firms enter the market, spacing themselves evenly around the circle and setting the same price; however, that additional step would extend our discussion substantially for little benefit in terms of our understanding of firm behaviour. We therefore concentrate solely on the entry decision, in which firms' fixed costs, F, have an important role to play.

In *Stage 2*, we propose an equilibrium in which the n firms in the market set the same price, p^*. Suppose that $n - 1$ firms have already chosen price p^*. The last firm, f, sets price, p_f. To simplify our notation, we suppose $x_f = 0$. Then, for the firm's marginal consumers, located at $x = \pm x_f^*$, the cost of buying from the neighbouring firms, $f - 1$ and $f + 1$, equals the cost of buying from firm f, so that:

$$p_f + (x_f^*)^2 = p^* + \left(x_f^* - \frac{1}{n} \right)^2 \qquad [29.22]$$

By yourself

X29.12 We use Expression 29.22 to obtain the number of firms, n, that enter the market.

(a) Confirm that $x^* = \frac{n}{2}(p^* - p_f + \frac{1}{n^2})$.

(b) Explain why firm f makes total sales:

$$q(p_f, p^*) = n\left(p^* - p_f + \frac{1}{n^2} \right) \qquad [29.23]$$

(c) Write an expression for the firm's profit, Π_f. Show that the first-order condition, $\frac{\partial \Pi_f}{\partial p_f} = 0$, is satisfied when $p_f = \frac{1}{2}(p^* + \frac{1}{n^2})$, and that for a symmetric equilibrium, $p_f = p^* = \frac{1}{n^2}$, so that each firm makes profits $\Pi_f^* = n^{-3} - F$.

(d) Firms continue entering the market until all profits are eliminated. Confirm that $\Pi_f = 0$ if $n = F^{-\frac{1}{3}}$, (where F is each firm's fixed costs); and that firms then set the price, $p^* = F^{\frac{2}{3}}$.

In Exercise X29.12, we require there to be a symmetric equilibrium in *Stage 2*, in which all firms choose the same price. It may seem that in this case we assume the result that we want, but by assuming that all other firms have set their price already, we demonstrate that firm F cannot do better than to choose the Nash equilibrium price, $p^* = \frac{1}{n^2}$. By the symmetry of the situation, no firm can increase its profits by deviating unilaterally from the Nash equilibrium price.

In Exercise X29.12d, we analyse firm entry behaviour in *Stage 1* of the game. We here assume that all firms make their decisions at the same time. Firms will only wish to enter if they believe that they will avoid losses, and this will be the case so long as the number entering, $n \leq F^{-\frac{1}{3}}$. When this condition is binding, entry stops. Note that were the fixed cost of entry, F, to increase, then the optimal number of firms in the market would decrease, reducing price competition, and the equilibrium price would increase. Similarly, as $F \rightarrow 0$, n increases, and the equilibrium price, $p^* \rightarrow 0$. In this case the market would approach perfectly competitive conditions.

29.2.2 The social optimum

We note that although a zero-profit condition must be satisfied for equilibrium, the equilibrium price $p^* > 0$. Firms are able to set price above marginal cost, and so firms, even though in equilibrium they do not make economic profits, still have some degree of market power. This comes from horizontal product differentiation and the differing transport costs consumers face when considering alternative suppliers. The zero-profit condition emerges because firms continue to enter the market so long as they can continue to make profits.

A social planner will impose a rather different solution. Given that the market is covered, the total quantity traded in the market does not depend on the market price: the value derived from consumption and the variable costs of production are unaffected by the equilibrium price. In contrast, the fixed cost of entry to the market, F, and the transport costs, T, will both depend upon the number of firms, n, entering the market. We can therefore write problem facing the planner as:

$$\min_{n} C = nF + 2n \int_{0}^{\frac{1}{2n}} z^2 dz$$

Fixed · Total transport costs to nearest firm

[29.24]

The second term in Expression 29.24 is the total transport cost. With each firm located at the centre of its market segment, of length $\frac{1}{n}$, no consumer has to travel further than $\frac{1}{2n}$. There are therefore $2n$ travel segments, with each consumer travelling a distance z within them, and facing a travel cost, z^2. We obtain the total travel costs within a segment by integrating over these costs. Applying the rules of integration:

Reverse of power rule of differentiation

$$\int_{0}^{\frac{1}{2n}} z^2 dz = \left[\frac{1}{3} x^3 \right]_{0}^{\frac{1}{2n}} = \frac{1}{3} \left[\left(\frac{1}{2n} \right)^3 - 0 \right] = \frac{1}{24n^3}$$

[29.25]

Difference between values at $(2n)-1$, 0

This allows us to rewrite Expression 29.24:

$$\min_{n} C = nF + \frac{1}{12n^2}$$

[29.26]

Partially differentiating with respect to n, and apply the standard first-order condition:

$$\frac{\partial C}{\partial n} = F - \frac{1}{6n^3} = 0$$

[29.27]

Solving this expression for n:

$$n^* = (6F)^{-\frac{1}{3}} \qquad\qquad [29.28]$$

The socially optimal number of firms, n^*, is therefore less than the number of firms entering the market when there is free entry. There is a tendency towards excessive entry, with firms able to enter (and avoid losses) through their ability to differentiate their products.[1]

29.3   Vertical differentiation

Vertical differentiation Spatial differentiation with agreement on the ranking of products.

With horizontal differentiation, people rank alternative products differently, according to their own, and the products', locations. We now consider the implications of vertical differentiation. Since everyone agrees on the ranking of the products, we treat the products as differing in underlying product quality. All potential buyers of the good can observe these quality differences, but they differ in their marginal valuations of quality, so that *WTP* varies across consumers. Within the model below, the distribution of valuations will determine each firm's market share, given prices and quality choices. Once again, we apply a two-stage structure to the games in which we are interested:

- in *Stage 1*, firms, $f = 1, 2$, choose the quality, θ_f, of their product; and
- in *Stage 2*, the firms choose the profit-maximizing prices, p_f, given the chosen qualities.

In more advanced analysis, we would also allow for firms deciding whether or not to enter the market, but the two-stage game is sufficient to demonstrate that under certain circumstances there is maximum product differentiation, while in other circumstances intense price competition drives the lower-quality firm out of the market.

We need to specify the structure of the market, to take account of there being vertical, rather than horizontal, differentiation:

- We assume that there is an index of product quality, θ_f. For convenience, we assume that $\theta_1 \leq \theta_2$, so that product 2 can never be of lower quality than product 1.
  - The marginal cost of production, c, is independent of the level of quality. As in previous examples, we assume $c = 0$.
  - Continuing our earlier analysis, with zero marginal costs, we treat each firm's price, p_f, as being reported net of marginal cost.
- People vary in their marginal valuation of quality, v_i: $v_i \sim \mathrm{U}[v_0, v_1]$, where $0 \leq v_0$ and $v_1 = 1 + v_0$.
  - People either demand $q_f = 1$ unit of the good, or else do not demand it at all. We write the surplus from consumption, U:

$$U(\theta_f; v_i) = \begin{cases} v_i\theta_f - p_f \text{ if } q_f = 1 \\ 0, \text{ if } q_1 = q_2 = 0 \end{cases} \qquad\qquad [29.29]$$

---

1   This is our only discussion of monopolistic competition. In the online student essay bank, Jessica Harris has written on the nature of product differentiation in retail markets, concentrating on the capacity of small, independent retailers to provide convenience, and so, where well managed, to compete in specific ways with large superstores. You can read Jessica's essay on the companion website for this book, at **www.palgrave.com/mochrie.**

- To ensure firstly that the range of marginal valuations of quality is large enough that more than one firm will enter the market, but also that it is not so large that two firms cannot cover the market, we also make two rather more technical assumptions:

$$2v_0 \leq v_1 \leq \frac{\theta_1 + 2\theta_2}{\theta_2 - \theta_1} v_0 \qquad [29.30]$$

Expression 29.30 means that we are restricting our attention to situations where the entry of two firms is efficient. We will not derive the second inequation in our analysis, but will give an intuitive argument for the first one.

29.3.1 Competition in prices

To find the perfect equilibrium of this model, we begin by considering the interaction between firms in *Stage 2*, where they compete in prices, (p_1, p_2), taking quality, (θ_1, θ_2), as given.

By yourself

X29.13 Define the marginal quality valuation, v^*, at which a potential customer will be indifferent between the products of quality θ_1 and θ_2, sold at prices p_1 and p_2. Show that $v^* = \frac{p_2 - p_1}{\theta_2 - \theta_1}$. Calculate the market shares, q_1 and q_2, that each firms enjoys.

X29.14 Given our assumptions about the costs of production, the firms seek to maximize their revenues, R_f. Firms decide on their prices at the same time, so that each seeks to maximize its conjectured revenues, R_f^e, by forming a conjecture about the other firm's price, p_{-f}^e, and then choosing the best reply, $p_f^*(p_{-f}^e)$.
(a) Write down each firm's conjectured revenues, R_f^e, as the product of its market share, q_f^e, and price, p_f.
(b) By partially differentiating each firm's conjectured revenue with respect to its own price, $\frac{\partial R_f^e}{\partial p_f}$, confirm that the best-reply functions can be written:

$$p_1^*(p_2^e) = \tfrac{1}{2}\left[p_2^e - v_0(\theta_2 - \theta_1)\right] \qquad [29.31a]$$
$$p_2^*(p_1^e) = \tfrac{1}{2}\left[p_1^e + v_1(\theta_2 - \theta_1)\right] \qquad [29.31b]$$

From Expression 29.31, we see that the goods are strategic complements, with the best replies linear and increasing in conjectures. As shown in Figure 29.5, the best replies both intersect the p_2 axis above the origin. With the best-reply line $p_1^*(p_2^e)$ steeper than $p_2^*(p_1^e)$, we can immediately see that if the range of possible qualities is small, so that $v_1 < 2v_0$, then p_1^* intersects the vertical axis above p_2^*. The lines will then intersect each other to the left of the vertical axis so that firm 1, selling the lower quality, is forced out of the market. Our assumption in Expression 29.30, that $v_1 \geq 2v_0$, prevents this from happening.

To find the Nash equilibrium in prices, we solve the system of equations, Expression 29.30, given that conjectures are consistent, so that $p_f^*(p_{-f}^e) = p_f^e$. Substituting the equilibrium prices, (p_1^*, p_2^*) into Expression 29.30:

$$2p_1^* - p_2^* = -v_0(\theta_2 - \theta_1) \qquad [29.32a]$$

$$-\tfrac{1}{2}p_1^* + p_2^* = \tfrac{1}{2}\left[v_1(\theta_2 - \theta_1)\right] \qquad [29.32b]$$

Adding together separately the left and right sides of these expressions:

$$\tfrac{3}{2}p_1^* = \tfrac{1}{2}(v_1 - 2v_0)(\theta_2 - \theta_1) \qquad [29.33]$$

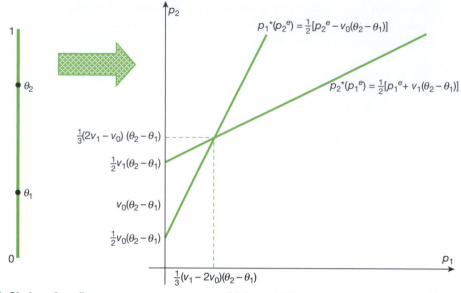

(a) Stage 1: Choice of quality   **(b) Stage 2: Choice of quality, given locations**

Figure 29.5 The two-stage game in quality and prices

Then multiplying through Expression 29.33 by $\frac{2}{3}$:

$$p_1^* = \tfrac{1}{3}(v_1 - 2v_0)(\theta_2 - \theta_1) \qquad\qquad [29.34]$$

By yourself

X29.15   Confirm that in equilibrium, firm 2 sets price, p_2^*:

$$p_2^* = \tfrac{1}{3}(2v_1 - v_0)(\theta_2 - \theta_1) \qquad\qquad [29.35]$$

X29.16   Show that:
(a) The firms' equilibrium outputs are (q_1^*, q_2^*):

$$q_1^* = \tfrac{1}{3}(v_1 - 2v_0); \text{ and } q_2^* = \tfrac{1}{3}(2v_1 - v_0) \qquad\qquad [29.36]$$

(b) The firms' equilibrium profits are (q_1^*, q_2^*):

$$R_1^* = \tfrac{1}{9}(v_1 - 2v_0)^2(\theta_2 - \theta_1); \text{ and } R_2^* = \tfrac{1}{9}(2v_1 - v_0)^2(\theta_2 - \theta_1) \qquad\qquad [29.37]$$

We see from Expressions 29.34–29.37 that in equilibrium prices, outputs and revenues all depend upon the maximum and minimum marginal valuations of quality, v_1 and v_0. It is quite easy to check that $q_1^* + q_2^* = v_1 - v_0$. Since we have assumed that $v_1 = 1 + v_0$, we can be certain that the market is covered. We also note that in equilibrium the revenues R_1^*, $R_2^* > 0$ (so long as $v_1 > 2v_0$).

A positive value for revenues means that firms make economic profits, and we would expect this to be noticed by other firms, which might then attempt to enter the market. Suppose that such an entrant were to choose a low quality, $\theta_0 < \theta_1$, and to try to undercut the incumbent firms with a very low price, targeting those potential customers with a low marginal valuation of quality. Were we to repeat our analysis of equilibrium pricing after entry had occurred, and given firms' choices of quality, we would find that it would be possible for the entrant to break even or to make profits only if people with the minimum marginal quality valuation, v_0, preferred their good to firm 1's offering, of quality v_1. This will only happen if the range of quality valuations is wide enough. We shall simply assert that the assumption in Expression 29.30 has been specified in such a way as to rule out this possibility. The two firms cover the market, and will not accommodate entry.

29.3.2 Competition in quality

Analysis of competition in *Stage 1* is very similar to the earlier discussion of horizontal differentiation. To analyse formally the effect of competition in quality, we would partially differentiate each firm's equilibrium price in *Stage 2*, p_f^*, with respect to its choice of quality, q_f, in *Stage 1*. Were we to do this, we would find that the standard first-order condition, $\frac{\partial p_f^*}{\partial q_f} = 0$ can never be satisfied, and would argue, as before, that we have to impose a corner solution, with maximum quality differentiation, so that $(\theta_1, \theta_2) = (\theta_{min}, \theta_{max})$, where θ_{min} represents the minimum possible value of quality, and θ_{max} the highest possible quality.

> **By yourself**
>
> **X29.17** Using the method outlined above, confirm that there will be maximum product differentiation in quality.

We can understand this claim in terms of diagrammatic analysis. In Figure 29.5, we have shown the best-reply lines and the Nash equilibrium in prices, all of which depend on the difference in qualities, $\theta_2 - \theta_1$. We can see the effect of an increase in θ_2 on the best-reply lines: their slope is not affected, but both move vertically upwards. We also see that with a wide enough range of valuations of marginal quality, $v_1 - v_0$, the equilibrium prices increase. As quality, θ_2, increases, holding θ_1 constant, there is greater quality differentiation, and in *Stage 2* price competition becomes less intense. Both firms charge higher prices and make greater profits.

> **By yourself**
>
> **X29.18** Repeat the argument above, but demonstrating that a decrease in quality, θ_1, also leads to decreased intensity of price competition, and thus allows higher prices and profits for both firms.

We can characterize the equilibrium outcome as a situation in which the market is served by two firms: a producer of a 'premium' product, of quality $\theta_2 = \theta_{max}$, the highest quality that can be produced, given the current technology, at the fixed marginal cost, $c = 0$; and a producer of a 'standard' product, of quality $\theta_1 = \theta_{min}$, the lowest quality that can be produced.

29.4   A role for advertising

With perfect information, there is of course no role for advertising. Relaxing that assumption, it is easy to identify several. We might wish to argue that advertising is *informative*. This can be seen in the advertisements placed on websites such as Craigslist, where potential sellers of a few items want to make potential buyers aware that they have goods and services to sell. Yet even there, we can see rudimentary attempts to make advertising *persuasive.* Similarly, even in brief listings estate agents regularly find the most favourable adjectives that might be applied in a description of a property. Persuasion can work on many levels. Many fast-moving consumer goods, bought regularly in small quantities, develop their advertising in order to promote a particular concept of the (ideal) product. Someone relying on choice heuristics is likely to find a branded product to be both available and, to the extent that the advertising is effective, representative. A third explanation would emphasize the *strategic* use of advertising. In many countries, the market for detergents is dominated by two businesses, Unilever and Procter & Gamble. These companies produce many brands, many of which receive strong advertising support. We might argue that this forms a barrier to entry. To the extent that consumers expect a good-quality detergent to be supported by advertising, should they notice a new brand when shopping but be unable to recall having seen or heard any advertising for it, they might be less likely to buy it. Through brand proliferation the incumbents are able to cover the market, and through advertising they are able to defend their positions.

At this point, we shall consider a simple model of advertising in which there is vertical differentiation of products, but potential purchasers do not know the quality of products. Within this model, advertising is essentially informative, although there will be strategic interactions between firms and potential customers. We assume that anyone considering the purchase of a good believes that only producers of high-quality brands will engage in advertising, in which case advertising functions as a signal of quality. We assume that people know the probability distribution of quality across firms. In the model of Section 29.3, for example, there is one premium product and one generic product. Having an initial belief about the probability of either product being of high quality, on exposure to advertising (or, more generally, to any marketing activities designed to support a branded product), potential buyers update those beliefs, assigning a higher probability to the product being of high quality. If they are unaware of marketing activity, the updating of beliefs will mean assigning a lower probability to the product being of high quality.

When we considered signalling in Section 28.3, we noted that it is necessary that the cost of generating the signal should vary with the underlying characteristic. It may seem that advertising fails that criterion. Any firm can advertise. We shall assume here that the effect of advertising is to encourage people to sample a product in the belief that it is of high quality (so that they will pay a high price for it). By sampling the product, customers determine its underlying quality with certainty (we ignore the possibility of self-perception biases). If they conclude that, in spite of the marketing support, it is of low quality, they will not purchase it again. In our model, for advertising to be effective it cannot generate so many sales in the first period that 'hit-and-run' entry supported by advertising is profitable, but it also cannot be so costly that businesses selling high-quality products are unable to recoup these signalling costs over time.

29.4.1   Advertising as a signal

We analyse a relatively simple model, shown in extensive form in Figure 29.6, in which we consider the interaction between a firm, F, and a potential customer, C, who is representative of all possible customers.

- At the start of the game (*Stage 0*), nature randomly determines the quality of the firm's product, measured in terms of its value, $v \in \{0, 1\}$, to potential customer, C.

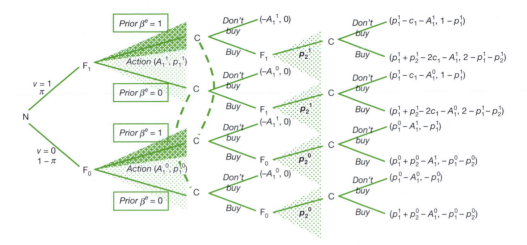

Figure 29.6 The advertising model

- We write the probabilities, $\Pr(v = 1) = \pi$; $\Pr(v = 0) = 1 - \pi$.
- Quality, v, is a characteristic. Firm F observes its value, while potential customer, C, only knows its underlying probability distribution, with prior belief, $\beta_0 = \pi$.
- We assume that all values are expressed net of the firm's marginal cost of low-quality output, so that $c_0 = 0$, but $0 < c_1 < 1$.
- *Stage 1*: Firm F sets an initial price, $p_1 \geq 0$, and advertising expenditure, $A_1 \geq 0$.
  - Potential customer, C, observes the pair (p_1, A_1) and updates the prior, β^e: $\beta^e \in \{0, 1\}$, so that the customer's beliefs are certain.
  - Consumers choose from the actions, {*Buy*, *Don't buy*}, with the choice being affected by beliefs, β^e.
  - Upon consuming the product, the customer becomes fully informed.
  - If the potential customer chooses *Don't buy*, then the game ends.
- *Stage 2*: The sub-game is played with complete information. Only those customers who buy the product in *Stage 1* will consider buying it in *Stage 2*.
  - Being fully informed, $WTP_2 = v$; firm F then sets price, p_2, to maximize profits.
  - Customers decide whether or not they wish to buy at this price.
  - At the end of the game, both players receive their payoffs.

29.4.2 The separating equilibrium of the game

This game has a slightly more complex structure than those we have studied in previous examples. Remember that in order to analyse an extensive game, we have to show every possible decision node, irrespective of whether or not it is likely to be reached in the equilibrium of the game, and so in the diagram there are several nodes where seemingly similar decisions are made. Since we have defined an extensive game of imperfect information, the appropriate solution concept is the perfect Bayesian equilibrium, and this requires consistency between belief and actions. In terms of the diagram, our objective here is to show that there is such an equilibrium in which potential customers turn out to be correct in believing that a firm with a high-quality product will choose an action pair in the upper (more darkly shaded) region of the action set; and also that that a firm with a low-quality product will choose an action pair in the lower (lighter) region of the action set.

By yourself

X29.19   We consider the sub-games of length 1.

   (a) Confirm that facing price p_2^1 for a product of quality $v = 1$, the customer, C, will choose to buy the product if $p_2^1 \leq 1$.

   (b) Confirm that facing price p_2^0 for a product of quality $v = 0$, the customer, C, will choose to buy the product if $p_2^0 = 0$.

X29.20   For the sub-games of length 2, beginning with firm F's pricing choice in *Stage 2*:

   (a) Confirm that if $v = 1$, in the perfect equilibrium $(p_2^1)^* = 1$.

   (b) If $v = 0$, show that the firm is indifferent among all prices $p_2^0 \geq 0$. [*Hint:* Think what customer C will choose to do if $p_2^0 > 0$.]

X29.21   Define the updating rule for the potential customer's beliefs as follows:

$$\beta^e = \begin{cases} 1, \text{ if } (p_1, A_1):p_1 \leq p_1^*, \ A_1 = A^* \\ 0, \text{ otherwise} \end{cases} \qquad [29.38]$$

   Assume that this updating rule is known to the firm. Confirm that in *Stage 1*:

   (a) If the potential customer observes:

      (i)   action pair (p_1^*, A_1^*), then if $p_1^* \leq 1$, the customer will choose *Buy*;

      (ii) action pair (p_1, A_1^*), with $p_1 < p_1^* \leq 1$, the customer will choose *Buy*.

      (iii) action pair (p_1^*, A_1), with $A_1 < A_1^*$, the customer will choose *Don't buy*.

   (b) Anticipating the customer's decision, then if $v = 1$:

      (i)   the firm chooses action pair (p_1^*, A_1^*) rather than (p_1, A_1^*);

      (ii) the firm chooses (p_1^*, A_1^*) rather than (p_1^*, A_1) if:

$$1 + p_1^* - A_1^* - 2c_1 \geq 0 \qquad [29.39]$$

   (c) But if $v = 0$, then the firm chooses action pair $(0, 0)$; unless $p_1^* \geq A_1^*$, in which case it would choose (p_1^*, A_1^*).

In the analysis presented in Exercises X29.19–X29.21, the outcome of *Stage 2* is quite straightforward. A firm with a high-quality product, whose quality $v = 1$, can make an economic profit $\Pi_2^1 = 1 - c_1$; while a firm with a low-quality product, whose quality $v = 0$, makes economic profit $\Pi_2^0 = 0$. This allows a seller of high-quality products to behave differently from a seller of low-quality ones in *Stage 1*. Remember that after sampling the product the customer is fully informed. A firm selling a high-quality product can therefore anticipate the economic profit in *Stage 2* by making a loss in *Stage 1*. Firms and potential customers are aware of this fact. A potential customer who notices a business apparently making a loss in the short term by promoting a new product might reasonably infer that the product quality is high, and that the firm expects to recoup its losses from *Stage 2* revenues. Making these inferences, potential customers are willing to sample the good, and, assuming that their inferences prove correct, to make repeat purchases.

   The arguments presented in Exercise X29.21 confirm that, given the customer's beliefs, the action profile in *Stage 1* maximizes payoffs. In Figure 29.7, we redraw the decision tree, reducing *Stage 2* to the equilibrium payoffs. Imposing the requirement that beliefs are consistent with actions, we ignore the two sub-histories of the game shown in light green, one in which the firm selling a high-quality product does not advertise, and the other in which the firm selling a low-quality product does advertise. We note three conditions, which we then bring together into a single expression:

- *Participation constraint (for a customer)*: Buying the high-quality good at price p_1^* must offer at least as high a payoff as staying out of the market: $p_1^* \leq 1$.

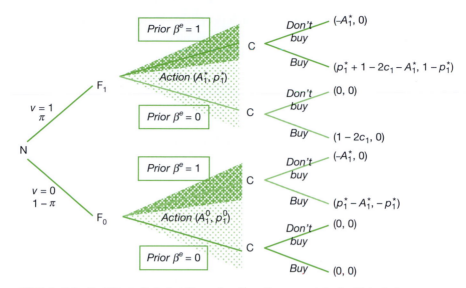

Figure 29.7 Anticipating Stage 2 during Stage 1, with actions consistent with beliefs

- *Incentive compatibility (for a firm with a product for which $v = 0$):* Mimicking the profit-maximizing strategy of a firm marketing a high-quality product in *Stage 1* cannot be profitable: $p_1^* - A_1^* \leq 0$.
- *Incentive compatibility (for a firm with a product for which $v = 1$):* Using advertising in *Stage 1* must be profitable: $1 + p_1^* - A_1^* - 2c_1 \geq 0$.

Amalgamating these three conditions:

$$A_1^* + 2c_1 - 1 \leq p_1^* \leq \min(1, A_1^*).$$

By yourself

X29.22 Confirm that when the cost $c_1 = 0.25$, there is a perfect Bayesian equilibrium of this game, in which $(A_1^*, p_1^*) = (0.75, 0.5)$.

We do not claim that this model explains all the uses of advertising, or more generally the marketing support that a firm makes available for products. Both the motivation and the predictions of the model seem reasonable, though. Given that some products are of high quality and some are not, businesses spend money promoting high-quality products. Such activities are informative, in the sense that without them people would either have to experiment or else to accumulate information about product qualities themselves. It is therefore possible that advertising activities reduce the costs of acquiring information. Nonetheless, these expenditures are wasteful, since if people had perfect information there would be no incentive for firms to engage in promotional expenditures.

29.5 Conclusions

We began the chapter by recalling one of the earliest studies of product differentiation in economics. Hotelling's spatial model anticipated many developments in game theory, which would only be fully explored fifty years after it was first set out. If we had started with other models, such as Chamberlin's analysis of monopolistic competition, we might well have concentrated on non-address models, in which people have a preference for variety. Rather than buying a standardized product, they like to buy small quantities of goods with different characteristics: a simple example would be the many different flavours of ice cream that are available from any ice-cream stall. Of the models that we have considered, the circular road is the closest to this approach; and in this model, rather than finding that firms used spatial differentiation strategically in order to create profit opportunities, we concluded that firms' entry into the market would continue until all profits were dissipated. Such an outcome was not socially optimal because more firms entered the market than would have entered had they not been able to differentiate themselves from each other.

Noting this point, we should reflect on some of the limitations of our study. We have treated product differentiation essentially as an environmental factor. Within a model of vertical differentiation, we might expect firms to have an incentive to invest in quality. Having the best-quality product in a market is likely to enable a firm to generate greater profits than the producer of a generic, relatively low-quality good. This seems relatively benign, since it suggests that product differentiation might be a spur to innovation, which we would not see in a standard model. In the same way, we have argued that advertising might be a signalling response to unobservable product differentiation, which is used by firms marketing high-quality products. Essentially, it is an investment to generate (and later defend) market share and so secure higher profits for the firm in future. Again, this seems to be a reasonable response to a problem of asymmetric information.

The circular road model reminds us that it is possible for firms to use product differentiation purely for their own benefit. It confirms, usefully, that firms might deviate from (socially) efficient behaviour while seeming to be engaged in intense competition. It also raises the question of whether or not it might be possible for firms to create apparent product differentiation where none exists. We have noted that in many markets for fast-moving consumer goods, brands exist, whose identity is the result of extensive marketing support; and it is possible to model such support as a strategic investment by the firm, designed to deter entry. This requires only a small variation on the model of advertising that we have developed. Suppose that potential customers continue to make inferences about product quality on the basis of observable marketing support. We noted above that many markets for detergents are dominated by two companies. An entrant with only a small advertising budget is unlikely to affect consumer perceptions to anything like the same extent as established businesses with their large advertising budgets. With the large companies also using brand proliferation, they cover the market, and engage in a form of non-price competition between products. To the extent that such activity supports higher prices than would otherwise emerge, such product differentiation may have social costs.

Summary

We distinguish between address models of product differentiation, studied in this chapter, and non-address models. In address models, there is an observable and measurable characteristic, which differentiates products.

In non-address models, products are different but there is no scale on which differences might be measured.

Hotelling's model of horizontal differentiation assigns all products to a location on a unit interval. We assume that every consumer has a preferred specification, and incurs transport costs when buying from any other location. With only two firms in the market, and quadratic transport costs, the Nash equilibrium exhibits minimum product differentiation.

Allowing for competition in both location and prices, we obtain the opposite result. Firms maximize product differentiation, reducing the extent of price competition, and thereby increasing their profits.

Hotelling's model has no equilibrium in pure strategies when more than two firms enter the market. To allow for entry, we used the model of the circular city, in which firms enter until all profits are exhausted. We demonstrated that there is a symmetric Nash equilibrium in which all firms' locations are equidistant, set the same price, and make zero economic profits. We also demonstrated that there is excessive entry in this model, since a social planner would permit fewer firms to enter, allowing them to make profits, but avoiding fixed costs of entry.

With address models, vertical differentiation occurs when there is agreement among consumers of quality rankings, but consumers differ in their *WTP* for quality (at the margin). We found that if differences in quality valuation are small, it would be possible for the producer of higher-quality goods to drive its competitor out of the market through intense price competition.

Assuming that two firms span the market, we showed that they will engage in maximum quality differentiation, which, by reducing competition in prices, increases firms' profits.

Lastly, we considered models of advertising as an (informative) signal. We developed a two-period model in which consumers treat advertising a signal of high-quality products. Able to recognize the quality of a product after first purchasing it, they will not make repeat purchases if the product turns out to be of low quality. This makes advertising more costly for low-quality firms, so that it can operate as a signal.

We obtained a perfect Bayesian equilibrium, in which firms, assigned a level of product quality by nature, make a decision about whether or not to advertise, as well as setting the initial price. Potential customers observe the advertising and infer whether or not the firm's product is of high quality. In equilibrium, advertising permits perfect separation, so that the belief that only high-quality products are advertised will be confirmed, and consumers will be willing to pay a higher price for advertised products in the second period as well.

Visit the companion website at **www.palgrave.com/mochrie** to access further teaching and learning materials, including lecturer slides and a testbank, as well as guideline answers and student MCQs.

chapter 30

Auctions

An *auction* is simply a way of organizing a sale so that potential buyers reveal their *WTP*, allowing the seller to maximize the expected revenue. After some introductory notes explaining how auctions operate, and noting that there are several forms which have been widely used for centuries, as well as innovations in auction design that reflect advances in the economic theory of auctions in the last thirty years, we set out an introductory analysis, concentrating on four widely used forms of auction: *English* (or *ascending*); *Dutch* (or *descending*); *first-price, sealed-bid*; and *Vickrey* (or *second-price, sealed-bid*).

We first consider auctions as strategic games of *perfect information*. We begin with analysis of Vickrey auctions, showing that there are some equilibria in which the auction is not won by the bidder with the highest valuation. Such

an outcome would be inefficient. We therefore consider whether it might be reasonable to impose restrictions on the strategies that bidders must adopt in equilibrium, showing that weak dominance is sufficient to ensure a unique, efficient equilibrium in which all bids are equal to the valuation. We then show that this approach does not permit the identification of a unique equilibrium for first-price auctions.

Continuing our analysis, we now consider auctions as strategic games of *imperfect information*, arguing that the strategy adopted by players in all four forms of auction is likely to be the same. From this, we are able to sketch the *revenue equivalence theorem*, an important result which states that across a wide range of auction forms, the seller expects to receive the same revenue, irrespective of the form of the auction.

30.1   Sales by auction

Auction Selling a good by inviting potential buyers to announce the amount they are willing to pay.

English (ascending) auction An auction in which bids are made verbally, ascending in value until no higher bid is received.

As applied from Chapter 1 onwards, the concept of a market presumes that exchanges between buyers and sellers are frequent. Such exchanges might involve differentiated products, but all products are recognizable varieties of a single good. A sale by auction, on the other hand, will often be used in situations where the item offered for sale is unique. In economic terms, an auction is a mechanism that identifies the potential buyers with the highest *WTP*. Until recently, probably the best-known and most widely used form of auction was the English auction or ascending auction. Large auction houses, such as Sotheby's or Christie's, have used this form for centuries. The sale by auction of high-value works of art is almost a form of entertainment, with the auctioneer obtaining higher and higher bids from a packed, and increasingly tense, saleroom until no more can be obtained. But whereas in 2013 the total value of sales at Christie's and Sotheby's reached a little over $11bn, in the same year the online auction site, eBay, a recent entrant to the market, launched in 1995, achieved over $50bn in sales (although this, in part, eBay's diversification into other activities).

By yourself

X30.1 eBay uses a proxy bid system. Describe how this works, and what a bidder has to do to win the auction.

We shall see below that auctions on eBay closely follow the form of the simple **Vickrey auction**. This is named after the Nobel-prizewinning economist, who suggested it in a paper in 1961. At the time, it was seen as little more than a theoretical curiosity. Vickrey suggested that auctions could be run by asking bidders to write down their valuation and then to place their bid in a sealed envelope, which would be opened only after the auction had closed, with the winner being required to pay the *second-highest* price. Vickrey argued that with this approach every bidder's optimal strategy would be to write down their true valuation of the good.

> **Vickrey auction** An auction conducted with written bids, in which the highest bidder wins, and pays an amount equal to the second highest bid.

Immediately, we can see that an auction on eBay differs from the Vickrey auction in several ways. While in both bidding is open for a fixed time interval, on eBay it is possible for bidders to revise their proxy bids. In addition, while the highest proxy bid remains secret, the second-highest bid becomes public, so that the actual process resembles an English auction, with bidders whose valuation is lower than the announced (second-highest) proxy bid unable to enter further bids. Such small differences in structure lead to substantial differences in both predicted (and observed) behaviour. For example, on Amazon's auction platform (now withdrawn), when a bid was made very close to the announced end of the auction, the auction period was immediately extended for long enough for other bidders to respond. As a result, late bids were much less frequent on Amazon than they are on eBay.

The emergence of online auctions is only one reason for economists paying more attention to auction markets. More generally, auctions are efficient mechanisms for the sale of any commodity for which there is no well-defined market. The early years of this century saw a sequence of auctions, managed by national governments, for the rights to operate 3G telephony services. Some were spectacularly successful: in the UK, winning bids in the auction held in 2000 totalled £22.5bn, while in Germany, in another auction held in 2000, they exceeded £30bn. (In comparison, the UK 4G auction raised about £2.4bn in 2013, and the German one £3.9bn in 2010.) Compared with other methods of allocating such rights, well-designed auctions now have a track record of attracting substantially greater revenues for sellers; however, there are also many examples of poorly designed auctions which have been bedevilled by problems such as a failure to attract sufficient bidders or collusion between bidders. Much recent work in auction theory has therefore been directed to improving design so that outcomes are more robust.

30.1.1 Common forms of auction

We have already introduced the English auction, in which bids are declared publicly and increase in value until the auctioneer cannot secure further bids. There are several ways of organizing these auctions. In Europe, it is normal either for bids to be announced by the auctioneers, with other bidders then responding, or for bidders to announce the prices that they are willing to pay. In Japan, such auctions are conducted with the asking price being raised automatically by some timing mechanism. Bidders indicate when they wish to quit the auction, and cannot be readmitted. In both kinds of auction, as we shall see, with perfect information bidders should remain in the auction until the sale price reaches their *WTP*.

There are situations, such as the sale of perishable goods, where being able to conclude the auction quickly is important. Go to a quayside at a fishing port early in the morning and you will see groups of men huddled around boxes of fish. The auctioneer starts with a high price and calls out decreasing offers. As soon as a bidder indicates willing-ness to pay the offer price, the auction stops. The advantage of this process is speed. Alternative forms of this mechanism again involve some sort of timed reduction in the asking price; this has been a feature of Dutch flower auctions for many years, and so this form of descending auction is commonly known as a Dutch auction.

> **Dutch (descending) auction** An auction conducted by open outcry, with the WTA descending; the first bid wins.

With both English and Dutch auctions, bidding is driven by a process of *open outcry*. An auction can also be conducted with bids being submitted remotely. Traditionally bids would be in writing, but now, as with eBay, electronic bidding has become much more widespread. Considering a traditional example, that of buying a house, if it seems that there are several willing purchasers one method of sale is for the seller to set a closing date by which every potential bidder must submit their *sealed bid*. After the auction closes, all of the bids are opened, and the winning bidder has to pay the price in the bid. (In some cases, in house sales, it may be that the winning bidder has not offered the highest price. For example, it might be that the highest bidder has included other terms, such as a particu-lar date of entry to the property, that are unacceptable to the seller.) Traditionally, in such contracts, the winning bidder has had to pay the full value of their bid, and so this form of auction is often called a first-price, sealed-bid auction.

> **First-price auction** An auction in which the highest bidder wins and pays their own bid.
>
> **Sealed-bid auction** An auction in which bids are submitted in writing.

In his seminal contribution to auction theory, Vickrey suggested the form of the second-price, sealed-bid auction, in which the seller requires the winning bidder to pay only the second-highest bid. As noted already, a slight variation of this rule is central to the operation of auctions on eBay. A similar form is also used by the US Treasury, which auctions short-term securities (Treasury Bills) through a system in which bidders pay the market-clearing price for all of the stock they are allocated, rather than the price that they have bid for individual units. As with the eBay example, such an auction is more complex than the simple Vickrey auction. There are multiple units being auctioned in a single transaction, but with the market-clearing price effectively the highest bid that was *not* accepted, the process is a straightforward generalization of the second-price form.

> **Second-price auction** An alternative name for a Vickrey auction.

30.2   Auctions with perfect information

We shall not treat sellers as strategic players, assuming instead that they set the rules of the auction, leaving the potential bidders to engage in strategic interactions. We shall also treat these auctions as strategic games in which players' strategies consist of exactly one action, a bid, chosen without knowing what the other players will choose. The important point of our analysis is the demonstration that even with all players knowing each other's preferences, there can be many Nash equilibria, given the requirement that players make their bids on the basis of beliefs about other players' bids, which turn out to be correct.

30.2.1 A two-player, two-action example

Consider a very simple example. Giselle has decided to sell her car through a Vickrey (second-price, sealed-bid) auction. There are only two possible bidders, Erica and Felicity, with *WTP*, $v_E = 18,000$ and $v_F = 15,000$ respectively. We assume that their bids, $b_I = \{0, v_I\}$, so that they must either bid their valuation, or else effectively enter no bid, in which case Giselle will keep the car and try to sell it in another way. There is no value derived from participation in the auction, either for the winner or the loser(s), but there is also no participation cost or entry fee.

By yourself

X30.2 Form the payoff matrix for this game in normal form, and confirm the best replies to bids of 0 and v_I. Show that for Erica, bidding $v^E = 18,000$ is a dominant strategy, whereas Felicity is then indifferent between actions. Hence confirm that there are two Nash equilibria, $(b_E{}^*, b_F{}^*) = (18,000, 0)$, and $(b_E{}^*, b_F{}^*) = (18,000, 15,000)$. Why does Giselle prefer the outcome in which Felicity bids her valuation? How could she make certain that this will happen?

X30.3 What would happen in this auction if Erica agreed that she would pay Felicity €6,000 so long as $b_F = 0$?

To obtain the car, Erica must bid; and upon bidding, she can be certain that she will win the auction. We can therefore be certain that this auction is an *efficient mechanism*, in the sense that Giselle will sell the car to the bidder with the highest valuation. Note that the terms of the sale will depend on the price that Felicity offers, and here Erica and Giselle have opposing interests. We assume that Giselle values the car at $v_G : v_G = 12,000$.

- If $b_F = 0$, Giselle would have to give Erica the car for free. Erica's payoff, $\pi_E(0) = 18,000$, while Giselle's payoff, $\pi_G(0) = -12,000$.
- If $b_F = 15,000$, then $(\pi_E, \pi_G) = (3,000, 3,000)$.

The sum of payoffs, $\pi_E(b_F) + \pi_G(b_F) = 6,000$, irrespective of Felicity's bid, but the distribution of payoffs varies considerably. We have defined a bid of $b_F = 0$ as not making a bid. To avoid having to give the car away when only Erica bids, Giselle could include in the rules of the auction a *reserve price*, $\underline{b}$, which would be the minimum that Erica has to pay, irrespective of Felicity's bid, b_F. In this case, any value, $\underline{b} : \underline{b} \geq v_G$, would ensure that Giselle would obtain a non-negative payoff. Indeed, were Giselle to know that the highest valuation, $v_{max} = 18,000$ (but not whether this is Erica's or Felicity's valuation), then should Giselle set the reserve price, $\underline{b} = 18,000$, Erica would have to bid (and pay) her full valuation. Giselle would then obtain the entire surplus.

If Giselle did not set a reserve price, she might also enter a bid herself. This is often considered unethical in more complex auctions, since it allows the seller to manipulate the final payment. In this case, though, with the range of bids deliberately restricted, if Giselle followed the rule that she could only bid her own valuation, so that $b_G = 12,000$, then this would simply ensure that she avoided making a loss. Entering a bid herself should have the same effect on the outcome as setting a reserve price.

For Erica to make a side-payment to Felicity conditional on Felicity not bidding would be difficult to justify in ethical terms. Such a payment would simply be a bribe to ensure that Erica wins the auction on the most favourable terms. Imposing a reserve price is a simple way for the seller to limit the effect of such collusion.

30.2.2   Bidding and efficiency

We extend our analysis, firstly by allowing players to make bids of any value, and secondly by increasing the number of bidders in the auction.

By yourself

X30.4   Assume that Giselle sets a reserve price, $\underline{b} = 12,000$, and announces an additional rule: that in the event of the two bids being equal, she will sell the car to Erica.
   (a) Obtain expressions for Erica's best replies for conjectured bids, b_F^e : (i) $b_F^e < 12,000$; (ii) $12,000 \leq b_F^e \leq 18,000$; (iii) $b_F^e = 15,000$; and (iv) $b_F^e > 15,000$.
   (b) Obtain expressions for Felicity's best replies for conjectured bids, b_E^e: (i) $b_E^e < 12,000$ (ii) $12,000 \leq b_E^e < 15,000$; (iii) $b_E^e = 15,000$; and (iv) $b_E^e > 15,000$.
   (c) Illustrate, on separate diagrams: (i) Erica's best replies; (ii) Felicity's best replies; and (iii) the Nash equilibria, where conjectures are consistent.
   (d) Confirm that there are Nash equilibria in which both Erica and Felicity bid in excess of their valuations, but that there is no Nash equilibrium in which they both bid in excess of Erica's valuation.

Remember that with the Nash equilibrium concept, the only requirement for equilibrium is that conjectures are consistent. Following this rule, we expect both players to enter bids that are either:

- between (1) the higher of the reserve price and their conjecture of the other bid and (2) their own *WTP*, so that they win the auction; or else
- less than their conjecture of the other bid, if this is greater than their own *WTP*, so that they lose the auction.

We illustrate these best replies graphically in Figure 30.1a and Figure 30.1b. As indicated above, the best reply to any conjecture is typically a range of bids. We believe that Erica and Felicity will only want to win if they will make a surplus by doing so (strictly, if they will avoid a loss, since they can bid their valuation and win the auction), and this determines when the range of best replies lies above or below the conjecture. From Figure 30.1c, we see that there are two areas in which there are consistent conjectures supporting Nash equilibria. In the first one, which is shaded darker, Erica's bid is higher than Felicity's. She wins the auction (and may make a surplus). Any action profile $(b_E{}^*, b_F{}^*)$ is a Nash equilibrium, satisfying the conditions:

$$\max(15,000, b_F{}^*) \leq b_E{}^*; b_F{}^* \leq 18,000 \tag{30.1}$$

As with the two-player, two-action example, every bidding profile satisfying Expression 30.1 is consistent with Felicity believing that it is better to lose, and not caring how low her bid is. We might extend the model slightly and say that if were there a cost to bidding, then

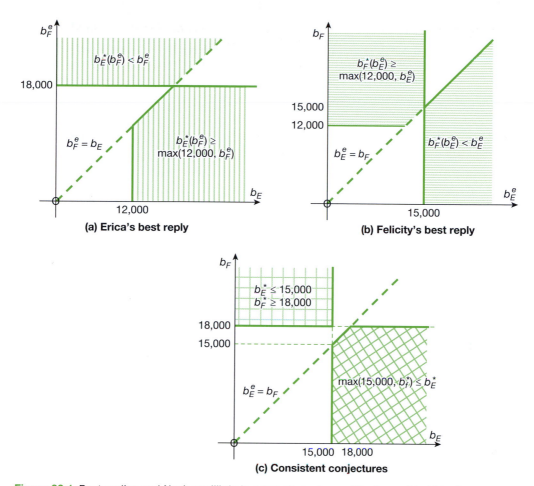

Figure 30.1 Best replies and Nash equilibria in a two-player game with all possible bid values

Felicity would certainly enter a bid of zero. Note that Felicity's belief that she will lose relies on Erica's bid being no less than Felicity's *WTP*.

The lighter-shaded area in Figure 30.1c consists of Nash equilibria in which Felicity's bid is high enough that Erica does not wish to win. In addition, Erica's bid has to be low enough that Felicity wants to win. Such an equilibrium requires:

$$b_E^* \leq 15{,}000; \; b_F^* \geq 18{,}000 \qquad\qquad [30.2]$$

For this outcome, Felicity must bid very aggressively, while Erica must be oddly accommodating. For Erica, making a bid b_E: $15{,}000 < b_E < 18{,}000$ has no cost. So, if Erica makes a bid in that range, and Felicity bids aggressively, she wins, but makes a loss. The Nash equilibrium is destroyed, because it would then be better for Felicity to reduce her bid. We conclude that for Felicity, any bid such that b_F: $b_F > v_F$ is *weakly dominated* by the bid $b_F^0 = v_F$. Comparing the strategies of bidding her *WTP* against bidding more than her *WTP*, Felicity can never increase her payoff by bidding more, but she can reduce it.

By yourself

X30.5   Show that should Erica bid less than her *WTP*, then there are (non-equilibrium) action profiles in which she would do worse than by bidding her *WTP*. Show that there are other (non-equilibrium) action profiles in which she would do worse by bidding more than her *WTP* than by bidding her *WTP*. What do you conclude about the strategy $b_E = v_E$ compared with all other strategies?

If we impose the requirement that strategies should be weakly dominant, then only one Nash equilibrium, $(b_E{}^*, b_F{}^*) = (v_E, v_F)$, survives. Erica and Felicity can never do better than by bidding their valuations. In this outcome, the underlying second-price, sealed-bid mechanism is efficient. Erica, who values the car more, obtains it, receiving a non-negative payoff. Felicity, who values the car less, does not obtain it, and definitely receives a zero payoff. Giselle will make the sale and, given the reserve price, will also receive a non-negative payoff. The transaction therefore leads to a Pareto improvement.

By yourself

X30.6   As before, a seller proposes to sell a car by second-price, sealed-bid auction. There are $n > 2$ potential bidders, indexed $i = 1, 2, \dots, n$ with valuations $v_1 > v_2 \dots > v_n > 0$, each choosing an action, b_i. In the event of the winning bids being equal, the seller will accept the winning bid made by the player with the lowest index.

(a) What is the payoff received by player 1: (i) when bid b_1 is the highest bid, and bid b_2 the second-highest bid; and (ii) when bid $b_1 < b_2$?

(b) Under what circumstances is bid b_i a winning bid? Under what circumstances would bid $b_i > 0$ be a best reply?

(c) Confirm that there are Nash equilibria in which: (i) $b_i = v_i$ for all n players; (ii) $b_1 = v_2$ and $b_i = 0$ for all of the other players; (iii) $b_1 > v_1$ and $b_i = v_1$ for all of the other players; (iv) $b_2 > v_1$ and $b_i = 0$ for all of the other players.

(d) Show that the strategy $b_i > v_i$ is weakly dominated by the strategy $b_i = v_i$.

(e) Show that the strategy $b_i < v_i$ is weakly dominated by the strategy $b_i = v_i$.

(f) Confirm that for there to be a Nash equilibrium in which player i wins, $b_i{}^* > v_1$ and $b_{\sim i}{}^* \leq v_i$; but that the strategies in this Nash equilibrium are weakly dominated by the strategies in the Nash equilibrium, $b_i{}^0 = v_i$.

30.2.3   Comparison with other auction forms

Ascending, or English, auctions have many properties in common with second-price, sealed-bid, or Vickrey, auctions. Indeed, the most important difference between them is in their form. Where it is clear that players have to decide their bidding strategy before playing a Vickrey auction game, during which they are called upon to make a sequence of bids, it might seem possible that bidders in an ascending auction would only finally decide upon their strategy as bidding progresses. Using arguments about signalling from Chapter 28, we can think of the auction as a game of imperfect information in which bidders' valuations are conditional on publicly revealed information, derived from the process of bidding. For example, in a Japanese auction, if they observed many bidders quitting at a given price, then the remaining bidders might revise their *WTP* downwards. Here, though, we restrict ourselves to games of perfect information.

By yourself

X30.7   Suppose that an object is brought to an ascending (English) auction. There are only two bidders, A and B, willing to pay $v_A = 3$ and $v_B = 2$. The auctioneer sets the initial bid $b_0 = 1$, and will require bid increases of 1 unit. After every point at which they have to make a decision, A has the choice of making another bid or of quitting the auction.

(a) Assume that A makes the initial bid. Draw a decision tree showing the game in extensive form and confirm that the sub-game perfect equilibrium action profile, $A* = \{Bid, Bid, Bid\}$; and that player A obtains the object by paying price $p = 3$, so that neither player makes a surplus.

(b) Repeat the exercise, assuming that B makes the initial bid. Confirm that the sub-game perfect equilibrium action profile, $A* = \{Bid, Bid, Stop\}$, and that player A obtains the object by paying price $p = 2$, making a surplus $v_A - p = 1$.

(c) Repeat the exercise, assuming that there is a Japanese auction. Show that B drops out when the required bid $p = 3$, so that the outcome is the same as in part (a).

X30.8   As in X30.6, a seller proposes to sell a car, but now by an English ascending auction. With $n > 2$ potential bidders, indexed $i = 1, 2, \dots, n$ with valuations $v_1 > v_2 \dots > v_n > 0$, and perfectly informed bidders, show that there are sub-game perfect equilibria: (a) in which player 1 makes an initial bid, $b_1 = v_2$, and every other bidder immediately stops bidding; and (b) in which some player, i, immediately bids $b_i = v_1 - 2$, bidder 1 announces $b_1 = v_1 - 1$, and bidding then stops.

These very simple examples demonstrate an obvious principle. If a player in these games has an opportunity to make a bid, $b : b < WTP$, then bidding is preferable to stopping (and immediately obtaining a zero payoff). We expect player 1 to win the auction, and to pay the price $p = v_2$, the second-highest valuation, exactly as with the Vickrey auction, confirming that in these circumstances, an English auction is efficient.

Given the argument that we have just developed, we assume that the analysis of first-price, sealed-bid and Dutch (descending) auctions is identical, at least in the context of perfect information. Since a Dutch auction stops as soon as a bid is made, the winning bidder has to pay the full amount of that bid, b_i. The bidding rule should be to bid when this maximizes the expected payoff, conditional on the bidder's knowledge of all other bidders' valuations. Similarly, in a first-price, sealed-bid auction, a bidder will only be called to make a payment on winning. Again, we expect the winning bid to maximize the expected payoff.

By yourself

X30.9   Suppose that Giselle decides to sell her car by a Dutch auction.

(a) Explain why Erica should be certain that she will win the auction if she follows the strategy $b_E : b_E \geq 15{,}000$.

(b) Confirm that Erica cannot make a surplus with the bid $b_E = 18{,}000$.

(c) Confirm that if Erica follows the strategy $b_E \geq 15{,}000$, then Felicity will be indifferent between all bids $b_F : b_F \leq b_E$.

X30.10   Generalizing the previous case, suppose that a seller proposes to sell a car by first-price, sealed-bid auction. There are $n > 2$ potential bidders, indexed $I = 1, 2, \dots, n$

(Continued)

with valuations $v_1 > v_2 \ldots > v_n > 0$, each choosing an action, b_i. In the event of the winning bids being equal, the seller will accept the winning bid made by the player with the lowest index.

(a) Suppose that player n conjectures that $b_1^e = \max\{b_i^e\} > v_n$. Write down player n's best reply.

(b) Suppose that player n conjectures that $b_1^e = \max\{b_i^e\} < v_n$. Write down the set of bids for which player n obtains a positive payoff upon winning.

(c) Confirm that there is no equilibrium in which bid $b_n > v_n$ and bidder n wins the auction.

(d) Confirm that there is no equilibrium in which $b_n < v_n$ and bidder n wins the auction.

(e) Hence or otherwise confirm that in equilibrium, $v_1 \geq b_1^* \geq v_2$; and $b_1^* = \max\{b_i^*\}$.

X30.11 Confirm that there are Nash equilibria in which:

(a) $b_1 = b_2 = v_2$; $b_3 = b_4 = \ldots = b_n = 0$;

(b) $b_1 = b_2 = \ldots = b_n = v_2$;

(c) $b_1 = b_2 = \frac{1}{2}(v_1 + v_2)$; $b_3 = b_4 = \ldots = b_n = 0$;

(d) $b_i = v_{i+1}$ for $i < n$; $b_n = v_n$.

The set of Nash equilibria for the first-price, sealed-bid auction has some fairly obvious characteristics. Remember that we only require consistency of conjectures. So, bidder 1 will expect to win the auction (and want to win it) if she believes that $\max\{b_i : i = 2, 3, \ldots, n\} \leq v_1$, while bidder i will be content to lose if he believes that $\max\{b_j : j \neq i\} \geq v_i$. In Exercise X30.11, we find that there are Nash equilibria in which bidders 1 and 2 make the same bid, a bid that lies between their *WTP*, v_1 and v_2.

We illustrate this outcome in Figure 30.2, for the case where Erica and Felicity bid for Giselle's car. In Figure 30.2a, the solid-line segment shows that Erica is willing to match Felicity's bid, so long as she expects Felicity's bid to be less than her own valuation of 18,000. The shaded area shows that if Erica believes that Felicity will bid more than that 18,000, she will enter a bid lower than Felicity's. In the same way, in Figure 30.2b, the dashed line indicates that Felicity will wish just to outbid Erica if Erica's bid is less than Felicity's *WTP*, while the shaded area indicates that if Erica bids more than Felicity's *WTP*, Felicity will choose to bid less than Erica. (Note that we cannot really draw the best reply for Felicity for bids less than her *WTP* unless we also make the assumption that there is a finite bid increment, in which case she bids the smallest amount more than Erica's bid.) Combining these observations, we are able to confirm that the set of consistent conjectures are found where Erica and Felicity bid the same amount, which is no more than Erica's and no less than Felicity's *WTP*, so that Erica wins the auction.

In this analysis, we cannot rely on the concept of weak dominance to identify a preferred Nash equilibrium. We can see that bidding *WTP* weakly dominates bidding more than *WTP*, since there will be occasions in which the higher bid will be enough to win the auction, and to generate a negative payoff rather than the zero payoff when $b_i = WTP$. But, by the same argument, bidding less than *WTP* (and winning the auction) also dominates bidding *WTP* (and winning), since if the next highest bid $b_j < WTP_i$, bidder i can reduce her bid and still win the auction. The outcome in which all bids are equal to the next highest *WTP*, effectively the outcome of the Vickrey auction, seems to have sensible properties, and we shall argue that a version of it emerges when we abandon the property of perfect information.

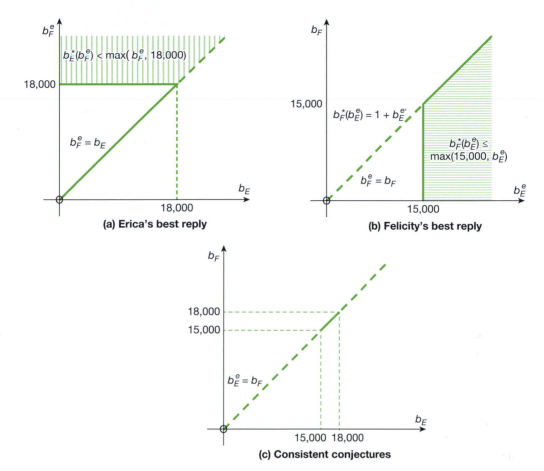

Figure 30.2 Best replies and Nash equilibria in a two-player Dutch auction with all possible bid values

30.3 Auctions with imperfect information

Treating an auction as a strategic game of imperfect information, for which we seek to obtain the set of Bayes–Nash equilibria, is a sensible next step. This is the correct formulation when we relax the assumption that every bidder knows the other bidders' valuation of the good, and instead assume that they will base their conjectures of the other bidders' strategies on their (limited) knowledge of the choice environment. As in Section 28.2.1, where we introduced Bayesian games, we specify:

- the players (in this case, all potential bidders, $i = 1, \dots, n$);
- the set of possible states of the world (here defined by the realization of each player's WTP, $v_i : \underline{v} \leq v_i \leq \overline{v}$);
- the set of *signals*, $S = \{\sigma_i\}$, or the information that each bidder has about the object being sold (with each player's signal, $\sigma_I = \sigma_i(v_1, \dots, v_n) = v_i$, so that each player knows his or her *WTP*);
- the range of actions available to them (the range of bids, $b_i \geq 0$);

- their payoff functions (determined by their *WTP*, v_i, whether or not they win the auction, and the payment, $p_i(b_1, \dots, b_n)$, made if they win); and
- their beliefs (about the distribution of other players' WTP_i, which are all independently and identically distributed).

For a Bayes–Nash equilibrium of an auction, each player's strategy consists of a bid, b_i^*, chosen to maximize their expected payoffs, $E[\pi_i(b_i|b_{\sim i}^*; \sigma_i|)]$ – that is, conditional upon the equilibrium bids of all of the other players, and their signals. As with any Nash equilibrium, unilateral deviation by any player from the equilibrium will not increase the expected payoff.

While this is a more formal statement of the structure of the game than we have seen before, there are two novel elements: that bidders' *WTP* are not common knowledge, but instead depend upon signals; and that bidders rely on beliefs about other players' *WTP*. We have assumed in the definition above that signals are sufficient information for each bidder to determine their own *WTP*, but that the bidders' *WTP* are unobservable. This means that the bidders have **private values**. For example, if we think of Giselle selling her car, Erica and Felicity might form their valuations after each had taken a test drive.

> **Private values**
> Personal valuations derived from private signals.

It is possible that differences in bids and valuations result from differences in beliefs, but the underlying valuation of the good is the same to all bidders. In such a case, we would have a **common-value** auction. For example, suppose that as well as taking a test drive, Felicity decides to take the car to a garage, where a mechanic inspects it and prepares a report alerting her to essential repairs that would need to be done before the car was safe to drive. While this signal is private, it reveals information that would be useful to Erica as well, and which would change her valuation of the car were it to be published.

> **Common values** A good with the same value to all bidders, for which estimates of value are inferred from signals.

By yourself

X30.12 Suppose that an art school regularly runs auctions of students' work at the end of their graduation show. Do you consider this to be a private-value auction or a common-value auction?

X30.13 Consider instead auctions of high-value, rare works of art. Remembering that these are often purchased by individuals or organizations as financial investments, discuss whether they should be treated as private-value or common-value auctions.

X30.14 Suppose that following the death of its previous owner, a painting by Raphael (a 16th Italian artist) comes to the market. A potential bidder obtains a report from an art historian indicating that the painting was probably completed by an assistant, rather than by the master. Why might this signal affect the bidder's *WTP*?

30.3.1 Weak dominance in Vickrey auctions

We have not yet defined in any detail the bidders' beliefs about other bidders' *WTP*, and we shall simply assume that they know that there is a common probability distribution, $F(v_j) = \Pr(v_j \le v_i)$. Assuming that all n values (and so all n signals) are independently and identically distributed, every bidder will conclude that the probability of having the highest *WTP* among the n bidders is the probability that all of the other $n - 1$ bidders have a lower *WTP*. That is, defining $\max\{v_j\}$ to be the highest *WTP* among the $n - 1$ other bidders:

$$\Pr(v_i \geq \max\{v_j\}) = [F(v_i)]^{n-1} \tag{30.3}$$

Our argument here relies on the fact that if an auction is efficient, then, in equilibrium, players' bids will be an increasing function of *WTP*. The rule $b_i = v_i$, which we found to work in the case of perfect information, clearly has that property. So let us treat it as a possible rule, and see whether it is possible to confirm that it would form part of a Nash equilibrium strategy. We shall assume that every bidder, $j \neq i$, has already adopted this strategy, so that $b_j = v_j$. Bidder i is free to choose any bid, v_i, and seeks to maximize the expected payoff:

$$\mathrm{E}[\pi_i(b_i)] = [F(b_i)]^{n-1}(v_i - \max\{v_j\}) \tag{30.4}$$

Since the payoff from losing the auction is zero, the expected payoff in Expression 30.4 is simply the product of the probability of, and the payoff received from, winning the auction.

By yourself

X30.15 Confirm that any strategy $b_i > v_i$ is weakly dominated by the strategy $b_i = v_i$. [*Hint:* Think of the payoff to winning when $b_i > \max\{v_j\} > v_i$.]

X30.16 Confirm that any strategy $b_i < v_i$ is weakly dominated by the strategy $b_i = v_i$. [*Hint:* Think of the payoff to losing when $v_i > \max\{v_j\} > b_i$.]

X30.17 Confirm that if $v_i > \max\{v_j\}$, then any bid $b_i^*: b_i^*(b_j^*) \geq \max\{v_j\}$ is a best reply; and that if $v_i < \max\{v_j\}$, then any bid $b_i^* : b_i^*(b_j^*) \leq \max\{v_j\}$ is a best reply. Hence demonstrate that there is a Nash equilibrium in which every bid $b_i^* = v_i$.

A second-price auction always has the property that changing strategy can only affect the payoff from participation if it changes the outcome of the auction, since the price paid depends on the second-highest, and not the winner's, bid. There are four possibilities:

- With strategy $b_i^* = v_i$, which wins the auction, all bids $b_i > v_i$ are also winning bids, but generate the same payoff as b_i^*.
- With strategy $b_i^* = v_i$ that wins the auction (with strictly positive payoff), then for strategies $b_i < v_i$ that win, the payoff will not change; but if they lose, the payoff falls to zero.
- With strategy $b_i^* = v_i$ that loses the auction, all bids $b_i < v_i$ are also losing bids, but generate the same (zero) payoff as b_i^*.
- With strategy $b_i^* = v_i$ that loses the auction (with strictly positive payoff), then for strategies $b_i > v_i$ that also lose, the payoff is still zero; but if they win, the payoff becomes negative.

A useful way of thinking about what happens here is to note that the equilibrium strategy, $b^*(v_i)$, is strictly increasing in v_i. We can think of someone who chooses another strategy as pretending to be a bidder with a different valuation. In equilibrium, we obtain preference revelation because no one can benefit from following another strategy.

30.3.2   Bidding in a first-price, sealed-bid auction

The argument we have just developed cannot hold with first-price auctions, since the payoff to winning varies with the strategy. Note that participants in first-price auctions only make positive surplus by bidding less than their *WTP*. We therefore develop the argument just introduced, that equilibrium strategies are a strictly increasing function of valuations, so no bidder benefits from pretending to have a different strategy in this type of auction.

To keep an example in front of us, we go back to Erica and Felicity bidding for Giselle's car. We now assume that Erica and Felicity do not know each other's *WTP*, and that each conjectures that the other will use bidding function $b : b_j = b(v_j)$. Note that we assume that they both use the same rule, b, to generate their bid from their valuation. They both expect to win the auction with any bid, $b_i : b_i > b(v_j)$, and in winning they obtain payoff $v_i - b_i$. For each of them, the probability of winning the auction is then $\Pr[b_j = b(v_j) < b_i]$.

We concentrate on Erica's strategy. Suppose Erica believes that Felicity's *WTP* is drawn from the uniform distribution, $v_F : 10{,}000 \leq v_F \leq 20{,}000$, with the cumulative distribution $\Pr[v_F \leq V] = \Theta_F(V) = \frac{V - 10{,}000}{10{,}000}$, and the probability density $\theta_F(V) = \frac{d\Theta_F}{dV} = \frac{1}{10{,}000}$. Now, with the bidding function, b, increasing in valuation, v_i, Erica can define the inverse function, $b^{-1} : b^{-1}(b_F) = v_F$. In deciding upon her own strategy, b_E, Erica concludes that she will win the auction with probability:

$$\Pr[v_F < b^{-1}(b_E)] = \frac{b^{-1}(b_E) - 10{,}000}{10{,}000} \tag{30.5}$$

Given that Erica and Felicity use the same bid function, Expression 30.5 is the probability of Felicity bidding less than Erica, given Felicity's bid function.

Erica therefore expects the payoff, π_E, from her strategy, b_E to be:

$$\mathrm{E}[\pi_E(b_E)] = (v_E - b_E)\left(\frac{b^{-1}(b_E) - 10{,}000}{10{,}000} \right) \tag{30.6}$$

The expected payoff in Expression 30.6 is the product of the bid–value margin and the probability of winning the auction. While the margin decreases as the bid b_E increases, the probability of winning increases. Erica's best reply is the bid $b_E{}^*$, which balances these effects at the margin, maximizing Expression 30.6.

We now consider what happens to Erica's expected payoff, $\mathrm{E}[\pi_E]$, as her *WTP*, v_E, increases. We may write the total derivative:

$$\frac{d\mathrm{E}[\pi_E]}{dv_E} = \frac{\partial \mathrm{E}[\pi_E]}{\partial v_E} + \frac{\partial \mathrm{E}[\pi_E]}{\partial b_E} \cdot \frac{db_E}{dv_E} \tag{30.7}$$

Should Erica's bid, b_E, have been chosen optimally, it must be that $\frac{\partial \mathrm{E}[\pi_E]}{\partial b_E} = 0$, and this allows us to simplify Expression 30.7:

$$\frac{d\mathrm{E}[\pi_E]}{dv_E} = \frac{\partial \mathrm{E}[\pi_E]}{\partial v_E} = \left(\frac{b^{-1}(b_E) - 10{,}000}{10{,}000} \right) \tag{30.8}$$

Expression 30.8 states that the rate of increase of Erica's expected payoff with her *WTP* is simply the probability of her winning the auction. We simplify Expression 30.8 further by remembering that in a Nash equilibrium conjectures are consistent; and since Erica and Felicity use the same bidding function, if $v_E = v_F$, the bids $b_E = b(v_E) = b(v_F) = b_F$. It follows that for Erica's bid, b_E, to be the winning bid, Felicity's valuation, $v_F < b^{-1}(b_E) = v_E$, so that:

$$\frac{dE[\pi_E]}{dv_E} = \frac{\partial E[\pi_E]}{\partial v_E} = \left(\frac{v_E - 10{,}000}{10{,}000}\right) \tag{30.9}$$

We now make one last assumption. Giselle, knowing that the lowest possible value of *WTP*, $\underline{v} = 10{,}000$, sets 10,000 as the reservation price. The effect is that should this be Erica's or Giselle's valuation, she would bid her full valuation, in which case $\pi(\underline{v}) = 0$. This permits us to integrate Expression 30.9, obtaining:

$$E[\pi_E] = \int_{10{,}000}^{v_E} \left(\frac{x - 10{,}000}{10{,}000}\right) dx \tag{30.10}$$

Substituting Expression 30.10 into Expression 30.6 and then rearranging it, we find an expression for the equilibrium bid:

$$b_E{}^* = v_E - \frac{\int_{10{,}000}^{v_E} \left(\frac{x - 10{,}000}{10{,}000}\right) dx}{\left(\frac{v_E - 10{,}000}{10{,}000}\right)} \tag{30.11}$$

By yourself

X30.18   Confirm that Expression 30.11 simplifies to give:

$$b_E{}^*(v_E) = \tfrac{1}{2}(10{,}000 + v_E) \tag{30.12}$$

Sketch a graph of $b_E{}^*$. Confirm that $b_E{}^*$ is the expected value of v_F given that $v_F \leq v_E$.

By expressing the optimal bid in terms of the bidder's value in Expression 30.12, we see the optimal shading of bids for this example. Erica's optimal bid, $b_E{}^*$ increases in her valuation. Were Erica to place the minimum value on the car, her optimal bid would be equal to the valuation. Should her valuation of the car be higher, her optimal bid would be the average of Erica's *WTP* and the minimum possible value. The optimal bid is then less than her *WTP*, and we call the difference the *shading* in the bid. If we think of Erica trying to work out how low she should bid so that Felicity will not try to change her strategy, the degree of shading should be such that Felicity will be indifferent between following the common bidding rule, *b*, and bidding more aggressively. Erica achieves this by assuming that she has the higher *WTP* and bidding the expected value of Felicity's *WTP*, given that assumption.

By yourself

X30.19   Suppose that there are several bidders in an auction. They all know that the others will wish to shade their bids. How would you expect the degree of shading of bids to increase as the number of bidders increases?

X30.20   Suppose that there are two bidders, whose valuations are drawn from a uniform distribution, $U[0, 1]$.

(a) What is the probability of bidder 1, whose valuation is v_1, winning the auction? Write down an expression for this bidder's expected payoff, and hence obtain the bid function associated with a symmetric equilibrium.

(b) Repeat part (a), but assume that there are N bidders.

(c) How would you explain the effect of increasing the number of bidders?

It should be unsurprising to discover that the larger the number of potential bidders in a first-price auction, the less the degree of shading will be. The rule in bidding, $b(v)$, is to assume that v is the highest *WTP* among the bidders, and then to bid the expected value of the second-highest *WTP* given this assumption. With more bidders, the expected value of the second-highest *WTP* will increase. Having more bidders in a first-price auction is therefore good for the seller, who expects bids to be closer to people's *WTP*.

30.4   Revenue equivalence

The *revenue equivalence theorem* is probably the best-known result in auction theory. As defined by Vickrey, the second-price, sealed-bid auction form emerged as an application of the underlying principle that in many circumstances the seller's expected revenue from an auction will not be affected by the form of auction being used. This is true for the four auction forms considered in this chapter, so long as we consider only private-value auctions. It does not necessarily apply to common-value auctions.

Here we only present a justification of the principles underlying the theorem. We begin by defining a *direct selling mechanism* as any game used to allocate the good among N potential bidders. As before, we denote by v_i both the value of the good to bidder i and the bidder's type, and the expected payoff to the bidder by $E[\pi_i]$. The expected payoff, $E[\pi_i]$ depends upon the probability of the bidder receiving the good, here $\theta_i(v_i)$, and the expected payment, P_i, given the bidder's value, v_i. We write:

$$E[\pi_i] = v_i\theta_i - P_i \qquad [30.13]$$

In the four forms of auction that we have considered, bidders only made payments on winning the auction. Expression 30.13 separates payment from winning, and so allows us to consider a wider range of mechanisms. For example, in *all-pay auctions*, all bidders make a payment to the seller, who then allocates the good to the person making the highest payment. We can also allow for bidders being charged participation fees, and for multi-stage auctions in which each bidder makes a sequence of bids, all of which are observed by other bidders.

To demonstrate the principle of the theorem, we develop the argument that in equilibrium no bidder will engage in out-of-equilibrium behaviour because $E[\pi_i]$ is at a maximum. To do this, we explore out-of-equilibrium behaviour, effectively treating bidder i as undertaking an impersonation of bidder j, when all other bidders are following the equilibrium strategy. In our example, this does not simply mean that Erica and Felicity might claim to have the other's *WTP*, but also that they might claim that their *WTP* is any value other than the true one. Specifically, pretending that $WTP_i = v_j$, bidder i will be given the good with probability θ_j and will expect to make payments P_j. We write bidder i's expected payoff under these circumstances as $E[\pi_{ji}]$. Then:

$$E[\pi_{ji}] = v_i\theta_j - P_j \qquad [30.14]$$

Here, we wish to argue that there is no type, j, for which bidder i finds that $E[\pi_{ji}] > E[\pi_i]$. This ensures that the selling mechanism then supports truthful revelation of preferences.

For bidder, j, for whom $WTP_j = v_j$, we can rewrite Expression 30.13 as:

$$E[\pi_j] = v_j\theta_j - P_j \qquad [30.15]$$

Combining Expressions 30.14 and 30.15 to eliminate the payments, we see that:

$$E[\pi_{ji}] = E[\pi_j] + (v_i - v_j)\theta_j \qquad [30.16]$$

so that for equilibrium, with player i never doing worse by following the equilibrium strategy:

$$E[\pi_i] \geq E[\pi_j] + (v_i - v_j)\theta_j \qquad [30.17]$$

Expression 30.17 has an intuitive interpretation in terms of the value of winning the auction. When bidder i impersonates bidder j, she receives exactly the same payoff as bidder j should her bid be unsuccessful. When she wins the auction, though, she obtains value v_i from being given the good, rather than v_j. If Expression 30.17 did not hold, bidder i would definitely prefer to impersonate bidder j, which would be inconsistent with our definition of equilibrium.

30.4.1 The equivalence theorem

It might seem obvious in our earlier examples that Erica and Felicity will not want to imitate the other's behaviour when there is a large, measurable difference in their *WTP*. But suppose player i is here considering a very small deviation from the equilibrium strategy. We represent this by writing $v_j = v_i + \delta v$. Adapting the notation slightly, Expression 30.17 may be rewritten as:

$$E[\pi(v_i)] \geq E[\pi(v_i + \delta v)] - \delta v.\theta(v_i + \delta v) \qquad [30.18a]$$

$$E[\pi(v_i + \delta v)] \geq E[\pi(v_i)] + \delta v.\theta(v_i) \qquad [30.18b]$$

In Expression 30.18, we have changed the notation slightly and written Expression 30.17 in two ways. If we have two bidders whose *WTP* are arbitrarily close, then in equilibrium neither will want to be mistaken for the other. We can rewrite Expression 30.16 in a single expression:

$$\theta(v_i + \delta v) \geq \frac{\mathrm{E}[\pi(v_i + \delta v)] - \mathrm{E}[\pi(v_i)]}{\delta v} \geq \theta(v_i) \qquad [30.19]$$

The expression in the middle should be recognizable as the average rate of change of the expected payoff over the finite interval, δv, which we have met before as a preliminary to defining the derivative function. Taking the limit as $\delta v \to 0$, Expression 30.19 becomes the rather simpler expression:

$$\frac{d\mathrm{E}[\pi_i]}{dv_i} = \theta_i \qquad [30.20]$$

This is a generalization of Expression 30.8, where we argued that in a simple first-price auction, the derivative of the payoff function with respect to bidder values was simply the probability of winning the auction. In that special case we integrated both sides, using the boundary condition $\pi(\underline{v}) = 0$ to obtain the payoff function analogous to:

$$\mathrm{E}[\pi_i] = \int_{\underline{v}}^{v_i} \theta(x) dx \qquad [30.21]$$

Expression 30.21 is sufficient to confirm revenue equivalence. It says that two elements define the expected payoff received by a bidder with value v_i in any auction mechanism. These are the expected payoff accruing to the member of the population who has the lowest possible value, $\pi(\underline{v})$, and the probability of any bidder being awarded the good, $\theta_i = \theta(v_i)$. There is nothing in Expression 30.21 relating to the form of the mechanism, which indicates that the expected revenue is independent of its form.

We have already presented arguments that in first- and second-price auctions, equilibrium bids and payoffs increase in *WTP*, and that the probability of any bidder being awarded the good is simply the probability of that bidder having the highest value among all the drawings from the underlying probability distribution. This means that the probability of a bidder being awarded the good, $\theta(v_i)$, is the same in both forms of auction; and so, given the definition in Expression 30.21, the expected payoff of any bidder is the same in these two mechanisms.

When we defined expected payoffs, $\mathrm{E}[\pi_i]$, in Expression 30.14, we defined them as being dependent on bidders' values, v_i, the probability of being awarded the good, θ_i, and the payment that each bidder expects to make, P_i. We have now argued that, except for the expected payment, all these terms will have the same value in both first- and second-price auctions. It follows that the expected payment, $P_i = v_i \theta_i - \pi_i$, will also be the same in both forms.

By yourself

X30.21   Rewrite Expression 30.16 in terms of value v_i, the difference in probabilities of the two bidders receiving the good and the difference in the expected payments. What interpretation would you place on this result?

X30.22   How can the seller's expected revenues be the same in first-price and second-price auctions when the mechanisms used are different?

X30.23 Suppose that bidder *j* considers impersonating bidder *i*. Write down an expression equivalent to Expression 30.14. Using this expression to substitute for π_j in Expression 30.15, confirm that the probability of being given the good increases with bidder *j*'s valuation.

X30.24 Consider the derivation of Expression 30.8. Give an intuitive explanation of its generalization in Expression 30.20.

30.4.2 The seller's expected revenue

Exercise X30.24 invites you to consider how revenue equivalence emerges across forms of auction. From the point of view of the seller, the shading of bids, which is an essential part of a first-price auction, has the same effect as the rule that the winning bidder will pay less than the sum bid in a second-price auction. We therefore demonstrate that the expected revenue from a first-price auction and from a second-price auction are indeed equal.

The most straightforward method of doing this begins by calculating the expected payment made by the winning bidder, for whom $WTP = v^*$, in a second-price auction. The payment made is determined by the second-highest value, which is also the highest of $(n - 1)$ values constrained to be less than v^*. We assume that values are independent, and identically distributed, with distribution function, $F(v)$.

By yourself

X30.25 Obtain expressions for the following:
  (a) The distribution function, G, for $n - 1$ independently distributed values, v_i, with distribution function, $F = F(v)$, which are all less than the value v^*.
  (b) The probability density function, $g(v) : g = \frac{dG}{dv}$.
  (c) The expected payment P^*, given that the winner's WTP is v^*.

X30.26 Assume that the distribution function, $F : F(v) = \frac{v - 10,000}{10,000}$, so that valuations are drawn from a uniform distribution, with $10,000 \leq v \leq 20,000$, and that there are only two bidders. Show that:
  (a) the distribution function, defined in X30.25, is $G : G(v) = F(v)$;
  (b) the probability density function $g : g(v) = \frac{1}{10,000}$; and
  (c) the expected payment is $P^* : P^*(v^*) = \dfrac{\displaystyle\int_{10,000}^{20,000} \frac{x}{10,000}\, dx}{\displaystyle\int_{10,000}^{20,000} \frac{dx}{10,000}} = \frac{1}{2}\,(v^* + 15,000)$.

X30.27 Assume that the distribution function $F : F(v) = v$, so that all valuations are drawn from a uniform distribution with $0 \leq n \leq 1$, and that there are n bidders. Show that:
  (a) the distribution function, defined in X30.25, is $G : G(v) = [F(v)]^{n-1} = v^{n-1}$;
  (b) the probability density function $g : g(v) = (n - 1)v^{n-2}$ and the expected payment is

$$P^* : P^*(v^*) = \dfrac{\displaystyle\int_0^{v^*} (n-1)x^{n-1}dx}{\displaystyle\int_0^{v^*} (n-1)x^{n-2}dx} = \left(\frac{n-1}{n}\right)v^*.$$

From Exercise X30.25, we obtain an expression for the expected payment, which can be simplified using elementary techniques of integration. In case these are not familiar to you, we note that the expected payments in Exercises X30.26 and X30.27 are the equilibrium bids made by a bidder in specific examples of first-price auctions. That is consistent with our argument, since bidders in first-price auctions expect to pay their bid (if they are correct in believing that they have the highest *WTP*), and so shade their bids, while winners in second-price auctions pay the second-highest bids. The optimal extent of shading is shown here to be the expected difference between the highest and second-highest ranked *WTP* values.

For any group of bidders, with given *WTP* values, the highest bidder expects to make the same payment in both forms of auction. Where the bidder can be quite certain about the payment that will be made upon winning a first-price auction, she will be uncertain about the price she will be asked to pay in a second-price auction, for that depends on the distribution of the other bidders' values as well as her own. Nonetheless, for any realization of the highest value, v^*, the seller expects to receive the same revenue, irrespective of the form of auction used.

By yourself

X30.28 Consider the special case where bidders' valuations are distributed according to a uniform distribution with supports $[\underline{v}, \overline{v}]$. The distribution function is then $F(v) = \frac{v - \underline{v}}{\overline{v} - \underline{v}}$ and the density function $f(v) = \frac{1}{\overline{v} - \underline{v}}$. The expected value of the 2nd order statistic (the 2nd highest of the n values drawn from the distribution) is then $v_{(2)} = \frac{2\underline{v} + (n - 1)\overline{v}}{n + 1}$.

   (a) What is the seller's expected revenue in a second-price auction, where the highest *WTP* is v^*?

   (b) Using revenue equivalence, how much will bidders be willing to offer in a first-price auction?

   (c) In an all-pay auction, bidders pay the amount that they bid, but only the highest bidder receives the object. Explain why revenue equivalence holds in this case, and use the result of part (b) to calculate optimal bids.

30.5　Conclusions

It is common for economists to refer to mechanism design as 'reverse game theory'. By this they mean that analysis of games generally begins from a problem of strategic interdependence and tries to explain the optimal behaviour of the players, using the Nash equilibrium concept or some refinement of it. With mechanism design, we start with a problem, in this chapter the one facing a seller of goods, who is attempting to obtain the highest price when there is no well-defined market and when the seller cannot identify the *WTP* of potential buyers. Any well-designed auction mechanism turns out to be efficient, in the sense that bidders have incentives to reveal their true *WTP* through their choice of bid. Instead of modelling the game to explain the outcome, in this case we design a game that generates the desired outcome.

Auctions have been used for many centuries, and we noted at the beginning of the chapter that there are several traditional forms. In that context our final result, revenue equivalence, is perhaps unsurprising, in that if sellers expected their revenues to depend upon the form of auction that they used, inefficient forms would gradually disappear. Of course, we have only introduced the simplest possible auctions (and models) in this chapter, and an important role of auction theory in recent years has been to improve the design of auctions so that they can be used in a wider range of circumstances and be more effective in the sense of increasing sellers' expected revenues. In this context the Vickrey auction was a very early innovation, but one which, while interesting to economists, had relatively limited practical applications until eBay incorporated elements of the second-price, sealed-bid form into its auctions. The volume of trade on eBay, and the behaviour of bidders, has made it an important subject for study in auction theory. For example, many experienced bidders do not reveal their true proxy value until seconds before the end of an auction, because keeping it private reduces substantially the likelihood of their losing out in a bidding war. Similarly, auction theory has provided governments with many important insights into the design of the sale of rights which have generated substantial revenues since the 1990s. Auctions continue to be an important area for research that deepens our understanding of how markets operate.

Summary

Among the most common forms of auction are the English (ascending, open outcry) auction, and the Dutch (descending) auction; and first-price, sealed-bid auctions. Vickrey proposed the second-price, sealed-bid auction as being broadly equivalent to the English auction.

In second-price auctions in which bidders have perfect information, including other bidders' *WTP*, there are Nash equilibria in which aggressive bidding by a bidder other than the one with the highest *WTP*, wins. The winning bid is then higher than the highest *WTP*. In such cases, the strategy of bidding *WTP* is weakly dominant for all players.

There is no unique weakly dominant Nash equilibrium for first-price auctions when bidders have perfect information. We showed that under certain circumstances (including an allocation rule for tied auctions) that the set of Nash equilibria would consist of all possible pairs of equal bids between the lower and the higher valuations.

Allowing for imperfect information (so that bidders do not know other bidders' valuations), then in second-price auctions the weakly dominant strategy of bidding valuations supports the only Nash equilibrium.

In first-price auctions, assuming that the bidding function is an increasing function of bidders' *WTP*, it is possible to derive the optimal bidding function, which shades the bid below *WTP* by the amount of the expected next-highest *WTP*.

Auctions are efficient mechanisms because the common bidding function means that no one wishes to appear to have a *WTP* other than the true value.

The rate of change of the expected payoff with respect to *WTP* is the probability of winning the auction, given the *WTP*. From this, we are able to define the expected payoff for any given valuation, and to show that the expected payment of bidders is determined only by the lowest-possible *WTP* and the probability of winning the auction.

This is sufficient to demonstrate revenue equivalence: that the expected revenue of the seller does not depend upon the form of the auction.

Visit the companion website at **www.palgrave.com/mochrie** to access further teaching and learning materials, including lecturer slides and a testbank, as well as guideline answers and student MCQs.

31

Afterword

The argument of this book runs to approximately a quarter of a million words. Even so, it is quite terse: in almost every chapter, it has been compressed, minimizing elaboration that might detract from the central points of the argument. We have repeatedly sought answers to a question that is easy to pose: how do people respond when they find themselves in a situation in which they command limited resources while their desires are effectively unbounded? The answer that we have explored in this book – the answer of almost all microeconomic analysis – is that people will use the available resources efficiently, so that no one applying the decision-making logic of microeconomic theory could fulfil their desires any more fully by allocating their resources in any other way. We rely throughout upon the equi-marginal principle: that across all of the possible uses of a resource, the ratio of marginal benefits to marginal costs will be the same.

Microeconomics should not simply be an explanation of the behaviour of a variety of seemingly independent actors, who must somehow husband their resources effectively. We also have to explain the operation of markets. Our arguments should predict how market outcomes will change as there are changes in some parameter values within the choice environment of individual participants. Setting out such predictions within the context of a coherent theory forms the core of the book. In Part II, we developed a model of an individual consumer's allocation of expenditure across goods, taking it to the point where we considered the effects of changes in the price of goods. Part III was largely the equivalent, in which we analysed the supply decisions of individual firms which face a perfectly competitive market. This was enough for us to obtain the market-clearing conditions, firstly in one perfectly competitive market; and then, in effect, in the linked product and factor markets of the general equilibrium models introduced in Part V. Both for markets and for individuals, we were able to predict how outcomes might change as prices change.

Parts VI and VII are framed rather differently. Rather than involving discussion of choice, they concentrate on behaviour. The discussion builds on the method of argument developed for the standard models. For example, in considering how to divide their time between labour and leisure, there is clearly no market in which people might trade leisure time. We instead model the problem in terms of the derivation of utility (or, using more natural language, pleasure) from the consumption of goods and services. People have to be able to buy goods and services, but also need leisure time to consume them. By providing labour services within the market, people can trade leisure time for the ability to purchase more goods and services. With the optimal time allocation between labour and leisure, the marginal value of labour time (or additional consumption capacity) matches the marginal cost of the loss of leisure. There is no tension between the analysis of choice and the analysis of behaviour, for behaviour involves choice, but among a more complex set of objects than alternative consumption bundles or factor input combinations.

Accepting that in the last fifty years there has been a shift in the focus of economic theory from understanding choice to understanding behaviour, the work of Gary Becker and George Akerlof has been exceptionally important. We have encountered some of their most prominent ideas already. Becker began his career by developing the existing theory of human capital very substantially. Arguing that through education, through training and through work itself, people are able to build up an intangible capital stock that has the effect of increasing their labour productivity, and thus their wages in future, Becker was able to provide a very useful and versatile framework for analysis of earnings. Of at least equal importance for the development of economic theory, Akerlof argued (in one of his earliest publications, 'The Market for Lemons') that in the presence of informational asymmetries, sellers of good-quality products will not necessarily be able to find willing buyers unless they are willing to accept a substantial discount on the true value of the goods they bring to market. Shortly after the publication of Akerlof's work, Michael Spence extended it, demonstrating how such sellers of good-quality products might bear the costs of signalling to overcome such asymmetries. Spence's argument gives us an alternative to Becker's explanation for wages increasing with education. If education were to be simply a signal of high productivity, an innate characteristic but one that cannot be observed by potential employers, it would have no intrinsic value. Education would then in effect be a form of quality certification.

Looking beyond these different characterizations of education, there is an important difference between Becker's and Akerlof's conceptualizations of the discipline of economics. For Becker, human behaviour is largely explicable in terms of the economic principles of resource allocation.[1] If people choose to engage in criminal activity, it is because the incentive structure that they face rewards them for doing so. While an addict might report feelings of compulsion in respect of specific behaviours, we might explain such behaviours in terms of the effect of past usage of the addictive good on the value of consumption of all goods, with forward-looking people willing to accept addiction as part of an inter-temporal utility-maximizing strategy. Families emerge as a rational response to the presence of economies of scale and scope in the production of household goods; and marriage is a legal contract, which either side might terminate if the value of an alternative outside option became greater than the value of remaining within the marriage.

The Beckerian approach – or, as he called it, the economic approach to human behaviour – deliberately aims to be comprehensive. It seeks to define economics as the primary mode of explanation of all social activity, and, for that reason, social scientists trained in disciplines other than economics have often been very critical of its assumption that the pursuit of

---

1 Becker's approach was lampooned by Alan Blinder's article, 'The Economics of Brushing Teeth'. Kieran Gillespie's essay, 'Relationships and University', also written, he assures me, as a parody, deliberately pushes economic analysis beyond all reasonable boundaries. Kieran's essay is available through the companion website for this book, at **www.palgrave.com/mochrie.**

self-interest effectively eclipses all other considerations. Among such social scientists, there is a concern that the Beckerian approach seeks to colonize their disciplines, subordinating other modes of enquiry and argument to the order and rigour of economic theory.[2]

If the Beckerian approach seeks to extend the *imperium* of economics, Akerlof seems much more to be the curious traveller, visiting other disciplines to extract new ways of thinking about economic phenomena. Akerlof has repeatedly drawn on ideas that have emerged within related disciplines and found ways of bringing them into economic models. Perhaps the end result differs from Becker's largely on semantic grounds, for Akerlof's models are clearly economic in character, even as they broaden the definition of what might be considered to be economic. Akerlof is willing to accept that social phenomena are in some sense real, and so have to be accommodated within economic theory, whereas Becker is at least tempted to suggest that they are entirely conventional, and that it is impossible to understand their true nature without applying the tools of economic enquiry.

We have seen in the chapter on behavioural economics that the commerce across the social sciences involves psychologists, organizational theorists and political scientists, as well as economists: it is not simply one-way traffic. Perhaps most notably, Herbert Simons, Daniel Kahneman, and Elinor Ostrom have made sufficiently important contributions to our understanding of economics, while working within these separate disciplines, that they have each (separately) been awarded the Nobel Memorial Prize for Economics. With their traditions of modelling the processes of individual and social decision making, other social sciences can easily extend our understanding of economic theory. Indeed, some of the most interesting developments in government policy in recent years have come from understanding how the framing of choices affects the decisions that people will make. For example, with ageing populations, many governments wish to encourage much greater saving for (long) retirements, rather than relying on public welfare. The appropriate design of savings vehicles can substantially increase their uptake. Economists such as Richard Thaler, who have sought to incorporate the knowledge developed in other social sciences in policy design, have played an important role in this area.

Such work goes well beyond mere explanation of behaviour, or indeed prediction of the effects of changes in behaviour in the context of a certain environment. Instead, it has been driven by the belief that socially desirable changes in behaviour might result from public interventions designed to affect people's understanding of their choice environment. Many governments consider pension saving to be problematic because people receive the benefits at some point in the distant future, and so are likely not to place a sufficiently high value on them at the time when they should first commit to a regular saving plan. Such people, as they approach the age at which they plan to retire, find that they will be excessively dependent upon social benefits. Behavioural analysis based on an understanding of the limitations of human cognitive capacity has argued that there is a form of status-quo bias in people's decision making. Even as simple a measure as changing the default position from non-membership of a savings scheme to membership of such a scheme, on the basis that people

---

2   For example, Becker's rational addiction model relies on people's demand for the good having the characteristic that any change in the choice environment, such as a reduction in the price of the good that leads to an immediate increase in demand, will also lead to an increase in demand in the future. Skye Madden's essay, in the online student essay bank, demonstrates what this means. You can read Skye's essay on the companion website for this book, at **www.palgrave.com/mochrie**.

will then be less likely to opt out of a scheme of which they are automatically members, can have substantial effects on individual behaviour. In effect, by changing the framing of the problem for pension savers, governments are able to change savers' behaviour.

Within the economics profession, understanding the nature of behaviour is an end in itself. Often, though, we develop economic theory with very practical objectives in mind, wishing to go beyond explanation of the operation of social institutions and to identify ways in which we might improve them. If we consider the range of applications of theory that have traditionally been at the heart of microeconomics, such as industrial organization, labour economics, public economics and welfare, law, education and health, management of natural resources, development, history, and environmental economics, then you may be able to recall from this book some examples drawn from almost all of these applications. All are amenable to the application of extensions of the standard theory; but all have been touched by the widening of analytical methods in the last fifty years, as we try to understand behaviour in the context of imperfect information and strategic interactions, making it amenable to the application of game theory. Throughout our discussion, whatever the application of theory, understanding, and shaping, behaviour has been important.

As we seek to understand economic phenomena, we expect to formulate alternative theories, which will generate competing economic policy recommendations. For example, if we treat education as a form of human capital formation, we recognize that principles for its public support might include equality of access, coupled with some form of risk sharing among participants to mitigate the uncertainty in individual returns. The government might guarantee loans for study, in the expectation that graduates as a group will be able to make repayments in full, while allowing those graduates who are not successful in the labour market effectively to default on their loans. On the other hand, suppose we see education as a signal of underlying productivity. The challenge for policy makers then is to ensure that the difference in education costs between groups of differing ability is large. Education, through some form of testing, can then be effective in separating these groups, even though the actual cost of participation is low for those people who wish to use it to signal their ability.

The validity of any theory is an empirical question, and in this book we have not considered the means by which the claims of economic theory can be tested and appraised. Perhaps unsurprisingly, given the nature of the standard theory, economists tend to rely upon the operation of statistical inference upon sampled, real economic data, in which a theory is only considered to receive support if there is significant evidence that its explanatory power is not zero. Importantly, therefore, economists seek to identify causal relationships associated with variation in objective, measurable data, rather than, for example, basing analysis upon survey evidence of intentions and motivations, where the sampled data is largely subjective. If we think about education and apply a human capital approach, we might predict positive returns to additional years of education, irrespective of the number of years. Applying a signalling approach, we would expect to see substantial differences in returns from the partial completion of a standardized course, such as an undergraduate degree, and the final award of credentials on full completion. Only full completion will be an effective signal. With appropriate statistical analysis, we can obtain evidence that is consistent with one or other of the alternative explanations of variation in wages.

We have defined data in this context as being essentially accidental – as being gathered through the observation of behaviour. Accompanying the increasing interest in behavioural economics in recent years, there has also been a considerable expansion in the scope of purposive data generation with the expansion of experimental economics. The idea of an experiment is simple: with substantial control over the choice environment, experimenters can observe how participants respond to changes in it. The simplest experiments explore behaviour in two-player, two-action games. It is also very easy to run auctions within an experimental context, to confirm that the predictions of the standard theory are (qualitatively) correct, and to explore behaviour in non-standard markets, such as voluntary contribution mechanisms for the provision of public goods. When making inferences about the ways in which people behave, laboratory experiments can have substantial problems. For example, it may be that in designing the choice environment the experimenters overlook some element that has a very substantial effect on decision making. In addition, there is always the problem of generalizing results. In a laboratory setting, for example, people may be aware that their actions are being observed and so change them to match what they believe the experimenter will consider appropriate.

Experiments tend to have value because they can generate data in a way that is largely reliable. They need not be confined to laboratories. We often find opportunities to rely on changes in government policy to observe the effects of natural experiments, in which we can identify changes in behaviour resulting from the policy changes. In recent years there has been an explosion of interest in field experiments, carried out, as far as possible, over an extended period of time, in which people are assigned on a random basis to one of a range of choice environments. Such randomized control trials have already generated substantial insights into behaviour, especially in developing countries where market mechanisms for resource allocation can be very limited so that there may be many opportunities for small-scale innovations to improve economic outcomes.

Building on our metaphor of trade, we might think of economics as being rather like an enclosed sea, such as the Baltic or the Mediterranean. Economists have colonized the coastal regions, with the areas of the discipline that we have mentioned above representing the great cities. The exchange of ideas between economists occurs within markets, both within the cities and between them. Beyond the entrance to the enclosed sea is the rest of social science, with which trade is possible, although there will often be cultural differences that make such trade difficult to sustain. This book is then like a ship, simple but seaworthy, allowing you to make a first voyage around the coast. If the voyage has been successful, then you will have returned to your home port, perhaps after a few rough passages, but with plenty of souvenirs collected on the voyage; and I hope that the prospect of further voyages, some of which might take you over the horizon to as yet unvisited regions, will be very appealing.

Glossary

Abatement cost The cost borne by the producer in reducing an externality.

Action profile (outcome) Combinations of actions that might be chosen by players.

Advances in technology (technological progress) Changes in the state of technology over time.

Adverse selection Asymmetric information exerts a negative externality on sellers of high-quality goods.

Anchor Information used as the starting point for making a decision.

Arrow's impossibility theorem No rank-order voting system can convert individual preferences into a satisfactory social preference ordering.

Artificial monopoly A firm's monopoly power if derived from legal restrictions that prevent entry.

Asymmetric information The situation in which players' information sets differ.

Attributes Observable signs, which can be manipulated by informed players and whose value is used by uninformed players to update priors.

Auction Selling a good by inviting potential buyers to announce the amount they are willing to pay.

Auctioneer A person who announces successive prices until declaring a set at which markets clear.

Availability The ease of recall of an item, taken as a measure of its relative frequency.

Average cost The production cost per unit of output.

Bayesian learning Revision (or updating) of a prior on receipt of information.

Bayesian prior A random variable, defining beliefs whose subjective probability distribution changes as information is received.

Bliss point The ideal consumption bundle.

Budget (affordability) constraint Those consumption bundles that cost the full amount of money available.

Budget (affordable) set All the consumption bundles that can be acquired for a cost less than income.

Capital input The monetary value of assets used in business.

Changes at the margin Very small changes in the level of an activity.

Characteristics Sources of utility embodied within a good.

Characteristics (of experience goods) Underlying (unobservable) qualities of a good, which nevertheless determine its value.

Cognitions Mental processes involved in knowledge acquisition.

Cognitive dissonance Mental tension caused by mutually incompatible cognitions.

Collusion Agreement between firms regarding their behaviour in order to increase their profits.

Common property resource An excludable resource to which members of a group have access.

Common values A good with the same value to all bidders, for which estimates of value are inferred from signals.

Compensated (Hicksian) demand The demand of the expenditure-minimizing consumer.

Competitive game A game in which increasing payoffs for one player require a reduction in others' payoffs.

Completeness A preference relation defined for every pair of consumption bundles.

Conjecture A belief about actions that competitors will choose.

Consistent conjectures All firms' beliefs about competitors' actions are correct.

Conspicuous consumption A public display of consumption to demonstrate wealth.

Constrained maximization Methods for solving problems of choice whereby solutions are drawn from a restricted set.

Consumption bundle A combination of quantities of the goods available to the consumer.

Consumption profile A list of total expenditure in a sequence of time periods.

Convexity Every preferred set is convex.

Coordination game A game with several equilibria, in which players realize gains by coordinating their actions.

Cost function The least possible expenditure required to produce any level of output, given input prices.

Costs of production The expenditure that is necessary in order to make sales.

Cournot conjecture The belief that a competitor's output will not vary with own output.

Demand function The relation between the price of a good and the quantity that a consumer buys.

Discount factor The ratio of the present value of money to its future value.

Dominant strategy The action that is the best reply to all actions other players might choose.

Dominant strategy equilibrium The Nash equilibrium in which every player's strategy is dominant.

Dutch (descending) auction An auction conducted by open outcry, with the WTA descending; the first bid wins.

Economic efficiency A state in which reallocation of resources cannot improve the outcome.

Economic efficiency in production A property of the cost-minimizing input bundle: changing inputs while holding expenditure constant causes costs to increase.

Economic surplus The difference between *WTP* and *WTA*; the social benefit from a transaction.

Elastic (or inelastic) demand A proportionate reduction in demand following a price rise that is greater than (less than) the proportionate price rise.

Elasticity of substitution The proportional change in the composition of a bundle that results from a small proportional change in the marginal rate of substitution.

Engel curve A graph of demand plotted against income.

English (ascending) auction An auction in which bids are made verbally, ascending in value until no higher bid is received.

Envelope A curve that forms boundary of other curves.

Equi-marginal principle A rule that, when the resource is being used as effectively as possible, the ratio of marginal benefits to costs will be the same across all alternative uses of the resource.

Eventually diminishing returns to scale Returns to scale that diminish only when output is high.

Excess demand A situation in which potential sellers offer less of a good than buyers wish to purchase.

Excess market demands A demand for a good that is beyond the quantity in the endowment.

Excess supply A situation in which potential sellers offer more of a good than buyers wish to purchase.

Exchange economy A model in which endowments take the form of bundles of goods, which are then traded.

Excludability A property of a good that allows its owner to prevent others from using it.

Expected utility A probability weighted sum of all possible values of utility scores from a lottery; the mean of utility.

Expected value A probability weighted sum of all possible values of a random variable; the mean value of the variable.

Expenditure function The least money required to reach an acceptable utility, given the prices of goods.

Expenditure share The proportion of money spent on a specific good.

Experience good A good whose nature can be confirmed only through use.

Extensive form of game A representation of a strategic game in which decisions can be made sequentially.

Externality The effect of one individual's decisions on another's payoffs.

Factor of production An asset hired by a firm in its production process.

Firm A business entity; often a limited company.

First-degree price discrimination Selling each unit of a good at a different price.

First-price auction An auction in which the highest bidder wins and pays their own bid.

Free-riding Obtaining access to a public good without contributing to the cost of its provision.

Fungible assets Assets such that individual units are perfect substitutes.

Future value The value of a sum of money available at the present time, evaluated at a certain time in the future.

Game A mathematical model of interactions between decision makers.

General equilibrium All market prices are determined at the same time, with simultaneous market clearing.

Giffen behaviour An increase in the price of a good leads to an increase in demand.

Heuristic A decision-making rule.

History The path through a decision tree, from the initial node to the payoffs.

Homogeneity of degree t The responsiveness of a function to scalar changes in inputs.

Horizontal differentiation Spatial differentiation such that consumers' preferences over characteristics differ.

Incentive compatibility A property of a mechanism such that participants reveal their true type.

Income effect The change in demand following a price increase that is associated with a loss of purchasing power.

Income elasticity of demand The responsiveness of a consumer's demand to a change in income.

Income expansion path A curve showing the most-preferred, affordable consumption bundles as income varies.

Income offer curve An alternative name for the income expansion path.

Incomplete information The situation in which a player in a game lacks information relevant to a decision.

Independence A quality of successive trials, such that the outcome of one cannot be (causally) related to the outcome of the others.

Indifference Equal ranking of outcomes, so that neither is seen as better than the other.

Indifference curve The representation of all equally preferred consumption bundles.

Indirect utility The greatest utility possible given prices and the money available to finance consumption.

Individual (firm) supply The quantity of output produced by a firm at a given price.

Individual demand The quantity of a good purchased at a given price.

Inferior good A good for which demand decreases with income.

Instantaneous utility The utility generated in a specific time period.

Inverse demand function The price a firm can set as a function of the quantity consumers demand.

Isocost line All of the input combinations that can be hired for a set price.

Isoprofit curve A contour of profit function, showing combinations of firm outputs for which one firm achieves a target profit.

Isoquant A curve that shows input combinations for which output is constant.

Labour input The number of hours of effort directed to production activity.

Law of small numbers The belief that a sample should have the distributional properties of the whole population.

Long run A period in which the use of all factors can be varied.

Loss aversion A desire to avoid losses.

Lottery A description of an experiment in terms of the values taken by a random variable, representing outcomes and their associated probability distribution

Marginal cost The rate at which costs change as output changes.

Marginal product The rate of change of output as usage of one input varies.

Marginal rate of substitution (MRS) The rate of decline in consumption of a good that compensates for the rising consumption of an alternative good.

Marginal rate of technical substitution The rate at which one factor input must be substituted for another in order to maintain output.

Marginal rate of transformation A rate at which output of one good falls as output of another increases.

Marginal utility The rate of change of utility as the quantity available of one good increases.

Marginal utility of a good The rate of change of utility as consumption of the good increases, consumption of other goods being held constant.

Market clearing A situation in which potential sellers offer the quantity of a good that buyers wish to purchase.

Market coverage Firms' strategies ensure that all consumers are in the market, with no unmet demand.

Market demand The total quantity of a good purchased in a market at a given price.

Market equilibrium The market price and the quantity traded such that the market supply equals the market demand

Market power A situation in which market participants, by their actions, can affect the quantity traded or the market price.

Market price The price at which all transactions completed in a market take place.

Market supply The total quantity of a good brought to market at a given price.

Markets An abstraction from the physical concept of a place and a time at which buyers and sellers of a good or a service meet to take part in exchanges.

Mechanism An incentive structure designed to elicit the truthful revelation of type or preferences.

Median voter A person at the centre point of a one-dimensional distribution of political beliefs.

Median voter theorem The claim that the manifestos of political parties are very similar on the basis that to win power each party requires the support of the median voter.

Method of equal gradients A method of solving problems of choice that explicitly applies the equi-marginal principle and resource constraints.

Minimax strategy The strategy of choosing the action that has the highest minimum payoff.

Mixed strategy A probability distribution over actions, used to choose a player's action.

Monopoly The firm is the only supplier in a market.

Monotonically increasing transformation A larger domain value leads to a larger image value.

Monotonicity If bundle Y has no less of any good than bundle Z, then Y is (weakly) preferred to Z.

Nash equilibrium An outcome in which all strategies are the best replies to other players' actions.

Natural monopoly A firm's monopoly power if derived from increasing returns in production.

Negative externality Externality with a harmful effect.

Network externality A benefit accruing to the user of a good or a service from its use by others.

Nominal income The money that is available to purchase goods and services.

Normal good A good for which demand increases with income.

Numeraire A good that serves as unit of value in the economy.

Oligopoly A market structure in which a few firms supply a good or service.

Open access resource A non-excludable but rivalrous resource.

Operant conditioning Learning based on the acquisition of rewards (or the experience of punishment) for behaviour.

Opportunity cost The quantity of goods forgone in order to increase consumption of some specific good.

Ordinary (Marshallian) demand The demand of the utility-maximizing consumer.

Parameter A value in a model that is fixed but indeterminate.

Pareto efficiency A division such that no further Pareto improvements exist.

Pareto improvement A division of endowment such that no one is worse off and at least one person is better off.

Pareto set (contract curve) All divisions are Pareto-efficient.

Partial equilibrium A market outcome that is determined by conditions in that market only.

Participation constraint Faced with a discrete choice, participation does not make the agent worse off.

Perfect Bayesian equilibrium Equilibrium of an extensive game with incomplete information, in which all players' revisions of priors and strategies are consistent.

Perfect complements A pair of goods for which the marginal rate of substitution is zero.

Perfect divisibility Technology that allows infinitesimally small increments in factor use.

Perfect information A situation in which a person has all the information she or he needs to make a decision.

Perfect market A market in which the assumptions of perfect competition all hold.

Perfect price discrimination Selling each unit of a good at the buyer's *WTP*.

Perfect substitutes A pair of goods for which the marginal rate of substitution is constant.

Perfectly elastic demand The demand falls to zero after any price rise.

Perfectly inelastic demand No change in demand after a price rise.

Pigovian tax A tax whose marginal rate is the marginal social cost less the marginal private cost.

Player A participant in a game.

Point elasticity The elasticity measure at a specific point on a curve.

Positional consumption Utility depends upon the level of consumption relative to other consumers' consumption.

Positive externality Externality with a beneficial effect.

Preference A ranking of two outcomes based on which one is considered better.

Preference ordering A complete ranking of all consumption bundles.

Present value The value of a sum of money available at some future date, as if available now.

Price discrimination Selling units of a good at different prices.

Price elasticity of demand The responsiveness of a consumer's demand to changes in prices.

Price offer path The set of all the most-preferred, affordable consumption bundles that are formed when the price of one good varies.

Price taker A firm that accepts the market price as given.

Price–cost margin A monopoly's ability to make profits from a marginal transaction.

Private cost The cost borne by an individual in making a decision that gives rise to an externality

Private good A good that is excludable and rivalrous.

Private values Personal valuations derived from private signals.

Probability distribution A function that measures the likelihood of particular events occurring.

Procedural (bounded) rationality Making choices using some prescribed decision making process.

Product uniformity The situation in which all units of a good are identical.

Production The process by which a firm takes factor inputs and turns them into goods and services.

Production function The relationship between inputs used and output.

Production possibility frontier A curve formed from just feasible output combinations.

Profit A firm's revenues from sales, less the costs of production.

Profits The difference between revenues and costs.

Prospect An alternative name for a lottery.

Prospect theory A behavioural theory of decision making when faced with uncertainty.

Public good A good that is both non-excludable and non-rivalrous.

Quantity leader The firm in an oligopoly that chooses its output level first.

Random variable A function whose value is determined by random events.

Randomness A quality of a trial such that all outcomes are equally likely to occur.

Reaction function The optimal choice as a function of conjectures about competitors' behaviour.

Real income The capacity to generate utility from consumption.

Reflexivity A preference relation that allows the bundle to be compared with itself.

Representativeness The probability of an outcome greater where the sample's distributional properties are the same as those of the population.

Returns to scale A measure of the responsiveness of output to the scale of inputs.

Revenue (total revenue) A firm's income from selling output.

Revenues The income that the seller obtains from sales of goods and services.

Risk aversion Behaviour that reflects a preference for a certain outcome rather than participation in lotteries.

Risk-loving Behaviour that reflects a preference for participation in lotteries rather than a certain outcome.

Risk neutrality Indifference between certain outcomes and participation in lotteries.

Risk premium The payment that a risk averse person will make to transfer the risk to someone else.

Rivalrousness A property of a good such that use by one person reduces the quantity available to others.

Satisficing Setting an acceptability target for a choice, and stopping a procedurally rational process as soon as the target is reached.

Scale of production Given constant technology, a measure of the extent of use of all input factors.

Scarcity The situation in which the quantity of a good or service that is sought is less than the amount that is available.

Sealed-bid auction An auction in which bids are submitted in writing.

Second-degree price discrimination Setting a different price for each buyer of the good.

Second-price auction An alternative name for a Vickrey auction.

Self-perception theory Justification of a choice by assertion of the existence of preferences.

Separation The outcome of a game in which a signal allows correct identification of types.

Short run A period in which the use of one factor is fixed.

Signal Manipulation of an attribute to convey information about a characteristic.

Social cost The cost of activity, including negative externalities.

Social planner An individual with authority to allocate resources to maximize social welfare.

Social preferences An aggregation of individual preferences over outcomes.

Social welfare function A function that weights individual preferences.

Spatial differentiation The distribution of goods' characteristics that can be measured.

State of technology A measure of the inputs required at any time to produce an output unit.

Strategic game of complete information A game in which a fixed group of players choose their actions at the same time, anticipating others' behaviour.

Strategic interdependence A situation in which the decisions of each participant affect all other participants' payoffs.

Strategy Actions that a player chooses, given that player's beliefs (about other players' actions).

Strategy (in extensive games) A listing of the actions that a player chooses (given previous actions) whenever called on to make a choice.

Sub-game The part of game that begins at the end of a sub-history, whose length is the number of decisions made in it.

Sub-game perfection An outcome such that the choice made at the end of every sub-history is optimal within the subsequent sub-game.

Sub-history The initial part of the history.

Subsistence The minimum consumption required for survival.

Substitution effect The change in demand following a price increase for a consumer with a fixed utility target.

Superior good A good for which demand increases more rapidly than income.

Technical efficiency Production using an input combination such that using less of any input produces a fall in output.

Technology The relative intensity of use of input factors in production.

Technology of production The combination of inputs used in producing a (unit) quantity of output.

Third-degree price discrimination Setting a different price for each class of buyer.

Total effect The change in demand following a price increase for a consumer with a fixed amount of money to spend.

Total product The output that a firm can produce when use of only one input varies.

Transitivity A preference relation that is consistent, and can therefore be applied successively.

Two-part tariff A charging structure based on an access fee plus usage fees.

Utility A measure of the strength of preference for a bundle, set by the preference ordering.

Utility possibility frontier A curve formed from utility combinations that are just feasible.

Variable A value in a model that is obtained by solving the model.

Vertical differentiation Spatial differentiation with agreement on the ranking of products.

Vickrey auction An auction conducted with written bids, in which the highest bidder wins, and pays an amount equal to the second highest bid.

Vickrey–Clarke–Groves mechanism (VCG) A mechanism that charges people for the costs that their choices impose on others.

Walrasian equilibrium A set of prices that ensures that all markets clear at the same time.

Weak preference Ranking two outcomes based on one being considered at least as good as the other.

(Weakly) preferred set All consumption bundles that are ranked at least as highly as the reference bundle.

Welfare loss of monopoly The cost to society of a good being produced by a monopoly rather than by a perfectly competitive industry.

Well-behaved preferences An ordering represented by infinite, convex, closed, nested preferred sets.

Willingness to accept (*WTA*) The minimum price for which a seller will sell one unit of a good.

Willingness to pay (*WTP*) The maximum price that a consumer will pay for one unit of a good.

Zero-sum game A game in which payoffs in all outcomes sum to zero: a purely competitive game.

Bibliography

Background reading in economics

Ariely, D. 2008. *Predictably Irrational.* London: Harper Collins.

Binmore, K. 1991. *Fun and Games.* Cambridge, MA: Houghton Mifflin.

Chang, H.-J. 2014. *Economics: the Users' Guide.* London: Pelican.

Dixit, A. and S. Skeath. 2015. *Games of Strategy.* New York: W. W. Norton.

Frank, R. 2008. *The Economic Naturalist: Why Economics Explains Almost Everything.* London: Virgin Books.

Harford, T. 2006. *The Undercover Economist.* London: Abacus.

Harford, T. 2008. *The Logic of Life.* London: Abacus.

Hill, R. and T. Myatt. 2010. *The Economics Anti-Textbook: a Critical Thinker's Guide to Microeconomics.* London: Zed Books.

Kay, J. 1996. *The Business of Economics.* Oxford: Oxford University Press.

Kay, J. 2004. *The Truth about Markets.* London: Penguin.

Keen, S. 2010. *Debunking Economics: the Naked Emperor Dethroned?* London: Zed Books.

Landsburg, S. 1995. *The Armchair Economist.* New York: Free Press.

Levitt, S. and S. Dubner. 2005. *Freakonomics.* London: Penguin.

Smith, D. 2012. *Free Lunch: Easily Digestible Economics.* London: Profile Books.

Wheelan, C. 2010. *Naked Economics: Undressing the Dismal Science.* New York: W. W. Norton.

Textbooks consulted in writing

Besanko, D. and R. Braeutigam. 2014. *Microeconomics,* 5th edn. Chichester: John Wiley.

Chiang, A. and K. Wainwright. 2005. *Fundamental Methods of Mathematical Economics.* Maidenhead: McGraw-Hill.

Cowell, F. 2006. *Microeconomics: Principles and Analysis.* Oxford: Oxford University Press.

Cullis, J. and P. Jones. 2009. *Microeconomics: a Journey through Life's Decisions.* Harlow: F. T. Prentice Hall.

Frank, R. and E. Cartwright. 2013. *Microeconomics and Behaviour.* Maidenhead: McGraw-Hill.

Estrin, S., D. Laidler and M. Dietrich. 2012. *Microeconomics.* Harlow: Pearson.

Gibbons, R. 1992. *A Primer in Game Theory.* Hemel Hempstead: Harvester Wheatsheaf.

Goolsbee, A., S. Levitt and C. Syverson. 2013. *Microeconomics.* New York: Worth Publishers.

Gravelle, H. and R. Rees. 2003. *Microeconomics.* Harlow: Pearson Education.

Hirshleifer, J., A. Glazer and D. Hirshleifer. 2005. *Price Theory and Applications.* Cambridge: Cambridge University Press.

Hoy, M., J. Livernois, C. McKenna, R. Rees, and T. Stengos. *Mathematics for Economics.* Cambridge, MA: MIT Press.

Jehle, G. and P. Reny. 2011. *Advanced Microeconomic Theory.* Harlow: Pearson Education.

Kreps, D. 1990. *A Course in Microeconomic Theory.* Harlow: Pearson Education.

Landsburg, S. 2014. *Price Theory and Applications.* Andover: Cengage.

Morgan, W., M. Katz and H. Rosen. 2009. *Microeconomics.* Maidenhead; McGraw-Hill.

Osborne, M. 2009. *An Introduction to Game Theory.* Oxford: Oxford University Press.

Perloff, J. 2011. *Microeconomics.* Cambridge, MA: Pearson Education.

Pindyck, R. and D. Rubinfeld. 2012. *Microeconomics.* Upper Saddle River, NJ: Pearson Education.

Renshaw, G. 2011. *Maths for Economics.* Oxford: Oxford University Press.

Sydsaeter, K., P. Hammond and A. Strøm. *Essential Mathematics for Economic Analysis.* Harlow: Pearson Education.

Tirole, J. 1988. *The Theory of Industrial Organization.* Cambridge, MA: MIT Press.

Varian, H. 1992. *Microeconomic Analysis.* London: W. W. Norton.

Varian, H. 2014. *Intermediate Microeconomics.* London: W. W. Norton.

Wilkinson, N. and M. Klaes. 2012. *An Introduction to Behavioral Economics.* London: Palgrave.

Journal articles and monographs

Ainslie, G. 1991. Derivation of Rational Economic Behavior from Hyperbolic Discount Curves. *American Economic Review* **81**(2): 334–340.

Akerlof, G. 1970. The Market for Lemons. *Quarterly Journal of Economics* **84**(3): 488–500.

Akerlof, G. 1982. Labor Contracts as Partial Gift Exchange. *Quarterly Journal of Economics* **97**(4): 543–569.

Allais. M. 1953. Le comportement de l'homme rationnel devant le risque, critique des postulats et axioms de l'école américaine. *Econometrica* **21**(4): 503–546.

Arrow, K. 1951. *Social Choice and Individual Values.* London: John Wiley.

d'Aspremont, C., J. Gabszewicz, and J.-F. Thisse. 1979. On Hotelling's 'Stability in Competition'. *Econometrica* **47**(5): 1145–1150.

Axelrod, R. 1985. *The Evolution of Cooperation.* New York: Basic Books.

Becker, G. 1962. *Human Capital.* Chicago, IL: University of Chicago Press.

Becker, G. 1993. *A Treatise on the Family*, 2nd edn. Cambridge, MA: Harvard University Press.

Becker, G. 1996. *Accounting for Tastes.* Cambridge, MA: Harvard University Press.

Becker, G. and K. Murphy. 1988. A Theory of Rational Addiction. *Journal of Political Economy* **96**(4): 675–700.

Becker, G., M. Grossman and K. Murphy. 1994. An Empirical Analysis of Cigarette Addiction. *American Economic Review* **84**(3): 396–418.

Bertrand, E. 2006. The Coasean Analysis of Lighthouse Financing: Myths and Realities. *Cambridge Journal of Economics* **30**(3): 389–402.

Camerer, C., G. Loewentstein and M. Rabin (eds). 2004. *Advances in Behavioral Economics.* New York: Russell Sage Foundation.

Cho, I. and D. Kreps. 1987. Signaling Games and Stable Equilibria. *Quarterly Journal of Economics* **102**(2): 179–221.

Coase, R. 1937. The Nature of the Firm. *Economica* **4**(16): 386–405.

Coase, R. 1960. The Problem of Social Cost. *Journal of Law and Economics* **3**(1): 1–60.

Coase, R. 1974. The Lighthouse in Economics. *Journal of Law and Economics* **17**(2): 357–376.

Davies, J. 1994. Giffen Goods, the Survival Imperative and the Irish Potato Culture. *Journal of Political Economy* **102**(3): 547–565.

Downs. A. 1957. *An Economic Theory of Democracy.* New York: Harper & Row.

Eaton, B. and M. Eswaran. 2009. Well-being and Affluence in the Presence of a Giffen Good. *Economic Journal* **119**(539): 1–23.

Ellsberg, D. 1961. Risk, Ambiguity and the Savage Axioms. *Quarterly Journal of Economics* **75**(4): 643–669.

Farber, H. 2008. Reference-Dependent Preferences and Labor Supply: the Case of New York Taxi Drivers. *American Economic Review* **98**(3): 1069–1082.

Farrell, J. and M. Rabin. 1996. Cheap Talk. *Journal of Economic Perspectives* **10**(3): 103–118.

Friedman, M. and L. Savage. 1948. The Utility Analysis of Choices Involving Risk. *Journal of Political Economy* **56**(4): 279–304.

Gabszewicz, J. and J.-F. Thisse. 1980. Entry (and Exit) in a Differentiated Industry. *Journal of Economic Theory* **22**(2): 327–338.

Genesove, D. 1993. Adverse Selection in the Wholesale Used Car Market. *Journal of Political Economy* **101**(4): 644–665.

Gruber, J. and B. Köszegi. 2001. Is Addiction Rational? Theory and Evidence. *Quarterly Journal of Economics* **116**(4): 1261–1303.

Hardin, G. 1968. The Tragedy of the Commons. *Science* **162**(3859): 1243–1248.

Hart, O. 1995. *Firms, Contracts and Financial Structure.* Oxford: Clarendon Press.

Hotelling, H. 1929. Stability in Competition. *Economic Journal* **39**(1): 41–57.

Hotelling, H. 1931. The Economics of Exhaustible Resources. *Journal of Political Economy* **39**(2): 137–175.

Jensen, R. and N. Miller. 2008. Giffen Behavior and Subsistence Consumption. *American Economic Review* **98**(4): 1553–1577.

Kahneman, D., J. Knetsch and R. Thaler. 1990. Experimental Tests of the Endowment Effect and the Coase Theorem. *Journal of Political Economy* **98**(6): 1325–1348.

Kahneman, D. and A. Tversky. 1979. Prospect Theory: an Analysis of Decision Under Risk. *Econometrica* **47**(2): 313–327.

Kahneman, D. and A. Tversky (eds). *Choices, Values and Frames.* Cambridge: Cambridge University Press.

Katz, M. and C. Shapiro. 1994. Systems Competition and Network Effects. *Journal of Economic Perspectives* **8**(2): 93–115.

Klemperer, P. 2004. *Auctions: Theory and Practice.* Princeton, NJ: Princeton University Press.

Köszegi, B. and M. Rabin. 2006. A Model of Reference-Dependent Preferences. *Quarterly Journal of Economics* **121**(4): 1133–1165.

Kreps, D. and R. Wilson. 1982. Sequential Equilibria. *Econometrica* **50**(4): 863–894.

Laibson, D. 1996. Golden Eggs and Hyperbolic Discounting. *Quarterly Journal of Economics* **112**(2): 443–477.

Liebenstein, H. 1950. Bandwagon, Snob and Veblen Effects in the Theory of Consumers' Demand. *Quarterly Journal of Economics* **64**(2): 183–207.

Machina, M. 1989. Dynamic Consistency and Non-Expected Utility Models of Choice Under Uncertainty. *Journal of Economic Literature* **27**(4): 1622–1668.

Milgrom, P. and K. Roberts. 1986. Price and Advertising Signals of Product Quality. *Journal of Political Economy* **94**(4): 796–821.

Myerson, R. 1981. Optimal Auction Design. *Mathematics of Operations Research* **6**(1): 58–73.

Nash, J. *1950*. Equilibrium Points in *n*-Person Games. *Proceedings of the National Academy of Sciences* **36**: 48–49.

Nash, J. 1951. Non-cooperative Games. *Annals of Mathematics* **54**(2): 286–295.

Nelson, P. 1974. Advertising as Information. *Journal of Political Economy* **82**(4): 729–754.

O'Donoghue, T. and M. Rabin. 1999. Doing It Now or Later. *American Economic Review* **89**(1): 103–124.

Olson, M. 1965. *The Logic of Collective Action: Public Goods and the Theory of Groups.* Cambridge, MA: Harvard University Press.

Pigou, A. 1920. *The Economics of Welfare.* London: Macmillan.

Plott, C. and K. Zeiler. 2005. The Willingness to Pay–Willingness to Accept Gap, the 'Endowment Effect,' Subject Misconceptions and Experimental Procedures for Eliciting Values. *American Economic Review* **95**(3): 530–545.

Posner, R. 1975. The Social Cost of Monopoly and Regulation. *Journal of Political Economy* **83**(4): 807–827.

Rabin, M. 1998. Psychology and Economics. *Journal of Economic Literature* **36**(1): 11–46.

Rawls, J. 1971. *A Theory of Justice.* Oxford: Oxford University Press.

Roemer, J. 2001. *Political Competition: Theory and Applications.* Cambridge, MA: Harvard University Press.

Roth, A. and A. Ockenfels. 2002. Last-Minute Bidding and the Rules for Ending Second-Price Auctions: Evidence from eBay and Amazon Auctions on the Internet. *American Economic Review* **92**(4): 1093–1103.

Rothschild, M. and J. Stiglitz. 1976. Equilibrium in Competitive Insurance Markets: An Essay on the Economics of Imperfect Information. *Quarterly Journal of Economics* **90**(4): 629–649.

Salop, S. 1977. The Noisy Monopolist: Imperfect Information, Price Dispersion and Price Discrimination. *Review of Economic Studies* **44**(3): 393–406.

Schelling, T. 1960. *The Strategy of Conflict.* Cambridge, MA: Harvard University Press.

Schelling, T. 1978. *Micromotives and Macrobehavior.* New York: W.W. Norton.

Shaked, A. and J. Sutton. 1982. Relaxing Price Competition through Product Differentiation. *Review of Economic Studies* **49**(1): 3–13.

Slade, M. 1995. Product Rivalry with Multiple Strategic Weapons: an Analysis of Price and Advertising Competition. *Journal of Economics and Management Strategy* **4**(3): 224–276.

Spence, M. 1974. *Market Signaling.* Cambridge, MA: Harvard University Press.

Stigler, G. and G. Becker. 1977. De gustibus non est disputandum. *American Economic Review* **67**(2): 76–90.

Skyrms. B. 2004. *The Stag Hunt and the Evolution of Social Structure.* Cambridge: Cambridge University Press.

Tversky, A. and D. Kahneman. 1973. Availability: A Heuristic for Judging Frequency and Probability. *Cognitive Psychology* **5**(2): 207–232.

Tversky, A. and D. Kahneman. 1974. Judgment Under Uncertainty: Heuristics and Biases. *Science* **185**(4157): 1124–1131.

Tversky, A. and D. Kahneman. 1981. The Framing of Decisions and the Psychology of Choice. *Science* **211**(4481): 453–458.

Vickrey, W. 1961. Counterspeculation, Auctions, and Competitive Sealed Tenders. *Journal of Finance* **16**(1): 8–37.

von Neumann, J. and O. Morgenstern. 1944. *Theory of Games and Economic Behavior.* Princeton, NJ: Princeton University Press.

Williamson, O. 1975. *Markets and Hierarchies: Analysis and Anti-Trust Implications.* New York: Free Press.

Index

Entries for figures are in **bold**. Entries for tables are in *italics*.